Mergers, Acquisitions, and Corporate Restructurings

Fourth Edition

MERGERS, ACQUISITIONS, AND CORPORATE RESTRUCTURINGS

FOURTH EDITION

PATRICK A. GAUGHAN

JOHN WILEY & SONS, INC.

This book is printed on acid-free paper.⊗

Copyright © 2007 by John Wiley & Sons, Inc. All rights reserved.

Published by John Wiley & Sons, Inc., Hoboken, New Jersey.
Published simultaneously in Canada.

For general information on our other products and services please contact our Customer Care Department within the U.S. at 877-762-2974, outside the U.S. at 317-572-3993 or fax 317-572-4002.

Wiley also publishes its books in a variety of electronic formats. Some content that appears in print, however, may not be available in electronic format.

For more information about Wiley products, visit our Web site at http://www.wiley.com.

Library of Congress Cataloging-in-Publication Data:

Gaughan, Patrick A.
    Mergers, acquisitions, and corporate restructurings / Patrick A.
Gaughan.—4th ed.
        p. cm.
    Includes index.
    ISBN: 978–0–471–70564–2 (cloth)
    1. Consolidation and merger of corporations. 2. Corporate
reorganizations. I. Title.
    HD2746.5.G38 2007
    658.1'6—dc22

                                        2006020848

Printed in the United States of America.

10 9 8 7 6 5 4 3

CONTENTS

Preface   xi
About the Web Site   xiii

Part 1   Background   1

1   Introduction   3
    Recent M&A Trends   3
    Definitions   12
    Valuing a Transaction   12
    Types of Mergers   13
    Reasons for Mergers and Acquisitions   14
    Merger Financing   14
    Merger Professionals   15
    Merger Arbitrage   16
    Leveraged Buyouts and the Private Equity Market   17
    Corporate Restructuring   18
    Merger Negotiations   19
    Merger Approval Procedures   21
    Short-Form Merger   22
    Freezeouts and the Treatment of Minority Shareholders   23
    Purchase of Assets Compared with Purchase of Stock   23
    Structuring the Deal   24
    Assumption of the Seller's Liabilities   24
    Advantages of Asset Acquisitions   24
    Asset Selloffs   25
    Reverse Mergers   25
    Holding Companies   26

2   History of Mergers   29
    Merger Waves   29
    What Causes Merger Waves?   29
    First Wave, 1897–1904   30
    Second Wave, 1916–1929   36
    The 1940s   39
    Third Wave, 1965–1969   40
    Trendsetting Mergers of the 1970s   47

Fourth Wave, 1984–1989   53
Fifth Wave   59
Summary   67

3   Legal Framework   **69**
Laws Governing Mergers, Acquisitions, and Tender Offers   70
Securities Laws   70
Other Specific Takeover Rules in the United States   84
International Securities Laws Relating to Takeovers   85
Business Judgment Rule   91
State Antitakeover Laws   92
Regulation of Insider Trading   98
Antitrust Laws   100
Recent Trends in Antitrust Enforcement in the United States   107
Measuring Concentration and Defining Market Share   109
European Competition Policy   114
Antitrust Remedies   114
Summary   116

4   Merger Strategy   **117**
Growth   117
Synergy   124
Operating Synergy   126
Diversification   136
Other Economic Motives   145
Hubris Hypothesis of Takeovers   157
Other Motives   163
Tax Motives   165
Summary   165

Part 2   Hostile Takeovers   **169**

5   Antitakeover Measures   **171**
Management Entrenchment Hypothesis versus Stockholder Interests Hypothesis 172
Preventative Antitakeover Measures   173
Changing the State of Incorporation   196
Active Antitakeover Defenses   197
Information Content of Takeover Resistance   231
Summary   233

6   Takeover Tactics   **234**
Preliminary Takeover Steps   236
Tender Offers   240

Open Market Purchases and Street Sweeps 258
Advantages of Tender Offers over Open Market Purchases 260
Arbitrage and the Downward Price Pressures Around M&A Announcements 263
Proxy Fights 263
Summary 281

Part 3 Going Private Transactions and Leveraged Buyouts **283**

7 Leveraged Buyouts **285**
Terminology 285
Historical Trends in LBOs 286
Costs of Being a Public Company 295
Management Buyouts 297
Conflicts of Interest in Management Buyouts 299
Financing for Leveraged Buyouts 309
Capital Structure of LBOs 314
Sources of LBO Financing 315
Returns to Stockholders from LBOs 317
Returns to Stockholders from Divisional Buyouts 317
Reverse LBOs 319
Empirical Research on Wealth Transfer Effects 324
Protection for Creditors 325
Summary 328

8 Trends in the Financing of Takeovers and Going Private Transactions **330**
Trends in Cash versus Stock Percentage of Takeover Financing 331
Shareholder Wealth Effects and Methods of Payment 335
Private Equity Market 340
Hedge Funds 348
Comparison of Private Equity Funds and Hedge Funds 352
Hedge Fund and Private Equity Fund Convergence 353
Junk Bonds Financing of Takeovers 355
Stapled Financing 373
Securitization and M&A Financing 374
Summary 375

9 Employee Stock Ownership Plans **378**
Historical Growth of ESOPs 378
Types of Plans 380
Characteristics of ESOPs 380
Leveraged versus Unleveraged ESOPs 381

Corporate Finance Uses of ESOPs   381
Voting of ESOP Shares   383
Cash Flow Implications   383
Valuation of Stock Contributed into an ESOP   384
Eligibility of ESOPs   384
Put Options of ESOPs   384
Dividends Paid   385
ESOPs versus a Public Offering of Stock   385
Employee Risk and ESOPs   387
Securities Laws and ESOPs   388
Tax Benefits of LESOPs   388
Balance Sheet Effects of ESOPs   389
Drawbacks of LESOPs   389
ESOPs and Corporate Performance   390
ESOPs as an Antitakeover Defense   392
ESOPs and Shareholder Wealth   393
ESOPs and LBOs   394
Summary   397

Part 4   Corporate Restructuring   **399**

10   Corporate Restructuring   **401**

Divestitures   403
Divestiture and Spinoff Process   413
Wealth Effects of Selloffs   421
Equity Carve-outs   434
Voluntary Liquidations, or Bustups   437
Tracking Stocks   439
Master Limited Partnerships and Selloffs   440
Summary   442

11   Restructuring in Bankruptcy   **443**

Types of Business Failure   443
Causes of Business Failure   444
Bankruptcy Trends   446
U.S. Bankruptcy Laws   452
Reorganization versus Liquidation   453
Reorganization Process   454
Benefits of the Chapter 11 Process for the Debtor   459
Company Size and Chapter 11 Benefits   459

Prepackaged Bankruptcy   462
Workouts   465
Corporate Control and Default   470
Liquidation   471
Investing in the Securities of Distressed Companies   471
Summary   477

12   Corporate Governance   479
Failed Corporate Governance: Accounting Scandals   479
Sarbanes-Oxley Act   481
Other Regulatory Changes   482
Corporate Governance   483
Summary   517

13   Joint Ventures and Strategic Alliances   519
Contractual Agreements   519
Comparing Strategic Alliances and Joint Ventures with Mergers
    and Acquisitions   520
Joint Ventures   520
Governance of Strategic Alliances   526
Summary   530

14   Valuation   531
Valuation Methods: Science or Art?   533
Managing Value as an Antitakeover Defense   533
Benchmarks of Value   534
How the Market Determines Discount Rates   545
Valuation of the Target's Equity   555
Takeovers and Control Premiums   555
Marketability of the Stock   557
Valuation of Stock-for-Stock Exchanges   566
Exchange Ratio   567
Fixed Number of Shares versus Fixed Value   575
International Takeovers and Stock-for-Stock Transactions   575
Desirable Financial Characteristics of Targets   575
Summary   583
Appendix   584

15   Tax Issues   588
Financial Accounting   588
Taxable versus Tax-Free Transactions   589
Tax Consequences of a Stock-for-Stock Exchange   591

Asset Basis Step-Up   594
Changes in the Tax Laws   595
Role of Taxes in the Merger Decision   596
Taxes as a Source of Value in Management Buyouts   598
Miscellaneous Tax Issues   599
Summary   600

Glossary   **601**

Index   **609**

PREFACE

The field of mergers and acquisitions continues to experience dramatic growth. Record-breaking megamergers have become commonplace across the globe. While megamergers used to be mainly an American phenomenon, the recently completed fifth merger wave became a truly international merger period. Starting in the 1990s and continuing into the next decade, some of the largest mergers and acquisitions (M&As) took place in Europe. This was underscored by the fact that the largest deal of all time was a hostile acquisition of a German company by a British firm.

While deal volume declined when the fifth wave ended it, the pace of M&A picked up again shortly thereafter. By the mid-2000s the nature of the M&A business changed even more. It became even more global with the emergence of the emerging market acquirer. In addition, deregulation combined with economic growth has greatly increased deal volume in Asia. M&A also grew markedly in Latin and South America.

Over the past quarter of a century we have noticed that merger waves have become longer and more frequent. The time periods between waves also has shrunken. When these trends are combined with the fact that M&A has rapidly spread across the modern world, we see that the field is increasingly becoming an ever more important part of the worlds of corporate finance and corporate strategy.

As the field has evolved we see that many of the methods that applied to deals of prior years are still relevant, but new rules are also in effect. These principles consider the mistakes of prior periods along with the current economic and financial conditions. It is hoped that these new rules will make the mergers of the 2000s sounder and more profitable than those of prior periods. However, while dealmakers have asserted that they will pursue such goals we would be remiss if we did not point out that when deal volume picked up dramatically such intentions seemed to fall by the wayside and M&A mistakes started to occur.

The focus of this book is decidedly pragmatic. We have attempted to write it in a manner that will be useful to both the business student and the practitioner. Since the world of M&As is clearly interdisciplinary, material from the fields of law and economics is presented along with corporate finance, which is the primary emphasis of the book. The practical skills of finance practitioners have been integrated with the research of the academic world of finance. In addition we have an expanded chapter devoted to the valuation of businesses, including the valuation of privately held firms. This is an important topic that usually is ignored by traditional finance references. Much of the finance literature tends to be divided into two camps: practitioners and academicians. Clearly, both groups have made valuable contributions to the field of M&As. This book attempts to interweave these contributions into one comprehensible format.

The increase in M&As activity has given rise to the growth of academic research in this area. This book attempts to synthesize some of the more important and relevant research studies and to present their results in a straightforward and pragmatic manner. Because of the voluminous research in the field, only the findings of the more important studies are highlighted. Issues such as shareholder wealth effects of antitakeover measures have important meanings to investors, who are concerned about how the defensive actions of corporations will affect the value of their investments. This is a good example of how the academic research literature has made important pragmatic contributions that have served to shed light on important policy issues.

We have avoided incorporating theoretical research that has less relevance to those seeking a pragmatic treatment of M&As. However, some theoretical analyses, such as agency theory, can be helpful in explaining some of the incentives for managers to pursue management buyouts. Material from the field of portfolio theory can help explain some of the risk-reduction benefits that junk bond investors can derive through diversification. These more theoretical discussions, along with others, are presented because they have important relevance to the real world of M&As. The rapidly evolving nature of M&As requires constant updating. Every effort has been made to include recent developments occurring just before the publication date. I wish the reader an enjoyable and profitable trip through the world of M&As.

Patrick A. Gaughan

ABOUT THE WEB SITE

As a purchaser of this book, *Mergers, Acquisitions, and Corporate Restructurings, 4th Edition*, you have access to the supporting Web site: www.wiley.com/go/mergers

The Web site contains files of exhibits that have the most current data.

The password to enter this site is: acquisition

MERGERS, ACQUISITIONS, AND CORPORATE RESTRUCTURINGS

FOURTH EDITION

1

BACKGROUND

1

INTRODUCTION

RECENT M&A TRENDS

The pace of mergers and acquisitions (M&As) picked up in the early 2000s after a short hiatus in 2001. The economic slowdown and recession in the United States and elsewhere in 2001 brought an end to the record-setting fifth merger wave. This period featured an unprecedented volume of M&As. It followed on the heels of a prior record-setting merger wave—the fourth. This one in the 1990s, however, was very different from its counterpart in the prior decade. The fifth wave was truly an international one and it featured a heightened volume of deals in Europe and, to some extent, Asia, in addition to the United States. The prior merger waves had been mainly a U.S. phenomenon. When the fourth merger wave ended with the 1990–91 recession, many felt that it would be a long time before we would see another merger wave like it. However, after a relatively short recession and an initially slow recovery, the economy picked up speed in 1993, and by 1994 we were on a path to another record-setting merger period. This one would feature deals that would make the ones of the 1980s seem modest. There would be many megamergers and many cross borders involving U.S. buyers and sellers, but also many large deals not involving U.S. firms. In the fifth wave the large-scale M&A business had become a global phenomenon. This was in sharp contrast to prior merger periods when the major players were mainly U.S. companies.

Starting in the early 1980s and the beginning of the fourth merger wave, we see the M&A area business mainly centered in the United States with the vast majority of transactions taking place within the continental United States. From a global perspective, the most pronounced increase in M&A volume in the fifth merger wave took place in Europe. After a short falloff at the end of the fourth merger wave, European M&A volume picked up dramatically starting in 1995, when it doubled (see Exhibit 1.1). The value of European deals peaked in 1999, when it equaled 38% of total global M&A deal value. There are several reasons why Europe became the scene for such an increased volume of deals. First, the same factors that caused M&A volume to pick up in the United States, such as the increase in worldwide economic demand, also played a key role in Europe. However, similar economic conditions prevailed in the 1980s, and Europe failed to produce a comparable increase in mergers as it did in the 1990s. The reasons why the European response was much different this time was that the European economy had structurally changed. The European Union had been established and artificial regulatory barriers were being dismantled. In the past, many European corporations were controlled by large blockholders such as those owned by individual families. However, by the fifth merger wave, these holdings had become somewhat less significant and more shares were in the hands of other parties who would be more receptive to M&As. The fact remains, though, that family control of European corporations still is greater than in the United States. Examples include the Benetton family, which controls the Italian clothing company of the same name; Francois Pinault, who controls a large French retail empire that includes Gucci; the German family-controlled Bertelsmann empire; and the Wallenberg family's holdings in Swedish companies such as Ericsson and ABB. As these holdings get passed on to later generations, the companies will more likely become takeover targets.

Exhibit 1.1 clearly shows that the fifth merger wave peaked in 1999 and the value of M&As declined significantly in 2001 and even more so in 2002. Similar trends are apparent in both Europe and the United States. The magnitude of the fifth wave deals is very apparent when we look at Table 1.1, which shows that all of the largest deals of all time occurred in the years 1998–2001. This table also reveals another interesting trend of this period. A disproportionate number of the deals came from certain sectors of the economy. In particular, telecommunications, media, and banking and finance featured a

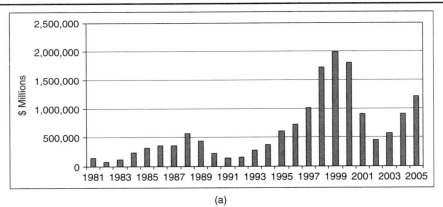

(a)

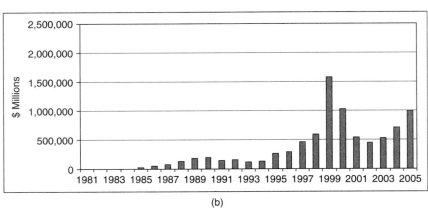

(b)

EXHIBIT 1.1   VALUE OF M&AS 1980–2004: (a) UNITED STATES AND (b) EUROPE
Source: Thomson Securities Financial Data.

Date Announced	Date Effective	Value of Transaction ($Million)	Target Name	Target Nation	Acquirer Name	Acquirer Nation
11/14/1999	6/19/2000	202,785.13	Mannesmann AG	Germany	Vodafone AirTouch PLC	United Kingdom
1/10/2000	1/12/2001	164,746.46	Time Warner	United States	America Online Inc.	United States
10/5/1999	—	113,643.77	Sprint Corp.	United States	MCI WorldCom	United States
11/4/1999	6/19/2000	89,167.72	Warner-Lambert Co.	United States	Pfizer Inc.	United States
4/18/1999	—	81,527.62	Telecom Italia SpA	Italy	Deutsche Telekom AG	Germany
12/1/1998	11/30/1999	78,945.79	Mobil Corp.	United States	Exxon Corp.	United States
1/17/2000	12/27/2000	75,960.85	SmithKline Beecham PLC	United Kingdom	Glaxo Wellcome PLC	United Kingdom
211/4/1999	—	75,563.15	Warner-Lambert Co.	United States	American Home Products Corp.	United States
10/28/2004	—	74,349.15	Shell Transport & Trading Co.	United Kingdom	Royal Dutch Petroleum Co.	Netherlands
4/6/1998	10/8/1998	72,558.18	Citicorp	United States	Travelers Group Inc.	United States

TABLE 1.1 TOP TEN WORLDWIDE M&AS BY VALUE OF TRANSACTION

Source: Thompson Financial, December 6, 2005.

disproportionate amount of total deal volume. These sectors were red hot in the 1990s. There are several reasons for this. One was the "irrational exuberance" that overwhelmed some of these sectors, such as parts of the technology sectors. We will discuss this further in Chapter 2. Other industries, such as banking, continued a process of consolidation that had begun in the prior decade when industry deregulation began.

The very important role of Europe in the M&A market is underscored by the fact that the largest deal in history was the $203 billion acquisition of Mannesmann AG by Vodafone Airtouch PLC in June 2000. The value of this deal was more than double the next largest European transaction, which was the $82 billion acquisition of Telecom Italia SPA by Deutsche Telekom AG (see Table 1.2).

In the Asian markets we see that with the exception of Australia, which has participated in both the fourth and fifth merger wave, Asian countries, including Japan, have generally not had much M&A activity within their borders (see Exhibit 1.2). In Japan, which is the world's second largest economy, this changed dramatically in 1999, when the country's deal volume skyrocketed. The number of deals slowed in the few years that followed but started to rebound in 2003. A similar trend is apparent in South Korea. Both nations had very restrictive and interlocked corporate structures that began to unravel toward the end of the 1990s—partly in response to the pressures of an economic downturn. As both economies began to restructure starting in the late 1990s, selloffs and acquisitions became more common.

In Exhibit 1.2 we have combined the deal volume data for China and Hong Kong, but both are significant. However, Table 1.3 shows the important role of Hong Kong, as the largest Asian deal was the August 2000 acquisition of Cable and Wireless HKT by Pacific Century CyberWorks—both Hong Kong firms. The deal is also noteworthy in that it was a hostile takeover. Pacific Century CyberWorks, led by Internet investor Richard Li, who is the son of Hong Kong tycoon Li Ka-shing, outbid Singapore Telecommunications Ltd. It is interesting that the combination of Cable and Wireless and Pacific Century CyberWorks created a telecom and media conglomerate that was second in size only to AOL Time Warner, which itself was the product of a failed megamerger.

As the Chinese economy continues to grow dramatically, it has begun to increasingly look outside its borders for acquisition candidates. The 2005 acquisition of IBM's PC business by Lenovo is an example. However, acquisitions of Chinese companies by non-Chinese firms are difficult and risky as that country is still in the early stages of becoming less centralized and more of a free market economy. Deal volume in Taiwan is relatively small, but that is mainly due to the comparatively smaller size of the economy. India remains a relatively small player in the worldwide M&A market, although this may change over the coming years.

After the United States, Europe, and Asia, the next largest M&A markets are Central and South America. In 2000, the highest deal volume year for M&A in many regions including South America, deal volume in South America was approximately equal to Australia, somewhat higher than Hong Kong and roughly double deal volume in South Korea. While deal volume in both South and Central America varies, the volume in South America has been roughly double that of Central America (see Exhibit 1.3 and Table 1.4).

Date Announced	Date Effective	Value of Transaction ($Million)	Target Name	Target Nation	Acquirer Name	Acquirer Nation
11/14/1999	6/19/2000	202,785.13	Mannesmann AG	Germany	Vodafone AirTouch PLC	United Kingdom
4/18/1999		81,527.62	Telecom Italia SpA	Italy	Deutsche Telekom AG	Germany
1/17/2000	12/27/2000	75,960.85	SmithKline Beecham PLC	United Kingdom	Glaxo Wellcome PLC	United Kingdom
10/28/2004		74,349.15	Shell Transport & Trading Co.	United Kingdom	Royal Dutch Petroleum Co.	Netherlands
1/26/2004	8/20/2004	60,243.38	Aventis SA	France	Sanofi-Synthelabo SA	France
7/19/1999		51,135.18	Total Fina SA	France	Elf Aquitaine	France
7/5/1999	3/27/2000	50,070.05	Elf Aquitaine	France	Total Fina SA	France
5/30/2000	8/22/2000	45,967.07	Orange PLC	United Kingdom	France Telecom SA	France
6/20/2000	12/8/2000	40,428.19	Seagram Co. Ltd.	Canada	Vivendi SA	France
9/24/1999		38,814.91	National Westminster Bank PLC	United Kingdom	Bank of Scotland PLC	United Kingdom

TABLE 1.2 TOP TEN EUROPEAN M&AS BY VALUE OF TRANSACTION

Source: Thompson Financial, December 6, 2005.

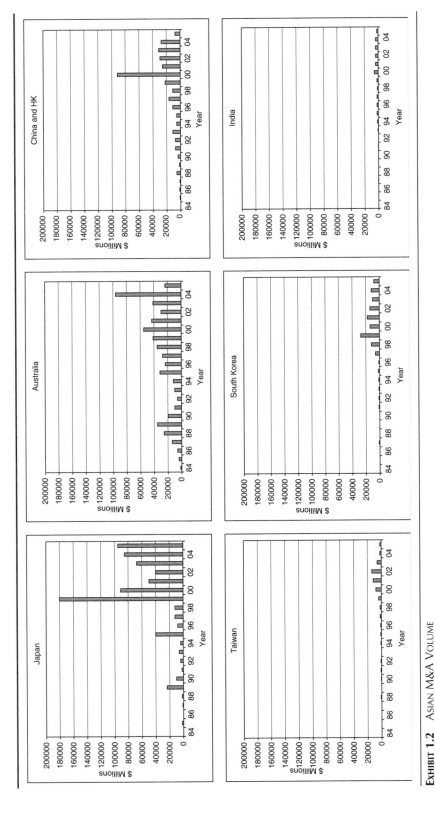

Exhibit 1.2 Asian M&A Volume
Source: Thompson SDC.

Date Announced	Date Effective	Value of Transaction ($Million)	Target Name	Target Nation	Acquirer Name	Acquirer Nation
2/29/2000	8/17/2000	37,442.15	Cable & Wireless HKT	Hong Kong	Pacific Century CyberWorks Ltd.	Hong Kong
10/4/2000	11/13/2000	34,007.71	Beijing Mobile, 6 others	China	China Telecom Hong Kong Ltd.	Hong Kong
3/19/2001	6/29/2001	11,510.99	Billiton PLC	United Kingdom	BHP Ltd.	Australia
5/16/2002	7/1/2002	10,335.27	CH Mobile HK(BVI)-Mobile	China	China Mobile (Hong Kong) Ltd.	Hong Kong
7/14/2003	12/31/2003	9,675.83	China Telecom- Fixed Line Asset	China	China Telecom Corp. Ltd.	China
3/26/2001	9/17/2001	8,491.12	Cable & Wireless Optus Ltd.	Australia	Sing.Tel.	Singapore
3/8/2005	6/17/2005	7,363.58	WMC Resources Ltd.	Australia	BHP Billiton Ltd.	Australia
11/16/2001	4/22/2002	6,868.85	LG Electronics Inc.-Electronics	South Korea	Shareholders	South Korea
10/28/2004		6,522.59	WMC Resources Ltd.	Australia	Xstrata PLC	Switzerland
1/7/2000	6/30/2000	6,447.97	Worldwide Semi- conductor	Taiwan	Taiwan Semiconductor Mnfr. Co.	Taiwan

TABLE 1.3 TOP TEN ASIAN M&AS BY VALUE OF TRANSACTION

Source: Thompson Financial, December 6, 2005.

Top Five Central American M&As by Value of Transaction

Date Effective	Value of Transaction ($Million)	Target Name	Target Nation	Acquirer Name	Acquirer Nation
2/7/2001	15,098.66	America Movil SA	Mexico	Shareholders	Mexico
8/6/2001	12,821.00	Banacci	Mexico	Citigroup Inc.	United States
3/22/2004	3,887.89	Grupo Financiero BBVA Bancomer	Mexico	BBVA	Spain
5/6/2003	3,692.04	Panamerican Beverages Inc.	United States	Coca-Cola FEMSA SA CV	Mexico
5/2/2002	3,217.45	America Telecom SA de CV	Mexico	Shareholders	Mexico

Top Five South American M&As by Value of Transaction

Date Effective	Value of Transaction ($Million)	Target Name	Target Nation	Acquirer Name	Acquirer Nation
6/24/1999	13,151.70	YPF SA	Argentina	Repsol SA	Spain
7/10/2000	10,213.31	Telecommunicacoes de Sao Paulo	Brazil	Telefonica SA	Spain
8/30/2004	7,758.01	John Labatt Ltd.	Canada	Ambev	Brazil
9/1/1997	6,200.67	Correo Argentino SA	Argentina	Investor Group	Argentina
1/23/1998	5,134.14	Argentina-Airports (33)	Argentina	Aeropuertos Argentina 2000	United States

TABLE 1.4   TOP FIVE M&AS BY VALUE OF TRANSACTION: (a) CENTRAL AMERICA AND (b) SOUTH AMERICA

Source: Thompson Financial, December 6, 2005.

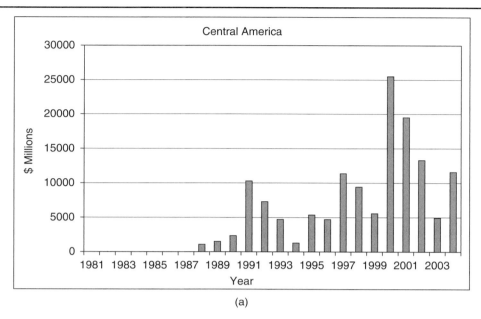

(a)

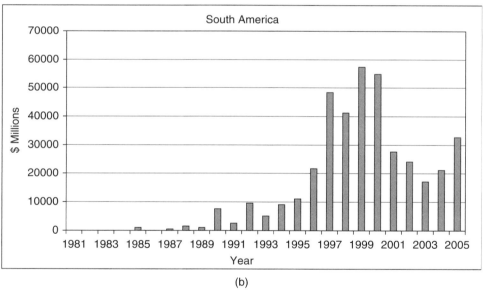

(b)

EXHIBIT 1.3   M&A VOLUME, 1981–2005: (a) CENTRAL AMERICA AND (b) SOUTH AMERICA
Source: Thompson Financial, May 13, 2005.

Having reviewed the recent trends in the field, let us being with our study of the subject of M&As. This will be begin with a discussion of the basic terminology used in the field.

DEFINITIONS

A *merger* is a combination of two corporations in which only one corporation survives and the merged corporation goes out of existence. In a merger, the acquiring company assumes the assets and liabilities of the merged company. Sometimes the term *statutory merger* is used to refer to this type of business transaction. It basically means that the merger is being done consistent with a specific state statute. The most common statute for mergers is the Delaware one, as so many companies are incorporated in that state.

A statutory merger differs from a *subsidiary merger,* which is a merger of two companies in which the target company becomes a subsidiary or part of a subsidiary of the parent company. The acquisition by General Motors of Electronic Data Systems, led by its colorful Chief Executive Officer Ross Perot, is an example of a subsidiary merger. In a *reverse subsidiary merger,* a subsidiary of the acquirer is merged into the target.

A merger differs from a *consolidation,* which is a business combination whereby two or more companies join to form an entirely new company. All of the combining companies are dissolved and only the new entity continues to operate. For example, in 1986, the computer manufacturers Burroughs and Sperry combined to form UNISYS. In a consolidation, the original companies cease to exist and their stockholders become stockholders in the new company. One way to look at the differences between a merger and a consolidation is that with a merger $A + B = A$, where company B is merged into company A. In a consolidation, $A + B = C$, where C is an entirely new company. Despite the differences between them, the terms *merger* and *consolidation,* as is true of many of the terms in the M&A field, are sometimes used interchangeably. In general, when the combining firms are approximately the same size, the term *consolidation* applies; when the two firms differ significantly by size, *merger* is the more appropriate term. In practice, however, this distinction is often blurred, with the term *merger* being broadly applied to combinations that involve firms of both different and similar sizes.

Another term that is broadly used to refer to various types of transactions is *takeover.* This term is vaguer; sometimes it refers only to hostile transactions, and other times it refers to both friendly and unfriendly mergers.

VALUING A TRANSACTION

Throughout this book we cite various merger statistics on deal values. The method used by Mergerstat is the most common method relied on to value deals. Enterprise value is defined as the base equity price plus the value of the target's debt (including both short and long term) and preferred stock less its cash. The *base equity price* is the total price less the value of the debt. The buyer is defined as the company with the larger market capitalization or the company that is issuing shares to exchange for the other company's shares in a stock-for-stock transaction.

TYPES OF MERGERS

Mergers are often categorized as horizontal, vertical, or conglomerate. A *horizontal merger* occurs when two competitors combine. For example, in 1998, two petroleum companies, Exxon and Mobil, combined in a $78.9 billion merger. If a horizontal merger causes the combined firm to experience an increase in market power that will have anti-competitive effects, the merger may be opposed on antitrust grounds. In recent years, however, the U.S. government has been somewhat liberal in allowing many horizontal mergers to go unopposed.

Vertical mergers are combinations of companies that have a buyer–seller relationship. For example, in 1993, Merck, the world's largest drug company, acquired Medco Containment Services, Inc., the largest marketer of discount prescription medicines, for $6 billion. The transaction enabled Merck to go from being the largest pharmaceutical company to also being the largest integrated producer and distributor of pharmaceuticals. This transaction was not opposed by antitrust regulators even though the combination clearly resulted in a more powerful firm. Ironically, regulators cited increased competition and lower prices as the anticipated result. Merck, however, might have been better off if the deal had been held up by regulators. Following this acquisition, and other copy-cat deals by competitors, great concerns were raised about Merck's effect on consumer drug choice decisions. While Merck saw the deal as a way to place its drugs in the hands of patients ahead of competitors, there was a backlash about drug manufacturers using distributors to affect consumer drug treatment choices. When this problem emerged, there were few benefits of the deal and Merck was forced to part with the distributor. This was a good example of a bidder buying a company in a similar business, one which it thought it knew well, where it would have been better off staying with what it did best—making and marketing drugs.

A *conglomerate merger* occurs when the companies are not competitors and do not have a buyer–seller relationship. One example would be Philip Morris, a tobacco company, which acquired General Foods in 1985 for $5.6 billion, Kraft in 1988 for $13.44 billion, and Nabisco in 2000 for $18.9 billion. Interestingly, Philip Morris, now called Altria, has used the cash flows from its food and tobacco businesses to become less of a domestic tobacco company and more of a food business. This is because the U.S. tobacco industry has been declining at an average rate of 2% per year (in shipments), although the international tobacco business has not been experiencing such a decline.

Another major example of a conglomerate is General Electric (GE). This company has done what many others have not been able to do successfully—manage a diverse portfolio of companies in a way that creates shareholder wealth. GE is a serial acquirer and a highly successful one at that. As we will discuss in Chapter 4, the track record of diversifying and conglomerate acquisitions is not good. We will explore why a few companies have been able to do this while many others have not.

REASONS FOR MERGERS AND ACQUISITIONS

As discussed in Chapter 4, there are several possible motives or reasons that firms might engage in M&As. One of the most common motives is expansion. Acquiring a company in a line of business or geographic area into which the company may want to expand can be quicker than internal expansion. An acquisition of a particular company may provide certain synergistic benefits for the acquirer, such as when two lines of business complement one another. However, an acquisition may be part of a diversification program that allows the company to move into other lines of business. In the pursuit of expansion, firms engaging in M&As cite potential synergistic gains as one of the reasons for the transaction. Synergy occurs when the sum of the parts is more productive and valuable than the individual components. There are many potential sources of synergy and they are discussed in Chapter 4.

Financial factors motivate some M&As. For example, an acquirer's financial analysis may reveal that the target is undervalued. That is, the value of the buyer may be significantly in excess of the market value of the target, even when a premium that is normally associated with changes in control is added to the acquisition price. Other motives, such as tax motives, also may play a role in an acquisition decision. These motives and others are critically examined in greater detail in Chapter 15.

MERGER FINANCING

Mergers may be paid for in several ways. Transactions may use all cash, all securities, or a combination of cash and securities. Securities transactions may use the stock of the acquirer as well as other securities such as debentures. The stock may be either common stock or preferred stock. They may be registered, meaning they are able to be freely traded on organized exchanges, or they may be restricted, meaning they cannot be offered for public sale, although private transactions among a limited number of buyers, such as institutional investors, are permissible.

If a bidder offers its stock in exchange for the target's shares, this offer may either provide for a fixed or floating exchange ratio. When the exchange ratio is floating the bidder offers a dollar value of shares as opposed to a specific number of shares. The number of shares that is eventually paid by the bidder is determined by dividing the value offered by the bidder's average stock price during a prespecified period. This period, called the pricing period, is usually some months after the deal is announced and before the closing of the transaction. The offer could also be defined in terms of a "collar" which provides for a maximum and minimum number of shares within the floating value agreement.

Stock transactions may offer the seller certain tax benefits that cash transactions do not provide. However, securities transactions require the parties to agree on the value of the securities. This may create some uncertainty and may give cash an advantage over securities transactions from the seller's point of view. For large deals, all-cash compensation may mean that the bidder has to incur debt, which may carry with it unwanted adverse risk consequences. Although such deals were relatively more common in the 1980s, securities transactions became more popular in the 1990s.

MERGER PROFESSIONALS

When a company decides it wants to acquire or merge with another firm, it typically does so by using the services of outside professionals. These professionals usually include investment bankers, attorneys, accountants, and valuation experts. Investment bankers may provide a variety of services, including helping to select the appropriate target, valuing the target, advising on strategy, and raising the requisite financing to complete the transaction. During the heyday of the fourth merger wave in the 1980s, merger advisory and financing fees were a significant component of the overall profitability of the major investment banks. Table 1.5 shows a ranking of M&A financial advisors.

Investment banks derive fees in various ways from M&As. They may receive advisory fees for their expertise in structuring the deal and handling the strategy—especially in hostile bids. These fees may be contingent on the successful completion of the deal. At that point investment bankers may receive a fee in the range of 1 to 2% of the total value of the transaction. Investment banks also may make money from financing work on M&As. In addition, the investment bank may have an arbitrage department that may profit in ways we will discuss shortly.

The role of investment banks changed somewhat after the fourth merger wave ended. The dealmakers who promoted transactions just to generate fees became unpopular. Companies that were engaged in M&As tended to be more involved in the deals and took over some of the responsibilities that had been relegated to investment bankers in the 1980s. More companies directed the activities of their investment bankers as opposed to merely following their instructions as they did in the prior decade. Managers of corporations decided that they would control their acquisition strategy and for a while this resulted in more strategic and better conceived deals. However, as we will see, managers themselves began to make major merger blunders as we moved through the fifth merger wave.

Rank	Financial Advisor	Total Invested Capital of Deals Worked ($ Billions)	Total Number of Deals
1	Goldman Sachs & Co.	528.218	192
2	Morgan Stanley	458.262	152
3	JP Morgan Chase & Co., Inc.	331.625	147
4	Merrill Lynch & Co., Inc.	296.304	125
5	Lehman Brothers Holdings, Inc.	294.455	113
6	UBS AG	279.358	137
7	Citigroup, Inc.	271.075	145
8	Credit Suisse First Boston, Inc.	238.222	137
9	Deutsche Bank Securities, Inc.	159.243	87
10	Bear, Stearns & Co., Inc.	125.521	50

TABLE 1.5 U.S. FINANCIAL ADVISOR RANKINGS, 1/1/05-12/31/05

Source: Mergerstat Review, 2006

Rank	Legal Advisor	Total Invested Capital of Deals Worked ($ Billions)	Total Number of Deals
1	Simpson Thacher & Bartlett LLP	385.5	118
2	Wachtell Lipton Rosen & Katz	315.5	65
3	Skadden, Arps, Slate, Meagher & Flom LLP	312.9	189
4	Sullivan & Cromwell LLP	299.7	119
5	Shearman & Sterling LLP	273.7	116
6	Weil Gotshal & Manges LLP	269.5	169
7	Cleary Gottlieb Steen & Hamilton LLP	261.6	79
8	Davis Polk & Wardell	239.6	76
9	Latham & Watkins LLP	232.5	208
10	Dewey Ballantine LLP	216.5	101

TABLE 1.6   U.S. LEGAL ADVISOR RANKINGS, 2005
Source: Mergerstat Review, 2006.

Given the complex legal environment that surrounds M&As, attorneys also play a key role in a successful acquisition process. Law firms may be even more important in hostile takeovers than in friendly acquisitions because part of the resistance of the target may come through legal maneuvering. Detailed filings with the Securities and Exchange Commission (SEC) may need to be completed under the guidance of legal experts. In both private and public M&As, there is a legal due diligence process that attorneys should be retained to perform. Table 1.6 shows the leading legal M&A advisors in 2000. Accountants also play an important role in M&As. They have their own accounting due diligence process. In addition, accountants perform various other functions such as preparing pro forma financial statements based on scenarios put forward by management or other professionals. Still another group of professionals who provide important services in M&As are valuation experts. These individuals may be retained by either a bidder or a target to determine the value of a company. We will see in Chapter 14 that these values may vary depending on the assumptions employed. Therefore, valuation experts may build a model that incorporates various assumptions, such as revenue growth rate or costs, which may be eliminated after the deal. As these and other assumptions vary, the resulting value derived from the deal also may change.

MERGER ARBITRAGE

Another group of professionals who can play an important role in takeovers is arbitragers (arbs). Generally, arbitrage refers to the buying of an asset in one market and selling it in another. Risk arbitragers look for price discrepancies between different markets for the same assets and seek to sell in the higher-priced market and buy in the lower one. Practitioners of these kinds of transactions try to do them simultaneously, thus locking in their gains without risk. With respect to M&A, arbitragers purchase stock of companies that may be taken over in the hope of getting a takeover premium when the deal closes. This is referred to as risk arbitrage, as purchasers of shares of targets cannot be certain the deal will be completed. They have evaluated the probability of completion and pursue deals with a sufficiently high probability.

The merger arbitrage business is fraught with risks. When markets turn down and the economy slows, deals are often canceled. This occurred in the late 1980s, when the stock market crashed in 1987 and the junk bond market declined dramatically. The junk bond market was the fuel for many of the debt-laden deals of that period. In addition, when merger waves end, deal volume dries up, lowering the total business available.

Some investment banks have arbitrage departments. However, if an investment bank is advising a client regarding the possible acquisition of a company, it is imperative that a *Chinese wall* between the arbitrage department and the advisors working directly with the client be constructed so that the arbitragers do not benefit from the information that the advisors have but that is not yet readily available to the market. To derive financial benefits from this type of *inside information* is a violation of securities laws.

The arbitrage business has greatly expanded over the past five to ten years. Several active funds specialize in merger arbitrage. These funds may bet on many deals at the same time. They usually purchase the shares after a public announcement of the offer has been made. Shares in these funds can be an attractive investment because their returns may not be as closely correlated with the market as other investments (except in cases of sharp and unexpected downturns).

LEVERAGED BUYOUTS AND THE PRIVATE EQUITY MARKET

In a leveraged buyout (LBO), a buyer uses debt to finance the acquisition of a company. The term is usually reserved, however, for acquisition of public companies where the acquired company becomes private. This is referred to as *going private* because all of the public equity is purchased, usually by a small group or a single buyer, and the company is no longer traded in securities markets. One version of an LBO is a *management buyout*. In a management buyout, the buyer of a company, or a division of a company, is the manager of the entity.

Most LBOs are buyouts of small and medium-sized companies or divisions of large companies. However, in what was then the largest transaction of all time, the 1989 $25.1 billion LBO of RJR Nabisco by Kohlberg Kravis & Roberts shook the financial world. The leveraged buyout business declined after the fourth merger wave but rebounded somewhat in the fifth wave (Exhibit 1.4). There are several reasons for this, including the collapse of the junk bond market. These issues are discussed at length in Chapters 7 and 8. However, the LBO business rebounded in the fifth merger wave and then took off in the mid-2000s. In 2005 and 2006, we saw the return of the mega-LBO. In addition, this business became a truly global one by that time.

LBOs utilize a significant amount of debt along with an equity investment. Often this equity investment comes from investment pools created by *private equity* firms. These firms solicit investments from institutional investors. The monies are used to acquire equity positions in various companies. Sometimes these private equity buyers acquire

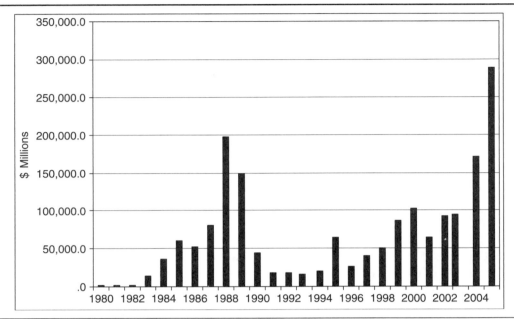

EXHIBIT 1.4   WORLDWIDE LEVERAGED BUYOUTS IN DOLLAR VALUE, 1980–2004
Source: Thomson Financial Securities Data.

entire companies, while in other instances they take equity positions in companies. Sometimes they may use some of their equity, which they may combine with a significant
amount of debt to pursue an LBO. The private equity business has grown significantly
in recent years. We will discuss this further in Chapter 8.

CORPORATE RESTRUCTURING

Users of the term *corporate restructuring* usually are referring to asset selloffs such as
divestitures. Companies that have acquired other firms or have developed other divisions through activities such as product extensions may decide that these divisions no
longer fit into the company's plans. The desire to sell parts of a company may come
from poor performance of a division, financial exigency, or a change in the strategic
orientation of the company. For example, the company may decide to refocus on its
core business and sell off noncore subsidiaries. This type of activity increased after the
end of the third merger wave as many companies that engaged in diverse acquisition
campaigns to build conglomerates began to question the advisability of these combinations. There are several forms of corporate selloffs, with divestitures being only one
kind. Spin-offs enjoyed increased popularity in the early 1990s, while equity carve-
outs provided another way that selloffs could be accomplished. The relative benefits
of each of these alternative means of selling off part of a company are discussed in
Chapter 10.

Other forms of corporate restructuring are cost and workforce restructuring. In the
1990s, we saw many companies engage in *corporate downsizing* as they strove to become

more efficient. This was encouraged by several factors, including the 1990–91 recession and the international competitive pressure of the globalization of world markets. Another form of corporate restructuring is *financial restructuring,* which refers to alterations in the capital structure of the firm, such as adding debt and thereby increasing financial leverage. Although this type of restructuring is important in corporate finance and is often done as part of the financing activities for M&As, it is not treated in this text as a form of corporate restructuring. Rather, the term *restructuring* is reserved for the more physical forms of restructuring such as divestitures.

MERGER NEGOTIATIONS

Most M&As are negotiated in a friendly environment. The process usually begins when the management of one firm contacts the target company's management, often through the investment bankers of each firm. The management of both firms keep the respective boards of directors up-to-date on the progress of the negotiations because mergers usually require the boards' approval. Sometimes this process works smoothly and leads to a quick merger agreement. A good example of this was the 1995 $19 billion acquisition of Capital Cities/ABC Inc. by Walt Disney Co. In spite of the size of this deal, there was a quick meeting of the minds by management of these two firms and a friendly deal was completed relatively quickly. Perhaps the speed with which these managers pushed this deal through was too fast, as the combination left much to be desired and the synergies between the two companies were often hard to see. A quick deal may not be the best. The AT&T acquisition of TCI is another good example of a friendly deal where the buyer did not do its homework and the seller did a good job of accommodating the buyer's (AT&T's) desire to do a quick deal at a higher price. Speed may help ward off unwanted bidders but it may work against a close scrutiny of the transaction.

Sometimes friendly negotiations may break down, leading to the termination of the bid or a hostile takeover. An example of a negotiated deal that failed and led to a hostile bid was the 1995 tender offer by Moore Corporation for Wallace Computer Services, Inc. Here negotiations between two archrivals in the business forms and printing business proceeded for five months before they were called off, leading to a $1.3 billion hostile bid. In other instances a bid is opposed by the target right away and the transaction quickly becomes a hostile one. A good example was the 2004 hostile bid by Oracle for PeopleSoft. This takeover battle was unusual for its protracted length. The battle went on for approximately a year before PeopleSoft finally capitulated and accepted a higher Oracle bid.

Except for hostile transactions, mergers usually are the product of a negotiation process between the managements of the merging companies. The bidding firm typically initiates the negotiations when it contacts the target's management to inquire whether the company is for sale and to express its interest in buying the target. This interest may be the product of an extensive search process to find the right acquisition candidates. However, it could be a recent interest inspired by the bidder's investment bank approaching it with a proposal that it believes would be a good fit for the bidder. For small-scale acquisitions, this intermediary might be a business broker.

Most merger agreements include a *material adverse change* clause. This clause may allow either party to withdraw from the deal if a major change in circumstances arises that would alter the value of the deal. This occurred in late 2005, when Johnson & Johnson (J&J) stated that it wanted to terminate its $25.4 billion purchase of Guidant Corporation after Guidant's problems with recalls of heart devices it marketed became more pronounced. J&J, which still felt the criticism that it had paid too much for its largest prior acquisition, Alza, which it acquired in 2001 for $12.3 billion, did not want to overpay for a company that might have unpredictable liabilities that would erode its value over time. J&J and Guidant exchanged legal threats but eventually agreed on a lower value of $21.5 billion. J&J's strategy of using the material adverse change clause to get a better price backfired, as it opened the door for Boston Scientific to make an alternative offer and eventually outbid J&J for Guidant with a $27 billion final offer.

Both the bidder and the target should conduct their own valuation analyses to determine what the target is worth. As discussed in Chapter 14, the value of the target for the buyer may be different from the value of that company for the seller. Valuations can differ due to varying uses of the target assets or different opinions on the future growth of the target. If the target believes that it is worth substantially more than what the buyer is willing to pay, a friendly deal may not be possible. If, however, the seller is interested in selling and both parties are able to reach an agreement on price, a deal may be possible. Other important issues, such as financial and regulatory approvals, if necessary, would have to be completed before the negotiation process could lead to a completed transaction.

When two companies engage in M&As they often enter into confidentiality agreements which allow them to exchange confidential information that may enable the parties to better understand the value of the deal. Following the eventual sale of Guidant to second bidder Boston Scientific for $27 billion, J&J sued Boston Scientific and Abbott Laboratories in September, 2006. J&J alleged that Guidant leaked confidential information to Abbott which had agreed to purchase Guidant's cardiac stent business for approximately $4 billion thereby reducing antitrust concerns. J&J alleged Guidant's release of this information violated its original agreement with J&J. This underscores another risk of M&A—the release of valuable internal information.

Disclosure of Merger Negotiations

Before 1988, it was not clear what obligations companies involved in merger negotiations had to disclose their activities. However, in 1988, in the landmark *Basic Inc. v. Levinson* decision, the U.S. Supreme Court made it clear that a denial that negotiations are taking place when the opposite is the case is improper. Companies may not deceive the market by disseminating inaccurate or deceptive information, even when the discussions are preliminary and do not show much promise of coming to fruition. The Court's position reversed earlier positions that had treated proposals or negotiations as being immaterial. The *Basic v. Levinson* decision does not go so far as to require companies to disclose all plans or internal proposals involving acquisitions. Negotiations between two potential merger partners, however, may not be denied. The exact timing of the disclosure is still not clear. Given the requirement to disclose, a company's hand may be forced by the pressure of market speculation. It is often difficult to confidentially continue such negotiations and planning for any length of time. Rather than let the information slowly leak, the company has an obligation to conduct an orderly disclosure once it is clear that confidentiality may be at risk or that prior statements the company has made are no longer accurate. In cases in which there is speculation that a takeover is being planned, significant market movements in stock prices of the companies involved—particularly the target—may occur. Such market movements may give rise to an inquiry from the exchange on which the company trades or from the National Association of Securities Dealers (NASD). Although exchanges have come under criticism for being somewhat lax about enforcing these types of rules, an insufficient response from the companies involved may give rise to disciplinary actions against the companies.

MERGER APPROVAL PROCEDURES

In the United States, each state has a statute that authorizes M&As of corporations. The rules may be different for domestic and foreign corporations. Once the board of directors of each company reaches an agreement, they adopt a resolution approving the deal. This resolution should include the names of the companies involved in the deal and the name of the new company. The resolution should include the financial terms of the deal and other relevant information such as the method that is to be used to convert securities of each company into securities of the surviving corporation. If there are any changes in the articles of incorporation, these should be referenced in the resolution.

At this point the deal is taken to the shareholders for approval. Friendly deals that are a product of a free negotiation process between the management of two companies are typically approved by shareholders. A recent exception to that was the refusal of a majority of the shareholders of VNU NV, a Dutch publishing company, to approve the 2005 $7 billion proposed acquisition of IMS Health, Inc., a pharmaceutical research publisher. VNU shareholders questioned the logic of the acquisition, and this left VNU in the difficult position of having to back out of the deal without having to pay IMS for the expenses it incurred. It is ironic that VNU shareholders turned down an acquisition of IMS, as this is just what IMS shareholders did in 2000 when its own shareholders turned down a sale of the company to the Tri-Zetto Group, Inc.

Following shareholder approval, the merger plan must be submitted to the relevant state official, usually the secretary of state. The document that contains this plan is called the *articles for merger or consolidation*. Once the state official determines that the proper documentation has been received, it issues a certificate of merger or consolidation. SEC rules require a proxy solicitation to be accompanied by a Schedule 14A. Item 14 of this schedule sets forth the specific information that must be included in a proxy statement when there will be a vote for an approval of a merger, sale of substantial assets, or liquidation or dissolution of the corporation. For a merger, this information must include the terms and reasons for the transaction as well as a description of the accounting treatment and tax consequences of the deal. Financial statements and a statement regarding relevant state and federal regulatory compliance are required. Fairness opinions and other related documents also must be included.

Special Committees of the Board of Directors

The board of directors may choose to form a special committee of the board to evaluate the merger proposal. Directors who might personally benefit from the merger, such as when the buyout proposal contains provisions that management directors may potentially profit from the deal, should not be members of this committee. The more complex the transaction, the more likely that a committee will be appointed. This committee should seek legal counsel to guide it on legal issues such as the fairness of the transaction, the business judgment rule, and numerous other legal issues. The committee, and the board in general, needs to make sure that it carefully considers all relevant aspects of the transaction. A court may later scrutinize the decision-making process, such as what occurred in the *Smith v. Van Gorkom* case (see Chapter 14). In that case the court found the directors personally liable because it thought that the decision-making process was inadequate, even though the decision itself was apparently a good one for shareholders.

Fairness Opinions

It is common for the board to retain an outside valuation firm, such as an investment bank or a firm that specializes in valuations, to evaluate the transaction's terms and price. This firm may then render a fairness opinion in which it may state that the offer is in a range that it determines to be accurate. This became even more important after the *Smith v. Van Gorkom* decision, which places directors under greater scrutiny. Directors may seek to avoid these legal pressures by soliciting a fairness opinion from an accepted authority.

According to one survey, for deals valued at less than $5 billion, the average fairness opinion fee was $600,000, whereas for deals valued at more than $5 billion, the average fairness opinion fee was $4.6 million.[1] These opinions may be somewhat terse and usually feature a limited discussion of the underlying financial analysis. As part of the opinion that is rendered, the evaluator should state what was investigated and verified and what was not. The fees received and any potential conflicts of interest should also be revealed.

Voting Approval

Upon reaching agreeable terms and receiving board approval, the deal is taken before the shareholders for their approval, which is granted through a vote. The exact percentage necessary for stockholder approval depends on the articles of incorporation, which in turn are regulated by the prevailing state corporation laws. Following approval, each firm files the necessary documents with the state authorities in which each firm is incorporated. Once this step is completed and the compensation has changed hands, the deal is completed.

SHORT-FORM MERGER

A short-form merger may take place in situations in which the stockholder approval process is not necessary. Stockholder approval may be bypassed when the corporation's

---

1. *The Daily Deal,* February 28, 2001. Source: CommScan/Computsoft Research Ltd., New York.

stock is concentrated in the hands of a small group, such as management, which is advocating the merger. Some state laws may allow this group to approve the transaction on its own without soliciting the approval of the other stockholders. The board of directors simply approves the merger by a resolution.

A short-form merger may occur only when the stockholdings of insiders are beyond a certain threshold stipulated in the prevailing state corporation laws. This percentage varies depending on the state in which the company is incorporated, but it usually is in the 90 to 95% range. Under Delaware law the short-form merger percentage is 90%.

FREEZEOUTS AND THE TREATMENT OF MINORITY SHAREHOLDERS

Typically, a majority of shareholders must provide their approval before a merger can be completed. A 51% margin is a common majority threshold. When this majority approves the deal, minority shareholders are required to tender their shares, even though they did not vote in favor of the deal. Minority shareholders are said to be *frozen out* of their positions. This majority approval requirement is designed to prevent a *holdout problem,* which may occur when a minority attempts to hold up the completion of a transaction unless they receive compensation over and above the acquisition stock price. This is not to say that dissenting shareholders are without rights. Those shareholders who believe that their shares are worth significantly more than what the terms of the merger are offering may go to court to pursue their *shareholder appraisal rights.* To successfully pursue these rights, dissenting shareholders must follow the proper procedures. Paramount among these procedures is the requirement that the dissenting shareholders object to the deal within the designated period of time. Then they may demand a cash settlement for the difference between the "fair value" of their shares and the compensation they actually received. Of course, corporations resist these maneuvers because the payment of cash for the value of shares will raise problems relating to the positions of other stockholders. Such suits are very difficult for dissenting shareholders to win. Dissenting shareholders may file a suit only if the corporation does not file suit to have the fair value of the shares determined, after having been notified of the dissenting shareholders' objections. If there is a suit, the court may appoint an appraiser to assist in the determination of the fair value.

PURCHASE OF ASSETS COMPARED WITH PURCHASE OF STOCK

The most common form of merger or acquisition involves purchasing the stock of the merged or acquired concern. An alternative to the stock acquisition is to purchase the target company's assets. In doing so, the acquiring company can limit its acquisitions to those parts of the firm that coincide with the acquirer's needs. When a significant part of the target remains after the asset acquisition, the transaction is only a partial acquisition of the target. When all the target's assets are purchased, the target becomes a corporate shell with only the cash or securities that it received from the acquisition as assets. In these situations, the corporation may choose to pay stockholders a liquidating dividend and dissolve the company. Alternatively, the firm may use its liquid assets to purchase other assets or another company.

STRUCTURING THE DEAL

Most deals employ a *triangular structure* utilizing a subsidiary corporation that is created by the buyer to facilitate the acquisition of the target. The acquirer creates a shell subsidiary whose shares are purchased with cash or stock of the parent. This cash or stock is then used to acquire either the assets or the stock of the target company. If the assets of the target are acquired, then the surviving target corporation is usually liquidated. If the shares of the target are acquired, the target corporation then merges with the subsidiary, which now has the assets and liabilities of the target. When the subsidiary survives the merger, this structure is sometimes referred to as a forward triangular merger. Another alternative is a reverse triangular merger, where the subsidiary is merged with the target and does not survive the merger but the target corporation does. The advantage of using subsidiaries and this triangular structure is that the acquirer gains control of the target without directly assuming the known, and potentially unknown, liabilities of the target.

ASSUMPTION OF THE SELLER'S LIABILITIES

If the acquirer buys all the target's stock, it assumes the seller's liabilities. The change in stock ownership does not free the new owners of the stock from the seller's liabilities. Most state laws provide this protection, which is sometimes referred to as *successor liability*. An acquirer may try to avoid assuming the seller's liabilities by buying only the assets rather than the stock of the target. In cases in which a buyer purchases a substantial portion of the target's assets, the courts have ruled that the buyer is responsible for the seller's liabilities. This is known as the *trust funds doctrine*. The court may also rule that the transaction is a *de facto* merger—a merger that occurs when the buyer purchases the assets of the target, and, for all intents and purposes, the transaction is treated as a merger. The issue of successor liability may also apply to other commitments of the firm, such as union contracts. The National Labor Relations Board's position on this issue is that collective bargaining agreements are still in effect after acquisitions. As we have noted, sellers try to separate the target corporation's liabilities from their own by keeping them in a different corporation through the use of a triangular deal structure that utilizes a subsidiary corporation.

ADVANTAGES OF ASSET ACQUISITIONS

One of the advantages of an asset acquisition, as opposed to a stock acquisition, is that the bidder may not have to gain the approval of its shareholders. Such approval usually is necessary only when the assets of the target are purchased using shares of the bidder and when the bidder does not already have sufficient shares authorized to complete the transaction. If there are not sufficient shares authorized, the bidder may have to take the necessary steps, which may include amending the articles of incorporation, to gain approval. This is very different from the position of the target company, where its shareholders may have to approve the sale of a substantial amount of the company's assets. The necessary shareholder approval percentage is usually the same as for stock acquisitions.

ASSET SELLOFFS

When a corporation chooses to sell off all its assets to another company, it becomes a corporate shell with cash and/or securities as its sole assets. The firm may then decide to distribute the cash to its stockholders as a liquidating dividend and go out of existence. The proceeds of the assets sale may also be distributed through a *cash repurchase tender offer*. That is, the firm makes a tender offer for its own shares using the proceeds of the asset sale to pay for shares. The firm may also choose to continue to do business and use its liquid assets to purchase other assets or companies. Firms that choose to remain in existence without assets are subject to the Investment Company Act of 1940. This law, one of a series of securities laws passed in the wake of the Great Depression and the associated stock market crash of 1929, applies when 100 or more stockholders remain after the sale of the assets. It requires that investment companies register with the SEC and adhere to its regulations applying to investment companies. The law also establishes standards that regulate investment companies. Specifically, it covers:

- Promotion of the investment company's activities
- Reporting requirements
- Pricing of securities for sale to the public
- Issuance of prospectuses for sales of securities
- Allocation of assets within the investment company's portfolio

If a company that sells off all its assets chooses to invest the proceeds of the asset sale in Treasury bills, these investments are not regulated by the Act. There are two kinds of investment companies: *open-end investment companies* and *closed-end investment companies*. Open-end investment companies, commonly referred to as mutual funds, issue shares that are equal to the value of the fund divided by the number of shares that are bought, after taking into account the costs of running the fund. The number of shares in a mutual fund increases or decreases depending on the number of new shares sold or the redemption of shares already issued. Closed-end investment companies generally do not issue new shares after the initial issuance. The value of these shares is determined by the value of the investments that are made using the proceeds of the initial share offering.

REVERSE MERGERS

A reverse merger is a merger in which a private company may go public by merging with an already public company that often is inactive or a corporate shell. The combined company may then issue securities and may not have to incur all of the costs and scrutiny that normally would be associated with an initial public offering. The private company then has greatly enhanced liquidity for its equity. Another advantage is that the process can take place quickly. In addition, the private company's shares are publicly traded after the deal, and that can be more attractive to other targets that the bidder may be pursuing. Most reverse mergers involve smaller companies that are looking for a less expensive way of going public. An example of a recent reverse merger was the March 2001 $229 million reverse merger involving Ariel Corporation and Mayan Network Corp. Under this deal, Mayan acquired Ariel. Mayan shareholders owned 90% of the combined company, while

Ariel shareholders owned the remaining 10%. One unusual aspect of this reverse merger was its size, as most such deals involve smaller firms. The deal presented benefits for both companies because it allowed Mayan, a company that only recently had signed up its first two customers, to tap public markets, while giving Ariel, whose stock price and financing were weak, an opportunity to improve its financial condition.[2]

HOLDING COMPANIES

Rather than a merger or an acquisition, the acquiring company may choose to purchase only a portion of the target's stock and act as a *holding company,* which is a company that owns sufficient stock to have a controlling interest in the target. Holding companies trace their origins back to 1889, when New Jersey became the first state to pass a law that allowed corporations to be formed for the express purpose of owning stock in other corporations. If an acquirer buys 100% of the target, the company is known as a *wholly owned subsidiary.* However, it is not necessary to own all of a company's stock to exert control over it. In fact, even a 51% interest may not be necessary to allow a buyer to control a target. For companies with a widely distributed equity base, effective working control can be established with as little as 10 to 20% of the outstanding common stock.

Advantages

Holding companies have certain advantages that may make this form of control transaction preferable to an outright acquisition. Some of these advantages are:

- *Lower cost.* With a holding company structure, an acquirer may be able to attain control of a target for a much smaller investment than would be necessary in a 100% stock acquisition. Obviously, a smaller number of shares to be purchased permits a lower total purchase price to be set. In addition, because fewer shares are demanded in the market, there is less upward price pressure on the firm's stock and the cost per share may be lower. The acquirer may attempt to minimize the upward price pressure by gradually buying shares over an extended period of time.
- *No control premium.* Because 51% of the shares were not purchased, the control premium that is normally associated with 51 to 100% stock acquisitions may not have to be paid.
- *Control with fractional ownership.* As noted, working control may be established with less than 51% of the target company's shares. This may allow the controlling company to exert certain influence over the target in a manner that will further the controlling company's objectives.
- *Approval not required.* To the extent that it is allowable under federal and state laws, a holding company may simply purchase shares in a target without having to solicit the approval of the target company's shareholders. As discussed in Chapter 3, this has become more difficult to accomplish because various laws make it difficult for the holding company to achieve such control if serious shareholder opposition exists.

---

2. Danny Forsten, "Mayan Snares Ariel in $229 Million Reverse Merger," *The Daily Deal,* 30 March 2001, p. 1.

Disadvantages

Holding companies also have disadvantages that make this type of transaction attractive only under certain circumstances. Some of these disadvantages are:

- *Multiple taxation.* The holding company structure adds another layer to the corporate structure. Normally, stockholder income is subject to double taxation. Income is taxed at the corporate level, and some of the remaining income may then be distributed to stockholders in the form of dividends. Stockholders are then taxed individually on this dividend income. Holding companies receive dividend income from a company that has already been taxed at the corporate level. This income may then be taxed at the holding company level before it is distributed to stockholders. This amounts to *triple taxation* of corporate income. However, if the holding company owns 80% or more of a subsidiary's voting equity, the Internal Revenue Service allows filing of consolidated returns in which the dividends received from the parent company are not taxed. When the ownership interest is less than 80%, returns cannot be consolidated, but between 70 and 80% of the dividends are not subject to taxation.
- *Antitrust issues.* A holding company combination may face some of the same antitrust concerns with which an outright acquisition is faced. If the regulatory authorities do find the holding company structure anticompetitive, however, it is comparatively easy to require the holding company to divest itself of its holdings in the target. Given the ease with which this can be accomplished, the regulatory authorities may be more quick to require this compared with a more integrated corporate structure.
- *Lack of 100% ownership.* Although the fact that a holding company can be formed without a 100% share purchase may be a source of cost savings, it leaves the holding company with other outside shareholders who will have some controlling influence in the company. This may lead to disagreements over the direction of the company.

Special Purchase Acquisition Vehicles

Special purchase acquisition vehicles (SPACs) are companies that raise capital in an initial public offering (IPO) where the funds are earmarked for acquisitions. Usually between 80% to 90% of the funds are placed in a trust which earns a rate of return while the company seeks to invest the monies in acquisitions. The remainder of the monies are used to pay expenses. Shareholders usually have the right to reject proposed deals. In addition, if the company fails to complete acquisitions the monies are returned to investors less expenses and plus an return earned in the capital.

Such investments can be risky for investors as it is possible that the company may not complete an acquisition. If that is the case investors could get back less monies than they originally invested. Even when the company does complete deals they do not know in advance what targets will be acquired.

The IPO offerings of SPACs are unique are differ in many ways from traditional IPOs. In addition to the differences in the nature of the company which we have discussed, they usually sell in "units" which include a share and one or two warrants which usually detach from the shares and trade separately a couple of weeks after the IPO. Because the market for these shares can be illiquid, they often trade at a discount—similar to many closed end funds. The post-IPO securities can be interesting investments as they represent shares in an entity which hold a known amount of cash but which trades at a value that may be less than this amount.

2

HISTORY OF MERGERS

In much of finance there is very little attention paid to the history of the field. Rather the focus usually is on the latest developments and innovations. This seems to be particularly the case in the United States, where there is less respect for that which is not new. It is not surprising then that we see that many of the mistakes and types of failed deals that occurred in earlier years tend to be repeated. The market seems to have a short memory and we see that a pattern of flawed mergers and acquisitions (M&As) tends to reoccur. It is for this reason that we need to be aware of the history of the field. Such an awareness will help us identify the types of deals that have been problematic in the past.

There have been many interesting trends in recent M&A history. These include the fact that M&A has become a worldwide phenomena as opposed to being mainly centered in the United States. Other trends include the rise of the emerging market acquirer, which has brought a very different type of bidder to the takeover scene. For these reasons we will devote special attention in this chapter to these important trends in recent M&A history.

MERGER WAVES

Five periods of high merger activity, often called merger waves, have taken place in the history of the United States. These periods were characterized by cyclic activity, that is, high levels of mergers followed by periods of relatively fewer deals. The first four waves occurred between 1897 and 1904, 1916 and 1929, 1965 and 1969, and 1984 and 1989. Merger activity declined at the end of the 1980s but resumed again in the early 1990s to begin the fifth merger wave. The various merger waves provoked major changes in the structure of American business. They were instrumental in transforming American industry from a collection of small and medium-sized businesses to the current form, which includes thousands of multinational corporations. This chapter focuses more closely on the later merger periods because they are, of course, more relevant to recent trends in the world of mergers.

WHAT CAUSES MERGER WAVES?

Research has showed that merger waves tend to be caused by a combination of economic, regulatory, and technological shocks.[1] The economic shock comes in the form of

---

1. Mark Mitchell and J. H. Mulherin, "The Impact of Industry Shocks on Takeover and Restructuring Activity," *Journal of Financial Economics*, 41, 1996, 193–229.

an economic expansion that motivates companies to expand to meet the rapidly growing aggregate demand in the economy. M&A is a faster form of expansion than internal, organic growth. Regulatory shocks can occur through the elimination of regulatory barriers that might have prevented corporate combinations. Examples include the changes in U.S. banking laws that prevented banks from crossing state lines or entering other industries. Technological shocks can come in many forms as technological change can bring about dramatic changes in existing industries and can even create new ones. Harford showed that these various shocks by themselves are generally not enough to bring about a merger wave.[2] He looked at industry waves, rather than the overall level of M&A activity, over the period 1981–2000. His research on 35 industry waves that occurred in this period showed that capital liquidity was also a necessary condition for a wave to take hold. His findings also found that misevaluation or market timing efforts by managers was not a cause of a wave, although it could be a cause in specific deals. The misevaluation findings, however, were contradicted by Rhodes-Kropf, Robinson, and Viswanathan, who found that misevaluation and valuation errors do motivate merger activity.[3] They measure these by comparing market to book ratios to true valuations. These authors do not say that valuation errors are the sole factor in explaining merger waves but that they can play an important role that gains in prominence the greater the degree of misevaluation.

FIRST WAVE, 1897–1904

The first merger wave occurred after the Depression of 1883, peaked between 1898 and 1902, and ended in 1904 (Table 2.1 and Exhibit 2.1). Although these mergers affected all major mining and manufacturing industries, certain industries clearly demonstrated a higher incidence of merger activity.[4] According to a National Bureau of Economic Research study by Professor Ralph Nelson, eight industries—primary metals, food products, petroleum products, chemicals, transportation equipment, fabricated metal products, machinery, and bituminous coal—experienced the greatest merger activity. These industries accounted for approximately two-thirds of all mergers during this period. The mergers of the first wave were predominantly horizontal combinations (Table 2.2 and Exhibit 2.2). The many horizontal mergers and industry consolidations of this era often resulted in a near monopolistic market structure. For this reason, this merger period is known for its role in creating large monopolies. This period is also associated with the first billion-dollar megamerger when U.S. Steel was founded by J. P. Morgan, who combined Carnegie Steel, founded by Andrew Carnegie and run by he and Henry Clay Frick, with Federal Steel, which Morgan controlled. However, Morgan also added other steel companies, such as American Tin Plate, American Steel Hoop, American Steel Sheet, American Bridge, American Steel and Wire, International Mercantile Marine, National Steel, National Tube, and Shelby Steel Tube. Combined together under the corporate

2. Jarrad Harford, "What Drives Merger Waves," *Journal of Financial Economics*, 77(3), September 2005, 529–560.
3. Matthew Rhodes-Kropf, David T. Robinson, and S. Viswanathan, "Valuation Waves and Merger Activity: The Empirical Evidence," *Journal of Financial Economics*, 77(3), September 2005, 561–603.
4. Ralph Nelson, *Merger Movements in American Industry: 1895–1956* (Princeton, NJ: Princeton University Press, 1959).

Year	Number of Mergers
1897	69
1898	303
1899	1,208
1900	340
1901	423
1902	379
1903	142
1904	79

TABLE 2.1   MERGERS, 1897–1904

Source: Merrill Lynch Business Brokerage and Valuation, *Mergerstat Review,* 1989.

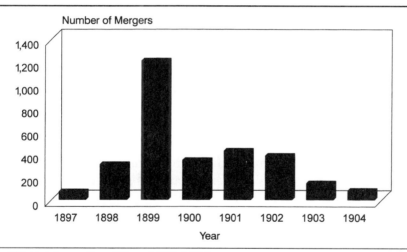

EXHIBIT 2.1   MERGERS OF THE FIRST WAVE, 1897–1904

Type of Merger	Percentage (%)
Horizontal	78.3
Vertical	12.0
Horizontal and Vertical	9.7
Total	100.0

TABLE 2.2   MERGERS BY TYPES, 1895–1904

Source: Neil Fligstein, *The Transformation of Corporate Control* (Cambridge, Mass.: Harvard University Press, 1990), p. 72.

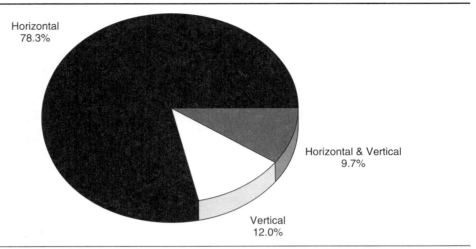

EXHIBIT 2.2   MERGERS OF THE FIRST WAVE BY TYPE
Source: Nelson 1959 and Neil Fligstein, *The Transformation of Corporate Control* (Cambridge, MA: Harvard University Press, 1990), p. 72.

umbrella of U.S. Steel, the company controlled one half of the U.S. steel industry.[5] The resulting steel giant merged 785 separate steel making operations. At one time, U.S. Steel accounted for as much as 75% of U.S. steel-making capacity.

Besides U.S. Steel, some of today's great industrial giants originated in the first merger wave. These include DuPont Inc., Standard Oil, General Electric, Eastman Kodak, American Tobacco Inc. (merged with Brown and Williamson in 1994, which in turn merged with RJ Reynolds in 2004), and Navistar International (formerly International Harvester but became Navistar in 1986 when it sold its agricultural business). While these companies are major corporations today with large market shares, some were truly dominant firms by the end of the first merger wave. For example, U.S. Steel was not the only corporation to dominate its market. American Tobacco enjoyed a 90% market share, and Standard Oil, owned by J. D. Rockefeller, commanded 85% of its market. In the first merger movement, there were 300 major combinations covering many industrial areas and controlling 40% of the nation's manufacturing capital. Nelson estimates that in excess of 3,000 companies disappeared during this period as a result of mergers.

By 1909, the 100 largest industrial corporations controlled nearly 18% of the assets of all industrial corporations. Even the enactment of the Sherman Antitrust Act (1890) did not impede this period of intense activity. The Justice Department was largely responsible for the limited impact of the Sherman Act. During the period of major consolidation of the early 1900s, the Justice Department, charged with enforcing the Act, was understaffed and unable to aggressively pursue antitrust enforcement. The agency's activities were directed more toward labor unions. Therefore, the pace of horizontal mergers and industry consolidations continued unabated without any meaningful antitrust restrictions.

---

5.   Ron Chernow, *The House of Morgan* (New York: Grove Press, 1990).

By the end of the first great merger wave, a marked increase in the degree of concentration was evident in American industry. The number of firms in some industries, such as the steel industry, declined dramatically, and in some sectors only one firm survived. It is ironic that monopolistic industries formed in light of the passage of the Sherman Act. However, in addition to the Justice Department's lack of resources, the courts initially were unwilling to literally interpret the antimonopoly provisions of the Act. For example, in 1895, the U.S. Supreme Court ruled that the American Sugar Refining Company was not a monopoly and did not restrain trade.[6] At this time, the Supreme Court was not concerned by the fact that the Sugar Trust controlled 98% of the sugar refining capacity in the United States. This favorable ruling gave the green light to companies such as DuPont, Eastman Kodak, General Electric, International Harvester, Standard Oil, and U.S. Steel to engage in M&A without being concerned about legal interference.[7] The courts initially saw the Sherman Act's focus to be on regulating stockholder trusts, in which investors would invest funds in a firm and entrust their stock certificates with directors who would ensure that they received dividends for their "trust certificates."

With a misguided focus on trusts, the law was not applied to hinder the formation of monopolies in several industries in the first merger wave. The trusts were formed by dominant business leaders, such as J. P. Morgan of the House of Morgan and John D. Rockefeller of Standard Oil and National City Bank, as a response to the poor performance of many of the nation's businesses as they struggled with the weak economic climate. They saw the structure of many industries, which included many small and inefficient companies, as part of the reason for this poor performance. They reorganized failing companies in various industries by forcing shareholders to exchange their equity in troubled companies for trust certificates in a holding company that would control the business in question but also many other competitors. With such control, J. P. Morgan was able to rein in intense competition that he saw was rendering companies in many industries weak. In doing so he was able to give investors confidence in the soundness of companies for which he and others were seeking to market securities. His main initial focus was the railroad industry, which at that time accounted for the majority of stocks traded on the New York Stock Exchange. Being an industry with large demands for capital, railroad companies aggressively marketed stocks and bonds through investment bankers across the United States and in Europe. However, railroad companies were prone to compete aggressively on rates and sought to drive each other to the brink of bankruptcy. Morgan hated such unrestrained competition and sought to reorganize this industry, and eventually others, using holding company trusts that would push aside aggressive competitor managers and replace them with those who would preside over a more orderly market. Morgan did not consider that consumers would suffer from these consolidations as his focus was on investors who would seek to benefit.

Trusts grew and came to dominate many industries. Among them were the American Cottonseed Oil Trust and the National Lead Trust, which dominated their respective industries. Morgan Bank, in turn, controlled First National Bank, the National Bank of

---

6. Joseph R. Conlin, *The American Past* (Fort Worth, TX: Harcourt Press, 1997), p. 500.
7. George Stigler, "Monopoly and Oligopoly by Merger," *American Economic Review*, 40, May 1950, 23–34.

Commerce, the First National Bank of Chicago, Liberty National Bank, Chase National Bank, Hanover National Bank, and the Astor National Bank.[8]

In addition to lax enforcement of federal antitrust laws, other legal reasons explain why the first merger wave thrived. For example, in some states, corporation laws were gradually relaxed. In particular, corporations became better able to secure capital, hold stock in other corporations, and expand their lines of business operations, thereby creating a fertile environment for firms to contemplate mergers. Greater access to capital made it easier for firms to raise the necessary financing to carry out an acquisition, and relaxed rules controlling the stockholdings of corporations allowed firms to acquire the stock in other companies with the purpose of acquiring them.

Not all states liberalized corporate laws. As a result, the pace of M&As was greater in some states than in others. New Jersey, in which the passage of the New Jersey Holding Company Act of 1888 helped liberalize state corporation laws, was the leading state in M&As, followed by New York and Delaware. The law enabled holding company trusts to be formed and the State of New Jersey became a mecca for this corporate form. This Act pressured other states to enact similar legislation rather than see firms move to reincorporate in New Jersey. Many firms, however, did choose to incorporate in New Jersey, which explains the wide variety of New Jersey firms that participated in the first merger wave. This trend declined dramatically by 1915, when the differences in state corporation laws became less significant.

The development of the U.S. transportation system was another of the major factors that initiated the first merger wave. Following the Civil War, the establishment of a major railway system helped create national rather than regional markets that firms could potentially serve. Transcontinental railroads, such as the Union Pacific–Central Pacific, which was completed in 1869, linked the western United States with the rest of the country. Many firms, no longer viewing market potential as being limited by narrowly defined market boundaries, expanded to take advantage of a now broader-based market. Companies now facing competition from distant rivals chose to merge with local competitors to maintain their market share. Changes in the national transportation system made supplying distant markets both easier and less expensive. The cost of rail freight transportation fell at an average rate of 3.7% per year from 1882 to 1900.[9] In the early 1900s, transportation costs increased very little despite a rising demand for transportation services.

Several other structural changes helped firms service national markets. For example, the invention of the Bonsack continuous process cigarette machine enabled the American Tobacco Company to supply the nation's cigarette market with a relatively small number of machines.[10] As firms expanded, they exploited economies of scale in production and distribution. For example, the Standard Oil Trust controlled 40% of the world's oil production by using only three refineries. It eliminated unnecessary plants and thereby achieved

---

8. Nell Irvin Painter, *Standing at Armageddon: The United States, 1877–1919* (New York: Norton, 1987), pp. 178–179.
9. Ibid.
10. Alfred D. Chandler, *The Visible Hand: The Managerial Revolution in American Business* (Cambridge, MA: Belknap Press, 1977), p. 249.

greater efficiency.[11] A similar process of expansion in the pursuit of scale economies took place in many manufacturing industries in the U.S. economy during this time. Companies and their managers began to study the production process in an effort to enhance their ability to engage in ever-expanding mass production.[12] The expansion of the scale of business also required greater managerial skills and led to further specialization of management.

As mentioned, the first merger wave did not start until 1897, but the first great *takeover battle* began much earlier—in 1868. Although the term *takeover battle* is commonly used today to describe the sometimes acerbic conflicts among firms in takeovers, it can be more literally applied to the conflicts that occurred in early corporate mergers. One such takeover contest involved an attempt to take control of the Erie Railroad in 1868. The takeover attempt pitted Cornelius Vanderbilt against Daniel Drew, Jim Fisk, and Jay Gould. As one of their major takeover defenses, the defenders of the Erie Railroad issued themselves large quantities of stock, even though they lacked the authorization to do so. At that time, because bribery of judges and elected officials was common, legal remedies for violating corporate laws were particularly weak. The battle for control of the railroad took a violent turn when the target corporation hired guards, equipped with firearms and cannons, to protect its headquarters. The takeover attempt ended when Vanderbilt abandoned his assault on the Erie Railroad and turned his attention to weaker targets.

In the late nineteenth century, as a result of such takeover contests, the public became increasingly concerned about unethical business practices. Corporate laws were not particularly effective during the 1890s. In response to many antirailroad protests, Congress established the Interstate Commerce Commission in 1897. The Harrison, Cleveland, and McKinley administrations (1889–1901) were all very pro-business and filled the commission with supporters of the very railroads they were elected to regulate. Not until the passage of antitrust legislation in the late 1800s and early 1900s, and tougher securities laws after the Great Depression, did the legal system attain the necessary power to discourage unethical takeover tactics.

Lacking adequate legal restraints, the banking and business community adopted its own voluntary code of ethical behavior. This code was enforced by an unwritten agreement among investment bankers, who agreed to do business only with firms that adhered to their higher ethical standards. Today Great Britain relies on such a voluntary code. Although these informal standards did not preclude all improper activities in the pursuit of takeovers, they did set the stage for reasonable behavior during the first takeover wave.

Financial factors rather than legal restrictions forced the end of the first merger wave. First, the shipbuilding trust collapse in the early 1900s brought to the fore the dangers of fraudulent financing. Second, and most important, the stock market crash of 1904, followed by the Banking Panic of 1907, closed many of the nation's banks and ultimately paved the way for the formation of the Federal Reserve system. As a result of a declining stock market and a weak banking system, the basic financial ingredients for fueling takeovers were absent. Without these, the first great takeover period came to a halt.

---

11. Alfred D. Chandler, "The Coming of Oligopoly and Its Meaning for Antitrust," in *National Competition Policy: Historian's Perspective on Antitrust and Government Business Relationships in the United States,* Federal Trade Commission Publication, August 1981, p. 72.
12. Robert C. Puth, *American Economic History* (New York: Dryden Press, 1982), p. 254.

Some economic historians have interpreted the many horizontal combinations that took place in the first wave as an attempt to achieve economies of scale. Through M&As, the expanding companies sought to increase their efficiency by lower per-unit costs. The fact that the majority of these mergers failed implies that these companies were not successful in their pursuit of enhanced efficiency. Under President Theodore Roosevelt, whose tenure in the executive office lasted from 1901 to 1909, the antitrust environment steadily became more stringent. Although he did not play a significant role in bringing an end to the first wave, Roosevelt, who came to be known as the *trustbuster*, continued to try to exert pressure on anticompetitive activities.

The government was initially unsuccessful in its antitrust lawsuits, but toward the end of Roosevelt's term in office it began to realize more successes in the courtrooms. The landmark Supreme Court decision in the 1904 Northern Securities case is an example of the government's greater success in bringing antitrust actions. Although President Roosevelt holds the reputation of being the trustbuster, it was his successor, William Howard Taft, who succeeded in breaking up some of the major trusts. It is ironic that many of the companies formed in the breakup of the large trusts became very large businesses. For example, Standard Oil was broken up into companies such as Standard Oil of New Jersey, which later became Exxon; Standard Oil of New York, which became Mobil and merged with Exxon in 1998; Standard Oil of California, which became Chevron, and acquired Texaco in 2001; and Standard Oil of Indiana, which became Amoco, and was acquired by BP in 1998. The recent mergers between some of the components of the old Standard Oil reflect the partial undoing of this breakup as the petroleum market has been global and these descendants of J.D. Rockefeller's old company now face much international competition.

SECOND WAVE, 1916–1929

George Stigler, the late Nobel prize–winning economist and former professor at the University of Chicago, contrasted the first and second merger waves as "merging for monopoly" versus "merging for oligopoly." During the second merger wave, several industries were consolidated. Rather than monopolies, the result was often an oligopolistic industry structure. The consolidation pattern established in the first merger period continued into the second period. During this second period, the American economy continued to evolve and develop, primarily because of the post–World War I economic boom, which provided much investment capital for eagerly waiting securities markets. The availability of capital, which was fueled by favorable economic conditions and lax margin requirements, set the stage for the stock market crash of 1929.

The antitrust environment of the 1920s was stricter than the environment that had prevailed before the first merger wave. By 1910, Congress had become concerned about the abuses of the market and the power wielded by monopolies. It also had become clear that the Sherman Act was not an effective deterrent to monopoly. As a result, Congress passed the Clayton Act in 1914, a law that reinforced the antimonopoly provisions of the Sherman Act. (For a discussion of the Sherman and Clayton Acts, see Chapter 3.) As the economy and the banking system rebounded in the late 1900s, this antitrust law became a somewhat more important deterrent to monopoly. With a more

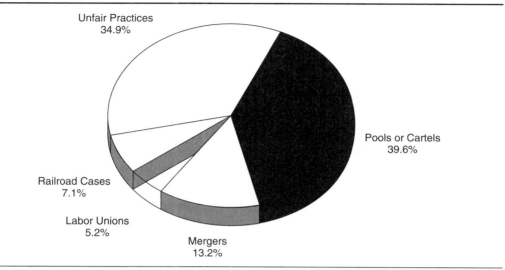

Unfair Practices
34.9%

Pools or Cartels
39.6%

Railroad Cases
7.1%

Labor Unions
5.2%

Mergers
13.2%

EXHIBIT 2.3   TYPES OF SHERMAN ACT CASES, 1901–20

Source: The Federal Antitrust Laws (Washington, D.C.: U.S. Government Printing Office, 1938), and Neil Fligstein, *The Transformation of Corporate Control* (Cambridge, MA: Harvard University Press, 1990), p. 79.

stringent antitrust environment, the second merger wave produced fewer monopolies but more oligopolies and many vertical mergers. In addition, many companies in unrelated industries merged. This was the first large-scale formation of conglomerates. However, although these business combinations involved firms that did not directly produce the same products, they often had similar product lines.

Armed with the Clayton Act and the Sherman Act, the government was in a better position to engage in more effective antitrust enforcement than had occurred during the first merger wave. Nonetheless, its primary focus remained on cracking down on unfair business practices and preventing cartels or pools, as opposed to stopping anticompetitive mergers (Exhibit 2.3). At this time widespread price-fixing occurred in many industries, which was thought to be a more pressing threat to competition than mergers, which now were mainly vertical or conglomerate transactions. Just as in the first merger wave, the second merger period witnessed the formation of many prominent corporations that still operate today. These include General Motors, IBM, John Deere, and the Union Carbide Corporation.

CASE STUDY

ALLIED CHEMICAL CORPORATION

Allied Chemical Corporation, one of the conglomerates formed in this period, consolidated control over five different companies: General Chemical, Barrett, Solvay Process, Semet-Solvay, and National Aniline and Chemical. Although these firms clearly had different product lines, they operated in related business areas: General Chemical was a combination of 12 producers of sulfuric acid; Barrett sold by-products of ammonia as well as coal tar products; Solvay Process was the country's largest producer of ash; Semet sold coal tar products; and National Aniline and Chemical was the nation's largest seller of dyestuffs. Consolidated under the single aegis of the Allied Chemical Corporation, these various different production processes united under a single management structure. Thus, Allied was able to exploit the various economies that existed across these production processes and their related marketing activities.[a]

[a]Jesse Markham, "Survey of the Evidence and Findings on Mergers," in *Business Concentration and Public Policy* (Princeton, NJ: Princeton University Press, 1995). See comments by George W. Stocking, pp. 208–209.

Between 1926 and 1930, a total of 4,600 mergers took place, and from 1919 to 1930, 12,000 manufacturing, mining, public utility, and banking firms disappeared. According to Earl Kintner, during the period from 1921 to 1933, $13 billion in assets were acquired through mergers, representing 17.5% of the nation's total manufacturing assets.[13] The continued development of a nationwide rail transportation system, combined with the growth of motor vehicle transportation, continued to transform local markets into national markets.

Competition among firms was enhanced by the proliferation of radios in homes as a major form of entertainment. This led to the increased use of advertising as a form of product differentiation. Marketers took advantage of this new advertising medium to start national brand advertising. The era of mass merchandising had begun. The public utility industry in particular experienced marked concentration. Many of these mergers involved public utility holding companies that were controlled by a relatively small number of stockholders. These utilities were often organized with a pyramidal corporate structure to provide profits for these stockholders and, according to the Federal Trade Commission (FTC), did not serve the public interest. The utility trusts were eventually regulated by the Public Utility Holding Company Act (PUHCA) of 1935. This law, which was designed to curb abuses, empowered the Securities and Exchange Commission (SEC) to regulate the corporate structure and voting rights of public utility stockholders. The act also gave the SEC the right to regulate the issuance of securities by utilities as well as their acquisition of assets or securities of other firms. The utilities' abuses of corporate power and fiduciary responsibilities were far more common at that time than they are today. This is why PUHCA was eliminated in 2005.

Although mergers affected industries across the board, the following industries experienced a disproportionate number of mergers:

- Primary metals
- Petroleum products
- Food products
- Chemicals
- Transportation equipment

Mergers were facilitated not only by the limited enforcement of antitrust laws but also by the federal government's encouragement of the formation of business cooperatives to enhance the nation's productivity as part of the war effort. Rather than compete with each

---

13. Earl W. Kintner, *Primer on the Law of Mergers* (New York: Macmillan, 1973), p. 9.

other during a time of war, the nation's firms, particularly those in manufacturing and mining, were urged to work together. Even after the war ended, however, the government maintained these policies through the 1920s.

The second merger wave bears some similarity to the fourth merger wave in that there was a significant use of debt to finance the deals that took place. Companies used a significant amount of debt in their capital structure, which provided the opportunity for investors to earn high returns but also brought downside risk if the economy slowed, as it soon did. One type of capital structure that became popular was the pyramid holding company, in which a small group of investors could control big businesses with a relatively small amount of invested capital.

The second merger wave ended with the stock market crash on October 29, 1929. "Black Thursday" would mark the largest stock market drop in history until the crash of October 1987. Although this collapse was not *per se* the cause of the Great Depression, it played a large role in it, for in contributing to a dramatic drop in business and investment confidence, business and consumer spending was further curtailed, thereby worsening the depression. After the crash, the number of corporate mergers declined dramatically. No longer focusing on expansion, firms sought merely to maintain solvency amid the rapid and widespread reduction in demand.

Investment bankers played key roles in the first two merger periods, exercising considerable influence among business leaders. They often vetoed a merger when they thought the deal was against the investment bank's policies or ethical interests by withholding funds from a firm seeking financing. The investment banks easily achieved controlling influence because a small number of them controlled the majority of the capital available for financing mergers and acquisitions. The investment banking industry was more concentrated in those years than it is today. The bulk of its capital was controlled by a small group of bankers who tended not to compete with each other. For example, one investment banker generally did not attempt to solicit business from another; each banker had his own clients, and those relationships tended not to change. This contrasts with the high degree of competition that exists in the industry today.

The number of mergers that took place during the first two waves demonstrates that investment banks generally supported merger activities. However, in the third merger period, the conglomerate era, the financial impetus for mergers would come from sources other than investment banks.

THE 1940s

Before we proceed to a discussion of the third merger period, we will briefly examine the mergers of the 1940s. During this decade, larger firms acquired smaller, privately held companies for motives of tax relief. In this period of high estate taxes, the transfer of businesses within families was very expensive; thus, the incentive to sell out to other firms arose. These mergers did not result in increased concentration because most of them did not represent a significant percentage of the total industry's assets. Most of the family business combinations involved smaller companies.

The 1940s did not feature any major technological changes or dramatic development in the nation's infrastructure. Thus, the increase in the number of mergers was relatively small. Nonetheless, their numbers were still a concern to Congress, which reacted by passing the Celler-Kefauver Act in 1950. This law strengthened Section 7 of the Clayton Act. (For further details on the Clayton Act, see the following section and Chapter 3.)

THIRD WAVE, 1965–1969

The third merger wave featured a historically high level of merger activity. This was brought about in part by a booming economy. During these years, often known as the conglomerate merger period, it was not uncommon for relatively smaller firms to target larger companies for acquisition. In contrast, during the two earlier waves, the majority of the target firms were significantly smaller than the acquiring firms. Peter Steiner reports that the "acquisition of companies with assets over $100 million, which averaged only 1.3 per year from 1948 to 1960, and 5 per year from 1961 to 1966, rose to 24 in 1967, 31 in 1968, 20 in 1969, 12 in 1970 before falling to 5 each year in 1971 and 1972."[14]

The number of mergers and acquisitions during the 1960s is shown in Table 2.3 and Exhibit 2.4. These data were compiled by W. T. Grimm and Company (now provided by Houlihan Lokey Howard & Zukin), which began recording M&A announcements on January 1, 1963. As noted, a larger percentage of the M&As that took place in this period were conglomerate transactions. The FTC reported that 80% of the mergers that took place in the ten-year period between 1965 and 1975 were conglomerate mergers.[15]

The conglomerates formed during this period were more than merely diversified in their product lines. The term *diversified firms* is generally applied to firms that have some subsidiaries in other industries but a majority of their production within one industry category. Unlike diversified firms, conglomerates conduct a large percentage of their business activities in different industries. Good examples were Ling-Temco-Vought (LTV), Litton Industries, and ITT. In the 1960s, ITT acquired such diverse businesses as Avis Rent a Car, Sheraton Hotels, Continental Baking, and other far-flung enterprises such as restaurant chains, consumer credit agencies, home building companies, and airport parking

Year	Mergers
1963	1,361
1964	1,950
1965	2,125
1966	2,377
1967	2,975
1968	4,462
1969	6,107
1970	5,152

TABLE 2.3 THIRD MERGER WAVE, 1963–70

14. Peter O. Steiner, *Mergers: Motives, Effects and Policies* (Ann Arbor: University of Michigan Press, 1975).
15. Federal Trade Commission, *Statistical Report on Mergers and Acquisitions* (Washington, D.C., 1977).

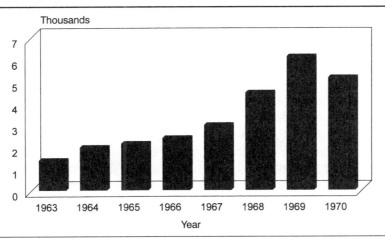

EXHIBIT 2.4 THIRD MERGER WAVE, MERGER AND ACQUISITION ANNOUNCEMENTS, 1963–70. THE THIRD MERGER WAVE PEAKED IN 1969. THE DECLINE IN THE STOCK MARKET, COUPLED WITH TAX REFORMS, REDUCED THE INCENTIVE TO MERGE.

firms. Although the third merger wave is associated with well-known conglomerate firms such as ITT and LTV, many corporations of varying sizes engaged in a diversification strategy. Many small and medium-sized firms also followed this fad and moved into areas outside their core business.

As firms with the necessary financial resources sought to expand, they faced tougher antitrust enforcement. The heightened antitrust atmosphere of the 1960s was an outgrowth of the Celler-Kefauver Act of 1950, which had strengthened the antimerger provisions of the Clayton Act of 1914. The Clayton Act made the acquisition of other firms' stock illegal when the acquisition resulted in a merger that significantly reduced the degree of competition within an industry. However, the law had an important loophole: It did not preclude the anticompetitive acquisition of a firm's assets. The Celler-Kefauver Act closed this loophole. Armed with tougher laws, the federal government adopted a stronger antitrust stance, coming down hard on both horizontal and vertical mergers. Expansion-minded firms found that their only available alternative was to form conglomerates.

The more intense antitrust enforcement of horizontal mergers was partially motivated by the political environment of the 1960s. During this decade, Washington policymakers, emphasizing the potential for abuses of monopoly power, worked through the FTC and the Justice Department to curb corporate expansion, which created the potential for monopolistic abuses. Prime advocates of this tougher antitrust enforcement were Attorney General John Mitchell and Assistant Attorney General Richard McLaren, the main architect of the federal government's antitrust efforts during the 1960s. In his book *Managing,* Harold Geneen, then chief executive officer of ITT, has described the difficulty his company had in acquiring companies when McLaren was in office.[16] McLaren opposed conglomerate acquisitions based on his fears of "potential reciprocity." This would occur, for example, if ITT and its other subsidiaries gave Hartford Insurance, a company ITT

---

16. Harold Geneen, *Managing* (New York: Avon, 1989), pp. 228–229.

acquired, a competitive edge over other insurance companies. ITT was forced to compromise its plans to add Hartford to its conglomerate empire. It was able to proceed with the acquisition only after agreeing to divest itself of other divisions with the same combined size of Hartford Insurance and to not acquire another large insurance company for ten years without prior Justice Department approval.

With the election of Richard M. Nixon toward the end of the decade, Washington policymakers advocated a freer market orientation. Nixon supported this policy through his four appointees to the U.S. Supreme Court, who espoused a broader interpretation of concepts such as market share. The tough antitrust enforcement of the Justice Department came to an end in 1972, as the Supreme Court failed to accept the Justice Department's interpretation of antitrust laws. For example, in some cases the Supreme Court began to use a broad international market view as opposed to a more narrow domestic or even regional market definition. Consequently, if as a result of a merger, a firm had a large percentage of the U.S. market or a region of the nation but a small percentage of the international market, it could be judged to lack significant monopolistic characteristics. By this time, however, the third merger wave had already come to an end.

Management Science and Conglomerates

The rapid growth of management science accelerated the conglomerate movement. Schools of management began to attain widespread acceptability among prominent schools of higher education, and the master of business administration degree became a valued credential for the corporate executive. Management science developed methodologies that facilitated organizational management and theoretically could be applied to a wide variety of organizations, including corporations, government, educational institutions, and even the military. As these management principles gained wider acceptance, graduates of this movement believed they possessed the broad-based skills necessary to manage a wide variety of organizational structures. Such managers reasonably believed that they could manage a corporate organization that spanned several industry categories. The belief that the conglomerate could become a manageable and successful corporate entity started to become a reality.

Industry Concentration and the Conglomerate Wave

Because most of the mergers in the third wave involved the formation of conglomerates rather than vertical or horizontal mergers, they did not appreciably increase industrial concentration. For this reason, the degree of competition in different industries did not significantly change despite the large number of mergers. Some 6,000 mergers, entailing the disappearance of 25,000 firms, took place; nonetheless, competition, or market concentration, in the U.S. economy was not greatly reduced. This clearly contrasts with the first merger wave, which resulted in a dramatic increase in industry concentration in many industries.

Shareholder Wealth Effects of Diversification During the Conglomerate Wave

In Chapter 4 we critically examine diversification strategies and their impact on shareholder wealth. However, while we are discussing the conglomerate wave, it is useful to briefly address some research that has attempted to assess the impact of these types of deals on shareholder wealth. Henri Servaes analyzed a large sample of firms over the years 1961–1976.[17] He showed that over this time period, the average number of business segments in which firms operated increased from 1.74 in 1961 to 2.7 in 1976. He then examined the Q ratios (ratios of the market value of securities divided by the replacement value of assets) of the companies in his sample and found that diversified firms were valued at a discount—even during the third merger wave when such diversifying deals were so popular. He found, however, that this diversification discount declined over time. Servaes analyzed the assertion that insiders derive private benefits from managing a diversified firm, which may subject the firm to less risk although at a cost that may not be in shareholders' interests. If managers derive private benefits that come at a cost to shareholders (the discount), then this may explain why companies with higher insider ownership were focused when the discount was high but began to diversify when the discount declined. At least they did not pursue their private benefits when it was imposing a cost on shareholders.

Price-Earnings Game and the Incentive to Merge

As mentioned previously, investment bankers did not finance most of the mergers in the 1960s, as they had in the two previous merger waves. Tight credit markets and high interest rates were the concomitants of the higher credit demands of an expanding economy. As the demand for loanable funds rose, both the price of these funds and interest rates increased. In addition, the booming stock market prices provided equity financing for many of the conglomerate takeovers.

The bull market of the 1960s bid stock prices higher and higher. The Dow Jones Industrial Average, which was 618 in 1960, rose to 906 in 1968. As their stock prices skyrocketed, investors were especially interested in growth stocks. Potential bidders soon learned that acquisitions, financed by stocks, could be an excellent "pain-free" way to raise earnings per share without incurring higher tax liabilities. Mergers financed through stock transactions may not be taxable. For this reason, stock-financed acquisitions had an advantage over cash transactions, which were subject to taxation.

Companies played the price-earnings ratio game to justify their expansionist activities. The *price-earnings ratio (P/E ratio)* is the ratio of the market price of a firm's stock divided by the earnings available to common stockholders on a per-share basis. The higher the P/E ratio, the more investors are willing to pay for a firm's stock given their expectations about the firm's future earnings. High P/E ratios for the majority of stocks in the market indicate widespread investor optimism; such was the case in the bull market of the 1960s. These high stock values helped finance the third merger wave. Mergers inspired by P/E ratio effects can be illustrated as follows.

Let us assume that the acquiring firm is larger than the target firm with which it is considering merging. In addition, assume that the larger firm has a P/E ratio of 25:1 and annual earnings of $1 million, with 1 million shares outstanding. Each share sells

17. Henri Servaes, "The Value of Diversification During the Conglomerate Wave," *Journal of Finance*, 51(4), September 1996, 1201–1225.

for \$25. The target firm has a lower P/E ratio of 10:1 and annual earnings of \$100,000, with 100,000 shares outstanding. This firm's stock sells for \$10. The larger firm offers the smaller firm a premium on its stock to entice its stockholders to sell. This premium comes in the form of a stock-for-stock offer in which one share of the larger firm, worth \$25, is offered for two shares of the smaller firm, worth a total of \$20. The large firm issues 50,000 shares to finance the purchase.

This acquisition causes the earnings per share (EPS) of the higher P/E firm to rise. The EPS of the higher P/E firm has risen from \$1.00 to \$1.05. We can see the effect on the price of the larger firm's stock if we make the crucial assumption that its P/E ratio stays the same. This implies that the market will continue to value this firm's future earnings in a manner similar to the way it did before the acquisition. The validity of this type of assumption is examined in greater detail in Chapter 14.

Based on the assumption that the P/E ratio of the combined firm remains at 25, the stock price will rise to \$26.25 (25 × \$1.05). We can see that the larger firm can offer the smaller firm a significant premium while its EPS and stock price rises. This process can continue with other acquisitions, which also result in further increases in the acquiring company's stock price. This process will end if the market decides not to apply the same P/E ratio. A bull market such as occurred in the 1960s helped promote high P/E values. When the market falls, however, as it did at the end of the 1960s, this process is not feasible. The process of acquisitions, based on P/E effects, becomes increasingly untenable as a firm seeks to apply it to successively larger firms. The crucial assumption in creating the expectation that stock prices will rise is that the P/E ratio of the high P/E firm will apply to the combined entity. However, as the targets become larger and larger, the target becomes a more important percentage of the combined firm's earning power. After a company acquires several relatively lower P/E firms, the market becomes reluctant to apply the original higher P/E ratio. Therefore, it becomes more difficult to find target firms that will not decrease the acquirer's stock price. As the number of suitable acquisition candidates declines, the merger wave slows down. Therefore, a merger wave based on such "finance gimmickry" can last only a limited time period before it exhausts itself, as this one did.

With its bull market and the formation of huge conglomerates, the term *the go-go years* was applied to the 1960s. When the stock market fell in 1969, it affected the pace of acquisitions by reducing P/E ratios. Exhibit 2.5 demonstrates how this decline affected some of the larger conglomerates.

Accounting Manipulations and the Incentive to Merge

Under accounting rules that prevailed at the time, acquirers had the opportunity to generate paper gains when they acquired companies that had assets on their books that were well below their market values. The gains were recorded when an acquirer sold off certain of these assets. To illustrate such an accounting manipulation, A. J. Briloff recounts how Gulf & Western generated earnings in 1967 by selling off the films of Paramount Pictures, which it had acquired in 1966.[18] The bulk of Paramount's assets were in the

---

18. A. J. Briloff, "Accounting Practices and the Merger Movement," *Notre Dame Lawyer,* 45(4), Summer 1970, 604–628.

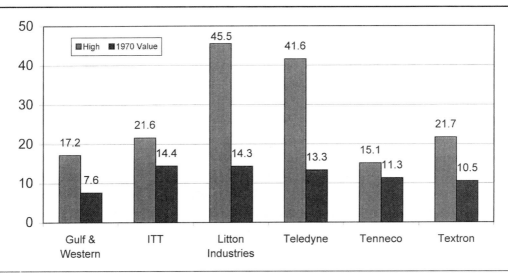

EXHIBIT 2.5 THIRD MERGER WAVE, CONGLOMERATE P/E RATIOS 1960, 1970. THE END OF THE THIRD MERGER WAVE WAS SIGNALED BY THE DRAMATIC DECLINE IN THE P/E RATIOS OF SOME OF THAT ERA'S LEADING CONGLOMERATES.

Source: Peter O. Steiner, *Mergers: Motives, Effects and Policies* (Ann Arbor: University of Michigan Press, 1975), p. 104.

form of feature films, which it listed on its books at a value significantly less than their market value. In 1967, Gulf & Western sold 32 of the films of its Paramount subsidiary. This generated significant "income" for Gulf & Western in 1967, which succeeded in supporting Gulf & Western's stock price.

Some believe that these accounting manipulations made fire and casualty insurance companies popular takeover targets during this period.[19] Conglomerates found their large portfolios of undervalued assets to be particularly attractive in light of the impact of a subsequent sale of these assets on the conglomerate's future earnings. Even the very large Hartford Insurance Company, which had assets of nearly $2 billion in 1968 (approximately $9.8 billion in 1999 dollars), had assets that were clearly undervalued. ITT capitalized on this undervaluation when it acquired Hartford Insurance.

Another artificial incentive that encouraged conglomerate acquisitions involved securities, which were used to finance acquisitions. Acquiring firms would issue convertible debentures in exchange for common stock of the target firm. Convertible debentures are debt securities that can be converted into a specific amount of common stock. In such a situation the target's earnings are added without an increase in common stock outstanding. If the stock price rose, however, the value of the convertible debentures would also rise because their conversion values rise. When convertible debentures are used to finance acquisitions, the earnings of the two firms are added together, but the stock of the target has been replaced by debt. Earnings per share rise because the target earnings are added to the acquiring firm, but the total shares outstanding initially remain the same.

---

19. Steiner, *Mergers: Motives, Effects and Policies*, p. 116.

This phenomenon is referred to as the *bootstrap effect*. If the same P/E ratio is applied to the merged firm, the stock price rises, thereby yielding a profit for the convertible debenture holders. Several laws enacted toward the end of the 1960s helped to end the third merger wave. In 1968, the Williams Act placed limits on the aggressiveness of tender offers and takeover attempts. Still a very influential piece of takeover regulation, the Williams Act is discussed in detail, along with tender offers, in Chapter 3. Although the Act limited some abusive takeover tactics, it did not stop hostile takeovers. Ironically, it may unintentionally have facilitated some hostile deals.

Decline of the Third Merger Wave

The decline of the conglomerates may be first traced to the announcement by Litton Industries in 1968 that its quarterly earnings declined for the first time in 14 years.[20] Although Litton's earnings were still positive, the market turned sour on conglomerates, and the selling pressure on their stock prices increased.

In 1968, Attorney General Richard McLaren announced that he intended to crack down on the conglomerates, which he believed were an anticompetitive influence on the market. In addition, Congress held hearings, led by Congressman Emmanuel Celler, on the adverse impact of conglomerates. This added to the downward pressure on the conglomerate stock prices. In 1969, passage of the Tax Reform Act ended some of the manipulative accounting abuses that created paper earnings that temporarily support stock prices. Specifically, it limited the use of convertible debt to finance acquisitions. Before enactment of this law, debt holders were willing to accept very low rates in exchange for the future capital gains on the sale of the convertible debentures. The low debt rates did not increase the riskiness of the corporation's capital structure because the associated fixed payments were low. The 1969 Tax Reform Act ended the use of low-rate convertible debt to finance acquisitions by stipulating that these bonds would be treated as common stock for the purpose of EPS computations. Consequently, EPS would not enjoy a paper increase because, for the purpose of its calculation, the number of common shares had, in effect, risen. This law also placed limits on the valuation of undervalued assets of targets that were to be sold at higher values to generate increased earnings. When the stock market fell in 1969, the P/E game could no longer be played. Indeed, many analysts thought that the conglomerate mergers helped collapse this market inasmuch as when securities attain values far in excess of the underlying economic basis for their valuation, a collapse is sure to follow. This is one lesson to be learned from the stock market crash of October 1987.

Performance of Conglomerates

Little evidence exists to support the advisability of many of the conglomerate acquisitions. Buyers often overpaid for the diverse companies they purchased. Many of the acquisitions were followed by poor financial performance. This is confirmed by the fact that 60% of the cross-industry acquisitions that occurred between 1970 and 1982 were sold or divested by 1989.

---

20. Stanley H. Brown, *Ling: The Rise, Fall and Return of a Texas Titan* (New York: Atheneum, 1972), p. 166.

There is no conclusive explanation for why conglomerates failed. Economic theory, however, points out the productivity-enhancing effects of increased specialization. Indeed, this has been the history of capitalism since the Industrial Revolution. The conglomerate era represented a movement away from specialization. Managers of diverse enterprises often had little detailed knowledge of the specific industries that were under their control. This is particularly the case when compared with the management expertise and attention that is applied by managers who concentrate on one industry or even one segment of an industry. It is not surprising, therefore, that companies like Revlon, a firm that has an established track record of success in the cosmetics industry, saw its core cosmetics business suffer when it diversified into unrelated areas such as health care.

TRENDSETTING MERGERS OF THE 1970s

The number of M&A announcements in the 1970s fell dramatically, as is shown in Table 2.4 and Exhibit 2.6. Even so, the decade played a major role in merger history. Several path-breaking mergers changed what was considered to be acceptable takeover behavior in the years to follow. The first of these mergers was the International Nickel Company (INCO) acquisition of ESB (formerly known as Electric Storage Battery Company).

INCO versus ESB Merger

After the third merger wave, a historic merger paved the way for a type that would be pervasive in the fourth wave: the hostile takeover by major established companies.

Year	Announcements
1969	6,107
1970	5,152
1971	4,608
1972	4,801
1973	4,040
1974	2,861
1975	2,297
1976	2,276
1977	2,224
1978	2,106
1979	2,128
1980	1,889

TABLE 2.4   MERGER AND ACQUISITION
ANNOUNCEMENTS, 1969–80

Source: Merrill Lynch Business Brokerage
and Valuation, *Mergerstat Review*, 1989.

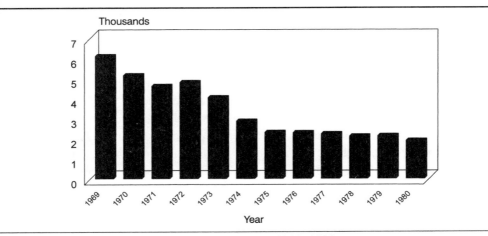

Thousands

Year

EXHIBIT 2.6 MERGER AND ACQUISITION ANNOUNCEMENTS, 1969–1980
Source: Merrill Lynch Business Brokerage and Valuation, *Mergerstat Review,* 1989.

In 1974, the Philadelphia-based ESB was the largest battery maker in the world, specializing in automobile batteries under the Willard and Exide brand names as well as other consumer batteries under the Ray-O-Vac brand name. Its 1974 sales were more than $400 million. Although the firm's profits had been rising, its stock prices had fallen in response to a generally declining stock market. Several companies had expressed an interest in acquiring ESB, but all these efforts were rebuffed. On July 18, 1974, INCO announced a tender offer to acquire all outstanding shares of ESB for $28 per share, or a total of $157 million. The Toronto-based INCO controlled approximately 40% of the world's nickel market and was by far the largest firm in this industry. Competition in the nickel industry had increased in the previous ten years while demand proved to be increasingly volatile. In an effort to smooth their cash flows, INCO sought an acquisition target that was less cyclical.

International Nickel Company ultimately selected ESB as the appropriate target for several reasons. As part of what INCO considered to be the "energy industry," ESB was attractive in light of the high oil prices that prevailed at that time. In addition, the possibility of a battery-driven car made a battery producer all the more appealing. International Nickel Company saw ESB's declining stock price as an inexpensive way to enter the booming energy field while helping smooth out the volatility of its own sales. Unfortunately, the acquisition of ESB did not prove to be a wise move for INCO. Although the battery business did have great potential, ESB was not a technological leader in the industry. It developed a low-maintenance auto battery while competitors marketed a maintenance-free product. It also lost market shares to the Duracell and Eveready long-life batteries, which it lacked. Because the takeover was an unfriendly acquisition, INCO did not have the benefit of a detailed financial analysis using internal data. Before INCO acquired ESB, major reputable corporations did not participate in unfriendly takeovers; only smaller firms and less respected speculators engaged in such activity. If a major firm's takeover overtures were rebuffed, the acquisition was discontinued. Moreover, most large investment banks refused to finance hostile takeovers.

At this time, the level of competition that existed in investment banking was putting pressure on the profits of Morgan Stanley, INCO's investment banker. Although it was seeking additional sources of profits, Morgan Stanley was also concerned that by refusing to aid INCO in its bid for ESB, it might lose a long-term client. Morgan Stanley, long known as a conservative investment bank, reluctantly began to change posture as it saw its market share erode because of the increasingly aggressive advance of its rivals in the investment banking business. Underwriting, which had constituted 95% of its business until 1965, had become less profitable as other investment banks challenged the traditional relationships of the underwriting business by making competitive bids when securities were being underwritten.[21]

Many banks, seeking other areas of profitability, expanded their trading operations. By the 1980s, trading would displace underwriting as the investment bank's key profit center.[22] This situation would change once again toward the end of the 1980s as fees related to M&As became an increasingly important part of some investment banks' revenues.

ESB found itself unprepared for a hostile takeover, given the novelty of this type of action. International Nickel Company gave it only a three-hour warning of its "take it or leave it" offer. ESB had installed some antitakeover defenses, but they were ineffective. It sought help from the investment bank of Goldman Sachs, which tried to arrange a friendly takeover by United Aircraft, but by September 1974, INCO's hostile takeover of ESB was completed.[23] The takeover of ESB proved to be a poor investment primarily because INCO, as a result of legal actions associated with antitrust considerations, was not given a free hand to manage the company. Not until 39 months after INCO had completed the acquisition did it attain the right to exercise free control over the company. Moreover, as noted previously, ESB's competitors were already aggressively marketing superior products. By 1981, ESB was reporting operating losses; INCO eventually sold it in four separate parts. INCO continued to be the world leader in the nickel business. Interestingly, it stepped into the role of white knight in 2006, when it made a bid for Canadian Falconbridge, Ltd, a leading copper, nickel, and zinc producer, which was the target of an unwanted 2005 bid from the Swiss mining company Xstrata.

This led to a long and complicated takeover battle involving several companies. Eventually, Inco was acquired for approximately $17 billion by the world's largest producer of iron ore, Brazilian Company CVRD.

Although the acquisition was not financially successful, it was precedent setting. It set the stage for hostile takeovers by respected companies in the second half of the 1970s and through the fourth merger wave of the 1980s. This previously unacceptable action—the hostile takeover by a major industrial firm with the support of a leading investment banker—now gained legitimacy. The word *hostile* now became part of the vocabulary of M&As. "'ESB is aware that a hostile tender offer is being made by a foreign company for

---

21. John Brooks, *The Takeover Game* (New York: Dutton, 1987), p. 4.
22. Ken Auletta, *Greed and Glory on Wall Street: The Fall of the House of Lehman* (New York: Random House, 1986). Auletta provides a good discussion of this trend at the investment bank of Lehman Brothers.
23. For an excellent discussion of this merger, see Jeff Madrick, *Taking America* (New York: Bantam Books, 1987), pp. 1–59.

all of ESB's shares,' said F. J. Port, ESB's president. 'Hostile' thus entered the mergers and acquisitions lexicon."[24]

Morgan Stanley received a $250,000 fee (1.3 million in 2006 $) for its advisory services. This fee, which did not involve the outright risk of the firm's capital and was considered attractive at the time, pales by comparison with today's merger advisory fees.

United Technologies versus Otis Elevator

As suggested previously, following INCO's hostile takeover of ESB, other major corporations began to consider unfriendly acquisitions. Firms and their chief executives who had inclined to be raiders but had been inhibited by public censure from the business community now became unrestrained. United Technologies was one such firm.

In 1975, United Technologies had recently changed its name from United Aircraft through the efforts of its chairman, Harry Gray, and president, Edward Hennessy, who were transforming the company into a growing conglomerate. They were familiar with the INCO-ESB acquisition, having participated in the bidding war for ESB as the unsuccessful white knight that Goldman Sachs had solicited on ESB's behalf. By mid-1975, Otis Elevator's common stock was selling for $32 per share, with earnings of $43.5 million on sales of $1.1 billion. Otis Elevator was an attractive target, with a book value of $38 per share and a stock price as high as $48 per share in 1973. United Technologies had never participated in a hostile takeover before its takeover of Otis Elevator.

At that time the growth of the elevator manufacturing business was slowing down and its sales patterns were cyclical inasmuch as it was heavily dependent on the construction industry. Nonetheless, this target was extremely attractive. One-third of Otis's revenues came from servicing elevators, revenues that tend to be much more stable than those from elevator construction. That Otis was a well-managed company made it all the more appealing to United Technologies. Moreover, 60% of Otis's revenues were from international customers, a detail that fit well with United Technologies' plans to increase its international presence. By buying Otis Elevator, United could diversify internationally while buying an American firm and not assuming the normal risk that would be present with the acquisition of a foreign company.

United initially attempted friendly overtures toward Otis, which were not accepted. On October 15, 1975, United Technologies bid $42 per share for a controlling interest in Otis Elevator, an offer that precipitated a heated battle between the two firms. Otis sought the aid of a white knight, the Dana Corporation, an auto parts supplier, while filing several lawsuits to enjoin United from completing its takeover. A bidding war that ensued between United Technologies and the Dana Corporation ended with United winning with a bid of $44 per share. Unlike the INCO-ESB takeover, however, the takeover of Otis proved to be an excellent investment of United's excess cash. Otis went on to enjoy greater than expected success, particularly in international markets.

United's takeover of Otis was a ground-breaking acquisition; not only was it a hostile takeover by an established firm, but also it was a successful venture. Indeed, Otis remains part of United today. Hostile takeovers were now an avenue through which

---

24. "Hostility Breeds Contempt in Takeovers, 1974," *Wall Street Journal*, 25, October 1989.

established firms could profitably expand. The larger U.S. companies began considering hostile takeovers as ways to enhance future profitability. The financial community now felt the competitive pressures to provide the requisite financing needed for these unfriendly takeover bids. The takeover business was quickly changing.

Colt Industries versus Garlock Industries

Colt Industries' takeover of Garlock Industries was yet another precedent-setting acquisition, moving hostile takeovers to a sharply higher level of hostility. The other two hostile takeovers by major firms had amounted to heated bidding wars but were mild in comparison to the aggressive tactics used in this takeover.

In 1964, the Fairbanks Whitney Company changed its name to Colt Industries, which was the firearms company it had acquired in 1955. During the 1970s, the company was almost totally restructured, with Chairman George Strichman and President David Margolis divesting the firm of many of its poorly performing businesses. The management wanted to use the cash from these sales to acquire higher-growth industrial businesses. By 1975, Colt Industries was a successful conglomerate with sales of $1 billion. Its target, Garlock Industries, manufactured packing and sealing products and had sales of approximately $160 million, with a rising EPS. At the time of Colt's offer, Garlock's common stock was selling for $20 per share and its book value exceeded $21 per share.

Having abandoned the option of a friendly takeover bid, Colt planned a surprise attack on Garlock. At that time a surprise attack was feasible because the Williams Act allowed a shorter waiting period for tender offers. Garlock had already initiated antitakeover defenses, such as staggered elections of directors and acquisitions that would absorb excess cash. Garlock also filed several lawsuits designed to thwart Colt's bid. They filed suit in federal court, for example, alleging that Colt Industries had failed to abide by federal securities disclosure laws. Their legal actions also alleged that the proposed Colt Industries–Garlock merger would violate antitrust laws. One of Garlock's most acerbic defenses was its use of public relations as an antitakeover defensive strategy. Garlock had employed the public relations firm of Hill and Knowlton, which was widely regarded as one of the leading firms in its field. The firm played on the Colt Industries name by placing advertisements in the *New York Times* and the *Wall Street Journal* in which it asserted that the sudden Colt tender offer, which it called a "Saturday-night special," was not in the stockholders' interests.

In the end the public relations defense, as well as all other defenses, proved ineffectual. Garlock accepted Colt's bid, and the Saturday-night special became an effective takeover tactic. The Colt–Garlock battle brought the level of bellicosity of takeover contests to an all-time high, and in the years that followed this aggressive behavior would only increase. Potential takeover targets now realized that no existing antitakeover defense could protect them from hostile bids; all companies were now vulnerable to such moves. The gloves were off in the battles to take over targets. Companies began scrambling to erect yet stronger defenses. Playing on these fears, investment bankers offered to sell their defensive skills to worried potential targets, and many were put on retainers as specialists in antitakeover defenses. The game had changed, and the hostile takeover had become an acceptable part of the world of modern corporate finance.

───────────────────────── CASE STUDY ─────────────────────────

LING-TEMCO-VOUGHT—GROWTH OF A CONGLOMERATE[a]

Ling-Temco-Vought (LTV) Corporation was one of the leading conglomerates of the third merger wave. The company was led by James Joseph Ling—the Ling of Ling-Temco-Vought. The story of how he parlayed a $2,000 investment and a small electronics business into the fourteenth largest industrial company in the United States is a fascinating one. Ling-Temco-Vought was a sprawling industrial corporation, which at its peak included such major enterprises as Jones & Laughlin Steel, the nation's sixth largest steel company; Wilson & Co, a major meat packing and sporting goods company; Braniff Airways, an airline that serviced many domestic and international routes; Temco and Vought Aircraft, both suppliers of aircraft for the military; and several other companies. The company originated in a small Texas electrical contracting business that Jimmy Ling grew, through a pattern of diverse acquisitions, into one of the largest U.S. corporations. The original corporate entity, the Ling Electric Company, was started in 1947 with a modest investment of $2,000, which was used to buy war surplus electrical equipment and a used truck. By 1956, Ling Electronics had enjoyed steady growth and embarked on one of its first acquisitions by buying L. M. Electronics. Various other electronic and defense contractors were then acquired, including the American Microwave Corporation, the United Electronics Company, and the Calidyne Company. Acquisitions such as these—companies that lacked the requisite capital to expand—were financed by Ling through a combination of debt and stock in his company, which traded on the over-the-counter market.

By 1958, this master dealmaker sold an offering of convertible debentures in a private placement that was arranged by the Wall Street investment bank of White Weld & Company. This type of securities offering was particularly popular with the dealmakers of the third wave because it did not have an immediate adverse impact on earnings per share, thus leaving the company in a good position to play the "P/E game." With its stock price trading in the $40s, Ling started the process of buying targets that were much bigger than the acquiring company by the 1958 stock-for-stock acquisition of Altec Companies, Inc., a manufacturer of sound systems.

After some other small acquisitions, Ling initiated his largest acquisition when he merged his company with the Texas Engineering and Manufacturing Company, Temco. This deal enabled Ling to accomplish a long-term goal when the merged company, Ling-Temco Electronics, became part of the *Fortune* 500. Shortly thereafter, Ling prevailed in a hostile takeover of the Vought Aircraft Company to form Ling-Temco-Vought.

Ling-Temco-Vought went through a period of lackluster financial performance, which forced Ling to restructure the company by selling off poorly performing divisions. In 1967, Ling successfully completed a tender offer for Wilson & Company, a firm twice the size of LTV. This deal vaulted LTV to number 38 on the *Fortune* 500 list. Wilson was composed of three subsidiaries: Wilson & Company, the meat packing business; Wilson Sporting Goods; and the Wilson Pharmaceutical and Chemical Corporation. Traders sometimes referred to these divisions as "meatball, golf ball, and goof ball." The next step Ling took in assembling this massive conglomerate was to buy the Great America Corporation, which was a holding company with investments in a variety of businesses such as Braniff Airlines and National Car Rental as well as banks and insurance companies. Although few beneficial commonalities appeared to be associated with this acquisition, Ling was able to exploit several, such as the insurance companies' writing insurance for a variety of LTV units and employees.

After an unsuccessful takeover of the Youngstown Sheet and Tube Company, Ling set his sights on the fourth largest steel producer in the United States, Jones & Laughlin Steel. Ling-Temco-Vought

[a]For an excellent discussion of the history of this company during the conglomerate era, see Stanley H. Brown, *Ling: The Rise and Fall of a Texas Titan* (New York: Atheneum, 1972).

bought Jones & Laughlin in an $85 tender offer for a company with a preannouncement price of $50. This $425 million bid was the largest cash tender offer as of that date and represented a 70% premium for a company in a low-growth industry. Unfortunately, the takeover of Jones & Laughlin drew the ire of Assistant Attorney General Richard McLaren, who saw it as another anticompetitive conglomerate acquisition. The Justice Department filed an antitrust lawsuit, which was bad news for any defendant because the government won a very high percentage of such cases. The market seemed to concur with this legal assessment because the stock price declined after the announcement. Because of the lawsuit, LTV was prevented from playing an active role in the management of Jones & Laughlin and taking steps to turn around the poorly performing steel company that had just announced its worst earnings performance in a decade. With the addition of Jones & Laughlin, LTV now had two major components of its empire—Braniff Airlines being the other one—reporting sizable losses. A settlement of the lawsuit was reached in which LTV agreed to sell off Braniff and the Okonite Company, a cable and wire manufacturer.

Although LTV was able to achieve a favorable settlement, its stock suffered, partly as a result of the lawsuit, the poor performance of its subsidiaries, and the overall decline in the market. These factors gave rise to pressures from dissident shareholders and bondholders to remove Ling from control of LTV. Ling was not able to survive these pressures and was demoted from his position as chief executive and eventually left LTV. The story of Jimmy Ling and the huge conglomerate that he built is one of a man who was ahead of his time. He was probably the most renowned of the great conglomerate builders of the third merger wave. Whereas the 1980s featured such raiders as Carl Icahn and Boone Pickens, Ling was joined in the third wave by other "conglomerators" such as Lawrence Tisch of Loews, Charles Bluhdorn of Gulf & Western, and Ben Heineman of Northwest Industries. Long before the 1980s, Ling had mastered the art of the LBO and hostile takeover. Unlike many of the raiders of the 1980s, however, Ling was opposed to trying to turn a quick profit on acquisitions by selling off assets. He bought companies with a more long-term strategy in mind, which, nonetheless, many criticized.

What was once LTV has undergone many changes since the 1960s. The company experienced financial troubles in the 1980s, as did many companies in the U.S. steel industry. It was acquired in 2002 by Wilber Ross, who rolled the company into the International Steel Group. This company was then sold by Ross to Mittal in 2004.

FOURTH WAVE, 1984–1989

The downward trend that characterized M&As in the 1970s through 1980 reversed sharply in 1981. Although the pace of mergers slowed again in 1982 as the economy weakened, a strong merger wave had taken hold by 1984. Table 2.5 shows the number of M&A announcements for the period from 1970 to 1989, and Exhibit 2.7 shows the decrease from 1974 to 1994. Here we merely highlight the major trends that differentiate this wave from the other three; the characteristics unique to each wave are discussed separately and in detail in various chapters of this book. The unique characteristic of the fourth wave is the significant role of hostile mergers. As noted previously, hostile mergers had become an acceptable form of corporate expansion by 1908, and the corporate raid had gained status as a highly profitable speculative activity. Consequently, corporations and speculative partnerships played the takeover game as a means of enjoying very high profits in a short time. Whether takeovers are considered friendly or hostile generally is determined by the reaction of the target company's board of directors. If the board

Year	Total Dollar Value Paid	Number
1970	16,414.9	5,152
1971	12,619.3	4,608
1972	16,680.5	4,801
1973	16,664.5	4,040
1974	12,465.6	2,861
1975	11,796.4	2,297
1976	20,029.5	2,276
1977	21,937.1	2,224
1978	34,180.4	2,106
1979	43,535.1	2,128
1980	44,345.7	1,889
1981	82,617.6	2,395
1982	53,754.5	2,346
1983	73,080.5	2,533
1984	122,223.7	2,543
1985	179,767.5	3,001
1986	173,136.9	3,336
1987	173,136.9	2,032
1988	246,875.1	2,258
1989	221,085.1	2,366

TABLE 2.5   MERGER AND ACQUISITION TRANSACTIONS, 1970–1989 ($ MILLIONS)

Source: Mergerstat Review, 1998.

approves the takeover, it is considered friendly; if the board is opposed, the takeover is deemed hostile.

Although the absolute number of hostile takeovers is not high with respect to the total number of takeovers, the relative percentage of hostile takeovers in the total value of takeovers is large. Exhibit 2.8 reflect the absolute number of tender offers for publicly traded companies as compared with the total number of M&As.

The fourth merger period may also be distinguished from the other three waves by the size and prominence of the M&A targets. Some of the nation's largest firms became targets of acquisition during the 1980s. The fourth wave became the wave of the *megamerger*. The total dollar value paid in acquisitions rose sharply during this decade. Exhibit 2.9 show how the average and median prices paid have risen since 1970. In addition to the rise in the dollar value of mergers, the average size of the typical transaction increased significantly. The number of $100 million transactions increased more than 23 times from 1974 to 1986. This was a major difference from the conglomerate era of the 1960s, in

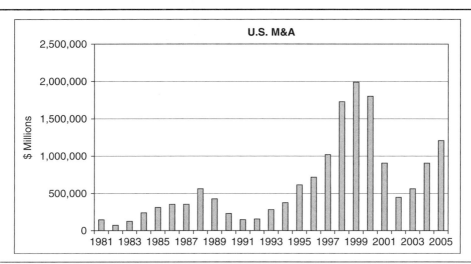

EXHIBIT 2.7 MERGER AND ACQUISITION TRANSACTIONS, 1981–2004
Source: Thompson Securities Financial Data.

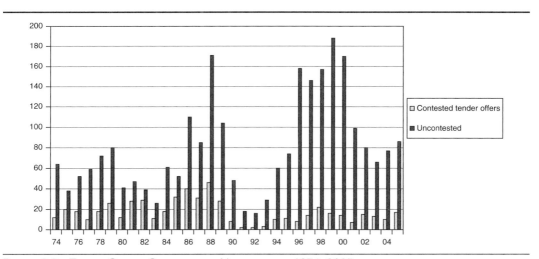

EXHIBIT 2.8 TENDER OFFERS: CONTESTED VS. UNCONTESTED, 1974–2005
Source: Mergerstat Review, 2006.

which the acquisition of small and medium-sized businesses predominated. The 1980s became the period of the billion-dollar M&As. The leading megamergers of the fourth wave are shown in Table 2.6.

M&A volume was clearly greater in certain industries. The oil industry, for example, experienced more than its share of mergers, which resulted in a greater degree of concentration within that industry. The oil and gas industry accounted for 21.6% of the total dollar value of M&As from 1981 to 1985. During the second half of the 1980s,

EXHIBIT 2.9 AVERAGE AND MEDIAN PURCHASE PRICE, 1970–2005
Source: Mergerstat Review, 2006; Table 1-4.

Year	Buyer	Target	Price ($Billions)
1988	Kohlberg Kravis	RJR Nabisco	25.1
1984	Chevron	Gulf Oil	13.3
1988	Philip Morris	Kraft	13.1
1989	Bristol Myers	Squibb	12.5
1984	Texaco	Getty Oil	10.1
1981	DuPont	Conoco	8.0
1987	British Petroleum	Standard Oil of Ohio	7.8
1981	U.S. Steel	Marathon Oil	6.6
1988	Campeau	Federated Stores	6.5
1986	Kohlberg Kravis	Beatrice	6.2

TABLE 2.6 TEN LARGEST ACQUISITIONS, 1981–1989

Source: Wall Street Journal, November 1988. Reprinted by permission of the
Wall Street Journal, copyright Dow Jones & Company, Inc. All rights reserved.

drugs and medical equipment deals were the most common. One reason some industries experienced a disproportionate number of M&As as compared with other industries was deregulation. When the airline industry was deregulated, for example, airfares became subject to greater competition, causing the competitive position of some air carriers to deteriorate because they could no longer compete effectively. The result was numerous acquisitions and a consolidation of this industry. The banking and petroleum industries experienced a similar pattern of competitively inspired M&As.

Role of the Corporate Raider

In the fourth wave, the term *corporate raider* made its appearance in the vernacular of corporate finance. The corporate raider's main source of income is the proceeds from takeover attempts. The word *attempts* is the curious part of this definition because the raider frequently earned handsome profits from acquisition attempts without ever taking ownership of the targeted corporation. The corporate raider Paul Bilzerian, for example, participated in numerous raids before his acquisition of the Singer Corporation in 1988. Although he earned significant profits from these raids, he did not complete a single major acquisition until Singer.

Many of the takeover attempts by raiders were ultimately designed to sell the target shares at a higher price than that which the raider originally paid. The ability of raiders to receive greenmail payments (or some of the target's valued assets) in exchange for the stock that the raider had already acquired made many hostile takeover attempts quite profitable. Even if the target refused to participate in such transactions, the raider may have succeeded in putting the company "in play." When a target goes into play, the stock tends to be concentrated in the hands of arbitragers, who readily sell to the highest bidder. This process often results in a company's eventually being taken over, although not necessarily by the original bidder.

Although arbitrage is a well-established practice, the role of arbitragers in the takeover process did not become highly refined until the fourth merger wave. Arbitragers, such as the infamous Ivan Boesky, would gamble on the likelihood of a merger being consummated. They would buy the stock of the target in anticipation of a bid being made for the company.

Arbitragers became a very important part of the takeover process during the 1980s. Their involvement changed the strategy of takeovers. Moreover, the development of this "industry" helped facilitate the rising number of hostile takeovers that occurred in those years.

Other Unique Characteristics of the Fourth Wave

The fourth merger wave featured several other interesting and unique characteristics. These features sharply differentiated this time from any other period in U.S. merger history.

Aggressive Role of Investment Bankers

The aggressiveness of investment bankers in pursuing M&As was crucial to the growth of the fourth wave. In turn, mergers were a great source of virtually risk-free advisory fees for investment bankers. The magnitude of these fees reached unprecedented proportions during this period. Merger specialists at both investment banks and law firms developed many innovative products and techniques designed to facilitate or prevent takeovers. They pressured both potential targets and acquirers into hiring them either to bring about or to prevent takeovers. Partially to help finance takeovers, the investment bank of Drexel Burnham Lambert pioneered the development and growth of the junk bond market. These previously lowly regarded securities became an important investment vehicle for financing many takeovers. Junk bond financing enabled expansionist firms and raiders to raise the requisite capital to contemplate acquisitions or raids on some of the more prominent corporations.

Increased Sophistication of Takeover Strategies

The fourth merger wave featured innovative acquisition techniques and investment vehicles. Offensive and defensive strategies became highly intricate. Potential targets set in place various preventive antitakeover measures to augment the active defenses that could deploy in the event that they received an unwanted bid. Bidders also had to respond with increasingly more creative takeover strategies to circumvent such defenses. These antitakeover strategies are discussed in detail in Chapter 5.

More Aggressive Use of Debt

Many of the megadeals of the 1980s were financed with large amounts of debt. This was one of the reasons small companies were able to make bids for comparatively larger targets. During this period the term *leveraged buyout* became part of the vernacular of Wall Street. Through LBOs, debt may be used to take public companies private. It often was the company's own management that used this technique in *management buyouts*. Although public corporations had been brought private before the fourth wave, this type of transaction became much more prominent during the 1980s.

Legal and Political Strategies

During this period new conflicts arose between the federal and the state governments. Besieged corporations increasingly looked to their state governments for protection against unwanted acquisition offers. They often were able to persuade local legislatures to pass antitakeover legislation, which brought the federal and state governments into direct conflict. Some representatives of the federal government, such as the SEC, believed that these laws were an infringement of interstate commerce. For their part, some state governments believed that such laws were based on their constitutionally granted state rights. Clearly, however, some state governments became protectors of indigenous corporations.

International Takeovers

Although most of the takeovers in the United States in the 1980s involved U.S. firms taking over other domestic companies, foreign bidders effected a significant percentage of takeovers although nothing compared to what would take place in the fifth merger wave. An example of one of the international megadeals of the fourth wave was the 1987 acquisition of Standard Oil by British Petroleum for $7.8 billion. Many of the deals were motivated by non-U.S. companies seeking to expand into the larger and more stable U.S. market. The United States offers a more stable political climate combined with the largest economy in the world. However, this period also featured a significant number of deals in which U.S. companies used acquisitions to expand beyond their national boundaries.

In addition to the normal considerations that are involved in domestic acquisitions, foreign takeovers also introduce currency valuation issues. If the dollar falls against other currencies, as it did in the 1990s relative to many currencies, stock in American corporations declines in value and the purchasing value of foreign currencies rises. A falling dollar may make U.S. acquisitions attractive investments for Japanese or European companies. The increased globalization of markets in the 1980s and 1990s brought foreign bidders to U.S. shores in increased numbers. Although American companies may also engage in acquisitions in foreign markets, as many have, a falling dollar makes such acquisitions more expensive.

Role of Deregulation

Certain industries were deregulated during the 1980s. Mitchell and Mulherin analyzed a sample of 1,064 M&As and other restructurings over the period 1982–1989.[25] They found that in industries that had undergone significant federal deregulation, such as air transport, broadcasting, entertainment, natural gas, and trucking, this deregulation was found to be a significant causal factor. They also noticed that all industries did not respond to deregulation in the same way. For example, the response in broadcasting was quicker than in air transport.

Why the Fourth Merger Wave Ended

The fourth merger wave ended in 1989 as the long economic expansion of the 1980s came to an end and the economy went into a brief and relatively mild recession in 1990. The economic slowdown led to the unraveling of a number of the high-profile leveraged deals of the fourth wave. In addition to the overall slowdown in the economy, other factors that led to the end of the wave included the collapse of the junk bond market, which had provided the financing for many of the LBOs of the period. These events are discussed in detail in Chapters 7 and 8.

FIFTH WAVE

Starting in 1992, the number of M&As once again began to increase (see Exhibit 2.10). Large deals, some similar in size to those that occurred in the fourth merger wave, began to occur once again. At this time the track record of many of the highly leveraged deals of the fourth wave, some of which were still in Chapter 11, was quite apparent. Managers vowed they would not duplicate the mistakes of the 1980s and focused more on strategic deals that did not unduly rely on leverage. Short-term, purely financial plays were also avoided. This all seemed to go according to plan—at least for a while.

During the 1990s, the U.S. economy entered into its longest postwar expansion and companies reacted to the increased aggregate demand by pursuing M&As, which are a faster way to grow than internal growth. At the same time, the stock market values of companies took off and various market indices reached new highs (see Exhibit 2.11).

25. Mark L. Mitchell and J. Harold Mulherin, "The Impact of Industry Shocks on Takeover and Restructuring Activity," *Journal of Financial Economics*, 41, June 1996, 193–229.

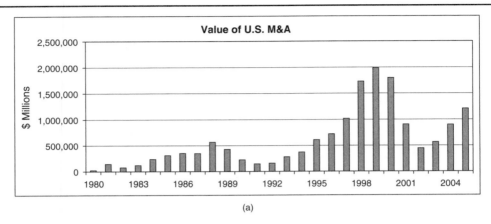

(a)

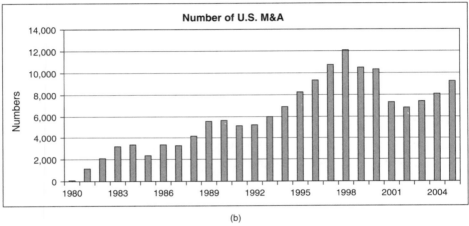

(b)

EXHIBIT 2.10   U.S. M&AS 1980–2005: (a) VALUE; (b) NUMBER

Source: Mergerstat Review, 2006; and Thomson Securities Financial Data.

While the expanding economy required that there be some adjustment in expected profitability, the high levels of the market became difficult to explain. We will revisit this issue a little later in this chapter.

Although the fifth merger wave featured many large megamergers, there were fewer hostile deals and more strategic mergers occurred. As the economy recovered from the 1990–91 recession, companies began to seek to expand and mergers once again were seen as a quick and efficient manner in which to do that. Unlike the deals of the 1980s, however, the transactions of the 1990s emphasized strategy more than quick financial gains. These deals were not the debt-financed bustup transactions of the fourth merger wave. Rather, they were financed through the increased use of equity, which resulted in less heavily leveraged combinations. Because the deals of the early 1990s did not rely on as much debt, there was not as much pressure to quickly sell off assets to pay down the debt and reduce the pressure of debt service. The deals that occurred were, at least initially, motivated by a specific strategy of the acquirer that could more readily be achieved by acquisitions and mergers than through internal expansion.

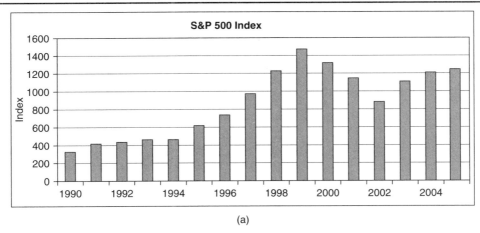

(a)

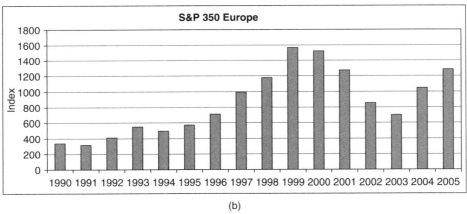

(b)

EXHIBIT 2.11   S&P INDEX IN THE UNITED STATES AND EUROPE: (a) S&P 500; (b) S&P 350 INDEX IN EUROPE
Source: Bloomberg, www.econstats.com/eqty/eqea_mi_1.htm

Industry Concentration During the Fifth Wave

Certain industries accounted for a disproportionate share of the total dollar volume of M&A in the United States during the fifth merger wave. In particular, banking and finance and communications and broadcasting accounted for 26.5% of all U.S. deals over the period 1993–2004. However, the percentage accounted for in these industries rose from a low of 7.5% in 1994 to a high of 41.9% of deals in 1999 (see Exhibit 2.12). This was caused by a combination of factors including the continued impact of deregulation and consolidation of the banking industry as well as the dramatic changes that were ongoing in telecom and Internet-related businesses. The fifth wave would have been different had it not been for the "inflating" yet short-lived impact of these sectors.

Fad of the Fifth Merger Wave: Roll-Ups and Consolidations of Industries

Each wave brought with it certain uniquely different transactions, and the fifth wave was no exception. In the mid-1990s, the market became enthralled with consolidating

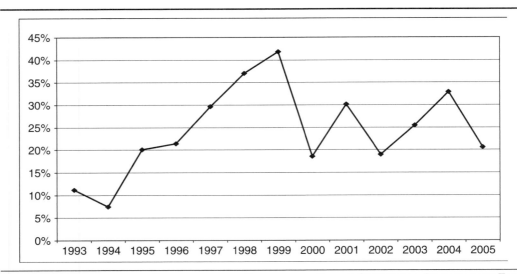

Exhibit 2.12   Broadcasting, Communications, Banking, and Finance Sectors as a Percentage of Total U.S. Transactions

Source: Mergerstat Review, 2006; Table 2-4.

Company Name	Industry
Metal USA	Metal service centers
Office Products USA	Office products
Floral USA	Florists
Fortress Group	Home building
U.S. Delivery Systems	Delivery
Comfort Systems USA	Air conditioning
Coach USA	Bus company
Waste Management	Waste removal
Republic Industries	Car dealerships

Table 2.7   Large Roll-Ups

deals—what were called roll-ups. Here fragmented industries were consolidated through larger-scale acquisitions of companies that were called consolidators. Certain investment banks specialized in roll-ups and were able to get financing and were issuing stock in these consolidated companies. Table 2.7 lists some of the more prominent consolidated companies. Roll-ups were concentrated in particular businesses such as the funeral printing, office products, and floral products businesses.

The strategy behind roll-ups was to combine smaller companies into a national business and enjoy economies of scale while gaining the benefits of being able to market to national as opposed to regional clients. There may have been some theoretical benefits to these combinations but the track record of many of these deals was abysmal. Many of the consolidated entities went bankrupt while others lost value and were sold to other companies. They were a fad that became popular while the market of the 1990s was caught up in a wave of irrational exuberance that was looking for investment opportunities.

Fifth Merger Wave in Europe, Asia, and Central and South America

The fifth merger wave was truly an international merger wave. As Exhibit 1.1 shows, the dollar value and number of deals in the United States increased dramatically starting in 1996. In Europe, the fifth wave really took hold starting in 1998. By 1999, the value of deals in Europe was almost as large as that of deals in the United States. Within Europe, Britain accounted for the largest number of deals followed by Germany and France. In Asia, merger value and volume also increased markedly starting in 1998. The volume of deals was significant throughout Asia, including not only Japan but all the major nations in Asia. Many of the Asian nations only recently have begun to restructure their tightly controlled economies and this restructuring has given rise to many sell-offs and acquisitions.

As discussed in Chapter 1, while the size of the M&A market in Central and South America is much smaller than Asia, which is in turn smaller than Europe and the United States, a significant volume of deals also took place in this region. The forces of economic growth and the pursuit of globalization affected all economies as the companies sought to service global markets. Expansion efforts that take place in one part of the globe set in motion a process that, if unrestrained by artificial regulation, has ripple effects throughout the world. This was the case in the fifth merger wave.

Performance of Fifth Merger Wave Acquirers

When the fifth merger wave began to take hold, corporate managers steadfastly stated that they would not make the same mistakes that were made in the fourth merger wave. Many maintained they would not engage in short-term, financially oriented deals, but would only focus on long-term, strategic deals. In fact, there is evidence that managers pursued deals that had modest positive effects for shareholders. In a large sample of 12,023 transactions with values greater than $1 million over the period 1980 and 2001, Moeller, Schlingemann, and Stulz found that the deals done at the beginning of the fifth wave enhanced shareholder value.[26] However, between 1998 and 2001, acquiring firm shareholders lost a shocking $240 billion! (See Exhibit 2.13.) These losses dramatically contrast with the $8 billion that was lost during the entire 1980s (inflation-adjusted values). From a societal perspective, one might wonder, did the gains of target shareholders more than offset the losses of acquiring firm shareholders? The answer is they did not even come close. Bidder shareholder losses exceeded those of target shareholders by $134 billion. However, from the bidder shareholder's perspective, these "offsetting" gains are irrelevant. To consider these gains would be like saying "lets pay this large premium for a given target and, sure, we will lose a large amount of money, but we will

---

26. Sara B. Moeller, Frederick P. Schlingemann, and Rene M. Stulz, "Wealth Destruction on a Massive Scale: A Study of Acquiring Firm Returns in the Recent Merger Wave," *Journal of Finance*, 60(2), April 2005, 757–783.

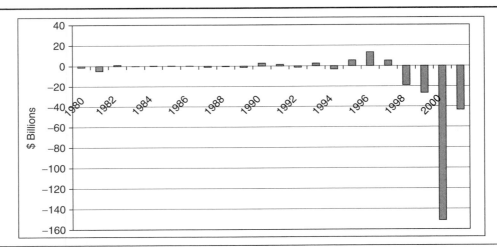

EXHIBIT 2.13   YEARLY AGGREGATE DOLLAR RETURN OF ACQUIRING FIRM SHAREHOLDERS, 1980–2001

Source: Sara B. Moeller, Frederik P. Schlingemann, and René M. Stulz, "Wealth Destruction on a Massive Scale? A Study of Acquiring Firm Returns to the Recent Merger Wave," *Journal of Finance,* 60(2), April 2005.

be giving target shareholders a large gain, at our expense, and from society's perspective, there may be a net gain on this deal."

The number of large losers is striking. Moeller et al. found that there were 87 deals over the period 1998–2001 that lost $1 billion or more for shareholders. Why were the acquirer's losses in the fifth wave as large as they were? One explanation was that managers were more restrained at the beginning and the middle of the fifth wave. They wanted to avoid the mistakes of the prior merger period. However, as the stock market bubble took hold, the lofty stock valuation went to managers' heads. This is evidenced by the dramatically higher P/E ratios that prevailed during this period (see Exhibit 2.14). Managers likely believed they were responsible for the high values their shares had risen

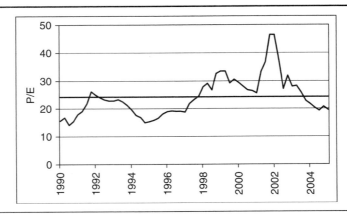

EXHIBIT 2.14   S&P 500 P/E RATIO: 1990–2005

Source: Standard & Poor's.

to. These hubris-filled executives thought that these high valuations were the product of their managerial expertise rather than the fact that their company, and most of the market, was riding an irrational wave of overvaluation. When such executives proposed deals to their board, they now carried the weight of the management's team "success" record. It is hard for a board to tell a CEO his or her merger proposals are unsound when they came from the same CEO who claims responsibility for the highest valuations in the company's history.

Privatization of State-Owned Enterprises

Many nations have sought to stimulate their economies and raise capital by selling off state-owned businesses. While this is not as relevant in developed economies such as the United States and Great Britain, it is much more important in less-developed countries in Asia, South and Central America, and Eastern Europe (see Exhibit 2.15). Many of these

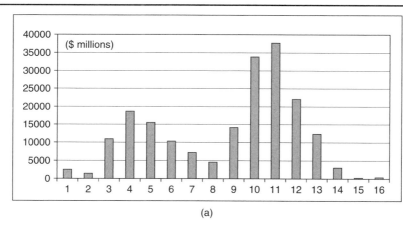

(a)

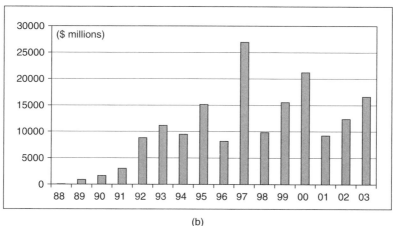

(b)

EXHIBIT 2.15 PROCEEDS FROM PRIVATIZATION, 1988–2003: (a) LATIN AMERICA AND THE CARIBBEAN; (b) EAST ASIA AND THE PACIFIC, EUROPE, AND CENTRAL ASIA

Source: http://rru.worldbank.org/Privatization/.

privatized businesses, when released from governmental control, were acquired by other firms or pursued their own takeovers. With the release of businesses from the public to the private sector the number of M&A potential bidders and targets swelled.

Emerging Market Acquirers

A new type of acquirer became more prominent in the fifth merger wave and in the 2000s—the emerging market bidder. Many of these acquiring companies were built through acquisitions of privatized businesses and consolidations of relatively smaller competitors in these emerging markets. Some grew to a substantial size and have targeted large Western companies (see Exhibit 2.16). One example of this is Mittal, which has used M&As across the world, many of them privatized steel businesses, to become the largest steel company in the world (see Table 2.8). Its clout was felt throughout the world in 2006, when it made a successful hostile bid for the second largest steel company—Arcelor. Mittal is but one example of this trend. Another is the Dubai-based Ports World, which in 2006 took over the venerable Peninsular & Oriental Navigation Co. (P&O) in a $6.8 billion acquisition. Still another is the Mubai-based Tata Group led by Ratan N. Tata. The company he created is an international conglomerate which includes one of the world's largest sellers of coffee and tea but also includes luxury hotels, soft drinks, and a telecommunications business. In october 2006, the company made a bid for the British owned Corus Group which would make the Tata Group one of the largest steel companies in the world.

Even before these 2006 deals, we had the 2005 $12 billion acquisition of Wind Telecommunications, owned by the Italian utility Enel SpA, being acquired by Egyptian billionaire Naguid Sawiris. Sawiris had made other deals in the Middle East and Asia but this was his first foray into Europe. The deal would not have been possible if

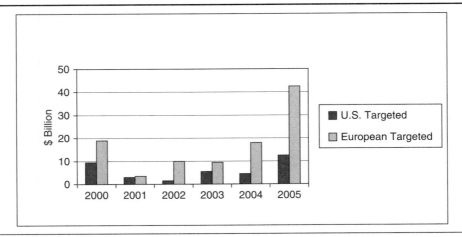

Exhibit 2.16   Emerging Market Acquisition Targets

Source: Jason Singer and Dennis K. Berman, "Companies Emerging Markets Show Clout in Global Deal Game," *Wall Street Journal,* February 13, 2006, A1.

Company	Steel Production (millions of tons)
Mittal Steel	65
Arcelor	52
Nippon Steel	34
JFE Steel	34
Posco	34
Baosteel	23
U.S. Steel	23

TABLE 2.8 LARGEST WORLDWIDE STEEL COMPANIES: 2004 PRODUCTION

Sources: Mittal Steel, Paul Glader, "Mittal, Arcelor Clash on Strategy in Takeover Battle," *Wall Street Journal*, March 10, 2006, A2.

he did not receive substantial funding from European banks. In the same year we had the acquisition of IBM's PC business by China's Lenovo.

The significance of the arrivals of large bids from emerging market companies is that the M&A business has now become truly a worldwide phenomena. While not that long ago most of the large bids came from U.S. bidders, the field has become truly globalized with large well-financed bidders coming from not only developed countries but also emerging markets. These emerging market companies have come to establish large worldwide market shares, making them highly credible bidders.

European Protectionism During the 2000s

Several European nations have difficulty allowing foreign bidders to acquire major national companies. In several instances European nations have stepped in to erect barriers to impede takeovers of national champions. For example, this was the case in 2006, when the French government arranged a hasty marriage between two French utilities, Suez SA and Gaz De France SA, as a way of fending off an unwanted bid from Italian utility Enel SpA. Spain also implemented a new takeover law to try to prevent German E.On AG's takeover of Spanish utility Endesa SA. The European Commission ruled that Spain violated European merger rules by applying conditions which violated the spirit of these rules. Many European countries want free markets to allow their own indigenous companies to expand beyond their own borders. At the same time they want the ability to prevent free market access when it comes to hostile bids by other nations. In several instances in the 2000s, nationalism has overpowered the pursuit of free markets.

SUMMARY

This chapter has described the ebb-and-flow development of corporate M&As in the United States, which was characterized by four main periods of intense merger activity called merger waves. The earlier merger waves were greatly influenced by the technolog-ical growth of the United States into a major industrial economy. The first merger wave included many horizontal combinations and the consolidations of several industries. The second wave included mainly horizontal deals but also many vertical transactions. The third wave was the conglomerate era, which refers to the acquisition of companies in different industries. The fourth merger wave was unique in that it featured the appear-ance of the corporate raider, who often used the junk bond market to finance highly leveraged deals. This debt financing also was used for other types of related financial transactions such as the LBO. Although corporate raiders existed before the 1980s, the fourth wave brought forth a raider armed with a larger arsenal of junk bond financing, which was used to attack some of America's largest corporations. In doing so, the raider permanently changed the outlook of corporate management, which previously had not been exposed to such formidable outside threats. When the junk bond market collapsed toward the end of the 1980s and the economy moved into a recession, it appeared that the hectic pace of M&A activity had come to an end. The lull in mergers, however, was short-lived and the volume of transactions picked up in 1992. This marked the start of the fifth merger wave. This period featured even larger megamergers than the transac-tions of the 1980s. In addition, the deals of the fifth merger wave were a worldwide phenomenon, with a large volume of mergers taking place in Europe and Asia. Deals of this period were different from many of those of the fourth merger wave. More of them were strategic mergers that involved companies seeking to expand into new markets or to take advantage of perceived synergies. However, things seemed to all go awry by 1998. Acquiring firms lost a total of $240 billion for their shareholders over the four-year period 1998–2001. The losses of the fifth wave dramatically eclipsed those of the fourth wave, which were a total of $8 billion.

After a slowdown in the early 2000s, the M&A business picked up steam again and became truly globalized. New potential targets and bidders came on the market as a result of increased privatizations—especially in Eastern Europe, Asia, and Central and South America. In addition, large bids started to come from emerging market companies as these firms established highly credible positions in various markets.

The remainder of this book more fully describes the recent developments of the world of M&As. The different dimensions of merger activity are explored in depth so that the reader will obtain a more complete understanding of the intricacies of this continually evolving field.

3

LEGAL FRAMEWORK

This chapter focuses mainly on the legal regulations governing mergers and acquisitions (M&A) in the United States. However, the rules for other countries are also discussed. It will be clear that there are many similarities in the takeover regulations of various countries although there are some important differences.

The legal requirements governing M&As in the United States differ depending on whether a transaction is a friendly merger or a hostile deal. Within each of these categories the rules vary depending on whether the transactions are cash or stock financed. The regulatory framework of each of these alternatives is:

- *Friendly merger—cash financed.* The bidder is required to file a proxy statement with the Securities and Exchange Commission (SEC) that describes the deal. Usually, the bidder has to file a preliminary statement first. If the SEC makes comments, the preliminary statement may be changed before it is finalized.
  The finalized proxy statement is then mailed to shareholders along with a proxy card that they fill out and return. Following this, the deal has to be approved at a shareholders' meeting, whereupon the deal can then be closed.
- *Friendly merger—stock financed.* This process is similar to a cash-financed merger except that the securities used to purchase target shares have to be registered. The bidder does this by filing a registration statement. Once this is approved, the combined registration/proxy statement can be sent to shareholders.
- *Hostile deal—cash tender offer.* The bidder initiates the tender offer by disseminating tender offer materials to target shareholders. Such offers have to be made pursuant to the requirements of the Williams Act. This law is discussed at length in this chapter. However, unlike the friendly transactions described above, the SEC does not have an opportunity to comment on the materials that are sent to shareholders prior to their dissemination. The SEC may do so, however, during the minimum offer period, which will be described later in this chapter.
- *Hostile deal—stock tender offer.* The bidder first needs to submit a registration statement and wait until it is declared effective prior to submitting tender offer materials to shareholders. The SEC may have comments on the preliminary registration statement that have to be resolved before the statement can be considered effective. Once this is done, the process proceeds similar to a cash tender offer.

LAWS GOVERNING MERGERS, ACQUISITIONS, AND TENDER OFFERS

Several laws regulate the field of M&A in the United States. These laws set forth the rules that govern the M&A process. Because target companies use some of these laws as a defensive tactic when contemplating a takeover, an acquiring firm must take careful note of legal considerations. The three main groups of laws are securities laws, antitrust laws, and state corporation laws.

SECURITIES LAWS

There are various securities laws that are important to the field of M&As. The more important parts of these laws are reviewed in this chapter, beginning with the filing of an 8K and then with a detailed discussion of the Williams Act.

Filing of an 8K

The Securities Exchange Act of 1934 requires that an 8K filing must be made within 15 calendar days after the occurrence of certain specific events. Such events include the acquisition and disposition of a significant amount of assets including companies. The filing will include information such as:

- Description of the assets acquired or disposed of
- Nature and amount of consideration given or received
- Identity of the persons from whom the assets were acquired
- In the case of an acquisition, the source of the funds used to finance the purchase
- Financial statements of the business acquired

Acquisitions are determined to involve a significant amount of assets if the equity interest in the assets being acquired, or the amount paid or received in an acquisition or disposition, exceeds 10% of the total book assets of the registrant and its subsidiaries. This percentage threshold can be important. For example, in the 1990s Tyco did many acquisitions for which it did not file an 8K due to this filing threshold. However, it did so many acquisitions that the combination was easily in excess of this percentage. Moreover, as the company grew through its acquisition program, more and larger acquisitions were "going under the radar" as it became more difficult to readily see the true extent of Tyco's acquisition program.

Filing of an S-4

When a public company has to issue new stock to acquire a target, it must register these shares by filing a disclosure form with the SEC. This usually is done through the filing of an S-4 form, which is slightly less detailed than the S-1 form that a company files when it first goes public.

Williams Act

The Williams Act, which was passed in 1968, is one of the most important pieces of securities legislation in the field of M&As. It had a pronounced impact on merger activity in the 1970s and 1980s. Before its passage, tender offers were largely unregulated, a situation that was not a major concern before 1960 because few tender offers were made. In the 1960s, however, the tender offer became a more popular means of taking control of corporations and ousting an entrenched management. In tender offers that used securities as the consideration, the disclosure requirement of the Securities Act of 1933 provided some limited regulation. In cash offers, however, there was no such regulation. As a result, the SEC sought to fill this gap in the law, and Senator Harrison Williams, as chairman of the Senate Banking Committee, proposed legislation for that purpose in 1967. The bill won congressional approval in July 1968. The Williams Act provided an amendment to the Securities Exchange Act of 1934, a legal cornerstone of securities regulations. This Act, together with the Securities Act of 1933, was inspired by the government's concern for greater regulation of securities markets. Both Acts have helped eliminate some of the abuses that many believed contributed to the stock market crash of October 1929.

Specifically, these laws provide for greater disclosure of information by firms that issue securities to the public. For example, the Securities Act of 1933 requires the filing of a detailed disclosure statement when a company goes public. In addition, the Securities Exchange Act of 1934 proscribed certain activities of the securities industry, including wash sales and churning of customer accounts. It also provided an enforcement agency, the SEC, which was established to enforce federal securities laws. In amending the Securities Exchange Act of 1934, the Williams Act added five new subsections to this law.

The Williams Act had four major objectives:

1. *To regulate tender offers.* Before the Williams Act was passed, stockholders of target companies often were stampeded into tendering their shares quickly to avoid receiving less advantageous terms.

2. *To provide procedures and disclosure requirements for acquisitions.* Through greater disclosure, stockholders could make more enlightened decisions regarding the value of a takeover offer. Disclosure would enable target shareholders to gain more complete knowledge of the potential acquiring company. In a stock-for-stock exchange, the target company stockholders would become stockholders in the acquiring firm. A proper valuation of the acquiring firm's shares depends on the availability of detailed financial data.

3. *To provide shareholders with time to make informed decisions regarding tender offers.* Even if the necessary information might be available to target company stockholders, they still need time to analyze the data. The Williams Act allows them to make more informed decisions.

4. *To increase confidence in securities markets.* By increasing investor confidence, securities markets can attract more capital. Investors will be less worried about being placed in a position of incurring losses when making decisions based on limited information.

Section 13(d) of the Williams Act

Section 13(d) of the Williams Act provides an early warning system for stockholders and target management, alerting them to the possibility that a threat for control may soon occur. This section provides for disclosure of a buyer's stockholdings, whether they have come from open market purchases, tender offers, or private purchases, when these holdings reach 5% of the target firm's total common stock outstanding. When the law was first passed, this threshold level was 10%; this percentage was later considered too high and the more conservative 5% was adopted. The disclosure of the required information, pursuant to the rules of Section 13(d), is necessary even when there is no tender offer. The buyer who intends to take control of a corporation must disclose the required information following the attainment of a 5% holding in the target. The buyer makes this disclosure by filing a Schedule 13D (see Exhibit 3.1). A filing may be necessary even though no one individual or firm actually owns 5% of another firm's stock. If a group of investors act in concert, under this law their combined stockholdings are considered as one group.

Schedule 13D

Section 13(d) provides for the filing of a Schedule 13D with the SEC, any exchange on which the issuer's stock is traded, as well as the issuer. The SEC filing is done through the SEC database—EDGAR (Electronic Data Gathering and Retrieval). The filing must be done within 10 days of acquiring 5% of the issuer's outstanding stock. Certain parties are exempt from this filing requirement, such as brokerage firms holding shares in street names or underwriters who happen to acquire shares for a limited period (up to 40 days).

Schedule 13D requires the disclosure of the following information:[1]

- The name and address of the issuing firm and the type of securities to be acquired. For example, a company may have more than one class of securities. In this instance, the acquiring firm must indicate the class of securities of which it has acquired at least 5%.
- Detailed information on the background of the individual filing the information, including any past criminal violations.
- The number of shares actually owned.
- The purpose of the transaction. At this point the acquiring firm must indicate whether it intends to take control of the company or is merely buying the securities for investment purposes.
- The source of the funds used to finance the acquisition of the firm's stock. The extent of the reliance on debt, for example, must be disclosed. Written statements from financial institutions documenting the bidder's ability to procure the requisite financing may be required to be appended to the schedule.

In addition to the above, the bidder must disclose all transactions in the target's shares that occurred over the 60-day period prior to the offer.

Amendments Required under Section 13(d)(2)

Section 13(d)(2) requires the "prompt" filing, with the SEC and the exchanges, by the issuer when there has been a "material change" in the facts that were set forth in Schedule 13D. As with much of the Williams Act, the wording is vague regarding what constitutes

---

1. Bryon E. Fox and Eleanor M. Fox, *Corporate Acquisitions and Mergers,* 2 (New York: Matthew Bender, 1994), p. 27.

SECURITIES AND EXCHANGE COMMISSION
Washington, D.C. 20549

SCHEDULE 13D

Under the Securities Exchange Act of 1934
(Amendment No. _____)*

(Name of Issuer)

(Title of Class of Securities)

(CUSIP Number)

(Name, Address and Telephone Number of Person Authorized to Receive Notices and Communications)

(Date of Event which Requires Filing of this Statement)

If the filing person has previously filed a statement on Schedule 13G to report the acquisition which is the subject of this Schedule 13D, and is filing this schedule because of Rule 13d-1(b)(3) or (4), check the following box ☐.

Check the following box if a fee is being paid with the statement ☐. (A fee is not required only if the reporting person: (1) has a previous statement on file reporting beneficial ownership of more than five percent of the class of securities described in Item 1; and (2) has filed no amendment subsequent thereto reporting beneficial ownership of five percent or less of such class.) (See Rule 13d-7.)

Note: Six copies of this statement, including all exhibits, should be filed with the Commission. See Rule 13d-1(a) for other parties to whom copies are to be sent.

*The remainder of this cover page shall be filled out for a reporting person's initial filing on this form with respect to the subject class of securities, and for any subsequent amendment containing information which would alter disclosures provided in a prior cover page.

The information required on the remainder of this cover page shall not be deemed to be "filed" for the purpose of Section 18 of the Securities Exchange Act of 1934 ("Act") or otherwise subject to the liabilities of that section of the Act but shall be subject to all other provisions of the Act (however, see the Notes).

SEC 1746 (2-87)

EXHIBIT 3.1   SAMPLE OF SCHEDULE 13D

a material change or even the time period that is considered prompt. However, Rule 13d-2 does specify that an increase or decrease of 1% is considered material. Generally, a filing within 10 days of the material change might be acceptable unless the change is so significant that a more timely filing is appropriate.[2] Such significance could be found in

---

2. Brent A. Olson, *Publicly Traded Corporations: Governance, Operation and Regulation* (New York: Thompson-West, 2005), p. 14-9.

SCHEDULE 13D

| CUSIP No. _____ | Page _____ of _____ Pages |

1	NAME OF REPORTING PERSON S.S. OR I.R.S. IDENTIFICATION NO. OF ABOVE PERSON	
2	CHECK THE APPROPRIATE BOX IF A MEMBER OF A GROUP*	(a) ☐ (b) ☐
3	SEC USE ONLY	
4	SOURCE OF FUNDS*	
5	CHECK BOX IF DISCLOSURE OF LEGAL PROCEEDINGS IS REQUIRED PURSUANT TO ITEMS 2(d) or 2(E)	☐
6	CITIZENSHIP OR PLACE OF ORGANIZATION	

	7	SOLE VOTING POWER
NUMBER OF SHARES BENEFICIALLY OWNED BY EACH REPORTING PERSON WITH	8	SHARED VOTING POWER
	9	SOLE DISPOSITIVE POWER
	10	SHARED DISPOSITIVE POWER

11	AGGREGATE AMOUNT BENEFICIALLY OWNED BY EACH REPORTING PERSON	
12	CHECK BOX IF THE AGGREGATE AMOUNT IN ROW (11) EXCLUDES CERTAIN SHARES*	☐
13	PERCENT OF CLASS REPRESENTED BY AMOUNT IN ROW (11)	
14	TYPE OF REPORTING PERSON*	

*SEE INSTRUCTIONS BEFORE FILLING OUT!

EXHIBIT 3.1   (continued)

the market's sensitivity and reliance on the new information as well as prior information disclosed in the original filing that now may be significantly different.

Remedies for Failure to Comply with Section 13(d)

If there is a perceived violation of Section 13(d), either shareholders or the target company may sue for damages. The courts are more mindful of the target's shareholders' rights under Section 13(d) than those of the target corporation itself because this section of the statute was designed for their benefit as opposed to protecting the interests of the target corporation. Courts have been more inclined to grant equitable relief, such as in the form of an injunction, as opposed to compensatory relief in the form of damages. They are more concerned about making sure the proper disclosure is provided to shareholders as opposed to standing in the way of an acquisition. In addition to the courts, the SEC may review the alleged violation of Section 13(d) and could see fit to pursue an enforcement action. Parties that are found guilty of violating Section 13(d) may face fines and possible disgorgement.

Schedule 13G

The SEC makes special provisions for those investors, usually institutional investors, who acquire 5% or more of a company's shares but who did not acquire more than 2% of those shares in the previous 12 months and who have no interest in taking control of the firm. Such investors are required to file the much less detailed Schedule 13G. Schedule 13G must be filed on February 14 of each year. These shareowners are sometimes called 5% *beneficial owners*.

Employee Stock Ownership Plans

The SEC may consider the trustee of an employee stock ownership plan to be a beneficial owner of the shares of stock in the plan. An employee stock ownership plan may have a trustee who is a bank advisor or an investment advisor. In making the determination of whether the trustee is the beneficial owner, the SEC would consider whether the trustee has discretionary authority to vote or dispose of the shares. If the trustee has such discretionary powers, there may be an obligation to file.

Section 14(d) and Regulation M-A

The Williams Act also provides for disclosure of various information in tender offers, principally through Section 14(d). These regulations apply to tender offers which, if successful, would result in the owner possessing five percent or more of a class of equity securities.

Schedule TO

Under the original wording of the law, disclosure came in the form of a Schedule 14D-1. A similar schedule, a Schedule 13E-4 was filed for tender offers done by the issuer itself. Since both schedules related to tender offers, either by the issuer or a third party, the SEC decided in January 2000 to combine the schedule into one filing, which is now called a Schedule TO. The Schedule TO refers to rules that are set forth in a new regulation—Regulation M-A. The schedule must be filed, at the time the offer is made, with the SEC and a copy must be hand delivered to the executive offices of the target company. A copy must also be hand delivered to other bidders, if any. In addition, the acquiring firm must not only telephone each of the exchanges on which the target company's stock is traded to notify them of the tender offer but also mail a copy of the Schedule TO to them. If the target's stock is traded on the over-the-counter market, similar notice must be provided to the National Association of Securities Dealers (NASD).

The bidder then will generally submit a press release to the media (see Exhibit 3.4). The Schedule TO can also be used to update information contained in the Schedule 13D filing and this will satisfy the reporting requirements of Section 13(d) of the Act.

Information Requested on Schedule TO

Disclosure requirements of Schedule TO are:

- *Item 1.* Summary term sheet—written in plain English.
- *Item 2.* The name of the target company, class of securities involved, and indication of any prior purchases of these securities.
- *Item 3.* The identity and background of the filing person (may be a corporation or partnership).
- *Item 4.* Terms of the transaction—this includes the number of shares being bid for, expiration date, tendering and withdrawal procedures, payment method, and tax consequences.
- *Item 5.* Description of past contacts, negotiations, or transactions with the target.
- *Item 6.* The purpose of the transaction.
- *Item 7.* Source of the funds used to complete transaction.
- *Item 8.* Indicate the number of shares bidder already owns.
- *Item 9.* Identity of persons and parties employed by bidder for the transaction.
- *Item 10.* Bidder's financial statements (two years).
- *Item 11.* Any agreements between the bidder and any of its officers that might be material to target company shareholders.
- *Item 12.* Any recommendations that bidder is making to the target shareholders.
- *Item 13.* If it is a going private transaction, state the purposes and reasons for the transaction and alternatives considered.
- *Item 14.* For a going private transaction, comment on its fairness.
- *Item 15.* Provide reports, opinions, and appraisals.

Commencement of the Offer

The time period of the tender offer may be crucially important in a contested takeover battle. Therefore, the date on which the offer is initially made is important. According to Rule 14d-2, the tender offer will begin on 12:01 A.M. on the date that any one of the following occurs:

- Publication of the tender offer
- Advertisement of the tender offer (such as through an advertisement in the *Wall Street Journal*)
- Submittal of the tender offer materials to the target

Following an announcement of an offer the bidder has five business days to disseminate the tender offer materials.

Position of the Target Corporation

The Williams Act originally only required the bidder to file a disclosure statement. In 1980, the Act was amended to require the target to comply with disclosure requirements.

SC TO-T 1 dsctot.htm SCHEDULE TO

UNITED STATES
SECURITIES AND EXCHANGE COMMISSION
Washington, D.C. 20549

SCHEDULE TO
(RULE 14d-100)

**Tender Offer Statement Pursuant to Section 14(d)(1) or 13(e)(1) of
the Securities Exchange Act of 1934**

PEOPLESOFT, INC.
(Name of Subject Company)

PEPPER ACQUISITION CORP.
ORACLE CORPORATION
(Name of Filing Persons–offeror)

COMMON STOCK, PAR VALUE $0.01 PER SHARE
(Title of Class of Securities)

712713106
(Cusip Number of Class of Securities)

**Daniel Cooperman
Senior Vice President, General Counsel and Secretary
Oracle Corporation
500 Oracle Parkway
Redwood City, California 94065
Telephone: (650) 506-7000**
(Name, Address and Telephone Number of Person Authorized to Receive Notices
and Communications on Behalf of Filing Persons)

Copies to:
**William M. Kelly
Davis Polk & Wardwell
1600 El Camino Real
Menlo Park, California 94025
Telephone: (650) 752-2000**

CALCULATION OF FILING FEE

Transaction Valuation*	Amount of Filing Fee**
$5,065,695,056	$409,815

*   Estimated for purposes of calculating the amount of filing fee only. Transaction value derived by multiplying $16,605,941 (number of shares of common stock of subject company outstanding as of May 27, 2003 (according to the Agreement and plan of Merger, dated June 1, 2003, by and among subject company, J.D. Edwards & Company and Jersey Acquisition Corporation filed with the J.D. Edwards & Company Form 8-K filed on June 3, 2003, with the Securities and Exchange Commission) by $16.00 (the purchase price per share offered by Offeror).

**   The amount of the filing fee, calculated in accordance with Rule 0-11 of the Securities and Exchange Act of 1934, as amended, and Fee Advisory #11 for Fiscal Year 2003 issued by the Securities and Exchange Commission on February 21, 2003, equals 0.008090% of the transaction valuation.

☐   Check box if any part of the fee is offset as provided by Rule 0-11(a)(2) and identify the filing with which the offsetting fee was previously paid. Identify the previous filing by registration statement number, or the Form or Schedule and the date of its filing.
Amount Previously Paid:	Not applicable.	Filing Party:	Not applicable.
Form *or* Registration No.:	Not applicable.	Date Filed:	Not applicable.

file://\\Amy\Economatrix%20Folder\Employee%20Folders\Current%20Employees\Iris\Schedule%20T   11/30/2005

EXHIBIT 3.2   SCHEDULE TO FOR ORACLE'S OFFER FOR PEOPLESOFT

Source: www.sec.gov/edgar.shtml.

The target company must now respond to the tender offer by filing a Schedule 14D-9 (Exhibit 3.3) within 10 days after the commencement date, indicating whether it recommends acceptance or rejection of the offer. If the target contends that it maintains no position on the offer, it must state its reasons. In addition to filing with the SEC, the target must send copies of the Schedule 14D-9 to each of the organized exchanges on

---

SECURITIES AND EXCHANGE COMMISSION
Washington, DC 20549

Schedule 14D-9

SOLICITATION/RECOMMENDATION STATEMENT
PURSUANT TO SECTION 14(d)(4) OF THE
SECURITIES EXCHANGE ACT OF 1934

PeopleSoft, Inc.
(Name of Subject Company)

Peoplesoft, Inc.
(Name of Person Filing Statement)

Common stock, Par Value $0.01 Per Share
(Title of Class of Securities)

712713106
(CUSIP Number of Class of Securities)

Craig Conway
President and Chief Executive Officer
PeopleSoft, Inc.
4460 Hacienda Drive, Pleasanton, California 94588-8618
(925) 225-3000

(Name, Address and Telephone Number of Person Authorized to Receive
Notice and Communications on Behalf of the person Filing Statement)

Copies To:

Donglas D. Smith, Esq.
Gibson, Dunn & Crutcher LLP
One Montgomery Street
San Francisco, California 94104
(415) 393-8200

□ Check the box if the filing relates solely to preliminary communications made before the commencement of a tender offer

---

file://\\Army\Economatrix%20Folder\Employee%20Folders\Current%20Employees\Iris\PeopleSoft,%20 . . .   11/30/2005

EXHIBIT 3.3   SCHEDULE 14D-9

Source: www.sec.gov/edgar.shtml.

which the target's stock is traded. If the stock is traded on the over-the-counter market, the NASD must also be sent a copy of this schedule.

Time Periods of the Williams Act

Minimum Offer Period

According to the Williams Act, a tender offer must be kept open for a minimum of 20 business days, during which the acquiring firm must accept all shares that are tendered.

However, it may not actually buy any of these shares until the end of the offer period. The minimum offer period was added to discourage shareholders from being pressured into tendering their shares rather than risk losing out on the offer. With a minimum time period, shareholders can take their time to consider this offer and compare the terms of the offer with that of other offers. The offering firm may get an extension on the 20-day offer period, if, for example, it believes there is a better chance of getting the shares it needs. The acquiring firm must purchase the shares tendered (at least on a pro rata basis) at the offer price unless the firm does not receive the total number of shares it requested in the terms of the tender offer. The acquirer may, however, still choose to purchase the tendered shares.

The tender offer may be worded to contain other escape clauses. For example, when antitrust considerations are an issue, the offer may be contingent on attaining the regulatory agencies' approval. Therefore, the offer might be so worded as to state that the bidder is not bound to buy if the Justice Department or the FTC objects to the merger. The mere presence of an investigation by the regulatory authorities might allow a bidder to refuse to purchase the tendered shares. For example, both Exelon and its target, PSE&G, had such escape clauses in their 2006 $12 billion merger agreement. Both companies had the right to walk away from the deal if the regulatory process required such significant assets sales that it affected the value the companies saw in the combination.

Withdrawal Rights

The Williams Act has been amended several times to enhance shareholders' rights to withdraw their shares from participation in the offer. In 1986, the SEC enacted Rule 14d-7, which allows shareholders to withdraw their shares any time during the entire period the offer remains open. The goal of this rule is to allow shareholders sufficient time to evaluate the offer or offers in the case of multiple bids.

Pro Rata Acceptance

In many instances tender offers are oversubscribed. For example, an offer to purchase 51% of a target company's stock may receive 80% of the total shares outstanding. Approximately five-eighths of each share submitted would be accepted if all 80% of the shares were tendered during the first 10 days of an offer to purchase 51% of the outstanding stock. If an additional 10% were submitted after the tenth calendar day of the offer, these shares would not be accepted unless the acquiring company decided to accept more shares than were stipulated in the 51% offer.

Definition of a Tender Offer

The Williams Act is purposefully vague regarding the definition of a tender offer. Not surprisingly, this vagueness gave rise to litigation as tender offer participants chose to adopt the definition of a tender offer that was most favorable to them. In *Kennecott Copper Corporation v. Curtiss-Wright Corporation,* the court found that open market purchases

AMERICAN HOME PRODUCTS CORPORATION

FIVE GIRALDA FARMS, MADISON, NEW JERSEY 07940, (201) 660-5000

EXECUTIVE OFFICES

FOR IMMEDIATE RELEASE:

Investor Contact: Media Contact:
John R. Considine   Louis V. Cafiero
(201) 660-6429   (201) 660-5013

**AMERICAN HOME PRODUCTS TO COMMENCE CASH TENDER
OFFER FOR AMERICAN CYANAMID AT $95 PER SHARE**

Madison, N.J., August 9, 1994 -- American Home Products
Corporation (NYSE:AHP) announced today that its Board of Directors has
formally approved the Company's previously announced offer to purchase
American Cyanamid Company for $95 per share in cash. In furtherance
of this offer, the Board authorized the commencement of a cash tender
offer for all of the outstanding stock of American Cyanamid at that
price, subject to customary conditions for an offer of this nature.

John R. Stafford, Chairman, President and Chief Executive Officer
of American Home Products, stated that "although we are starting our
tender offer, we are confident that American Cyanamid's Board of
Directors will recognize the inherent value of our offer to their
stockholders, and we hope they will quickly accept our invitation to
begin meaningful discussions for a negotiated transaction."

American Home Products also announced that it was commencing
litigation designed to eliminate the applicability to its offer of
certain of American Cyanamid's anti-takeover and other defensive
provisions. In addition, American Home Products stated that it
intends to solicit other American Cyanamid stockholders to join it in
calling for a special stockholders meeting to act on matters relating
to the American Home Products offer.

#####

EXHIBIT 3.4 AMERICAN HOME PRODUCTS PRESS RELEASE

---

without a deadline and for which no premium was offered did not constitute a tender offer.[3] However, in *Wellman v. Dickinson* the court set forth the *Eight Factor Test*.[4]

These factors are listed here and are revisited in Chapter 6:

1. Active and widespread solicitation of public shareholders for shares of an issuer.
2. Solicitation is made for a substantial percentage of an issuer's stock.
3. Offer to purchase is made at a premium over the prevailing market price.
4. Terms of the offer are firm rather than negotiated.

---

3. *Kennecott Copper Corp. v. Curtiss-Wright Corp.*, 584 F.2d 1195 (CA2 1978).
4. *Wellman v. Dickinson*, 475 F. Supp. (SD NY 1979), *aff'd* 632 F.2d 355 (CA2 1982), *cert. denied*, 460 U.S. 1069 (1983).

5. Offer is contingent on the tender of a fixed number of shares and possibly specifying a maximum number of shares.

6. Offer is open for only a limited time period.

7. Offeree is subject to pressure to sell stock.

8. Public announcements of a purchasing program that precede or are coincident with a rapid accumulation of shares.[5]

In *Hanson Trust PLC v. SCM Corp.*, the Second Circuit has recognized that the *Wellman* factors are relevant to determining whether certain actions by a bidder constitutes a tender offer.[6] However, the court stopped short of saying that these factors are a "litmus test." This court preferred to consider whether offerees would be put at an informational disadvantage if official tender offer procedures are not followed. Other courts have put forward more basic tests. In a district court opinion in *S-G Securities, Inc. v. Fuqua Investment Co.*, the court concluded that a tender offer exists if the following occurs:[7]

- A bidder publicly announcing its intention to acquire a substantial block of a target's shares for the purposes of acquiring control of the company
- A substantial accumulation of the target's stock by the bidder through open market or privately negotiated purchases

---

CASE STUDY

SUN OIL VERSUS BECTON DICKINSON

The Becton Dickinson Corporation is a medical products company that is located in Bergen County, New Jersey. The company was run by Fairleigh S. Dickinson Jr. until 1973. He was the son of the founder of the company, Fairleigh Dickinson Sr., who also founded Fairleigh Dickinson University. Fairleigh Dickinson Jr. had turned over the day-to-day control to a management team headed by Wesley Howe and Marvin Ashe. As time passed, disagreements occurred between Fairleigh Dickinson Jr. and Howe and Ashe. For example, they disagreed on certain personnel decisions and on other strategic decisions such as the acquisition of National Medical Care—a Boston-based medical care company. Fairleigh Dickinson Jr. opposed this particular acquisition because the equity offered for the purchase would dilute his shareholdings and his ownership percentage. The pattern of disagreements came to a head in a board of directors' meeting in which Ashe and Howe called for the removal of Fairleigh Dickinson Jr. as chairman of the board of directors.

While the internecine conflicts were ongoing at Becton Dickinson, Sun Oil, Inc., a Philadelphia-based corporation, was pursuing an expansion program that would help them diversify outside the petroleum industry. They were working with their investment banker, Salomon Brothers, to find suitable non-oil acquisition candidates. Given its position in its industry, they found Becton Dickinson an attractive takeover target. Salomon Brothers, the investment banker for both Sun Oil and Fairleigh Dickinson Jr., was more easily able to reach an understanding between the two parties, which provided for Fairleigh Dickinson Jr. to sell his 5% holdings in Becton Dickinson to Sun Oil at the appropriate time.

---

5. This last factor was added after the *Wellman v. Dickinson* decision.

6. *Hanson Trust PLC v. SCM Corp.*, 744 F.2d 47 (2d Cir. 1985).

7. *S-G Securities, Inc. v. Fuqua Investment Co.*, 466 F. Supp. 1114 (D. Mass. 1978).

Sun Oil obtained commitments from 33 financial institutions to buy 20% of the outstanding shares of Becton Dickinson. On one day couriers were sent to these institutions to purchase these shares. Following the stock purchase, Sun Oil informed the New York Stock Exchange and Becton Dickinson of their actions. They did not file a 14D-1 but did file a 13D.

In a lawsuit that followed, the court ruled that the manner in which the shares were purchased did not constitute a tender offer. In doing so, the court set forth the basis for what has now become known as the Eight Factor Test. The court did rule that Sun Oil had violated the Williams Act by not filing a 13D when it had reached its understanding with Fairleigh Dickinson to purchase his 5%.

Materials That Shareholders Receive

Shareholders receive an "Offer to Purchase" and a "Letter of Transmittal." The Offer to Purchase sets forth the terms of the offer. Chief among these terms are the number of shares to be purchased, the offer price, and the length of time the offer will remain open. The Offer to Purchase may be many pages in length (e.g., 30 pages) and may contain much additional information for shareholders to consider, such as withdrawal rights, a discussion of tax considerations, and more details on the terms of the offer.

Method of Tendering Shares

Stockholders tender their shares through an intermediary, such as a commercial bank, or trust company, which is referred to as the paying agent. As stockholders seek to participate in the tender offer, they submit their shares to the paying agent in exchange for cash or securities, in accordance with the terms of the offer. Attached to their shares must be a letter of transmittal.

The agent accumulates the shares but does not pay the stockholders until the offer expires. In the event that the offer is extended, the paying agent holds the shares until the new offer expires, unless instructed otherwise by the individual stockholders. The bidder may extend an undersubscribed tender. In fact, it is not unusual for an offer to be extended several times as the bidder tries to get enough shares to ensure control. If the bidder decides to extend the offer, it must announce the extension no later than 9:00 A.M. on the business day following the day on which the offer was to have expired. At that time the bidder must disclose the number of shares that have already been purchased. As noted, shareholders have the right to withdraw their shares at any time during the offer period. The fact that they originally tendered them in response to the offer does not limit their ability to change their mind or tender these same shares to a competing offer after they withdraw them.

Changes in the Tender Offer

The Williams Act allows a modification in the offer period if there is a material change in the terms of the offer. The length of the extension in the offer period depends on the significance of the change, which generally is considered a *new offer*. A new offer ensures the stockholders a 20-day period to consider the offer. A higher price might be considered such a significant change. A less significant change results in an *amended offer*, which provides for a 10-day minimum offer period. An increase in the number of shares to be purchased might be considered an amended offer.

Best Price Rule and Other Related Rules

Under Section 14(d)(7), if the bidder increases the consideration offered, the bidder must pay this increased consideration to all those who have already tendered their shares at the lower price. The goal of this section is to ensure that all tender shareholders are treated equally, regardless of the date within the offer period that they tender their shares. Under SEC Rule 14d-10, a bidder may offer more than one type of consideration. In such cases, however, selling stockholders have the right to select the type of consideration they want.

Bidder Purchases Outside of Tender Offer

Under Rule 10b-13, a bidder may not purchase shares outside the tender offer on terms that are different from those of the tender offer. There may be exceptions to this rule if the SEC agrees to exempt the transactions based on its belief that the purchases are not manipulative, fraudulent, or deceptive. Such purchases, however, are permitted in the event that the tender offer concludes or is withdrawn.

Payment Following Completion of the Offer

The law provides that the tendered shares must be either paid for promptly after the offer is terminated or returned to the shareholders. This prompt payment may be frustrated by other regulatory requirements, such as the Hart-Scott-Rodino Act. The bidder may postpone payment if other regulatory approvals must still be obtained after the Williams Act offer period expires.

Mini-Tender Offers

Mini-tender offers are bids for less than five percent of a company's stock. Such offers are much less regulated as bidders, and are not required to comply with the disclosure requirements for larger tender offers. Investors who accept such offers need to know that they are not entitled to pro-rata acceptance and do not have withdrawal rights. These offers may not contain a premium and may even be below the market price. Therefore, investors need to be wary of them.

Taking Control after a Successful Tender Offer

It is common that after a successful tender offer the target and the bidder agree that the bidder may elect a majority of the board of directors. This would allow the bidder to take control of the board of directors without calling a meeting of the shareholders. However, when antitakeover defenses that limit the ability of an offeror to appoint members to the board are in place, this process may be more difficult. If this is not the case, the board change may go smoothly. If the target agrees to the change in control of the board, it must communicate to the SEC and its shareholders information about the new directors similar to that which would normally be disclosed if they were nominees in an election of directors.

De-listing the Target

Following a takeover and merger of a target into the bidder, a bidder/target may then file to have the target's shares de-listed from the exchanges on which it was traded. An application then needs to be filed with and approved by the SEC.

Competing Tender Offers

An initial tender offer often attracts rival tender offers in takeover battles. Because the law was designed to give stockholders time to carefully consider all relevant alternatives, an extension of the offer period is possible when there is a competing offer. The Williams Act states that, in the event of a new tender offer, stockholders in the target company must have at least 10 business days to consider the new offer. In effect, this 10-day consideration period can extend the original offer period. Consider, for example, that we are 16 days into the first offer when a new bidder makes a tender offer for the target firm; then target shareholders have at least 10 days to decide on the original offer. As a result, the original offer period is extended six more days, or a total of 26 days. If, however, the new offer occurred on the fourth day of the first offer period, there would not be an extension of the original offer period.

Applicability of U.S. Tender Offer Rules to Takeovers of Non-U.S. Companies

The U.S. tender offer rules apply to U.S. companies when they make bids for the shares of foreign companies if the target's shares are registered in the United States pursuant to the Securities Exchange Act. Exemptions may be had in cases where the foreign issuer's U.S. shareholders comprise less than 10% of the total shares outstanding.

OTHER SPECIFIC TAKEOVER RULES IN THE UNITED STATES

There are certain other takeover rules that may be relevant to certain takeovers. For example, in the utility sector, there is the Public Utility Holding Company Act (PUHCA), passed in 1935, which imposed geographical limitations on utility mergers, while also placing restrictions on their investments in utilities' investments in non-energy companies. This law was overseen by the SEC. However, the Energy Policy Act liberalized these outmoded rules. The Federal Energy Regulatory Commission was formed and took a role in reviewing utility deals.

Takeovers that are determined to be threats to U.S. national security can be halted by the president. Such deals are reviewed by the Committee on Foreign Investment in the United States (CFIUS), a 12-member interagency panel that includes the Secretaries of State, Defense, Treasury, and Commerce, which makes a recommendation to the president. This panel does not review all deals, and most dealmakers and their advisors, when they believe there may be a potential security issue, contact the committee so as not to have a problem after the fact. Potential opposition to deals related to CFIUS was a key factor in China's Cnnoc Ltd. dropping its $18.5 billion all-cash offer for Unocal in August 2005 and for the Dubai-owned Ports World's amendment of its 2006 $6.8 billion offer for

Britain's Peninsular and Oriental Steam Navigation Co., which held contracts to manage six U.S. ports.

Stock Exchange Regulations

Various stock exchanges have implemented regulations that affect control transactions such as takeovers, antitakeover defenses, and proxy contests. The most prominent exchange in the United States is the New York Stock Exchange (NYSE), which charges companies $300 million per year to be listed. To enhance the integrity of the exchange, the NYSE has adopted rules such as ones requiring shareholder approval for transactions such as the issuance of shares equal to 20% or more of a listed company's outstanding shares. It also, for example, requires shareholder approval for stock sales that will lead to a change in control of the company. In instituting such rules, the exchange seeks to walk the fine line between attracting companies to the exchange and not wanting to alienate them and have them leave for venues such as NASDAQ, and maintaining the integrity of its market.

Regulation of Proxy Solicitation

State corporation laws require annual shareholder meetings. In order to achieve a quorum, the company solicits proxies from shareholders. Bidders attempting to take over a company may also solicit proxies from shareholders. Section 14(a) of the Securities Exchange Act regulates these solicitations. As part of these regulations, a solicitor must file a proxy statement and a Schedule 14A, which must also be given to security holders. According to Rule 14a-6, proxy materials must be filed with the SEC 10 days before they are used. An exception exists for more noncontroversial events such as annual meetings. However, in no case must the materials be used prior to being submitted. In light of the substantial mailing costs that security holders who have their own proposals may incur, the law requires the issuer to provide a supporting statement (up to 500 words), which is included with management proxy proposals. Only a very small percentage of such security holder solicitations are successful.

INTERNATIONAL SECURITIES LAWS RELATING TO TAKEOVERS

In this section we will highlight some of different takeover laws that exist in countries other than the United States. A comprehensive discussion of these various laws is beyond the scope of this book. However, some of them are discussed to give the reader a flavor of their variety but also the extent to which many have similar provisions to U.S. takeover rules.

Europe

Great Britain

British takeover regulation is a form of self-regulation by the corporate sector and the securities industry. This regulation is based on the Code of Takeovers and Mergers, a collection of standards and regulations on takeovers and mergers, and is enforced by the

Panel on Takeovers and Mergers. This panel is composed of members of the Bank of England, London Stock Exchange members, and various other financial leaders. Its chief responsibility is to ensure that a "level playing field" exists, that is, that all investors have equal access to information on takeover offers. The panel also attempts to prevent target firms from adopting antitakeover measures without prior shareholder approval. Some of the more important provisions of the British code are:

- Investors acquiring 30% or more of a company's shares must bid for the remaining shares at the highest price paid for the shares already acquired.
- Substantial partial offers for a target must gain the approval of the target and the panel.
- Antitakeover measures, such as supermajority provisions or the issuance of options to be given to friendly parties, must be approved by the target's shareholders.

The unique aspect of the British system is that compliance is voluntary; the panel's rulings are not binding by law. Its rulings are considered most influential, however, and are commonly adopted. If the panel detects a violation and lack of compliance with its rules by a party involved in a takeover, it may refer the matter to the Financial Services Authority (FSA), which is the main financial regulator in the United Kingdom. Mergers that may be anticompetitive may be referred to the Competition Commission.

Pursuant to Britain's Companies Act, buyers of 3% or more of a target's shares must notify the target within two days of acquiring that position. Rule 2.5 of this country's Share Acquisition Rules requires the bidder to make a public announcement of offers. In the case of hostile bids, the target must respond with its position within 14 days of the bid.[8]

European Union

The European Commission had sought one set of rules for all European nations, including the United Kingdom, rather than separate rules for each country that might be involved in cross-border deals. Such an accord has been under discussion for almost two decades. Agreement on a joint takeover directive was finally reached after 15 years of debate and was made effective as of May 2006. As of that date each EU member country had to implement the directive into its national laws. While the original form of the takeover directive included many shareholder rights provisions, it has been diluted by countries that wanted to give their indigenous companies a greater ability to oppose hostile takeovers from bidders from other countries—even if they were from EU member states. The main opposition to a common set of rules came from Germany and Sweden.

In order to protect minority shareholders the directive contains a requirement to make a mandatory offer after a bidder purchases a certain number of shares. This bid must be made at an equitable price and must be submitted to shareholders with certain disclosures relating to the offer and bidder. Target shareholders must have no less than two weeks to evaluate the bid. The directive contains provisions to limit the use of poison pills and

---

8. Charles Mayo, "UK: England and Wales," in *Mergers and Acquisitions: 2005/06* (London: Practical Law Company, 2005/06).

shares with multiple voting rights to oppose hostile bids. However, member states may choose to opt out of the provisions that they find not in their interests and substitute their own national rules. Their individual national rules are still relevant depending on the particular circumstances.

France

In France, bids are regulated by the Financial Markets Authority and bidders, acting through financial representatives, such as banks, must submit disclosures to this entity. Filings must be made within five trading days of crossing various shareholding thresholds starting with 5% and moving up to two-thirds of outstanding shares.[9] Bidders acquiring additional shares must disclose their holdings on a daily basis. Offers for French companies are required to remain open for 25 trading days but not longer than 35 trading days.

Germany

In general, Germany tends to be more supportive of management and more accepting of antitakeover defenses. This position is partly due to the shock of the takeover of Mannesman by Vodafone. Takeovers are regulated by several laws including the Takeover Act. They are supervised by the Federal Office of Supervision of Financial Services (Bundesanstalt fur Finanzdienstleistungsaufsicht or BaFin). In Germany, mandatory offers for the complete company are required when a bidder acquires a threshold number of shares. Offers must be kept open for 28 days but no more than 60 days. Targets must respond within two weeks of receiving the offer. Offers must be publicized in approved national newspapers. Hostile bids are not common in Germany due to the large cross holdings that have been assembled over many years including major holdings by banks that tend to be supportive of management.

Ireland

Takeovers in Ireland are regulated by the Takeover Panel Act of 1997, which established the Takeover Panel that oversees takeovers.[10] Acquisitions of shares of 5% or more require a disclosure. Additional disclosure is required for purchase of 1% or more of a target's shares. In Ireland, there is a 21-day minimum offer period. In hostile bids the target must respond within 14 days.

Netherlands

In the Netherlands takeovers must be made pursuant to the Securities Act, which is enforced by The Authority for Financial Markets. Acquisitions of shareholdings at various thresholds, starting at 5%, require disclosure. Bids must be kept open for at least 20 days

---

9. Pierre Servan-Schreiber, Armand W. Grumberg, and Arash Attar, "France," in *Mergers and Acquisitions: 2005/06* (London: Practical Law Company, 2005/06).

10. John Given and Cian McCourt, "Ireland," in *Mergers and Acquisitions: 2005/06* (London: Practical Law Company, 2005/06).

but, in effect, rules make this period 23 days.[11] For hostile bids the target's board must disclose its position four days prior to a shareholder meeting that may be called to address the bid.

Spain

In both Spain and France hostile bids are common. Bidders acquiring 5% or more of a target's stock must notify the National Securities Market Commission. This body then suspends the trading of the target's stock. The bidder must make a formal announcement of the bid, such as in at least two national newspapers and the Commission's Official Gazette, within five days of making the offer.[12] Offers may be kept open for as long as four months.

Russian Tender Offer Rules

In mid-2006, Russia adopted a broad takeover reform law. It provided for both a minority put option and minority squeeze out. The law provided for mandatory tender offers after crossing an odd mix of share thresholds of 30%, 50%, and 70%. It also requires bidders to attain anti-monopoly approval before completing 100% stock acquisitions. Mandatory tender offers have minimum price requirements with shareholders having an option to choose cash in case of securities offers. The minimum price cannot be lower than the stock's price in the prior six-month trading period. Offers must be filed with the Russian Federal Service for the Financial Markets.

Canada

Securities regulation in Canada is fragmented, with each Canadian province and territory having its own securities commission. The most important of these 13 securities commissions is the Ontario Securities Commission. The Ontario Securities Act provides for similar regulation of takeovers as provided under the Williams Act. Takeover bids for 20% or more of a particular class of securities are subject to the regulation. The minimum offer period, called the *minimum deposit period* in Canada, is 35 business days. Shareholders have withdrawal rights, bids may be extended, and oversubscribed bids may be completed on a pro rata basis, although specific conditions apply to each action. Like the United States, and many other nations, Canada has regulations that allow the government to intervene to stop transactions larger than $250 million if the government believes that national security is threatened by the deal.

Asia

As noted in Chapters 1 and 2, the M&A business is rapidly evolving in many Asian markets. As these markets continue to restructure, their laws evolve to accommodate the volume of deals.

---

11. Maarten Muller and Johan Kleyn, "The Netherlands," in *Mergers and Acquisitions: 2005/06* (London: Practical Law Company, 2005/06).
12. Francisco Pena and Fernando de las Cuevas, "Spain" in *Mergers and Acquisitions: 2005/06* (London: Practical Law Company, 2005/06).

Japan

The takeover market in Japan has been undergoing major changes in recent years. These changes have taken pace while some major takeover battles have occurred. One was the takeover battle between Mitsubishi Tokyo Financial Group, UFJ, and Sumitomo. Japanese courts have reached decisions similar to those of courts in the State of Delaware. In response to heightened takeover pressures, Japanese corporations have adopted various antitakeover defenses including poison pills.

Tender offers are regulated by the Securities Exchange Law. Tender offers must be kept open for 20 days but not more than 60. A new Company Law is expected to go into place in May 2006. In May 2005, the Ministry of Economy, Trade, and Industry and the Ministry of Justice jointly issued certain guidelines for the usage of anti-takeover defenses. These guidelines are not necessarily legally binding but it is expected companies will follow them. The guidelines recommend that defenses should be disclosed when installed and that should facilitate the enhancement of shareholder value. They also state that defense should be related to the magnitude of the threat to shareholder value.

In enforcing takeover laws, Japanese courts have reached decisions somewhat similar to what one would expect to see in Delaware courts. These decisions allow for the use of antitakeover defenses but with an eye toward enhancing shareholder value and not in a way that would hurt shareholders and merely entrench management.

Korea

The Korean Commercial Code contains a broad variety of laws governing Korean companies, including those that relate to the incorporation of businesses but also takeover regulations and other control share transactions. Under Korea's Securities Exchange Law, when a shareholder acquires a stock position of 5%, that shareholder is required to report this holding to this country's Financial Supervisory Commission within five business days of reaching that percent holding. An additional report is required for further share purchases of 1% or more. The acquiring shareholder is subject to a "cooling-off period" in which it must wait five days after acquiring the stock position before exercising the voting rights associated with the stock. As a result of an effort by Dubai-based Sovereign Asset Management Ltd. to remove the chairman of a Korean refiner, SK Corp, Korean laws were changed to now require holders of 5% or more to "disclose their intentions" if they are interested in pursuing changes in management.

Korea's Securities Exchange Law requires that a tender offer statement be filed when such a bid is initiated. This law used to mandate a three-day waiting period between the filing of the report and the offer being effective, but this was recently eliminated. Tender offer rules apply equally to offers from outside parties as well as self-tenders. Violators of these laws are subject to both administrative and criminal penalties.

Many Korean companies are protected by rules that allow for large golden parachutes as well as a requirement that two-thirds shareholder approval be received before changes in the board of directors can take place.

China

With the advent of communism in the 1950s in China, shareholdings disappeared. China began the slow process of returning to some form of a free market economy in the 1980s. The Shanghai Exchange was founded in 1990, and then all trading was required to be done on this and then other organized exchanges. Interim trading rules were established in 1993. This was followed by the Securities Law of China, which went into effect in July 1999. This law provided for acquisitions of public companies through agreement between the parties as well as through bids.

The Securities Law requires that owners of 5% or more of a public company's shares disclose this holding to the Chinese Securities Regulatory Commission, the exchange on which the shares are traded, and to the issuing company within three days of acquiring this position. Once a 30% holding is achieved, the holder of the shares is prohibited from purchasing more shares unless it makes a bid for the entire company.

Taiwan

Taiwan's takeover rules are set forth in the Tender Offer Rules for Public Issuance Companies. Tender offer rules have been in effect since 1995, but they have had little impact due to the paucity of such offers, which is in part due to the fact that many companies are controlled by large family shareholding positions. Revisions of these rules took effect in 2005. These rules require that bidders make a public announcement prior to initiating an offer. They also provide for greater disclosure in such tender offers. Under prior rules target shareholders could withdraw shares for the entire offer period, but those withdrawal rights have been limited if the terms of the offer have been met during the offer period.

India

Takeovers are regulated by the Company Court and the Department of Company Affairs. For companies that are publicly traded, the Securities Exchange Board of India supervises the transaction.[13] India has a Takeover Code that sets forth the rules governing takeovers. The bidder's investment bank is required to make a public announcement of the offer. This announcement includes the typical disclosures required in most countries. Offers have to remain open for 20 days. In India, companies have developed some of the various takeover defenses we see in the United States, such as poison pills and greenmail.

Australia

The Uniform Companies Code that was passed in 1961 provided regulations for takeovers. Various changes in the law were made since then and they culminated with the Corporate Law Economic Reform Program (CLERP), which went into effect in March 2000 and amended the Corporations Law. CLERP law makes the Corporations and Securities Panel the sole entity responsibility for ruling on various takeover-related disputes during the bid period. This transferred such responsibility from the courts during this time period.

---

13. Shardul Shroff, "India," in *Mergers and Acquisitions: 2005/06* (London: Practical Law Company, 2005/06).

The Act made compulsory takeovers necessary when a bidder purchased 75% of the value of a company's outstanding stock. Also, bids that seek to acquire 20% or more of a company's stock are allowed as long as they are followed by subsequent bids for the remaining stock of the company. The law also sets forth disclosure rules relating to bids while also requiring supplementary disclosures. Acquisitions of shares equal to or greater than 5% require disclosure of this holding. Bids must remain open for at least one month but no more than one year. In addition, the Act places limits on the use of certain antitakeover defenses and some, such as greenmail, are not allowed.

BUSINESS JUDGMENT RULE

The *business judgment rule* is the standard by which directors of corporations are judged when they exercise their fiduciary duties in the course of an attempted takeover. Under this standard it is presumed that directors acted in a manner that is consistent with their fiduciary obligations to shareholders. Thus, any party contesting this presumption must conclusively demonstrate that their fiduciary duties were violated. Specific court decisions have highlighted certain relevant issues regarding how directors must act when employing antitakeover defenses. Through these decisions, standards such as the *Revlon duties* and the *Unocal standard* have been developed.

Unocal Standard

In *Unocal v. Mesa Petroleum,* the Delaware Supreme Court reviewed the actions of the Unocal board of directors as they implemented an antitakeover strategy to thwart the unwanted tender offer by Mesa Petroleum, led by its colorful chief executive officer, T. Boone Pickens.[14] This strategy included a self-tender offer in which the target made a tender offer for itself in competition with the offer initiated by the bidder. In reaching its decision, the court noted its concern that directors may act in their own self-interest, such as in this case, in which they were allegedly favoring the self-tender as opposed to simply objectively searching for the best deal for shareholders. In such instances directors must demonstrate that they had reason to believe that there was a danger to the pursuit of a corporate policy that was in the best interest of shareholders. In addition, they must show that their actions were in the best interest of shareholders. Subsequent courts have refined the Unocal Standard to feature a two-part responsibility that includes:

1. *Reasonableness test.* The board must be able to clearly demonstrate that their actions were reasonable in relation to their perceived beliefs about the danger to their corporate policies.
2. *Proportionality test.* The board must also be able to demonstrate that their defensive actions were in proportion to the magnitude of the perceived danger to their policies.[15]

Once these Unocal standards are satisfied, the normal presumptions about director behavior under the business judgment rule apply.

---

14. *Unocal Corp. v. Mesa Petroleum Co.,* 493 A.2d 946 (Del. 1985).
15. *Moore Corp. v. Wallace Computer Services,* 907 F. Supp. 1545, 1556 (D. Del. 1995).

Revlon Duties

In *Revlon, Inc. v. MacAndrews and Forbes Holdings,* the Delaware Supreme Court ruled on what obligations a target board of directors has when faced with an offer for control of their company.[16] In this transaction, which is discussed further in Chapter 5 in the context of lockup options, the court ruled that certain antitakeover defenses that favored one bidder over another were invalid. The court determined that rather than promoting the auction process, which should result in maximizing shareholder wealth, these antitakeover defenses, a lockup option and a no-shop provision, inhibited rather than promoted the auction process. *Revlon duties* come into play when it is clear that the sale or breakup of the company is inevitable. At that time, directors have a responsibility to maximize the gains for their shareholders. That is, they have a responsibility to shift their focus away from actions that they normally would take to preserve the corporation and its strategy to actions that will result in the greatest gains for shareholders, such as making sure they get the highest bid possible for shareholders.

In reaching its decision rendering the lockup options and no-shop provisions invalid, the court did not go so far as to say that the use of the defenses was invalid *per se.* The use of defenses that might favor one bidder over another could be consistent with the board's Revlon duties if they promoted the auction process by enabling one bidder to be more competitive with another bidder, thereby causing offer prices to rise. However, defenses that hinder the auction process are not valid.

STATE ANTITAKEOVER LAWS

Many non-Americans are confused and dismayed by the sometimes conflicting combination of federal laws and state laws that characterizes the U.S. legal system. Indeed, under current federal and state takeover laws, it is possible that conforming to some aspects of the federal laws means violating certain state laws. The line of demarcation between federal takeover laws and their state counterparts has to do with the focus of each. Federal laws tend to be directed at securities regulation, tender offers, and antitrust considerations, whereas state laws govern corporate charters and their bylaws. Currently, a broad array of inconsistent state laws exists across the United States. Many of these laws were passed in response to pressure by particular corporations who found themselves the object of interest by potential acquirers. The usual scenario is that a local firm petitions the state legislature to pass an antitakeover law or amend the current one to make it more difficult for a local corporation to be taken over. The political pressure that is brought to bear on the state legislatures comes in the form of allegations that a takeover by a "foreign raider" will mean a significant loss of jobs as well as other forms of community support, such as charitable donations by the local corporation.

The system of differing state laws is not unique to the United States. The EU has worked to have a common set of merger rules but has only achieved approval of a set of limited rules. Given that EU countries have the right to opt out of the new EU merger

---

16. *Revlon, Inc. v. MacAndrews & Forbes Holdings, Inc.,* 506 A.2d 173, CCH Fed. Sec. L. Rep. ¶ 92,348 (Del. 1986).

rules, and then apply their own differing country-specific laws, the situation in the EU is in some respects somewhat analogous to what we have in the United States.

Genesis of State Antitakeover Laws in the United States

State antitakeover laws were first developed in the late 1960s and early 1970s. These statutes typically required that disclosure materials be filed following the initiation of the bid. The problem with these "first-generation" state antitakeover laws was that they applied to firms that did only a small amount of business in that state. This seemed unfair to bidding corporations. Thus, the stage was set for a legal challenge.

Key Court Decisions Relating to Antitakeover Laws

Certain court decisions have defined the types of state antitakeover laws that are acceptable and those that are not. These decisions, which were recorded in the 1980s, are still relevant today.

Edgar v. MITE

The constitutionality of these first-generation antitakeover laws was successfully challenged in 1982, in the famous *Edgar v. MITE* decision.[17] In this decision the U.S. Supreme Court ruled that the Illinois Business Takeover Act was unconstitutional. The Illinois law permitted the state to block a nationwide tender offer for a state-affiliated target corporation if the bidder failed to comply with the disclosure laws of Illinois. The challenge to the Illinois law caused states with similar laws to question their constitutionality and redevelop their provisions. The states still wanted to inhibit takeovers, which they thought were not in the best interest of the states, but now they had to adopt a different approach, which came in the form of the "second-generation" laws. The second-generation state antitakeover laws had a narrower focus than the first-generation laws. They tended to apply only to those firms that were incorporated within the state or that conducted a substantial part of their business activities within state boundaries. They were not directed at regulating disclosure in tender offers, as the first-generation laws were. Rather, they focused on issues of corporate governance, which traditionally are the domain of state corporation laws.

Dynamics v. CTS

The *Edgar v. MITE* decision delivered a severe blow to the first-generation laws. Many opponents of antitakeover legislation attacked the second-generation laws, which they believed were also unconstitutional. These legal actions resulted in the *Dynamics v. CTS* decision of April 1987.[18] In this case, the CTS Corporation used the Indiana law to fight off a takeover by the Dynamics Corporation. Dynamics challenged the law, contending that it was unconstitutional. In *Dynamics v. CTS,* the U.S. Supreme Court ruled that the

---

17. *Edgar v. MITE Corporation*, 102 S. Ct. 2629 (1982).
18. *Dynamics Corporation of America v. CTS Corporation*, 637 F. Supp. 406 (N.D. Ill. 1986).

Indiana antitakeover law was constitutional. This law allows stockholders to vote on whether a buyer of controlling interest can exercise his or her voting rights. The CTS decision gave the Supreme Court's approval to the second-generation state takeover laws. Since the April 1987 CTS decision, many states have adopted antitakeover laws. Today most states have some kind of law regulating takeovers.

Amanda Acquisition Corporation v. Universal Foods Corporation

In November 1989, the U.S. Supreme Court refused to hear a challenge to the Wisconsin antitakeover law.[19] The Court's unwillingness to hear this challenge further buttressed the legal viability of state antitakeover laws. The Wisconsin law requires a bidder who acquires 10% or more of a target company's stock to receive the approval of the other target shareholders or wait three years to complete the merger. The three-year waiting period makes heavily leveraged buyouts, which were typical of the fourth merger wave, prohibitively expensive.

The Supreme Court decision arose out of a legal challenge by the Amanda Acquisition Corporation, which is a subsidiary of the Boston-based High Voltage Engineering Corporation. Amanda challenged the Wisconsin law that prevented it from proceeding with a tender offer for the Milwaukee-based Universal Foods Corporation. The directors of Universal Foods opposed the takeover and reacted by using what has been called the Just Say No defense. Amanda Acquisition Corporation charged that the Wisconsin law was an interference with interstate commerce and was harmful to shareholders. The Supreme Court failed to agree and refused to hear the challenge to the law. The Court's position in this case reaffirms the *Dynamics v. CTS* decision that upheld the constitutionality of the Indiana antitakeover law in 1987.

Components of Second-Generation Laws

Most second-generation laws incorporate some or all of the following provisions:

- Fair price provision
- Business combination provision
- Control share provision
- Cash-out statute

Fair Price Provision

A fair price provision requires that in a successful tender offer all shareholders who do not decide to sell will receive the same price as shareholders who do accept the offer. These provisions are designed to prevent the abuses that may occur in two-tiered tender offers. With two-tiered bids, a high price is offered to the first-tier tenders, whereas a lower price or less advantageous terms (such as securities of uncertain value instead of cash) are offered to the members of the second tier.

---

19. *Amanda Acquisition Corp. v. Universal Foods Corp.*, 877 F.2d 496 (7th Cir. 1989).

Business Combination Provision

This provision prevents business agreements between the target company and the bidding company for a certain time period. For example, the wording of a business combination provision may rule out the sales of the target's assets by the bidding company. These provisions are designed to prevent leveraged hostile acquisitions. When an acquiring company assumes a large amount of debt to finance a takeover, it may be relying on the sales of assets by the target to pay the high interest payments required by the debt. The law is designed to prevent the transformation of local firms, with a low-risk capital structure, into riskier leveraged companies.

Control Share Provision

The State of New York adopted the first control share statute in 1985. A control share provision requires that acquiring firms obtain prior approval of current target stockholders before the purchases are allowed. These provisions typically apply to stock purchases beyond a certain percentage of the outstanding stock. They are particularly effective if the current share ownership includes large blocks of stock that are held by groups of people who are generally supportive of management, such as employee stockholders.

Cash-Out Statute

This provision, like the fair price requirement, is designed to limit tender offers. It typically requires that if a bidder buys a certain percentage of stock in a target firm, the bidder is then required to purchase all the remaining outstanding shares at the same terms given to the initial purchase. This provision limits acquiring firms that lack the financial resources for a 100% stock acquisition. It also limits leveraged acquisitions because it may require the bidder to assume an even greater amount of debt with the associated high debt service. Bidders might therefore be discouraged because of their inability to obtain financing for a 100% purchase or simply because they do not believe their cash flow will service the increased debt.

Delaware Antitakeover Law

The Delaware antitakeover law is probably the most important of all the state antitakeover laws because more corporations are incorporated in Delaware than in any other state. General Motors, Exxon Mobil, Wal-Mart and DuPont are among the 308,492 companies that have incorporated in Delaware. One-half of all New York Stock Exchange companies are incorporated there, along with 60% of the *Fortune* 500 companies.

There is a clear preference on the part of companies to incorporate in Delaware. It has often been assumed that the reason for the preference for Delaware is that it has a well-developed body of law and a sophisticated court system.[20] Delaware's court system utilizes very knowledgeable judges to decide corporate lawsuits as opposed to juries.

---

20. Stephen J. Massey, "Chancellor Allen's Jurisprudence and the Theory of Corporate Law," *Delaware Journal of Corporate Law*, 683,702(79), 1992.

Another explanation for the preference for Delaware is that Delaware's incorporation fees are cheaper than all but eight other states (although the $150,000 that Delaware charges may not be that significant for a *Fortune* 500 company). Still the fee difference is not significant enough to explain the preference for Delaware[21] Other desirable characteristics of Delaware which contribute to its popularity is the fact that companies and their shareholders do not need to be a resident of the state to incorporate there. In addition, non-Delaware businesses do not have to pay Delaware corporate taxes even if they are incorporated in that state.

The Delaware antitakeover law was passed in 1988, but was made retroactive to December 23, 1987, the date before corporate raider Carl Icahn acquired 15% of Texaco Corporation. The law was passed in response to an intense lobbying effort by companies seeking to adopt a protective statute. They threatened that if such a protective statute was not passed, they would reincorporate in states that did have antitakeover laws. The fact that incorporation fees account for nearly 20% of the Delaware state budget underscored the importance of this threat.[22] The choice of the effective date testifies to the power of this lobbying effort. The law stipulates that an unwanted bidder who buys more than 15% of a target company's stock may not complete the takeover for three years except under the following conditions:[23]

- If the buyer buys 85% or more of the target company's stock. This 85% figure may not include the stock held by directors or the stock held in employee stock ownership plans.
- If two-thirds of the stockholders approve the acquisition.
- If the board of directors and the stockholders decide to waive the antitakeover provisions of this law.

Being primarily a business combination statute, the law is designed to limit takeovers financed by debt. Raiders who have financed their takeovers by large amounts of debt often need to sell off company assets and divisions to pay off the debt. The need to pay off the debt quickly becomes significant in the case of the billion-dollar takeover, as in the 1980s, when interest payments were as much as half a million dollars per day. Although the Delaware law might discourage some debt-financed takeovers, it is not very effective against cash offers. Moreover, even debt-financed offers at a very attractive price may be sufficiently appealing for stockholders to waive the antitakeover provisions of the law.

Why Do State Antitakeover Laws Get Passed?

Most state antitakeover laws get passed as a result of lobbying efforts of companies that are concerned about being taken over. For example, the Pennsylvania antitakeover law was passed partly as a result of the efforts of Armstrong World Industries of Lancaster, Pennsylvania, which was concerned about being taken over by the Belzberg family of Canada. Harcourt Brace Jovanovich and Gillette promoted the respective Florida and

21. Jill E. Fisch, "The Peculiar Role of the Delaware Court in the Competition for Corporate Charters," Fordham University Law School, Research Paper 00–02, May 2000.
22. Robert A. G. Monks and Well Morow, *Corporate Governance* (Cambridge, MA: Blackwell Business, 1995), p. 35.
23. Section 203 of the Delaware General Corporation Law.

Massachusetts control share statutes. Burlington Industries promoted North Carolina's antitakeover law, whereas Dayton-Hudson and Boeing promoted antitakeover laws in Minnesota and Washington, respectively. Ironically, some indigenous companies are so aggressive in promoting such laws that they even draft the statute for lawmakers. The result is a patchwork of many different state laws across America.

Wealth Effects of State Antitakeover Laws

In a study of 40 state antitakeover bills introduced between 1982 and 1987, Karpoff and Malatesta found a small but statistically significant decrease in stock prices of companies incorporated in the various states contemplating passage of such laws.[24] They even found that companies doing significant business in these states also suffered a decline in stock prices. Szewczyk and Tsetsekos found that Pennsylvania firms lost $4 billion during the time this state's antitakeover law was being considered and adopted.[25] It should be kept in mind, however, that these effects are short-term effects based on the reactions of traders in the market during that time period.

State Antitrust Actions

Later in this chapter we will discuss federal antitrust laws. However, in this section on state laws we should point out that many states have their own antitrust laws. The wording of these laws is often similar to that of the federal laws. In addition, the states have the power, under federal law, to take action in federal court and to block mergers they believe are anticompetitive, even when the Justice Department or the FTC fails to challenge the merger. The states' ability to do so was greatly enhanced by a 9-to-0 U.S. Supreme Court ruling in April 1990. The ruling came as a result of California officials' challenge to the $2.5 billion takeover of Lucky Stores, Inc. by American Stores Company in June 1988. The ruling, written by Justice John Paul Stevens, overturned a 1989 U.S. Court of Appeals Ninth Circuit ruling in 1989, which held that the Clayton Act did not permit California to block the Lucky Stores and American Stores merger. California obtained a stay of the ruling from Chief Justice Sandra Day O'Connor in August 1989. This prevented combining the operations of Lucky Stores, the state's largest supermarket chain, with Alpha Beta, owned by American Stores and the state's fourth largest supermarket chain, until the matter was finally adjudicated. California's argument that the merger would cost the California consumers $440 million per year in grocery bills was found to be compelling by the U.S. Supreme Court.[26] This ruling opens the door for states to be active in opposing mergers on antitrust grounds when the federal government decides to adopt a pro-business stance and to limit its antitrust enforcement. It also makes antitrust enforcement less sensitive to the political makeup of the executive branch of the federal government.

---

24. Johnathan M. Karpoff and Paul Malatesta, "The Wealth Effects of Second Generation State Takeover Legislation," *Journal of Financial Economics,* 25(2) December 1989, 291–322.
25. S.H. Szewczyk and G.P. Tsetsekos, "State Intervention in the Market for Corporate Control: The Case of Pennsylvania Senate Bill 1310," *Journal of Financial Economics,* February 1992, 3–23.
26. *California v. American Stores Co.,* 697 F. Supp. 1125 (C.D. Cal. 1988).

CASE STUDY

TIME-WARNER-PARAMOUNT

In March 1989, Time, Inc. entered into a merger agreement with Warner Communications, Inc. The deal was a planned stock-for-stock exchange that would be put before the shareholders of both companies for their approval. Paramount Communications, Inc. then entered the fray with a hostile tender offer for Time. This offer was structured by Paramount to be higher than the valuation that was inherent to the original Time-Warner agreement. Time then responded with a tender offer for Warner that featured a cash offer for 51% of Warner followed by a second-step transaction using securities as consideration.

Paramount sued and contended that the original merger agreement between Time and Warner meant that there was an impending change in control, thereby bringing the Revlon duties of the directors into play. In *Paramount Communications, Inc. v. Time, Inc.*, the court rejected Paramount's argument that there would be a change in control.[a] The court was impressed by the fact that both companies were public and their shares were widely held. Based on such reasoning, the court concluded that this was not an acquisition in which one company was acquiring another but rather a strategic merger. Therefore, Revlon duties were not triggered, and the normal business judgment rule standard applied.

The significance of this decision is that the announcement of a strategic merger between two companies is not a signal that either of the companies is for sale. Therefore, the directors do not have to consider other offers as if there were an auction process. This implies that if there is an unwanted bid, the directors may consider the use of antitakeover measures to avoid the hostile bid while they go ahead with the strategic merger.

[a]Paramount Communications, Inc. v. Time, Inc., 571 A.2d 1140 (Del. 1989).

REGULATION OF INSIDER TRADING

The SEC rules specify remedies for shareholders who incur losses resulting from insider trading. Insiders are bound by SEC Rule 10b-5, which states that insiders must "disclose or abstain" from trading the firm's securities. Insider trading regulation was buttressed by the passage of the Insider Trading and Securities Fraud Enforcement Act of 1988. This law imposed maximum penalties of up to $1 million and up to 10 years in prison while also setting up a bounty program whereby informants could collect up to 10% of the insider's profits. It also established the possibility of top management's being liable for the insider trading of subordinates. The 1988 law followed the passage of the Insider Trading Sanctions Act of 1984, which gave the SEC the power to seek treble damages for trading on inside information. This law provided a dual-pronged approach for regulators, who now could seek civil remedies in addition to the criminal alternatives that were available before the passage of the 1984 Act. Illegal insider trading may occur, for example, if insiders, acting on information that is unavailable to other investors, sell the firm's securities before an announcement of poor performance. Other investors, unaware of the upcoming bad news, may pay a higher price for the firm's securities. The opposite might be the case if insiders bought the firm's stock or call options before the announcement of a bid from another firm. Stockholders might not have sold the shares to the insiders if they had known of the upcoming bid and its associated premium.

Who Are Insiders?

Insiders may be defined more broadly than the management of a company. They may include outsiders such as attorneys, investment bankers, financial printers, or consultants who can be considered "temporary insiders." Under Rule 10b-5, however, the U.S. Supreme Court held that outside parties who trade profitably based on their acquired information did not have to disclose their inside information. This was the case in the 1980 *Chiarella v. United States,* in which a financial printer acquired information on an upcoming tender offer by reviewing documents in his print shop.[27] If an individual misappropriates confidential information on a merger or acquisition and uses it as the basis for trade, however, Rule 10b-5 will apply. The rule is applicable only to SEC enforcement proceedings or criminal actions, but not to civil actions, under the Insider Trading Sanctions Act of 1984, which permits the recovery of treble damages on the profits earned or the loss avoided.

A classic example of illegal insider trading was the famous Texas Gulf Sulphur case. In 1963, Texas Gulf Sulphur discovered certain valuable mineral deposits, which it did not disclose for several months; actually, the firm publicly denied the discovery in a false press release. Meanwhile, officers and directors bought undervalued shares based on their inside information. The SEC successfully brought a suit against the insiders. The short swing profit rule prohibits any officer, director, or owner of 10% of a company's stock from a purchase and sale, or a sale and purchase, within a six-month period. Profits derived from these transactions must be paid to the issuer even if the transactions were not made on the basis of insider information.

Insider Trading Scandals of the 1980s

The world of M&As has been plagued with several notorious insider trading scandals in which some of the field's leading participants were convicted of insider trading violations. Each of the major cases provided information that led to the subsequent conviction of other violators.

In June 1986, Dennis Levine, an investment banker at Drexel Burnham Lambert, pleaded guilty to securities fraud, tax evasion, and perjury. He had acquired information on upcoming merger deals through payments to other investment bankers. Levine was an important link in the conviction of Ivan Boesky, a leading risk arbitrager on Wall Street. Boesky would, for example, purchase the securities of firms that he anticipated would be taken over. If he bought these securities before any increase in the target's price, he could realize significant profits. Boesky had illegally acquired insider information from investment bankers on deals before a public announcement of a merger or acquisition. Information provided in turn by Boesky and others, such as Boyd Jefferies, a broker at Jefferies and Company (who had already pleaded guilty in April 1987 to breaking securities laws), led to Michael Milken's guilty plea to six felony counts in 1990. Milken was later fined and sentenced to a 10-year prison term. Milken, the leading figure in the junk bond market, was the government's most significant conviction in its campaign to

---

27. *Chiarella v. United States,* 445 U.S. 222, 100 S. Ct. 1108, 63 L.Ed.2d, 348 (1980).

stamp out insider trading. His legal problems were one of the major factors that led to the collapse of Drexel Burnham Lambert and the junk bond market.

Do Insider Trading Laws Effectively Deter Insider Trading?

One research study by Nejat Seyhun has questioned the effectiveness of laws in curbing insider trading.[28] In addition, Lisa Muelbroek empirically confirmed that stock price run-ups before takeover announcements do reflect insider trading.[29] Other research seems to indicate that such laws may have a significant deterrent effect. Jon Garfinkel examined insider trading around earnings announcements and found that after the passage of the Insider Trading and Securities Fraud Enforcement Act, insiders appeared to adjust the timing of their transactions so that the trades occurred after the release of the relevant information.[30] The fact that the laws and the enforcement activity do seem to have a positive effect does not negate the fact that insider trading seems to remain a part of merger and acquisition activity of public companies.

ANTITRUST LAWS

The ability to merge with or acquire other firms is limited by antitrust legislation. Various antitrust laws are designed to prevent firms from reducing competition through mergers. Many mergers are never attempted, simply because of the likelihood of governmental intervention on antitrust grounds. Other mergers are halted when it becomes apparent that the government will likely oppose the merger.

The U.S. government has changed its stance on the antitrust ramifications of mergers several times since 1890. As noted previously, in recent years the government's attitude has been evolving toward a freer market view, which favors a more limited government role in the marketplace. Although many horizontal mergers were opposed during the 1980s, many others proceeded unopposed. This is in sharp contrast to the government's earlier position in the 1960s. During that period, mergers and acquisitions involving businesses only remotely similar to the acquiring firm's business were often opposed on antitrust grounds. This situation encouraged large numbers of conglomerate mergers, which generally were not opposed.

Sherman Antitrust Act

The Sherman Antitrust Act, which was originally passed in 1890, is the cornerstone of all U.S. antitrust laws. The first two sections of the law contain its most important provisions:

> **Section 1.** This section prohibits all contracts, combinations, and conspiracies in restraint of trade.

---

28. Nejat H. Seyhun, "The Effectiveness of Insider Trading Regulations," *Journal of Law and Economics,* 35, 1992, 149–182.
29. Lisa Muelbroek, "An Empirical Analysis of Insider Trading," *Journal of Finance,* 47(5), December 1992, 1661–1700.
30. Jon A. Garfinkel, "New Evidence on the Effects of Federal Regulations on Insider Trading: The Insider Trading and Securities Fraud Enforcement Act," *Journal of Corporate Finance,* 3, April 1997, 89–111.

Section 2. This section prohibits any attempts or conspiracies to monopolize a particular industry.

The Sherman Act made the formation of monopolies and other attempts to restrain trade unlawful and criminal offenses punishable under federal law. The government or the injured party can file suit under this law, and the court can then decide the appropriate punishment, which may range from an injunction to more severe penalties, including triple damages and imprisonment. The first two sections of the Sherman Act make it immediately clear that it is written broadly enough to cover almost all types of anticompetitive activities. Surprisingly, however, the first great merger wave took place following the passage of the law. This first merger wave, which took place between 1897 and 1904, was characterized by the formation of monopolies. The resulting increased concentration in many industries, combined with the formation of many powerful monopolies, revealed that the Act was not performing the functions its first two sections implied.

The apparent ineffectiveness of the Sherman Act was partly due to the law's wording. Specifically, it stated that all contracts that restrained trade were illegal. In its early interpretations, however, the court reasonably refused to enforce this part of the law on the basis that this implies that almost all contracts could be considered illegal. The court had difficulty finding an effective substitute. Court rulings such as the 1895 Supreme Court ruling that the American Sugar Refining Company was not a monopoly in restraint of trade made the law a dead letter for more than a decade after its passage. The lack of government resources also made it difficult for the government to enforce the law. While a dead letter under President McKinley, the law started to have more impact on the business community under the pressure of trustbusting President Theodore Roosevelt and his successor, William Howard Taft. In an effort to correct the deficiencies associated with the wording of the law and the lack of an enforcement agency, the government decided to make a more explicit statement of its antitrust position. This effort came with the passage of the Clayton Act.

Clayton Act

The goal of the Clayton Act was to strengthen the Sherman Act while also specifically proscribing certain business practices. Some of its more prominent provisions are:

Section 2. Price discrimination among customers was prohibited except when it could be justified by cost economies.

Section 3. Tying contracts were prohibited. An example of a tying contract would be if a firm refused to sell certain essential products to a customer unless that customer bought other products from the seller.

Section 7. *The acquisition of stock in competing corporations was prohibited if the effect was to lessen competition.*

Section 8. Interlocking directorates were prohibited when the directors were on the boards of competing firms.

The Clayton Act did not prohibit any activities that were not already illegal under a broad interpretation of the Sherman Act. The Clayton Act, however, clarified which business practices unfairly restrain trade and reduce competition. The bill did not address the problem of the lack of an enforcement agency charged with the specific responsibility for enforcing the antitrust laws.

Section 7 is particularly relevant to M&As: "No corporation shall *acquire* the whole or any part of the stock, or the whole or any part of the assets, of another corporation where in any *line of commerce* in any *section of the country* the effect of such an acquisition may be to substantially lessen competition or tend to create a *monopoly*."

This section reflects four main aspects of the Clayton Act:

1. *Acquisition.* Originally, the Clayton Act prohibited only the acquisition of *stock* in a corporation if the effect was to lessen competition. However, the marketplace quickly exposed a loophole in the wording of the section. The loophole involved the acquisition of the assets of a target company. This was later amended, with the law covering both stock and asset acquisitions.

2. *Line of commerce.* Through the use of the term *line of commerce*, the Act adopted a broader focus than just a particular industry. This broader focus allows antitrust agencies to consider the competitive effects of a full range of a firm's business activities.

3. *Section of the country.* The Act can be applied on a regional rather than a national basis. Through this provision, the antitrust authorities can look at regional market shares rather than national market shares. Therefore, a firm that dominated a regional market and enjoyed a monopoly in that section of the country could be found in violation of this law. The antitrust authorities often require the violating firm to divest the operations in the affected region in order to diminish their market power in that area.

4. *Tendency to lessen competition.* The wording of this part of Section 7 is quite vague. It states that a firm may lessen competition or tend to create a monopoly. This vague wording is intentionally designed to take into account the possibility that the effect on competition may not be immediate. This wording gives the antitrust authorities the power to act if there is only a reasonable probability that competition will be lessened. This almost assumes that if a firm has the power to limit competition, it will do so. Therefore, the law seeks to prevent these activities before they occur. This view of business behavior changed considerably over the past two decades.

Federal Trade Commission Act of 1914

One weakness of the Sherman Act was that it did not give the government an effective enforcement agency to investigate and pursue antitrust violations. At that time the Justice Department did not possess the resources to be an effective antitrust deterrent. In an effort to address this problem, the Federal Trade Commission Act, which was passed in 1914, established the FTC. The FTC was charged with enforcing both the Federal Trade Commission Act and the Clayton Act. In particular, it was passed with the intention of creating an enforcement arm for the Clayton Act. The main antitrust provision of the Act is Section 5, which prohibits unfair methods of competition. Although the FTC was given the power to initiate antitrust lawsuits, it was not given a role in the criminal enforcement of antitrust violations. The Act also broadened the range of illegal business activities beyond those mentioned in the Clayton Act.

Celler-Kefauver Act of 1950

Section 7 of the Clayton Act was written broadly enough to give the antitrust authorities wide latitude in defining an antitrust violation. However, through a loophole in the Clayton Act, corporations were engaging in acquisitions even when these acquisitions represented a clear lessening of competition.

As noted, the Clayton Act was originally worded to prohibit the acquisition of another corporation's stock when the effect was to lessen competition. Historically, corporations and raiders have continually found loopholes in the law. Many firms were able to complete acquisitions by purchasing a target firm's assets rather than its stock. Under the original wording of the Clayton Act, this would not be a violation of the law. This loophole was eliminated by the passage of the Celler-Kefauver Act of 1950, which prohibited the acquisition of assets of a target firm when the effect was to lessen competition. The Celler-Kefauver Act also prohibited vertical mergers and conglomerate mergers when they were shown to reduce competition. The previous antitrust laws were aimed at horizontal mergers, which are combinations of firms producing the same product. The Celler-Kefauver Act set the stage for the aggressive antitrust enforcement of the 1960s.

Hart-Scott-Rodino Antitrust Improvements Act of 1976

The Hart-Scott-Rodino Act requires that the FTC and the Justice Department be given the opportunity to review proposed M&As in advance. According to the Act, an acquisition or merger may not be consummated until these authorities have reviewed the transaction. These two agencies must decide which of the two will investigate the particular transaction. The law prevents consummation of a merger until the end of the specified waiting periods. Therefore, failure to file in a timely manner may delay completion of the transaction.

The Hart-Scott-Rodino Act was passed to prevent the consummation of transactions that would ultimately be judged to be anticompetitive. Thus, the Justice Department would be able to avoid disassembling a company that had been formed in part through an anticompetitive merger or acquisition. The law became necessary because of the government's inability to halt transactions through the granting of injunctive relief while it attempted to rule on the competitive effects of the business combination. When injunctive relief was not obtainable, mandated divestiture, designed to restore competition, might not take place for many years after the original acquisition or merger. The Hart-Scott-Rodino Act was written to prevent these problems before they occurred. The Hart-Scott-Rodino law adds another layer of regulation and a waiting period for tender offers beyond what was already in place with the Williams Act. Whether antitrust approval actually slows down a tender offer depends on the actual length of time it takes to receive the antitrust green light.

Size Requirements for Filing

Various amendments of the Hart-Scott-Rodino were implemented with the 21st Century Acquisition Reform and Improvement Act of 2000, which went into effect in 2001. As a result, filing requirements vary based on either the size of the entities or the size of the transaction. After that date, transactions valued at $50 million or more must file while those valued below $50,000 are exempt. If either party has assets or sales of at least $100 million and the other party has assets or sales of at least $10 million and the transaction is valued under $200 million, then a filing is required. Transactions over $200 million must be reported. This law eliminated a 15% of voting securities filing threshold.

Filing Fees

Companies must pay filing fees that vary depending on the size of the deal. Deals valued less than $100 million must pay $45,000. These fees vary up to $280,000 for those in excess of $500,000.

Who Must File

The original wording of the Hart-Scott-Rodino Act is somewhat vague, leading some people to believe that it did not apply to certain business entities, such as partnerships. The Act requires that persons or corporations file if they meet the firm and purchase size criteria previously described.

Type of Information to Be Filed

The law requires the filing of a 16-page form. Business data describing the business activities and revenues of the acquiring and the target firms' operations must be provided according to Standard Industrial Classification (SIC) codes. Most firms already have this information because it must be submitted to the U.S. Bureau of the Census. In addition, when filing, the acquiring firm must attach certain reports it may have compiled to analyze the competitive effects of this transaction.

This presents an interesting conflict. When a transaction is first being proposed within the acquiring firm, its proponents may tend to exaggerate its benefits. If this exaggeration comes in the form of presenting a higher market share than what might be more realistic, the firm's ability to attain antitrust approval may be hindered. For this reason, when the firm is preparing its premerger reports, it must keep the antitrust approval in mind.

Antitrust Premerger Review Time Periods

The time periods for review vary, depending on whether the offer is an all-cash offer or includes securities in the compensation package.

All-Cash Offers

In an all-cash offer, the regulatory authorities have 15 days in which to review the filing. However, the agency may decide that it needs additional information, which is known as a *second request*, before it can make a judgment on the antitrust ramifications of the merger or acquisition. It may therefore take another 10 days before it decides whether to challenge a transaction. The request for additional information usually indicates that the deal will not receive antitrust approval. In all-cash offers, the waiting period begins when the acquirer files the required forms.

Securities Offers

In offers that include securities in the compensation package, the initial review period is 30 days. If the regulatory authorities request additional information, they may take an additional 30 days to complete the review. For offers that are not all-cash offers, the waiting period starts when both firms have filed the necessary forms. A bidding firm may request an early termination of the waiting period if it believes that the transaction does not create any antitrust conflicts. Early terminations have been much more common in recent years. An early termination, however, is totally up to the discretion of the regulatory agencies.

The waiting period is designed to provide the antitrust agency with an opportunity to identify those transactions that might reduce competition. The reasoning is that it is far easier to prevent a deal from occurring than to disassemble a combined firm after the merger has been completed. If the antitrust agencies determine that there is an antitrust problem, they normally file suit to prevent the merger. Target firms may use the waiting period as a defensive tactic. Targets of hostile bids may be purposefully slow to report the required information. Firms that receive favorable friendly bids, however, may choose to expedite the selling process by responding quickly.

Impact of Notice of Government Opposition

If the Justice Department files suit to block a proposed acquisition, that usually is the end of the deal. Even if the bidder and the target believe that they might ultimately prevail in the lawsuit, it may not be in either company's interest to become embroiled in a protracted legal battle with the government that may last years. Such was the case in 1995, when Microsoft dropped its bid for financial software maker Intuit. At that time this deal would have been the largest software acquisition in history, with Intuit's equity being valued in the range of $2.3 billion. Another example was Blockbuster, which dropped its 2005 bid for rival movie-rental chain Hollywood Entertainment when it encountered resistance from the FTC. It dropped a similar bid in 1999 for the same reasons. Ironically, this industry has been shrinking due to competition from the video-on-demand segment of the cable industry as well as the mail order vendors in this industry. Based upon changes that have taken place in the 2000s, this deal may not have been as problematic as antitrust authorities believed in the 1990s.

A bidder may perceive that a strategic acquisition may provide synergistic benefits within a certain window of opportunity. However, if an indefinite delay is imposed before the companies can take action to realize these benefits, they typically will terminate the deal rather than risk incurring the significant acquisition costs with a more uncertain prospect of ever reaping these benefits. In the time it would take for the lawsuit to run its course, the competitive environment could change significantly, closing the window of opportunity. Sometimes the bidder may be able to convince the Justice Department to agree to take steps to speed up the trial, but even a more speedy trial may take many months to complete. In the case of the computer industry, for example, even six months can erase competitive opportunities.

Deadlines for Filing

A bidder must file under the Hart-Scott-Rodino Act as soon as it announces a tender offer or any other offer. The target is then required to respond. This response comes in the form of the target's filing, which must take place 15 days after the bidder has filed.

Federal Trade Commission Rules on Creeping Acquisitions

The FTC has set forth various rules that refine the Hart-Scott-Rodino Act. These rules address the aforementioned creeping acquisition case. They also eliminate the need for repeated filings for each share acquisition beyond the original one that may have required a filing. These rules indicate that a purchaser does not have to file for additional purchases if during a five-year period after the expiration of the original filing requirement period the total share purchases did not reach 25% of the outstanding shares of the issuer. If there are continued purchases after the 25% level that had required an additional filing, the purchaser does not have to file again until the 50% threshold is reached.

FTC Rules for Second Requests and Speed of Takeover Completion

A second request is often dreaded by M&A participants as it means delays and significant increases in expenses. Such requests often require as many as a million pages of documents to be provided by the companies. In 2006, the FTC announced new rules that give companies the option to agree to extend the deadline for an FTC decision to 30 days after the company has certified it is in compliance with the FTC's data requests. In these circumstances, the FTC agrees to place certain limits such as confining the data requested to two years and limit the number of employees whose files can be searched to 35.

Exemptions to the Hart-Scott-Rodino Act

Certain acquisitions supervised by governmental agencies, as well as certain foreign acquisitions, are exempt from the requirements of the Hart-Scott-Rodino Act. The *investment exception* permits an individual to acquire up to 10% of an issuer's voting securities as long as the acquisition is solely for the purposes of investment. The investment exception is designed to exempt those buyers of securities who are passive investors and have no interest in control. It allows investors to buy a large dollar amount of voting securities in a particular company without having to adhere to the Hart-Scott-Rodino filing requirement.

Another exception is the *convertible securities exception*, Securities that are convertible into voting securities are exempt from the filing requirements of the Hart-Scott-Rodino Act, as are options and warrants. In addition to these exceptions purchases by brokerage firms are also exempt, assuming that these purchases are not being made for the purpose of evading the law.

Antitrust Approval of International Mergers

For mergers of companies that do a substantial business outside the United States, the merger partners must address international antitrust guidelines as well as domestic ones. This was underscored when Ernst & Young and KPMG announced in February 1998 to abandon their plans to merge because of the fact that the European antitrust authorities had begun an investigation of the anticompetitive ramifications of the deal. The announcement of this investigation followed the European Commission's efforts in 1997 to block the Boeing and McDonnell Douglas merger until they obtained certain concessions from Boeing. Both Ernst & Young and KPMG are global companies with offices in most major countries. Later in this chapter we will discuss European competition policy further and some of the deals, such as the 2001 GE—Honeywell merger, which the European Commission opposed.

Enforcement of Antitrust Laws: Justice Department and Federal Trade Commission Interaction

Both the Justice Department and the FTC share the responsibility for enforcing U.S. antitrust laws. When the Justice Department brings a suit, it is heard in federal court, whereas when the FTC initiates an action, it is heard before an administrative law judge at the FTC and the decision is reviewed by the commissioners of the FTC. If a defendant wants to appeal an FTC decision, it may bring an action in federal court. Both the Justice Department and the FTC may take steps to halt objectionable behavior by firms. The Justice Department may try to get an injunction, whereas the FTC may issue a cease-and-desist order. Criminal actions are reserved for the Justice Department, which may seek fines or even imprisonment for the violators as well as the costs of bringing the action. Readers should not infer that the government are the sole parties who may bring an antitrust action. Individuals and companies may also initiate such actions. Indeed, it is ironic that such private actions constitute a significant percentage of the total antitrust proceedings in the United States.[31]

It is important to note that although much attention has been devoted to antitrust enforcement actions, the majority of deals do not incite enforcement actions. For example, during the period from 1993 to 1996, enforcement actions occurred in only 0.4% of all the transactions filed under the Hart-Scott-Rodino Act.[32]

RECENT TRENDS IN ANTITRUST ENFORCEMENT IN THE UNITED STATES

Antitrust enforcement was relatively relaxed in the 1990s. This posture became somewhat stiffer in the 1990s. One of the most notable deals to be opposed in the late 1990s was

---

31. Lawrence White, *Private Antitrust Litigation: New Evidence, New Learning* (Cambridge, MA, MIT Press, 1989).
32. Malcolm B. Coate, "Merger Enforcement at the Federal Trade Commission," unpublished working paper, January 1998, p. 4.

the $8.3 billion takeover of Northrop Grumman Corp. by Lockheed Martin Corp. Each of the two deal partners was the product of a prior major merger, with Northrop and Grumman merging in 1994 in a $2.17 billion deal and Lockheed and Martin Marietta merging in 1995 in a $10 billion deal. The defense industry was undergoing a general consolidation as competitors sought to gain efficiencies to cope with the post–Cold War defense environment. In December 1996, Boeing Co. bought McDonnell Douglas Corp. for $14 billion, and in 1997 Raytheon acquired the defense business of Hughes Electric Corp. for $12.5 billion. There were several other acquisitions in the industry involving whole companies or defense-related divisions of companies, such as Loral's 1993 acquisition of IBM's defense business and the 1994 merger between FMC and Harsco-BMY. In the face of the contracting competitive environment, the Lockheed Martin–Northrop Grumman deal was vigorously opposed by Raytheon. The Justice Department also began to be concerned and initiated an extensive investigation, which led to a suit to block the deal. This action signaled that the consolidations that were symptomatic of the fifth merger wave, particularly in industries such as the defense industry, but also possibly in telecommunications and banking, could not continue indefinitely before reaching a point of being objectionable. One of the lessons from the failure of this deal to gain antitrust approval is that when an industry is consolidating, it is important not to be one of the later deals that cause the quantitative measures of concentration to reach objectionable levels. The shrewder competitors may anticipate the eventual consolidation of the industry and merge or acquire early, whereas later would-be dealmakers may find themselves the target of an antitrust enforcement action.

The stronger antitrust enforcement was apparent in the government's challenges to the Microsoft acquisition of Intuit and its subsequent challenge to Microsoft underscored a somewhat activist antitrust enforcement process. This became clear in 1997, when the Staples, Inc. acquisition of Office Depot was stopped. In 1998, there were several other major challenges to mergers, including the proposed $1.72 billion acquisition of AmeriSource Corporation by McKesson Corporation and the $2.41 billion proposed acquisition of Bergen Brunswig Corporation by Cardinal Health, Inc. These companies were four of the largest wholesalers in the industry. One of the largest proposed deals of all time, which was halted by the Justice Department in 2000, was the $115 billion acquisition of Sprint by MCI WorldCom. Among the concerns of regulators was the belief that long-distance rates would rise if the big three firms became the big two. The Justice Department also was concerned about a possible adverse impact on the Internet. Even if the deal were able to vault the Justice Department hurdle, there was no assurance that it would have received approval from the European Commission.

Antitrust regulators analyze each deal on a case-by-case basis. While they have opposed deals such as the WorldCom/MCI acquisition of Sprint, they have also allowed other deals in which there are a limited number of competitors.[33] This was the case when the FTC allowed the 2004 merger between the number-two and -three cigarette manufacturers. In reaching its decision, the FTC took into account the fact that RJ Reynolds, although the

---

33. Statement of the Federal Trade Commission, "R.J. Reynolds Tobacco Holdings, Inc./British American Tobacco p.l.c.," File No. 041 0017, June 24, 2004.

number-two cigarette maker, had lost market share to smaller aggressive competitors. The FTC looked at more than overall cigarette market shares; it also looked at market segments, such as discount brands, where competitors have steadily eaten away at Reynolds' and Brown and Williamson's market shares. The FTC also considered the companies' long-term prospects when it noted that Brown and Williamson had a "very small share among smokers under 30. '

CASE STUDY

REQUIRED DIVESTITURES AS PART OF THE ANTITRUST APPROVAL PROCESS: GLAXO-SMITHKLINE MERGER

Rather than prevent a merger, antitrust regulatory authorities may approve a deal subject to the companies' divesting certain business units. A recent example was the qualified permission that the FTC gave Glaxo Wellcome PLC in December 2000 to acquire SmithKline Beecham PLC. The permission was given only on the condition that the companies would sell six businesses to rival drug companies. Glaxo and SmithKline agreed to sell their antiemetic drug, Kytril, to F. Hoffman LaRoche.[a] It also sold the U.S. marketing and distribution rights for an antibiotic (ceftazidime) to Abbott Laboratories while also selling the world rights to certain antiviral drugs to Novartis Pharma AG. In cases such as this, the companies have to determine whether the costs of selling valued units and product rights to rivals, which will make the rivals only more formidable competitors, are more than offset by the gains from the merger. In this instance, Glaxo-SmithKline clearly decided that the gains outweighed the costs. It is noteworthy that this is another cost of the deal—one that may not necessarily be known at the time the parties enter into an agreement. It is very much dependent on the actions of the antitrust regulatory authorities, which in turn are only partially predictable.

[a]Janet Seiberg, "Glaxo-Smith Kline's $73 B merger wins FTC Approval," *The Daily Deal*, December 19, 2001, p. 10.

MEASURING CONCENTRATION AND DEFINING MARKET SHARE

A key factor that the Court has relied on in deciding antitrust cases has been the market share of the alleged violator of antitrust laws and the degree of concentration in the industry. The Justice Department's method of measuring market share and concentration has varied over the years. The varying standards have been set forth in various merger guidelines.

The 1968 Justice Department Merger Guidelines

In 1968, the Justice Department issued merger guidelines that set forth the types of mergers that the government would oppose. Through these guidelines, which were used to help interpret the Sherman Act and the Clayton Act, the Justice Department presented its definitions, in terms of specific market share percentages, of highly concentrated and less highly concentrated industries. The guidelines used concentration ratios, which are the market shares of the top four or top eight firms in the industry. Under the 1968 guidelines, an industry was considered to be highly concentrated if the four largest firms held at least 75% of the total market. The guidelines for horizontal acquisitions that could give rise to a challenge are set forth in Table 3.1 in terms of market shares of the merger partners.

Market	Acquiring Company	Acquired Company
Highly concentrated	4%	4% or more
	10%	2% or more
	15%	1% or more
Less highly concentrated	5%	5% or more
	10%	4% or more
	15%	3% or more
	20%	2% or more
	25%	1% or more

TABLE 3.4   1968 JUSTICE DEPARTMENT MERGER GUIDELINES

The issuance of these guidelines made antitrust enforcement more mechanistic. Companies considering a merger with another firm could be better able to ascertain in advance the position of the Justice Department on the merger. Moreover, the Justice Department used these guidelines to determine its enforcement policies.

The 1982 Justice Department Guidelines

The limitations of such a rigid antitrust policy began to be felt in the 1970s; a policy that allowed more flexibility was clearly needed. Such a policy was instituted in 1982 through the work of William Baxter, head of the antitrust division of the Justice Department. Baxter was both a lawyer and an economist. Using his economics training, he introduced certain quantitative measures into the antitrust enforcement process, making it more mechanistic, predictable, and consistent with prevailing economic theory. Chief among these measures was the *Herfindahl-Hirschman (HH) Index* to American antitrust policy.[34] The HH Index is the sum of the squares of the market shares of each firm in the industry.

$$HH = \sum_i^n s_i^2$$

where: s_i = the market share of the ith firm.

Using this index rather than simple market shares of the top four or top eight firms in the industry provides a more precise measure of the impact of increased concentration that would be brought on by a merger of two competitors. It is important to note, however, that when using the HH Index (or even concentration ratios), the assumption that each of the merged firms would maintain their market shares needs to be carefully

---

34. Lawrence J. White, "Economics and Economists in Merger Antitrust Enforcement," in Patrick A. Gaughan and Robert Thornton, eds., *Developments in Litigation Economics* (Amsterdam: Elsevier/JAI, 2005), pp. 205–216.

examined. The postmerger combined market share needs to be considered even when this may be difficult.

Properties of the HH Index

The Herfindahl-Hirschman Index possesses certain properties that make it a better measure of merger-related market concentration than simple concentration ratios:

- The index increases with the number of firms in the industry.
- The index sums the squares of the firms in the industry. In doing so, it weights larger firms more heavily than smaller firms. Squaring a larger number will have a disproportionately greater impact on the index than squaring a smaller number. Moreover, a merger that increases the size differences between firms will result in a larger increase in the index than would have been reflected using simple concentration ratios.
- Because larger firms have greater impact on the index, the index can provide useful results even if there is incomplete information on the size of the smaller firms in the industry.

In evaluating market concentration:

- Postmerger HH less than 1,000: *Unconcentrated market.* This is unlikely to cause an antitrust challenge unless there are other anticompetitive effects.
- Postmerger HH between 1,000 and 1,800: *Moderately concentrated market.* If a merger increases the HH index by less than 100 points, this is unlikely to be a problem, but if it raises the index by more than 100 points, there may be concentration-related antitrust concerns.
- Postmerger HH above 1,800: *Highly concentrated market.* If a merger only raises the index by less than 50 points, this is unlikely to be objectionable. Increases of greater than 50 points "raise significant antitrust concerns."

Example of the HH Index

Consider an industry composed of eight firms, each of which has a 12.5% market share. The Herfindahl-Hirschman Index then is equal to:

$$\text{HH} = \sum_{i=1}^{8} Si^2 = 8(12.5)^2 = 1{,}250$$

If two of these equal-sized firms merge, the index is computed to be:

$$\text{HH} = 625 + 937.5 = 1562.5$$

1984 Justice Department Guidelines

On June 14, 1984, the Justice Department again revised its merger guidelines in an attempt to further refine its antitrust enforcement policies. The department recognized that its prior guidelines, including the more accurate HH Index, were too mechanistic and inflexible. In an attempt to enhance the flexibility of its policies, the department allowed the consideration of *qualitative* information in addition to the quantitative measures it had been employing. This qualitative information would include factors such as the efficiency of firms in the industry, the financial viability of potential merger candidates, and the ability of U.S. firms to compete in foreign markets.

The 1984 merger guidelines also introduced the 5% test. This test requires the Justice Department to make a judgment on the effects of a potential 5% increase in the price of each product of each merging firm. This test is based on the assumption that there may be an increase in market power resulting from the merger. If so, the merged firms may have the ability to increase prices. The test attempts to examine the potential effects of this increase on competitors and consumers.

One macroeconomic measure that provides an indication of the responsiveness of consumers and competitors is the concept of *elasticity.* The price elasticity of demand provides an indication of the consumers' responsiveness to a change in the price of a product. It is measured as follows:

- $e > 1$ *Demand is elastic.* The percentage change in quantity is more than the percentage change in price.
- $e = 1$ *Unitary elasticity.* The percentage change in quantity is equal to the percentage change in price.
- $e < 1$ *Inelastic demand.* The percentage change in quality is less than the percentage change in price.

If demand is inelastic over the 5% price change range, this implies greater market power for the merged firms; if, however, demand is elastic, consumers are not as adversely affected by the merger.

The 1982 and 1984 merger guidelines recognized the possibility of efficiency-enhancing benefits from mergers. Although they do not have the force of law, the 1968 merger guidelines were found to warrant some legal consideration.

The 1992 Merger Guidelines

The current position of the Justice Department and the FTC is set forth in the jointly issued 1992 merger guidelines, which were revised in 1997. They are similar to the 1984 guidelines in that they also recognize potential efficiency-enhancing benefits of mergers. However, these guidelines indicate that a merger will be challenged if there are anticompetitive effects, such as through price increases, even when there are demonstrable efficiency benefits. Clearly, mergers that lead to an anticompetitive increase in market powers will be challenged.

The 1992 guidelines provide a clarification of the definition of the relevant market, which often is a crucial issue of an antitrust lawsuit. They state that a market is the smallest group of products or geographic area where a monopoly could raise prices by a certain amount, such as by 5%. Like the 1984 guidelines, they also use the HH Index to measure the competitive effects of a merger.

The 1992 guidelines set forth a five-step process that the enforcement authorities follow:

1. Assess whether the merger significantly increases concentration. This involves a definition of the relevant market, which may be an issue of dispute.
2. Assess any potential anticompetitive effects of the deal.
3. Assess whether the potential anticompetitive could be mitigated by entry into the market by competitors. The existence of barriers to entry needs to be determined.
4. Determine if there could be certain offsetting efficiency gains that may result from the deal and that could offset the negative impact of the anticompetitive effects.
5. Determine whether either party would fail or exit the market but for the merger. These possible negative effects are then weighed against the potential anticompetitive effects. The 1997 revisions highlight the antitrust authorities' willingness to consider the net antitrust effects of a merger. Adverse anticompetitive effects may be offset by positive efficiency benefits. The merger participants need to be able to demonstrate that the benefits are directly related to the merger. It is recognized that such benefits may be difficult to quantify in advance of the deal, but their demonstration may not be vague or speculative. Practically, the merger-specific efficiencies offset only minor anticompetitive effects, not major ones.

CASE STUDY

RJ REYNOLDS, INC./BROWN AND WILLIAMSON

The 2004 merger between cigarette makers RJ Reynolds and Brown and Williamson is a useful case study to highlight the fact that simple market shares can be of limited benefits when analyzing the antitrust ramifications of a merger. In analyzing the combination of the number-two, RJ Reynolds, and number-three, Brown and Williamson, U.S. cigarette makers, the Federal Trade Commission (FTC) concluded the deal would not result in a damaging increase in the combined company's market power. By far the largest company in the U.S cigarette market is Philip Morris USA, which is owned by Altria. In analyzing the market, the FTC noted important trends such as the rising market share of companies outside of the top four who had long dominated the U.S. market (Lorillard being number four in market share). There were several rapidly growing upstarts who had made inroads into certain parts of this industry including the discount segment. Both RJ Reynolds and Brown and Williamson had suffered market share losses in the premium and discount segments. Indeed the FTC noted that Brown and Williamson, which enjoyed a high percent of its sales from the discount segment, had lost significant sales to the new discounters.[a] Between 1998 and 2004, Brown and Williamson's total market share fell from 15% to 10% while RJ Reynolds' market share fell from 24% to 20% over the same time period. In citing the Horizontal Merger Guidelines, the FTC concluded that the industry was highly concentrated by simply looking at the market share of the top four; such "market share and concentration data provide only the starting point for analyzing the competitive impact of a merger." The combination of these two companies was one of two firms that had suffered over the prior decade and were merging to try to halt their declining positions rather than gain competitive advantages or exercise market power at consumers' expense.

[a]Statement of Chairman Timothy J. Muris, Commissioner Swindle, and Commissioner Timothy B. Leary, RJ Reynolds Tobacco Holdings, Inc./British American Tobacco plc, File No. 041 0017.

EUROPEAN COMPETITION POLICY

In December 1989, the European Union adopted what is referred to as the *merger regulation*. This policy went into effect in September 1990 and was amended in 1998. The regulation focused on mergers, but also joint ventures, that have an impact on the degree of competition beyond one nation's borders. Under the regulation, mergers with significant revenues within the European Commission (EC) must receive EC approval. Unlike the U.S. system, in which antitrust regulators must go to court to block a merger, the EC's regulatory system is not dependent on the courts.

The EC's antitrust regulators had outright rejected only 13 deals in the 1990s and 3 in 2000, even though this period featured the high volume of M&As from the fifth merger wave. However, they actively review many deals and may possibly offer their approval only after the participants take certain corrective action. In the year 2000, the EC rejected the $115 billion merger between WorldCom and Sprint. It is ironic that a merger between WorldCom, a company with headquarters in Clinton, Mississippi, and Sprint, a company located in Kansas City, Kansas, was blocked by the 13-member EC. Other large deals that were halted included the $17 billion merger between three of the world's largest aluminum companies, Alcan Aluminum of Canada, Pechiney of France, and the Alusuisse-Lonza Group of Switzerland, as well as the $40 billion General Electric–Honeywell merge. The European opposition to the GE-Honeywell deal, a merger that was not opposed in the United States, raised many eyebrows as some felt the European Union was using its competition policy to insulate European companies from competition with larger U.S. rivals. This conflict led to a round of discussions to make the competition policies in both markets more consistent. Under the leadership of its antitrust chief, Mario Monti, a former Italian economics professor, the EC antitrust regulators, based in Brussels, used an economic doctrine known as *collective dominance* when reviewing the impact that mergers may have on the level of competition within the EC. This refers to the ability of a group of companies to dominate a particular market.

Now that Monti has left this position, EC antitrust regulators under the new leadership of Nellie Kroes, seem to have taken a more pro-business approach to antitrust enforcement. They now seem to be adopting a stance that is more similar to U.S. antitrust enforcement, where there is less emphasis on governments protecting competitors and more of a focus on consumer effects. The current orientation of the Brussels-based regulators is to encourage companies that believe they are the object of anticompetitive activities to take their claims to courts while regulators mainly focus on the adverse impact such activities have on consumers.

ANTITRUST REMEDIES

There are two broad types of remedies for economic conditions that regulatory authorities find anticompetitive. These remedies are relevant for situations that do or do not involve M&As. They come in two broad types: structural and behavioral. An example of a structural remedy would be a required divestiture of an acquired division that had anticompetitive effects. This has been the preferred solution of the EC to merger-related antitrust problems.[35] This was the case when Perrier was purchased by Nestle. Before the EC would approve the deal, Nestle/Perrier had to transfer one of Perrier's brands, Volvic, to a competitor. Behavioral, or nonstructural, remedies focus on specific business practices. An example of this involved the merger of Vodafone and Mannesmann, which created concerns about the ability of regional European mobile companies to compete with the combined Vodafone/Mannesmann, which then controlled mobile operations in many EU states. The EC's solution was to allow the merger only if Vodafone/Mannesmann granted competitor mobile operators access to their networks that would allow these competitors to offer seamless mobile service through regions that Vodafone/Mannesmann controlled.[36]

CASE STUDY

VIACOM-PARAMOUNT–QVC

On September 12, 1993, the Paramount board of directors approved a merger with Viacom that was valued at $69.14 per share. The friendly merger between these two companies was interrupted on September 20 by an unwanted bid from QVC valued at $80 per share. QVC announced that two of its largest shareholders, Liberty Media and the Comcast Corporation, each agreed to put up $500 million to help finance the QVC offer. One of the unique characteristics of this takeover battle was that each side enlisted merger partners to provide financing in exchange for certain considerations.

Viacom responded with a $600 million investment from Blockbuster Entertainment and a $1.2 investment from NYNEX. QVC then received some financial support from the acquisition of Tele-Communication, Inc. by Bell Atlantic. Tele-Communications was in the process of acquiring Liberty Media. On October 17, Advance Publications and Cox Enterprises agreed to provide $500 million each to help finance QVC's bid. Armed with the financial support of its various merger partners, QVC announced a two-stage tender offer for Paramount valued at $80 per share. The first step was a cash offer for 51%, to be followed by a closeout transaction using stock. The Paramount board authorized its management to meet with QVC on October 5, but it was not until November 1 that they met with QVC.

Viacom reacted to the QVC tender offer with an $85 cash offer, which Paramount accepted. Concerns about potential antitrust conflicts were allayed by QVC when it announced on November 11 that it would sever its association with Liberty Media, which would be sold to Bell South for $1 billion. Bell South would then provide the $500 that Liberty Media was contributing to the QVC bid. On November 12, QVC then announced that it was topping the Viacom bid with its own $90 per share offer.

The takeover battle then moved to the courts, where QVC came out the victor, with the Delaware Chancery Court ruling that the Paramount board acted improperly in not exercising its Revlon duties

---

35. Mario Monti, "The Commission Notive on Merger Remedies," in Francois Leveque and Howard Shelanski, eds., *Merger Remedies in American and European Union Competition Law* (Cheltenham, UK, Edward Elgar, 2003), pp. 3–12.
36. Massimo Motta, Michele Polo, and Helder Vasconcelos, "Merger Remedies in the European Union: An Overview," in Francois Leveque and Howard Shelanski, eds., *Merger Remedies in American and European Union Competition Law* (Cheltenham, UK, Edward Elgar, 2003), pp. 106–134.

and allowing defensive measures, such as lockup options, termination fees, and lucrative stock options, to give Viacom an advantage.

This decision was upheld on December 9 by the Delaware Supreme Court. Paramount was then forced to withdraw its support for the Viacom bid, and the auction process began. QVC upped its bid to $88.50 and Paramount's board recommended acceptance, but Viacom came back with an even higher $10 billion offer that ultimately won the takeover contest.

SUMMARY

To more fully understand the world of M&As, it is necessary to understand the laws that regulate the process. In the United States, these laws are divided into three categories: securities law, antitrust laws, and state corporation laws. The leading securities law for M&As is the Securities Exchange Act of 1934, of which the Williams Act is an amendment. The Williams Act regulates tender offers, which are important to takeovers—particularly hostile deals. The law is designed to provide shareholders with more information about bidders as well as the time to analyze this information. Section 13D of the law regulates the disclosure required of purchase of more than 5% of the outstanding stock of a company. When companies initiate a tender offer in the United States, they must file a Schedule TO, which regulates the disclosure necessary to tender offers.

Takeover laws vary by nation. However, many, such as those in Europe and Asia, have similar characteristics to the U.S. laws that have been the focus of much litigation over two large merger waves. For many years, the EU has tried to agree on a common set of merger rules, but the takeover directive that was eventually agreed to was watered down to allow member states to opt out of the rules and apply their own national takeover laws.

The two main antitrust laws in the United States, the Sherman Antitrust Act and the Clayton Act, were two of the early antitrust laws. These laws were augmented by the Federal Trade Commission Act and the Celler-Kefauver Act. However, the interpretation of these laws has varied over the course of modern U.S. history. It has varied from being very intense during the 1950s and 1960s to being relatively relaxed in the 1980s. The 1990s, however, exhibited signs of a movement back toward somewhat more aggressive antitrust enforcement. In addition to the aforementioned antitrust laws, the Hart-Scott-Rodino Act is a law that is directed toward M&As. It is designed to provide a clear sign of opposition to a takeover if such a transaction would possibly be anticompetitive.

State corporation laws play an important role in M&As. In particular, many state antitakeover laws provide protection against hostile takeover for corporations located within states. These laws sometimes even cover corporations that are incorporated in a state other than the one that has passed a particular law. State antitakeover laws are divided into four categories: fair price laws, business combination statutes, control share statutes, and cash-out laws.

4

MERGER STRATEGY

This chapter focuses on the strategic motives and determinants of mergers and acquisitions (M&As). It begins with a discussion of two of the most often cited motives for mergers and acquisitions—faster growth and synergy. Proponents of a deal will often point to an ability to grow faster and/or anticipated synergy as the justification for a specific purchase price. The different types of synergy, operating and financial synergy, are explored in this chapter. It will be seen that operating synergy, including both economies of scale and economies of scope, has the most economically sound basis. Financial synergy is a more questionable motive for a merger or an acquisition.

Companies often merge in an attempt to diversify into another line of business. The history of mergers is replete with diversification transactions. The track record of these diversifications, with notable exceptions, is not very impressive. However, certain types of diversifying transactions, those that do not involve a movement to a very different business category, have a better track record. Companies experience greater success with horizontal combinations, which result in an increase in market share, and even with some vertical transactions, which may provide other economic benefits. Unfortunately, a less noble motive such as hubris, or pride of the management of the bidder, also may be a motive for an acquisition. This determinant, along with others, such as improved management and tax benefits, may serve as the motivation for a deal. These motives, with their respective shareholder wealth effects, are analyzed.

GROWTH

One of the most fundamental motives for M&As is growth. Companies seeking to expand are faced with a choice between internal or organic growth and growth through M&As. Internal growth may be a slow and uncertain process. Growth through M&As may be a much more rapid process, although it brings with it its own uncertainties. Companies may grow within their own industry or they may expand outside their business category. Expansion outside one's industry means diversification. Because diversification has been a controversial topic in finance, it is discussed separately later in this chapter. In this section we focus on growth within a company's own industry.

If a company seeks to expand within its own industry they may conclude that internal growth is not an acceptable alternative. For example, if a company has a window of opportunity that will remain open for only a limited period of time, slow internal growth may not suffice. As the company grows slowly through internal expansion, competitors may respond quickly and take market share. Advantages that a company may have can dissipate over time or be whittled away by the actions of competitors. The only solution may be to acquire another company that has the resources, such as established offices and facilities, management, and other resources, in place. There are many opportunities that must be acted on immediately lest they disappear. It could be that a company has developed a new product or process and has a time advantage over competitors. Even if it is possible to patent the product or process, this does not prevent competitors from possibly developing a competing product or process that does not violate the patent. Another example would be if a company developed a new merchandising concept. Being first to develop the concept provides a certain limited time advantage. If not properly taken advantage of, it may slip by and become an opportunity for larger competitors with greater resources.

CASE STUDY

JOHNSON & JOHNSON—GROWTH THROUGH ACQUISITIONS STRATEGY

Johnson & Johnson is a manufacturer and marketer of a wide range of health care products. Over the period 1995–2005, the company engineered over 50 acquisitions as part of its growth through acquisitions strategy (see Table A). This strategy is similar to that pursued by companies in other rapidly changing, innovation-filled industries such as the computer software industry. Rather than internally try to be on the forefront of every major area of innovation, Johnson & Johnson, a $55 billion company, has sought to pursue those companies who had developed successful products. In doing so they do not waste time with unsuccessful internal development attempts and only go after those products and companies that have demonstrated success. However, the company has to pay a premium for such deals. This strategy has sometimes simply meant that Johnson & Johnson would buy its competitors rather than try to surpass them using internal growth. For example, in 1996 it acquired Cordis in the medical stent business for $1.8 billion. When this deal failed to place J&J in the lead in this market segment, Johnson & Johnson resorted to M&A again by its $25.4 billion bid (initial bid) for market leader Guidant. This acquisition would have been the largest deal in

Company Acquired	Primary Focus	Date	Size in Billions
Guidant	Implants	2005	25.4
Alza	Drug delivery	2001	12.3
Centocor	Immune-related diseases	1999	6.3
Depuy	Orthopedic devices	1998	3.6
Scios	Cardiovascular diseases	2003	2.4
Cordis	Vascular diseases	1996	1.8
Inverness Med. Tech.	Diabetes self-management	2001	1.4
Neutrogena	Skin and hair care	1994	0.9
Closure	Topical wounds	2005	0.4
Biopsys Medical	Breast cancer	1997	0.3
Peninsula Pharmaceuticals	Life-threatening infections	2005	0.3

TABLE A   JOHNSON & JOHNSON'S GROWTH THROUGH ACQUISITIONS STRATEGY: 1994–2005

Johnson & Johnson's long history of M&A. However, it lowered its bid when Guidant's litigation liabilities became known and then was outbid by Boston Scientific. Following the collapse of the Guidant deal, the cash rich J&J acquired Pfizer's consumer products division for $16 billion.

Another example of using M&As to facilitate growth is when a company wants to expand to another geographic region. It could be that the company's market is in one part of the country but it wants to expand into other regions. Alternatively, perhaps it is already a national company but seeks to tap the markets of other nations, such as a U.S. firm wanting to expand into Europe. In many instances, it may be quicker and less risky to expand geographically through acquisitions than through internal development. This may be particularly true of international expansion, where many characteristics are needed to be successful in a new geographic market. The company needs to know all of the nuances of the new market and to recruit new personnel and circumvent many other hurdles such as language and custom barriers. Internal expansion may be much slower and difficult. Mergers, acquisitions, joint ventures, and strategic alliances may be the fastest and lowest-risk alternatives.

Achieving Growth in a Slow-Growth Industry through Acquisitions

Corporate managers are under constant pressure to demonstrate successful growth. This is particularly true when the company and the industry have achieved growth in the past. However, when the demand for an industry's products and services slows, it becomes more difficult to continue to grow. When this happens, managers often look to M&A as a way to show growth. It often is hoped that such acquisitions will lead not only to revenue growth but also to improved profitability through synergistic gains. Unfortunately, it is much easier to generate sales growth by simply adding the revenues of acquisition targets than it is to improve the profitability of the overall enterprise. In fact, one can argue that although acquisitions bring with them the possibility of synergistic gains, they also impose greater demands on management, which now runs an even larger enterprise. Management needs to make sure that the greater size in terms of revenues has brought with it commensurate profits and returns for shareholders. If not, then the whole growth through M&A strategy has not improved shareholder's positions and investors would have been better off if management had resigned themselves to be a slower growth company.

CASE STUDY

FLAVOR AND FRAGRANCE INDUSTRY—USING ACQUISITIONS TO ACHIEVE GROWTH IN A SLOW-GROWTH INDUSTRY (IFF'S ACQUISITION OF BUSH BOAKE ALLEN)

The growth in the flavor and fragrance industry slowed significantly in the 1990s. Companies in this industry sold products to manufacturers and marketers of various other products. As the demand for the end users' products slowed, the demand for intermediate products such as flavors also slowed. Food manufacturers rely on various suppliers, including flavor developers, to come up with new or improved products. The frozen food business is a case in point.

With the advent of the microwave oven, this business grew dramatically. However, when the proliferation of this innovation reached its peak, the growth in the frozen food business also slowed. Companies that sold to frozen food manufacturers experienced the impact of this slowing demand in the form of a slower demand for their products and increased pressure placed on them by manufacturers for price concessions that would enable the manufacturers to improve their own margins. Faced with the prospect of slow growth, International Flavors and Fragrances, Inc. (IFF), one of the largest companies in this industry, acquired competitor Bush Boake Allen, which was about one-third the size of IFF. On the surface, however, the acquisition of Bush Boake Allen increased the size of IFF by one-third, giving at least the appearance of significant growth in this slow-growth industry.

Is Growth or Increased Return the More Appropriate Goal?

It is virtually taken without question that a major goal for a company's management and board is to achieve growth. While the advisability of this goal is often unquestioned, managers need to make sure that the growth is one that will generate good returns for shareholders. Too often management may be able to continue to generate acceptable returns by keeping a company at a given size, but instead choose to pursue aggressive growth.[1] Boards need to critically examine the expected profitability of the revenue derived from growth and determine if the growth is worth the cost. Consider the case of Hewlett-Packard in the post-Fiorina era. Having made a highly questionable $19 billion mega-acquisition of Compaq in 2002, Hewlett-Packard finds itself managing several business segments in which it is a leader in only one—printers. The company had revenues in excess of $80 billion. If, as an example, its goal was to grow at 10% per year, it would have to generate approximately $8 billion in new revenues each year. In effect, it would have to create another large company's worth of revenues each year to satisfy management's growth goals. When we consider the fact that much of its business comes from the highly competitive PC market with its weak margins coupled with steady product price *deflation,* one has to wonder where the growth will come from and at what price. Would the company be better off downsizing and having separate, but more manageable and focused, businesses? Would it be better off leaving the PC business, as the founder of the business, IBM, did in mid-2005 when it sold its PC division to Chinese computer manufacturer Lenovo?

International Growth and Cross-Border Acquisitions

Companies that have successful products in one national market may see cross-border acquisitions as a way of achieving greater revenues and profits. Rather than seek potentially diminishing returns by pursuing further growth within their own nation, cross-border deals may be an advantageous way of tapping another market. A cross-border deal may enable an acquirer to utilize the country-specific know-how of the target, including its indigenous staff and distribution network. The key question, as it is with every acquisition, is whether the risk-adjusted return from the deal is greater than what can be achieved with the next best use of the invested capital.

---

1. Andrew Campbell and Robert Park, *The Growth Gamble* (London: Nicholas Brealey International), 2005.

With the advent of the European Common Market, cross-country barriers have been reduced. This has given rise to a spate of cross-border deals in Europe. Certain Asian markets continue to be resistant to foreign acquirers (although there are signs that this is changing); thus the volume of cross-border deals in this region is probably significantly less than what it will be in the future if and when these artificial market restrictions become more relaxed.

Exchange rates can play an important role in international takeovers. When the currency of a bidder appreciates relative to that of a target, a buyer holding the more highly valued currency may be able to afford a higher premium, which the target may have difficulty passing up. Harris and Ravenscraft, using a sample drawn from the period 1970–1987, showed that foreign acquirers paid 10% higher premiums.[2] They attributed the higher premiums to currency valuation differences. Interestingly, they also found that approximately one-half of the foreign deals could be attributed to factors related to research and development.

CASE STUDY

INTERNATIONAL GROWTH AND THE HOTEL INDUSTRY

In January 2006, the Hilton Hotels Corp. announced a $5.7 billion offer to purchase the international hotel business unit owned by Hilton Group PLC. This acquisition offer came with a touch of irony as the two businesses were one prior to 1964, when Hilton parted ways with its international hotel business. The move to expand outside the United States came partly in response to the international expansion efforts of two of Hilton's main rivals—Marriott International, Inc. and Starwood Hotels and Resorts Worldwide Inc.

The combination united the hotels operating under the Hilton name and allows Hilton to offer an international network of properties across the globe. The chain traces its roots to Conrad Hilton in 1919, when he bought his first hotel. The company was split in 1964 and as part of that division the two units agreed not to compete with one another. However, market opportunities in the 1960s were very different from those of the 2000s. The current world market is much more globalized. Hotel businesses that can offer a true global network can leverage their customer base in one market to generate sales in another. For example, some American travelers familiar with the Hilton brand and seeking comparable services when abroad might more likely stay at a Hilton property than another that they were unfamiliar with.

The merger also comes at a time when the hotel business is undergoing many changes. Hotel chains have been selling properties and focusing more on brand marketing and hotel management. Hotels work to develop a brand that they often franchise to owners who will maintain the property consistent with the standards they seek to maintain. In 2005, for example, Hilton sold off "more than 20 hotels for more than $1 billion."[a] The acquisition of many more properties comes at a time when Hilton and others are selling off properties. This implies that this deal may also be followed by some property sales while retaining the newly acquired hotels within the now international Hilton network.

[a]Peter Sanders, "Hilton Hotels Seek Global Reach," Wall Street Journal, December 30, 2005, A3.

---

2. Robert S. Harris and David Ravenscraft, "The Role of Acquisitions in Foreign Direct Investment: Evidence from the U.S. Stock Market," Journal of Finance, 46, 1991, 825–844.

As with all types of acquisitions, we need to consider the market reactions to international M&As and compare them to intracountry deals. Doukas and Travlos found that, unlike many domestic acquisitions, acquirers enjoyed positive (although not statistically significant) returns when they acquired targets in countries in which they did not previously have operations. Interestingly, the returns were negative (although also not statistically significant) when the acquirers already had operations in these foreign countries.[3] When the company is already in the market, and presumably has already exploited some of the gains that can be realized, then investors may be less sanguine about the gains that may be realized through an increased presence in this same region.

Another study compared the shareholder wealth effects of acquisitions of U.S. firms by non-U.S. bidders and the opposite—acquisitions of non-U.S. companies by U.S. bidders. Cakici, Hessel, and Tandon analyzed the shareholder wealth effects from 195 acquisitions, over the period 1983–1992, of non-U.S. companies that bought U.S. targets.[4] They then compared these effects to a sample of 112 deals in which U.S. companies acquired non-U.S. firms. The non-U.S. acquirers generated statistically significant returns of just under 2% over a ten-day window, whereas the U.S. acquirers realized the negative returns that we often generally see from acquisitions.

Still another research study by Markides and Oyon, using a sample of 236 deals, compared acquisitions by U.S. firms of European (189) versus Canadian targets (47). They found positive announcement effects for acquisitions of continental European targets but not for acquisitions of British or Canadian target firms.[5] These negative shareholder wealth effects for acquisitions of Canadian firms were also found by Eckbo and Thorburn, who considered 390 deals involving Canadian companies over the period 1962–1983.[6]

The fact that acquisitions of non-U.S. targets by U.S. companies may be more risky than deals involving all-U.S. targets is underscored by a large sample study by Moeller and Schlingemann.[7] They analyzed 4,430 deals over the period 1985–1992. They found that U.S. bidders who pursued cross-border deals realized lower returns than acquisitions where the bidders chose U.S. targets.

The fact that we live in an increasingly globalized world puts pressure on corporations to be truly global. The fastest way to achieve such "globalness" is through acquisitions of companies in other international markets. Entering new markets presents unique additional risks, which may explain the spotty track record of many U.S. acquirers of non-U.S. companies. Hopefully, additional research will shed some light on the extent to which there is a learning effect from such international deals that may improve their track record.

3. John Doukas and Nicholas G. Travlos, "The Effect of Corporate Multinationalism on Shareholder's Wealth," *Journal of Finance*, 43, December 1988, 1161–1175.
4. Nusret Cakici, Chris Hessel, Kishore Tandon, "Foreign Acquisitions in the United States: Effect on Shareholder Wealth of Foreign Acquiring Firms," *Journal of Banking & Finance*, 20, 1996, 307–329.
5. C. Markides and D. Oyon, "International Acquisitions: Do They Create Value for Shareholders?" *European Management Journal*, 16, 1998, 125–135.
6. Epsen Eckbo and K. S. Thorburn, "Gains to Bidder Firms Revisited: Domestic and Foreign Acquisitions in Canada," *Journal of Financial and Quantitative Analysis*, 35(1), March 2000, 1–25.
7. Sara B. Moeller and Frederick P. Schlingemann, "Are Cross-Border Acquisitions Different from Domestic Acquisitions? Evidence on Stock and Operating Performance for U.S. Acquirers," *Journal of Banking and Finance*, (forthcoming).

CASE STUDY

INTERNATIONAL DIVERSIFICATION IN THE AUTOMOBILE INDUSTRY

Over the past two decades, many of the major automobile companies have engaged in a pattern of cross-border acquisitions as they have sought to exploit markets outside of their own borders. Indeed this form of expansion has been going on much longer than the past couple of decades. However, when the pace of M&As from two of the largest merger waves took hold, the automobile industry responded like so many others and pursued their own deals.

As we look back on many of these deals, we see that many were major disappointments. Probably the most notable flop was Daimler's 1998 takeover of Chrysler. Chrysler was profitable at the time it was acquired by Daimler, but the market was changing around that time, and following the deal, sales of many of its profitable cars and SUVs declined as consumer tastes changed. Led by its hubris-filled CEO, Jurgen Schremp, Daimler Chrysler would never admit the deal was a failure even as it generated staggering losses in 2001.[a] The distracted Daimler worked to fix the problems at Chrysler, which it did, but only at the expense of "taking their eye off the ball" at Mercedes, their highly successful luxury brand.[b] Quality problems began to emerge in various Mercedes autos, such as the E and M class sedans, and Mercedes began to lose ground to its chief rival—BMW. Indeed Daimler's losing deal with Chrysler was not its only flop. Its investment in Mitsubishi was also fraught with problems.

Daimler was not the only auto company to lose from its international deals. General Motors pursued a number of international acquisitions as it sought to expand its presence throughout the world. Many of these were major losers. Perhaps the most embarrassing for GM was its investment in Fiat, which gave the troubled Italian automaker the right to require GM to pay $2 billion to Fiat if GM wanted to end their alliance. As Fiat's financial problems mounted, GM was forced to pay $2 billion at a time it was experiencing many other financial problems.[c] In addition, other GM global deals were also troubled. Its investments in the Russian auto market were fraught with difficulties.

Ford experienced its share of M&A woes. It acquired targets in Europe so as to expand its presence in that market while also providing the number-two U.S. auto maker with luxury brands such as Jaguar. While Jaguar is a world-renowned brand and serves as a key component to Ford's Premier Auto Group, it has failed to generate profits for Ford. At a time when Ford labored under burdensome union agreements and intense foreign competition in its main market, the United States, it was forced to continually invest in its failed acquisition, Jaguar, which regularly lost money for Ford.

Japanese automakers declined to use acquisitions as the key to their U.S. expansion strategy. Nonetheless, they continued to gain market share from the major U.S. auto companies. Toyota and Honda opened plants in the United States, where they enjoyed major cost advantages compared with U.S. car companies as Toyota's and Honda's plants were not unionized and had labor costs that were a fraction of U.S. auto makers. Toyota, a company that for years studied Ford's and GM's manufacturing practices, used its organic internal growth strategy to steadily take over market share from its higher-cost U.S. rivals. Since U.S. automakers were beset with very costly labor agreements, they were not attractive targets for the Japanese, who could steadily expand in the United States using new plants they would build far from Detroit and using a cost structure that gave them important advantages over their U.S. rivals.

[a]Bill Vlasic and Bradley A. Stertz, *Taken for a Ride: How Mercedes-Benz Drove Off with Chrysler* (New York: William Morrow), 2000.
[b]Patrick Gaughan, *Mergers: What Can Go Wrong and How to Prevent It* (Hoboken: NJ: John Wiley & Sons), 2004, pp. 306–316.
[c]"G.M. Warned of a Cut in Debt Rating," *New York Times*, February 15, 2005, late ed., Business/Financial Desk, sec. C, col. 5, p. 2.

SYNERGY

The term *synergy* is often associated with the physical sciences rather than with economics or finance. It refers to the type of reactions that occur when two substances or factors combine to produce a greater effect together than that which the sum of the two operating independently could account for. For example, a synergistic reaction occurs in chemistry when two chemicals combine to produce a more potent total reaction than the sum of their separate effects. Simply stated, synergy refers to the phenomenon of $2 + 2 = 5$. In mergers this translates into the ability of a corporate combination to be more profitable than the individual parts of the firms that were combined.

The anticipated existence of synergistic benefits allows firms to incur the expenses of the acquisition process and still be able to afford to give target shareholders a premium for their shares. Synergy may allow the combined firm to appear to have a positive *net acquisition value* (NAV).

$$NAV = V_{AB} - [V_A + V_B] - P - E \tag{4.1}$$

where:

V_{AB} = the combined value of the two firms

V_B = the value of B

V_A = the value of A

P = premium paid for B

E = expenses of the acquisition process

Reorganizing equation 4.1, we get:

$$NAV = [V_{AB} - (V_A + V_B)] - (P + E) \tag{4.2}$$

The term in the brackets is the synergistic effect. This effect must be greater than the sum of P + E to justify going forward with the merger. If the bracketed term is not greater than the sum of P + E, the bidding firm will have overpaid for the target. What are to be considered synergistic effects? Some researchers view synergy broadly and include the elimination of inefficient management by installing the more capable management of the acquiring firm.[8] Although it is reasonable to define synergy in this manner, this chapter defines the term more narrowly and treats management-induced gains separately. This approach is consistent with the more common uses of the term *synergy*.[9]

The two main types of synergy are operating synergy and financial synergy. *Operating synergy* comes in two forms: revenue enhancements and cost reductions. These revenue

8. Paul Asquith, "Merger Bids, Uncertainty and Stockholder Returns," *Journal of Financial Economics* 11(1–4), April 1983, 51–83; and Michael Bradley, Anand Desai, and E. Han Kim, "The Rationale Behind Interfirm Tender Offers: Information or Synergy," *Journal of Financial Economics* 11(1–4), April 1983, 183–206.
9. Michael Jensen and Richard Ruback, "The Market for Corporate Control: The Scientific Evidence," *Journal of Financial Economics* 11(1–4), April 1983, 5–50.

enhancements and efficiency gains or operating economies may be derived in horizontal or vertical mergers. *Financial synergy* refers to the possibility that the cost of capital may be lowered by combining one or more companies.

CASE STUDY

ALLEGIS—SYNERGY THAT NEVER MATERIALIZED

The case of the Allegis Corporation is a classic example of synergistic benefits that had every reason to occur but failed to materialize. The concept of Allegis was the brainchild of CEO Richard Ferris, who has risen through the ranks of United Airlines.

Ferris's dream was to form a diversified travel services company that would be able to provide customers with a complete package of air travel, hotel, and car rental services. Accordingly, United Airlines paid $587 million for Hertz Rent a Car from RCA in June 1986—a price that was considered to be a premium. In addition to buying Pan American Airways Pacific routes, Ferris bought the Hilton International hotel chain from the Transworld Corporation for $980 million. The Hilton International purchase on March 31, 1987, was also considered to be expensive.

United Airlines had already acquired the Westin International hotel chain in 1970 for only $52 million. On February 18, 1987, United Airlines changed its name to Allegis Corporation. Allegis' strategy was to offer customers "one-stop" travel shopping. With one telephone call they could book their air travel, hotel reservations, and car rental within the same corporate umbrella. Allegis hoped to weave the network together through a combination of cross-discounts, bonus miles, and other promotional savings and the introduction of a new computer system called Easy Saver. Through Easy Saver, customers could check prices and book reservations through the Allegis network. All travel services could be charged on an Allegis credit card. Travel agents using United Airlines' Apollo computer reservation system, the largest in the airline industry, would pull up Allegis's air, hotel, and car services before any other competitor's products.

Despite the concept's appeal, customers and the market failed to respond. At a time when the stock market was providing handsome returns to investors, the Allegis stock price fell; in February 1987, its stock price was in the low-to-mid-$50 range. The market did respond, however, when Coniston Partners, a New York investment firm, accumulated a 13% stake in the travel company. Coniston planned to sell off the various parts of the Allegis travel network and distribute the proceeds to the stockholders. On April 1, 1987, Allegis announced a large recapitalization plan proposal that would have resulted in the company's assuming $3 billion worth of additional debt to finance a $60 special dividend. The recapitalization plan was intended to support the stock price while instilling stockholder support for Allegis and away from the Coniston proposal. The United Airlines Pilots Union followed up Allegis's recapitalization plan proposal with its own offer to buy the airline and sell off the nonairline parts.

The pressure on CEO Ferris continued to mount, leading to a pivotal board of directors meeting. According to Chairman of the Board Charles Luce, the board, watching the company's stock rise, "thought the market was saying that Allegis was worth more broken up and that the current strategy should be abandoned." Although the outside directors had supported Ferris during the company's acquisition program, they now decided that Ferris was an obstacle to restructuring the company. "There comes a point," said Luce, "when no board can impose its own beliefs over the opposition of the people who elected it." Ferris was replaced by Frank A. Olsen, chairman of Allegis's Hertz subsidiary.[a]

[a]Arthur Fleisher Jr., Geoffrey C. Hazard Jr., and Miriam Z. Klipper, *Board Games: The Changing Shape of Corporate America* (Boston: Little, Brown, 1988), p. 192.

Allegis is one of many examples of management wanting to create a "one-stop shop" for consumers that the market failed to embrace. Sears's diversifying acquisitions (see Case Study at the end of this chapter) and Citicorp's related acquisitions are other examples of such failures. Boards that should know better seem to be too passive and allow managers to waste resources on these failed empire-building efforts.

OPERATING SYNERGY

Revenue-Enhancing Operating Synergy

Revenue-enhancing operating synergy may be more difficult to achieve than cost reduction synergies. It may come from new opportunities that are presented as a result of the combination of the two merged companies.[10] There are many potential sources of revenue enhancements, and they may vary greatly from deal to deal. They may come from a sharing of marketing opportunities by cross-marketing each merger partner's products. With a broader product line, each company could sell more products and services to their product base.

Cross-marketing has the potential to enhance the revenues of each merger partner, thereby enabling each company to expand its revenues quickly. The multitude of ways in which revenue-enhancing synergies may be achieved defies brief descriptions. It may come from one company with a major brand name lending its reputation to an upcoming product line of a merger partner. Alternatively, it may arise from a company with a strong distribution network merging with a firm that has products of great potential but questionable ability to get them to the market before rivals can react and seize the period of opportunity. Although the sources may be great, revenue-enhancing synergies are sometimes difficult to achieve. Such enhancements are more difficult to quantify and build into valuation models. This is why cost-related synergies are often highlighted in merger planning, whereas the potential revenue enhancements may be discussed but not clearly defined. It is easier to say we have certain specific facilities that are duplicative and can be eliminated than to specifically show how revenues can be increased through a combination of two companies. Potential revenue enhancements often are vaguely referred to as merger benefits but are not clearly quantified. This is one reason some deals fail to manifest the anticipated benefits. The reason can be found in poor premerger planning caused by failing to specifically quantify revenue enhancements. Probably the most dramatic example of such vague and generally poor merger planning is the largest deal of all time—the disastrous 2002 merger of AOL and Time Warner.

Cost-Reducing Operating Synergies

Merger planners tend to look for cost-reducing synergies as the main source of operating synergies. These cost reductions may come as a result of *economies of scale*—decreases in per-unit costs that result from an increase in the size or scale of a company's operations.

---

10. Mark N. Clemente and David S. Greenspan, *Winning at Mergers and Acquisitions: The Guide to Market-Focused Planning and Integration* (New York: John Wiley & Sons, 1998), p. 46.

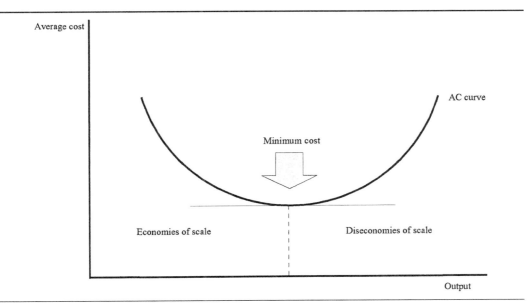

Average cost

AC curve

Minimum cost

Economies of scale

Diseconomies of scale

Output

EXHIBIT 4.1 ECONOMIES AND DISECONOMIES OF SCALE.

Manufacturing firms, especially capital-intensive ones, typically operate at high per-unit costs for low levels of output. This is because the fixed costs of operating their manufacturing facilities are spread out over relatively low levels of output. As the output levels rise, the per-unit costs decline. This is sometimes referred to as *spreading overhead.* Some of the other sources of these gains arise from increased specialization of labor and management and the more efficient use of capital equipment, which might not be possible at low output levels. This phenomenon continues for a certain range of output, after which per-unit costs may rise as the firm experiences diseconomies of scale. Diseconomies of scale may arise as the firm experiences higher costs and other problems associated with coordinating a larger-scale operation. The extent to which diseconomies of scale exist is a topic of dispute for many economists. Some economists cite as evidence the continued growth of large multinational companies, such as Exxon and General Electric. These firms have exhibited extended periods of growth while still paying stockholders an acceptable return on equity. Others contend that such firms would be able to provide stockholders a higher rate of return if they were smaller, more efficient companies.

Exhibit 4.1, which depicts scale economies and diseconomies, shows that an optimal output level occurs when per-unit costs are at a minimum. This implies that an expansion through the horizontal acquisition of a competitor may increase the size of the acquiring firm's operation and lower per-unit costs.

CASE STUDY

CONSOLIDATION IN THE CRUISE INDUSTRY AND THE PURSUIT OF ECONOMIES AND OTHER SYNERGIES

Several examples of M&As motivated by the pursuit of scale economies have occurred in the cruise industry, which has undergone a series of consolidating M&As. Examples include the 1989 acquisition of Sitmar Cruises by Princess Cruises and the 1994 merger between Radisson Diamond Cruises and Seven Seas Cruises, which enabled the combined cruise lines to offer an expanded product line in the form of more ships, beds, and itineraries while lowering per-bed costs. The cruise industry has learned that a sales force of a given size can service a greater number of ships and itineraries. As cruise lines combine, they find that they do not need to maintain the same size administrative facilities and sales forces. For example, each cruise line has its own network of district sales managers who call on travel agencies within an area. When one cruise line buys another, one company's sales force may be able to service the combined itineraries of both groups of ships. This enables the acquiring company to purchase the target's projected revenues with less than the target's historical cost structure.

Another example of scale economies related to these cruise mergers is the use of marketing expenditures. Partly because of the size of its fleet, Princess Cruises is able to maintain a national television advertising campaign. A cruise line needs to be of a certain minimum size for a national television advertising campaign to be feasible. By buying Sitmar, which offered similar cruises and was of similar size, Princess was better able to market its "Love Boat" theme nationally while the television show that featured their ships was quite popular. They were also able to expand capacity quickly through this acquisition while at the same time ordering new ships to be built. When the new ships arrived, they sold off some of the older Sitmar ships. The Sitmar acquisition served its purpose by providing an avenue for quick expansion to take advantage of a window of opportunity. In the cruise industry, the smaller cruise companies have difficulty competing with the bigger lines because they are not large enough to be able to spread out the costs of a national and print television campaign across a large enough number of ships to make such marketing costs effective. They then are relegated to other forms of marketing that do not have the same effectiveness as television in generating consumer awareness. Therefore, acquisitions are one way to develop a larger revenue base to support the use of the more expensive marketing media used by larger competitors. The marketing advantages combined with cost economies help explain the consolidation-through-mergers phenomena we have witnessed in this industry over the 1980s and 1990s. This consolidation has resulted in two large rivals—Carnival and Royal Caribbean.

Carnival, originally a low-priced, mass-market cruise line, has become the largest company in the industry through a broad acquisition program. Interestingly, it has been able to acquire "upper end" cruise lines such as Seaborne, without experiencing any negative effects on the quality and reputational integrity of the high-price cruise line. This was possible because Carnival marketed the brands separately and did not change the way they were marketed much after they were acquired. The synergistic benefits are accrued to Carnival in a behind-the-scenes manner that was seamless to the traveler.

The 2003 merger of P&O's Princess Cruises and Carnival firmly placed the combined company in the leadership position of this industry. This is why Royal Caribbean, the number-two company in this industry, fought hard to outbid Carnival for this valued target. The resulting Carnival includes Cunard Line, Carnival, Costa Cruises, Holland American, Seaborne, Windstar, and now Princess.

There is empirical support spanning a long time period for the assertion that M&As are used to achieve operating economies. For example, Lictenberg and Siegel detected improvements in the efficiency of plants that had undergone ownership changes.[11] In fact, they found that those plants that had performed the worst were the ones that were most likely to experience an ownership change. There is also more recent research that supports

---

11. Frank Lictenberg and Donald Siegel, "Productivity and Changes in Ownership of Manufacturing Plants," *Brookings Papers on Economic Activity*, 3, 1987, 643–683.

these findings. Shahrur examined the returns that occurred around the announcement of 463 horizontal mergers and tender offers over the period 1987–1999. He noticed positive combined bidder/target returns and interpreted these findings to imply that the market saw the deals as efficiency enhancing.[12] These results are also consistent with the market reactions (positive return of 3.06% over a three-day window) detected in Fee and Thomas's analysis of a large sample of 554 horizontal deals over the period 1980–1997.[13]

It should not, however, be concluded that simply because some evidence exists that mergers are associated with operating economies, mergers are the best way to achieve such economies. That proposition is not supported by economic research.

Another concept that is closely related to and sometimes confused with economies of scale is *economies of scope,* which is the ability of a firm to utilize one set of inputs to provide a broader range of products and services. A good example of scope economies arises in the banking industry. In the banking industry, scope economies may be as important as economies of scale in explaining M&As.[14] The pursuit of these economies is one of the factors behind the consolidation within the banking industry that occurred in the fifth merger wave.

When financial institutions merge, they can share inputs to offer a broader range of services, such as a trust department, consumer investment products unit, or economic analysis group. Smaller banks might not be able to afford the costs of these departments. Inputs such as a computer system may be shared to process a wide variety of loans and deposit accounts. Whether these benefits are either the true reason or a sufficient reason for the increased number of banking mergers that have taken place in the recent period of deregulation is a very different issue.[15] The many bank mergers that occurred during the fourth merger resulted in a new breed of bank in the industry—the superregional bank. The acquisition of other regional banks largely accounts for the growth of the superregional banks of the 1980s. These superregional banks, such as the Bank One Corporation, Barnett Bank, and NationsBank, grew to the point where they were competitive with the larger money center banks in the provision of many services. Other banks, such as the Bank of New England, expanded too rapidly through acquisitions and encountered financial difficulties.

In the 1990s, certain of the superregionals, such as NationsBank and First Union, continued to expand and became two of the largest banks in the United States. However, in the fifth wave, the banking industry continued to consolidate and the superregionals were merged with, or acquired by, even larger banks. First Union Bank acquired First Fidelity in 1996 at a time it was acquiring several other mid-sized banks. Between 1997 and 1998, NationsBank acquired Boatman's Bank, Signet Banking Corp. and Barnett Banks, Inc. Later in 1998, NationsBank itself merged with Bank of America. In 2001, First Union merged with Wachovia in a $13.6 billion deal.

12. Husayn Shahrur, "Industry Structure and Horizontal Takeovers: Analysis of Wealth Effects on Rivals, Suppliers and Corporate Customers," *Journal of Financial Economics*, 76, 2005, 61–98.
13. C. Edward Fee and Shawn Thomas, "Sources of Gains in Horizontal Mergers: Evidence from Customer, Supplier, and Rival Firms," *Journal of Financial Economics,* December 2004, 423–460.
14. Loretta J. Mester, "Efficient Product of Financial Services: Scale and Scope Economies," *Review, Federal Reserve Bank of Philadelphia,* January/February 1987, 15–25.
15. Patrick A. Gaughan, "Financial Deregulation, Banking Mergers and the Impact on Regional Business," *Proceedings of the Pacific Northwest Regional Economic Conference, University of Washington*, Spring 1988.

The pace of consolidation in the U.S. banking system has continued steadily for the past quarter of a century. This consolidation wave is also taking place in Europe although at a slower pace as intercountry barriers, even within the EU, have somewhat limited the ability to merge. Banks are able to lend more profitably when they can borrow at lower money market rates and lend at higher long-term rates. When the spread between these two rates narrows, as it did in 2006, it puts greater pressure on smaller and regional banks to be cost efficient and have multiple revenue sources. This gives larger banks a cost advantage over smaller institutions and has caused many regional banks to sell to larger firms. This was the case in March 2006, when North Fork Bancorp sold out to the much larger Capital One Financial Corp. for $14.6 billion.

The track record of banking M&As is generally good as there are considerable opportunities for economies of scale and scope. We also have the benefit of being able to offer bank customers a truly national, if not international, bank. What is not clear, however, are the costs in the form of potentially poorer customer service. Will that create an opportunity for smaller, more nimble banks to attack the market shares of the larger banking behemoths the way Jet Blue and Southwest Airlines have done to their larger rivals in the airline industry? One major difference between these industries, however, is that most large banks are profitable, whereas the large airlines often are not.

Cost Economies in Banking Mergers: United States Compared with Europe

An example of successful cost reductions was the 1991 acquisition of Manufacturers Hanover Trust by Chemical Bank in 1991. When the deal was announced, the companies declared that they anticipated savings of approximately $650 million. However, the actual savings derived from closing unnecessary branches and eliminating redundant overhead proved to be approximately $100 million greater. The success of this deal was one factor that led Chemical Bank to merge with Chase Manhattan in a $13 billion deal in 1995. This bank would continue to merge with other major financial institutions to create one of the biggest banks in the world. In September 2000, J. P. Morgan and Chase Manhattan combined. Just four years after that, in 2004, J. P. Morgan Chase merged with Bank One.

The banking industry has consolidated significantly over the past 25 years since the industry was deregulated. Studies of fourth merger wave bank mergers do not show significant gains from combining banks.[16] For example, Houston and Ryngaert analyzed 152 bank mergers over the period 1985–1991 and found average bidder announcement returns of −2.25% while target returns were 14.77%.[16] A later study by the same authors, using 184 mergers over the period 1985–1992, found −0.24% and 20.4% for bidder and target returns respectively.[17] While evidence from the fourth merger wave is not impressive, there is more recent evidence that bank mergers do realize synergistic gains and that mergers in this industry do not take place just to create empires for CEOs. For example, Becher analyzed 558 U.S. bank mergers over the period 1980–1997.[18] Over the

16. J. F. Houston and M. D. Ryngaert, "The Overall Gains from Large Bank Mergers," *Journal of Banking and Finance*, 18, 1155–1176.
17. J. F. Houston and M. D. Ryngaert, "Equity Issuance and Adverse Selection: A Direct Test Using Conditional Stock Offers," *Journal of Finance*, 52, 197–219.
18. David Becher, "The Valuation Effects of Bank Mergers," *Journal of Corporate Finance*, 6, 2000, 189–214.

full time period he found that bidder returns were not dramatically different from zero while shareholders of target banks enjoyed positive returns. However, over the 1990s, the fifth merger wave, the picture improved and both bidder and target returns were positive. He concluded that these banking industry deals brought real benefits to shareholders of both companies and not just for the CEO.

There have been several studies that have found that European banks may be more successful than their U.S. counterparts at realizing cost economies following mergers. Using event studies, Cybo-Ottone and Murgia found positive abnormal returns for European bank merger announcements.[19] This implies the markets see benefits, and the most obvious benefits from bank mergers would be cost economies. More directly, however, Vander Vennett found evidence of falling average operating costs in 492 European Union bank mergers over the period 1988–1993.[20] Other studies have focused on specific European countries. For example, Humphrey and Vale found a 2% reduction in operating costs following Norwegian bank mergers.[21] Resti found somewhat similar benefits for Italy while Hayes and Thompson did the same for England.[22] Some studies found few benefits from Spanish bank mergers.[23] While Valverde and Humphrey generally found the same type of neutral results for 22 Spanish bank mergers over the period 1986–2000, they did detect the presence of cost benefits for larger deals and deals where the bank had more prior experience from mergers.[24] This implies that in this market there is more of a learning effect and banks "learn by doing." The Valverde and Humphrey result is interesting when we consider that many studies of U.S. bank mergers found lower gains for the 1980s while finding greater benefits for the 1990s. This may also imply some learning effect in the U.S. market.

CASE STUDY

WACHOVIA—PURSUIT OF SCOPE ECONOMIES IN 2005

As we have discussed, over the past 20 years, the bank we now know as Wachovia grew from a medium-sized bank to the fifth largest bank in the United States. By 2005, Wachovia commanded a huge base of depositors but not the product line width of some of its large competitors. With its large depositor base, Wachovia had a great amount of capital to lend but not enough business opportunities, such as through consumer loans, to lend these monies out. In 2000, the Charlotte,

---

19. Alberto Cybo-Ottone and Maurizio Murgia, "Mergers and Shareholder Wealth in European Banking," *Journal of Banking and Finance*, 24, 2000, 831–859.

20. R. Vander Vennett, "The Effects of Mergers and Acquisition on Efficiency and Profitability of EC Credit Institutions," *Journal of Banking and Finance*, 20, 1997, 1531–1558.

21. D. B. Humphrey and B. Vale, "Scale Economies, Bank Mergers and Electronic Payments: A Spline Function Approach," *Working Paper*, 2002, Central Bank of Norway, Oslo, Norway.

22. A. Resti, "Regulation Can Foster Mergers. Can Mergers Foster Efficiency?: The Italian Case" *Journal of Economics and Business*, 50, 157–169. M. Hayes and S. Thompson, "The Productivity Effects of Banking Mergers: Evidence from the U.K. Building Societies," Journal of Banking and Finance, 23, 1999, 825–846.

23. J. L. Raymond, "Economias de Escala y Fusiones en el Sector de Cajas de Ahorros," *Papeles de Economia Espanola*, 58, 1994, 113–125 ; I. Fuentes and T. Sastre, "Mergers and Acquisitions in the Spanish Banking Industry: Some Empirical Evidence," *Working Paper, 9924*, 1999, Bank of Spain, Madrid, Spain.

24. Santiago Carbo Valverde and David Humphrey, "Predicted and Actual Costs From Individual Bank Mergers," *Journal of Economics and Business*, 56, 2004, 137–157.

North Carolina–based bank had sold off its credit card and mortgage divisions due to their poor performance. They used the monies from the sale of these business units to help finance Wachovia's $13.6 billion merger with First Union in 2001. However, they still needed to be able to offer customers services that other major banks offered—credit cards and mortgages. In order to do that, Wachovia entered into agreements with MBNA for credit cards and Countrywide Financial Corp. for mortgages.

In late 2005, Wachovia elected not to renew its five-year agreement with MBNA and started to offer credit cards directly. In September 2005, Wachovia decided to use M&A to accelerate its returns to the consumer finance business by buying Westcorp, Inc. for $3.9 billion (Westcorp. has a significant auto lending business). This acquisition quickly made Wachovia into the ninth largest auto lender in the United States—a position more consistent with its overall size in the market. At the same time, Wachovia also internally expanded its own mortgage lending business while acquiring AmNet, a small West Coast mortgage company, for $83 million.[a] Through a combination of internal development and M&A, Wachovia quickly was able to achieve economies of scope.

The acquisition of Westcorp is a relatively modest deal when compared to the bold acquisition of MBNA, the largest credit card issuer in the United States, by the Bank of America in June 2005 for $35 billion. While Wachovia had pursued some negotiations for MBNA, a company that it was familiar and therefore somewhat comfortable with, the price tag of this deal was more than Wachovia wanted to pay for a business that is much more risky than traditional banking. In buying smaller companies, Wachovia quickly acquired the expertise it needed in specialized areas, such as Westcorp's skills in auto lending, while not risking the capital needed to do a megadeal. With these moves, Wachovia has achieved a broader product line without all of the risk that the Bank of America assumed with its MBNA deal. Only time will tell which deal will be the wiser move.

[a]David Enrich, "Wachovia Re-Enters the Consumer Finance," *Wall Street Journal*, December 14, 2005, p. B3B.

Synergy and Acquisition Premiums

In Chapter 14 we discuss the concept of acquisition premiums, which typically are paid in control share acquisitions. This premium is a value in excess of the market value of a company that is paid for the right to control and proportionately enjoy the profits of the business. Bidders often cite anticipated synergy as the reason for the payment of a premium. Given the track record of some acquisitions that have not turned out as anticipated, the market sometimes questions the reasonableness of this synergy, especially when it is used as the justification for an unusually high premium. Synergy requires that the bidder receive gains, such as in the form of performance improvements, that offset the premium.[25] It is hoped that these gains will be realized in the years following the transaction. In order for the premium payment (P) to make sense, the present value of these synergistic gains (SG) must exceed this amount. This relationship is expressed as follows:

$$P < [SG_1/(1 + r) + SG_2/(1 + r)^2 + \cdots\cdots + SG_n/(1 + r)^n] \qquad (4.3)$$

where r = discount rate and n = number of periods.

One of the complicating factors in rationalizing the payment of a significant premium is that the premium is usually paid up front, with the gains coming over the course of time.

---

25. See Mark L. Sirower, *The Synergy Trap* (New York: Free Press, 1997), pp. 44–81.

The further into the future these gains are realized, the lower their present value. In addition, the higher the discount rate that is used to convert the synergistic gains to present value, the more difficult it is to justify a high premium. If the bidder also anticipates that there will be a significant initial period before the gains begin manifesting themselves, such as when the bidder is trying to merge the two corporate cultures, this pushes the start of the gains further into the future. If a bidder is using a high discount rate and/or does not expect gains to materialize for an extended period of time, it is hard to justify a high premium. Moreover, the higher the premium, the more pressure the combined company is under to realize a high rate of growth in future synergistic gains.

The best situation is when the business is able to realize both revenue enhancement and cost reduction. When a bidder has paid a significant premium, it implicitly assumes more pressure to realize greater revenue enhancement and more cost reductions. The higher the premium, the more of both are needed.

Throughout the process the bidder needs to be aware of the actual and anticipated response of competitors. Enhanced revenues may come at the expense of competitors' revenues. It may not be realistic to assume that they will stand still and watch a competitor improve its position at their expense through acquisitions. When a company can demonstrate such performance improvements through M&As, competitors may respond with their own acquisition programs. Once again, the myriad different responses may be somewhat difficult to model, but they, nonetheless, need to be carefully considered. Although it has already been mentioned, it is so important that it is worth mentioning again how easy it is to build a financial model that shows whatever result one wants to see. Assumptions can be built into the valuation models that are developed in Chapter 14 to show both revenue enhancement and cost reductions. As the merged business takes steps to realize the theorized financial gains, it may discover that the financial model building process was the easiest part, whereas working through all the other steps necessary to realize the actual gains proves to be the most difficult task.

Financial Synergy

Financial synergy refers to the impact of a corporate merger or acquisition on the costs of capital to the acquiring firm or the merging partners. The extent to which financial synergy exists in corporate combinations, the costs of capital should be lowered. Whether the benefits of such financial synergy are really reasonable, however, is a matter of dispute among corporate finance theorists.

As noted, the combination of two firms may reduce risk if the firms' cash flow streams are not perfectly correlated. If the acquisition or merger lowers the volatility of the cash flows, suppliers of capital may consider the firm less risky. The risk of bankruptcy would presumably be less, given the fact that wide swings up and down in the combined firm's cash flows would be less likely.

Higgins and Schall explain this effect in terms of *debt coinsurance*.[26] If the correlation of the income streams of two firms is less than perfectly positively correlated,

---

26. Robert C. Higgins and Lawrence C. Schall, "Corporate Bankruptcy and Conglomerate Mergers," *Journal of Finance,* 30, March 1975, 93–113.

the bankruptcy risk associated with the combination of the two firms may be reduced. Under certain circumstances one of the firms could experience conditions that force it into bankruptcy. It is difficult to know in advance which one of two possible firms would succumb to this fate. In the event that one of the firms fails, creditors may suffer a loss. If the two firms were combined in advance of these financial problems, however, the cash flows of the solvent firm that are in excess of its debt service needs would cushion the decline in the other firm's cash flows. The offsetting earnings of the firm in good condition might be sufficient to prevent the combined firm from falling into bankruptcy and causing creditors to suffer losses.

The problem with the debt-coinsurance effect is that the benefits accrue to debtholders at the expense of equity holders. Debtholders gain by holding debt in a less risky firm. Higgins and Schall observe that these gains come at the expense of stockholders, who lose in the acquisition. These researchers assume that total returns that can be provided by the combined firm are constant (R_T). If more of these returns are provided to bondholders (R_B), they must come at the expense of stockholders (R_S):

$$R_T = R_S + R_B \qquad (4.4)$$

In other words, Higgins and Schall maintain that the debt-coinsurance effect does not create any new value but merely redistributes gains among the providers of capital to the firm. There is no general agreement on this result. Lewellen, for example, has concluded that stockholders gain from these types of combinations.[27] Other studies, however, fail to indicate that the debt-related motives are more relevant for conglomerate acquisitions than for nonconglomerate acquisitions.[28] Studies have showed the existence of a coinsurance effect in bank mergers. Penas and Unal examined 66 bank mergers and looked at the effects of these deals on 282 bonds.[29] They found positive bond returns for both targets (4.3%) as well as acquiring banks (1.2%). One explanation that may play a role is that larger banks may be "too big to fail" as regulators would not want to allow a larger bank to fail outright and would step in to provide assistance.

Higgins and Schall show that the stockholders' losses may be offset by issuing new debt after the merger. The stockholders may then gain through the tax savings on the debt interest payments. Galais and Masulis have demonstrated this result.[30] The additional debt would increase the debt-equity ratio of the postmerger firm to a level that stockholders must have found desirable, or at least acceptable, before the merger. With the higher debt-equity ratio, the firm becomes a higher risk–higher return investment.

As noted previously, a company may experience economies of scale through acquisitions. These economies are usually thought to come from production cost decreases, attained by operating at higher capacity levels or through a reduced sales force or a

27. Wilbur G. Lewellen, "A Pure Rationale for the Conglomerate Merger," *Journal of Finance,* 26(2), May 1971, 521–545.
28. Pieter T. Elgers and John J. Clark, "Merger Types and Shareholder Returns: Additional Evidence," *Financial Management,* 9, issue 2, Summer 1980, 66–72.
29. ./Maria Fabiana Penas and Haluk Unal, "Gains in Bank Mergers: Evidence from the Bond Markets," *Journal of Financial Economics,* 74, 2004, 149–179.
30. Dan Galais and Ronald W. Masulis, "The Option Pricing Model and the Risk Factor of Stock," *Journal of Financial Economics,* 3(1/2), January/March 1976, 53–81.

shared distribution system. As a result of acquisitions, *financial* economies of scale are also possible in the form of lower flotation and transaction costs.[31]

In financial markets, a larger company has certain advantages that may lower the cost of capital to the firm. It enjoys better access to financial markets, and it tends to experience lower costs of raising capital, presumably because it is considered to be less risky than a smaller firm. Therefore, the costs of borrowing by issuing bonds are lower because a larger firm would probably be able to issue bonds offering a lower interest rate than a smaller company. In addition, there are certain fixed costs in the issuance of securities, such as Securities and Exchange Commission (SEC) registration costs, legal fees, and printing costs. These costs would be spread out over a greater dollar volume of securities because the larger company would probably borrow more capital with each issue of bonds.

The analysis is similar in the case of equity securities. Flotation costs per dollar raised would be lower for larger issues than for smaller issues. In addition, the selling effort required may be greater for riskier issues than for less risky larger firms. It is assumed in this discussion that larger firms are less risky and bear a lower probability of bankruptcy and financial failure. If a larger firm, which might result from a combination of several other firms, is so inefficient, however, that profits start to fall, the larger combination of companies could have a greater risk of financial failure. Levy and Sarnat have developed a model to show the diversification effect that occurs when two or more imperfectly correlated income streams combine to lower the probability of default. This lower risk level induces capital holders to provide capital to the combined firm or conglomerate at lower costs than they would have provided to the individual, premerger components. Their analysis presents the financial synergistic benefits as an economic gain that results from mergers.

CASE STUDY

FINANCIAL SYNERGY—FLORIDA POWER & LIGHT AND CONSTELLATION ENERGY

Regardless of the debate about the reasonableness of some of the assumptions related to financial synergy, deals based on financial synergy continue to take place. For example, in December 2005, the boards of both FPL Group, Inc. and Constellation Energy Group, Inc. approved a $11 billion stock-for-stock swap. The FPL Group, Inc. includes the Florida Power & Light utility, which is the source of nearly three-quarters of its profits.[a] One of the bases for the merger was the benefits that Constellation would receive from being part of FPL, which is considered by the bond rating agencies to be less risky than Constellation. Based on this lower risk perception FPL commanded an A rating while Constellation's was in the BBB range. One of the reasons for the difference in risk profile and debt ratings is the relative mix of business at the two power companies. FPL is more of a traditional

[a]Rebecca Smith and Dennis Berman, "FPL, Constellation Reach Agreement on $11 Billion Deal, *Wall Street Journal,* December, 19, 2005, p. A3.

---

31. Haim Levy and Marshall Sarnat, "Diversification, Portfolio Analysis and the Uneasy Case for Conglomerate Mergers," *Journal of Finance*, 25(4), September 1970, 795–802.

power company with the bulk of its profits coming from the power generation and distribution business. Constellation, however, derives most of its profits from the unregulated areas such as power trading, which are considered more risky—especially after the Enron debacle. Therefore, even though Constellation is a power utility, its traditional power generation and supply business provides it with only a small percent of its total profits. Ironically, Constellation's competitors in the power trading business are divisions of major investment banks such as Bear Stearns, Goldman Sachs, and Morgan Stanley. These financial institutions are much better situated to access capital on preferential terms and command an A rating in the credit markets. The combination of the two power companies formed one of the largest generators of power in the United States. More important, the combination will enable the Constellation part of the combined business to access additional capital to expand into the unregulated part of the business at lower costs. If the additional risk does not pull down the FPL through its association with the more risky Constellation, the lower capital costs may enhance the company's profit opportunities.

DIVERSIFICATION

Diversification means growing outside a company's current industry category. This motive played a major role in the acquisitions and mergers that took place in the third merger wave—the conglomerate era. During the late 1960s, firms often sought to expand by buying other companies rather than through internal expansion. This outward expansion was often facilitated by some creative financial techniques that temporarily caused the acquiring firm's stock price to rise while adding little real value through the exchange. The legacy of the conglomerates has drawn poor, or at least mixed, reviews. Indeed, many of the firms that grew into conglomerates in the 1960s were disassembled through various spinoffs and divestitures in the 1970s and 1980s. This process of *deconglomerization* raises serious doubts as to the value of diversification based on expansion.

Although many companies have regretted their attempts at diversification, others can claim to have gained significantly. One such firm is General Electric (GE). Contrary to what its name implies, for many years now GE is no longer merely an electronics-oriented company. Through a pattern of acquisitions and divestitures, the firm has become a diversified conglomerate with operations in insurance, television stations, plastics, medical equipment, and so on.

During the 1980s and 1990s, at a time when the firm was acquiring and divesting various companies, earnings rose significantly. The market responded favorably to these diversified acquisitions by following the rising pattern of earnings.

Diversification and the Acquisition of Leading Industry Positions

Part of the reasoning behind GE's successful diversification strategy has been the types of companies it has acquired. General Electric sought to acquire leading positions in the various industries in which it owned businesses. Leading is usually interpreted as the first or second rank according to market shares. It is believed by acquirers like GE that the number-one or number-two position provides a more dominant position, which affords advantages over the smaller competitors. These advantages can manifest themselves in a number of ways, including broader consumer awareness in the marketplace as leading positions in distribution. Corporations in the secondary ranks, such as numbers four or five, may sometimes be at such a disadvantage that it is difficult for them to generate rewarding returns. Companies within the overall company framework that do not hold a leading position, and do not have reasonable prospects of cost-effectively acquiring such a position, become candidates for divestiture. The released resources derived from such a divestiture can then be reinvested in other companies to exploit the benefits of their dominant position or used to acquire leading companies in other industries.

CASE STUDY

GE—WHAT TO DO WHEN YOU CAN'T ACHIEVE A LEADING POSITION

While the General Electric Company has enjoyed great success with acquisitions in many different industries, it has experienced significant difficulty turning a profit in the insurance industry. This was underscored in November 2005, when General Electric (GE) announced that it would sell its reinsurance business to Swiss Re for $8.5 billion. GE's CEO at that time, Jeffrey Immelt, successor to the well-known Jack Welch, indicated that the insurance business was "a tough strategic fit for GE." That business had lost over $700 million in the five years prior to the sale and had required the infusion of $3.2 billion more of GE capital. However, even with the strong financial support of GE, its reinsurance business could not move up in industry rankings relative to leaders Munich Re, Swiss Re, and General Re. However, the deal allowed Swiss Re, which would then have total revenues of $34 billion, to overtake Munich Re, which had 2004 sales of just under $29 billion. These two companies are clearly the market leaders as their sales are more than double their nearest rivals, General Re ($10.6 billion) and Hanover Re ($10.1 billion). GE, which marketed its reinsurance business under the name GE Insurance Solutions, had $8.2 billion in total 2004 sales.

For GE this was an admission of failure by a very successful company. GE cut its losses and sold the reinsurance business to another company that was better at it than they were. GE has done this before when an acquisition has failed to achieve expected goals. For example, in 1982, it sold off its Trane air conditioning business, which, with its 10% market share, was an "also ran" by GE standards and was more trouble that it was worth.[a] In many ways this is a sign of good management as managers need to know when to cut their losses and focus on areas in which they can achieve greater returns rather than continue with a failing business just to avoid having to admit mistakes to shareholders. Given the volume of deals that GE does, all of them are not going to be a success. The key is to quickly recognize and admit mistakes and refocus on the winners.

[a]Patrick A. Gaughan, *Mergers: What Can Go Wrong and How to Prevent It* (Hoboken: NJ: John Wiley & Sons), 2004, pp. 51–52.

"Portfolio" Management of Business Units

There are several other examples of very diversified companies that have enjoyed significant success by pursuing the strategy of trying to acquire a leading position in each business category they are in. In the 1990s, Allied Signal, based in Morris Township, New Jersey, was a good example of a diversified manufacturer that has enjoyed impressive earnings growth and a high market valuation. CEO Larry Bossidy managed the performance of the different business units contained within Allied Signal and sold off units that did not fit or did not exhibit at least the potential for a profit margin in excess of 15%. During Bossidy's tenure he reduced the number of business units while retaining and expanding those that were more profitable. The units contained within large, diversified companies, such as GE and Allied Signal, are, in a sense, a portfolio of investments made by a corporation. These investments generate a rate of return that in turn is passed to investors in the form of dividends and capital gains (or losses). In 1999, Allied Signal, itself a product of a 1985 merger between Allied Corporation and the Signal Companies, would merge with Honeywell to create a huge industrial giant.

One conglomerate that attracted much attention in the fifth wave and thereafter was Tyco. Seemingly modeled by its CEO, Dennis Kozlowski, to be another GE, Tyco combined many acquisitions to form a very large conglomerate that operated in four main business segments: security and electronics, fire protection and flow control, health care and flow control, and financial services. Clearly, financial services has little to do with health care or security and fire protection. The market initially liked Tyco's acquisition program although accounting issues, such as doing many small acquisitions that were below the 10% materiality reporting threshold, may have clouded the true volume of Tyco's deals. Tyco sold off its CIT financial services business shortly after it was acquired! By January 2006, the company had a market capitalization of $62 billion but a weak stock price. It finally succumbed to market pressures and announced that it was selling off its electronics and health care businesses, thus breaking up the conglomerate.

By expanding through the acquisition of a number of firms, the acquiring corporation may attempt to achieve some of the benefits that investors receive by diversifying their portfolio of assets. The portfolio theory research literature in finance has attempted to quantify some of the risk-reduction benefits that an investor may enjoy through diversification. This research clearly supports the intuitive belief of investors that "putting all one's eggs in one basket" is not a wise decision. However, when this strategy is applied to capital assets and whole corporations, it loses some of its appeal. A company often will pursue diversification outside its own industry when management is displeased by the current volatile level of earnings. A volatile income stream makes it more difficult to pay regular dividends and creates an unstable environment for long-term planning. Financial markets may interpret a falloff in earnings that results in a reduction or cancellation of a quarterly dividend as a negative sign. Having a diverse corporation that spans a number of different business areas may help facilitate dividend stability.

CASE STUDY

ACHIEVING A NUMBER-ONE OR -TWO RANKING IS NOT A PANACEA

Simply achieving a number-one or -two ranking in an industry is not sufficient to guarantee success. This was demonstrated in the farm equipment business. In 1994, Case Corp. found itself mired in a distant third position in farm equipment business with little hope of catching the leader, John Deere Corp. The success that companies like General Electric had in using a dominant position in various markets to outpace smaller rivals surely was not lost on the management of Case when it decided to merge with the number-two company in the business, New Holland. The 1999 $4.6 billion merger created CNH Global—a company with sales of almost $11 billion. However, merely being in the number-two position did not prevent the combined company from losing further ground to John Deere. Since the merger, CNH has had trouble generating profits and continues to try to cut costs and integrate the two companies better to realize economies that may yield greater profits.

Diversification to Enter More Profitable Industries

One reason management may opt for diversified expansion is its desire to enter industries that are more profitable than the acquiring firm's current industry. It could be that the parent company's industry has reached the mature stage or that the competitive pressures within that industry preclude the possibility of raising prices to a level where extranormal profits can be enjoyed.

One problem that some firms may encounter when they seek to expand by entering industries that offer better profit opportunities is the lack of an assurance that those profit opportunities will persist for an extended time in the future. Industries that are profitable now may not be as profitable in the future. Competitive pressures serve to bring about a movement toward a long-term equalization of rates of return across industries. Clearly, this does not mean that the rates of return in all industries at any moment in time are equal. The forces of competition that move industries to have equal returns are offset by opposing forces, such as industrial development, that cause industries to have varying rates of return. Those above-average-return industries that do not have imposing barriers to entry will experience declining returns until they reach the cross-industry average.

Economic theory implies that in the long run only industries that are difficult to enter will have above-average returns. This implies that a diversification program to enter more profitable industries will not be successful in the long run. The expanding firm may not be able to enter those industries that exhibit persistently above-average returns because of barriers that prevent entry and may be able to enter only the industries with low barriers. When entering the low-barrier industry, the expanding company will probably be forced to compete against other entrants who were attracted by temporarily above-average returns and low barriers. The increased number of competitors will drive down returns and cause the expansion strategy to fail.

CASE STUDY

MONTANA POWER—FAILED CORPORATE TRANSFORMATION

The story of Montana Power is one of a company that existed for decades as a stable, but slow-growth, power utility. During the 1990s, its management began the process of transforming it into a telecommunications company. The end result was a disaster.

Montana Power was founded in 1912. It moved into oil and gas in the 1930s and then expanded into coal in the 1950s. Its initial entry into the telecommunications business began in the 1980s, when it took advantage of the breakup of AT&T. It slowly began to expand its position in the telecommunications business by laying more fiber and building more of its own network.

In February 2001, the company eventually sold off its "boring" power utility business for $1.3 billion and invested the proceeds into the high-flying telecommunications business, which was called Touch America. The energy distribution business was sold to NorthWestern Corporation for $612 million in cash plus the assumption of $488 million in debt.[a] The monies from the sale were invested in Touch America's telecom business. In August 2000, PanCanadian Petroleum Ltd. agreed to purchase

[a]"Montana Power and Northwestern in $612 Million Deal," New York Times, October 3, 2000.

Montana Power's oil and gas business for $475 million.[b] This acquisition increased PanCanadian's oil field capacity by providing it with properties in Alberta, Montana, and Colorado. It was indicated by PanCanadian that the accrued fields had reserves of 550 billion cubic feet of gas and 20 million barrels of crude oil. In the summer of 2000, Touch America then entered into a deal to buy Quest's in-region long-distance network, which regulatory constraints forced Quest to divest pursuant to an agreement related to its acquisition of U.S. West—one of the seven superregionals that were formed in the breakup of AT&T. This $200 million deal gave Touch America long-distance operations in 14 states with sales of approximately $300 million in revenues and 250,000 customers.[c]

After the selloff of the power utility business, Montana Power changed its name to Touch America Holdings, Inc. The company was traded on the New York Stock Exchange. For a while it was highly touted by the market and the industry.[d] Touch America started off as a growing company in a growing industry while being largely debt free. Initially, it seemed that the combination of rapid growth without debt pressures made Touch America seemed highly desirable. However, all was not well in the telecom sector and Touch America's fate declined with the industry. While its 2001 results were impressive, in the second and third quarters of 2002 the company generated losses of $32.3 million and $20.9 million. This occurred even though revenues increased. At the time Touch America sold off its utility business its stock was as high as $65 per share. By the third quarter of 2003, the stock had fallen to $0.53 per share and was de-listed.[e]

Like many companies in the telecom sector, Touch America had invested heavily in network expansion and fiber laying throughout the 1990s and early 2000s. Billions of dollars were spent on laying fiber-optic cable as telecom and non-telecom companies expanded. The result is that 360 networks held over 87,000 miles of fiber-optic cable linking urban areas in North America, Asia, and South America.[f] Touch America was one such company. The overcapacity in the industry helped fuel increased competition and declining margins. Only the more savvy companies would survive and newcomer Touch America was not one of them. Touch America finally filed for Chapter 11 bankruptcy protection on June 19, 2003, but assets were eventually put up for sale despite the objections of various creditors.

[b]"PanCanadian Will Acquire Oil and Gas Assets," New York Times, August 29, 2000.

[c]"Unit of Montana Power Is Buying Quest Phone Business," New York Times, March 17, 2000.

[d]Steve Skobel, "Rising Starts," Telecom Business, July 1, 2001.

[e]Matt Gouras, "Touch America Trading Suspended: Company Made Disastrous Move Into Telecommunications," Associated Press Newswires.

[f]Lucy I. Vento, "Who Will Profit from the U.S. Fiber Network Glut," Business Communications Review, September 1, 2001.

Financial Benefits of Diversification

One possible area of benefits of diversification that has been cited is the coinsurance effect. This occurs when firms with imperfectly correlated earnings combine and derive a combined earnings stream that is less volatile than either of the individual firms' earnings stream. The covariance is a statistical measure of the linear association between two variables. If the covariance between earnings of two potential merger candidates is negative, there might be an opportunity to derive coinsurance benefits from a combination of such firms. What the merger partners have to determine is if these coinsurance "benefits" truly provide benefits to shareholders beyond what they can achieve on their own. When they purchased their shares in the companies in question, shareholders presumably were aware of the pattern of earnings at the companies. They reconciled the pattern of those earnings, and the investment returns these securities provided, with those of other securities in their portfolio. It is questionable that the managers of the merger candidates are truly providing a benefit for shareholders that they could not achieve on their own and at a lower cost. Mergers motivated by financial diversification may provide benefits for the management, who may be then able to demonstrate a less volatile earnings stream. Whether this is truly a benefit for shareholders is a separate issue.

Empirical Evidence on Acquisition Programs of the 1960s

The conglomerate wave of the 1960s provided abundant evidence of the effects of large-scale diversifications into unrelated fields. During this period many firms diversified. Using a large sample of firms, Henri Servaes showed that in 1961, 55% percent of the firms he studied operated in only one business segment, whereas by 1976 that percent declined to 28%.[32] Over that same time period the percent of companies that operated in four or more business segments increased from 8 to 30.

These types of diversifications have attracted much criticism. Some evidence, however, indicates that, at least initially, the market responded favorably to the announcements of such acquisition programs. Schipper and Thompson have analyzed the wealth effects of firms that announced acquisition programs.[33] Specifically, they considered what impact an announcement of an acquisitions program had on the value of the acquiring firm. They examined announcements of such programs before 1967 to 1970 because regulatory changes such as the Williams Act and the Tax Reform Act of 1969 took place in these years. These regulatory changes created certain impediments to the types of acquisitions that occurred in the 1960s. The study found that during this period acquisition programs were capitalized as positive net present value programs. Exhibit 4.2 shows that cumulative abnormal returns for the acquiring firm's stock responded positively to the acquisition program announcement. These results indicate that, at least before the regulatory changes of the late 1960s, the market had a positive view of acquisition programs, many of which involved substantial diversification. The favorable response of the market to the diversifying acquisitions of that time helps explain why the third takeover wave was as significant as it was. Another study by Scherer and Ravenscraft also showed that investors who bought shares of the 13 conglomerates in their sample, which included many of the more notable ones, such as ITT, Gulf & Western, Textron, and Teledyne, prior to the start of the conglomerate boom outperformed the market, but those who purchased them after the merger wave took hold earned returns below the market.[34]

Although Schipper and Thompson have shown that the market had a positive reaction to the announcement of the diverse acquisition programs of the 1960s, the poor performance of many of these acquisitions during the years that followed, which was noted in the Scherer and Ravenscraft study, has shown that the market may have been overly optimistic

32. Henri Saerves, "The Value of Diversification During the Conglomerate Merger Wave," *Journal of Finance*, 51(4), September 1996, 1201–1225.
33. Katherine Schipper and Rex Thompson, "The Value of Merger Activity," *Journal of Financial Economics*, 11(1–4), April 1983, 85–119.
34. David Ravenscraft and Frederick Scherer, "Mergers and Managerial Performance," in John Coffee, Louis Lowenstein, and Susan Rose Ackerman, eds., *Knights, Raiders and Targets* (New York: Oxford University Press, 1988), pp. 194–210.

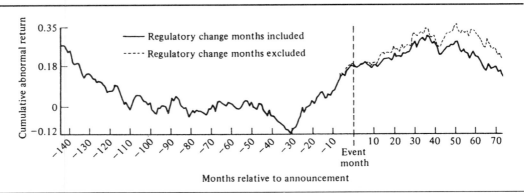

EXHIBIT 4.2 CUMULATIVE ABNORMAL RETURNS RELATIVE TO ACQUISITION PROGRAMS OF ACQUIRING FIRMS
Source: Katherine Schipper and Rex Thompson, "Evidence on the Capitalized Value of Merger Activity for Acquiring Firms," *Journal of Financial Economics,* April 1983, p. 100.

in its initial assessment of the likelihood of conglomerate acquisitions to be successful. The subsequent undoing of many of these deals, sometimes through bustup takeovers, has confirmed the questionable nature of this expansion strategy.

Positive Evidence of Benefits of Conglomerates

Many studies question the risk-reduction benefits of conglomerates. However, some studies cast the wealth effects of conglomerates in a better light. For example, one study by Elger and Clark has shown that returns to stockholders in conglomerate acquisitions are greater than in nonconglomerate acquisitions.[35]

The study, which examined 337 mergers between 1957 and 1975, found that conglomerate mergers provided superior gains relative to nonconglomerate mergers. The researchers reported these gains for both buyer and seller firms, with substantial gains registered by stockholders of seller firms and moderate gains for buying company stockholders. This finding was supported by later research by Wansley, Lane, and Yang. They focused on 52 nonconglomerate and 151 conglomerate mergers. It was also found, however, that returns to shareholders were larger in horizontal and vertical acquisitions than in conglomerate acquisitions.[36]

Is There a Diversification Discount?

Using the aforementioned large sample drawn from the 1960s, Henry Servaes compared the Tobin's q's of diversified firms to those which were not diversified. He found no evidence that diversification increased corporate values. On the contrary he found that the Tobin's q's for diversified firms were significantly lower than those for multisegment

---

35. Peter T. Elgers and John J. Clark, "Merger Types and Shareholder Returns: Additional Evidence," *Financial Management*, 9, issue 2, Summer 1980, 66–72.

36. James Wansley, William Lane, and Ho Yang, "Abnormal Returns to Acquired Firms by Type of Acquisition and Method of Payment," *Financial Management*, 12(3), Autumn 1983, 16–22.

companies. Other research has found that the diversification discount was not restricted to the conglomerate era. A study conducted by Berger and Ofek, using a large sample of firms over the 1986–1991 sample period, found that diversification resulted in a loss of firm value that averaged between 13% and 15%.[37] This study estimated the imputed value of a diversified firm's segments as if they were separate firms. The results found that the loss of firm value was not affected by firm size but was less when the diversification occurred within related industries. The loss of firm value results were buttressed by the fact that the diversified segments showed lower operating profitability than single-line businesses. The results also showed that diversified firms overinvested in the diversified segments more than single-line businesses. This implies that overinvestment may be a partial cause of the loss of value associated with diversification.

Value-reducing effects of diversification were detected by Lang and Stulz.[38] Using a large sample of companies (in excess of 1,000), Lang and Stulz found that greater corporate diversification in the 1980s was inversely related to the Tobin's q of these firms. Like Berger and Ofek, when these findings are combined with those of Lang and Stulz, we see that diversification often lowers firm values. This conclusion, however, is not universally accepted by finance researchers. Villalonga believes that the diversification discount is merely an artifact of the data used by these researchers.[39] He states that the data used by these researchers were artificially restricted by Financial Accounting Standards Board definition of segments as well as requirements that only segments that constitute 10% or more of a company's business are required to be reported. Using a data source that is not affected by this problem, Villalonga finds a diversification premium, as opposed to a discount.

Other studies have tackled the problem differently. Comment and Jarrell analyzed a sample of exchange-listed firms from 1978 to 1989. They found that increased corporate focus or specialization was consistent with shareholder wealth maximization.[40] They concluded that the commonly cited benefits of diversification, economies of scope, go unrealized and that the access to greater internal capital does not appear to affect the diversified firm's propensity to pursue external capital. One "benefit" of diversification that was found was that diversified firms tend to be targets of hostile takeovers less frequently than their less diversified counterparts. Nonetheless, diversified firms were more active participants, as both buyers and sellers, in the market for corporate control.

Related versus Unrelated Diversification

Diversification does not mean conglomerization. That is, it is possible to diversify into fields that are related to the buyer's business. An example of a related diversification

37. P. G. Berger and E. Ofek, "Diversification's Effect on Firm Value," *Journal of Financial Economics*, 37(1), January 1995, 39–65.
38. Larry Lang and Rene Stulz, "Tobin's q, Corporate Diversification and Firm Performance," *Journal of Political Economy*, 102(6), December 1994, 1248–1280.
39. Belen Villalonga, "Diversification Discount or Premium? New Evidence from the Business Information Tracking Series," *Journal of Finance*, 59(2), April 2004, 479–506.
40. R. Comment and G. Jarrell, "Corporate Focus and Stock Returns," *Journal of Financial Economics,* 37(1), January 1995, 67–87.

occurred in 1994, when Merck purchased Medco. Merck is one of the largest pharmaceutical companies in the world and Medco is the largest marketer of pharmaceuticals in the United States. The two businesses are different in that one company is a manufacturer and the other company is a distributor. Nonetheless, the two companies are both in the broadly defined pharmaceutical industry, and each has a greater knowledge of the other's business than an outside firm would have. In addition, there may be a more reliable expectation of economies of scale and scope in related diversifications because a buyer may be better able to leverage its current resources and expertise if it says closer to its current business activities. However, while these two companies were leaders in their respective segments of the drug industry, their combination did not yield synergistic benefits. Merck assumed that in the world of managed care, owning a company such as Medco would provide it competitive advantages. Indeed, shortly after the Merck-Medco merger, in 1994, some of Merck's competitors thought the same, as Roche acquired Syntex Corp. for $5.3 billion and Eli Lilly bought PCS Health Systems for $4.1 billion. Unfortunately, relatedness was not enough to ensure success and Merck and Medco had to later undo the deal after concluding that they did not understand the regulatory environment that would not allow Medco to influence the usage by physicians and consumers of its drugs. This eliminated certain synergistic benefits.

It is not always clear when another business is related. One example put forward by Young and Morck is the 3M Corp.[41] 3M is well known for its brand of Scotch tape. However, the company also extends this success to marketing of other related products such as Post-it notes as well as other tape products such as VCR tapes. This company was able to extend its brand name to other products whose manufacturing and marketing has some commonalities to its main business activities.

The track record of related acquisitions is significantly better than that of unrelated acquisitions. Morck, Shleifer, and Vishny found that the market punished shareholders in companies that engaged in unrelated acquisitions, whereas shareholders in companies that made related acquisitions did significantly better.[42] Their study of 326 acquisitions between 1975 and 1987 presented a more favorable picture of this type of diversification. Rather, a particular form of diversification, unrelated diversification, showed poor results. They measured relatedness by determining if the two firms had at least one of their top three lines of business in the same Standard Industrial Classification (SIC) code. Not all the research on related diversification shows the same results. For example, the result found by Agrawal, Jaffe, and Mandelker was the opposite of the result of Morck, Shleifer, and Vishny. Their result showed that unrelated acquisitions outperformed related acquisitions.[43] The market performance of diversified firms is discussed later in this chapter.

---

41. Bernard Young and Robert Morck, "When Synergy Creates Real Value," in *Mastering Strategy*, University of Michigan Business School Web site paper.
42. Randall Morck, Andrei Shleifer, and Robert Vishny, "Do Managerial Objectives Drive Bad Acquisitions?" *Journal of Finance*, 45(1), March 1990, 31–48.
43. A. Agrawal, J. F. Jaffe, and G. N. Mandelker, "The Post-Merger Performance of Acquiring Firms: A Reexamination of an Anomaly," *Journal of Finance*, 47(4), September 1992, 1605–1671.

CASE STUDY

LVMH—IS LUXURY RELATED?

If the track record of related diversifications is better than unrelated, then how do we define *related*? This is not that obvious and, unfortunately, is open to interpretation. If it is misinterpreted, it can result in losses for shareholders. One such example was LVMH's fifth merger wave expansion strategy. LVMH, which stands for Louis Vuitton, Moet, and Hennessy, led by its flamboyant CEO Bernard Arnault, seems to see any connection to luxury to be related. The Paris-based company went on an acquisition binge that focused on a wide variety of companies that marketed products or services to upper-end customers. This led them to acquire such major brand names as Chaumet jewelry, Dom Perignon (part of Moet), Fendi, Givenchy, Donna Karan, Loewe leather goods, Sephora, TAG Heuer, Thomas Pink shirts, and Veuve Cliquot champagne. The company has become a clearinghouse for luxury products, but the combination of various different acquired companies has provided few, if any, synergies. Many of the acquired businesses, such as Fendi and Donna Karan, while major international brands, generated few profits. In November 1999, LVMH stretched the luxury-related connection by buying fine art auctioneer Phillips De Pury & Luxembourgh for $115 million. However, in doing so Arnault violated several rules of merger success. First, he acquired a company that was a distant third behind Sotheby's and Christie's. Second, he stretched the definition of related so far that there were no possible synergies. Finally he acquired a company that needed a large cash infusion with little potential for it to be recouped. As with many other failed deals, CEO Arnault went unchecked by his directors and shareholders paid the price. LVMH eventually admitted this failure and sold off the art auctioneering company at a loss. Clearly, defining *related* as any luxury good or service was a faulty strategy. Relatedness is a subjective concept and the more narrow the definition, the more likely the deal will be successful.

OTHER ECONOMIC MOTIVES

In addition to economies of scale and diversification benefits, there are two other economic motives for M&As: horizontal integration and vertical integration. *Horizontal integration* refers to the increase in market share and market power that results from acquisitions and mergers of rivals. *Vertical integration* refers to the merger or acquisition of companies that have a buyer–seller relationship.

Horizontal Integration

Combinations that result in an increase in market share may have a significant impact on the combined firm's market power. Whether market power actually increases depends on the size of the merging firms and the level of competition in the industry. Economic theory categorizes industries within two extreme forms of market structure. On one side of this spectrum is pure competition, which is a market that is characterized by numerous buyers and sellers, perfect information, and homogeneous, undifferentiated products. Given these conditions, each seller is a price taker with no ability to influence market price. On the other end of the industry spectrum is monopoly, which is an industry with one seller. The monopolist has the ability to select the price-output combination that maximizes profits. Of course, the monopolist is not guaranteed a profit simply because it is insulated from direct competitive pressures. The monopolist may or may not earn a profit, depending on the magnitude of its costs relative to revenues at the optimal "profit-maximizing" price-output combination. Within these two ends of the industry structure spectrum is monopolistic competition, which features many sellers of a some-what differentiated product. Closer to monopoly, however, is oligopoly, in which there are a few (i.e., 3 to 12) sellers of a differentiated product. Horizontal integration involves a movement from the competitive end of the spectrum toward the monopoly end.

CASE STUDY

HORIZONTAL INTEGRATION—MOBIL MERGER WITH EXXON

In December 1998, Exxon announced that it was merging with the Mobil Oil Company. The $82 billion merger created the world's largest oil company. Both companies were vertically inte-grated with substantial oil reserves and a broad retail network. In spite of their substantial size, the companies were able to convince regulators that the new oil behemoth would not stifle competition.

One of the difficulties in a merger between companies of the size of these two firms is the postmerger integration. To achieve the synergistic gains that they predicted to the media at the time of the deal, the companies must be able to successfully integrate the varied resources of the two companies. At the time of the deal the companies stated that they predicted merger savings on the order of $3.8 billion. In what was a little unusual for such megamergers, less than two years later the combined Exxon-Mobil announced that merger savings would be approximately 20% higher—$4.6 billion. The success of this deal, along with concerns that they would be left at a competitive disadvantage, led several of their competitors to do their own deals. (See Table A.)

Company	Revenue ($ Billions)	Oil Reserves (million barrels)	Gas Reserves (million barrels)
Exxon-Mobil	$160.6	11,260	9,498
Royal Dutch Shell	105.4	9,775	10,093
BP-Amoco	83.5	7,572	8,125
Chevron-Texaco	66.5	8,264	2,860

TABLE A   REVENUE OF MERGER COMPANIES IN THE OIL INDUSTRY

With the greatly increased size of the combined Exxon-Mobil entity, the deal set off a series of horizontal combinations in the industry. One of the measures of economic power in the industry is the ownership of reserves. This led British Petroleum (BP) to buy the Atlantic Richfield Company (ARCO) in 1999 for $26.8 billion. In the next year Chevron bought Texaco for $36 billion. Even with these combinations, Exxon-Mobil still led the industry by a wide margin. The success of this deal was underscored when in 2006 Exxon-Mobil announced the highest annual profits of any corporation in history. The company's 2005 annual profits were $36 billion on sales of $371 billion and a market capitalization of $377 billion, making it the largest company in the world using a variety of measures!

Market Power

Market power, which is sometimes also referred to as monopoly power, is defined as the ability to set and maintain price above competitive levels. Because in the long run sellers in a competitive industry only earn a normal return and do not earn "economic rent," competitive firms set price equal to marginal cost. Market power refers to the ability to set price in excess of marginal cost. Abba Lerner developed what has been known as the

Lerner Index, which measures the magnitude of the difference between price and marginal cost relative to price. Simply having a positive difference between price and marginal cost, however, does not guarantee profits because fixed costs could be sufficiently high that the firm generates losses.

$$\text{Lerner Index} = (P - MC)/P \tag{4.5}$$

where:

    P = price

    MC = marginal cost

There are three sources of market power: product differentiation, barriers to entry, and market share. Through horizontal integration, a company is able to increase its market share. It could be the case that even with a substantial increase in market share, the lack of significant product differentiation or barriers to entry could prevent a firm from being able to raise its price significantly above marginal cost. If an industry does not possess imposing barriers to entry, raising price above marginal cost may only attract new competitors who will drive price down toward marginal costs. Even in industries that have become more concentrated, there may be a substantial amount of competition. In addition, if prices and profits rise too high, new entrants may enter such contestable markets quickly, raising the degree of competition.

Social Costs of Increased Concentration

The costs to society that result from increased concentration are a function of the state of competition that exists after the horizontal mergers. If the industry structure formed approximates monopoly, the social costs may be significant. This can be seen by the fact that in pure competition each firm is a price taker, and competitive firms produce an output where price equals marginal costs. In a monopoly, a firm maximizes profits by setting marginal revenue equal to marginal costs. The rule is the same for the competitive firm, but in the instance of monopoly, marginal revenue is less than price. The end result is that a competitive industry has lower prices and higher output levels than a monopolized version of the same industry. This is seen in Exhibit 4.3. If a competitive pricing rule is used ($P = MC$), an output level equal to X_c results, with price equal to P_c. If such an industry were to become so concentrated that a monopoly resulted, a lower output level equal to X_m, and a higher price equal to P_m, would result. The end result is that consumers would pay higher prices in the monopolized industry and would have a lower total output available. One way to see the effect on society is to consider a concept that economists call deadweight loss or welfare loss—that is, the loss of *consumer surplus* and *producer surplus.* Consumer surplus is the difference between the price paid and the height up to the demand curve for all units bought by consumers. The height up to the demand curve reflects the maximum that consumers would be willing to pay for each unit. This maximum declines as consumers purchase more units. Producer surplus is the difference between the height up to the supply curve and the price that producers receive for each unit. The supply curve reflects the producers' cost conditions. In a competitive market, the supply curve is the horizontal summation of the individual marginal cost curves of each producer above the average cost curve. In such a market, the height up

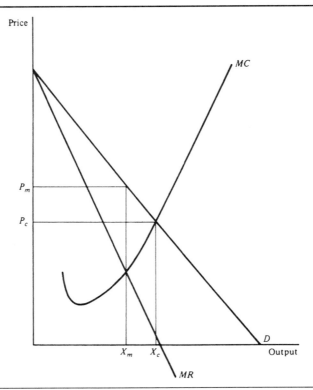

EXHIBIT 4.3   CONSUMERS BENEFIT MORE FROM A COMPETITIVE MARKET. THEY BUY MORE OUTPUT (X_c) THAN IN A MONOPOLIZED MARKET (X_m), AND PAY LESS ($P_c < P_m$).

to the supply curve reflects the costs of producing additional units. Producers should not accept less than the marginal costs of producing each additional unit. The upward-sloping shape of the supply curve reflects diminishing returns in production.

Gains from trade occur for both parties: Consumers pay less than the maximum they would have been willing to pay for all units up to X_e, and producers receive a price greater than the additional costs of producing each unit for all units up to X_e. The total gains from trade are depicted in Exhibit 4.4, and the combined total of the two triangular areas depicts consumer surplus (CS) and producer surplus (PS).

The welfare loss in monopoly occurs because fewer units are sold, and each is sold for a higher price than in competition. Given that trading ends at an output level of X_m instead of X_c, a loss of consumer and producer surplus results. The combined loss of consumer and producer surplus is the deadweight or welfare loss. The upper shaded triangle in Exhibit 4.5 refers to the loss of consumer surplus, and the lower shaded triangle shows the loss of producer surplus.

The obvious practical question that arises is whether horizontal mergers result in a welfare loss to society. Economists have written many theoretical papers that purport to measure the welfare loss.[44] In reality, these are interesting exercises, but they have failed to provide

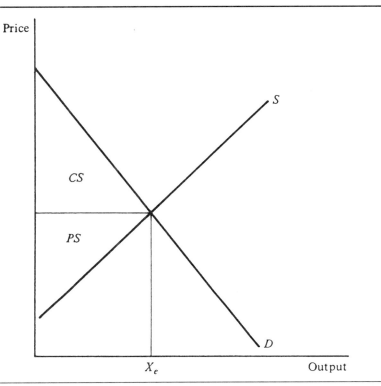

EXHIBIT 4.4   A FREE MARKET SYSTEM BRINGS ABOUT AN EXCHANGE BETWEEN SUPPLIERS AND DEMANDERS IN WHICH THE GAINS FROM TRADE ARE MAXIMIZED. CONSUMER GAINS ARE DENOTED BY CONSUMER SURPLUS (CS) AND SUPPLIER GAINS ARE DENOTED BY PRODUCER SURPLUS (PS).

a convincing quantitative measure of the deadweight loss in the extreme case of monopoly. Neither do they provide guidance for the intermediate cases of oligopoly, which are more relevant to the horizontal mergers that have occurred throughout the world.

It is important to note, however, that there is no real basis for assuming that a deadweight loss occurs when firms combine horizontally but the industry structure falls short of being monopolized. The mere fact that a more concentrated industry structure results does not imply that competition has declined. The final outcome might be a number of strong competitors who engage in a heightened state of competition characterized by competitively determined prices and differentiated products. If so, the argument for a deadweight loss resulting from increased concentration is weakened. The existence of a welfare loss resulting from the formation of oligopolies should be considered on an individual, industry-by-industry basis.

Empirical Evidence on the Monopoly Hypothesis

There is little empirical evidence that firms combine to increase their monopoly power. Much of the evidence that elucidates this question is indirect. A doctoral dissertation by Robert S. Stillman in 1983 showed that competitors failed to react when other firms

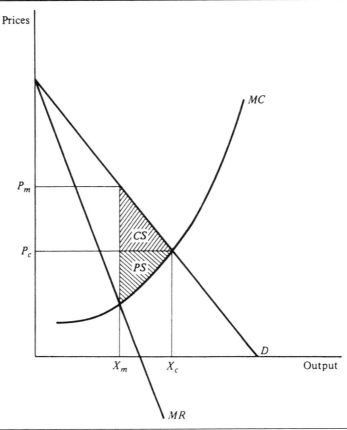

EXHIBIT 4.5 | THE DEADWEIGHT LOSS OR WELFARE LOSS OF MONOPOLY DERIVES FROM THE LOSS OF THE GAINS FROM TRADE. THE LOSS OF THE CONSUMER AND PRODUCER SURPLUS IS SHOWN IN THE SHADED REGION. X_m UNITS ARE TRADED INSTEAD OF X_c. THE MARKETPLACE LOSES THE GAINS FROM TRADE (CS AND PS) ON THE UNITS THAT ARE NOT TRADED.

in the same industry announced a combination.[45] The analysis considered the value of the stock of firms in the affected industry when events took place that increased the probability of mergers in that industry. It also considered the fact that product prices might rise after horizontal mergers, benefiting other firms in the industry. With higher product prices, resulting from a more concentrated industry, the equity values of the firms in the industry should also rise. The study examined a small sample of 11 mergers that were challenged on antitrust grounds under Section 7 of the Clayton Act. No statistically significant abnormal returns for 9 of the 11 mergers were found. Of the other two, one showed positive abnormal returns and the other showed ambiguous results. These results fail to support the view that firms merge in an effort to seek monopoly power. A similar study, also based on a doctoral thesis, was conducted by B. Epsen Eckbo

45. Robert S. Stillman, "Examining Antitrust Policy Towards Mergers," Ph.D. dissertation, University of California at Los Angeles, 1983. This dissertation was later published in the *Journal of Financial Economics,* 11(1), April 1983, 225–240.

on a larger sample of 126 horizontal and vertical mergers in the manufacturing and mining industries.[46] Approximately half of Eckbo's sample were horizontal mergers. An average of 15 rival firms existed in each industry category. If the market power hypothesis delineated previously was valid, negative abnormal returns would be observed for firms in industries that had announced mergers that were challenged on antitrust grounds. The reasoning is that the merger is less likely when there is an antitrust challenge. When challenges take place, negative abnormal returns should be associated with the announcement of the challenge.

Eckbo found statistically insignificant abnormal returns. The study also showed that firms initially showed positive and statistically significant abnormal returns when the mergers were first announced but failed to show a negative response after the complaint was filed. Like Stillman's results, Eckbo's research does not support the belief that firms merge to enjoy increases in market power. Curiously, Eckbo's results reveal that "stockholders of bidder and target firms in challenged (horizontal) mergers earn larger abnormal returns than do the corresponding firms in unchallenged mergers."[47] Eckbo concludes that the gains found in mergers are not related to increases in market power but rather are motivated by factors such as efficiency gains.

Eckbo conducted another study of the market power hypothesis in which he compared the level of competition in Canada, a country that, until 1985, had more relaxed antitrust enforcement policies. He refuted the hypothesis that the probability of a merger being anticompetitive was greater in Canada than in the United States. One conclusion that could be drawn from this research is that the more rigid antitrust enforcement that has sometimes been pursued in the United States, and which was pursued in Europe during the Mario Monti era, is unnecessary. However, this is a complex issue that cannot be decided based on one study. Although the Stillman and Eckbo studies of the early 1980s provide little support for the pursuit of market power as a motive for M&As, other recent research implies that market power may be a motive for some deals. Specifically, Kim and Singal found that mergers in the airline industry during the late 1980s resulted in higher prices on routes served by merging firms compared with a control group of routes that were not involved in control transactions.[48] Indeed, some critics of deregulation have cited the unfettered ability of previously regulated competitors to merge and the subsequent increase in airfares as an example of failure of deregulation. Their study took into account many factors such as the existence of financially distressed firms as well as possible premerger excess supply and any postmerger quality improvements. Even after all these factors were taken into account, they showed that market power and its associated price increases dominated any postmerger efficiency effects to result in a welfare loss.

More recent research implies that horizontal mergers increase buyer power of the merging firms in instances where the suppliers are concentrated. This was theoretically demonstrated by Snyder as well as by Stole and Zwiebel, who theorized that merged

46. B. Epsen Eckbo, "Horizontal Mergers, Collusion and Stockholder Wealth," *Journal of Financial Economics,* 11(1), April 1983, 241–273.
47. *Ibid.*
48. E. Han Kim and Vijay Singal, "Mergers and Market Power: Evidence from the Airline Industry," *American Economic Review,* 83(3), June 1993, 549–569.

buyers could lower their costs of inputs that they purchase from concentrated supplier industries.[49] This was supported by recent empirical work. Fee and Thomas analyzed a sample of 554 horizontal transactions over the period 1980–1997.[50] They found no significant stock market reactions by customers, which implies that the market perceived no change in market power as a result of the deals. However, they noticed negative stock market reactions by suppliers which implies that the merged companies gain some buying power relative to their suppliers. These results were also supported by Shahrur analysis sample of 463 horizontal mergers and tender offers over the period 1987–1999.[51] He found that efficiency considerations were the main factor driving the horizontal deals as opposed to the achievement of market power. His results lend support to the Eckbo findings some two decades earlier.

Horizontal Integration, Consolidation, and Roll-Up Acquisition Programs

The 1990s featured a consolidation within certain industries. Many of these deals involved larger companies buying smaller rivals in a series of acquisitions. The acquired companies are then combined into an ever-growing larger company. Such deals are sometimes referred to as *roll-up acquisitions.*

The market of the 1990s liked roll-ups, although not as much as they were enamored with Internet companies. The typical market that was attractive to consolidators was one that featured many relatively smaller competitors in an industry that was fragmented and unconcentrated. Many of the targets in such industries, such as those in the bus transportation or the funeral home business, were closely held. The owners lacked liquidity and being acquired by a large public company enabled them to convert their illiquid closely held shares into a more liquid asset. Consolidators were able to convince the market that the large-scale acquisition of these smaller targets would enable the combined company to realize scale economies while also enhancing sales through a greater ability to service national clients. The scale economies were supposed to have many sources including increased buying power that a national company would have compared to a small regional firm. A whole host of roll-up companies were formed in the United States during the fifth wave with names such as Coach USA, Metals USA, and Floral USA.

For many of the privately held sellers, the dream of liquidity combined with an attractive premium proved to be a nightmare. This was the case in the funeral home industry, where big consolidators like Service Corp and Leowen encountered financial problems and Leowen eventually had to file for Chapter 11 bankruptcy protection. Many consolidators were only good at one thing—doing deals. They were not good managers and it took the market a long time to come to this realization.

49. C.M. Snyder, "Why Do Large Buyers Pay Lower Prices? Intense Supplier Competition," *Economic Letters*, 58, 205–209; and L. A. Stole and J. Zwiebel, "Organizational Design and Technology Choice Under Intrafirm Bargaining," *American Economic Review*, 42, 1996, 943–963.

50. C.E. Fee and S. Thomas, "Sources of Gains in Horizontal Takeovers: Evidence from Customer, Supplier, and Rival Firms," *Journal of Financial Economics*, 74, 2004, 423–460.

51. Husayn Shahrur, "Industry Structure and Horizontal Takeovers: Analysis of Wealth Effects on Rivals, Suppliers and Corporate Customers," *Journal of Financial Economics*, 76, 2005, 61–98.

CASE STUDY

WORLDCOM

One classic example of a consolidation acquisition program was the acquisitions of WorldCom, formerly LDDS, over the second half of the 1980s and 1990s. WorldCom, based in Jackson, Mississippi, was formed through a series of more than 40 acquisitions, culminating in the $37 billion acquisition of MCI in 1998. Many of these deals were acquisitions of regional long-distance telecommunication resellers who added more minutes to WorldCom's market clout while bringing a regionally based sales force to service the acquired market. It is ironic that WorldCom was a telecommunications business owned by ITT that was later acquired by LDDS. ITT was a conglomerate that underwent a series of downsizing transactions (see Chapter 10), whereas LDDS went on to grow horizontally to become the second leading long-distance company in the U.S. market. In paying a high price for MCI, which enabled it to outbid British Telecom, WorldCom asserted that it would realize significant cost savings from combining these two long-distance companies.

WorldCom is a classic example of a company run by a CEO, Bernie Ebbers, who was a good dealmaker but a bad manager. The company's board was asleep at the wheel and allowed its CEO to pursue deals when the company was already of a sufficient size. They also allowed him to continue to run the company when he was clearly out of his element. He continued to pursue deals but the company became so large that meaningful deals, such as the proposed acquisition of Sprint, were halted by antitrust regulators. It has been alleged that management resorted to illegal means to try to manufacturer profits that it could not otherwise achieve. The end result of this acquisition program was an inefficient company that spiraled into the largest bankruptcy of all time.

Many of the roll-up deals of the 1990s fell into bankruptcy when the market euphoria and economic expansion of that period came to an end. Some, such as Coach USA, a company put together by consolidator Simon Harter, were sold to other buyers. Others, such as Wayne Huizinga's Waste Management and Blockbuster Video, and Jonathan Ledecky's Cort Business Services, survived the collapse of the roll-ups. Still others such as Westinghouse thrived.

CASE STUDY

WESTINGHOUSE

There are numerous other examples of consolidating roll-up acquisition programs that became popular in the 1990s. Westinghouse's sales and acquisitions are a good example of a company deciding to unload businesses that it thought had few growth prospects and acquire a greater market share in a growth business. Specifically, Westinghouse sold off its defense business and, in the face of better-financed rivals, decided in November 1997 to sell its power generation business to Siemens AG for $1.53 billion. Westinghouse realized that becoming a leading player in the international power generation market was a costly proposition. To achieve such a position, it would have to invest a large amount of capital without the prospect of high growth to offset the costs. Instead it sold off such capital-demanding businesses and used the proceeds to continually expand its presence in broadcasting. Siemens, however, decided to focus on power generation, and the acquisition of Westinghouse's power generation business helped enhance its already strong position in the world market.

Although television may be the glamorous side of broadcasting, Westinghouse used roll-up acquisitions to steadily expand its radio station network, which already had a presence in this business through Westinghouse's Group W stations. The $5.4 billion acquisition of CBS in August 1995 was a costly major acquisition. Following that, Michael Jordan, Westinghouse's CEO, added two large chains of radio stations. The first was Infinity Broadcasting, which owned 83 radio stations. This was followed by the $2.6 billion acquisition of American Radio Systems Corp., which owned 98 radio stations. The company continued to sharpen its focus on broadcasting with the sale of its Thermo-King, which marketed refrigerated transport equipment, to Ingersoll Rand for $2.56 billion. In 1997, Westinghouse changed its named to CBS corporation. This entity merged with Viacom in 1999, and both operated under the CBS name in 2005. The combined business then spun off most ot its cable and movie businesses which operated in a new business under the Viacom name.

Vertical Integration

Vertical integration involves the acquisition of firms that are closer to the source of supply or to the ultimate consumer. An example of a movement toward the source of supply was Chevron's acquisition of Gulf Oil in 1984. Chevron bought Gulf primarily to augment its reserves, a motive termed *backward integration*. In the same year, Mobil bought Superior Oil for similar reasons. Mobil was strong in refining and marketing but low on reserves, whereas Superior had large oil and gas reserves but lacked refining and marketing operations. An example of *forward integration* would be if a firm with large reserves bought another company that had a strong marketing and retailing capability.

CASE STUDY

MERCK'S ACQUISITION OF MEDCO—AN EXAMINATION OF VERTICAL INTEGRATION

In July 1993, Merck & Co., the largest pharmaceutical company in the world at that time, acquired Medco Containment Services for $6.6 billion. Medco was the largest prescription benefits management company. With the drug industry experiencing the effects of managed care, pharmaceutical companies had to adapt to new means of distribution. Merck realized that the decisions of what treatments and what drugs should be used in patients' care were increasingly being influenced by the managed care environment rather than by physicians. In the world of managed care, it was no longer sufficient to market just to physicians. The successful pharmaceutical companies of the future would be companies that were able to adapt to the changed distribution system.

This vertical integration move by Merck was not lost on its rival drug companies. Shortly after the Medco acquisition, other drug companies began their own acquisitions so as not to leave Merck with better channels to the ultimate consumer. Toward that end, in 1994, Eli Lilly bought PCS Health Systems for $4.1 billion, while Roche Holdings bought Syntex Corp. for $5.3 billion. This is an example of copycat acquisitions as Merck's competitors instinctively reacted to a perceived competitive advantage that Merck may have achieved. Copycat acquisitions are very common. The automobile industry did the same with its forward and backward vertical integration strategies as well as its international expansion programs. All of these have yielded questionable results for many of these companies.

Merck and also its copycat competitors, however, did not do their homework. Regulatory concerns arose regarding Merck's possibly unduly influencing consumers' prescription alternatives through Medco. Merck was forced to eventually undo this acquisition.

Another example of forward integration took place in the securities industry when Shearson Lehman Brothers bought E. F. Hutton. Shearson was attracted by E. F. Hutton's strong network of retail brokers. This vertical combination was motivated by a movement toward the consumer. It is also an example of a previously vertically integrated firm that wanted to expand its access to the consumer. Before the merger, Shearson Lehman had a large network of retail brokers. After the merger, however, it acquired a retail capacity to rival all competitors, including Merrill Lynch. Although this strategy of combining seemingly complementary and closely related businesses appeared to make sense, it also was later undone and the firms were sold off.

Motives for Vertical Integration

A firm might consider vertically integrating for several reasons. As seen in the case of the Mobil–Superior Oil combination, companies may vertically integrate to be assured of a *dependable source of supply.* Dependability may be determined not just in terms of supply availability but also through quality maintenance and timely delivery considerations. Having timely access to supplies helps companies to provide their own products on a reliable basis. In addition, as companies pursue *just-in-time* inventory management, they may take advantage of a vertically integrated corporate structure to lower inventory costs.

It is popularly believed that when a company acquires a supplier it is obtaining a cost advantage over its rivals. The thinking is that it will not have to pay the profit to suppliers that it was previously paying when it was buying the inputs from independent suppliers. This raises the question: What is the appropriate *internal transfer price?* It is the price carried on the company's books when it acquires its supplies or inputs from a supplier that it now controls and may be a subsidiary. If the price for these inputs is less than the prevailing market price, the parent company will appear to be more profitable than it really is. The reason is that the lower costs and higher profits for the parent company come at the cost of lower profitability for the subsidiary. This is a paper transfer, however, and does not result in increased value to the combined firm.

Although the establishment of an accurate transfer price helps dismiss the illusion that supplies derived from a newly acquired supplier come at a lower cost, there may be other cost savings from acquiring a supplier. These savings may come in the form of lower *transactions costs.*[52] By acquiring a supplier and establishing a long-term source of supply at prearranged costs, the acquiring firm may avoid potential disruptions that might occur when agreements with independent suppliers end. When the buyer owns the supplier, it may be better able to predict future supply costs and avoid the uncertainty that normally is associated with renegotiation of supply agreements.

Still another reason for vertical integration could arise from the need to have *specialized inputs.* These may be custom-designed materials or machinery that might have little or no market value other than to the buyer. The buyer may then be at the mercy of these companies if they choose not to provide the products. It may be difficult to switch to other suppliers if there are fixed costs associated with the initial manufacture of the

---

52. Dennis Carlton and Jeffrey Perloff, *Modern Industrial Organization*, 2nd ed. (New York: HarperCollins, 1994), p. 502.

materials. Other suppliers may be unwilling to produce the specialized products unless the buyer compensates for the initial costs or enters a long-term supply agreement that allows the supplier to amortize the up-front costs. One way to eliminate this problem is to acquire the supplier. The buyer can then have access to these specialized inputs and be in an even better position to oversee the maintenance of the company's own standards of manufacturing. In Chapter 13, however, we will explore whether some of these goals can be better accomplished through lower costs, joint ventures, or strategic alliances.

Another interesting example of vertical integration occurs in the marketing of automobiles. Automobile manufacturers have long realized that they may need to provide potential buyers with financial assistance, in the form of less expensive and more readily available credit, to sell more cars. For this reason, General Motors (GM) formed General Motors Acceptance Corporation (GMAC). General Motors Acceptance Corporation provides low-cost credit to many car buyers who might not be able to get the financing necessary to buy a new car. Companies such as GMAC are able to sell commercial paper at money market rates and use the difference between these rates and the financing rates it charges to car buyers to help sell cars while making profits on financing. However, in the 2000s, automakers needed to try to maintain market share to keep their costly plants and labor force generating revenues and were forced into costly financing programs that competitors, such as Toyota, avoided.

CASE STUDY

VERTICAL INTEGRATION IN THE AUTOMOBILE INDUSTRY

For a period of time all of the U.S. automakers were vertically integrated, both backward and forward, in one form or another. General Motors, the number-one auto company in the world for many years, owned its own supplier, Delphi, which is the largest parts supplier in the automobile business. GM spun off this entity in 1999. Ford had been in the auto supply business for many years going back to the decision of Henry Ford to create his own parts supplier and release his reliance on suppliers such as those controlled by the Dodge brothers. Ford spun off this entity in 2000 when it formed Visteon. Unfortunately, due to the tight hold the United Auto Workers (UAW) had on these two companies, they could not sever their financial obligations to the workers at these companies. Ford was forced to take back many of Visteon's employees in 2005. When Delphi filed for bankruptcy, it reminded GM that it must honor obligations to its workers.

There are many suppliers of parts, and by buying a large percent of their parts from their own captive suppliers, both Ford and GM, in effect, were purchasing parts at higher prices than what they would otherwise pay if they were dealing with suppliers who did not have the same burdensome labor agreements with the UAW. Both Ford and GM, and other automakers, pressure their suppliers to be very competitive in their prices. The combination of intensely competitive pricing, combined with high labor costs, did not make this an attractive business for Ford and GM.

At one time, Chrysler, Ford, and GM all were vertically integrated forward through their purchases of car rental companies. In 1989, Chrysler bought Thrifty Rent-A-Car, which in turn bought Snappy Rent-A-Car in 1990. In addition, Chrysler solidified its presence in the car rental business by buying Dollar Rent-A-Car in 1990. Lee Iacocca termed the combination a "natural alliance." However, what was "natural" in 1990 became "unnatural" just a few years later.

Similarly, in 1988, GM acquired a 45% interest in National Car Rental. The company also owned an interest in Avis—the number-two company in the industry. Ford acquired Hertz, the number-one company in the car rental industry, in 1987 from Allegis for $1.3 billion.

The automakers thought that the purchase of the larger buyers of their cars, car rental companies, would lock in demand for their products. In addition, the entry of these automakers into the car rental business is also an example of "copy cat" acquisitions as one auto manufacturer did not want to let another one gain market share at its expense. Market share has always been a major focus in the auto industry as the industry has a huge investment in capital in its plants as well as relatively fixed obligations to workers that are not flexible due to the pressures from the UAW. These burdensome agreements with the UAW caused the companies to lose market shares to non-U.S. manufacturers, such as Toyota and Honda, who built nonunion plants in the United States that enjoyed major cost advantages over their U.S. rivals.

Unfortunately for the U.S. automakers, the sales gained from deals with the car rental industry were not very profitable. Car rental companies, being large buyers, purchase at attractive prices and require the manufacturers to buy back these autos after a period such as one year, so that they can maintain a relatively modern fleet of vehicles. The terms of these sales were not good for U.S. car companies as they used such sales, along with heavily discounted promotional sales and rebate offers, to try to offset their shrinking market shares. Foreign automakers, such as Toyota, Nissan, and Honda, steered clear of this part of the market and focused on gaining market share while maintaining profitability.

As U.S. automakers began to rethink the benefits of forward vertical integration, they began to extricate themselves from the car rental business. GM took a $300 million charge related to National Car Rental and had to write down the goodwill on its balance sheet stemming from National. In 1995, it sold National to Lobeck for $1.3 billion. In 1997, Chrysler did an equity carve-out of its car rental business for $387.5 million. Finally, in 2005, Ford sold off Hertz to a private equity group. Ironically, Hertz was a profitable business, valued at approximately $15 billion. However, at that time Ford was losing money and market share and had to sell off this asset to try to consolidate its business.

By the middle of the 2000s, the U.S. automakers have reversed many of their vertical integration efforts (to the extent the UAW agreement allows them to). Clearly, their moves to vertically integrate were not a success.

HUBRIS HYPOTHESIS OF TAKEOVERS

An interesting hypothesis regarding takeover motives has been proposed by Roll.[53] He considers the role that hubris, or the pride of the managers in the acquiring firm, may play in explaining takeovers. The hubris hypothesis implies that managers seek to acquire firms for their own personal motives and that the pure economic gains to the acquiring firm are not the sole motivation or even the primary motivation in the acquisition.

Roll uses this hypothesis to explain why managers might pay a premium for a firm that the market has already correctly valued. Managers, he claims, have superimposed their own valuation over that of an objectively determined market valuation. Roll's position is that the pride of management allows them to believe that their valuation is superior to

---

53. Richard Roll, "The Hubris Hypothesis of Corporate Takeovers," *Journal of Business*, 59(2), April 1986, 197–216.

that of the market. Implicit in this theory is an underlying conviction that the market is efficient and can provide the best indicator of the value of a firm. Many would dispute this point. As evidence, Roll draws on a wide body of research studies. This evidence is described in the following section.

Empirical Evidence

Roll states that if the hubris hypothesis explains takeovers, the following should occur for those takeovers motivated by hubris:

- The stock price of the acquiring firm should fall after the market becomes aware of the takeover bid. This should occur because the takeover is not in the best interests of the acquiring firm's stockholders and does not represent an efficient allocation of their wealth.
- The stock price of the target firm should increase with the bid for control. This should occur because the acquiring firm is not only going to pay a premium but also may pay a premium in excess of the value of the target.
- The combined effect of the rising value of the target and the falling value of the acquiring firm should be negative. This takes into account the costs of completing the takeover process.

A number of studies show that the acquiring firm's announcement of the takeover results in a decline in the value of the acquirer's stock. Dodd found statistically significant negative returns to the acquirer following the announcement of the planned takeover.[54] Other studies have demonstrated similar findings.[55] Not all studies support this conclusion, however. Paul Asquith failed to find a consistent pattern of declining stock prices following the announcement of a takeover.[56]

There is more widespread agreement on the positive price effects for target stockholders who have been found to experience wealth gains following takeovers. Bradley, Desai, and Kim show that tender offers result in gains for target firm stockholders.[57] Admittedly, the hostile nature of tender offers should produce greater changes in the stock price than in friendly takeover offers. Most studies, however, show that target stockholders gain following both friendly and hostile takeover bids. Varaiya showed that bidders tend to overpay.[58]

In a study that examined the relationship between the bid premium and the combined market values of the bidder and the target, it was found that the premium paid by bidders was too high relative to the value of the target to the acquirer. The research on the combined effect of the upward movement of the target's stock and the downward movement

---

54. P. Dodd, "Merger Proposals, Managerial Discretion and Stockholder Wealth," *Journal of Financial Economics*, 8, June 1980, 105, 138.
55. C. E. Eger, "An Empirical Test of the Redistribution Effect of Mergers," *Journal of Financial and Quantitative Analysis*, 18, December 1983, 547–572.
56. Paul Asquith, "Merger Bids, Uncertainty and Stockholder Returns," *Journal of Financial Economics*, 11, April 1983, 51–83.
57. Michael Bradley, Anand Desai, and E. Han Kim, "The Rationale Behind Interfirm Tender Offers: Information or Synergy," *Journal of Financial Economics*, 11(1), April 1983, 183–206.
58. Nikhil P. Varaiya, "Winners Curse Hypothesis and Corporate Takeovers," *Managerial and Decision Economics*, 9, 1989, 209.

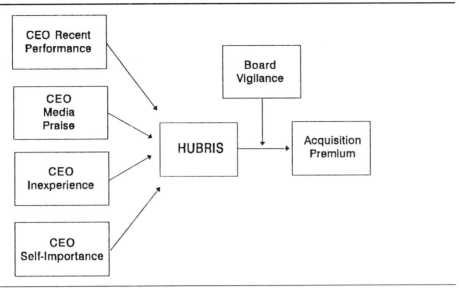

EXHIBIT 4.6 MODEL OF CEO HUBRIS AND ACQUISITION PREMIUMS
Source: Mathew L. A. Hayward, and Donald C. Hambrick, "Explaining Premiums Paid for Large Acquisitions: Evidence of CEO Hubris," unpublished manuscript, July 1995.

of the acquirer's stock does not seem to provide strong support for the hubris hypothesis. Malatesta examined the combined effects and found that "the evidence indicates that the long-run sequence of events culminating in merger has no net impact on combined shareholder wealth."[59] It could be countered, however, that Malatesta's failure to find positive combined returns does support the hubris hypothesis. More recent research seems to support the hubris hypothesis.[60] Using a sample of 106 large acquisitions, Hayward and Hambrick found CEO hubris positively associated with the size of premiums paid. Hubris was measured by the variables such as the company's recent performance and CEO self-importance (as reflected by media praise and compensation relative to the second highest paid executive). The study also considered independent variables such as CEO inexperience, as measured by years in that position, along with board vigilance, as measured by the number of inside directors versus outside directors (see Exhibit 4.6).

Other studies provide support for the hubris hypothesis for takeover of U.S. firms by foreign corporations. Using shareholder wealth effect responses similar to those theorized by Roll, in a sample of 100 cross-border deals over the period 1981 to 1990, Seth, Song, and Pettit found that hubris played an important role in these deals.[61] Other factors, such as synergy and managerialism, also played a role. Managerialism is somewhat similar to hubris, in that both may involve overpaying for a target. In managerialism,

59. Paul Malatesta, "Wealth Effects of Merger Activity," *Journal of Financial Economics*, 11(1), April 1983, 178–179.
60. Mathew L. A. Hayward and Donald C. Hambrick, "Explaining Premiums Paid for Large Acquisitions: Evidence of CEO Hubris," unpublished manuscript, July 1995.
61. Anju Seth, Kean P. Song, and Richardson Pettit, "Synergy, Managerialism or Hubris? An Empirical Examination of Motives of Foreign Acquisitions of U.S. Firms," *Journal of International Business Studies*, 31(3), 3rd Quarter, 2000, 387–405.

however, the bidder's management knowingly overpay so as to pursue their own gains even though it comes at the expense of their shareholders—to whom they have a fiduciary obligation.

Roll did not intend the hubris hypothesis to explain all takeovers. He merely proposed that an important human element enters takeovers when individuals are interacting and negotiating the purchase of a company. Management's acquisition of a target may be motivated purely by a desire to maximize stockholder wealth. However, other motives may include a desire to enter a target's industry or to become "the largest firm in the business." The extent to which these motives may play a role will vary from takeover to takeover. It is therefore of some interest that much evidence does support the hubris hypothesis. Surely the questionably high premiums paid for some firms, such as Federated Stores and RJR Nabisco, imply some element of hubris. The fact that Campeau Corporation was forced to declare bankruptcy not long after the acquisition of Federated Stores lends support to the view that it overpaid in the highly leveraged deal.

--- CASE STUDY ---

VIVENDI AND MESSIER'S HUBRIS—ANOTHER FAILED CORPORATE TRANSFORMATION

Vivendi Universal SA (Vivendi) is a colorful case study involving a stodgy French water utility run by a CEO who wanted to be a high-flying leader of an international media company. He eventually transformed this water utility into a media giant. The only problem was that he sacrificed shareholders' interests to do so. Shareholders picked up the tab for his grandiose dreams and when they failed he walked away with too much of their money in his pockets and in the pockets of others he brought in to help with his schemes.

Vivendi's roots come from being a 100-year-old water utility that was housed in an entity that they eventually called Vivendi Environment SA. When the division was eventually sold off as part of the bustup of the company, it raised 2.5 billion euros. This was be a relatively small amount compared to the losses that Messier's media empire would generate.

If Vivendi's financial performance was good, no one would question that apparent lack of synergy between Vivendi's water and entertainment industry assets. Unfortunately, the combination of the two produced very poor results. The company lost 23 billion euros in 2002, which followed a 13.6 billion euro loss in 2001. This was the largest corporate loss in French history. Vivendi cannot be proud that its 2002 23.6 billion euro loss narrowly passed the prior record of 23 billion euros that was held by French Telecom. As the situation worsened in 2002, major shareholders pushed for action—they were just a few years too late.

CEO Messier was not satisfied with being the CEO of a water utility. Messier had a dealmaker's background. He was formerly an investment banker at Lazard LLC, where he spent six years of his business career. If you put an investment banker at the helm of a water utility, odds are that he is going to engage in *investment banker–like activities*. Messier, originally a utility CEO, became an entertainment CEO by engaging in major acquisition of entertainment companies.

One of Messier's big deals was to buy Seagram Universal in 2000. This sale gave the Bronfmans, major shareholders in Seagram, 88.9 million shares in Vivendi, which constituted 8.9% of the company.[a] This acquisition marked Vivendi's major foray into the media industry by buying a company that itself was a combination between the liquor and soft drinks company, Seagram, and the Universal movie studios. It is quite ironic that Messier would buy Seagram Universal as this company was formed by the acquisition engineered by young Edgar Bronfman when he took a leadership position at Seagram. He used the assets and cash flows of the Seagram family business to finance its venture into the entertainment sector. This deal went through its own rocky period as the movie business proved to be not as exciting to Seagram's shareholders as it was to the young Mr. Bronfman.

Messier's acquisition plans did not stop with Seagram Universal. He then bought Canal Plus—a pay-cable French TV network. They also owned shares in British Sky Broadcasting. He then purchased Barry Diller's USA Networks in December 2001 for $10.3 billion, only to see its value drop like many other Messier purchases. The deal brought together the Universal Studios Group with the entertainment assets of the USA Networks to form what they called Vivendi Universal Entertainment. As with so many other acquisitions, Vivendi stated that it hoped to realize significant synergies that would improve content, ratings, and subscriber fees.[b]

Messier paid 12.5 billion euros for Canal Plus. This was even though there were significant limitations on the ability of any buyer to make significant changes at the European cable company to make the programming more profitable. Canal Plus was not profitable and had approximately 2.8 billion euros in debt.[c] Messier also bought a 44 percent stake in Cegetel—a French phone company that owned 80% of SFR, France's second biggest mobile phone operator. In addition, the company also purchased Houghton Mifflin, a book publisher, for $2.2 billion that included $500 million in debt. Vivendi also owned an equipment division that held U.S. Filter Corporation.

In the midst of his acquisition binge, Messier, the CEO of this water/worldwide media company, moved to New York in September 4, 2001. To say that Messier was filled with hubris seems to be an understatement. He himself concedes that this may be a normal characteristic of a CEO. In his book he stated: "Don't ask a CEO to be modest. The costume does not fit him. A strong ego, not to say an outsized one, is more becoming, although each has its way of wearing." We would have to say that when this ego leads the company down the path of billions in losses, it can be very draining on the value of investors' portfolios. Messier loved the limelight—especially the lights of New York—much to the chagrin of his French management and shareholders.

When Vivendi began to rack up huge losses, shareholders and creditors began to call for an end of the acquisition binge and the ouster of its colorful CEO. After a new, more conservative management team was put in place, the company began the slow and costly process of disassembling the media and utility conglomerate that the hubris-filled Messier had built.

[a]"The Bronfman Family Feels Messier's Pain," *New York Times*, April 25, 2002.
[b]Vivendi Universal Press Release, December 17, 2001.
[c]"Messier's Mess," *Economist*, June 6, 2002.

Winner's Curse Hypothesis of Takeovers

The winner's curse of takeovers is the ironic hypothesis that states that bidders who overestimate the value of a target will most likely win a contest. This is due to the fact that they will be more inclined to overpay and outbid rivals who more accurately value the target. This result is not specific to takeovers but is the natural result of any bidding contest.[62] One of the more public forums where this regularly occurs is the free

---

62. M. Baserman and W. Samuelson, "I Won the Auction but I Don't Win the Prize," *Journal of Conflict Resolution*, 27, 1983, 618–634.

agent markets of sports such as baseball and basketball.[63] In a study of 800 acquisitions from 1974 to 1983, Varaiya showed that on average the winning bid in takeover contests significantly overstated the capital market's estimate of any takeover gains by as much as 67%.[64] He measured overpayment as the difference between the winning bid premium and the highest bid possible before the market responded negatively to the bid. This study provides support for the existence of the winner's curse, which in turn also supports the hubris hypothesis.

Do Bad Bidders Become Good Targets?

Given that many acquisitions have failed to live up to expectations, the questions arises: Does the market punish companies that make bad acquisitions? Using a sample of 1,158 companies, Mitchell and Lehn examined their control transactions from 1980 to 1988.[65] They determined that companies that make acquisitions that cause their equity to lose value are increasingly likely to become takeover targets. That is, they found that "the likelihood of becoming a takeover target is significantly and inversely related to the abnormal stock price performance with the firm's acquisitions."[66] Their analysis shows that takeovers may be both a problem and a solution. Takeovers that reduce market value may be bad deals, assuming the market correctly assesses them, and this is a problem. The deals market, however, may take care of the problem through another takeover of the "bad bidder." The Mitchell and Lehn analysis also implies that just looking at the returns to acquirers, which research has shown may be zero or slightly negative, obscures the picture because it aggregates good deals and bad deals. When the negative market impact of bad deals is taken into account, it becomes clear that good acquisitions should have a positive impact on share values, whereas bad deals should cause the stock price of these acquirers to lag behind the market.

Executive Compensation and Corporate Acquisition Decisions

One theory of acquisitions that is closely related to the hubris hypothesis is the theory that managers of companies acquire other companies to increase their size, which in turn allows them to enjoy higher compensation and benefits.[67] Khorana and Zenner analyzed the role that executive compensation played in the corporate acquisition decisions of 51 firms that made 84 acquisitions between 1982 and 1986.[68] For companies that engaged in acquisitions, they found a positive relationship between firm size and executive compensation but not for those that did not. However, when they separated good acquisitions from bad acquisitions, they found that good acquisitions increased compensation whereas

---

63. J. Cassing and R. Douglas, "Implication of the Auction Mechanism in Baseball's Free Agent Draft," *Southern Economic Journal,* 47, July 1980, 110–121.

64. Nikhil Varaiya, "The Winner's Curse Hypothesis and Corporate Takeovers," *Managerial and Decision Economics* 9 (1988), pp. 209–219.

65. Mark L. Mitchell and Kenneth Lehn, "Do Bad Bidders Become Good Targets?" *Journal of Political Economy,* 98(2), 1990, 372–398.

66. Ibid., p. 393.

67. William Baumol, *Business Behavior, Value and Growth,* 2nd ed. (New York: Macmillan), 1959.

68. Ajay Khorana and Marc Zenner, "Executive Compensation of Large Acquirers in the 1980s," *Journal of Corporate Finance,* 4, 1988, 209–240.

bad deals did not have a positive effect on compensation. When the fact that bad deals may result in departures from the firm is taken into account, there is even a negative relationship between bad acquisitions and executive compensation.

More recent evidence from the fifth merger wave provides evidence that CEOs receive compensation for doing deals. Grinstein and Hribar conducted a study using a database of 327 large deals drawn from the period 1993 to 1999.[69] In examining proxy statements that identified the components of CEO compensation, they found that in 39% of the cases the board of directors' compensation committee cited completing deals as one of the reasons why the compensation was at the level it was.

OTHER MOTIVES

Improved Management

Some takeovers are motivated by a belief that the acquiring firm's management can better manage the target's resources. The bidder may believe that its management skills are such that the value of the target would rise under its control. This leads the acquirer to pay a value for the target in excess of the target's current stock price.

The improved management argument may have particular validity in cases of large companies making offers for smaller, growing companies. The smaller companies, often led by entrepreneurs, may offer a unique product or service that has sold well and facilitated the rapid growth of the target.

The growing enterprise may find that it needs to oversee a much larger distribution network and may have to adopt a very different marketing philosophy. Many of the decisions that a larger firm has to make require a different set of managerial skills than those that resulted in the dramatic growth of the smaller company. The lack of managerial expertise may be a stumbling block in the growing company and may limit its ability to compete in the broader marketplace. These managerial resources are an asset that the larger firm can offer the target.

Little significant empirical research has been conducted on the importance of improved management motive. The difficulty is determining which takeovers are motivated solely by this factor, because improved management usually is just one of several factors in the acquirer's decision to make a bid. It is difficult to isolate improved management and to explain its role in the bidding process. The argument that takeover offers by large companies for smaller, growing companies are motivated in part by managerial gains may be reasonable.

For large public firms, a takeover may be the most cost-efficient way to bring about a management change. Proxy contests may enable dissident stockholders to oust the incumbent management, whom they may consider incompetent. One problem with this process is that corporate democracy is not very egalitarian. It is costly to use a proxy fight to replace an incumbent management team. The process is biased in favor of management, who may also occupy seats on the board of directors. It is therefore difficult to win a proxy battle. The proxy process is explained in detail in Chapter 6.

---

69. Yaniv Grinstein and Paul Hribar, "CEO Compensation and Incentives: Evidence from M&A Bonuses," *Journal of Financial Economics*, 2003, 535–554.

Improve Research and Development

Research and development (R&D) is critically important to the future growth of many companies, particularly pharmaceutical companies. This was one of the reasons for the consolidation that occurred in the pharmaceutical industry in the fifth merger wave. For example, the $73 billion megamerger between Glaxo Wellcome and SmithKline Beecham in 1999, which formed the largest company in that industry, merged the R&D budgets of two companies. This was estimated to equal an annual total of $4 billion, which was, at that time, more than double the R&D budgets of some of their larger rivals such as Pfizer and Merck. In response, other companies began to look for their own merger targets so as to remain competitive in pharmaceutical R&D. This helps explain the successful 2000 acquisition by Pfizer of Warner-Lambert. Not only did this deal give Pfizer enhanced R&D, it filled up its drug pipeline including the addition of the largest selling drug in the world—Lipitor.

Improve Distribution

Companies that make a product but do not have direct access to consumers need to develop channels to ensure that their product reaches the ultimate consumer in a profitable manner. Vertical mergers between manufacturers and distributors or retailers often give competitor manufacturers cause for concern in that they worry about being cut off from distribution channels. Locking in dependable distribution channels can be critical to a firm's success.

CASE STUDY

MERCK—INTERNAL DEVELOPMENT: AN ALTERNATIVE TO ACQUISITION OF RESEARCH AND DEVELOPMENT

During the fifth merger wave, widespread consolidation took place in the pharmaceutical industry. One of the motives for such deals was the need to come up with new drugs and the mounting costs of such research and development (R&D). Such factors help explain the megamergers that took place between Glaxo Wellcome and SmithKline Beecham in 1999 and the merger between Pfizer and Warner-Lambert in 2000. However, not all the industry leaders decided that merging was the best way to enhance product development.

One prominent example is the internal development program that was pursued by Merck as an alternative to M&As. Part of the problem that continually faces pharmaceutical companies is that patents, which allow developers to recoup the substantial costs of drug development, eventually expire, subjecting the company to competition with generic "knockoffs." For example, two of Merck's big sellers were Vasotec, an antihypertensive drug that was scheduled to come off patent protection in August 2000, and Mevacor, an anticholesterol drug that would lose patent protection in December 2001.[a] Amid the consolidation going on in its industry in the fifth wave, Merck was left with the choice to continue to use internal resources to come up with replacement drugs or to engage in expensive acquisitions to replace the drugs about to come off patent protection. Merck decided to go it alone. Using internal R&D it came up with a

[a]Gardiner Harris, "With Big Drugs Dying, Merck Didn't Merge—It Found New Ones," *Wall Street Journal*, January 10, 2001.

number of promising replacement drugs such as the anti-inflammatory cyclooxygenase-2 (COX-2) inhibitor—Vioxx.

For a while Merck's decision not to acquire R&D externally raised many questions. Merck had enjoyed impressive revenue growth in the 1980s, but this growth slowed in the first half of the 1990s. By the beginning of 2001, Merck was again among the industry leaders in revenue growth and profitability while maintaining its independence. This growth was stunted in 2005–2006 when it encountered a massive wave of Vioxx-related lawsuits.

TAX MOTIVES

Whether tax motives are an important determinant of M&As has been a much debated topic in finance. Certain studies have concluded that acquisitions may be an effective means to secure tax benefits. Gilson, Scholes, and Wolfson have set forth the theoretical framework demonstrating the relationship between such gains and M&As.[70] They assert that for a certain small fraction of mergers, tax motives could have played a significant role. Hayn, however, has empirically analyzed this relationship and has found that "potential tax benefits stemming from net operating loss carry forwards and unused tax credits positively affect announcement-period returns of firms involving tax-free acquisitions, and capital gains and the step-up in the acquired assets' basis affect returns of firms involved in taxable acquisitions."[71] Moreover, whether the transaction can be structured as a tax-free exchange may be a prime determining factor in whether to go forward with a deal. Sellers sometimes require tax-free status as a prerequisite of approving a deal.

SUMMARY

We have seen that there are a wide variety of motives and determinants of M&As. One of the most basic motives for M&As is growth. Mergers and acquisitions provide a means whereby a company can grow quickly. Often the only alternative is to grow more slowly through internal expansion. Competitive factors, however, may make such internal growth ineffective. Firms may acquire another firm with hope of experiencing economic gains. These economic gains may come as a result of economies of scale or economies of scope. *Economies of scale* are the reductions in per-unit costs that come as the size of a company's operations, in terms of revenues or units production, increases. *Economies of scope* occur when a business can offer a broader range of services to its customer base.

Some of these gains are reported as motives for horizontal and vertical acquisitions. Horizontal deals involve mergers between competitors, whereas vertical transactions involve companies that have a buyer–seller relationship. Although the pursuit of monopolistic power is sometimes believed to be a cause of horizontal mergers, the research in this area often fails to show that the other companies in the market perceive

---

70. Ronald Gilson, Myron S. Scholes, and Mark A. Wolfson, "Taxation and the Dynamics of Corporate Control: The Uncertain Case for Tax-Motivated Acquisitions," in John Coffee, Louis Lowenstein, and Susan Rose Ackerman, eds., *Knights, Raiders and Targets* (New York: Oxford University Press, 1988), pp. 273–299.
71. Carla Hayn, "Tax Attributes as Determinants of Shareholder Gains in Corporate Acquisitions," *Journal of Financial Economics,* 23(1), June 1989, 121–153.

that a real increase in market power will be achieved in many cases. Vertical transactions may sometimes provide valuable benefits, but they sometimes generate unforeseen adverse effects.

Other gains may come in the form of financial benefits when a larger firm that resulted from the combination of two or more smaller firms has better access to capital markets. This improved access could come in the form of a lower cost of capital. However, this latter motive has been the subject of considerable debate in finance. Its importance and validity is still disputed.

Another motivation for M&As may take the form of improved management. A bidding firm may be able to pay a premium for a target because of the anticipated gains it will experience when it applies its superior management skills to the target's business. The bidder, however, may falsely believe that it can extract higher returns than what the market believes are possible from the target. Hubris, rather than objective analysis, may motivate a takeover. The presence of hubris may increase the likelihood that a buyer may end up with the winner's curse. These last two motives are examples of the ever-present human element that permeates takeovers. Ideally, sound analysis should not be replaced by the individual motivations of managers. The human element, however, cannot be discounted as an important part of the world of M&As.

Various other motives exist for M&As, including accelerating the R&D process through acquiring companies that are strong in that area. Other targets may have good distribution systems that make them attractive. The motives are many and can vary from deal to deal.

The role of taxes as a determinant of M&As has been much debated. Some studies indicate it is only important in a relatively small number of deals, whereas other studies indicate that its role is much more important.

CASE STUDY

SEARS—A FAILED DIVERSIFICATION STRATEGY

In 1992, Sears, Roebuck and Co. announced that it was divesting its financial services operations and was going to refocus on the retail operations for which it is world famous. This ended the company's expensive and aggressive foray into the financial services business. The overall company was first formed in 1886 by Alvah Roebuck and Richard Sears. At the turn of the century it created a financial division that handled credit it extended to its customers. In the 1930s, it formed an insurance division, Allstate, which offered automobile insurance. In the 1950s, the company formed Sears Roebuck Acceptance Corporation, which handled short-term financial management activities for the company.

Around this time the company also began offering its own credit card. Therefore, financial services was nothing new to Sears. However, these activities were complementary to the overall retail operations of the company, except for perhaps Allstate's insurance sales and its later expansion into mutual fund activities and purchase of California Financial Corporation, a large savings and loan.

Major Expansion into Financial Services

In the late 1970s, the management of Sears was disappointed with the weak performance of the company's retail business. It was losing ground to Wal-Mart, a company that had steadily grown at the expense of traditional rivals such as Sears. Rather than try to fix the problem, management decided that they would not be able to achieve their desired return in the retail business and that the way to achieve their financial goals was to expand into a supposedly more lucrative business—financial services. In 1981, Sears bought Coldwell Banker & Co. for approximately $175 million in stock and cash and Dean Witter Reynolds, Inc. for a little over $600 million in stock and cash. In making these acquisitions, Sears's management believed it had acquired leaders in their respective fields. Coldwell Banker was the largest real estate brokerage firm in the United States, whereas Dean Witter was one of the larger stock brokerage firms.

ANTICIPATED SYNERGY: CROSS-SELLING TO EACH OTHER'S CUSTOMERS

Sears's management believed that there would be great cross-selling opportunities for the respective units that were now under the Sears umbrella. Sears was reported to have had over 25 million credit card holders. Each was considered a potential customer for the securities and real estate sales. The synergistic gains would materialize as soon as the cross-selling would take place. Unfortunately, as with many mergers that were based in part on such cross-selling hopes, the different divisions were not successful in achieving these overly optimistic goals.

ANTICIPATED SYNERGY: SELLING FINANCIAL SERVICES THROUGH RETAIL STORES

Sears was thwarted from going so far into financial services that it operated like a bank. Based on the success of its other financial services efforts, perhaps these regulatory strictures prevented the company from investing even more resources in an unsuccessful area than it already had. Nonetheless, Sears tried to market its financial services through financial services centers that it operated in more than 300 of its retail stores. These centers failed to become profitable. This strategy of selling houses and stocks at places usually reserved for lawn mowers and washing machines hurt the company's ability to keep pace with rivals that specialized in more targeted endeavors.

CORPORATE GOVERNANCE: A MANAGEMENT-DOMINATED BOARD AND AN INSTITUTIONAL INVESTOR REVOLT

Gillan, Kensinger, and Martin chronicled the battle between the CEO of Sears, Edward Brennan, and institutional investors, championed by Robert Monks of the LENS fund.[a] Management held almost a majority of the board while board members also held positions on each other's boards, creating a very chummy atmosphere. Insiders chaired important board committees. Gillan and colleagues concluded that Sears was a "firm lacking management accountability." While the market began to seriously question Sears's diversification strategy, management and the board initially circled the wagons and tried to aggressively oppose external dissent. Eventually, in 1991, the number of insiders was reduced to only one.

MARKET REACTION AND SHAREHOLDER RETURNS

The market often is skeptical of claimed synergies when deals are announced. Investors often express this skepticism by showing little reaction or by selling pressure, which may cause the stock price of a bidder to fall after the announcement of a proposed merger. With Sears, however, this was not the case. The market responded positively to the diversifying acquisitions made by Sears. The market eventually caught on and the stock price, relative to that of its industry peers, weakened. There is a lesson here that although securities markets may be somewhat (certainly

[a]Stuart Gillan, John W. Kensinger, and John Martin, "Value Creation and Corporate Diversification," *Journal of Financial Economics*, 56(1), January 2000, 103–137.

not perfectly) efficient in the long run, they can efficiently react in the wrong direction. Efficiency merely states that the market react quickly to news such as a merger. This does not mean that the reaction is correct or rational but merely that it occurs quickly. Gillan and colleagues measured the shareholder returns of Sears relative to the market and the industry. They found that a $100 investment in Sears on January 1, 1981, would be worth $746, whereas a similar investment in a hypothetical portfolio designed to mimic the composition of businesses within Sears would have been worth $1,256. Clearly, shareholders who invested in Sears incurred a significant opportunity cost.

2

HOSTILE TAKEOVERS

5

ANTITAKEOVER MEASURES

Corporate takeovers reached new levels of hostility during the 1980s. This heightened bellicosity was accompanied by many innovations in the art of corporate takeovers. Although hostile takeover tactics advanced, the methods of corporate defense were initially slower to develop. As a result of the increased application of financial resources by threatened corporations, however, antitakeover defenses became quite elaborate and more difficult to penetrate. By the end of the 1980s, the art of antitakeover defenses became very sophisticated. Major investment banks organized teams of defense specialists who worked with managements of larger corporations to erect formidable defenses that might counter the increasingly aggressive raiders of the fourth merger wave. After installing the various defenses, teams of investment bankers, along with their law firm counterparts, stood ready to be dispatched in the heat of battle to advise the target's management on the proper actions to take to thwart the bidder. By the 1990s, most large U.S. corporations had in place some form of antitakeover defense. The array of antitakeover defenses can be divided into two categories: preventative and active measures. Preventative measures are designed to reduce the likelihood of a financially successful hostile takeover, whereas active measures are employed after a hostile bid has been attempted.

This chapter describes the more frequently used antitakeover defenses. The impact of these measures on shareholder wealth, a controversial topic, is explored in detail. Opponents of these measures contend that they entrench management and reduce the value of stockholders' investment. They see the activities of raiders as an element that seeks to keep management "honest." They contend that managers who feel threatened by raiders will manage the firm more effectively, which will in turn result in higher stock values. Proponents of the use of antitakeover defenses argue, however, that these measures prevent the actions of the hostile raiders who have no long-term interest in the value of the corporation but merely are speculators seeking to extract a short-term gain while sacrificing the future of the company that may have taken decades to build. Thus, proponents are not reluctant to take actions that will reduce the rights of such short-term shareholders because they believe that they are not equal, in their eyes, to long-term shareholders and other *stakeholders,* such as employees and local communities. The evidence on shareholder wealth effects does not, however, provide a consensus, leaving the issue somewhat unresolved. Some studies purport clear adverse shareholder wealth effects, whereas others fail to detect an adverse impact on the shareholders' position. This chapter includes the results of most of the major studies in this field so that readers can make an independent judgment.

MANAGEMENT ENTRENCHMENT HYPOTHESIS VERSUS STOCKHOLDER INTERESTS HYPOTHESIS

The *management entrenchment hypothesis* proposes that nonparticipating stockholders experience reduced wealth when management takes actions to deter attempts to take control of the corporation. This theory asserts that managers of a corporation seek to maintain their positions through the use of active and preventative corporate defenses. According to this view, stockholder wealth declines in response to a reevaluation of this firm's stock by the market.

The *shareholder interests hypothesis*, sometimes also referred to as the convergence of interests hypothesis, implies that stockholder wealth rises when management takes actions to prevent changes in control. The fact that management does not need to devote resources to preventing takeover attempts is considered a cost savings. Such cost savings might come in the form of management time efficiencies savings, reduced expenditures in proxy fights, and a smaller investor relations department. The shareholder interests hypothesis can also be extended to show that antitakeover defenses can be used to maximize shareholder value through the bidding process. Management can assert that it will not withdraw the defenses unless it receives an offer that is in the shareholders' interests.

The shareholder wealth effects of various antitakeover measures, both preventative and active, are examined with an eye on the implications of the validity of these two competing hypotheses. If the installation of a given antitakeover defense results in a decline in shareholder wealth, this event lends some support to the management entrenchment hypothesis. If, however, shareholder wealth rises after the implementation of such a defense, the shareholder interests hypothesis gains credence. Given that the evidence from the various shareholder wealth effects studies of antitakeover measures is somewhat conflicting, the reader is presented with the evidence from several studies and can make his or her own determination of which theory is valid. However, other research studies on these hypotheses, which do not involve antitakeover defenses, have also been conducted. Some of this additional evidence is initially presented so that the reader may also consider it along with the antitakeover defenses evidence.

Morck, Shleifer, and Vishny examined the validity of these two competing hypotheses separate from a consideration of antitakeover defenses.[1] They considered the entrenchment of managers along with several other relevant factors, such as management's tenure with the company, personality, and status as a founder, and other factors such as the presence of a large outside shareholder or an active group of outside directors. The study examined the relationship between Tobin's q—the market value of all of a company's securities divided by the replacement costs of all assets—as the dependent variable, and the shareholdings of the board of directors in a sample of 371 of the *Fortune* 500 firms in 1980. They found that Tobin's q rises as ownership stakes rise. The positive relationship was not uniform in that it applied to ownership percentages between 0 and 5% as well as to those above 25%, whereas a negative relationship applied for those between 5 and 25%. The positive relationship for all ownership percentages, except the 5 to 25% range,

1. R. Morck, A. Shleifer, and R. W. Vishny, "Management Ownership and Market Valuation: An Empirical Analysis," *Journal of Financial Economics,* 20(1/2), January/March 1988, 293–315.

provides some support for the shareholder interests hypothesis, because higher ownership percentages imply greater entrenchment, which in turn was shown to be associated with higher values of securities except the intermediate range of 5 to 25%. The conflicting results for the intermediate 5 to 25% range notwithstanding, Morck, Shleifer, and Vishny have provided some weak support for the shareholder interest hypothesis that the reader can consider while evaluating the numerous antitakeover defenses studies that are discussed throughout this chapter. We will return to the issue of equity holding of directors in Chapter 12 when we discuss corporate governance.

PREVENTATIVE ANTITAKEOVER MEASURES

Preventative antitakeover measures have become common in corporate America. Most *Fortune* 500 companies have considered and developed a plan of defense in the event that the company becomes the target of a hostile bid. Some of these plans are directed at reducing the value that a bidder can find in the firm. The value-enhancing characteristics of a target are outlined in Chapter 14. These include characteristics such as high and steady cash flows, low debt levels, and low stock price relative to the value of the firm's assets. The presence of these factors may make a firm vulnerable to a takeover. Therefore, some preventative measures are designed to alter these characteristics of the firm in advance, or upon completion of a hostile takeover, so that the financial incentive a raider might have to acquire the target is significantly reduced.

Early Warnings Systems: Monitoring Shareholding and Trading Patterns

One of the first steps in developing a preventative antitakeover defense is to analyze the distribution of share ownership of the company. Certain groups of shareholders, such as employees, tend to be loyal to the company and probably will vote against a hostile bidder. Institutional investors usually invest in the security to earn a target return and may eagerly take advantage of favorable pricing and terms of a hostile offer. If a company is concerned about being a target of a hostile bid, it may closely monitor the trading of its shares. A sudden and unexpected increase in trading volume may signal the presence of a bidder who is trying to accumulate shares before having to announce its intentions. Such an announcement will usually cause the stock price to rise, so it is in a bidder's interest to accumulate as many shares as possible before an announcement.

Types of Preventative Antitakeover Measures

In effect, the installation of preventative measures is an exercise in wall building. Higher and more resistant walls need to be continually designed and installed because the raiders, and their investment banking and legal advisors, devote their energies to designing ways of scaling these defenses. These defenses are sometimes referred to as shark repellants.

Among the preventative measures that are discussed in this chapter are:

- *Poison pills.* These are securities issued by a potential target to make the firm less valuable in the eyes of a hostile bidder. There are two general types of poison pills: flip-over and flip-in. They can be an effective defense that has to be taken seriously by any hostile bidder.

- *Corporate charter amendments.* The target corporation may enact various amendments in its corporate charter that will make it more difficult for a hostile acquirer to bring about a change in managerial control of the target. Some of the amendments that are discussed are supermajority provisions, staggered boards, fair price provisions, and dual capitalizations.
- *Golden parachutes.* The attractive severance agreements sometimes offered to top management may be used as a preventative antitakeover measure. Alone, they may not prevent a takeover. However, they may help enhance the effect of some of the preceding measures and create a disincentive to acquire the target. These defenses, however, are far less powerful than poison pills and corporate charter amendments.

First-Generation Poison Pills: Preferred Stock Plans

Poison pills were invented by the famous takeover lawyer Martin Lipton, who used them in 1982 to defend El Paso Electric against General American Oil and again in 1983 during the Brown Foreman versus Lenox takeover contest. Brown Foreman was the fourth largest distiller in the United States, marketing such name brands as Jack Daniels whiskey, Martel cognac, and Korbel champagne, and generating annual sales of $900 million. Lenox was a major producer of china. Lenox's shares were trading at approximately $60 per share on the New York Stock Exchange. Brown Foreman believed that Lenox's stock was undervalued and offered $87 a share for each share of Lenox. This price was more than 20 times the previous year's per share earnings of $4.13. Such an attractive offer is very difficult to defeat. Lipton suggested that Lenox offer each common stockholder a dividend of preferred shares that would be convertible into 40 shares of Brown Foreman stock if Brown Foreman took over Lenox. These convertible shares would be an effective antitakeover device because, if converted, they would seriously dilute the Brown family's 60% share ownership position.

The type of poison pill Lenox used to fend off Brown Foreman is referred to as a *preferred stock plan.* Although they may keep a hostile bidder at bay, these first-generation poison pills had certain disadvantages. First, the issuer could only redeem them after an extended period of time, which might be in excess of ten years. Another major disadvantage is that they had an immediate adverse impact on the balance sheet. This is because when an analyst computes the leverage of a company, the preferred stock may be added to the long-term debt, thus making the company more heavily leveraged and therefore more risky in the eyes of investors after the implementation of the preferred stock plan.

In recent years Brown Forman has pursued acquisitions that make much more strategic sense. In 2000, it bought 45% of Finland's Finlandia Vodka and bought the remaining 55% in 2004. In 2006, it purchased the Chambord brand (the main component of Kir Royale cocktails), from French liquor firm Charles Jacquin et Cie.

Second-Generation Poison Pills: Flip-Over Rights

Poison pills did not become popular until late 1985, when their developer, Martin Lipton, perfected them. The new pills did not involve the issuance of preferred stock so that, by being easier to use, the pills would be more effective. They would also eliminate any adverse impact that an issue of preferred stock might have on the balance sheet. Preferred stock is considered to be a fixed-income security by financial analysts. An increase in the amount of preferred stock would generally be interpreted as increased financial leverage and risk.

The perfected pills came in the form of rights offerings that allowed the holders to buy stock in the acquiring firm at a low price. Rights are a form of call option issued by the corporation, entitling the holders to purchase a certain amount of stock for a particular price during a specified time period. The rights certificates used in modern poison pills are distributed to shareholders as a dividend and become activated after a triggering event. A typical triggering event could be one of the following:

- An acquisition of 20% of the outstanding stock by any individual, partnership, or corporation
- A tender offer for 30% or more of the target corporation's outstanding stock

Flip-over poison pills seemed to be a potent defense until they were effectively overcome in the takeover of the Crown Zellerbach Corporation by the Anglo-French financier Sir James Goldsmith (see Case Study: Goldsmith versus Crown Zellerbach).

CASE STUDY

GOLDSMITH VERSUS CROWN ZELLERBACH CORPORATION

Crown Zellerbach was a San Francisco–based forest products company with substantial holdings of forest-related assets. Sir James Goldsmith saw great value in Crown Zellerbach's assets at a time when the market failed to reflect its worth. "I do believe in forests. I do believe in forest lands. Everybody says they are a disaster. But they're still making profits. And forest lands will one day be as valuable as they were."[a] Crown Zellerbach's chairman, William T. Creason, who was concerned about the company's vulnerability to a takeover from a raider such as Goldsmith, adopted an elaborate set of antitakeover defenses designed to maintain the company's independence. These measures were as follows (use of the antitakeover measures, other than poison pills, are described later in this chapter):

- *Formation of a defensive team.* Crown Zellerbach formed a well-rounded defensive team that included the prestigious investment bank Salomon Brothers and attorney Martin Lipton. Crown Zellerbach also included the publicist Gershon Kekst, whose involvement highlights the important role public relations may play in takeover contests.
- *Updating of the stockholders list.* The corporation updated its stockholders list so that if a takeover battle ensued, it would be in a position to quickly contact important institutional and individual investors.
- *Staggering the board of directors.* The board of directors' elections were staggered to make it more difficult to take control of the board.
- *Enactment of the antigreenmail amendment.* An antigreenmail amendment was enacted in Crown Zellerbach's corporate charter to preempt the possibility that a raider would make a bid in the hope of attracting greenmail compensation.
- *Addition of a supermajority provision.* This alteration of the corporate charter required a two-thirds majority vote on future bylaw changes.
- *Issuance of a poison pill.* Crown Zellerbach's poison pill allowed stockholders to buy $200 worth of stock in the merged concern for $100. This significant discount for current Crown Zellerbach stockholders would make the company less valuable. As noted previously,

the pill was issued in the form of rights that were activated when either an acquirer bought 20% of Crown Zellerbach's stock or an acquirer made a tender offer for 30% of Crown Zellerbach stock. The rights became exercisable after a bidder bought 100% of the company's stock.

The rights were thought to be such a formidable obstacle to a raider that no bidder would trigger them. Because of the large financial incentives involved, however, the market developed a means of evading the effects of the defenses. This innovative tactic was first developed by the team representing Sir James Goldsmith. Designed to enable Crown to still make a deal with a favored suitor, the rights, trading independently of the shares, could be redeemed or canceled by the board by buying them back from shareholders for 50 cents each. But once a raider had acquired 20% of Crown's stock, the rights could no longer be redeemed and would not expire for ten years.

The pill's consequences were so devastating, it was hoped Goldsmith would hold short of the 20% threshold. But what if he kept buying? Would the pill be any defense against his gaining control on the open market? Lipton warned: "The plan wouldn't prevent takeovers; it would have no effect on a raider who was willing to acquire control and not obtain 100% ownership until after the rights expired."[b] Goldsmith's tactic entailed buying just over 50% of Crown Zellerbach stock. He bought this stock gradually but stopped purchasing once he had a controlling interest in the company. The rights were issued when Goldsmith bought more than 20%, but they never became exercisable because he did not buy 100%.

The ironic part of this takeover was that Goldsmith used Crown Zellerbach's poison pill against Crown Zellerbach. After the rights were issued, the company found it more difficult to pursue other options such as a friendly bidder, sometimes referred to as a white knight. The fact that these wealth-reducing rights were outstanding lowered the interest of potential white knights. This actually made Crown Zellerbach more vulnerable. Crown Zellerbach's management, after a protracted but futile struggle, was forced to agree to a takeover by Goldsmith.

[a]Moira Johnson, *Takeover* (New York: Penguin, 1986), p. 55.
[b]Ibid., p. 121.

Household International and the Legality of Poison Pills

Various legal challenges have been made to the modern versions of poison pills. One such challenge involved the poison pills issued by Household International Corporation (see Case Study: Dyson-Kissner-Moran versus Household International). In a November 1985 ruling in the Delaware Supreme Court, the court upheld the legality of Household's use of a poison pill. The court's position was that the pills did not necessarily keep bidders away; rather, they gave target corporations the opportunity to seek higher bids.

CASE STUDY

DYSON-KISSNER-MORAN VERSUS HOUSEHOLD INTERNATIONAL

Household International Inc. was a large financial services company located in Prospect Heights, IL. Although its main operations were in the financial services industry, it possessed diversified holdings, which included Household Finance, National Car Rental, and a retail food business. John Moran, one of the largest shareholders and the director of Household, planned to make a bid to take over Household through his New York–based investment company, Dyson-Kissner-Moran. Dyson-Kissner-Moran was estimated to be 1% the size of the larger Household International. It never made a hostile bid for Household, but it did engage in negotiations to buy the company. The other directors, unwilling to allow Household International to be acquired by Moran's investment company, decided to try to prevent the acquisition by adopting a poison pill that would be activated when a bidder bought more than 20% of Household. Moran believed that management and the directors adopted the pill to preserve their own positions. Therefore, represented by the famous takeover lawyer Joseph Flom, Moran sued Household on August 17, 1984, in Delaware, where Household was incorporated. He lost at the Chancery Court level but appealed to the Delaware Supreme Court. In November 1985, however, the Delaware Supreme Court upheld the legality of Household's poison pill. The Household decision was extremely important because it helped establish the legality of poison pills as an antitakeover defense. This decision has had great impact because so many corporations are incorporated in Delaware.[a]

[a] Moira Johnson, *Takeover* (New York: Penguin, 1986), p. 55.

After the use of poison pills was upheld in the courts, large corporations rushed to adopt their own poison pill defenses. In the 1990s, poison pill defenses were commonplace (see Exhibit 5.1).

Third-Generation Poison Pills: Flip-In Poison Pills

Flip-over poison pills have the drawback that they are effective only if the bidder acquires 100% of the target; they are not effective in preventing the acquisition of a controlling but less than 100% interest in the target. Given that most acquirers want to obtain 100% of the target's stock so as to have unrestricted access to the target's resources, flip-over provisions may prevent many, but not all, control transactions. Flip-in poison pills were an innovation designed to deal with the problem of a bidder who was not trying to purchase 100% of the target. With the flip-over provisions, a bidder could avoid the impact of the pill simply by not buying all of the target's outstanding stock.

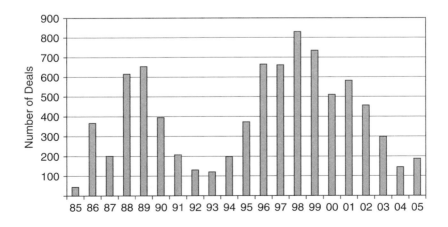

Exhibit 5.1 Poison Pill Adopted, 1985–2005
Source: Thomson Financial Securities Data.

Flip-in provisions allow holders of rights to acquire stock in the target, as opposed to *flip-over* rights, which allow holders to acquire stock in the acquirer. The flip-in rights were designed to dilute the target company regardless of whether the bidder merged the target into his company. They can be effective in dealing with raiders who seek to acquire a controlling influence in a target while not even acquiring majority control. Controlling ownership can often be achieved with stockholdings less than 51%. This is particularly true of widely held corporations in which most stockholders have a small percentage of the outstanding stock. The presence of flip-in rights makes such controlling acquisitions very expensive.

A flip-over plan may also contain flip-in provisions, thus combining the advantages of a flip-over plan, which is used against a 100% hostile acquisition, with a flip-in plan, which is used against a control share acquisition that is not a 100% share acquisition.

Back-End Plans

Another variant on the poison pill theme are *back-end plans,* also known as *note purchase rights plans.* The first back-end plan was developed in 1984. Under a back-end plan, shareholders receive a rights dividend, which gives shareholders the ability to exchange this right along with a share of stock for cash or senior securities that are equal in value to a specific "back-end" price stipulated by the issuer's board of directors. These rights may be exercised after the acquirer purchases shares in excess of a specific percentage of the target's outstanding shares. The back-end price is set above the market price, so back-end plans establish a minimum price for a takeover. The board of directors, however, must in good faith set a reasonable price.

Back-end plans were used to try to limit the effectiveness of two-tiered tender offers. In fact, the name *back-end* refers to the back end of a two-tiered offer. However, given that two-tiered offers are considered coercive and in conflict with the Williams Act, they are now less relevant.

Voting Plans

Voting plans were first developed in 1985. They are designed to prevent any outside entity from obtaining voting control of the company. Under these plans the company issues a dividend of preferred stock. If any outside entity acquires a substantial percentage of the company's stock, holders of preferred stock become entitled to supervoting rights. This prevents the larger block holder, presumably the hostile bidder, from obtaining voting control of the target. The legality of these plans has been successfully challenged in court. Therefore, they are not very commonly used.

Mechanics of Issuing Poison Pills

Poison pills are issued by distributing to common stockholders a dividend of one right for each share of stock they own. Rights holders receive the right to purchase one share of stock during the exercise period, which is typically ten years in length. Rights plans are usually authorized by the board of directors without shareholder approval. Until the occurrence of the first triggering event, such as a bidder's announcement of intentions to purchase of 20% of the issuer stock or to make an offer for 30% of its shares, the rights trade with the common shares and no separate rights certificates are issued. Once this triggering event occurs, however, the rights detach and become exercisable. At that time rights certificates are mailed to shareholders. However, the exercise price of these rights is set so high they really have no value as it would not make any sense to exercise them. However, the second trigger occurs when the bidder closes on the purchase of the target's shares. The rights now convey upon the holder the right to purchase shares at "50% off" prices.

As noted previously, the issuer may redeem the rights after the first trigger for a nominal amount, such as $0.02 per right, if it decides that it is advantageous. For example, if the issuer receives a bid that it finds desirable, the existence of the rights may be an impediment to an advantageous deal and the issuer may want to remove them. However, once the second trigger has occurred, the rights are no longer redeemable by the board.[2]

Blank Check Preferred Stock

Although a board of directors may have authority to issue rights, its ability to issue shares is dictated by the corporate charter. For this reason, it is standard practice for boards to create and reserve a certain amount of preferred stock that can be issued in the event that the rights become exercisable.[3] This prevents the board from having to solicit shareholder approval to amend the charter to allow for the issuance of shares to satisfy the rights. Such a request for shareholder approval would be tantamount to a referendum on the poison pill itself. It would also mean additional delay and uncertainty and would effectively weaken the poison pill defense.

Dead Hand, Slow Hand, and No Hand Provisions

Poison pills can be deactivated by the target's board of directors. Bidders can try to use this feature to offset the poison pill by initiating a tender offer that is contingent on the removal of the pill. The higher the premium offered, the more pressure on the board to remove the pill defense. Dead hand provisions give the power to redeem the poison pill to the directors who were on the target's board of directors when the pill was adopted or who were appointed by such directors. Even if these directors are ousted, they retain the voting power to control the pill's redemption. Courts in several states have not been receptive to dead hand provisions.[4] For example, dead hand provisions have been ruled invalid in states such as Delaware.[5]

Slow hand provisions place a limit on the time period where only prior directors can redeem the pill. Limitation periods are typically 180 days.[6] Some states, such as

---

2. R. Matthew Garms, "Shareholder By-Law Amendments and the Poison Pill: The Market for Corporate Control and Economic Efficiency," *Journal of Corporation Law*, 24(2), Winter 1994, 436.

3. Arthur Fleischer, Jr. and Alexander Sussman, *Takeover Defense*, 5th ed. (New York: Aspen, 1995), pp. 5–105.

4. *Carmody v. Toll Bros., Inc.*, 723 A. 2d 1180 (Del Ch. 1988).

5. *Quickturn Design Systems v. Mentor Graphic Corp.*, 721 A.2d 1281 (Del. 1999).

6. *Special Study for Corporate Counsel on Poison Pills*, William A. Hancock editor (Chesterfield, Ohio: Business Laws), 2002, 101.010.

Pennsylvania, allow slow hand provisions. No hand provisions limit the period for redemption to a certain time frame.

Shadow Pill

A bidder cannot simply look at a target company and conclude from the fact that it may not have a poison pill in place that it will not have to face such a defense. Targets may simply adopt a pill after a bid has taken place. For large companies, this can be done in a single day at a board of directors' meeting during which the members approve the pill.[7] This is a fact that bidders should be aware of when weighing a target's defenses.

Court Rulings Limiting the Use of Poison Pills

Certain courts have issued rulings in lawsuits emanating from specific takeover battles that have placed limits on how pills may be used. In 1988, British publisher Robert Maxwell successfully challenged the publisher Macmillan's poison pill defense. A Delaware court ruled that Macmillan's poison pill defense unfairly discriminated against Maxwell's offer for the New York publishing firm. The court concluded that poison pills should be used to promote an auction. In the court's view, Macmillan's pill prevented an effective auction. Also in 1988, a Delaware court reached a similar decision when it ruled that Interco's poison pill unfairly favored Interco's own recapitalization plan while discriminating against the Rales tender offer. (This case is discussed later in this chapter.)

Corporate Governance and "Chewable" Pills

Certain activist shareholders, such as some arbitragers and hedge funds, as well as activist pension funds, such as CALPERs, have challenged some poison pills as devices that serve to entrench poor managers. Only the board of directors, not shareholders, have the right to redeem the pill. The power of the board alone to redeem the pill has given rise to many protests by shareholder activists. One version of a poison pill that attempts to limit this sole power is a *chewable* pill. These are pills that disappear, or are brought to a shareholder vote, if the company receives a certain type of offer such as a certain price or type of consideration.

Impact of Poison Pills on Stock Prices

Several studies have examined the impact of poison pill provisions on stock prices. A study by Malatesta and Walking considered what effect the announcement of the adoption of a poison pill had on 132 firms between 1982 and 1986.[8] They found that poison pill defenses appeared to reduce stockholder wealth and that, on average, the firms that announced poison pill defenses generated small but statistically significant, abnormal

7. John C. Coates, "Takeover Defense in the Shadow of the Pill: A Critique of the Scientific Evidence," *Texas Law Review* (December 2000).
8. Paul H. Malatesta and Ralph A. Walking, "Poison Pills Securities: Stockholder Wealth, Profitability and Ownership Structure," *Journal of Financial Economics,* 20(1/2), January/March 1988, 347–376.

negative stock returns (−0.915%) during a two-day window around the announcement date. When these firms abandoned their poison pill plans, they showed abnormal positive returns.

Malatesta and Walking's results provide some support for the managerial entrenchment hypothesis in that the firms adopting the pills tended to have below-average financial performance. They also found that, on average, the managerial ownership percentage was significantly less for firms that adopted poison pills compared with industry averages. This supports the management entrenchment hypothesis. The findings of Malatesta and Walking were supported by Michael Ryngaert in his study of 380 firms that had adopted poison pill defenses between 1982 and 1986.[9] Ryngaert found statistically significant stock price declines from firms that adopted pill defenses and that were perceived as takeover targets. Ryngaert also analyzed the impact on the target firm's stock of legal challenges to the pill defense. He noted negative excess stock returns in 15 of 18 promanagement court decisions (upholding the legality of the pill) and positive excess returns in 6 of 11 proacquirer decisions (invalidating the pill). Ryngaert's research also touched on the effectiveness of poison pills as an antitakeover defense. He found that hostile bids are more likely to be defeated by firms that have a poison pill in place. Thirty-one percent of the pill-protected firms remained independent after receiving unsolicited bids, compared with 15.78% for a control group of non–pill-protected firms that also received unsolicited bids. Moreover, in 51.8% of the unsolicited bids, pill-protected firms received increased bids, which Ryngaert attributes to the presence of the pill defense. This finding is consistent with other research such as the Georgeson study that is discussed next.

CASE STUDY

ORACLE HELD AT BAY BY PEOPLESOFT'S POISON PILL

In June 2003, the second largest U.S. software maker (behind Microsoft), Oracle Corp., initiated a $7.7 billion hostile bid for rival and third largest, PeopleSoft, Inc. Both firms market "back-office" software that is used for supply management as well as other accounting functions. Lawrence Ellison, Oracle's very aggressive CEO, doggedly pursued PeopleSoft, which brandished its powerful poison pill defense to keep Ellison at bay. The takeover battle went on for approximately a year and a half; all the while PeopleSoft was able to prevent Oracle from completing its takeover due to the strength of its poison pill.

PeopleSoft's board rejected Oracle's offer as inadequate and refused to remove the poison pill. Oracle then pursued litigation in Delaware to force PeopleSoft to dismantle this defense. Over the course of the takeover contest Oracle increased its offer from an initial share offer price of $19 to $26 and then lowered it to $21 and then back up to $24. PeopleSoft also used a novel defense when it offered its customers, in the event of a hostile takeover by Oracle, a rebate of up to five times the license fee they paid for their PeopleSoft software. PeopleSoft defended this defense by saying that the hostile bid made it difficult for PeopleSoft to generate sales; as customers were worried that if they purchased PeopleSoft software it would be discontinued by Oracle in the event of a

---

9. Michael Ryngaert, "The Effects of Poison Pill Securities on Stockholder Wealth," *Journal of Financial Economics,* 20, January/March 1988, 377–417.

takeover, as Oracle had its own competing products and no incentive to continue the rival software. Ironically, Oracle really wanted PeopleSoft's customer base, not its products or even many of its employees.

The takeover contest became very hostile with the management of the companies launching personal attacks against each other. PeopleSoft's management called Ellison the "Darth Vader" of the industry. PeopleSoft's own board eventually got so fed up with this way of handling the contest that it asked the company's CEO, Craig Conway, to step down.

The battle went on for approximately a year and a half but eventually PeopleSoft succumbed in January 2005. One week later Oracle began sending payoff notices to thousands of PeopleSoft's employees. While the poison pill did not help these employees directly, PeopleSoft's shareholders benefited by the higher $10.3 billion takeover price. Employees indirectly benefited as the prolonged contest allowed many of them to make alternative employment plans. This takeover contest featured an effective use of a poison pill defense and also showed just how useful it can be in increasing shareholder value. However, while it underscored the effectiveness of poison pills, it also showed that even a poison pill will not necessarily hold off a determined bidder who is willing to pay higher and higher prices.

Impact of Poison Pills on Takeover Premiums

Two often-cited studies concerning the impact of poison pills on takeover premiums were conducted by Georgeson and Company (now Georgeson Shareholders), a large proxy solicitation firm. In a study released in March 1988, the firm showed that companies protected by poison pills received 69% higher premiums in takeover contests than unprotected companies. The study compared the premiums paid to pill-protected companies with those paid to companies without pill protection. Protected corporations in the Georgeson sample received premiums that were 78.5% above where the company's stock was trading six months before the contest. Nonprotected corporations received 56.7% premiums. The firm did a later study in November 1997 analyzing transactions from 1992 to 1996. The results were similar, although the difference between premiums was less. Premiums paid to pill-protected companies averaged eight percentage points, or 26% higher than those without pill protection. As Exhibit 5.2 shows, the difference was greater for small capitalization companies than for large capitalization companies.

The positive impact of poison pills on takeover premiums that was found in both Georgeson studies has also been confirmed by academic research. Comment and Schwert also found that poison pills are associated with higher takeover premiums.[10] More generally, Varaiya found that antitakeover measures were one of the determinants of takeover premiums.[11]

The Georgeson studies contradicted the previously widely held belief that poison pills are bad for stockholders. Some of this research has demonstrated that poison pills cause

---

10. Robert Comment and G. William Schwert, "Poison or Placebo: Evidence on the Deterrence and Wealth Effects of Modern Antitakeover Measures," *Journal of Financial Economics*, 39, 1995, 3–43.
11. Nikhil P. Varaiya, "Determinants of Premiums in Acquisition Transactions," *Managerial and Decision Economics*, 8, 1987, 175–184.

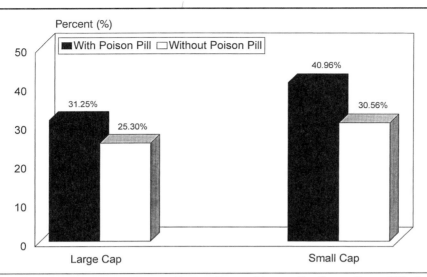

EXHIBIT 5.2 TAKEOVER PREMIUM AND POISON PILLS, BY TARGET MARKET CAP (LARGE CAP ≥ $1B; SMALL CAP < $1B)
Source: Poison Pills and Shareholder Value: 1992–1996, Georgeson & Company, November 1997.

stock prices to decline, presumably because pill-protected companies are more difficult takeover targets. Therefore, there is a lower likelihood that this type of company will be the object of a takeover bid. However, the Georgeson studies show that, in the event of a bid, the premium will be higher.

Poison Pills and the Auction Process

The fact that poison pills result in high takeover premiums has been supported by other research on the relationship between poison pills and the auction process.[12] One of the reasons poison pills result in higher premiums is that they facilitate the auction process. Bradley, Desai, and Kim have shown that auctions result in an added takeover premium of 11.4%,[13] whereas Comment and Schwert found added premiums equal to 13%. Poison pill defenses are often circumvented when the bidder increases its bid or makes an attractive all-cash offer. All-cash offers have been associated with 12.9% higher premiums.[14] In the face of increased prices brought about by an auction that may have been combined with more attractive compensation, such as an all-cash offer, target boards are often pressured to deactivate the poison pill.

---

12. Robert Comment and G. William Schwert, "Poison or Placebo? Evidence on the Deterrence and Wealth Effects of Modern Antitakeover Measures," *Journal of Financial Economics,* 39, September 1995, 3–43.
13. Michael Bradley, Anand Desai, and E. Han Kim, "Synergistic Gains From Corporate Acquisitions and Their Division Between the Shareholders of the Target and Acquiring Firms," *Journal of Financial Economics,* 21, May 1988, 3–40.
14. Yen-Sheng Huang and Ralph A. Walking, "Target Abnormal Returns Associated With Acquisition Announcements: Payment, Acquisition Form, and Managerial Resistance," *Journal of Financial Economics,* 19, December 1987, 329–349.

Conclusion of Research on Shareholder Wealth Effects of Poison Pills

The consensus of the research is that the implementation of poison pill defenses tends to be associated with negative, although not large, excess returns to the target's stock. We must remember, however, that these studies focus on a narrow time period around the date when the adoption of the pill plan was announced. Pill-protected firms that ultimately are acquired may exhibit higher returns as a result of the pill defense. These higher premiums were not reflected in this body of research.

Poison Puts

Poison puts are a unique variation on the poison pill theme. They involve an issuance of bonds that contain a *put option* exercisable only in the event that an unfriendly takeover occurs. A put option allows the holder to sell a particular security to another individual or firm during a certain time period and for a specific price. The issuing firm hopes that the holders' cashing of the bonds, which creates large cash demands for the merged firm, will make the takeover prospect most unattractive. If the acquiring firm can convince bondholders, however, not to redeem their bonds, these bond sales may be avoided. In addition, if the bonds are offered at higher than prevailing interest rates, the likelihood of redemption will not be as high.

Corporate Charter Amendments

Changes in the corporate charter are common antitakeover devices. The extent to which they may be implemented depends on state laws, which vary among states. Corporate charter changes generally require shareholder approval. The majority of antitakeover charter amendments are approved. Only in extreme cases of poor management performance do stockholders actively resist antitakeover amendments. This is partly because management is generally much more organized in its lobbying efforts than those shareholders who may oppose the proposed charter changes. Another important reason that shareholders tend to approve these amendments is that the majority of shareholders in large U.S. corporations are institutions, which have in the past been known to side with management. Some evidence suggests that this tendency is starting to change. Moreover, institutions as a whole are not unified in their support of management.

Brickley, Lease, and Smith point out that certain types of institutional investors, such as banks, insurance companies, and trusts, are more likely to vote in favor of management's proposals than other institutions, such as mutual funds, public pension funds, endowments, and foundations.[15] They believe that the latter category of investors is more independent of management in that they do not generally derive income from the lines of business controlled by management. When the charter amendment proposal clearly reduces shareholder wealth, institutions in general are more clearly found to be in opposition to the amendment.

---

15. James A. Brickley, Brickley, Ronald Lease, and Clifford Smith, "Ownership Structure and Voting on Antitakeover Amendments," *Journal of Financial Economics,* 2091/20, January/March 1988.

The process of proxy approval of shareholder amendments is discussed in Chapter 6. A later study by Brickley, Lease, and Smith explored the circumstances under which managers are more constrained by the voting process.[16] They found that although there is a high rate of passage of proposals put forward by management, managers tend to make such proposals only when they are highly likely to pass. In addition, in a study of 670 antitakeover corporate charter amendments involving 414 firms, they showed that managers are more constrained by voting when the following conditions apply: (1) in small companies with more concentrated ownership, (2) in companies that have large outside blockholders, (3) when information about possible adverse shareholder wealth effects has attracted media attention, and (4) in companies that have stringent voting rules.

Some of the more common antitakeover corporate charter changes are:

- Staggered terms of the board of directors
- Supermajority provisions
- Fair price provisions
- Dual capitalizations

Staggered Board Amendments

The majority of U.S. public companies have staggered boards—also called classified boards. The staggered board defense varies the terms of the board of directors so that only a few, such as one-third, of the directors may be elected during any given year. This may be important in a takeover battle because the incumbent board may be made up of members who are sympathetic to current management. Indeed, boards may also contain members of management. When a bidder has already bought majority control, the staggered board may prevent him from electing managers who will pursue the bidder's goals for the corporation, such as the sale of assets to pay down the debt incurred in the acquisition process. Staggered boards require shareholder approval before they can be implemented.

Under Delaware law, classified directors cannot be removed before their term expires. Nonclassified board members, however, can be removed by majority voting from the shareholders. Like many other corporate charter amendments, staggered boards are not a sufficiently powerful defense to stop a determined bidder, Rather, they are usually one of a collection of defenses that together can make a takeover difficult and costly to complete.

Staggered Board Research

The impact of staggered boards on shareholder wealth has been the subject of research for over 20 years. Some early studies, such as the one conducted by DeAngelo and Rice, seemed to find some evidence of negative shareholder wealth effect. They studied a sample of 100 different firms, of which 53 had a staggered board.[17] However,

---

16. James A. Brickley, Ronald C. Lease, and Clifford W. Smith, "Corporate Voting: Evidence from Corporate Charter Amendment Proposals," *Journal of Corporate Finance,* 1, 1994.

17. Harry DeAngelo and Eugene Rice, "Antitakeover Charter Amendments and Stockholder Wealth," *Journal of Financial Economics,* 11, 1983, 329–360.

their sample included other forms of antitakeover amendments although staggered boards made up a significant percentage of the amendments considered. These results were also tempered by low statistical significance. Other early research by Ruback failed to find a statistically significant relationship between a negative stock price effect and staggered board provisions.[18] His research showed a negative 1% decline in stock prices resulting from passage of staggered board provisions; these results were not statistically significant.

A later study by Bhagat and Jefferis considered 344 companies that adopted classified boards along with other defenses.[19] They did not find evidence of significant shareholder wealth effects following the adoption of several defenses including staggered boards. However, once again, this study did not exclusively focus on staggered boards alone but rather a grouping of various different preventative antitakeover defense.

More recent research of Bebchuk and Cohen found a negative relationship between firm value, as measured by Tobin's q, and the implementation of a staggered board.[20] They focused on the period between 1995 and 2002. This study implies that staggered boards lower firm values.

Supermajority Provisions

A corporation's charter dictates the number of voting shares needed to amend the corporate charter or to approve important issues such as mergers. Other transactions that may require stockholder approval are corporate liquidation, lease of important assets, sale of the company, or transactions with interested parties or substantial shareholders. The definition of a substantial shareholder may vary but it most often means a stockholder with more than 5 to 10% of the company's outstanding shares.

A supermajority provision provides for a higher than majority vote to approve a merger—typically 80% or two-thirds approval. The more extreme versions of these provisions require a 95% majority. Supermajority provisions may be drafted to require a higher percentage if the size of the bidder's shareholding is larger. They are more effective when management, or other groups that tend to be very supportive of management on issues such as mergers, hold a sufficient amount of stock to make approval of a merger more difficult. For example, if management and an employee stock ownership plan (ESOP) hold 22% of the outstanding stock and the corporation's charter requires 80% approval for mergers, it will be very difficult to complete a merger if the 22% do not approve.

Supermajority provisions generally contain escape clauses, sometimes called *board out clauses,* which allow the corporation to waive or cancel the supermajority provision. The most common escape clause provides that the supermajority provisions do not affect mergers that are approved by the board of directors or mergers with a subsidiary. Most of

18. Richard Ruback, "An Overview of Takeover Defenses," in Alan J. Auerbach, ed., *Mergers and Acquisitions* (Chicago: National Bureau of Economic Research, University of Chicago Press, 1987), pp. 49–67.
19. Sanjai Bhagat and Richard H. Jefferis, "Voting Power in the Proxy Process: The Case of Antitakeover Charter Amendments," *Journal of Financial Economics,* 1991, 193–225.
20. Lucian A. Bebchuk and Alma Cohen, "The Costs of Entrenched Boards," *Journal of Financial Economics*, 78(2), November 2005, 409–432.

these escape clauses are carefully worded so that the members of the board of directors who are interested parties may not vote with the rest of the board on related issues. An example of the interested party qualification would be the raider who holds 12% of a target company's stock, which has allowed the raider to command one or more seats on the board of directors. The escape clause would prevent this raider from exercising his or her votes on issues of approving a merger offer.

Supermajority provisions are most frequently used in conjunction with other anti-takeover corporate charter changes. Corporations commonly enact supermajority provisions along with or after they have put other antitakeover charter amendments into place. If the supermajority provisions require a supermajority to amend the corporate charter, it is more difficult for a raider to erase the other antitakeover provisions once the supermajority provision is in place. Supermajority provisions are more effective against partial offers. Offers for 100% of the target tend to negate the effects of most supermajority provisions. Exceptions may occur when certain groups loyal to the target hold a percentage greater than the difference between 100% and the supermajority threshold.

Legality of Supermajority Provisions

The courts have upheld the legality of supermajority provisions when these provisions have been adopted *pursuant to shareholder approval.* For example, in *Seibert v. Gulton Industries Inc.,* the court upheld a supermajority provision requiring 80% voting approval to approve a takeover by a 5% shareholder.[21] The provision required the supermajority approval before the bidder reached the 5% threshold. The courts have pointed out the obvious fact that shareholders themselves adopted the supermajority provisions and clearly possess the ability to "unadopt" them if they so choose.

Supermajority Provision Shareholder Wealth Effects

Early research on the shareholder wealth effects of antitakeover amendments, many of which included supermajority provisions, found some initial negative effects around the announcement of their implementation. DeAngelo and Rice[22] and Linn and McConnell[23] both conducted studies in 1983 and failed to find significant negative price effects for the various antitakeover amendments considered. These results are somewhat contradicted, however, by Jarrell and Poulsen, who point out that these other studies considered only the earlier versions of supermajority provisions, which do not include an escape clause.[24] They found that the later supermajority provisions, which included such escape clauses, were associated with a statistically significant negative 5% return. However, those supermajority provisions without escape clauses did not show significant negative returns.

21. *Seibert v. Gulton Industries, Inc.,* No. 5631.5 Del. J. Corp. L. 514 (Del. Ch. June 21, 1974), *aff'd without opinion* 414 A.2d 822 (Del. 1980).

22. Harry DeAngelo and Eugene Rice, "Antitakeover Charter Amendments and Stockholder Wealth," *Journal of Financial Economics,* 11, April 1983, 275–300.

23. Scott C. Linn and John J. McConnell, "An Empirical Investigation of the Impact of Antitakeover Amendments on Common Stock Prices," *Journal of Financial Economics,* 11(1–4), April 1983, 361–399.

24. Gregg A. Jarrell and Annette B. Poulsen, "Shark Repellents and Stock Prices: The Effects of Antitakeover Amendments Since 1980," *Journal of Financial Economics,* 19(1), September 1987, 127–168.

In 1987, a study shed light on the effectiveness of classified boards and supermajority provisions. Pound examined two samples of 100 firms each; one group had supermajority provisions and classified boards, whereas the control group had neither. His results showed that the frequency of takeovers was 28% for the group with the antitakeover amendments in place but 38% for the nonprotected control group.[25] These findings were also supported in a study by Ambrose and Megginson, who found that companies with supermajority amendments were insignificantly less likely to be the target of a takeover bid.[26]

Fair Price Provisions

A fair price provision is a modification of a corporation's charter that requires the acquirer to pay minority shareholders at least a fair market price for the company's stock. This may be stated in the form of a certain price or in terms of the company's price-earnings (P/E) ratio. That is, it may be expressed as a multiple of the company's earnings per share. The P/E multiple chosen is usually derived from the firm's historical P/E ratio or is based on a combination of the firm's and the industry's P/E ratio. Fair price provisions are usually activated when a bidder makes an offer. When the fair price provision is expressed in terms of a specific price, it usually states that stockholders must receive at least the maximum price paid by the acquirer when he or she bought the holdings.

Many state corporation laws already include fair price provisions. Fair price amendments to a corporation's charter augment the fair price provisions of the state's laws. In states in which fair price provisions exist, corporate fair price provisions usually provide for higher prices for stockholders in merger offers. The target corporation may waive most fair price provisions.

Fair price provisions were most useful when the target firm is the object of a two-tiered tender offer. The requirement for the bidder to pay a minimum, fair price helps negate the pressure a two-tiered offer tries to impose. However, as we have already noted, two-tiered offers are no longer as important to takeovers. Given that fair price provisions are a relatively weak antitakeover defense, it is not surprising that research on their shareholder wealth effects does not reveal major effects following implementation.

Shareholder Wealth Effects of Fair Price Provisions

Research on the impact of fair price provisions on stockholder wealth has thus far failed to show a significant relationship between fair price amendments and stock prices. Jarrell and Poulsen reported a small but statistically insignificant (negative) −0.65% change in stock prices in response to the implementation of fair price amendments.[27] This means that although they found the expected sign (negative), their results were not sufficiently

25. John Pound, "The Effectiveness of Antitakeover Amendments on Takeover Activity," *Journal of Law and Economics,* 30, October 1987, 353–367.
26. Brent W. Ambrose and William L. Megginson, "The Role of Asset Structure, Ownership Structure and Takeover Defenses in Determining Acquisition Likelihood," *Journal of Financial and Quantitative Analysis*, 27, 1992, 575–589.
27. Gregg A. Jarrell and Annette B. Poulsen, "Shark Repellents and Stock Prices: The Effects of Antitakeover Amendments Since 1980," *Journal of Financial Economics,* 19(1), September 1987, 127–168.

robust to state confidently that there is any relationship between the fair price provisions and stock prices. The main effort seems to be a restructuring of the offer with a blended price as opposed to a two-tiered structure. Some evidence appears to contradict Jarrell and Poulsen's mild negative stock price effect. For example, McWilliams found a positive stock price effect associated with the adoption of fair price provisions.[28]

Dual Capitalization

Dual capitalization is a restructuring of equity into two classes of stock with different voting rights. This equity restructuring can take place only with shareholder approval. There are various reasons to have more than one class of stock other than to prevent a hostile takeover. For example, General Motors (GM) used its Class E shares to segregate the performance and compensation of shareholders of its EDS division. GM also had Class H shares for its Hughes Aircraft division. General Motors has long since parted ways with these diversifications. Another example of a dual classification is the Ford Motor Company, which has both Class A and Class B shares with the Class B shares having 16.561 votes per share as opposed to Class A shares, which have one vote per share. The greater voting rights of the Class B shares allow those shareholders to command 40% of the voting power in the company.

From an antitakeover perspective, however, the purpose of dual capitalization is to give greater voting power to a group of stockholders who might be sympathetic to management's view. Management often increases its voting power directly in a dual capitalization by acquiring stock with greater voting rights. A typical dual capitalization involves the issuance of another class of stock that has superior voting rights to the current outstanding stock. The stock with the superior voting rights might have 10 or 100 votes for each share of stock. This stock is usually distributed by the issuance of superior voting rights stock to all stockholders. Stockholders are then given the right to exchange this stock for ordinary stock. Most stockholders choose to exchange the supervoting rights stock for ordinary stock because the super stock usually lacks marketability or pays low dividends. However, management, who may also be shareholders, may not exchange their supervoting rights stock for ordinary stock. This results in management increasing its voting control of the corporation.

Why Do Dual Class Recapitalizations Get Approved?

Companies must first receive the approval of shareholders before they can create a dual class recapitalization. However, if the end result of such recapitalizations is to concentrate voting power in the hands of a small group who usually are insiders, one may wonder, why would shareholders willingly agree to such equity structures? The answer is straightforward—shareholders seek the financial gain from the higher dividends and may not value control that highly. Research also shows that companies that pursue dual class recapitalizations seem to do better in some ways (not as well in others) than some other groups of firms, leveraged buyout (LBO) firms, which also change their capital structure

---

28. Victoria B. McWilliams, "Managerial Share Ownership and the Stock Price Effects of Antitakeover Amendment Provisions," *Journal of Finance*, 45(5), December 1990, 1627–1640.

while increasing control in the hands of management. Lehn, Netter, and Poulsen showed that, for the firms in the sample, which covered the period 1977–1987, dual class firms spend more on capital expenditures although LBO firms showed better financial performance.[29]

CASE STUDY

TRUMP VERSUS GRIFFIN

A classic battle for control involving superior voting rights stock was waged in 1988 between real estate tycoon Donald Trump and television personality Merv Griffin. Griffin, fresh with cash from the sale of the "Wheel of Fortune" and "Jeopardy" television shows to Coca-Cola for $250 million, set his sights on Donald Trump's Resorts casino. The Resorts Corporation was originally the Mary Carter Paint Company, but changed its name to Resorts in 1968. It is a diversified business that includes a helicopter and plane airline, a hotel in the Bahamas, and the 700-room Resorts International hotel and casino. Resorts was Atlantic City's first casino hotel.

Donald Trump, in addition to owning a significant stake in Resorts, also owned the Trump Plaza and the Trump's Castle casinos. In 1990, he constructed the 1,260-room Taj Mahal casino, which cost an estimated $1 billion. Because casino licensing regulations provide that an individual may hold only three casino licenses, Trump decided that Resorts was the most likely candidate for sale.

Resorts had two classes of stock: Class A and Class B. Class A shares only had 1/100 votes per share, whereas each Class B share had one vote for each share. Class A shares sold for as much as $75 in 1986, while Class B shares were not traded on an organized exchange. Trump had 88% of the voting shares in Resorts. Although he did have effective voting control of Resorts, he was under pressure to divest one casino. Griffin, aware of Trump's position, made a bid for Resorts at $35 per share. Given his superior voting rights stock, Trump remained in control of Resorts. He could not have been compelled to sell, although he had to face the choice of selling one casino to take ownership of the Taj Mahal. Trump eventually sold his interest in Resorts and tendered his superior voting rights stock to Merv Griffin.

The Resorts deal was played out vividly in the media, given the notoriety of the two protagonists. The acquisition proved to be a disaster for Merv Griffin, who discovered that Resorts needed a greater than anticipated level of capital investment. Resorts was forced to file Chapter 11 not long after the acquisition.[a]

[a]Pauline Yoshihashi and Neil Barsky, "Merv Griffin's Plunge into Casino Gambling Could Prove a Loser," *Wall Street Journal*, February 10, 1989, p. A1.

Shareholder Wealth Effects of Dual Capitalizations

Jarrell and Poulsen examined 94 firms that recapitalized with dual classes of stock that had different voting rights between 1976 and 1987.[30] Forty of the firms were listed on the New York Stock Exchange, with 26 on the American Stock Exchange and 31 traded

---

29. Kenneth Lehn, Jeffrey Netter, and Anne Poulsen, "Consolidating Corporate Control: Dual Class Recapitalizations versus Leveraged Buyouts," *Journal of Financial Economics*, October, 1990, 557–580.

30. Gregg Jarrell and Annette Poulsen, "Dual Class Recapitalizations as Antitakeover Mechanisms," *Journal of Financial Economics*, 20, January/March 1988, 129–152.

over-the-counter. The study found significant abnormal negative returns equal to 0.82% for a narrow time period around the announcement of the dual capitalization. Jarrell and Poulsen also reported that the greatest negative effects were observed for firms that had high concentrations of stock held by insiders (30 to 50% insider holdings). Dual capitalization will be more effective in consolidating control in the hands of management when management already owns a significant percentage of the firm's stock. The fact that negative returns were higher when management already held more shares implies that when management entrenchment was more likely (which in turn implies that the potential for a successful bid was lower), the market responded by devaluing the shares.

Shum, Davidson, and Glascock found that, although the implementation of dual capitalizations may not generate significant shareholder wealth effects, when their implementation causes the original shareholders to lose control without receiving compensation in return, there were negative effects.[31] Bacon, Cornett, and Davidson found out that how the market reacted to dual capitalizations depended on how many independent directors were on the board.[32] When independent directors dominated, the market response was positive. This implies that the market believes that if a largely independent board approved the dual capitalizations, then the defense furthered shareholder's interests and did not entrench management.

Antigreenmail Provisions

Antigreenmail charter amendments restrict the ability of a target corporation to pay greenmail to a potential hostile bidder. Some amendments allow the payment if shareholders extend their approval. Other variations allow for the payment of some ceiling amount such as the market price. In the case of a takeover battle, which generally causes stock prices to rise, this may still provide a hostile shareholder a profit from his activities. Greenmail is discussed later in this chapter with active antitakeover defenses.

Restrictions on Ability to Call an Election

Unless there are specific restrictions in the corporate charter, most states require corporations to call a special shareholder meeting if a certain percentage of the shareholders request it. Such meetings may be used as a forum whereby insurgents try to gain control of the company. At shareholder meetings, takeover defenses such as poison pills may be dismantled. These meetings may also be used to promote proxy fights. Given the opportunities for bidders that shareholder meetings present, companies may try to amend the charter to limit the ability to call meetings. Some of the more extreme restrictions limit the ability to call a meeting to the board of directors or only if a certain high percentage of the shareholders request it. In addition, there may be limitations imposed on the type of issues that may be raised at the shareholder meeting.

---

31. C. M. Shum, W. N. Davidson III, and J. L. Glascock, "Voting Rights and the Market's Reaction to Dual Class Common Stock," *Financial Review,* 32(2), 275–288.
32. Curtis J. Bacon, Marcia M. Cornett, and Wallace N. Davidson III, "The Board of Directors and Dual Class Recapitalizations," *Financial Management,* 26(3), 1997, 5–22.

Antitakeover Amendments and Managerial Ownership Research

McWilliams conducted a study on the impact of managerial share ownership and the shareholder wealth effects of antitakeover amendments.[33] She examined 763 amendments that were adopted by 325 New York Stock Exchange and American Stock Exchange firms. McWilliams's research was partially motivated by a desire to explain why several earlier research studies fail to find a statistically significant share price response with the adoption of antitrust amendments. These earlier studies did not consider managerial share ownership, which varies by firm.

McWilliams's results show a negative relationship between managerial share ownership and the adoption of antitakeover amendment proposals (with the exception of fair price provisions). The stock price reaction to amendment proposals was positive when managerial share ownership was near zero and became negative as these ownership percentages rose. She concludes that the market is interpreting these proposals as lowering the likelihood of a takeover when proposed by companies that have high managerial share ownership.

Golden Shares

With the privatization of many state-owned companies, some governments are reluctant to totally embrace the free market ownership of these enterprises. In Europe and Asia some governments resorted to golden shares, which are shares that are owned by the government that give the government certain control, such as in the form of significant voting rights, over the companies once they are privatized. Governments have claimed that this is necessary, particularly when they see there are strategic interests at stake and they fear those interests would be compromised if some outside shareholders gained control of the businesses. An alternative to actual shares are laws that are passed to limit the number of shares or votes any one outside shareholder can control. Golden shares were used in the privatization of British Aerospace and British Telecom. They have been criticized by the European Commission as putting limits on the free movement of capital.

Golden Parachutes

Golden parachutes are special compensation agreements that the company provides to upper management. The word *golden* is used because of the lucrative compensation that executives covered by these agreements receive. Although companies typically maintain that they adopt such agreements for reasons other than the prevention of takeovers, they may have some antitakeover effects. These effects may occur whether the parachutes are used in a preventative or an active manner. They may be used in advance of a hostile bid to make the target less desirable, but they may also be used in the midst of a takeover battle. It should be kept in mind, particularly for large takeovers, that the golden parachute payments are a small percentage of the total purchase price. This implies that the antitakeover effects of these benefits may be relatively small. Many CEOs of corporations believe that

---

33. Victoria McWilliams, "Managerial Share Ownership and the Stock Price Effects of Antitakeover Amendment Proposals," *Journal of Finance*, 45(5), December 1990, 1627–1640.

golden parachutes are a vital course of action in a takeover contest. One problem corporations face during a takeover battle is that of retaining management employees. When a takeover has been made, a corporation's management is often besieged by calls from recruiters. Managers who are insecure about their positions are quick to consider other attractive offers. Without a golden parachute agreement, the managers might be forced to litigate to realize certain compensation in the event that they were terminated following a change in control. Therefore, some corporations adopt golden parachutes to alleviate their employees' concerns about job security. Jensen contends that properly constructed golden parachutes should result in management possessing sufficient incentives to negotiate higher takeover premiums for shareholders.[34] He states, "These control related contracts are beneficial when correctly implemented, because they help reduce the conflict of interest between shareholders and managers at times of takeover and therefore make it more likely that the productive gains stemming from changes in control will be realized."[35]

Shareholder Wealth Effects of Golden Parachute Agreements

A study by Lambert and Larker provides some support for Jensen's view. They found that stock prices rose 3% when companies announced the adoption of golden parachutes.[36] Other studies have provided a basis for the market's positive stock price response. In a sample of 146 firms that adopted golden parachutes between 1975 and 1988, Machlin, Choe, and Miles found that the number of multiple takeover offers was significantly greater for firms that possessed golden parachute agreements than for those firms without such agreements.[37] They also found a positive relationship between the size of the golden parachute agreement and the magnitude of the takeover premium. Other research has found negative shareholder wealth effects following the adoption of golden parachute agreements but these results were not statistically significant.[38]

Some studies find that the shareholder wealth effects of golden parachutes are dependent on when they are adopted. Hall has found that the effects are negative if they are adopted when a firm is in play but are neutral when that is not the case.[39] Some studies show that the adoption of golden parachutes increases the likelihood that the company will be a takeover target.[40] However, Schnitzer has shown that this effect is less likely when the management team is efficient.[41]

---

34. Michael Jensen, "Takeovers: Causes and Consequences," in Patrick A. Gaughan, ed., *Readings in Mergers and Acquisitions* (Oxford: Basil Blackwell, 1994), pp. 15–43.

35. Jensen, "Takeovers," p. 32.

36. Richard A. Lambert and David F. Larker, "Golden Parachutes, Executive Decision Making and Shareholder Wealth," *Journal of Accounting Economics,* 7, 1985, 179–203.

37. Judith Machlin, Hyuk Choe, and James Miles, "The Effects of Golden Parachutes on Takeover Activity," *Journal of Law and Economics,* 36(2), 1993, 861–876.

38. P. L. Hall and D. C. Anderson, "The Effect of Golden Parachutes on Shareholder Wealth and Takeover Probabilities," *Journal of Business Finance and Accounting,* 23, April 1997, 445–463; and Damian J. Mogavero and Michael F. Toyne, "The Impact of Golden Parachutes on Fortune 500 Stock Returns: A Reexamination of the Evidence," *Quarterly Journal of Business and Economics,* 34, 1995, 30–38.

39. P. L. Hall, "An Examination of Stock Returns to Firms Adopting Golden Parachutes Under Certain Conditions," *American Business Review,* 16(1), 123–130.

40. J. A. Born, E. A. Trahan, and H. J. Faria, "Golden Parachutes, Incentive Aligners, Management Entrenchers, or Takeover Bids Signals?" *Journal of Financial Research,* 16(4), 299–308.

41. M. Schnitzer, "Breach of Trust in Takeovers and the Optimal Corporate Charter," *Journal of Industrial Economics,* 43(3), 1995, 229–260.

Mechanics of Golden Parachutes

A typical golden parachute agreement provides for lump-sum payments to certain senior management on either voluntary or involuntary termination of their employment. This agreement is usually effective if termination occurs within one year after the change in control. The agreements between the employee and the corporation may have a fixed term or may be an *evergreen* agreement, in which the term is one year but is automatically extended for an additional year if there is not a change in control during a given year. Monies to fund golden parachutes are sometimes put aside in separate accounts referred to as *rabbi trusts*. Rabbi trusts provide assurance to the employee that the monies will be there for the payment of the parachutes.

The amount of compensation is usually determined by the employee's annual compensation and years of service. For example, the agreement could provide for the terminated employee to receive some multiple of a recent year's annual salary, possibly also including incentive and bonuses, for a certain number of years.

Golden parachutes are usually triggered by some predetermined ownership of stock by an outside entity. Lambert and Larker found that the trigger control percentage of stocks acquired by a bidder was an average 26.6% for the firms they studied.[42] However, some corporations have control trigger percentages below 10%—well below the Lambert and Larker sample average. Lambert and Larker also showed that the participants in golden parachutes plans are narrowly defined. In their sample, golden parachute agreements covered only 9.7% of the executives. These agreements are extended to executives who do not have employment contracts. They are effective even if the managers leave the corporations voluntarily after a change in control.

Golden parachutes are not usually applied broadly. One unusual exception is what are known as *silver parachutes,* compensation agreements given to most employees in the firm, including lower-level employees. The most common type of silver parachute is a one-year severance pay agreement.

Legality of Golden Parachutes

Golden parachutes have been challenged in court by stockholders who contend that these agreements violate directors' and management's fiduciary responsibilities. The problem arises because golden parachutes generally do not have to be approved by a stockholder vote before implementation. The courts have held that the actions of directors in enacting golden parachute agreements were within their purview under the Business Judgment Rule.[43] As discussed in Chapter 3, this rule holds that management's actions are valid as long as they are enacted while management is acting in the stockholders' best interests. The fact that management's actions may not maximize stockholder wealth, in retrospect, is irrelevant according to this rule.

Courts have generally refused to distinguish between golden parachute agreements and other types of executive compensation arrangements.[44] Part of the reason courts have not

---

42. Lambert and Larker, "Golden Parachutes, Executive Decision Making and Shareholder Wealth," *Journal of Accounting and Economics*, 7, 179–203.
43. *Buckhorn Inc. v. Ropak Corp.*, 656 F. Supp. 209 (S.D. Ohio), *aff'd by summary order* 815 F.2d 76 (6th Cir. 1987).
44. *Royal Crown Cos. v. McMahon*, 359 S.E. 2d 379 (Ga. Ct. App. 1987), *cert. denied* (Ga. September 8, 1987).

been persuaded by the self-dealing argument of golden parachute critics is because the agreements are typically approved by a compensation committee of the board of directors, which should be dominated by disinterested directors and not those who would expect to profit from the parachutes.[45] When the golden parachute agreements are triggered by the manager's own actions, however, courts have invalidated them or at least granted a preliminary injunction against their use.[46]

Criticism of Golden Parachutes

Some shareholder rights activists believe that golden parachutes are a burden on both the corporation and the stockholders. Some critics cite moral hazard concerns, and golden parachutes could be considered a form of self-dealing on the part of management and one of the more flagrant abuses of the modern takeover era. The magnitude of these compensation packages, they state, is clearly excessive. Critics contend that managers of companies that were poorly managed and have experienced a declining stock price end up being rewarded for that mismanagement. The golden parachute that was given to Michael Bergerac, former chairman of Revlon Corporation, after his resignation at the end of the unsuccessful defense against corporate raider Ronald Perelman was estimated to have provided Bergerac with a compensation package in excess of $35 million. This package included stock options worth $15 million. This is not an isolated situation. While these excessive payments raised eyebrows at the time, as we moved into the fifth merger wave and the years that followed the problem only got worse.

The excessiveness of golden parachute agreements has given rise to the term *golden handcuffs,* which reflects the belief that golden parachutes serve only to entrench management at the expense of stockholders. This belies their role as an antitakeover device. If the compensation package is very large, some raiders might be put off from making a bid for the company. As noted previously, although a large golden parachute agreement may be a mild deterrent, it is not considered an effective antitakeover tool. In conjunction with other, stronger devices, however, these agreements may have some role as a deterrent.

The tax treatment of golden parachutes can be complex. However, Congress, in the tax reform acts of 1984 and 1986, imposed penalties on golden parachute payments. These penalties feature the payment of a nondeductible 20% tax, to be paid by the employee, for "excessive" golden parachute payments. Generally, the excess is defined as the amount greater than a typical annual compensation. In addition, the employer corporations are denied tax deductions for excessive golden parachutes. Excessive is defined as being three times the average salary of the employee in the previous five-year period.

Golden Parachutes and Huge Acquisition Payouts of the 2000s

What started out as golden parachutes in the 1980s gave rise to a system that awarded CEOs with huge payouts when their companies were sold. One example was the

---

45. *E. Tate & Lyle PLC v. Staley Continental, Inc.,* Fed. Sec. L. Rep. 93, 764 (Del. Ch. CCH 93, 764) (Del. Ch. May 9, 1988); *Nomad Acquisition Corp. v. Damon Corp.,* CCH Fed. Sec. L. Rep. 94,040 (Del. Ch. September 16, 1988).
46. John C. Coffee, "Shareholders versus Managers: The Strain in the Corporate Web," in John Coffee, Louis Lowenstein, and Susan Rose Ackerman, eds., *Knights, Raiders and Targets* (New York: Oxford University Press, 1988), pp. 71–134.

$165 million given to James Kilts, CEO of Gillette, after its sale to Procter & Gamble Co. in 2005. Another was the $102 million that Bruce Hammonds was reported to receive in connection with MBNA's acquisition by Bank of America, and the $92 million that Bruce Hammonds is reported to have received in connection with the 2005 sale of his company, Georgia Pacific, to Koch Industries. Even companies known for poor performance still have similar payouts for their CEOs when they are finally sold. For example, AT&T CEO David Dorman is reported to have received $55 million in connection with the sale of his company to SBC Communications. Given AT&T's long history of poor performance and horrendous deals, such a high compensation level is difficult to explain.

The system has given rise to a new breed of CEO, who joins companies that have underperformed and tries to sell the business to a buyer. An example was Michael Capellas, who received $14 million in connection with the sale of Compac to Hewlett-Packard followed by $39 million for the sale of MCI to Verizon. These new CEOs join companies for a relatively short period and then "flip" them.

CHANGING THE STATE OF INCORPORATION

Because states have antitakeover laws that vary in degrees of protection, a company may choose to relocate its legal corporate home so it is protected by another state's laws that have stronger antitakeover provisions. This is usually accomplished by a company's creating a subsidiary in the new state and then merging the parent into the subsidiary. Reincorporating in another state that has stronger antitakeover laws, however, will not ensure a firm's independence. For example, Singer moved its state of incorporation from Connecticut to New Jersey, a state that has a strong antitakeover law. The move did not prevent Singer from ultimately being taken over by raider Paul Bilzerian. Nonetheless, reincorporating may make a takeover more difficult for the raider. This stronger bargaining position may help the target get a better price for the shareholders.

Shareholder Wealth Effects of Reincorporation

Netter and Poulsen examined the shareholder wealth effects of reincorporation announcements for 36 firms in 1986 and 1987.[47] They divided their sample into two groups: 19 firms that reincorporated from California and the remaining 17 firms. They point out that California is a shareholder rights state whose corporation laws protect shareholder interests. Among the rights provided are mandatory cumulative voting, a prohibition against classified boards, and other shareholder rights such as the ability to remove directors without cause or to call special meetings. Netter and Poulsen reasoned that if there were stock price effects, they would be greater in reincorporations from California to Delaware. Their results failed to reveal any shareholder wealth effects either from the 36 reincorporations in their sample or from the California subsample. On the basis of their study, we may conclude that the greater flexibility provided to management by incorporating in Delaware will not reduce shareholder wealth.

---

47. Jeffrey Netter and Annette Poulsen, "State Corporation Laws and Shareholders: The Recent Experience," *Financial Management,* 18(3), Autumn 1989, 29–40.

ACTIVE ANTITAKEOVER DEFENSES

Installing the various preventative antitakeover defenses will not guarantee a company's independence. It may, however, make the takeover more difficult and costly. Some bidders may decide to bypass a well-defended target in favor of other firms that have not installed formidable defenses. Nonetheless, even those firms that have deployed a wide array of preventative antitakeover defenses may still need to actively resist raiders when they become targets of a hostile bid. The second half of this chapter describes some of the various actions a target may take after it receives an unwanted bid or learns that it is about to be the target of such a bid. The target may become aware of this in several ways, such as through the results of its stock watch or market surveillance programs or through required public filings such as a Hart-Scott-Rodino filing.

The following actions are discussed in the second half of this chapter:

- *Greenmail.* Share repurchases of the bidder's stock at a premium.
- *Standstill agreements.* These agreements usually accompany a greenmail payment. Here the bidder agrees not to buy additional shares in exchange for a fee.
- *White knight.* The target may seek a friendly bidder, or white knight, as an alternative to the hostile acquirer.
- *White squire.* The target may place shares or assets in the hands of a friendly firm or investor. These entities are referred to as white squires.
- *Capital structure changes.* Targets may take various actions that will alter the company's capital structure. Through a *recapitalization,* the firm can assume more debt while it pays shareholders a larger dividend. The target can also simply assume more debt without using the proceeds to pay shareholders a dividend. Both alternatives make the firm more heavily leveraged and less valuable to the bidder. Targets may also alter the capital structure by changing the total number of shares outstanding. This may be done through a new offering of stock, placement of shares in the hands of a white squire, or an ESOP. Instead of issuing more shares, some targets buy back shares to ensure they are not purchased by the hostile bidder.
- *Litigation.* Targets commonly sue the bidder, and the bidder often responds with a countersuit. It is unusual to see a takeover battle that does not feature litigation as one of the tools used by either side.
- *Pac-Man defense.* One of the more extreme defenses occurs when the target makes a counteroffer for the bidder. This is one of the more colorful takeover defenses, although it is seldom used.

The coverage of these active antitakeover defenses is similar to the coverage of the preventative measures. The use of each action is described, along with the research on its shareholder wealth effects. Bear in mind that a target may choose to use several of these defenses together as opposed to selecting merely one. It is difficult, therefore, for research studies to isolate the shareholder wealth effects of any specific defense. In addition, some of the research, using different data sets drawn from different time periods with varying market conditions, reach conflicting conclusions. As the market changes and adapts to the various defenses, their effectiveness—and therefore their impact on stock prices—also varies. These problems were also apparent in the research studies on the preventative measures. Once again, readers will have to draw their own conclusions about the impact of these defenses on stockholders and other stakeholders.

Greenmail

The term *greenmail* refers to the payment of a substantial premium for a significant shareholder's stock in return for the stockholder's agreement that he or she will not initiate a bid for control of the company. Greenmail is a form of *targeted share repurchases,* which is a general term that is more broadly applied to also include other purchases of stock from specific groups of stockholders who may not ever contemplate a raid on the company.

One of the earlier reported instances of greenmail occurred in July 1979, when Carl Icahn bought 9.9% of Saxon Industries stock for approximately $7.21 per share. Saxon repurchased Icahn's shares for $10.50 per share on February 13, 1980.[48] This stock buyback helped launch Icahn on a career as a successful corporate raider. Icahn was not the first greenmailer, however. That distinction may belong to Charles Bluhdorn, chairman of Gulf & Western Industries, "who was an early practitioner when Cannon Mills in 1976 bought back a Gulf & Western holding."[49] While many of the corporate raiders from the fourth merger wave have left the M&A business, Icahn has actually risen in prominence and has become the leader of large hedge funds in the 2000s. Greenmail brought significant profits to those who were able to successfully pursue the practice. The Bass Brothers were said to have earned $400 million on the Texaco-Getty deal, whereas Icahn reportedly received $6.6 million for his stake in American Can, $9.7 million on Owens Illinois, $8.5 million on Dan River Mills, and $19 million on Gulf & Western.[50] Saul Steinberg's 1984 attempted takeover of Disney earned him not only an impressive payout of $325 million for his share holdings but also another $28 million for his expenses.

CASE STUDY

ICAHN VERSUS HAMMERMILL PAPER CORPORATION

One classic example of greenmail occurred following Carl Icahn's announcement that he owned more than 10% of Hammermill Paper Corporation's common stock. Hammermill was a high-quality manufacturer of paper products for more than 80 years.[a] During late 1979, Hammermill stock was valued at approximately $25 per share, a low valuation because the stock's book value was approximately $37 per share. Analysts thought that even this valuation was too low inasmuch as many of Hammermill's assets, such as its timberlands, were carried on the firm's books below their actual value. Icahn suggested that Hammermill be liquidated because its per-share liquidation value would exceed the cost of a share of stock. Hammermill's management, busily engaged

[a]Jeff Madrick, *Taking America* (New York: Bantam, 1987), pp. 242–243.

---

48. "Icahn Gets Green as Others Envy Him," *Wall Street Journal*, November 13, 1989, p. B1.
49. Ibid.
50. John Brooks, *Takeover* (New York: Dutton, 1987), p. 186.

in rejuvenating the company, vehemently opposed liquidation. Both parties ultimately filed suits against each other while they pursued a proxy contest. Icahn lost the proxy battle and Hammermill eventually paid Icahn $36 per share for each of his 865,000 shares. Icahn was reported to have made a $9 million profit on an investment of $20 million.[b] The payment of greenmail raises certain ethical issues regarding the fiduciary responsibilities of management and directors, both of whom are charged with maximizing the value of stockholder wealth. Management critics, however, state that managers use tools such as greenmail to pursue their own goals, which may conflict with the goal of maximizing stockholder wealth.

[b]Ibid.

Legality of Differential Payments to Large-Block Shareholders

The courts have ruled that differential payments to large-block shareholders are legal as long as they are made for valid business reasons.[51] However, the term *valid business reasons* is so broad that it gives management considerable latitude to take actions that may favor management more than stockholders. Managers may claim that to fulfill their plans for the corporation's future growth, they need to prevent a takeover of the corporation by any entity that would possibly change the company's direction.

The interpretation of legitimate business purposes may involve a difference in business philosophies between the incumbent management and a bidder. It may also simply be that managers are seeking to preserve the continuity of their business strategies. Although some managers think that the court's broad views on this matter may serve to entrench management, others see the court's position as one that helps preserve management's ability to conduct long-term strategic planning. Many corporate managers believe that the court's position allows them to enact the necessary defenses to fend off takeovers by hostile bidders who might acquire the corporation simply to sell off assets and achieve short-term returns. Considerable debate surrounds the issue of short-term versus long-term motives of corporate bidders.

The legality of greenmail itself was upheld in a legal challenge in the Texaco greenmail payment to the Bass Brothers. The Delaware Chancery Court found that the 1984 payment of $1.3 billion, which was a 3% premium, to the Bass Brothers was a reasonable price to pay for eliminating the potentially disruptive effects that the Bass Group might have posed for Texaco in the future.[52] The Delaware Chancery Court's approval of the greenmail payment and dismissal of a shareholder class action were upheld by the Delaware Supreme Court. The important decision clearly established a precedent for the legality of greenmail in the all-important Delaware court system. However, other states, such as California, have not been as supportive of the practice of greenmail. The board of Disney was sued by shareholders who objected to the company's alleged greenmail payments to Steinberg. The court issued an injunction, and when the case was finally settled in 1989, both Steinberg's Reliance Corp. and Disney itself had to pay damages.

51. C. M. Nathan and M. Sobel, "Corporate Stock Repurchases in the Context of Unsolicited Takeover Bids," *Business Lawyer*, July 1980, 1545–1566.
52. *Good v. Texaco, Inc.*, No. 7501 (Del. Ch. February 19, 1985), *aff'd sub nom. Polk v. Good*, 507 A.2d 531 (Del. 1986).

Shareholder Wealth Effects of Greenmail

One of the leading studies on the effects of greenmail payments on stockholder wealth was conducted by Bradley and Wakeman. Their study considered 86 repurchases from insiders or individuals who were unaffiliated with the firms from 1974 to 1980. The Bradley and Wakeman study showed that privately negotiated purchases of a single block of stock from stockholders who were unaffiliated with the company reduced the wealth of nonparticipating stockholders.[53] Repurchases from insiders, however, were associated with increases in shareholder wealth. Bradley and Wakeman's research therefore supports the management entrenchment hypothesis. In revealing that stockholders lose money as a result of targeted share repurchases from outsiders, the study implies that these targeted share repurchases are not in the stockholder's best interest. It further implies that, by engaging in these repurchases, management is doing stockholders a disservice. Other research, such as a study by Dann and DeAngelo that is discussed further in the context of standstill agreements, also found negative shareholder wealth effects for nonparticipating shareholders when the company announced target share repurchases.[54]

In 1986, Wayne Mikkelson and Richard Ruback[55] analyzed 111 repurchases and found that only 5% occurred after the announcement of a takeover attempt. One-third of the repurchases took place after less overt attempts to change control such as formulation of preliminary plans for acquisitions or proxy fights. Almost two-thirds of the repurchases occurred without any overt indication of an impending takeover. It is interesting that the Mikkelson and Ruback study showed that the downward impact of the targeted share repurchases was more than offset by the stock price *increases* caused by purchasing the stock. Mikkelson and Ruback found a combined overall impact on stock prices of 17%! Their study supports the stockholder interests hypothesis in that it finds that the target share repurchases actually benefit incumbent stockholders. It therefore conflicts with the Bradley and Wakeman results and so has added more fuel to this debate. Mikkelson and Ruback's analysis also showed that the payment of greenmail was not associated with a lower probability of a change in control. They showed that the frequency of control changes following targeted share repurchases was three times higher than a control sample of firms that did not engage in such repurchases.

More recent research, using data derived from targeted share repurchases from 1974 to 1983, failed to provide support for the management entrenchment hypothesis.[56] Bhagat and Jefferis found that the performance of firms that pay greenmail was no worse than the performance of firms in a control group that did not engage in greenmail payments. This does not support the view that firms that engage in greenmail are poor performers who are seeking shelter from the normal market processes that might bring about a change

---

53. Michael Bradley and L. MacDonald Wakeman, "The Wealth Effects of Targeted Share Repurchases," *Journal of Financial Economics,* 11, April 1983, 301–328.

54. Larry Dann and Harry DeAngelo, "Standstill Agreements, Privately Negotiated Stock Repurchases, and the Market for Corporate Control," *Journal of Financial Economics,* 11(1–4), April 1983, 275–300.

55. Wayne Mikkelson and Richard Ruback, "Targeted Share Repurchases and Common Stock Returns," Working Paper No. 1707–86, Massachusetts Institute of Technology, Sloan School of Management, June 1986.

56. Sanjai Bhagat and Richard H. Jefferis, "The Causes and Consequences of Takeover Defense: Evidence from Greenmail," *Journal of Corporate Finance,* 1, 1994, 201–231.

in management. The differences between these results and that of Bradley and Wakeman are mainly attributable to different samples considered.

Ang and Tucker found that managers who pay greenmail are often let go by the corporations in the years that follow the repurchase.[57] They find that the likelihood of this occurring is directly related to the magnitude of the premium they pay to the selling shareholders.

Corporate Finance of Share Repurchases

It is important to note that share repurchases are a common occurrence and usually take place for reasons having nothing to do with takeovers or threats of M&As. Companies may use share repurchases as a way of providing a return to shareholders. In this sense they are an alternative to dividends. Companies with excess cash may choose to pay a higher dividend or issue a special one-time dividend. Another alternative would be to purchase shares at a price that will be attractive to its shareholders. Kahle examined over 700 repurchases during the first half of the 1990s.[58] She found that companies that had higher cash flow to asset ratios were more likely to do share repurchases as opposed to increasing their dividends. Interestingly, she noted that companies often do not repurchase all of the shares they announce they intend to. Grinstein and Michaely, in their study of 79,000 firm years over the period 1980–1996, noticed that firms that have done repurchases were more likely to do such repurchases in the future as opposed to dividend increases.[59]

Research studies have attempted to determine the primary reason why companies engage in share repurchases. One study by Bena, Nagar, Skinner, and Wong found a relationship between the dilutive effects of issuances of stock options by S&P 500 companies and the propensity of companies to repurchase shares.[60] Fenn and Liang, in their study of over 1,100 companies during the 1990s, found a similar relationship between repurchases and the issuance of employee stock options.[61]

From an accounting perspective, repurchased shares are recorded at their cost. They are reflected in the financial statements through a reduction of total stockholders equity. Treasury shares may be "retired," resulting in a subsequent reduction of the common stock and paid-in capital accounts, or they may be reissued. Any difference in the reissuance proceeds from the cost of those treasury shares results in an adjustment to paid-in capital

Decline of Greenmail

For a variety of reasons, greenmail has become uncommon. For one, the pace of hostile takeover activity has declined dramatically in the 1990s, thus reducing the need to

---

57. James S. Ang and Allen R. Tucker, "The Shareholder Effects of Corporate Greenmail," *Journal of Financial Research*, 11(4), 1988, 265–280.

58. Kathleen Kahle, "When a Buyback Isn't a Buyback: Open Market Repurchases and Employee Options," *Journal of Financial Economics*, 63(2), February 2002, 235–261.

59. Grinstein and Michaely, *Journal of Finance*, June 2005.

60. Daniel Bena, Venky Nagar, Douglas Skinner, and M.H. Wong, "Employee Stock Options, EPS Dilution and Share Repurchases," *University of Chicago Working Paper*, February 2002.

61. George Fenn and Nellie Liang, "Corporate Payout Policy and Managerial Stock Incentives," *Journal of Financial Economics*, 60(1), April 2001, 45–72.

engage in greenmail payments. In addition, federal tax laws imposed a 50% tax penalty on gains derived from greenmail payments. Under this law, greenmail is defined as consideration paid to anyone who makes or threatens to make a tender offer for a public corporation. In order for the payment to be considered greenmail, the offer must not be available to all shareholders. Furthermore, although various legal decisions have upheld the legality of greenmail, defendants in greenmail-inspired lawsuits have been sufficiently uncertain of the outcome to be willing to pay large settlements. For example, in 1989, Disney and Saul Steinberg were reported to have paid $45 million to settle a lawsuit with shareholders, prompted by an alleged greenmail payment in 1984 that included a $59.7 premium.[62] Donald Trump was reported to have paid $6.5 million to settle a lawsuit involving an alleged greenmail payment that included an $18 million premium. In addition, companies have adopted antigreenmail amendments to their corporate charters that limit the company's ability to pay greenmail. Research has showed that such amendments are usually adopted as part of a package of different antitakeover amendments.[63] While some research has found that antitakeover amendments may have negative shareholder wealth effects, Eckbo showed that in a subsample of a larger study he did on antitakeover amendments in general, the passage of antigreenmail amendments was associated with a positive market response.[64] The combined effects of the declining volume of hostile takeovers, tax penalties, antigreenmail charter amendments, and fear of litigation costs have caused greenmail to virtually disappear from the 1990s takeover scene.

Evolution of the Greenmailer

We really do not have greenmail like we had in the fourth merger wave, as the greenmailer has evolved into a new form of activist shareholder and is practicing his art somewhat differently. We now have large shareholders who assume major stock positions in corporations and, instead of seeking to be bought out at a premium lest they launch a hostile takeover, these activist investors are taking a different tack in the 2000s. Usually operating from a hedge fund they control, they assume a stock position like their greenmailer counterparts did in the 1980s, but they now use this position to pressure the company to bring about changes that will increase the value of their holdings. For example, Icahn, considered by many a greenmailer in the 1980s, became a hedge fund manager and pursued Time Warner Corporation in 2005 and 2006 to implement value-enhancing changes. He recommended various courses of action, such as share buybacks and corporate restructuring, to the media company. Nelson Peltz, a hostile takeover artist form the 1980s, did the same through his Trian fund and its holdings in Wendy's International. Kirk Kerkorian, through his Tracinda Corp., has amassed holdings in GM, which have varied within the 7 to 10% range in 2005 and 2006. Using the leverage of being GM's largest shareholder, Kerkorian has tried to pressure the auto giant to take bold

62. Bhagat and Jefferis, 1994, p. 229.
63. Sanjai Bhagat and Richard Jefferis, "Voting Power in the Proxy Process: The Case of Antitakeover Charter Amendments," *Journal of Financial Economics*, 30, 1991, 193–225.
64. Espen Eckbo, "Valuation Effects of Antigreenmail Prohibitions," *Journal of Financial and Quantitative Analysis*, 25, December 1990, 491–505.

actions to improve its market position and overall profitability.[65] One of the differences between the actions of these investors and their 1980s greenmailer counterparts is that the side effect of their actions may more likely result in gains for all shareholders in the companies they target. They generally are not seeking specific profits just for themselves but major changes in corporate policy that will inure to the benefit of themselves but also other shareholders. While it may not be largesse or a concern for the greater good that motivates these activist shareholders, the pressures they exert on corporations may serve to keep managers of their targets more focused on improving performance.

Standstill Agreements

A standstill agreement occurs when the target corporation reaches a contractual agreement with a potential acquirer whereby the would-be acquirer agrees not to increase its holdings in the target during a particular time period. This has been found to be legal under Delaware law.[66] Such an agreement takes place when the acquiring firm has established sufficient stockholdings to be able to pose a threat to mount a takeover battle for the target. Many standstill agreements are accompanied by the target's agreement to give the acquirer the right of first refusal in the event that the acquirer decides to sell the shares it currently owns. This agreement is designed to prevent these shares from falling into the hands of another bidder who would force the target to pay them standstill compensation or, even worse, to attempt to take over the target. Another version of a standstill agreement occurs when the acquirer agrees not to increase its holdings beyond a certain percentage. In other words, the target establishes a ceiling above which the acquirer may not increase its holdings. The acquiring firm agrees to these various restrictions for a fee. Like greenmail, standstill agreements provide compensation for an acquirer not to threaten to take control of the target. In fact, standstill agreements often accompany greenmail.

Shareholder Wealth Effects of Standstill Agreements

Standstill agreements usually accompany greenmail payments, so it is hard to separate their effects from each other when conducting research studies. Nonetheless, Dann and DeAngelo examined 81 standstill agreements between 1977 and 1980.[67] They found that standstill agreements and negotiated stock purchases at a premium were associated with negative average returns to nonparticipating stockholders. On average, stock prices fell 4%. The Dann and DeAngelo study supports the management entrenchment hypothesis and, as such, is inconsistent with the stockholder interests hypothesis with respect to nonparticipating stockholders.

The Mikkelson and Ruback study considered the impact of greenmail payments that were accompanied by standstill agreements.[68] They found that when negative returns were associated with targeted share repurchases, they were much greater when these

---

65. Joseph White, "Kerkorian Aide Presses for Speed in GM Overhaul," *Wall Street Journal*, January 11, 2006, p. 1.
66. *Alliance Gaming Corp. v. Bally Gaming International, Inc.*, 1995 W.L 523453 (Del. Ch. 1995).
67. Larry Y. Dann and Harry DeAngelo, "Standstill Agreements and Privately Negotiated Stock Repurchases and the Market for Corporate Control," *Journal of Financial Economics,* 11, April 1983, 275–300.
68. Wayne Mikkelson and Richard Ruback, "Targeted Share Repurchases and Common Stock Returns," Working Paper No. 1707–86, Massachusetts Institute of Technology, Sloan School of Management, June 1986.

purchases were accompanied by standstill agreements. We may therefore conclude that these two antitakeover devices often, but certainly not always, tend to have a complementary negative impact on stock prices that is greater than the negative effect we would expect if just one of them were implemented.

CASE STUDY

GILLETTE—STANDSTILL AGREEMENTS AND GREENMAIL

In 1986, Gillette was being pursued by Ronald Perelman, who had previously taken over the Revlon Corporation. When it appeared that he was about to make a tender offer for Gillette, Gillette responded by paying Revlon $558 million in return for Revlon agreeing not to make a $65 tender offer to stockholders. One unique aspect of this deal was that Gillette even paid greenmail to the investment bank that represented Revlon. Gillette paid Drexel Burnham Lambert $1.75 million in return for an agreement not to be involved in an acquisition or attempted acquisition of Gillette for a period of three years. This is testimony to the activist role that investment banks played in the takeovers of the 1980s. Gillette was worried that, having seen Gillette's vulnerability, Drexel Burnham Lambert would approach another potential suitor.

The payment of greenmail usually is only a temporary fix, as is confirmed by the fact that another bidder, Coniston Partners, initiated an attempt to take control of Gillette by means of a proxy fight. During the legal proceedings that followed the acerbic proxy fight between Gillette and Coniston, it was revealed that Gillette had entered into standstill agreements with ten different companies:[a] Colgate Palmolive, Ralston Purina, Anheuser-Busch, PepsiCo, Metromedia, Citicorp Industrial Corporation, Salomon Brothers (acting on its own behalf), Kidder, Peabody, Kohlberg Kravis & Roberts, and Forstmann Little.

Gillette eventually reached a settlement with Coniston in which Coniston conceded to a standstill agreement in return for Gillette's agreement to buy back shares from Coniston and other shareholders. A total of 16 million shares were purchased at a price that was above the market price at that time of $45.[b] The Gillette case study is an example of some of the benefits of raiders that Holderness and Sheehan reported.[c] Gillette had been the target of several raiders, including Revlon's CEO, Ronald Perelman. He had agreed to a standstill agreement with Gillette after an aborted takeover attempt in November 1986. Although Perelman had a standstill agreement with Gillette, he renewed his interest in acquiring the firm in late 1987, when it appeared that other bidders were showing interest in the razor manufacturer.

The constant pressure that Gillette was under appeared to have beneficial effects. Gillette responded to the various takeover threats by cutting costs and thinning out its workforce. Gillette also enacted various restructuring measures, which included reducing and eliminating weak operations within the firm.[d] By 1990, the firm had laid off a total of 2,400 workers and had sold several weak businesses. Gillette's common stock responded to the increased efficiencies by showing a 50% total return in 1989, up from the 24% average annual return the firm's stock yielded during the prior ten years.[e] At least in the case of Gillette, the Holderness and Sheehan hypothesis on the beneficial

[a]"Trial Discusses Identity of 10 Firms Gillette Company Contacted as White Knights," *Wall Street Journal,* June 27, 1988, p. 16.

[b]Alison Leigh Cowan, "Gillette and Coniston Drop Suit," *New York Times,* August 2, 1988, p. D1.

[c]Clifford Holderness and Dennis Sheehan, "Raiders or Saviors? The Evidence of Six Controversial Raiders," *Journal of Financial Economics,* 14(4), December 1985, 555–581.

[d]"How Ron Perelman Scared Gillette into Shape," *Business Week,* October 12, 1987, p. 40.

[e]Anthony Ramirez, "A Radical New Style for Stodgy Old Gillette," *New York Times,* February 25, 1990, p. 5.

effects of raiders seems to be borne out. By 2004, Gillette had annual sales of $10.5 billion and net income of $1.7 billion derived from various leading products such as its line of shavers and the market leader Duracell battery. An improved Gillette was acquired by Procter & Gamble in 2005.

White Knights

When a corporation is the target of an unwanted bid or the threat of a bid from a potential acquirer, it may seek the aid of a *white knight*—that is, another company that would be a more acceptable suitor for the target. The white knight will then make an offer to buy all or part of the target company on more favorable terms than those of the original bidder. These favorable terms may be a higher price, but management may also look for a white knight that will promise not to disassemble the target or lay off management or other employees. It is sometimes difficult to find a willing bidder who will agree to such restrictive terms. The target often has to bargain for the best deal possible to stay out of the first bidder's hands. The incumbent managers of the target maintain control by reaching an agreement with the white knight to allow them to retain their current positions. They may also do so by selling the white knight certain assets and keeping control of the remainder of the target. A target company may find a white knight through its own industry contacts or through the assistance of an investment banker who will survey potential suitors. The potential white knight might request favorable terms or other consideration as an inducement to enter the fray. However, if this consideration is given only to the white knight and not to the hostile bidder, and if it is so significant an advantage that it could cause the hostile bidder to withdraw, the deal with the white knight may be a violation of the target's Revlon duties.

Takeover Tactics and Shareholder Concentration: United States Compared with Europe

In the United States the majority of equity of U.S. companies is held by institutional investors, although individuals do own a significant number of total shares outstanding. In Britain the majority of equity is held by institutions. While institutions as a whole own the majority of equity in general, particular institutions tend not to own large percentages of specific companies. This is quite different from continental Europe, where even public companies have high concentrations of shares in the hands of specific groups or individuals. Franks and Mayer have noted that 80% of the largest public companies in Germany and France have a single shareholder who owns at least 25%.[69] The shareholder concentration is usually in the hands of a single individual or family or another corporation. More than half of the companies they studied have a single largest shareholder. Often this corporate shareholding is in the form of pyramids, where one company owns shares in another company, which in turn owns shareholders in another, and so on. In addition, many large companies in continental Europe are private and are not traded on public markets. Franks and Mayer have also noted that in Austria, Belgium, Germany, and Italy

---

69. J. Franks and C. Mayer, "Ownership and Control," in H. Siebert, ed., *Trends in Business Organization: Do Participation and Cooperation Increase Competitiveness?* (Coronet Books, 1995).

a single shareholder, individual or group of investors, controls more than 50% of voting rights. In 50% of Dutch, Spanish, and Swedish companies, more than 43.5%, 34.5%, and 34.9%, respectively, of votes are controlled by a single shareholder. Fifty-seven percent of the 250 largest companies that trade on the Paris exchange have been reported to be family controlled in the late 1990s.[70] In contrast, the median blockholder in the United Kingdom controls only 9.9% of votes, and in the United States the median size of block-holding of companies quoted on NASDAQ and the New York Stock Exchange is just above the disclosure level of 5% (8.5% and 5.4%). Their analysis also reviewed the holdings of the second and third largest shareholders. They concluded that share ownership is much more concentrated in continental Europe than it is in Britain and the United States.

The relevance of this to takeovers is that public appeals to shareholders, appeals that are much more common in the United States in the form of tender offers, are less successful in continental Europe due to the dominating presence of specific major shareholders. It is difficult to implement a hostile takeover when large blocks may be in the hands of controlling shareholders unless they want to sell. The concentration of shares is an additional problem that a hostile bidder may face in Europe that usually would not be as much a factor in the United States.

CASE STUDY

TYCO AS WHITE KNIGHT FOR AMP

In 1998, Allied Signal Corp. launched a $10 billion hostile takeover bid for AMP, Inc. AMP, Inc. was an electronic connector maker with just under $6 billion in revenues and $500 million in net income. The Harrisburg, PA–based company was a diversified firm with approximately half of its revenues coming from outside the United States—from both Europe and Asia. AMP, Inc. tried to remain independent, but when this did not look like it was going to be successful, the company decided to seek a white knight. AMP, Inc.'s decision was partially forced by a favorable court ruling Allied Signal received giving it the green light to launch a proxy fight to gain control of AMP's board of directors.

AMP, Inc. agreed to sell to Tyco, the industrial conglomerate we discussed in Chapter 4 that makes its headquarters in Hamilton, Bermuda. At the time of the AMP deal, Tyco had sales in excess of $12 billion and net income in excess of $1 billion. The deal was a stock-for-stock swap that was valued at $11.3 billion. This transaction basically doubled the size of Tyco, which had generated rapid growth in the 1990s, mainly through acquisitions. Tyco's stock, which traded at a higher multiple than that of many industrial companies (P/E of 32), was attractive at that time to AMP, which was vulnerable to a takeover due to declines in its revenues and net income, which caused its stock price to weaken. This deal was one of several that Tyco did as part of the growth through acquisitions strategy. This strategy was reversed in 2006 as the company finally responded to pressures from the market to break up this diversified conglomerate.

Shareholder Wealth Effects of White Knight Bids

Research results show that white knight bids are often not in the best interests of bidding firm shareholders. One study of 100 white knights over a 10-year period between 1978

---

70. Peter Gumbel, "Putting on Heirs: A New Generation is Leading Europe's Biggest Family Firms Toward New Profits—and Risks," *Time*, March 24, 2003.

and 1987 showed that white knight shareholders incurred losses in shareholder wealth.[71] These results were confirmed in another study of 50 white knights covering the period from 1974 to 1984. The explanation for these negative shareholder wealth effects is that such bids are not part of a planned strategic acquisition and do not yield net benefits for the acquiring firm's shareholders. In addition, the white knights are bidders in a contested auction environment where prices tend to be higher than nonauction acquisitions. Research has shown that competition has a negative effect on shareholder wealth of bidding firms.[72] This negative effect is even greater for subsequent bidders.

CASE STUDY

T. BOONE PICKENS AND MESA PETROLEUM VERSUS CITIES SERVICE—MULTIPLE WHITE KNIGHTS

Just as the fourth merger wave was about to take hold, T. Boone Pickens was involved in a few classic takeover battles. One such contest was Pickens's bid for the Cities Service Oil Company. In June 1982, Pickens, the CEO of Mesa Petroleum, made a bid for the Cities Service Oil Company. Although not part of the Seven Sisters, the seven largest oil companies in the United States at that time, Cities Service was approximately 20 times as large as Mesa Petroleum. Mesa had been carrying an investment in Cities Service since 1979 and had chosen this time to make a bid for the larger oil company. Pickens thought that Cities Service possessed valuable assets but was badly managed. Cities Service is a case study of what was wrong with Big Oil's management. Based in Tulsa, Oklahoma, Cities Service was a large company. By 1982, it ranked thirty-eighth in the Fortune 500 companies and was the nineteenth largest oil company in the country. It was unusually sluggish, even by the less-demanding standards of the oil industry, and had been for 50 years. Its refineries and chemical plants were losers, and although it had 307 million barrels of oil and 3.1 trillion cubic feet of gas reserves, it had been depleting its gas reserves for at least ten years. Although it had leases on 10 million acres, it was finding practically no new oil and gas. Cities Service's problems were hidden by its cash flow, which continued in tandem with the Organization of Petroleum Exporting Countries (OPEC) price increases. The stock, however, reflecting management's record, sold at approximately a third of the value of its underlying assets. The management did not understand the problem or did not care; either condition is terminal.[a]

Mesa Petroleum made a $50-per-share bid for Cities Service. Cities Service responded with a Pac-Man defense in which it made a $17-per-share bid for the smaller Mesa Petroleum. The Cities Service offer was not a serious one because Mesa's stock had been trading at $16.75 before the Cities offer, which therefore did not contain a premium. Cities Service asked Gulf Oil to be its white knight. Pickens, a critic of the major oil companies, was equally critical of Gulf Oil. Gulf made a $63-per-share bid for Cities Service. Cities saw Gulf as a similar type of oil company and one that would be much friendlier to Cities management than Mesa. At that time Gulf was the third largest oil company in the United States. Cities accepted Gulf's bid. Mesa ended up selling its shares back to Cities for $55 per share, which resulted in an $11-per-share profit for Mesa, or a

[a]T. Boone Pickens, *Boone* (Boston: Houghton Mifflin, 1987), p. 150.

---

71. Ajeyo Banerjee and James E. Owers, "Wealth Reduction in White Knight Bids," *Financial Management*, 21(3), Autumn 1992, 48–57.
72. Michael Bradley and L. MacDonald Wakeman, "The Wealth Effects of Targeted Share Repurchases," *Journal of Financial Economics*, 11, April 1983, 301–328.

total of $40 million. However, Gulf had second thoughts about the Cities acquisition: Gulf would have taken on a significant amount of debt if it had gone through with the merger. In addition, Gulf was concerned that the Federal Trade Commission might challenge the merger on antitrust grounds. Much to Cities Service's surprise and chagrin, Gulf dropped its offer for Cities. Cities Service stock dropped to $30 a share following the announcement of Gulf's pullout. Cities Service management was highly critical of Gulf and stated that its action was reprehensible. Cities Service then had to look for another white knight. Occidental Petroleum, led by the well-known Armand Hammer, made an initial offer of $50 per share in cash for the first 49% of Cities stock and securities of somewhat uncertain value for the remaining shares. Cities rejected this bid as inadequate, and Occidental upped its offer to $55 in cash for the front end and better quality securities for the back end. Cities Service then agreed to sell out to its second white knight.

White Squire Defense

The white squire defense is similar to the white knight defense. In the white squire defense, however, the target company seeks to implement a strategy that will preserve the target company's independence. A *white squire* is a firm that consents to purchase a large block of the target company's stock. The stock selected often is convertible preferred stock. The convertible preferred shares may be already approved through a blank check preferred stock amendment of the company's charter. The target may need to receive the approval of shareholders even if the shares are blank check preferred stock. The New York Stock Exchange, for example, requires that shareholder approval be received if such shares are issued to officers or directors or if the number issued equals 20% of the company's shares outstanding. The white squire is typically not interested in acquiring control of the target. From the target's viewpoint, the appeal is that a large amount of the voting stock in the target will be placed in the hands of a company or investor who will not sell out to a hostile bidder. The deal may be structured so that the shares given to the white squire may not be tendered to the hostile bidder. Sometimes, however, a potential white squire is given incentives to go ahead with the transaction such as a seat on the board. Other possible incentives could be a favorable price on the shares or a promise of generous dividends. In an effort to insure that the white squire does not become hostile, the white squire may have to agree in advance to vote with the target and not against it.

A classic example of a white squire defense was Carter Hawley Hale's (CHH's) sale of convertible preferred stock to the General Cinema Corporation in 1984. The stock sold to General Cinema had voting power equal to 22% of (CHH's) outstanding votes. (CHH's) believed this was necessary to prevent a takeover by the Limited Corporation in 1984. (CHH's) accompanied this white squire defense with a stock repurchase program that increased the voting power of General Cinema's stock to 33% of (CHH's) voting shares.

CASE STUDY

PORSCHE AG ACQUIRERS WHITE SQUIRE STAKE IN VOLKSWAGEN AG

In 2005, Porsche acquired shares in Volkswagen, which is Europe's largest automaker. As of October 2005, the Stuttgart, Germany–based Porsche had just under 19% of Volkswagen's stock.

This made Porsche the largest shareholder in Volkswagen. Volkswagen of Lower Saxony had made strategic errors by trying to market luxury brands under the Volkswagen brand, which had normally been associated with more modest-priced, mass-market autos. This failed strategy was tied to losses in North America. In November 2005, Volkswagen finally admitted this error and decided to stop marketing the Phaeton, its attempt at a luxury car, in the U.S. market.

Germany has a law that caps voting rights of shareholders at the 20% voting level. This has been controversial within the European Union, which had been pressuring Germany to overturn the law. In 2005, Volkswagen's poor performance had attracted private equity firms to accumulate shares in the vulnerable company. Part of the reason why Porsche came to Volkswagen's aid was a desire to keep Volkswagen a German company. This is not an unusual occurrence in the very protectionist-minded Germany.

Porsche was a likely candidate to become a white knight as Ferdinand Porsche designed the first Volkswagen bug in the 1930s. His grandson, Ferdinand Piech, serves on Volkswagen's board. In addition to family ties, Volkswagen is a parts supplier for Porsche and the two companies share plants that make SUVs. This purchase of the Volkswagen shares, however, raises corporate governance issues as Porsche had an excellent return on equity while Volkswagen's return was poor. It was hard to justify the investment from Porsche's shareholders' point of view.

We would be remiss if we did not note that, in spite of the problems Volkswagen encountered trying to market upscale cars when it was known as a mid-market auto company, Volkswagen announced in 2005 that it would begin marketing the Bugatti Veyron (just after announcing it was withdrawing the Phaeton from the U.S. market). The two-seated Veyron boasts a 1,000 horsepower engine and a $1 million price tag. The car went through a painful seven-year development process and Volkswagen readily admits it will not directly make money.[a] It seems that one of the prices that is paid for having had Mr. Piech as CEO, with his Porsche roots, is failed attempts to turn a successful mid-market car manufacturer into a high-end automaker.

[a]Stephen Power, "Million-Dollar Baby: World's Most Expensive Car," *Wall Street Journal*, December 14, 2005, D1.

Merger Agreement Provisions

Targets may seek to enter into agreements with friendly parties, such as white knights, that provide these parties with certain benefits that give them an incentive to participate in the merger process. These incentives, which may come in the form of lockup options, topping fees, or bustup fees, may work to the target's benefit by making a takeover by a hostile bidder more difficult and expensive.

Lockup Transactions

A lockup transaction is similar to a white squire defense. In the case of lockups, the target is selling assets to another party instead of stock. Sometimes the term *lockup transaction* is also used more generally to refer to the sale of assets as well as the sale of stock to a friendly third party. In a lockup transaction, the target company sells assets to a third party and thus tries to make the target less attractive to the bidder. The target often sells those assets it judges the acquirer wants most. This may also come in the form of *lockup options,* which are options to buy certain assets or stock in the event of a change in control. These options may be written so that they become effective even if a bidder acquires less than 51% of the target.

In some instances, lockup options have been held to be invalid. The court's position has been that, in limiting the desirability of the target to the original bidder, lockup options may effectively preempt the bargaining process that might result during the 20-day waiting period for tender offers required by the Williams Act. An example of such an invalid option was Marathon Oil's option that it gave to U.S. Steel in 1981 to buy its Yates Oil Field at a fixed price in an attempt to avoid a takeover by Mobil Oil Corporation. This option would be exercisable in the event that Marathon was taken over. It would have an important impact on future bidding contests because it was one of Marathon's most valued assets. The court invalidated this option on the grounds that it violated the spirit of the Williams Act. An appeals court later affirmed this ruling. U.S. Steel ended up acquiring Marathon Oil when Mobil's bid was stopped on antitrust grounds.

An example of the legal viability of lockup options came in subsequent takeover battles involving lockup options that were partially fought in the same Delaware Chancery Court. In the 1988 takeover contest between J. P. Stevens and West Point–Pepperell, both textile manufacturers, the court ruled that the financial enticements that J. P. Stevens offered another bidder, Odyssey Partners, were legal. The enticements included $17 million toward Odyssey's expenses and an additional $8 million if the bidding prices rose significantly. These enticements may be considered small compared with the $1.2 billion offer for J. P. Stevens. The key to the court's thinking is whether the lockup option or the financial incentives given to one bidder but not the other help facilitate the bidding process or limit it. The belief is that the bidding process will bring about higher bids and thereby maximize stockholder wealth. Chancellor William T. Allen of the Delaware Chancery Court wrote in his opinion, "The Board may tilt the playing field if, but only if, it is in the stockholders' interest to do so."[73]

In the fifth merge wave, the Delaware Supreme Court invalidated Viacom's lockup option to purchase 24 million shares of Paramount Communications treasury stock at a negotiated, preacquisition price if QVC acquired Paramount.[74] The option would have enabled Viacom to sell the shares to QVC, thereby increasing QVC's price.

CASE STUDY

REVLON VERSUS PANTRY PRIDE

In 1985, Ronald Perelman, CEO of Pantry Pride, made an offer for Revlon, Inc. MacAndrews and Forbes Holdings, the parent company of Pantry Pride, had built a diversified company with acquisitions between 1978 and 1984 that included a jewelry company, a cigar company, a candy manufacturer, and Pantry Pride—the supermarket chain. Charles Revson had built Revlon into one of the nation's largest cosmetics companies. Revson's successor, Michael Bergerac, a former head of the conglomerate ITT and protégé of Harold Geneen, expanded Revlon considerably through large acquisitions in the health care field. In terms of its revenues, Bergerac's Revlon was more of a health care company than a cosmetics company. In terms of assets, Revlon was approximately five times the size of Pantry Pride.

---

73. "When Targets Tilt Playing Fields," *New York Times*, April 21, 1988, p. D2.
74. *Paramount Communications, Inc. v. QVC Network, Inc.* 637 A.2d. (Del. 1994).

Revlon's acquisition strategy had not fared well for Bergerac, and Revlon's earnings had been declining. Perelman decided to make a bid for Revlon, his goal being to sell off the health care components and keep the well-known cosmetics business. Pantry Pride made a cash tender of $53 a share. It financed its offer for the significantly larger Revlon by borrowing $2.1 billion. Revlon's board of directors had approved a leveraged buyout (LBO) plan by Forstmann Little at $56 cash per share. When Pantry Pride increased its offer to $56.25, Revlon was able to get Forstmann Little to increase its offer to $57.25 by giving Forstmann Little a lockup option to purchase two Revlon divisions for $525 million. This was reported by Revlon's investment banker to be $75 million below these divisions' actual value.[a] This option would be activated if a bidder acquired 40% of Revlon's shares.

Delaware's Chancery Court ruled that in agreeing to this lockup agreement, the board of directors had breached its fiduciary responsibility. The court believed that this option effectively ended the bidding process and gave an unfair advantage to Forstmann Little's LBO. However, in its ruling, the court did not declare lockup options illegal. It stated that the options may play a constructive role in the bargaining process and thus increase bids and shareholder wealth.

[a]Dennis Block, Nancy Barton, and Stephen Radin, *Business Judgment Rule* (Englewood Cliffs, NJ: Prentice-Hall, 1988), p. 101.

The prevailing wisdom is that lockup options are used by management to entrench themselves. This surely is the case in some instances. However, in a study of 2,067 deals over the period from 1988 to 1995, of which 8% had lockup options, Birch found that announcement returns for targets were higher when lockup options were present, whereas acquirer returns were lower.[75] This implies that, on average, target shareholders may benefit from such arrangements.

Although the J. P. Stevens and West Point–Pepperell decision outlined the legally legitimate uses of lockup agreements, a subsequent decision in the Delaware Supreme Court further underscored the illegitimate uses of these agreements. The court ruled that a lockup agreement between Macmillan Inc. and Kohlberg Kravis & Roberts (KKR), that allowed KKR to buy certain valuable Macmillan assets even if the agreement between KKR and Macmillan fell through, was merely designed to end the auction process and to preempt bidding, which would maximize the value of stockholder wealth. The court stated that a lockup could be used only if it maximized stockholder wealth. In this case, the lockup was used to drive away an unwanted suitor, Maxwell Communications Corporation. The court's position remains that a lockup may be used only to promote, not inhibit, the auction process.[76]

Termination, Breakup, and Topping Fees

Termination or breakup fees as well as topping fees can occur when a target agrees to compensate a bidder if the target company is taken over by a company other than the initial bidder. These fees may come in the form of compensation for some of the bidder's

75. Timothy R. Birch, "Locking Out Rival Bidders: The Use of Lockup Options in Corporate Mergers," *Journal of Financial Economics*, 60(1), April 2001, 103–141.
76. "Delaware High Court Rules a Company Can't Use 'Lockup' Just to Stop a Suitor," *Wall Street Journal*, May 8, 1989.

costs incurred in the bidding process. It is sometimes used to encourage a bidder who may be reluctant to engage in a costly bidding process with an uncertain outcome. These fees are somewhat of a disincentive for a raider because they are liabilities of the target and, therefore, are a cost that will have to be assumed if its takeover is successful. That is why we discuss them in this chapter, although they really should not be considered antitakeover defenses in the sense of other formidable defenses such as poison pills.

The largest breakup fee was the payment of approximately $1.8 billion that American Home Products (now called Wyeth Corp.) received from Pfizer Corp. in 2000 for the cancellation of its 1999 merger agreement with Warner-Lambert. Pfizer prevailed in a bidding contest for Warner-Lambert, but American Home Products received these monies as an agreed-upon "consolation prize." While this is a substantial sum, the acquisition of Warner-Lambert, which Pfizer followed with the acquisition of Pharmacia, placed Pfizer firmly in the lead position in the worldwide pharmaceutical industry. The acquisition also gave Pfizer rights to the anticholesterol drug, Lipitor, which became the largest selling drug in the world with 2004 sales of approximately $13 billion. This sales level was close to the total 2004 sales level of all of Wyeth. Pfizer was also able to receive a favorable tax treatment for this payment. For example, Guidant paid J&J a $622 million termination fee when it chose not to merge with J&J and instead combine with Boston Scientific.

Termination fees have become quite common. In the fourth merger wave termination fees were relatively uncommon. However, between 1997 and 1999, two-thirds of the M&A bids featured termination fee clauses.[77] One view of these fees is that they deter bids and therefore help entrench managers. Another view is that they give the target leverage that allows it to extract higher bids from acquirers. Micah Officer analyzed a sample of 2,511 merger bids and tender offers over the period 1988 to 2000. He found an average termination fee of just $35.24 million although the median was just $8 million.[78] The mean termination fee was 5.87% of the equity being acquired. He found an average increased premium of 4% when the bids featured termination fees. The finding of higher premiums was supported by a study by Bates and Lemmon, who analyzed a sample 3,307 deals and found that takeover premiums for firms with termination fees was 3.1% higher.[79] They also found that bids with termination fee clauses had a higher probability of completion.

No-Shop Provisions

No-shop provisions are agreements that may be part of an overall acquisition agreement or letter of intent in which the seller agrees not to solicit or enter into negotiations to sell to other buyers. Targets may try to reach such an agreement with a white knight and use the existence of the no-shop provision as the reason they cannot negotiate with a hostile bidder.

This was done by Paramount Communications when it was trying to avoid a hostile takeover by QVC. As in this case, the courts tend to not look kindly on these provisions

---

77. Micah S. Officer, "Termination Fees in Mergers and Acquisitions," *Journal of Financial Economics*, 69(3), September 2003, 431–468.
78. Officer, 2003, 431–468.
79. Thomas W. Bates and Mitchell L. Lemmon, "Breaking Up Is Hard to Do? An Analysis of Termination Fee Provisions and Merger Outcomes," *Journal of Financial Economics*, 69(3), 469–504.

because they often have the effect of inhibiting the auction process. Although the court was highly critical of the no-shop provision in the Paramount–QVC takeover contest, it is not illegal under Delaware law.

Capital Structure Changes

A target corporation may initiate various changes in its capital structure in an attempt to ward off a hostile bidder. These defensive capital structure changes are used in four main ways:

1. Recapitalize.
2. Assume more debt:
    a. Bonds
    b. Bank loan
3. Issue more shares:
    a. General issue
    b. White squire
    c. Employee stock option plan (ESOP)
4. Buy back shares:
    a. Self-tender
    b. Open market purchases
    c. Targeted share repurchases

Recapitalize

In the late 1980s, recapitalization became a more popular, albeit drastic, antitakeover defense. After a recapitalization, the corporation is in dramatically different financial condition than it was before it. A recapitalization plan often involves paying a superdividend to stockholders, which is usually financed through assumption of considerable debt. For this reason, these plans are sometimes known as *leveraged recapitalizations.* When a company is recapitalized, it substitutes most of its equity for debt while paying stockholders a large dividend. In addition to the stock dividend, stockholders may receive a stock certificate called a *stub,* which represents their new share of ownership in the company.

In a recapitalization, total financial leverage usually rises dramatically. Studies have shown that, on average, total debt to total capitalization ratios increase from 20% to 70%.[80]

Recapitalization as an antitakeover defense was pioneered in 1985 by the Multimedia Corporation with the assistance of the investment bank of Goldman Sachs. Multimedia, a Greenville, SC, broadcasting company, initiated a recapitalization plan after the original founding family members received unsolicited bids for the company in response to their LBO offer. In addition to a cash payout, Multimedia stockholders saw the value of their stub increase from an original value of $8.31 to $52.25 within two

---

80. Atul Gupta and Leonard Rosenthal, "Ownership Structure, Leverage and Firm Value: The Case of Leveraged Recapitalizations, *Financial Management*, 20, Autumn 1991, 69–83; and Punett Handa and A. R. Radhakrishnan, "An Empirical Investigation of Leveraged Recapitalizations With Case Payout as a Takeover Defense," *Financial Management*, 20, Autumn 1991, 38–68.

years.[81] The success of the Multimedia deal led to several other recapitalizations, such as FMC Corp, Colt Industries, and Owens Corning, several of which were completed in the following two years.

One attraction of a recapitalization plan is that it allows a corporation to act as its own white knight. Many companies in similar situations would either seek an outside entity to serve as a white knight or attempt an LBO. The recapitalization plan is an alternative to both. In addition, the large increase in the company's debt, as reflected in the examples shown in Table 5.1, makes the firm less attractive to subsequent bidders. A recapitalization may defeat a hostile bid because stockholders receive a value for their shares that usually is significantly in excess of historical stock prices. This amount is designed to be superior to the offer from the hostile bidder.

Another feature of recapitalization that is most attractive to the target company's management is that it may give management a greater voting control in the target following the recapitalization. The target company may issue several shares of common stock to an ESOP.[82] It may also create other security options that may give management enhanced

Company		Before Recapitalization	After Recapitalization
Multimedia	Long-term debt	73.2	877.7
	New worth	248.7	d576.4
	Book values/share	14.9	d52.4
FMC Corporation	Long-term debt	303.2	1787.3
	Net worth	1123.1	d506.6
	Book value/share	7.54	d11.25
Colt Industries	Long-term debt	342.4	1643.1
	Net worth	414.3	d1078.0
	Book value/share	2.55	d36.91
Owens-Corning	Long-term debt	543.0	1645.2
	Net worth	944.7	d1025.0
	Book value/share	31.7	d25.94
Holiday Corporation	Long-term debt	992.5	2500.0
	Net worth	638.7	d850.0
	Book value/share	27.1	d31.2
Harcourt Brace Jovanovich	Long-term debt	790.3	2550.0
	Net worth	531.5	d1050.0
	Book value/share	13.5	d21.0

TABLE 5.1   COMPARATIVE EFFECTS OF RECAPITALIZATION

Source: Robert Kleinman, "The Shareholder Gain from Leveraged Cash Outs: Preliminary Evidence," *Journal of Applied Corporate Finance*, 1(1), Spring 1988, 50.

---

81. "The New Way to Halt Raiders," *New York Times*, May 29, 1988, p. D4.
82. Ralph C. Ferrara, Meredith M. Brown, and John Hall, *Takeovers: Attack and Survival* (Salem, NC: Butterworth, 1987), p. 425.

voting power. Other stockholders, however, will receive only one share in the recapitalized company (the stub) as well as whatever combination of debt and cash has been offered. The company is required to make sure that all nonmanagement stockholders receive at least a comparable monetary value for their common stockholdings as did management. After the recapitalization the concentration of shares in the hands of insiders tends to significantly increase.

Many recapitalizations may require stockholder approval before they can be implemented, depending on the prevailing state laws and the corporation's own charter. When presenting a recapitalization plan to stockholders, corporations often seek approval for a variety of other antitakeover measures that are proposed as part of a joint antitakeover plan. Some of the other measures discussed previously, such as fair price provisions or staggered boards, might be included here.

In addition to possible restrictions in the company charter and state laws, companies may be limited from using the recapitalization defense by restrictive covenants in prior debt agreements. The corporation enters into these legal agreements when it borrows from a bank or from investors through the issuance of corporate bonds. Such agreements place limitations on the firm's future options so as to provide greater assurance for the lenders that the debt will be repaid. The language of these restrictive covenants might prevent the company from taking on additional debt, which might increase the probability that the company could be forced into receivership.

Comparison between Recapitalization Plans and LBOs

There are a number of similarities between LBOs and recapitalization plans. Some are:

- *Tax advantages of debt.* In a recapitalization plan, the firm assumes a considerable amount of debt and thereby substitutes tax-deductible interest payments for taxable dividend payments. Dividend payments are often suspended following the payout of a larger initial dividend. The effect of an LBO is similar. Firms going private in an LBO assume considerable debt to finance the LBO. This has the effect of sheltering operating income for the time period in which the debt is being paid.
- *Concentration of ownership in management's hands.* In an LBO, management usually receives a percentage of ownership as part of the LBO process. When the debt is repaid, this ownership position may become quite valuable, even after warrants held by debtholders are exercised. In a recapitalization plan, management often receives new shares instead of the cash payout that stockholders receive. Managers of firms involved in defensive recapitalization prefer this arrangement because the concentration of ownership in their hands helps prevent a takeover.

Kleinman points out that in view of the similarities between LBOs and recapitalizations, it is not surprising that good LBO and recapitalization candidates have much in common, such as:

- A stable earnings stream that can be used to service debt.
- Low pre-LBO or pre-recapitalization plan debt levels. A low level of debt on the balance sheet gives the firm greater ability to assume more debt.
- A strong market position.

- A product line that is not vulnerable to a high risk of obsolescence.
- A business that does not need high levels of research and development or capital expenditures.
- The high debt service may not allow for such investments.
- A high borrowing capacity as reflected by the collateral value of the firm's assets.
- Assets and/or divisions that can be readily sold to help pay the debt.
- Experienced management with a proven track record, an important characteristic because the added pressure of the high debt service does not leave a high margin for error.[83]

Use of Recapitalization Plans Protected by Poison Pills

The recapitalization plan is the company's own offer, which is presented to stockholders as an alternative to a hostile raider's offer. Before 1988, companies used poison pills to try to counteract the bidder's tender offer while presenting their own unencumbered recapitalization plan. In November 1988, a Delaware Chancery Court struck down the combined use of these defenses.[84] In a case involving a challenge to the use by Interco of a recapitalization plan and a poison pill in opposition to a hostile bid from the Rales Brothers, the court ruled that both offers should be presented on an equal footing to shareholders as opposed to having the poison pill directed at the tender offer while not affecting the company's own recapitalization plan offer.

CASE STUDY

SANTA FE VERSUS HENLEY

In 1989, the Santa Fe Corporation used what was at that time the largest recapitalization plan ever implemented as a defensive tactic to prevent a takeover by the Henley Group. Henley was a conglomeration of assorted companies spun off from the Allied Signal merger. They were managed by Michael Dingman, who prided himself in bringing poorly performing companies to profitability. The term *Dingman's dogs* was sometimes used to describe these poor performers.[a] In February 1988, following the Henley Group's extended attempt to take over Santa Fe, as well as overtures from other would-be bidders such as Olympia and York, Santa Fe announced a major recapitalization plan. The plan featured the payout of a $4.7 billion dividend to stockholders, which was to be financed through the selloff of assets and the assumption of considerable debt. Santa Fe agreed to pay a $25 dividend to stockholders combined with a $5 subordinated debenture for each of its 156.5 million shares. The cash portion of this payout came to $4 billion. The debentures had a face value of $783 million and a 16% coupon rate. The repayment of the debentures was structured so that no payments would be made for five years. This requirement was designed to reduce the demands on Santa Fe's already stretched cash flows.

[a]Kathleen Deveney, Stewart Toy, Edith Terry, and Tom Ichniowski, "Santa Fe Keeps Throwing the Raiders Off Track," *Business Week*, February 15, 1988, p. 28.

---

83. Robert Kleinman, "The Shareholder Gains from Leveraged Cash Outs," *Journal of Applied Corporate Finance*, 1(1), Spring 1998, 47–48.
84. "Interco Defense Against Rales Is Struck Down," *Wall Street Journal*, November 2, 1988, p. 83.

Santa Fe raised approximately $2.25 billion from assets sales. These included the Southern Pacific Railroad, pipelines, timberlands, and other real estate, as well as other subsidiaries. In addition, Santa Fe borrowed $1.9 billion. Santa Fe's financial leverage increased dramatically. The debt–total capital ratio rose from 26% to 87% following the recapitalization plan. This higher financial leverage represents a greater degree of risk for the corporation.

Shareholder Wealth Effects of Recapitalization Plans

The shareholder wealth effects of recapitalization plans differ depending on the reason for the recapitalization. If it is a recapitalization that is done for reasons other than to defend against a takeover, such as to change the company's capital structure to increase stockholder return, the shareholder wealth effects tend to be positive. For example, Handa and Ranhakrishnan found that for the 42 recapitalizations that they studied, shareholder returns were 23% for the period between 60 and 15 days prior to the event with some other days of positive returns before day 0 for the group of firms in their sample that were actual takeover targets.[85] For firms that were not actual takeover targets there was no runup in prices and some days of negative returns before the recapitalization. Gupta and Rosenthal found similar positive returns for the period leading up to the announcement of the recapitalization (26.7%) for firms that were in play and lower but positive returns (15.1%) for those that were not in play.[86] These results are somewhat intuitive. Defensive recapitalizations usually generate a substantial amount of cash than can be used as an alternative to the offer from the hostile bidder. These shareholder wealth effects, however, are initial stock market reactions. Whether the recapitalization is good for the long-term welfare of the corporation is another issue. Dennis and David found that 31% of the 29 recapitalizations that they studied that did leveraged recapitalizations encountered subsequent financial distress.[87] Nine either filed Chapter 11 or had to restructure claims out of court. They attributed many of these problems to industry-wide troubles, as well as poor proceeds from asset sales. This was the case, for example, in the Interco recapitalization, which we discuss in a separate case study (see Case Study: Interco—The Problems with Recapitalization). Interco believed it would generate greater proceeds from assets sales, which could be used to pay down debt. These overly optimistic assessments were not shared by the market.

Assume More Debt

Although the assumption of more debt occurs in a recapitalization plan, the firm can also directly add debt without resorting to the implementation of recapitalization to prevent a takeover. A low level of debt relative to equity can make a company vulnerable to a takeover. A hostile bidder can utilize the target's borrowing capacity to help finance the acquisition of the target. Although some may interpret a low level of debt to be beneficial

85. Punett Handa and A. R. Radhakrishnan, "An Empirical Investigation of Leveraged Recapitalizations With Case Payout as a Takeover Defense," *Financial Management*, 20, Autumn 1991, 38–68.
86. Atul Gupta and Peonard Rosenthal, "Ownership Structure, Leverage and Firm Value: The Case of Leveraged Recapitalizations, *Financial Management*, 20, Autumn 1991, 69–83.
87. David J. Dennis and Diane K. David, "Causes of Financial Distress Following Leveraged Recapitalizations," *Journal of Financial Economics*, 37, February 1995, 129–157.

to the corporation, by lowering its risk, this can also increase the company's vulnerability to a takeover. However, additional debt can make the target riskier because of the higher debt service relative to the target's cash flow. This is something of a *scorched earth defense* because preventing the acquisition by assuming additional debt may result in the target's future bankruptcy.

CASE STUDY

INTERCO—THE PROBLEMS WITH RECAPITALIZATION

Interco's recapitalization plan and the company's subsequent financial problems is a highly instructive case study. It highlights not only the problems of too much leverage but also of overoptimistic projections that often underlie both takeover and recapitalization failures.

In the fall of 1988, St. Louis–based Interco, a diverse manufacturer of well-known products such as London Fog rainwear, Converse shoes, and Ethan Allan and Broyhill furniture, found itself the object of a hostile bid from the Rales Brothers. Steven and Michael Rales, relatively little-known investors from Washington D.C., had offered $74 per share in a $2.73 billion all-cash tender offer. Interco responded with a recapitalization plan defense. This defense was coupled with a poison pill, however. As is explained elsewhere in this chapter, the use of a poison pill to shield a recapitalization plan was found to be illegal by a Delaware Chancery Court. Nonetheless, the recapitalization plan proved sufficient to counter the Rales Brothers' offer. Although the recapitalization plan ensured Interco's independence, it did so at a drastic price. The plan, in part developed by merger strategists Bruce Wasserstein and Joseph Perella, increased Interco's debt service obligations beyond the firm's ability to pay. The result was a cash flow crisis that culminated in the firm's eventual default on June 15, 1990. Holders of junk bonds issued in the recapitalization process eventually had to accept equity in exchange for their bonds to avoid further losses that would result from bankruptcy.[a]

It Sold Off Businesses...
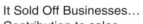

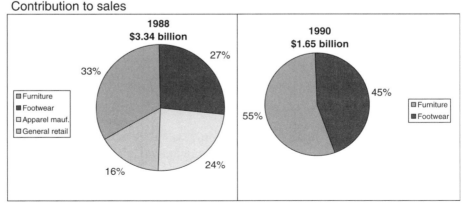

EXHIBIT A   INTERCO'S RECAPITALIZATION PROBLEMS

Source: George Anders and Francine Schwadel, "Wall Streeters Helped Interco Defeat Raiders—But at a Heavy Price," *Wall Street Journal,* July 11, 1990, p. A7. Reprinted by permission of the *Wall Street Journal,* copyright © 1990 Dow Jones & Company Inc. All rights reserved worldwide.

[a]Michael Quint, "Interco Pact Includes Conversion of Bonds to Stock," *New York Times,* August 1, 1990, p. D22.

The expected success of the Interco recapitalization plan was contingent on the accuracy of the forecasts developed for asset sales and revenues from the company's operations. This plan, labeled Project Imperial, was reported by the *Wall Street Journal* to have been developed by "a few number crunching financial people with very little oversight from top officials at either Interco or Wasserstein-Perella."[b] The *Journal* reported that ten-year projections of cash flows and earnings were made by a team of financial analysts, one of whom was only one and a half years out of college, without the benefit of much basic research. Several scenarios were considered, but the worst case showed a 20% annual return following the recapitalization.

The firm of Wasserstein-Perella earned $5.5 million for its work in the antitakeover defense of Interco. The plan it developed called for the sale of divisions such as the Ethan Allen furniture chain for approximately $500 million. However, the eventual sale price proved to be only $388 million. The Central Hardware division was valued at $312 million in the recapitalization plan but brought only $245 million when it was sold. Record annual profits of $70 million were forecasted for divisions such as Converse shoes, whereas fiscal 1990 profits proved to be only $11 million. Given the volatile and competitive nature of the athletic shoe industry, the continual generation of increasing profit levels would be a most difficult task for any company in this industry (Exhibit A).

The fate of the Interco recapitalization plan is symbolic of much of what went wrong in the world of leveraged mergers during the late 1980s. Seemingly sophisticated financial analysis could be developed to make risky leveraged deals appear attractive. The art of financial valuation, as practiced by some, has therefore fallen into much criticism.[c]

[b] George Anders and Francine Schwadel, "Wall Streeters Helped Interco Defeat Raiders—But at a Heavy Price," *Wall Street Journal,* July 11, 1990, p. 1.
[c] Data for this case were drawn from research by George Anders and Francine Schwadel of the *Wall Street Journal.*

The target can acquire the additional debt in two ways: (1) It can borrow directly from a bank or other lender, or (2) it can issue bonds. If the target has to wait for SEC approval for the bonds to be issued, it might be taken over before the debt issuance is completed. Companies with this defense in mind can prepare for it by obtaining prior SEC approval to issue bonds and taking advantage of SEC Rule 415, which is called the *shelf registration rule.* This rule allows the corporation to register with the SEC all those securities offerings it intends to make within the upcoming two years.

Issue More Shares

Another antitakeover option available to the target company is to issue more shares. Issuing more shares would change the company's capital structure because it increases equity while maintaining the current level of debt. By issuing more shares, the target company makes it more difficult and costly to acquire a majority of the stock in the target. The notion of increasing the number of shares to make it more difficult for a raider to obtain control has been around for some time. Matthew Josephson, in his book *The Robber Barons,* points out how this tactic was used to prevent Cornelius Vanderbilt from obtaining control of the Erie Railroad: "This explains how the 'Erie Gang' or the Erie Lackawanna Railroad successfully prevented the New York Central Railroad, a precursor to today's Conrail, and Cornelius Vanderbilt from taking control of Erie. Every time Vanderbilt came close to getting a majority, Erie would issue more shares."[88] On the negative side, issuing more shares dilutes stockholder equity. It is reasonable to expect the company's stock price to decline in the face of this stock issuance. This downward movement in the company's stock price is the market's reflection of the costs of this issuance. In the presence of these clear costs to stockholders, many states specifically require that corporations receive adequate compensation in return for the newly issued shares. When the shares are issued and not given to a particular group or company, they are called a *general issue*. However, because these shares might fall into hostile bidders' hands, the target often issues these shares directly into friendly hands. Such is the case in a white squire defense, where the target both increases the number of shares necessary to obtain control and makes sure that these newly issued shares will not fall into the hostile bidder's hands.

As an example of a defensive share issuance, in 1999, Gucci, which was incorporated in the Netherlands (for tax reasons) but operated out of Italy, issued more shares as a defense against a hostile bid from LVMH. Gucci sold a 40% stake in the company to Francois Pinault, the owner of Pinault-Printemps. Pinault had pledged to convert Gucci into a major rival of LVMH. Gucci stated that it would use the $3 billion from Pinault to shop for more luxury brands, which would better enable it to compete with LVMH in the luxury goods market. As we discussed in Chapter 4, LVMH controlled Givenchy, Donna Karan, Fendi, and Christian Dior as well as several other luxury brands. Ironically, up to this point Gucci's largest shareholder was LVMH, which owned a 20% stake in the company.

Share Issuance and ESOPs

Another option that the target may consider is to issue the stock to the ESOP. To make it easy for the ESOP to purchase these shares, the ESOP may borrow using the corporation's guarantee. The company may also make tax-deductible contributions into the ESOP that may then be used to repay the loan. In using ESOPs as a defensive tactic, the target must make sure that the price paid by the ESOP for the target's securities is "fair." If the company pays too high a price, the transaction could be judged improper according to the federal employee benefit laws. If the ESOP is allowed to buy the shares at too low a price, directors could be charged with violating their fiduciary duties to non-ESOP shareholders. Employee stock ownership plans are discussed in greater detail in Chapter 9.

In light of the passage of the Delaware antitakeover law, leveraged "bustup" acquisitions can be impeded by placing 15% of a firm's outstanding shares in an ESOP. In December 1989, Chevron Corporation, to prevent a takeover by cash-rich Penzoil Corporation, issued 14.1 million shares to create an ESOP. Chevron borrowed $1 billion to repurchase the newly issued shares.[89] Before the issuance of these shares, employees had held 11% of Chevron's outstanding shares through a profit-sharing program. In an effort to offset the dilution effects of the share issuance, having perceived that the takeover threat had passed, Chevron announced a program of stock repurchases in 1990.

---

88. Matthew Josephson, *The Robber Barons* (New York: Harcourt Brace, 1931).
89. "Chevron Purchasing Shares to Replace Stock Used for ESOP," *Wall Street Journal*, February 13, 1990, p. A.5.

Chevron survived this takeover threat and grew into one of the larger companies in the oil industry. This was accomplished partly through its $35 billion acquisition of Texaco in November 2000.

CASE STUDY

SHAMROCK HOLDINGS INC. VERSUS POLAROID CORPORATION

In 1988, when Polaroid was the target of an unwanted takeover offer from Shamrock Holdings Inc., it used the employee stock ownership plan (ESOP) stock issuance defense. Shamrock Holdings Inc. was a Burbank, California, television and radio company owned by the Roy Disney family. It bought 6.9% percent of Polaroid and expressed interest in acquiring control of the company. Polaroid created an ESOP for the purpose of avoiding this takeover. It then placed 10 million newly issued shares, which constituted 14% of the outstanding stock of Polaroid, into the ESOP.

Polaroid considered this an effective defense because the ESOP would likely exercise its voting power to oppose an acquisition by Shamrock and to maintain current management. Polaroid, a Delaware-based corporation, had its defense bolstered by the ESOP stock issuance inasmuch as a bidder must buy 85% of a Delaware-incorporated target to be able to take control and sell off assets. (See Chapter 3.) With the ESOP stock issuance, only 86% of the outstanding stock remained in public hands.

Polaroid would go on to have a troubled history. The camera company fell behind the leading edge companies in this industry and had to file for Chapter 11 bankruptcy protection in 2001. In 2005 it was acquired by one of its licensees, Petters Group Worldwide, for $426 million.

Buy Back Shares

Another way to prevent a takeover is for the target to buy back its own shares. Such share repurchases can have several advantages for a target corporation, namely:

- Share repurchases can divert shares away from a hostile bidder. Once the target has acquired certain shares, these shares are no longer available for the bidder to purchase.
- Share repurchases can also divert shares away from the hands of arbitragers. Arbitragers can be of great assistance to a hostile bidder because they acquire shares with the explicit purpose of earning high returns by selling them to the highest bidder. This is often the hostile acquiring corporation. By preventing some of the target's shares from falling into the hostile bidder's hands, the target can make the acquisition process more difficult.
- The acquisition of the target's own shares can allow the corporation to use up its own resources. The bidder can use these resources to finance the target's own acquisition. For example, if the target uses some of its excess cash reserves to acquire its own shares, the acquirer cannot use this cash to pay off some of the debt incurred in the acquisition.
- Similar reasoning can be applied to share repurchases by the target, which are financed through debt. By borrowing, the target is using up its own borrowing capacity, which could have been used to finance some of the acquisition. This can be effective in deterring bids by raiders who are relying on the heavy use of leverage.

- The acquisition of shares can be a necessary first step in implementing a white squire defense. If the target has enough SEC-authorized shares available, it must first acquire them through share repurchases.

Federal securities laws limit the ability of a target to repurchase its own shares after it has become the recipient of a target offer. These laws require the target to file with the SEC and to provide certain disclosures, including the number of shares to be repurchased, the purpose of the transaction, and the source of funding. Although share repurchases have several clear advantages for a target corporation, they are not without drawbacks. Share repurchases may be an instinctive first reaction by an embattled target CEO who is striving to maintain the company's independence. By repurchasing the company's shares, however, the CEO is withdrawing outstanding shares from the market. With fewer shares outstanding, it may be easier for the acquirer to obtain control because the bidder has to buy a smaller number of shares to acquire 51% of the target.

One solution to this dilemma is to use targeted share repurchases. This strategy takes shares out of the hands of those who would most likely sell them to the hostile bidder. If, at the same time, these shares are placed in friendly hands, the strategy can be successful. When CHH combined a buyback of 17.5 million shares in 1984 with a sale of stock to General Cinema Corporation, it was implementing a similar strategy to prevent The Limited from obtaining control of CHH.

General Cinema was able to help CHH to survive two hostile takeover attempts by The Limited in 1984 and 1986. It could not help the company, which used an aggressive acquisition program to build itself into the sixth largest department store chain in the United States, to avoid bankruptcy. CHH had acquired such venerable names as Bergdorf Goodman, Thalhimer, Walden Books, and the Wanamaker chains. They were able to show higher and higher acquired revenues but not profits. When its results flagged it began to sell off assets. It separated one business unit, the Neiman Marcus Group, which contained Neiman Marcus and Bergdorf Goodman. As part of its reward for assisting CHH, General Cinema became the controlling shareholder of the Neiman Marcus Group when CHH filed for Chapter 11 and was eventually liquidated. The failure of this company, which was a major force in the Southern California market, is summed up by the following saying that was heard on Wall Street and in the media during the waning days on the company—"God gave them Southern California and they blew it." This failed merger strategy is one of many examples of companies that enjoyed significant success in their own markets but that incurred large losses by pursuing losing M&As.

Implementing a Share Repurchase Program

A target can implement a share repurchase plan in three ways:

1. General nontargeted purchases
2. Targeted share repurchases
3. Self-tender offer

General nontargeted purchases simply buy back a certain number of shares without regard to their ownership. Targeted share repurchases, however, are designed to take shares out of the hands of stockholders who may sell their shares to the hostile bidder.

A self-tender occurs when the target makes a tender offer for its own securities. Regulations governing self-tenders are different from those that apply to tender offers by an outside party. Self-tenders are regulated by Section 13 of the Securities and Exchange Act of 1934. A company engaging in a self-tender has two main sets of filing requirements. According to Rule 13e-1, the target may not buy its own securities following a tender offer by a hostile bidder unless it first files with the SEC and announces its intentions. The target firm must disclose the following:

- Name and class of securities
- Identity of purchaser
- Markets and exchanges that will be used for the purchases
- Purpose of the repurchase
- Intended disposition of the repurchased shares[90]

The target corporation is also bound by Rule 14d-9, which requires that the company file a Schedule 14D-9 with the SEC within 10 days of the commencement of the tender offer. The 14D-9 filing, which is also required in the case of a hostile bid, requires management to indicate its position on the self-tender.

Discriminatory Self-Tenders: Unocal versus Mesa

In February 1985, T. Boone Pickens announced a bid from his investor group, Mesa Partners II, for Unocal Corporation.[91] Mesa had just purchased 8% of the larger Los Angeles–based oil company. Pickens's company, Mesa Petroleum, was flush with cash from successful prior offers for Gulf and Phillips Petroleum. Pickens made $800 million on his bid for Gulf and $90 million on the offer for Phillips.[92] Pickens has stated that these gains were not greenmail, based on his long-held position of refusing to accept a higher payment for his shares unless other shareholders could participate in the buyout by the target. Pickens increased the pressure on Phillips by increasing his holdings to 13% of Unocal's outstanding shares. He found Unocal an attractive target because of its low debt level and significant size (revenues of $11.5 billion). Mesa increased its credibility by amassing a war chest of $4 billion in financing through the help of its investment banker, Drexel Burnham Lambert. In April 1985, Pickens bid for just over 50% of Unocal at $54 per share. Unocal, led by Chairman Fred Hartley, responded with a discriminatory self-tender offer for 29% of Unocal's outstanding shares. Hartley wanted to defeat the Pickens bid but did not want to give his foe greenmail. His self-tender offer therefore contained a provision that Mesa Partners II could not participate in Unocal's offer. Pickens appealed to the Delaware Chancery Court to rule on what he believed was a clearly unfair offer by Unocal. The Delaware Chancery Court agreed that Unocal's offer was illegal, a ruling that was later reversed by the Delaware Supreme Court. The Delaware Supreme Court concluded on May 17, 1985, that Unocal's offer was within the board of directors' rights according to the business judgment rule. The court found that Mesa's offer was a "grossly inadequate two-tiered coercive tender offer coupled with the threat of greenmail." The

---

90. Brown, Ferrara, and Hall, *Takeovers,* p. 78.
91. *Unocal v. Mesa,* 493 A.2d 949 (Del. 1985).
92. Jeff Madrick, *Taking America* (New York: Bantam, 1987), p. 282.

higher court held that Unocal's response to this type of offer was within its rights as provided by the business judgment rule. The Delaware Supreme Court ruling forced Pickens to capitulate; he agreed to a standstill agreement. Ironically, this ruling led to the SEC's review of discriminatory self-tenders, which eventually resulted in a change in tender offer rules making such discriminatory self-tenders illegal.

The *Unocal* decision has become a standard guide for directors in the use of anti-takeover measures. In applying *Unocal*, courts now look to see if the defensive measures being used are proportional to the threat perceived. In a later decision clarifying this, the Delaware Supreme Court noted that the defensive response must not be "draconian" and within a "range of reasonableness."[93] In this decision, the Delaware Supreme Court noted that in applying Unocal, a court must go through a two-step process. The first step is to determine if the defensive measures go so far as to be coercive or preclusive and halt a takeover contest that might otherwise be in shareholder's interests. The second step is to see if the defensive measures taken are reasonable in light of the perceived threat. In the case of Unitrin's response to American General's hostile bid, the Delaware Supreme Court found that the first prong of the test was satisfied but it took issue with Unitrin's repurchase program, although it was not troubled by its poison pill or bylaw change requiring advance notice of an offer.

Market Reaction to the Unocal Decision

Kamma, Weintrop, and Weir analyzed the market reaction to the Delaware Supreme Court decision expanding the board of directors' authority to take a broad range of actions to keep a company independent.[94] The market responded by lowering the probability of a potential target receiving a takeover premium in a successful hostile bid. Kamma, Weintrop, and Weir examined a sample of 124 firms that were targets of stock purchases that warranted Schedule 13D filings on May 10 and May 24, 1985. They divided these firms into two groups: 24 firms that were clearly targets of hostile bids and the remaining 100 firms that were not. These subsamples were further subdivided into Delaware and non-Delaware firms. The study results revealed that the 14 "hostile Delaware firms" earned abnormal negative returns of 1.51%. The other group of firms failed to show a statistically significant abnormal performance. Kamma, Weintrop, and Weir's results support the subsequent SEC action that made discriminatory repurchases illegal and show that such discriminatory repurchases result in a decline in stockholder wealth.

CASE STUDY

POLAROID'S $1.1 BILLION STOCK BUYOUT

In 1988, the Polaroid Corporation found itself the object of an unwanted bid from Roy E. Disney and his company, Shamrock Holdings, Inc. Polaroid had rejected Disney's overtures and instituted

---

93. *Unitrin, Inc. v. American General Corp.*, 651 A. 2d 1361, 1388 (Del 1995).
94. Sreenivas Kamma, Joseph Weintrop, and Peggy Weir, "Investors Perceptions of the Delaware Supreme Court Decision in *Unocal v. Mesa*," *Journal of Financial Economics*, 20, January/March 1988, 419–430.

various defenses, including the placement of stock into an employee stock ownership program (ESOP). However, Disney did not give up his bid to take over the camera manufacturer.

In January 1989, Polaroid announced a plan to buy back $1.1 billion worth of stock. Ironically, the stock repurchase would be financed by the sale of a large block of stock to a private investor group. The private investor group's ownership in Polaroid would rise from 8.5% to 13% due to the combined effect of both the increased number of shares and the fact that fewer shares would be outstanding as a result of the buyback. The group would pay $300 million for Polaroid preferred stock, which would be convertible into common stock at $50 per share. This would give the group, which included institutional investors such as the California State Teachers Retirement System, 8 million new shares. "If Polaroid bought back stock at its current level, it could buy 27 million shares, reducing the 71.6 million shares outstanding to 44.6 million."[a]

Polaroid used the combination of a stock sale and a stock repurchase to take shares off the market, where they might fall into a raider's hands, and to place more shares into friendly hands. The combined effect was to make a takeover by Disney or any other raider more difficult. In light of the poor performance of Polaroid, which we discussed earlier, one wonders how the company's fortunes might have been different if it was less insulated from pressures of the takeover market.

[a]"$1.1 Billion Polaroid Buyback," *New York Times,* January 31, 1989, p. D1.

Corporate Restructuring as a Takeover Defense

Corporate restructuring is another of the more drastic antitakeover defenses. It may involve selling off major parts of the target or even engaging in major acquisitions. Defensive restructuring has been criticized as a case of "Do unto yourself as others would do unto you." Given the anticipated criticism, management usually employs this defense only as a last resort.

Defensive corporate restructuring can be both a preventative defense and an active antitakeover defense. If a firm believes it may become a takeover target, it may restructure to prevent this occurrence. Takeovers also occur in the midst of a takeover battle when the target feels that only drastic actions will prevent a takeover.

An example of a successful use of corporate restructuring as a defense against an unwanted bid occurred in 1986, when Lucky Stores sold three units and spun off a fourth to shareholders to prevent a takeover by raider Asher Edelman. The proceeds of the assets sales were used to finance a self-tender for 27% of its own shares.

It is often difficult for an incumbent management to justify restructuring to prevent an acquisition because management must take considerable liberty with stockholders' resources. Management should be able to convince stockholders, however, that such drastic changes in the nature of the target's business as well as the rejection of the bidder's proposed premium are both in their best interests.

Defensive restructuring may take the following forms:

- Take the corporation private in an LBO.
- Sell off valued assets.
- Acquire other companies.
- Liquidate the company.

Going private is often the reaction of a management that does not want to give up control of the corporation. Going private and LBOs are discussed in detail in Chapter 7. They can be justified from the stockholders' point of view when they result in higher premiums than rival bids. However, if the buyers in the going-private transaction are managing directors, the offer price must be one that is clearly fair. Fairness may be judged as a significant premium that is higher than the premium offered by other bidders.

The sale of valued assets to prevent a takeover is a highly controversial defensive action. The idea is that the target will sell off the assets the acquirer wants, and so the target will become less desirable in the eyes of the hostile bidder. As a result, the bidder may withdraw its offer. This is essentially a lockup transaction. Stockholders have often strongly opposed these actions and have sometimes successfully sued to prevent their completion. If, on the other hand, the target can establish that it received fair and reasonable value for the assets and that their loss did not lower the overall value of the firm after taking into account the receipt of the proceeds from the sale, the target may be on firmer legal ground.

A target may acquire another company to prevent its own takeover for several reasons. First, it may seek to create an antitrust conflict for the acquirer. This will then involve the acquisition of a company in one of the bidder's main lines of business. This tactic was somewhat more effective when the Justice Department exercised stricter antitrust enforcement. However, even if there is a reasonable likelihood that the takeover will be opposed on antitrust grounds, this defense can be deactivated by the sale of the acquired business following the acquirer's acquisition of the target. In its filings with the Justice Department and the Federal Trade Commission (FTC), the acquirer can clearly state its intentions to sell the target's new acquisitions. This may result in an approval of the acquisition pending the acquirer's ability to sell off the necessary parts of the target. A classic case of acquisitions designed to ward off bidders by creating antitrust conflicts occurred when Marshall Field and Company made a series of acquisitions in 1980 in areas where potential bidders were present. These acquisitions were motivated not by any economic factor but only to keep Marshall Field independent. The result was a financially weaker Marshall Field and Company. The company was eventually acquired by Target Corp., which later sold it to May Department Stores in 2004 for $3.24 billion.

A target might want to acquire another concern to reduce its appeal in the eyes of the acquirer. If the target is a highly profitable, streamlined company, this state of financial well-being may be quickly changed by acquiring less profitable businesses in areas in which the acquirer does not want to be. If these acquisitions involve the assumption of greater debt, this increased leverage may also make the target less appealing.

One final restructuring option available for the target company is liquidation. In liquidation the target sells all of its assets and uses the proceeds to pay a liquidating dividend to stockholders. The payment of the dividend is restricted by a variety of legal constraints that protect the rights of the firm's creditors. Therefore, the liquidating dividend needs to be calculated after financial adjustments have been made to take into account outstanding obligations that have to be satisfied. In the best interests of stockholders, this dividend payment must exceed the offer of the hostile bidder. This may be possible, however, in instances in which the target believes that, perhaps because of inordinately low securities market prices, the premium above market price offered by the bidder is below that of the liquidation value of the company.

Litigation as an Antitakeover Defense

Litigation is one of the more common antitakeover defenses. In the early stages of the hostile takeover era (the mid-1970s), it was an effective means of preventing a takeover. However, its power in this area has somewhat diminished. Today litigation is only one of an array of defensive actions a target will take in hopes of preventing a takeover. Lipton and Steinberger cite four goals of antitakeover-related litigation:

1. To choose a more favorable forum
2. To preclude the raider from taking the initiative and suing first
3. To delay the bidder while the target pursues a white knight
4. To provide a psychological lift to the target's management[95]

One of the first legal maneuvers the target might try is to request that a court grant an injunction that will prevent the takeover process from continuing. Such an injunction coupled with a restraining order might bar the hostile bidder from purchasing additional stock until the bidder can satisfy the court that the target's charges are without merit.

The temporary halting of a takeover can delay the acquisition, giving the target time to mount more effective defenses. The additional time can also allow the target to seek a white knight. Litigation and the grant of injunctive relief may provide the necessary time to allow a bidding process to develop. Other bidders will now have time to properly consider the benefits of making an offer for the target. The bidding process should result in higher offers for the target. Another major benefit of litigation is to give the bidder time to raise the offer price. The target might indirectly give the bidder the impression that if the offer price and terms were improved, it would drop the litigation.

The more common forms of defensive litigation are:

- *Antitrust.* This type of litigation was more effective during the 1960s and 1970s, when the U.S. Justice Department practiced stricter enforcement of the antitrust laws. However, given the Department's probusiness stance over the past two decades, it has become much more difficult to establish an antitrust violation.
  In 2005, the EU instituted new rule changes that allow, if not encourage, companies to take their antitrust complaints to local national courts instead of before the understaffed EU. This may open the door for greater use of private antitrust litigation in Europe.
- *Inadequate disclosure.* This type of lawsuit often contends that the bidder has not provided complete and full disclosure as required under the Williams Act. The target might argue that, in not providing full and complete disclosure, the acquirer has either not given stockholders adequate information or has provided information that presents an inaccurate picture of the acquirer or the acquirer's

---

95. Martin Lipton and Erica H. Steinberger, *Takeovers and Freezeouts* (New York: Law Journal Seminar Press, 1987), pp. 6–144.

intention. The target in these types of lawsuits commonly maintains that the bidder did not convincingly state how it would raise the requisite capital to complete the purchase of all the stock that was bid for. The bidder usually contends that the disclosure is more than adequate or agrees to supplement his or her filings.

- *Fraud.* This is a more serious charge and is more difficult to prove. Except in more extreme circumstances, it cannot be relied on to play a major role in the target's defense.

CASE STUDY

WALT DISNEY COMPANY'S DEFENSIVE ACQUISITION OF ARVIDA

In 1984, the Walt Disney Company became the target of a hostile bid by Saul Steinberg and Reliance Group Holdings. Financed by Drexel Burnham Lambert, Steinberg made a credible offer to take over the venerable motion picture company. In an effort to ward off this hostile bid, Walt Disney sought to acquire other firms by offering Disney stock in exchange for the target's stock. In May 1984, Disney began negotiations to purchase the Arvida Corporation from the Bass Brothers. The Bass Brothers had bought this real estate concern in an LBO from the bankrupt Penn Central Corporation in 1978. Disney thought that Arvida was a natural fit because it was a real estate development firm; Disney owned extensive real estate in Florida, much of which was undeveloped. Disney, lacking the expertise to develop its real estate assets, sought this expertise in Arvida. Moreover, the acquisition of Arvida, financed by Disney stock, reduced Steinberg's holdings from 12.1% to 11.1%.[a]

One of the problems with defensive acquisitions financed by the issuance of stock is that the acquiring company may be concentrating shares in the hands of other substantial shareholders. As a result of this stock purchase, the Bass Brothers owned 5.9% of Disney stock. This problem may be alleviated if the new stockholders sign a standstill agreement and promise to support management's position in future stockholder votes. In this particular case, the Basses refused to sign such an agreement.

Disney would go on to play a prominent role in the world of M&As, when in 1996 it acquired Capital Cities/ABC for $19 billion in what was one of the largest acquisitions of its time.

[a]John Taylor, *Storming the Magic Kingdom* (New York: Ballantine, 1987), p. 89.

Litigation Research

In a 1985 study of attempted and completed takeovers that involved litigation between 1962 and 1980, Jarrell found that litigation occurred in one-third of all tender offers.[96] As noted previously, litigation may be beneficial for target shareholders even when it does not result in the acquirer's retraction of the bid. Litigation may result in a bid being delayed or forcing the bidder to raise his offer.

Jarrell found that 62% of the offers that had litigation had competing bids, whereas only 11% of those that did not have litigation had competing offers. He also found that, although it seems reasonable that litigation would cause bidders to raise their offer price to encourage the target to drop the litigation and avoid the legal expenses (as well as the possibility that the bid might be permanently halted), there was no evidence of

---

96. Gregg Jarrell, "Wealth Effects of Litigating by Targets: Do Interests Diverge in a Merge?" *Journal of Law and Economics,* 28, April 1985, pp. 151–177.

a significant price effect. On average, a stock price decline took place when litigation was initiated. This decline occurred both for firms that were eventually acquired and for those that remained independent. However, unacquired stock returns fell 23.4%, whereas acquired returns declined slightly more than 21%.

Jarrell also found that when an auction for the firm resulted following the initiation of litigation, there was an additional 17% premium above the first offer relative to nonauctioned firms. When litigation results in the bidder's withdrawing its offer, however, target company stockholders suffer major losses. They incur both the loss of a premium, which averaged 32% for Jarrell's sample of firms, as well as the costs of litigation. We can conclude that litigation may bring benefits for targets, but if the bid is withdrawn, it may also result in significant losses for target stockholders.

Pac-Man Defense

The *Pac-Man defense,* so-named after the popular video game in which characters try to eat each other before they are eaten themselves, is one of the more colorful defenses employed by target companies. It occurs when the target makes an offer to buy the raider in response to the raider's bid for the target. Because of its extreme nature, this defense is considered a "doomsday machine." One of the more famous uses of this defense came when the Martin Marietta Corporation made an offer to buy Bendix following Bendix's unwanted $43 tender offer for Martin Marietta in the summer of 1982.

The Pac-Man defense is often threatened but it is seldom used. Before the Bendix–Martin Marietta takeover battle, two companies had used it in a vain effort to maintain their independence. In 1982, NLT Corporation ended up merging with its bidder—American General Corporation. As stated earlier, Cities Service tried the Pac-Man defense in response to T. Boone Pickens's bid from Mesa Petroleum. Although the defense halted Mesa's bid and helped to convince Mesa to accept greenmail, Cities Service was nonetheless put in play and ended up selling out to Occidental Petroleum.

In another early use of the Pac-Man defense, Houston Natural Gas Corporation (which later became Enron Corporation) used a 1984 bid for the raider to try to fend off the Coastal Corporation. It was not successful because Houston Natural Gas sold off nearly half its assets to maintain its independence. The Heublein Corporation, however, threatened to use the Pac-Man defense when it was confronted by General Cinema Corporation and was able to scare away General Cinema.

CASE STUDY

E-II HOLDINGS VERSUS AMERICAN BRANDS—SUCCESSFUL USE OF THE PAC-MAN DEFENSE

A successful use of the Pac-Man defense occurred in January 1988, when E-II Holdings made an offer for American Brands Corporation.[a] In January 1988, Donald Kelly, chairman of E-II Holdings, announced a $6 billion bid for American Brands, a firm in Old Greenwich, Connecticut. By 1988,

[a]"Takeovers Are Back But Now the Frenzy Is Gone," *Business Week,* February 9, 1988, p. 24; Pamela Sebastian, "American Brands Offer to Buy Debt at E-II Holdings Gets Tepid Response," *Wall Street Journal,* February 24, 1988, p. 8; Stephen Labaton, "American Brands Set to Buy E-II," *New York Times,* 1 February 1988, p. 1.

megamerger offers in the billions of dollars were not unusual. Kelly took this occasion as an opportunity to announce a 4.6% stake in American Brands while revealing his plans to dismantle American Brands following a takeover. Kelly had previously taken E-II Holdings private through an LBO in which he was aided by Kohlberg Kravis & Roberts.

E-II Holdings was a diverse consumer products group of companies formed from the spinoff of 15 companies following the acquisition of Beatrice. It had lost $1.2 billion for nine months before the offer for American Brands. A total of $132 million of this loss came from interest costs, and $147.5 million was a result of the October 1987 stock market crash. E-II Holdings was heavily leveraged and would have to incur significant debt to buy American Brands.

American Brands' main businesses were tobacco, spirits, office products, and financial services. Among its popular brand names are Master Locks, Jim Beam bourbon, Titleist golf equipment, and Pall Mall cigarettes. Its financial condition was in sharp contrast to that of E-II Holdings. It had strong credit lines compared with the debt-laden E-II Holdings. Its chairman, William J. Alley, had been finetuning the company into good financial condition by selling off businesses that were not in the categories outlined. American Brands had recently showed record sales of $9.2 billion, which provided an income of $1.1 billion. This represented increases of 26% and 33%, respectively.

Many people speculated that Kelly was gambling and that Alley would respond with a Pac-Man defense. Kelly was rumored to have been looking for a buyer to purchase E-II Holdings. One way to get such a buyer would be to force an unwilling buyer's hand. Alley responded with an offer for E-II Holdings of $2.7 billion. The acquisition was completed, and American Brands took ownership. In the months that followed, American Brands began to disassemble E-II by selling off product lines such as Samsonite luggage and Culligan water-treatment operations. American Brands indicated that it planned to keep only five or six of the companies it acquired.

"Just Say No"

In the most basic form of antitakeover defense, the target refuses to be taken over, simply hiding behind its poison pills and other defenses and stating that it will not deactivate them and will not bring the offer before the shareholders. In the *just say no* defense, the target may refuse to take any measures, even providing more cash to shareholders, by stating that it has more optimistic plans for the future of the company.

The Universal Foods Corporation, a manufacturer of products such as french fries and cheese, used the just say no defense in 1989, when it turned down an offer from the High Voltage Engineering Corporation. When High Voltage Engineering offered $38 per share, Universal responded that its investment banker, Goldman Sachs, had determined that this offer was inadequate. Universal's board of directors decided that profits were rising and that this was not the time to sell the company. Martin Lipton, the originator of the just say no defense, advised his client, Universal Foods, to reject the offer and not take any other action. Universal compromised by raising its dividend from 18 cents per share to 22 cents. The company's defense, especially its poison pill, was challenged in court. In March 1989, a federal court judge in Wisconsin ruled that if the company's executives believed that the offer was inadequate, they were in a position to determine an accurate value for the company.

Just Say No Reconciled with Revlon Duties

The just say no defense allows directors to reject a bid as inadequate or not in the company's long-term interests without putting the company up for sale in an auction. The just say no defense is a post-Revlon concept that target company directors often rally toward when confronted with an unwanted takeover bid. The leading case in support of this concept is *Paramount Communications v. Time, Inc.*[97] In this attempted takeover, Time, Inc.'s directors rejected Paramount's bid in favor of Warner Communications, Inc. It may be the case that this finding will be relevant only in situations where a target corporation has a well-developed long-term strategy that it is pursuing, as with the merger with Warner, and that other target corporations that lack such a long-term strategy involving an alternative merger would not fit the *Paramount v. Time* decision.[98] If future decisions determine that is the case, then target directors may not be able to liberally apply the just say no defense.

The just say no defense may be challenged by higher offers that will counter the board of directors' position that the future value of the company is worth more to stockholders than the offer price. There will always be some price that will leave the board of directors with no choice but to approve the offer.

INFORMATION CONTENT OF TAKEOVER RESISTANCE

Throughout this chapter we have reviewed a variety of antitakeover defenses and have analyzed the shareholder wealth effects of several of these defenses. Looking at defenses more globally, Pound has studied the information content of takeover bids and the resistance of the target to the takeover.[99] Pound used consensus earnings forecasts as a proxy for the market's expected value of the targets as standalone entities. The effect of different types of takeover contests and defenses on the market's value of the target was assessed by considering whether the consensus changed. These tests were conducted for three samples: targets of friendly bids, targets of hostile bids that were ultimately acquired, and targets of hostile bids that remained independent. Pound observed that the consensus forecasts were unchanged after the initial takeover bid. He therefore concluded that the bids themselves do not convey important information. The unchanged forecasts also imply that the bid did not reveal to the marketplace a previously undiscovered case of undervaluation.

Pound found the resistance to a takeover to be associated with a downward revision of the average earnings forecasts of approximately 10%. This was the case both for firms that were acquired and for those that remained independent. Pound concluded that the market interprets the resistance as a negative signal about future performance.

---

97. *Paramount Communications, Inc. v Time, Inc*, 571 A. 2d 1140 (Del. 1989).
98. Brent A. Olson, *Publicly Traded Corporations: Governance & Regulations* (New York: Thompson West, 2005).
99. John Pound, "The Information Effects of Takeover Bids and Resistance," *Journal of Financial Economics,* 22(2), December 1988, 207–227.

CASE STUDY

BENDIX VERSUS MARTIN MARIETTA

One of the most colorful takeover battles in U.S. economic history was the contest between the Bendix Corporation and the Martin Marietta Corporation. Bendix was led by its chairman, William Agee, who got his training in acquisitions while chief financial officer of Boise Cascade Corporation. Boise Cascade was a forest products company that transformed itself into a conglomerate through diverse acquisitions in the 1960s. Agee joined Bendix in 1972 as executive vice president, reporting to Michael Blumenthal, who left to become Secretary of the Treasury in the Carter Administration. At the age of 38 years, Agee was named chairman of the company, which had two main lines of business, auto products, such as ignition systems and brakes, and aviation products for the defense industry.

In August 1982, after an aborted takeover attempt of RCA, Agee began his bid for Martin Marietta, a company that was an established presence in the defense industry, particularly in aerospace products such as missile systems. Bendix made a $43 tender offer for 45% of Martin Marietta (Bendix already had just under 5% of Martin Marietta), which was previously selling for $33 per share. Martin Marietta rejected the offer and initiated its own $75-per-share tender offer for Bendix, which had been previously selling for $50 per share.

Although Bendix, a Delaware corporation, bid for Martin Marietta first, Martin Marietta was incorporated in Maryland and that state's corporation laws required any bidder to give the target ten days' notice before calling an election of the board of directors. This gave Martin Marietta an apparent advantage over Bendix because Martin Marietta could complete its tender offer for Bendix, following the necessary 20-day Williams Act waiting period that affected both offers, change Bendix's board of directors, and call off Bendix's tender offer before Bendix could do the same at Martin Marietta. Arthur Fleisher, of the firm Fried, Frank, Harris, Shriver, and Jacobson, had advised Agee that Bendix's corporate charter's election rules should be amended to remove this advantage, but that was never done.

Each firm engaged in various defenses, including litigation. Bendix adopted golden parachutes; Martin Marietta searched for a white knight. They found a gray knight, Harry Gray, chairman of United Technologies Corporation, who agreed to make a backup tender offer for Martin Marietta if its offer for Bendix failed.

Agee counted on the 23% of the company's stock that was held in an ESOP that was managed by Citibank's trustee. Martin Marietta's tender offer was two-tiered, with better consideration being offered for the first tier. Citibank concluded that its fiduciary's responsibilities were with the financial well-being of the ESOP shareholders and not based on any other loyalty to Bendix. Many of the employees, however, did not agree with this assessment.

Although Agee may have believed that he could have reached agreement with Martin Marietta to drop its offer, Martin Marietta could not count on United Technologies to simply walk away, so it went ahead with its bid for Bendix and raised the offer price. The absurdity of the deal was that it looked as if both companies would end up buying each other, with each company being debt-laden after the transaction.

Bendix contacted Edward Hennessy, then chairman of Allied Signal, to be its white knight. Hennessy bid for Bendix and won control of the company. He then reached agreement with Thomas Pownall, CEO of Martin Marietta, to exchange shares. Martin Marietta remained independent but highly leveraged. Hennessy ended up with valuable Bendix assets.

SUMMARY

The art of takeover defense has evolved over the past quarter of a century to become a sophisticated process. It may be classified into two broad groupings: preventative and active takeover defenses. Preventative defenses are those that a potential target puts in place in advance of a possible hostile bid. One of the most commonly used of these preventative defenses is the poison pill. Two versions of poison pills are found. Flip-over poison pills allow target shareholders to purchase shares in the bidder's company at a significant discount, typically 50%, if the bidder purchases 100% of the target. Flip-in poison pills allow target shareholders to purchase shares in the target at a discount if the bidder acquires a certain number of the target's shares or makes an offer for a minimum number of shares. Poison pills are one of the more effective defenses but even this defense can often be circumvented by a sufficiently attractive offer. Such an offer puts pressure on the board of directors to withdraw the pill lest they become targets of a lawsuit from shareholders alleging breach of their fiduciary duties.

Other preventative takeover defenses include a variety of corporate charter amendments, antigreenmail such as supermajority provisions, fair price provisions, dual capitalizations, blank check preferred stock, and staggering the elections of the board of directors. Much research has been conducted to determine what impact the implementation of these and other antitakeover defenses has on shareholder wealth.

If the preventative antitakeover defenses are not successful in fending off an unwanted bid, the target may still implement active defenses. These defenses include greenmail and standstill agreements. Greenmail, which is the payment of a premium for the bidder's shares, has become less popular as a result of tax law changes. Greenmail is typically accompanied by a standstill agreement, wherein the bidder agrees, in exchange for a fee, not to purchase target shares beyond some agreed-upon threshold. The target may also engage in more drastic active antitakeover defenses, including capital structure changes, physical restructuring, or changing the state of incorporation. One popular form of capital structure changes, recapitalization, increases the target's leverage, and therefore its risk level, while using the proceeds to pay a superdividend to shareholders as an alternative to the hostile bid. Courts have ruled that the combination of recapitalization plans with poison pills, which uses the pill to prevent the successful hostile bid while the recapitalization plan remains unaffected by the pill, is illegal. An even more drastic defense is the Pac-Man defense, in which the target makes an offer for the bidder. Although very colorful, this defense has been implemented only a few times. At the opposite end of the spectrum of severity is litigation, which is very commonly used. Its effectiveness varies, but research has showed that when it does not result in the withdrawal of an offer, it tends to be associated with higher premiums. The business judgment rule allows the use of various takeover defenses when they work to promote the bidding process and promote shareholder wealth. When such defenses are used to inhibit the auction process, they are generally found to be illegal. The development of takeover defenses will continue to evolve as bidders refine their aggressive tactics to circumvent defenses. With the resurgence of takeovers in the 1990s, this should continue to be an importance area of corporate finance.

6

TAKEOVER TACTICS

During the fourth merger wave of the 1980s, increasingly powerful takeover tactics were required to complete hostile acquisitions because potential targets erected ever-stronger antitakeover defenses. Before this period, comparatively simple tactics had been sufficient to force a usually surprised and bewildered target into submission. As hostile takeovers reached new heights of intensity, targets became more wary, and bidders were required to advance the sophistication of their takeover tactics. When the pace of takeovers slowed at the end of the fourth merger wave, hostile takeovers also became less frequent. Nonetheless, after a lull at the end of the fourth merger wave that lasted a few years, hostile takeovers started to increase in frequency. They became commonplace in the fifth merger wave and remain so.

This chapter analyzes the evolution of takeover tactics over the past quarter of a century and discusses how they are used and their relative effectiveness. It will become clear that the options for the hostile bidder are fewer in number compared with the broad variety of defenses that targets implement in advance of and during a hostile bid. The bidder is typically left with the choice of three main tactics: a bear hug, a tender offer, and a proxy fight. Each tactic has its strengths and weaknesses. In addition, each may be implemented in varying manners to increase the likelihood of success. The options and their shareholder wealth effects are the focus of this chapter.

Of the main takeover tactics, bear hugs are the least aggressive and often occur at the beginning of a hostile takeover. When the target is not strongly opposed to a takeover, a bear hug may be sufficient. However, for a determined and firmly entrenched bidder, it is unlikely that a bear hug will be sufficient to complete the takeover. However, a bear hug may be a precursor to an eventual tender offer.

The most frequently used hostile takeover tactic is the tender offer (see Exhibit 6.1). The laws regulating tender offers, which are fully discussed in Chapter 3, are approached here from the viewpoint of the impact of takeover rules on the hostile bidder's tactics. For example, we describe under what circumstances a bidder has actually made a legal tender offer and thereby becomes bound by the filing requirements of the Williams Act. It is shown that such factors may determine the success of the bid. The legal environment determines the rules within which a bidder must structure a tender offer. How these rules affect tender offer tactics is discussed from a strategic viewpoint.

The tender offer process, along with different variations such as two-tiered tender offers and partial tenders, are also described in this chapter. We also consider the shareholder

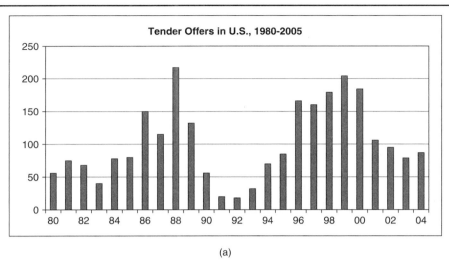

(a)

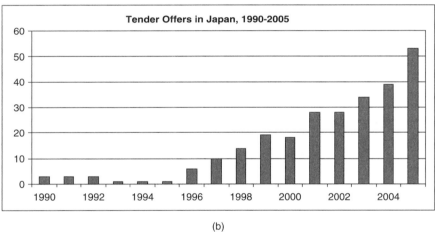

(b)

EXHIBIT 6.1 TENDER OFFERS 1980–2005
Source: Thompson Securities Financial Data

wealth effects of the different types of tender offers and other takeover tactics, just as in Chapter 5, where the impact of the various antitakeover measures on shareholder wealth was discussed.

Another broad category of takeover tactics covered in this chapter is proxy fights. This tactic is discussed in a manner similar to the discussion of tender offers. The corporate election process through which proxy fights are waged is considered in detail. The different types of proxy fights, such as battles for seats on the board of directors and contests that seek to produce a managerial change in the corporation, are described. Although this chapter focuses mainly on the tactics a hostile bidder may employ, an effort is also made to show the proxy fight process from the target's point of view, with a discussion of management's options. Once again, the shareholder wealth effects of this takeover tactic are analyzed through a review of the research literature in this field.

PRELIMINARY TAKEOVER STEPS
Establishing a Toe Hold

An initial step that is often pursued before using the various takeover tactics that are at the disposal of a hostile bidder is to begin an initial accumulation of the target's shares. In doing so, the bidder seeks to establish a toe hold from which to launch its hostile bid. One of the advantages of such share purchases is that if the market is unaware of its actions, the bidder may be able to avoid the payment of a premium. This lowers the average cost of the acquisition. In addition, it may provide the bidder with some of the same rights that other shareholders have, thus establishing a fiduciary duty, which the board would now have to the bidder in its dual role as the hostile bidder and as the target shareholder. This is why target defenses that relate to share acquisitions are exclusionary and usually leave out the accumulator/hostile bidder. This is often a subject of litigation between the company and the bidder.

It is interesting to note that there is some evidence that, despite the theoretical benefits of establishing a toe hold prior to initiating a tender offer, most bidders do not utilize toe hold share accumulations. Arturo Bris found that only about 15% of the firms in his sample of 327 hostile deals in the United States and Britain (70% in the United States) acquired a toe hold.[1] Bidders have to disclosure their holdings within ten days after acquiring 5% of a target's stock. This allows them to possibly accumulate a significantly higher percent of shares than the 5% level set forth in the Williams Act. Surprisingly, in addition to the fact that most bidders do not establish a toe hold, most hold fewer shares than they could anonymously accumulate. Jennings and Mazzeo as well as Betton and Eckbo all report that raiders tend to have toeholds well below the 5% reporting threshold.[2]

The fact that toe holds are not used even more frequently and fully is surprising in light of the research of Betton and Eckbo, who showed that toe holds result in lower tender offer premiums.[3] This is doubly surprising when the lower cost is considered along with Walking's finding that toe holds increase the probability of a tender offer's success.[4]

Given the fact that many bidders chose to not acquire toe holds, or to accumulate smaller positions than they could have cost-effectively achieved, there may be a logical explanation. Goldman and Qian approached the problem from a theoretical perspective and their analysis implies that bidders may be more rational than what some have given them credit for.[5] Most of the analysis in this area just focused on the benefits of establishing a toe hold while not considering all of the potential costs, including those that

---

1. Arturo Bris, "When Do Bidders Purchase a Toe Hold? Theory and Tests," Yale University Working Paper, October 1998.
2. R. H. Jennings and M.A. Mazzeo, "Competing Bids, Target Management Resistance, and the Structure of Takeover Bids," *Review of Financial Studies*, 6(4), 883–909; and S. Betton and B.E. Eckbo, "Toeholds, Bid Jumps and the Expected Payoff in Takeovers," *Review of Financial Studies*, 13(4), 2000, 841–882.
3. Sandra Betton and B. Espen Eckbo, "Toeholds, Bid-jumps and Expected Payoffs in Mergers," *Review of Financial Studies*, 69, 2000, 841–882.
4. R. Walking, "Predicting Tender Offer Success: A Logistic Analysis," *Journal of Financial and Quantitative Analysis*, 20, 1985, 461–478.
5. Eitan Goldman and Jun Qian, "Optimal Toeholds in Takeover Contests," *Journal of Financial Economics*, 77, August 2005, 321–346.

might occur in the event that the bid was a failure. Their analysis implies that when bids fail due to management entrenchment, the costs that this adverse result imposes on failed bidders may cause them to be more cautious about establishing larger toe hold positions.

Casual Pass

Before initiating hostile actions, the bidder may attempt some informal overture to the management of the target. This is sometimes referred to as a casual pass. It may come from a member of the bidder's management or from one of its representatives, such as its investment banker. A casual pass may be used if the bidder is unsure of the target's response. If the target has been the subject of other hostile bids that it has spurned, or if the target has publicly stated its desire to remain independent, this step may provide few benefits. In fact, it can work against the bidder because it provides the target with advance warning of the bidder's interest. In most takeover battles, the target tries to buy more time while the bidder seeks to force the battle to a quick conclusion. Managers of potential target companies are often advised by their attorneys to not engage in loose discussions that could be misconstrued as an expression of interest. They are often told to unequivocally state that the target wants to remain independent.

Bear Hugs

A bidder will sometimes try to pressure the management of the target before initiating a tender offer. This may be done by contacting the board of directors with an expression of interest in acquiring the target and the implied intent to go directly to stockholders with a tender offer if these overtures are not favorably received. This strategy—known as the *bear hug*—may also be accompanied by a public announcement of the bidder's intent to make a tender offer. The bear hug forces the target's board to take a public position on the possible takeover by this bidder. Such offers carry with them the implication that if it is not favorably received, it will be immediately followed by a tender offer directly to shareholders. A bear hug also puts pressure on the board of directors because it must be considered lest the board be regarded as having violated its fiduciary duties.

CASE STUDY

RAIDERS OR SAVIORS?

Raiders have been much maligned in the media. As noted previously, critics have contended that they are short-term speculators who have no long-term interest in the future of the company. They believe that the payment of greenmail to such short-term speculators can only injure the firm's future viability. This view, however, has been challenged by the results of a study by Holderness and Sheehan. They analyzed the activities of six popular raiders, Carl Icahn, Irwin Jacobs, Carl Lintner, David Murdock, Victor Posner, and Charles Bluhdorn, between 1977 and 1982.[a] Their analysis showed that stock prices rose significantly after the announcement that they had first purchased

[a]Clifford G. Holderness and Dennis P. Sheehan, "Raiders or Saviors? The Evidence of Six Controversial Raiders," *Journal of Finance and Economics,* 14(4), December 1985, 555–581.

shares in a target firm. They learned that the traditional view of "raiding" was not supported by the activities of these investors over a two-year period that had followed each purchase. Holderness and Sheehan define raiders as those who would use their position as significant shareholders to try to expropriate assets from the firm. They contend that if this were the case, share prices would have declined after the initial share repurchase. Instead, the market responded with an increase in its valuation of the firm. This suggests that the market does not view these investors as expropriating raiders. Their analysis of instances in which these raiders were the recipients of repurchase offers by the target shows that the announcement of the repurchases yielded negative returns. Similar to findings of Mikkelson and Ruback, however, when the aggregate effects of the initial stock purchase, intermediate events, and the eventual share repurchase are combined, the overall effects are positive and statistically significant.[b]

Holderness and Sheehan see part of the reason for the positive stock price effect on the announcement of share repurchases as the result of an improved management effect. They believe that the market may anticipate that these raiders either will play a direct role in the management of the firm or will seek to change management. Indeed, in 10 of the 73 target firms studied, they found that the raiders played a direct role in the management of the firm.

One final conclusion that Holderness and Sheehan draw from their analysis is that these six investors managed to purchase undervalued stocks. They attribute this "superior security analyst's acumen" either to the possession of nonpublic information or to a greater ability to analyze public information. They see the positive stock price effects around the initial announcement of the purchases as support for this view of raiders.

[b]Wayne H. Mikkelson and Richard Ruback, "Targeted Repurchases and Common Stock Returns, *The Rand Journal of Economics*, 22, Winter 1991, 544–561.

CASE STUDY

AIG'S BEAR HUG FOR AMERICAN GENERAL

An example of an effective bear hug occurred on April 3, 2001, when American International Group, Inc. (AIG) joined the bidding for American General Corp., posing an alternative to the offer by Prudential PLC. In a letter directly to Robert Devlin, chairman of the board of American General, M. R. Greenberg, chairman of AIG, pointed out that the market was not enthusiastic about Prudential PLC's bid:

> As I explained when we spoke today, we have been observing closely the market's reaction to the announcement of your intent to merge American General with Prudential PLC. It appears clear that the exceptionally steep price drop experienced by Prudential's stock reflects investors' serious concern about the transaction. In light of the events, we are submitting an alternative for a combination of American General with AIG. We would like to begin discussions with you and your board to reach a satisfactory agreement.[a]

The letter goes on to outline AIG's offer, which featured higher consideration for American General's shareholders. The letter ended with the following sentences:

> You can be assured that we will do everything in our power to see this transaction through to completion. We are prepared to meet immediately with you and your board to work toward that end.

The two-page letter was clear and to the point. It basically stated that AIG's offer was better for shareholders than the Prudential bid was, that there was synergy between the two companies, and that AIG was prepared to take necessary aggressive actions to complete the deal. AIG's aggressive bear hug resulted in a successful takeover.

[a]Letter from AIG, Inc. to American General Corp. April 3, 2001.

Once a bear hug becomes public, arbitragers typically accumulate the target's stock. Depending on the companies involved, they may even want to sell the bidder's shares short based on the fact that when bidders make takeover offers, the bidder's shares may decline after the announcement. The accumulation of shares by arbitragers may make large share block purchases easier for the initiator of the bear hug or any other bidder. This often puts the company in play, which makes continued independence more difficult. Investors who have been accused of greenmail in the past, such as Carl Icahn and Boone Pickens, were active users of the bear hug. Its effectiveness in the fifth merger wave was somewhat reduced by the increased potency of poison pills. However, we did see bear hugs during that wave and in the 2000s. For example, in 2004, the Jones Apparel Group, Inc., marketer of brands such as Anne Klein, Nine West, Evan Picone, and Norton McNaughton, initiated a bear hug for the Maxwell Shoe Company, which markets a variety of shoes including Anne Klein footwear under a license agreement with Jones Apparel. Jones Apparel presented Maxwell with a $20-a-share, all-cash offer that was a premium over the $18.40 stock price on February 24, 2004. At the same time that the offer was submitted to Maxwell, Jones made the offer public. By making the offer public, Jones Apparel brought pressure from public shareholders who it then made aware of the offer. Maxwell's board rejected the offer saying that it was inadequate. Jones then pursued a tender offer directly to shareholders at a higher price of $22.50 per share. Maxwell's board continued to resist, and in June 2004 was able to agree on a $23.25-per-share offer that amounted to a total of $346 million agreed-upon price for the shoe marketer. This semi-hostile takeover was one of several the company engaged in. The acquisition program, however, failed to create value. In 2006 Jones Apparel hired Goldman Sachs to try to find a buyer for the firm. The ensuing auction proved fruitless as the company announced in August 2006 that it could not find a buyer willing to pay an attractive price.

A stronger version of the standard bear hug occurs when one bidder offers a specific price in order to, among other reasons, establish a range for damages in possible stockholder lawsuits that might follow the target management's rejection of the bid. This tactic increases the pressure on the target's board, which might be the object of the lawsuits. The typical response of an unreceptive target board is to acquire a fairness opinion from an investment bank that will say that the offer is inadequate. This gives the board of directors a "legitimate" reason to reject the offer. If the bidder makes a public announcement while engaging in a bear hug, the bidder is bound to file pursuant to Rule 14d-2 of the Williams Act and is required to disseminate tender offer materials or abandon the offer within five days. If the target discloses the offer, the bidder is not required to file.

From a strategic point of view, if the bidder sees a realistic possibility of a negotiated transaction, the bear hug may be an attractive alternative to a tender offer. It is a less expensive and less time-consuming way to conduct a "hostile" acquisition. It may also reduce the adverse consequences that sometimes are associated with hostile deals, such as the loss of key target employees and a deterioration of employee morale following the acquisition. If the target strongly opposes the acquisition, however, the bear hug may be unsuccessful, leaving the bidder to pursue other methods such as a tender offer.

Bidders who are reluctant to engage in a costly tender offer begin to use the bear hug as an initial, less expensive takeover tool. The advantage is that the pressure placed on the target's board of directors may be sufficient to complete the takeover.

TENDER OFFERS

Because the Williams Act is the key piece of federal legislation that regulates tender offers, it is ironic that the law does not even define the term. Instead, it has been left to the courts to formulate an exact definition. This ambiguity has naturally led to some confusion regarding what constitutes a tender offer. In some instances, bidders, believing that their actions were not a tender offer, have failed to follow the rules and procedures of the Williams Act. This occurred in the landmark case, discussed in Chapter 3, involving the bid by Sun Oil, Inc. for the Becton Dickinson Company. In late 1977, Sun Oil structured a deal with Fairleigh S. Dickinson, founder of the New Jersey private college of the same name, to purchase shares that Fairleigh Dickinson, his family, and other related parties held. Because the company did not file the proper disclosure statements at the time this agreement was reached, the court ruled that it had violated the Williams Act under the definition of a group as offered by the law. In deciding the case, the federal district court ruled that the establishment of an agreement between Dickinson and the Sun Oil to sell shares to Sun and to have Dickinson become chairman of Becton Dickinson following its acquisition by Sun Oil warranted a disclosure filing. In arriving at its decision, the court established a definition of a tender offer, naming eight factors that are characteristic of a tender offer.[6] These factors, which were covered in Chapter 3, are listed in Table 6.1.

The eighth point was not relevant to the *Wellman v. Dickinson* case and was not discussed in this ruling. It is derived from an earlier ruling. Not all eight factors must be

---

1. Active and widespread solicitation of public shareholders for the shares of an issuer.

2. Solicitation made for the substantial percentage of an issuer's stock.

3. Offer to purchase made a premium over the prevailing market price.

4. Terms of the offer firm rather than negotiated.

5. Offer contingent on the tender of a fixed number of shares, often subject to a fixed maximum number to be purchased.

6. Offer open only a limited period of time.

7. Offeree subject to pressure to sell his stock.

8. Public announcements of a purchasing program concerning the target company precede or accompany rapid accumulation of larger amounts of the target company's securities.

TABLE 6.1   TENDER OFFER EIGHT-FACTOR TEST

Source: Larry D. Soderquist, *Understanding Securities Laws* (New York: Practicing Law Institute, July 1987), p. 236.

---

6. *Wellman v. Dickinson*, 475 F. Supp. 783 (SD NY 1979).

present for an offer to be judged a tender offer. The court did not want the eight factors to constitute an automatic litmus test for tender offers. Rather, in deciding whether the circumstances of a given stock purchase constitute a tender offer, the eight factors are considered together, along with any other relevant factors.

CASE STUDY

VODAFONE-MANNESMAN $203 BILLION HOSTILE TAKEOVER

It is ironic that the largest deal of all time was a hostile takeover by a British company, Vodafone, of a German firm, Mannesmann. The $203 billion, year 2000 deal was reminiscent of the hostile deals that occurred in the United States during the fourth merger wave. The lucrative all-stock offer from the British telecommunications firm brought a sharp hostile response from the German conglomerate. The battle featured very different rivals. Vodafone began in 1985 and owned Britain's largest mobile telephone network. The company had experience with megadeals, having acquired Air-Touch Communications, Inc. in 1999 for $62.8 billion. AirTouch was a minority partner in many of Mannesmann's telecommunications ventures.

Mannesmann invaded the British mobile phone market by buying Orange PLC for $33 billion in October 1999. The German conglomerate had been around for over a century, originally having been established by two brothers as a manufacturer of seamless steel pipe. Over time it evolved into other areas such as auto parts, electronics, and telecommunications. As of the date of its offer, Mannesmann was the biggest single manufacturer of mobile phones in Europe.

Mannesmann initially attempted to negotiate a friendly deal in which its shareholders would own the majority of the combined company. Vodafone was unwilling to accept such an offer and warned that it would take its deal directly to Mannesmann's shareholders. Mannesmann's shares were widely distributed and were held by investors throughout the world, including the United States. Nationalistic appeals would not work here. Moreover, while other countries came to the defense of a local company rather than allow it to be taken over by "foreigners," that did not occur in this deal. Unlike in France and Italy, where the government clearly opposed a takeover by a foreign bidder, the German government took a more free market approach. When Mannesmann eventually lost its independence, the Germany government began to change its free market stance and became more protective of German corporations.

Mannesmann's only hope of staying independent depended on enlisting the aid of a white knight—Vivendi of France. Vivendi is a conglomerate with substantial telecommunications assets. It had a 44% stake in Cegatel, which is a holding company that owns the French mobile phone company SFR, as well as Cegatel 7, which is a fixed-line telephone company in France that had not been doing very well. Mannesmann's strategy, which its CEO denied was a defensive move, collapsed when Vivendi announced an alliance with Vodafone. Vivendi was rewarded after the acquisition for its alliance with Vodafone when Vodafone agreed to sell its 15% stake in Cegatel to Vivendi. This acquisition brought Vivendi's ownership in Cegatel to 59%. The deal was a stock-for-stock swap and it featured intense negotiation on the issue of how much of the combined company would be controlled by Mannesmann shareholders who strongly opposed holding a minority interest in the combined company. This opposition enabled them to end up holding almost half of the combined entity.

Open Market Purchases

The courts have generally found that open market purchases do not by themselves represent a tender offer. Generally, they do require that the purchaser file a Schedule TO.

One version of open market purchases is a *creeping tender offer,* which is the process of gradually acquiring shares in the market or through private transactions. Although under certain circumstances these purchases may require a Schedule TO filing, the courts generally do not regard such purchases as a legal tender offer. Courts have repeatedly found that the purchase of stock from sophisticated institutional investors is not under the domain of the Williams Act.[7] However, the courts have maintained that a publicly announced intention to acquire control of a company followed by a rapid accumulation of that firm's stock is a tender offer.[8]

History of the Tender Offer

The tender offer was the most frequently used tool of hostile takeovers in the 1980s, whereas the proxy fight was the weapon of choice in earlier years. Early on, tender offers were first recognized as a powerful means of taking control of large corporations in the acquisition by International Nickel Company (INCO) of the Electric Storage Battery (ESB) Corporation in 1973 (see Chapter 2). INCO employed its tender offer strategy with the help of its investment banker, Morgan Stanley & Company. As noted in Chapter 2, this takeover was the first hostile takeover by a major, reputable corporation, and the fact that a major corporation and the leading investment bank chose to launch a hostile takeover helped give legitimacy and acceptability to hostile takeovers.

Tender offers had been used even before the ESB acquisition. As early as the 1960s, there was much concern that less reputable businesspeople would use tender offers to wrest control of companies from their legitimate owners. Tender offers were not considered acceptable practice within the corporate community. Moreover, banking institutions, including both investment banks and commercial banks, generally did not provide financing for tender offers. Nonetheless, the effectiveness of tender offers was increasingly being recognized, and in the late 1960s their use began to increase. Tender offers also became popular outside the United States and represented an important hostile takeover method in Great Britain. In response to the fear of the corporate and financial community that the use of tender offers was growing out of control, the New York Stock Exchange and the American Stock Exchange imposed certain limitations on them. Even so, their numbers continued to rise—from 8 in 1960 to 45 in 1965.

As their use proliferated, a swell of opposition developed on Capitol Hill. Spearheaded by Senator Harrison Williams, the Williams Act was passed in 1968 (see Chapter 3). This law initially had a dampening effect on the number of tender offers, which declined from 115 in 1968 to 34 in 1970. Eventually the market adjusted to the regulations of the new law, and the number rose to 205 in 1981. One reason for the strong rebound following the passage of the Williams Act may have been that, although the law made abusive tender offer practices illegal, it gave a certain legitimacy to the method by providing rules to regulate their use. The clear implication was that if tender offers were made in

---

7. *Stromfeld v. Great Atlantic & Pacific Tea Company,* 484 F. Supp. 1264 (SD NY 1980), *aff'd* 6464 F.2d 563 (2nd Cir. 1980); *Kennecott Cooper Corp. v. Curtiss Wright Corp.,* 584 F.2d 1195 (2d Cir. 1978).

8. *S-G Securities, Inc. v. Fuqua Investment Company,* 466 F. Supp. 1114 (D. Mass. 1978).

accordance with federal laws, they were a reasonable business practice. The Williams Act also helped increase the premium associated with tender offers. The average cash takeover premium paid to target stockholders had increased from 32% before the passage of the law to 53% after its enactment.

Overall, the Williams Act facilitated the development of the art of takeover defenses. Before this legislation was passed, tender offers could be so structured that stockholders could be forced to make a quick decision on them. The Williams Act provided management with an extended offer period before the bidder could purchase the shares, giving the targets time to mount increasingly effective takeover defenses.

The Williams Act helped facilitate the popularity of tender offers and the high volume of hostile takeovers that occurred in the fourth merger wave. Exhibit 6.1 shows that the volume of tender offers rose dramatically in the fourth merger wave but fell off dramatically when that wave came to an end and the economy fell into a recession. However, Exhibit 6.1 also shows that the volume of tender offers rose sharply at the start of the fifth merger wave and has stayed relatively high since then.

Reason for Using a Tender Offer

A company usually resorts to a tender offer when a friendly negotiated transaction does not appear to be a viable alternative. In using a tender offer, the bidder may be able to circumvent management and obtain control even when the managers oppose the takeover. The costs associated with a tender offer, such as legal filing fees and publication costs, make the tender offer a more expensive alternative than a negotiated deal. The initiation of a tender offer usually means that the company will be taken over, although not necessarily by the firm that initiated the tender offer. The tender offer may put the company in play, which may cause it to be taken over by another firm that may seek to enter the bidding contest for the target. The auction process may significantly increase the cost of using a tender offer. It also tends to increase the returns enjoyed by target shareholders.

Success Rate of Tender Offers

Most offers are not contested (see Exhibit 6.2). Based on experience in the years from 1990 to 2005, the success rate of total contested tender offers for publicly traded companies was 55% on a weighted average basis.[9] The targets that were not acquired by a bidder either went to a white knight or remained independent. White knights accounted for a significant percent of the instances in which targets fought off the original hostile bidder. Bidders have to take the fact that approximately half of the contested deals will be unsuccessful from their perspective into account when they launch a hostile bid. We have to also keep in mind that in this discussion we are defining success as being able to ultimately take over the target that is resisting the offer. We are not defining success as an eventual takeover and a deal that is also a financial success based upon years of profitable, post-takeover -00-performance. If this were done the success rate would be lower.

---

9. *Mergerstat Review*, 2004.

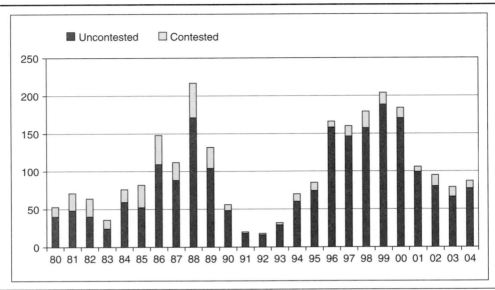

EXHIBIT 6.2 CONTESTED VS. UNCONTESTED TENDER OFFERS, 1980–2004
Source: Mergerstat Review, 1998 and 2005.

Cash versus Securities Tender Offers

The firm that is initiating a tender offer may go with an all-cash tender offer or may use securities as part or all of the consideration used for the offer. Securities may be more attractive to some of the target stockholders because under certain circumstances the transaction may be considered tax free. The bidding firm may create a more flexible structure for target shareholders by using a double-barreled offer, which is an offer in which the target shareholders are given the option of receiving cash or securities in exchange for their shares. If securities are used in the transaction, they must be registered with the Securities and Exchange Commission (SEC) under the Securities Act of 1933. The securities must also be issued in compliance with the relevant state's blue sky laws, which regulate the issuance and transfer of securities.

The SEC review process may also slow down the tender offer. The acquiring firm is encumbered by the waiting periods of the Williams Act and the Hart-Scott-Rodino Act (see Chapter 3). The use of securities may add another waiting period while the firm awaits the SEC review. The SEC's Division of Corporate Finance has designed a system of selective review whereby it responds to repeat issuers more expeditiously.[10] This system permits only a brief review of firms that may have already gone through a thorough review process for prior issues of securities. In these cases, the securities registration and review process may present little or no additional delays beyond the Williams Act and Hart-Scott-Rodino waiting periods.

---

10. Martin Lipton and Erica H. Steinberger, *Takeovers and Freezeouts* (New York: Law Journal Seminar Press, 1987, updated 1994), pp. 1–12.

Ten-Day Window of the Williams Act

As noted in Chapter 3, the Williams Act requires that purchasers of 5% of the outstanding shares of a company's stock register with the SEC within ten days by filing a Schedule TO. The filing of this schedule notifies the market of the purchaser's intentions and alerts stockholders to an impending tender offer. It is in the bidder's interest to purchase shares as quickly as possible during the ten-day period after the acquirer reaches the 5% threshold. If the bidder is able to purchase securities during this period, the stock price may be lower than it would be following the notification to the market of the bidder's intentions. The filing gives the stockholders notice that a bidder may be about to make a bid. This implies a dramatic increase in the demand for the securities and makes them more valuable. Stockholders will demand a higher price to part with their stock, knowing that an upcoming bid and its associated premium may be forthcoming. The ten-day window gives the bidder an opportunity to purchase a larger amount of stock without having to pay the postfiling premium—assuming, however, that rumors have not already anticipated the content of the filing. It is difficult to purchase large amounts of stock and keep the identity of the purchaser secret.

The 10-day window may be turned into a 12-day window if the initial purchases are made on a Wednesday. This would require the purchaser to file on a Saturday. The SEC usually allows the purchaser to file on the next business day, which would be two days later, on Monday.

Response of the Target Management

How should the target company respond to a tender offer? Target company stockholders often view tender offers as a favorable development because they tend to bring high offer premiums. The appropriate response of the target company's management is not always clear. If resistance will increase shareholder returns, then this may be a more appropriate course of action. Such resistance might be used as leverage to try to get the bidder to increase its offer. This assumes, however, that the company believes that an increased offer is more advantageous than the gains that shareholders could realize if the company remained independent.

By resisting the bid, the target may be able to force the bidder to raise its offer. The target may also be able to attract other bidders to start an auction process. We have seen that the winners of such auctions are often afflicted with the winner's curse, which inures to the target shareholders' advantage. Multiple bidders usually translate into higher premiums and somewhat greater leverage for the target.

The risk that the target takes when it resists the bid is that the bid may be withdrawn. If the premium offered reflects a value that is in excess of that which could be realized for shareholders by keeping the company independent, then resistance reduces value. Each takeover contest is different and different circumstances apply. If the target's independence presents lower value for its own shareholders, but synergistic gains mean that the target is much more valuable when combined with the bidder, then it would seem that there should be a basis for a sale at a premium that is attractive for target shareholders.

When evaluating the level of resistance, target managers need to assess their options well in advance of an actual bid. If the target's board and management believe that the company would be an attractive target, they may install defenses in advance of any bid so that the company cannot be acquired at values less than what they believe the company is worth. The installation of such defenses conveys information to the market that the target may not be receptive to a hostile offer. If the target has already fought off prior hostile bids this is also additional information for the market. It is difficult for any target board and management team to take the position that no offer, no matter how high, would be acceptable. However, there are cases where managers may not explicitly say the company would never be for sale at any price, but where their intentions seem to convey that view. Obviously, this is not in shareholders' interests.

Tender Offers and Keeping Management Honest

Supporters of hostile tender offers view them as a monitoring mechanism that keeps management honest and limits agency costs.[11] Without the possibility of a hostile tender offer, managers might be free to take actions that would maximize their own welfare but would fail to produce stock prices that maximize the wealth of equity holders. Knowledge that tender offers can be an effective means of taking control may keep management wary and conscious of the value of the firm's stock. The effectiveness of tender offers makes the possibility of a successful hostile bid most real. In this way, tender offers help to deal with the agency problem of corporations (see Chapter 7).

Individual stockholders have neither the incentive nor the resources to launch a tender offer. A hostile bidder, however, may have both resources and incentive. The bidder may compare the value of the company under its management and may decide that it exceeds the company's current market value by a sufficient margin to be able to offer stockholders a significant premium and still profit from the takeover. When presented with a takeover bid, shareholders have the opportunity to consider the bidder's valuation, compare it with the value that has been realized by management, and select the one that maximizes their return.

Creation of a Tender Offer Team

The bidding firm assembles its team of essential players and coordinates its actions throughout the tender offer process. The team may be composed of the following members outside the corporation's own management and in-house counsel:

- *Investment bank.* The investment bank will play a key role in providing the requisite financing and advisory services through the tender offer. The investment bank may provide bridge financing, which allows the bidder to "buy now and pay later." It also may ultimately finance the bid by issuing securities such as junk bonds or through securing loan agreements. The investment bank's merger expertise is most important in cases of actively fought hostile acquisitions in which the target employs more sophisticated defensive maneuvers.

---

11. Frank H. Easterbrook and Daniel R. Fischel, *The Economic Structure of Corporate Law* (Boston: Harvard University Press, 1991), pp. 171–172.

- *Legal advisors.* Attorneys who are knowledgeable in the tactics and defenses employed to evade tender offers may be an invaluable source of advice, both legal and strategic, for the bidder. During the 1990s, a larger number of law firms began to play prominent roles in merger and acquisition advising. This differed from the 1980s, when two law firms dominated this market.
- *Information agent.* The information agent is typically one of the major proxy soliciting firms. The information agent is responsible for forwarding tender offer materials to stockholders. Proxy firms may also actively solicit the participation of stockholders in tender offers by means of a telephone and mail campaign.
- *Depository bank.* The depository bank handles the receipt of the tender offers and the payment for the shares tendered. The bank makes sure that shares have been properly tendered. An ongoing tabulation is kept for the bidder, allowing the probability of success to be determined throughout the tender offer.
- *Forwarding agent.* The bidder may decide to retain a forwarding agent in addition to the depository bank. The forwarding agent enhances the resources of the depository bank and transmits tenders received to the depository bank. A forwarding agent is particularly useful when there is a concentration of shares in a given area that is not well serviced by the depository bank.

Two-Tiered Tender Offers

A two-tiered tender offer is sometimes referred to as a *front end–loaded* tender offer. It provides for superior compensation for a first-step purchase, followed by inferior compensation for the second tier or the *back end* of the transaction. The technique is designed to exert pressure on stockholders who are concerned that they may become part of a second tier and that they may receive inferior compensation if they do not tender early enough to become part of the first tier. If sufficient shares are tendered in the first tier and if the merger or acquisition is approved, the remaining shareholders can be "frozen out" of their positions and may have to tender their shares for the inferior compensation. The compensation for the two tiers may be broken down into a first-tier, all-cash offer at a higher price for 51% of the target and a second-tier offer at a lower price that may provide noncash compensation such as debentures. The noncash compensation in the form of debentures is often considered inferior when its value is less clear and less exact relative to cash consideration. The two-tiered pricing strategy is often considered coercive to stockholders because it attempts to stampede them into becoming part of the first tier.

During the early 1980s, the two-tiered offer was a popular weapon of the hostile bidder. As the fourth merger wave progressed, however, hostile bidders, having gained access to large amounts of capital through the junk bond market, found that the all-cash, any-and-all offer was a more effective offensive strategy. The target's board of directors finds it difficult to resist the appeal of the all-cash offer; that is, directors find it hard to justify turning down such an offer at a fixed price that includes a significant premium. When bidders had easy access to junk bond funds, they could more readily finance the higher all-cash premiums. This situation changed toward the end of the 1980s, when the junk bond market declined. All-cash offers became far fewer and were often replaced by offers that were financed by more equity and less high-risk debt. This made it more difficult for smaller bidders to participate in major megadeals. However, when the fifth merger wave began to gain momentum in 1997, there was once again a rise in the cash component of transactions.

Regulation of Two-Tiered Tender Offers

Those who oppose the two-tiered bid maintain that it is too coercive and unfair to shareholders in the second tier, who are entitled to equal treatment under the Williams Act. Two-tiered offers may be coercive in that shareholders in the front end receive better compensation than back-end shareholders. Although courts have ruled that two-tiered tender offers are not illegal *per se*, calls for horizontal equity, equal treatment for all shareholders, gave rise to changes in state corporation laws. In many states these statutes have been amended to try to bring about equitable treatment for all tendering shareholders. These amendments included fair price provisions and redemption rights.

Fair price provisions may require that all shareholders, even those in the second tier, receive a fair price. This price may be equal to the prices paid to the first-tier shareholders. Redemption rights may allow shareholders to redeem their shares at a price similar to the price paid to the first tier.

Corporations also reacted to the use of two-tiered offers in the 1980s. Many have amended their corporate charters to include fair price provisions. Jarrell and Poulsen have reported a dramatic rise in the adoption of fair price provisions in corporate charters in response to the increased use of front end–loaded offers.[12] They found that 354 adoptions of fair price amendments took place between 1983 and 1984, which is in sharp contrast to the total of 38 amendments passed between 1979 and 1982. Jarrell and Poulsen attribute this increase to the greater incidence of two-tiered bids in the early 1980s. These corporate charter amendments, a process that began in earnest in the 1980s, however, combined with the passage of specific state laws, have limited the effectiveness of two-tiered bids.

In Europe, tender offer regulations are somewhat similar to the United States but may impose additional restrictions on the bidder. For example, in England, a bidder who owns 30% or more of a company's voting outstanding shares must make an offer for all of the remaining shares at the highest price it paid to acquire its stock position. This renders partial bids and two-tiered offers ineffective.

Effect of Two-Tiered Tender Offers on Stockholder Wealth

The charge that two-tiered tender offers are coercive and cause decreases in stockholder wealth remains an open issue. A study by Comment and Jarrell failed to detect such a decline in stockholder wealth resulting from two-tiered bids.[13] They examined 210 cash

---

12. Greg Jarrell and Annette Poulsen, "Shark Repellents and Stock Prices: The Effects of Antitakeover Amendments Since 1980," *Journal of Financial Economics*, 19(1), September 1987, 127–168.
13. Robert Comment and Greg Jarrell, "Two-Tiered and Negotiated Tender Offers," *Journal of Financial Economics*, 19(2), December 1987, 283–310.

tender offers between 1981 and 1984 and found far fewer two-tiered offers than any-and-all offers. Their results also showed that stockholders do as well when confronted with a front end–loaded bid than when they have an any-and-all offer. Comment and Jarrell attribute this finding to management's ability to enter into a negotiated transaction with the bidder and achieve equal gains in stockholder wealth when offered two-tiered bids as compared with receiving any-and-all offers. They found that the average premium for the 144 any-and-all offers was 56.6%, whereas the average premium for the 39 two-tiered offers in their sample was 55.9%. It is interesting that the Comment and Jarrell results were not caused by fair price provisions because only 14 of the 210 tender offers in their sample were for firms that had fair price amendments in place. Their sample period predates the passage of many of the fair price amendments. They conclude that there is no need for regulatory changes that prohibit two-tiered bids because they do not appear to have had an adverse impact on shareholder wealth.

Any-and-All versus Partial Tender Offers

Before initiating a tender offer, the bidder must decide whether to make an offer for any-and-all shares tendered or to structure the offer so that only a certain percentage of the outstanding shares are bid for. Generally, the any-and-all offer is considered a more effective takeover tactic and is therefore more difficult to defend against. Partial offers are not considered as valuable because of the risk of oversubscription. In an oversubscribed offer, shares are accepted on a pro rata basis unless the buyer agrees to accept all shares tendered. Stockholders incur the risk that they will not receive the full premium for all the shares they would like to tender. This is not the case in an any-and-all offer.

A partial offer that is designed to take control of the target without a second-step closeout transaction is less attractive to stockholders because they may be left holding shares that have a reduced value after the partial buyout is completed. If some or all of their shares are not included in the shares purchased by the bidder, their price may decline as the market assesses the likelihood of an eventual second-step transaction. If a second-step transaction eventually does occur, it may not contain the same premium as the first-step transaction because the first-step transaction contained a control premium. After the first-step transaction is completed, control is usually established, and the remaining shares may be less valuable to the bidder. First-step transactions are often for cash, which has a clear, fixed value, whereas second-step transactions often use debt or equity securities as consideration. The debt securities may be considered more risky inasmuch as the bidder may have incurred considerable debt to finance the all-cash first-step transaction. As noted previously, stockholders may differ with the bidder on the value of the debt securities in the second-step offer. The bidder sometimes tries to ameliorate these concerns by structuring the all-securities second-step transaction so that it constitutes a tax-free exchange. This advantage for the second-step shareholders may partially offset the higher premium that the first-step shareholders received.

Second-step shareholders also have to be concerned about the bidder's ability to purchase the remaining shares in the second tier. The bidder may be straining its financial resources to take control through the first-step transaction and may later be unable to complete the purchase of the remaining shares. For example, William Farley ran out of money after purchasing 95% of West Point–Pepperell. He had expected to complete the $2.5 billion takeover of West Point–Pepperell through the issuance of junk bonds by his investment banker, Drexel Burnham Lambert, but Drexel Burnham Lambert's financial difficulties, coupled with the decline of the junk bond market, prevented it. Farley was unable to service the debt he held as a result of the 95% share purchase. He realized a lower than expected price for a division of West Point–Pepperell, Cluett, Peabody & Co. ($350 million plus a $60 million note from the buyer).[14] The combined effect of these developments was his eventual default in March 1990.

Transactions are sometimes structured in three steps. A bidder using a three-step transaction is sometimes referred to as a *three-piece suitor*. The general process for such transactions involves the bidder making an initial stock purchase followed by a second-step tender offer. Once control is established and a majority of the shareholders have tendered their shares in the tender offer, a third-step freezeout purchase of the minority shareholders who have not tendered their shares is conducted.

Empirical Evidence on the Effects of Tender Offers

One of the early studies that comprehensively focused on the shareholder wealth effects of tender offers was conducted by Asquith as an outgrowth of his doctoral dissertation at the University of Chicago.[15] Asquith examined 211 successful and 91 unsuccessful merger bids between 1962 and 1976 and considered the impact of the bids on daily excess returns to stockholders in the affected companies. Daily excess returns reflect stock returns that are in excess of that which would be expected by the stock's risk level as measured by its Beta. Beta is a measure of systematic or diversifiable risk. This concept is covered in most corporate finance textbooks.

Asquith's results indicate a strong positive cumulative excess return for targets of successful bids when considering a 60-day window before and after the offer. In is interesting that the market was efficient in anticipating the offer, as reflected by the fact that most of the nearly 20% cumulative excess return was reached before the announcement date (press day). Unsuccessful targets lose most of their almost 10% gains by the end of the 60-day period after the announcement.

According to Asquith, acquiring firms in successful bids experience relatively small gains that persist 60 days after the takeover. Those potential acquirers in unsuccessful takeovers display a 25% cumulative excess return 60 days after the attempted takeover (Exhibits 6.3 and 6.4).

The Asquith study was published roughly a quarter of a century ago. However, its basic findings regarding the wealth effects of tender offers on bidders still are somewhat relevant to today's M&A market. However, later research has shown that these

---

14. Robert Johnson, "William Farley's Quest for Status Threatens to Topple His Empire," *Wall Street Journal*, April 30, 1990, p. Al.
15. Paul Asquith, "Merger Bids and Stock Returns," *Journal of Financial Economics*, 11(1–4), April 1983, 51–83.

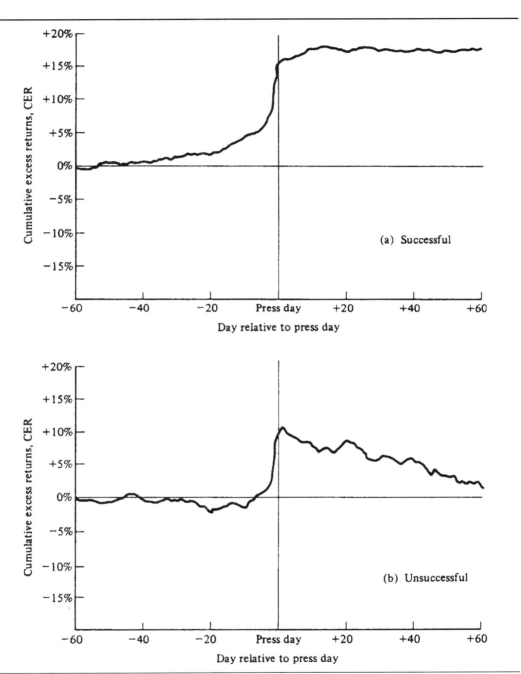

EXHIBIT 6.3 AVERAGE CUMULATIVE EXCESS RETURNS FOR 211 SUCCESSFUL AND 91 UNSUCCESSFUL TARGET FIRMS FROM 60 DAYS BEFORE UNTIL 60 DAYS AFTER THE MERGER DAY IN THE PERIOD 1962–76

Source: Paul Asquith, "Merger Bids and Stock Returns," *Journal of Financial Economics* 11, (1–4) April 1983, 70.

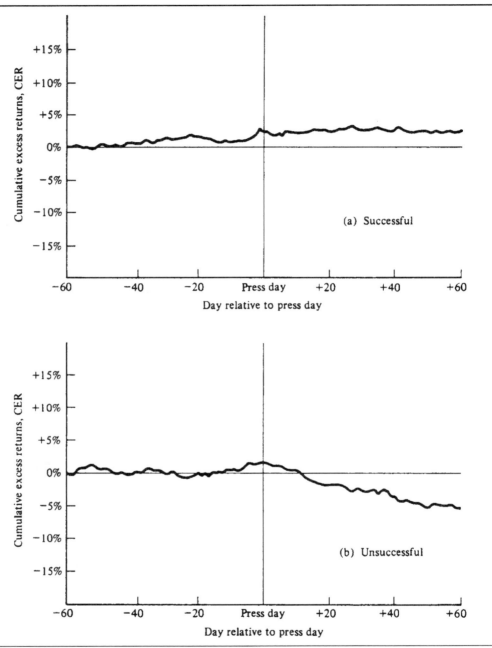

EXHIBIT 6.4 AVERAGE CUMULATIVE EXCESS RETURNS FOR 196 SUCCESSFUL AND 89 UNSUCCESSFUL BIDDING FIRMS FROM 60 DAYS BEFORE UNTIL 60 DAYS AFTER THE MERGER DAY IN THE PERIOD 1962–76

Source: Paul Asquith, "Merger Bids and Stock Returns," *Journal of Financial Economics* 11, (1–4) April 1983, 71.

initial responses may not always be indicative of the long-term performance of the bidder.[16] One explanation for the positive initial stock market response is that bidders and the market may perceive tender offer targets to be undervalued and thus good buys. Perhaps these targets are companies that have been poorly managed and do not trade at prices consistent with their potential values. However, we have seen that over time, the performance of these bidders for these companies tends to erode. Indeed, Rau and Vermaelen have identified one group of bidders in particular who tend to do progressively poorly over time. These are what they refer to as *glamour* firms. They define glamour firms to be firms with low book to market ratios. The low book to market ratios imply that the market may be keen on these firms and they may trade at "popular" values but these values are not reflected in the book value of their assets. They theorize that managers of such glamour companies, perhaps afflicted by hubris enhanced by the glamour status, may overestimate their ability to manage the target. Exhibit 6.5 shows the book to market rankings of glamour and value acquirers relative to broad market averages. The figure shows that glamour acquirers lose their glamour status following acquisitions as reflected by the rising trend in the upper panel of this figure.

Wealth Effects of Unsuccessful Tender Offers

Although the premium associated with a successful bid may increase the target shareholder's wealth, the question exists whether the increase in the target's shares caused by the announcement of a bid persists when the bid fails. Bradley, Desai, and Kim analyzed the returns to stockholders by firms that either received or made *unsuccessful* control-oriented tender offers between 1963 and 1980.[17] They defined a control-oriented tender offer as one in which the bidding firm holds less than 70% of the target's shares and is attempting to increase its holdings by at least 15%. They considered a total of 697 tender offers. This study measured the impact of the tender offers by examining the cumulative abnormal returns to both the target and the bidding firm. *Abnormal returns* are those that cannot be fully explained by market movements. Returns are defined using the market model in equation 6.1:

$$R_{it} = \alpha_i + \beta_{mt} R_{mit} + \varepsilon_{it} \qquad (6.1)$$

where:

R_{it} = the cumulative dividend monthly stock return for the ith firm in month t

R_{mit} = the return on an equally weighted market portfolio month t relative to the announcement of offer

∞, β = the regression parameters

ε_{it} = a stochastic error term with a mean of zero

16. T. Loughran and A. Vijh, "Do Long Term Shareholders Benefit from Corporate Acquisitions,"*Journal of Finance*, 52(5), December 1997, 1765–1790; and P. Raghavendra Rau and Theo Vermaelen, "Glamor, Value and the Post-Acquisition Performance of Acquiring Firms," *Journal of Financial Economics*, 49, 1998, 223–253.

17. Michael Bradley, Anand Desai, and E. Han Kim, "The Rationale Behind Interfirm Tender Offers: Information or Synergy," *Journal of Financial Economics*, 11, April 1983, 183–206.

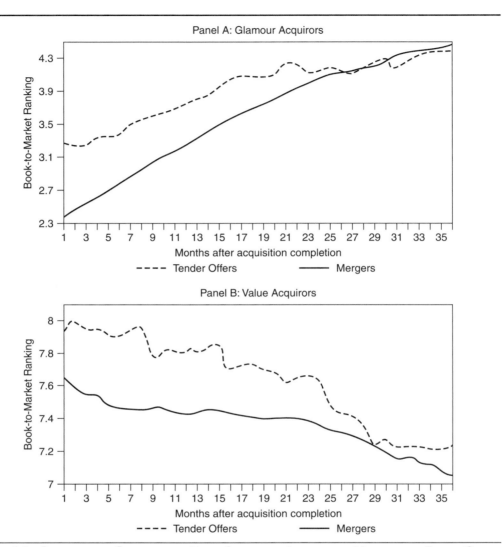

EXHIBIT 6.5 EVOLUTION OF GLAMOUR AND VALUE STATUS FOR ACQUIRERS IN MERGERS AND TENDER OFFERS. THIS GRAPHS SHOWS THE AVERAGE BOOK TO MARKET DECILE RANKINGS FOR VALUE AND GLAMOUR ACQUIRERS IN MERGERS AND TENDER OFFERS, RESPECTIVELY. ACQUIRERS ARE RANKED IN DECILES RELATIVE TO THE UNIVERSE OF NYSE, AMEX, AND NASDAQ FIRMS EVERY MONTH FOR 36 MONTHS AFTER THE ACQUISITION COMPLETION

Source: P. Raghavendra Rau and Theo Vermaelen, "Glamour, Value and the Post-Acquisition Performance of Acquiring Firms," *Journal of Financial Economics*, 49, 1998, 232.

Abnormal returns for firm i and month t are defined as follows:

$$AR_{it} = R_{it} - \alpha_i - \beta_{mt}R_{mit} \tag{6.2}$$

These abnormal returns can then be summed for a defined time period to arrive at cumulative abnormal returns (CAR). CARs are used as a guide to abnormal effects in a wide variety of M&A event studies.

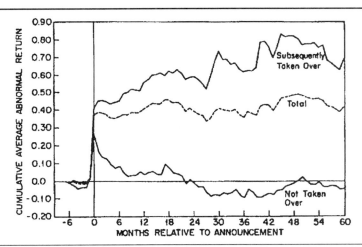

EXHIBIT 6.6 CUMULATIVE ABNORMAL RETURNS TO UNSUCCESSFUL TARGET FIRMS—TOTAL SAMPLE, AND "SUBSEQUENTLY TAKEN OVER" AND "NOT TAKEN OVER" SUBSAMPLES, IN THE PERIOD 1963–1980

Source: Michael Bradley, Anand Desai, and E. Han Kim, "The Rationale Behind Interfirm Tender Offers: Information or Synergy," *Journal of Financial Economics,* 11 April 1983, 192.

One goal of the study was to ascertain whether there were permanent wealth effects from tender offers on the target firm and the acquiring firm. These effects are discussed separately in the following sections.

Target

The results show that target shareholders realize positive abnormal returns surrounding the month of the announcement of the tender offer. The cumulative abnormal returns "show a positive revaluation of the target shares which does not dissipate subsequent to the rejection of the offer."[18] In their total sample of unsuccessful tender offers, 76.8% of the firms were taken over and 23.2% were not. A review of Exhibit 6.6 shows that this positive effect is the case for those that are eventually taken over, whereas it is very different for those that are not taken over.

Bidder

The Bradley study reveals interesting results regarding the impact of tender offers on acquiring firms. As Exhibit 6.7 shows, the cumulative abnormal returns for bidding firms remain nonnegative when the target is independent and there is no change in control. When the target is acquired by another bidder and the bidder in question loses the tender offer, the value of the bidding firm falls significantly. Bradley and colleagues interpret this effect as the market's perception that the bidding firm has lost an opportunity to acquire a valuable resource. This effect is sometimes caused by competitors acquiring resources that will provide a competitive advantage over the firm that lost the bid.

---

18. Ibid., p. 192.

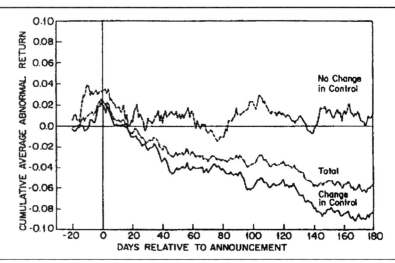

EXHIBIT 6.7   CUMULATIVE ABNORMAL RETURNS TO UNSUCCESSFUL BIDDING FIRMS—TOTAL SAMPLE, AND "NO
CHANGE IN CONTROL" AND "CHANGE IN CONTROL" SUBSAMPLES, IN THE PERIOD 1963–1980

Source: Michael Bradley, Anand Desai, and E. Han Kim, "The Rationale Behind Interfirm Tender Offers:
Information or Synergy," *Journal of Financial Economics,* 11 April 1983, 200.

The Bradley study traced the time frame for the wealth effects on unsuccessful bidders
and found that, for their sample of tender offers between 1963 and 1980, the average
gap between the announcement of the unsuccessful bid and the subsequent successful
tender offer was 60.6 days. Almost all the decline in the value of a portfolio of successful
bidding firms had occurred by day 21. The value of the portfolio declined 2.84% by
day 21.

Tender Offer Premiums and Director Independence

Independent directors are those who are not employees and who do not have any other
relationship with the corporation. Finance theorists have long contended that the more
independent a board is, the greater the return to shareholders.[19] Cotter, Shivdasani, and
Zenner studied 169 tender offers between 1989 and 1992.[20] Their results supported Fama
and Jensen's hypothesis. They found that targets of tender offers experience shareholder
gains that are 20% higher when the board is independent compared with less independent
tender offer targets. They also found that bid premium revisions were also higher when
the board was more independent. These findings suggest that independent directors are
more active supporters of shareholder value than nonindependent directors. Cotter and
colleagues extended their research to determine the source of the increased shareholder
gains. Their results suggest that the higher target gains come at the expense of returns

19. Eugene Fama and Michael Jensen, "Separation of Ownership and Control," *Journal of Law and Economics,* 26,
1983, 301–325.
20. James Cotter, Anil Shivdasani, and Marc Zenner, "Do Independent Directors Enhance Target Shareholder Wealth
During Tender Offers?" *Journal of Financial Economics,* 43(2), February 1997, 195–218.

to bidder shareholders. This conclusion is consistent with other studies that we discuss throughout this text.

Are "Bad Bidders" More Likely to Become Targets?

The impact of poor acquisitions was discussed in Chapter 4 in the context of conglomerate or diversification mergers that performed poorly. It was also discussed in Chapter 2 in the context of the acquisitions that occurred in the third merger wave. The issue of how a firm is affected by a poor acquisition is of interest to stockholders in the bidding firm as they consider whether they should favor a certain acquisition.

In 1988, Mitchell and Lehn analyzed the effects of poor acquisitions on acquiring firms.[21] They found that the probability of becoming a takeover target was inversely related to the cumulative average returns associated with the firm's acquisitions. They used a logistic regression, which is an econometric technique in which the dependent variable may vary between 0 and 1. In this case, the 0 or 1 represents the probability of whether a firm became a target. Some studies of the impact of acquisitions on acquiring firms show a zero or negative impact while providing clear benefits for the target firm. Mitchell and Lehn contend that the market differentiates between good and bad acquiring firms. Although they found returns to acquirers to be approximately zero, they observed that subsamples of good acquirers outperformed acquiring firms that pursued failed acquisition strategies, or what Mitchell and Lehn refer to as bad bidders. For example, as shown in Exhibit 6.8, acquiring firms that did not subsequently become targets themselves showed clearly positive returns over a 60-day window around the acquisition announcement. Acquiring firms that became targets of either friendly or hostile acquisitions showed clearly negative returns. In other words, acquisitions by companies that become targets, especially hostile targets, cause the acquiring company's stock price to fall, whereas acquisition by companies that do not become targets results in an increase in the acquiring firm's stock price.

Mitchell and Lehn's explanation for the returns depicted in Exhibit 6.8 is twofold. Acquiring companies that become targets make acquisitions that the market expects will reduce the combined profitability of these companies. That is, the market is saying that this is a bad acquisition. The second possible explanation for this phenomenon is that the acquiring company is overpaying for the target. It could be that at some lower price the acquisition would be a better one.

The authors of this study went on to trace the relationship between the acquisitions and subsequent divestitures. They found a statistically significantly negative stock price response (average of 24%) to acquisitions that were subsequently divested. For acquisitions that were not divested, they found a small, not statistically significant, positive stock price response (average of 1.9%). The import of this result is that it seems that at the time of the acquisition announcement, the market is making a prediction regarding which acquisitions are good and which are bad. Mitchell and Lehn's analysis suggests that the market is an efficient predictor of the success of acquisitions.

---

21. Mark L. Mitchell and Kenneth Lehn, "Do Bad Bidders Become Good Targets?" *Journal of Applied Corporate Finance*, 3(2), Summer 1990, 60–69.

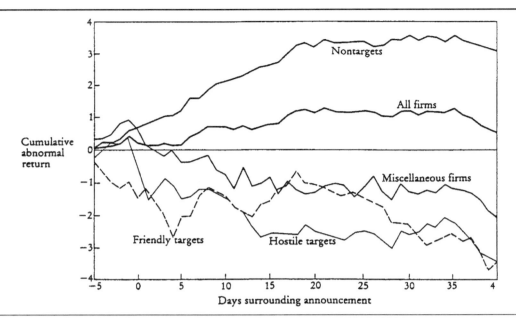

EXHIBIT 6.8 STOCK PRICE REACTIONS TO ACQUISITION ANNOUNCEMENTS, 1982–1986

Source: Mark L. Mitchell and Kenneth Lehn, "Do Bad Bidders Become Good Targets?" *Journal of Applied Corporate Finance* 3(2), Summer 1990 60–69.

OPEN MARKET PURCHASES AND STREET SWEEPS

A hostile bidder may accumulate stock in the target before making a tender offer. As noted previously, the purchaser usually tries to keep these initial purchases secret to put as little upward pressure as possible on the target's stock price. To do so, the acquisitions are often made through various shell corporations and partnerships whose names do not convey the true identity of the ultimate purchaser.

Upon reaching the 5% threshold, the purchaser has ten days before it is necessary to make a public disclosure. This time may be used to augment the bidder's stockholdings. If a bidder engages in an aggressive purchasing program, it is not unusual for the bidder to acquire up to 20% of a target. The larger the purchaser's position in the target, the more leverage the firm has over the target. This leverage may enable the bidder to launch a tender offer that has a high probability of success, given the stockholdings the bidder already possesses. The bidder is also in a better position, as a result of the number of votes he already controls, to make a credible threat of a proxy fight. Even if the bidder fails to take control of the board of directors, it may be able to place representatives on the board. This could make operations more difficult for management and enable the bidder to force the company to take actions that favor the bidder, such as paying additional dividends.

Significant stockholdings accumulated through open market purchases may be sufficient to offset defenses such as supermajority voting provisions. They may also be used as a negotiating tool to convince the target to agree to a "friendly tender offer" and to discourage potential white knights from making a bid for the target. The would-be white knight knows that it will have to deal with an unwanted substantial stockholder even if it succeeds in obtaining majority control of the target. The hostile bidder may not want to relinquish its stockholding without receiving a high premium, which may be tantamount to greenmail. The white knight is then faced with the unappealing prospect of paying a premium to the other target shareholders and greenmail to the hostile bidder.

The open market purchase of stock may be a precursor to a tender offer, but it may also be an effective alternative to a tender offer. When a hostile bidder concludes that the tender offer may not be successful, it may decide not to initiate one. The result may be large-scale open market purchases of stock. The goal of these purchases may be to try to acquire enough stock to take control of the target. The hostile bidder's investment bank assists the bidder by providing the necessary financing for these purchases and by locating large blocks of stock to be bought. These share purchases may be made through secret accumulations by the bidder's investment bank through various corporations or partnerships. Once the 5% threshold is crossed, the bidder still has ten days to file a Schedule TO. The purchases, however, are sometimes difficult to keep secret because they may also be subject to the filing requirements of the Hart-Scott-Rodino Act.

The use of street sweeps as an effective takeover tactic was pioneered in 1985 by Hanson Trust PLC. In that year Hanson Trust terminated its tender offer for SCM Corporation and immediately bought 25% of SCM's outstanding stock from arbitragers. The 25% holding was accumulated in just six transactions. This block of stock, which brought Hanson Trust's holdings up to 34.1%, was purchased in response to SCM's defensive leveraged buyout (LBO) proposal. The buyout was prevented by Hanson Trust's stock acquisition because under New York law (where SCM was incorporated), major transactions such as LBOs must be approved by a two-thirds majority. Hanson's 34.1% position prevented SCM from obtaining the requisite two-thirds approval level.

Hanson Trust PLC took advantage of the fact that in a takeover contest larger blocks of stock begin to be concentrated in the hands of arbitragers. This creates an attractive alternative to a tender offer. An astute investment bank advising a bidder knows that a larger holding can be amassed through a small number of transactions.

The Hanson Trust street sweep was challenged in court.[22] The court of appeals ruled that Hanson Trust's open market purchase of stock after its cancellation of its tender offer was not bound by the requirements of the Williams Act. However, pursuant to Rule 14b-5, an offeror that has initiated an active tender offer is prohibited from purchasing shares outside of that tender offer as long as it is still active. This was not the case with the Hansen purchases, as it had ended its tender offer. The Hansen ruling established a precedent that made street sweeps legal and not in violation of the Williams Act (see Case Study: *Campeau Corp. versus Allied Stores*). The ruling also highlights a loophole in the Williams Act that renders targets vulnerable to street sweeps following an attempted tender offer because of the concentration of shares in the hands of arbitragers, which increases the probability of success for a street sweep.

---

22. *Hanson Trust PLC v. SCM Corp.*, 774 F.2d 47 (2d Cir. 1985).

CASE STUDY

CAMPEAU CORPORATION VERSUS ALLIED STORES—A LOOK AT THE EFFECTIVENESS OF STREET SWEEPS

One notable example of the effectiveness of street sweeps occurred in 1986, when Campeau Corporation, a real estate concern in Toronto, abandoned its tender offer for Allied Stores and immediately purchased 48% of Allied's stock on the open market. Robert Campeau, chairman of the Campeau Corporation, had become involved in a bidding war with Edward J. DeBartolo, who runs a closely held corporation with real estate interests in more than 50 shopping malls, hotels, condominiums, and office buildings. DeBartolo had entered into a partnership with raider Paul Bilzerian, and together they made a $3.56 billion tender offer at $67 per share for Allied. This offer topped Campeau's $66-per-share offer. Realizing that his tender offer would not be successful, Campeau canceled the offer and, within 30 minutes of the cancellation, bought 25.8 million shares of Allied, or 48% of the outstanding stock. The stock acquisition was made possible by the work of Jeffries Group, Inc., the brokerage firm that assembled the block of stock. Lipton and Steinberger report that the Jefferies Group had offered the block to the competing bidders before selling it to Campeau.[a]

The street sweep was challenged by the SEC, which argued that the 48% stock purchase was a continuation of Campeau's tender offer. A settlement was reached, and the legal challenge to the street sweep was abandoned.

[a]Martin, Lipton and Erica H. Steinberger, *Takeovers and Freezeouts* (Washington, D.C.: Law Journal Seminar Press, 1987), pp. 1–43.

ADVANTAGES OF TENDER OFFERS OVER OPEN MARKET PURCHASES

Open market purchases may at first seem to provide many advantages over tender offers. For example, they do not involve the complicated legal requirements and costs associated with tender offers. (The bidder must be concerned that the open market purchases will be legally interpreted as a tender offer.) The costs of a tender offer may be far higher than the brokerage fees incurred in attempting to take control through open market purchases of the target's stock. As noted previously, Smiley estimated that the total cost of tender offers averaged approximately 13% of the post–tender offer market price of the target's shares.[23]

Open market purchases also have clear drawbacks that are not associated with tender offers. A bidder who purchases shares in the open market is not guaranteed that he will be able to accumulate sufficient shares to acquire clear control. If 51% clear control is not achieved, the bidder may become stuck in an undesirable minority position. One advantage of a tender offer is that the bidder is not bound to purchase the tendered shares unless the desired number of shares has been tendered. The bidder who becomes mired in a minority position faces the following alternatives:

- *Do a tender offer for additional shares.* In this case, the bidder incurs the tender offer expenses in addition to the costs of the open market purchasing program.

---

23. Robert Smiley, "Tender Offers, Transactions Costs and the Theory of the Firm," *Review of Economics and Statistics*, 58, 1976, 22–32.

- *Begin a proxy fight.* This is another costly means of acquiring control, but the bidder, after having already acquired a large voting position, is now in a stronger position to launch a proxy fight.
- *Sell the minority stock position.* These sales would place significant downward pressure on the stock price and may result in significant losses.

Large-scale open market purchases are also difficult to keep secret. Market participants regard the stock purchases as a signal that a bidder may be attempting to make a raid on the target. This may then change the shape of the target's supply curve for its stock by making it more vertical above some price.[24] This can make a street sweep effective but expensive. Other shareholders may also have the idea that a higher price may be forthcoming and may be reluctant to sell unless a very attractive offer is made. This threshold price may be quickly reached as the available supply of shares on the market, which may be relatively small compared with the total shares outstanding, becomes exhausted. As stockholders come to believe that a bid may be forthcoming, they have an incentive to *hold out* for a higher premium. The holdout problem does not exist in tender offers because the bidder is not obligated to purchase any shares unless the amount requested has been tendered. If the requested amount has not been tendered at the end of the expiration date of the offer, the bidder may cancel the offer or extend it.

A street sweep may be more effective when a bidder is able to locate large blocks of stock in the hands of a small group of investors. In cases in which there have been offers for the company or speculation about impending offers, stock often becomes concentrated in the hands of arbitragers. Although these investors are often eager to sell, they will often only do so at a high price. The existence of large blocks of stock in the hands of *arbitragers* may enable a bidder to amass a significant percentage of the target's stock, perhaps enough to gain effective control of the company, but only if the bidder is willing to pay a possibly painful price. Often the cost will make this method of acquisition prohibitively expensive.

Arbitragers and Takeover Tactics

Arbitragers are firms that accumulate shares of companies that are targeted for acquisitions. If a given deal is completed, arbitragers will profit from the difference between the purchase price and the takeover price. The arbitrager may also hedge its investment by selling the acquirer's stock short. The most famous, or really infamous, arbitrager was Ivan Boesky, who in the 1980s was the most well-known practitioner of this craft. However, while he claimed the success he enjoyed from merger arbitrage came from his ability to judge the dealmakers themselves, he really purchased insider information from investment bankers such as Martin Siegel of Kidder Peabody.

A simple expression of a risk arbitrager's annualized return (RAR) is shown in equation 6.3:

$$RAR = GSS/I \times (365/IP) \qquad (6.3)$$

---

24. Lloyd R. Cohen, "Why Tender Offers? The Efficient Markets Hypothesis, the Supply of Stock and Signaling," *Journal of Legal Studies,* 19(1), January 1990, 113–143.

where:
   RAR = risk arbitrage return
   GSS = gross stock spread
     I = investment by arbitrager
    IP = investment period (days between investment and closing date)

The gross stock spread is shown in equation 6.4:

$$GSS = OP - MP \qquad (6.4)$$

where:
   OP = offer price
   MP = market price

As an example, assume that Company A makes a \$50-per-share offer for Company B, which now trades at \$45 per share. The gross stock spread is \$5. Also assume that the deal is expected to close in 90 days. If the deal closes, then the risk arbitrager's return would be:

$$RAR = (\$50 - \$45)/\$45 \times (365/90)$$

$$= 45.1\%$$

This is an impressive annual return. Practitioners in this area wish the reality of this business were as lucrative and simple as the above example.

Arbitragers have to consider a variety of risk factors when they evaluate takeovers that they are gambling will be completed. A host of different factors can halt a deal. These include the defensive actions of the target but also regulatory factors such as gaining antitrust approval. For companies that have a significant international business, such as in Europe as well as the United States, they must get antitrust approval of both the U.S. and the EU antitrust authorities. In addition, some deals may take a number of months before they close. The arbitrager's gain comes from the premium that will be received if the deal is completed. For deals that take an extended time to complete, arbitragers have to also consider dividends that will be paid on the shares during the waiting period.

Research has showed that arbitragers often enjoy attractive returns. For example, Dukes, Frohlich, and Ma found annualized arbitrager returns of 220% in their sample of 761 tender offers over the period 1971 through 1985.[25] This has been supported by other research. Jindra and Walking found annualized returns in excess of 100% in their sample of 361 cash tender offers over the period 1971 through 1995.[26]

From the bidder's perspective, the fact that shares become concentrated into the hands of arbitragers is a positive development. These shareholders have no loyalty to the target and actually want the deal to be completed. The greater their holdings, the more the bidder can count on being able to readily purchase the necessary shares to complete the deal.

---

25. William Dukes, Cheryl Frohlich, and Christopher Ma, "Risk Arbitrage in Tender Offers: Handsome Rewards—And Not For Insiders Only," *Journal of Portfolio Management,* 18, 1992, 47–55.

26. Jan Jindra and Ralph Walking, "Arbitrage Spreads and the Market Pricing of Proposed Acquisitions," Working Paper, Ohio State University, 1999.

ARBITRAGE AND THE DOWNWARD PRICE PRESSURES AROUND M&A ANNOUNCEMENTS

Research has shown that the stock price of acquirers tends to decline, especially those which use stock to finance bids, around the date of an announcement of an offer. Mitchell, Pulvino, and Stafford analyzed 2,130 mergers over the period 1994—2000 and found out that approximately one half of this downward effect was caused by the short selling actions of arbitragers.[27] Arbitragers will buy the target's shares, which puts upward price pressure of the target's stock while often selling that bidder's shares in an effort to lock in a specific gain. One of the interesting results of their research was that they found the these price effects were relatively short lived.

PROXY FIGHTS

A *proxy fight* is an attempt by a single shareholder or a group of shareholders to take control or bring about other changes in a company through the use of the proxy mechanism of corporate voting. Proxy contests are political processes in which incumbents and insurgents compete for shareholder votes through a variety of means including mailings, newspaper advertisements, and telephone solicitations. In a proxy fight, a bidder may attempt to use his voting rights and garner support from other shareholders to oust the incumbent board and/or management.

Proxy Fight Data

The number of proxy fights increased significantly toward the end of the fourth merger wave. For example, they rose from 21 in 1987 to 36 in 1988 and to a peak of 41 in 1989, followed by 35 in 1990 (Exhibit 6.9). The rise in proxy contests at the end of the fourth merger wave coincided with the collapse of the junk bond market, which made tender offer financing more difficult to find. Just as the number of mergers and acquisitions fell dramatically in the early 1990s, so did proxy fights, which declined steadily through 1993 but rebounded starting in 1994. Contested solicitation volume rose steadily through 2001 and has remained relatively high since then.

To know how the proxy device may be used to take control of a target company, we need a basic understanding of the workings of the corporate election process.

Corporate Elections

Corporate elections for seats on the board of directors are typically held once a year at the annual stockholders' meeting. The board of directors is particularly important to the corporation because the board selects the management, who in turn run the corporation on a day-to-day basis. The date and time of the stockholders' meeting is stipulated in the company's articles of incorporation. The date is usually chosen to coincide with the

---

27. Mark Mitchell, Todd Pulvino, and Erik Stafford, "Price Pressure Around Mergers," *Journal of Finance*, 59 (1), February 2004, 31–63.

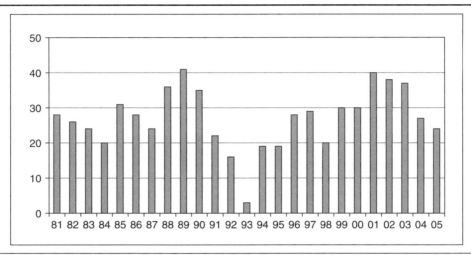

EXHIBIT 6.9   NUMBER OF CONTESTED PROXY SOLICITATIONS, 1981–2005
Source: 2005 Annual Meeting Season Wrap-Up Corporate Governance, Georgeson Shareholder Communications, Inc.

end of the company's fiscal year, when the annual report and the summary of the firm's financial results are available for the stockholders' review. SEC rules require that the annual report be sent to stockholders before the annual meeting. Because it takes time to produce the annual report, the annual meeting is usually held four to five months after the close of the firm's fiscal year.[28]

Shareholder elections tend to be characterized by considerable voter apathy. Some theorists contend that shareholders who supply capital to corporations should not necessarily have an interest in managing the company's affairs.[29] They assert that shareholders may adopt the easier route of voting with their feet, that is, by selling their shares when the firm and its management do not perform up to expectations. In their view, the sale of the shares is a far less expensive option than a collective action to alter the course of the company or to take control away from management. Moreover, they believe that the federal proxy laws, which require extensive disclosure, add further burdensome costs to dissenting groups, which creates a disincentive to engage in a proxy fight.

Smaller individual shareholders are naturally apathetic, given their share of ownership in the company, but, surprisingly, larger institutional shareholders often display similar apathy. Institutional shareholders are increasingly dominating equity markets. In the late 1980s, they accounted for more than 42.7% of the total equity holdings in the United States.[30] This percentage has continued to rise through the 2000s, and now it is typical

---

28. Herbert A. Einhorn and J. William Robinson, *Shareholder Meetings* (New York: Practicing Law Institute, 1984), p. 27.
29. Frank Easterbrook and Daniel Fischel, "Voting in Corporate Law," *Journal of Law and Economics,* 23, 1983, 395–427.
30. Carolyn K. Brancato and Patrick A. Gaughan, *Institutional Investors and Their Role in Capital Markets*, Columbia University Center for Law and Economics Monograph, 1988.

that institution investors can command at least half of the outstanding shares of a company. However, institutional investors have often sided with management. Indeed, some corporations pressure institutions to side with them against insurgents.[31]

While institutions have become somewhat more active, the evidence still indicates that, despite their ability to collectively wield considerable power and control proxy contests, they do not often choose to use this power. Considering that the institutional money managers' primary goal is to maximize the value of their portfolios, it is not surprising that they show little interest in the day-to-day running of the companies in which they invest. Not until the firm's performance flags do they look to divest their holdings.

The sale of an institution's large holdings may depress the stock price. In such an event, the institution may be locked into its position and thereby create an incentive for great activism by institutions. The active monitoring of individual companies by institutions, however, is hampered by the fact that it may hold equity in hundreds of companies. The large number of firms held in an institution's portfolio precludes micromanagement of their holdings. The fact that institutions may be temporarily locked into some of their positions, and the difficulties in micromanagement of their portfolios, helps explain why institutions are not active investors.

Voting by Proxy

Approximately 80% of annual shareholder meetings are held in the spring at a site selected by management. Not all interested stockholders find it possible to attend the stockholders' meeting to execute their votes, simply because they have other commitments or because they are scattered throughout the world. The voting process has been made easier through the use of proxies. Under the proxy system, shareholders may authorize another person to vote for them and to act as their proxy. Most corporate voting is done by proxies.

CASE STUDY

ICAHN VERSUS TEXACO—THE ROLE OF INSTITUTIONAL INVESTORS

Institutional investors account for approximately one-half, and in many cases, more than half, of the equity holdings of large corporations.[a] The percentage has been steadily rising for the past few decades. Given the significant holdings they account for, combined with the fact that a small number of institutions may control larger percentages of a company's stock, these investors may be the key to the success of a proxy contest. Historically, however, they have been loyal supporters of management. One example of this loyalty was the 1988 unsuccessful proxy contest that Carl Icahn waged to gain 5 seats on Texaco's 14-member board of directors. At that time Texaco was in bankruptcy after its disastrous lawsuit with Penzoil. Icahn favored various strategic

[a]Carolyn Brancato and Patrick A. Gaughan, "The Growth of Institutional Investors in U.S. Capital Markets," The Institutional Investor Projects: Columbia University School of Law, November 1988.

---

31. Robert Monks and Nell Minow, "Article on the Employee Benefit Research Institute Report on Proxy Voting," Institutional Shareholders Services, Washington, D.C.

changes, including asset sales, such as the sale of Texaco Canada and Caltex Petroleum. He even interposed himself as a possible buyer by initiating his own $60-per-share tender offer for the large oil company, which would be partially financed through the sale of $5.3 billion of Texaco assets.[b]

In spite of his intensive lobbying, including the able assistance of the leading proxy solicitation firm D. F. King, Icahn failed to win the crucial support of the institutional investors. He lost the battle by a 41.3% to 58.7% margin in Texaco's favor. The key to Texaco's win was Icahn's failure to receive support from the institutions holding large blocks of Texaco stock. Icahn's abortive attempt to take control of the company was not without benefits for the bidder. Texaco acquiesced to his pressure by announcing two special dividends of $8 per share. Texaco was also forced to redeploy $7 billion in assets, including the sale of Deutsche Texaco and Texaco Canada. This seems to be a common occurrence in "failed" proxy fights. After an insurgent or activist shareholder mounts pressure on the company's management, a process begins that usually results in changes in the way the company is run.

This proxy contest is instructive for several reasons. First, it highlights the crucial role that institutions may play; Icahn failed to garner sufficient institutional support and thereby lost the contest. Second, it highlights the problematic nature of proxy contests, in which a well-financed insurgent, aided by the best proxy advisors and a substantial share position of 14.9% of Texaco's equity, may fail to be successful. However, even in failure, Icahn remained a credible threat and was able to accomplish several of the structural changes he sought.

[b]Mark Stevens, *King Icahn* (New York: Dutton, 1993), p. 254.

Calling a Stockholders' Meeting

The ability to call a stockholders' meeting is very important to a bidder who is also a stockholder in the target firm. Upon establishing an equity position in the target, the hostile bidder may want to attempt to remove the board of directors and put in place a board that is favorable to the bidder. Such a board may then approve a business combination or other relationship with the bidding firm. The meeting may also be used to have the stockholders approve certain corporate actions, such as the deactivation of antitakeover defenses or the sale of certain assets and the payment of a dividend from the proceeds of this sale. If the next annual meeting is not scheduled for several months, the bidder may want to call a meeting sooner. The ability to call a special meeting, at which the issue of a merger or a new election may be considered, is determined by the articles of incorporation, which are governed by the prevailing state corporation laws. Most state laws allow meetings to be called if a certain percentage of shareholders request it. As an antitakeover defense, companies sometimes try to amend the corporate charter so that there are limitations on the ability of certain types of shareholders to call a special meeting.

Record Date

The corporation must notify all *stockholders of record* of an election. Only those stock-holders recorded on the stock transfer books as owners of the firm's stock on the record date may vote at the election. The record date is used for other purposes as well, such as to decide who will receive dividends or notice of a particular meeting. The record date is important because the firm's stock may trade actively, with the owners changing continually. The record date is usually no more than 60 days, but no less than 10 days, from the meeting date. As the owners of stock change, the record date specifies which stockholders will be able to vote. Stockholders who buy the stock before the meeting but after the meeting date do not receive notice of the meeting. If the stock is held under a *street name,* such as a brokerage firm, the stockholder may relinquish the right to receive notice of events such as meetings.

A stock price will often fall after the record date in a proxy contest.[32] This reflects that the market considers a stock less valuable when it does not carry the right to participate in an upcoming proxy contest. Presumably, this reflects some of the value of the right of voting participation in proxy fights.

Shares Held in Street Names

Stock may be held in street names for a variety of reasons. Stockholders who turn over their portfolios often may keep their stocks in their brokerage firm's name to expedite the registration of their securities. Many stockholders decide they do not want to be bothered with keeping their share certificates and simply leave their shares with the broker, who keeps them in the firm's name. A stockholder may be required to leave the purchased shares with the stockbroker if they were used as collateral in a margin purchase. The shareholdings are left with the broker in case the value of the collateral, the shares, falls. The stockholder will then get a margin call, and the shares might be sold if the shareholder cannot provide more collateral.

Bidders who are considering taking control of a company may want to keep the shares in the name of their brokerage firm to conceal the true identity of the owner of the shares. If the market anticipates an upcoming bid, the share price may rise. Keep in mind that under the Williams Act, bidders must make sure that they register their cumulative holdings, should they rise to the 5% level, with the SEC.

Approximately 70% of all corporate stock is held in street names, 30% in the name of brokerage firms and the remaining 40% in bank nominee names.[33] Often shareholders do not give their brokers voting instructions. When this happens brokers often choose to vote for the directors proposed by management. On average, at any given shareholder meeting, brokers may control approximately a quarter of the votes. There have been calls for new rules to be adopted which would prevent brokers from voting when they have not received specific instructions. Such a proposal to eliminate the "broker voting rule", however, was put forward at the New York Stock Exchange in 2006 and was not approved.

The physical exchange of shares is not the *modus operandi* of stock sales and purchases. Most brokerage firms do not hold the shares entrusted to them at the brokerage firm; rather, they keep them at a *depository.* One of the largest depositories in the United States is the Depository Trust Company located in New York City. When the shares are held in a depository, they are usually in the depository's name. Although the issuing corporation may obtain the names of the owners of the shares from the depository, this

---

32. Ronald C. Lease, John J. McConnell, and Wayne E. Mikkelson, "The Market Value of Control in Publicly Held Corporations," *Journal of Financial Economics,* 11, 1983, 439–472.
33. James Heard and Howard Sherman, *Conflicts of Interest in the Proxy System* (Washington, D.C.: Investor Responsibility Research Center, 1987), p. 74.

list may not be very helpful. The depository will show the street names for those shares held by brokerage firms. This may not indicate, however, who the real beneficial owners are. Efforts have been made in recent years to require that the depository list reflect the true owners of the firm's stock.

Different Types of Proxy Contests

Typically, there are two main forms of proxy contests:

1. *Contests for seats on the board of directors.* An insurgent group of stockholders may use this means to replace management. If the opposing slate of directors is elected, it may then use its authority to remove management and replace them with a new management team. In recent years we have seen insurgents who believe they may lack the power to unseat directors, try to organize a campaign to have shareholders withhold their votes as a way of recording their disapproval. A large percentage of shareholders did this in an election at Disney as a way a showing this disapproval of the extremely well paid CEO Michael Eisner.

2. *Contests about management proposals.* These proposals concern the approval of a merger or acquisition. Management may oppose the merger, and the insurgent group of stockholders may be in favor. Other relevant proposals might be the passage of antitakeover amendments in the company's charter. Management might be in favor, whereas the insurgent group might be opposed, believing that its opposition will cause the stock price to fall and/or reduce the likelihood of a takeover.

Regulation of Proxy Contests

The SEC regulates proxy contests, and its staff monitors the process to ensure that the participants comply with proxy regulations. Proxy solicitations are made pursuant to Section 14(a) of the 1934 Act and require that any solicitation be accompanied by the information set forth in Schedule 14A. All materials that are used to influence the outcome of the contest must be submitted to the SEC examiners in advance. This includes newspaper announcements, materials being mailed to shareholders, and press releases. If the examiners find some of these materials objectionable, they may require that the information be reworded or include additional disclosure.

The writing in proxy fight proposals tends to be much more direct and heated than what one normally finds in securities filings.[34] The SEC allows this as a way for both parties to get their message across to shareholders. Under Rule 14a-7 the corporation is required to provide its shareholder list to the dissidents so that they can communicate directly to shareholders.

SEC rules require a proxy solicitation to be accompanied by a Schedule 14A. Item 14 of this schedule sets forth the specific information that must be included in a proxy statement when there will be a vote for an approval of a merger, sale of substantial assets, or liquidation or dissolution of the corporation. For a merger, this information must include the terms and reasons for the transaction as well as a description of the

---

34. Edward Shea, *The McGraw-Hill Guide to Acquiring and Divesting Businesses* (New York: 1999), pp. 335–336.

accounting treatment and tax consequences of the deal. Financial statements and a statement regarding relevant state and federal regulatory compliance are required. Fairness opinions and other related documents also must be included.

In an effort to strike back against the use of proxy fights by insurgents, companies sometimes petition the SEC to have it issue a "no action" letter. A no action letter disallows a shareholder proposal. The SEC is empowered to do this under Section 14(a)8 of the Securities and Exchange Act. Such a letter may be issued if it can be demonstrated that the proposal is clearly not in the interests of other shareholders, serves only the personal interests of its proponent, or if it is designed to redress a personal claim of grievance of the shareholder.

Proxy Contests: From the Insurgents' Viewpoint

In a proxy contest, an insurgent group attempts to wrest control of the target by gathering enough supporting votes to replace the current board with board members of the group's choosing. The following characteristics increase the likelihood that a proxy fight will be successful:

- *Insufficient voting support for management.* Management normally can count on a certain percentage of votes to support its position. Some of these votes might be through management's own stockholdings. As we have noted, management can usually count on the voting support of brokers who have not received specific instructions from shareholders. Without a strong block of clear support for management among the voting shareholders, management and the incumbent board may be vulnerable to a proxy fight.
- *Poor operating performance.* The worse the firm's recent track record, the more likely other stockholders will vote for a change in control. Stockholders in a firm that has a track record of declining earnings and a poor dividend record are more likely to support an insurgent group advocating changes in the way the firm is managed.
- *Sound alternative operating plan.* The insurgents must be able to propose changes that other stockholders believe will reverse the downward direction of the firm. These changes might come in the form of asset sales with the proceeds paid to stockholders by means of higher dividends. Another possibility could be a plan that provides for the removal of antitakeover barriers and a receptive approach to outside offers for the sale of the firm.

Target Size and Proxy Fight Success

It is often easier and less expensive for insurgents in corporations that have a smaller market capitalization to control a sufficient number of shares to be able to influence, if not control, the outcome of a proxy fight. For larger corporations, this can be more difficult. An example would be Time Warner (formerly AOL Time Warner), which as of January 2006 had a market capitalization in excess of $83 billion. To control even 10% of the outstanding shares of this company requires approximately $8 billion. In 2005 and 2006, Carl Icahn and certain other institutional investors amassed Time Warner shareholding in excess of 3% of total shares outstanding. Icahn and Steve Case, the former AOL CEO, both lobbied Time Warner not to do more deals, such as a combination or venture with Internet Google, but to seriously consider breaking the company up into several units. It is ironic that Case, one of the major movers of the original AOL–Time Warner combination, would years later lobby the market to break up the combination that he helped to form. In early 2006, Icahn ended his proxy battle without getting Time Warner to agree to break up the company, but his strong pressure did cause management to agree to many of his proposals. However, clearly the size of the total market capitalization of Time Warner helped insulate management from even as determined a foe as Icahn.

Companies with larger market capitalizations are more insulated from proxy fight threats than smaller companies where an insurgent, such as a hedge fund, can control a much larger percentage of shares while still not concentrating too much of its capital in this one investment. Given that this is the case, management does not have to be as responsive to pressures of insurgents.

Effectiveness of Shareholder Activism

In 1989, Pound conducted a study of the effectiveness of shareholder activism by examining various countersolicitations by shareholders who opposed management's antitakeover proposals. Pound analyzed a sample of 16 countersolicitation proxy fights by shareholder groups that occurred in the 1980s. He reported the following results:[35]

- Countersolicitations were unsuccessful more often than they were successful. Dissidents in Pound's sample were successful only 25% of the time.
- When shareholders approved the contested provisions, the net-of-market share values of the company dropped an average of 6%. The range of stock price reactions was between 23 and 230%. Pound found that when the amendments were defeated, stock prices rose.
- The majority of the countersolicitations that Pound examined were preceded by a direct attempt to take control. In 8 of 16 countersolicitations in his sample, the dissidents had made an outright offer to take control of the company. In another 7 cases, the dissidents had purchased a large stake in the firm. In only 1 of the 16 cases was there no attempt to take control.

CASE STUDY

TORCHMARK VERSUS AMERICAN GENERAL

Insurgents may lose a proxy fight and still achieve some of their objectives. A hotly contested battle for control may set in motion a process that may bring about major changes in the way a firm is managed or even the sale of the firm. The 1990 proxy battle for American General is a case in point. Torchmark Corporation had attempted to place 5 new members on American General's 15-member

---

35. John Pound, "Shareholder Activism and Share Values," *Journal of Law and Economics* (October 1989), pp. 357–379; also in Patrick A. Gaughan, ed., *Readings in Mergers and Acquisitions* (Boston: Basil Blackwell, 1994), pp. 235–254.

board of directors. Torchmark, a small insurance company located in Birmingham, Alabama, was approximately one-sixth the size of the larger insurance company. Torchmark criticized what it thought was the poor performance of American General compared with the performance of Torchmark. As is typical of proxy fights, Torchmark conducted this critical campaign through full-page advertisements in the major financial media. The advertisement placed in the *New York Times* cited the relatively higher growth in dividends, stock prices, earnings per share, and return on equity of Torchmark. American General won its proxy contest with Torchmark, which had sought to take over American General. Its success may be partially attributed to support from institutional investors, who controlled approximately 70% of American General's shares.[a]

Institutions, however, were disappointed with American General's relatively poor performance. In response to criticism, American General's management announced an increase in its quarterly dividend from $0.39 to $0.80 per share. In addition, at their victorious annual meeting in May 1990, CEO Harold Hook announced that the company, which was vulnerable to a hostile takeover because of its lagging stock price (approximately $40 per share before the meeting), would be put up for sale. As discussed earlier in this chapter, American General was eventually taken over by AIG.

[a]Michael Allen and Randall Smith, "Sale of American General Sought in Spite of Vote," *Wall Street Journal*, May 3, 1990, p. A3.

Proxy Fight Process

It is easier to understand the proxy fight process if it is broken down into discrete steps such as the following:

Step 1. Starting the Proxy Fight. A proxy fight for control of a company may begin when a bidder, who is also stockholder, decides to attempt to change control at the upcoming stockholders' meeting. An insurgent group of stockholders may have the right to call a special meeting at which the replacement of management may be formally considered. A proxy fight might also come as a result of a management proposal for a major change, such as the sale of the firm or the installation of certain antitakeover defenses.

Step 2. The Solicitation Process. In advance of the stockholders' meeting, the insurgent stockholder group attempts to contact other stockholders to convince them to vote against management's candidates for the board of directors or to vote for an acquisition or against certain antitakeover amendments. The process of contacting stockholders is usually handled by the proxy solicitor hired by the insurgent group. Management may have a proxy firm on retainer and, if the proxy battle is particularly contentious, may choose to hire other proxy firms. These proxy firms, which may have their own lists of stockholders compiled from various sources, may use a staff of workers to repeatedly call stockholders to convince them of the merits of their client's position. Materials are then distributed to the beneficial owners of the stock. The depositories will submit a list of shareholders and their holdings to the issuing corporation.

The issuing corporation will try to deal directly with the beneficial owners of the shares. An insurgent group may sue to have the issuing corporation share this information with the insurgent stockholders so as to have the interested parties on a more equal footing. When the shares are registered in the names of banks and trust companies, these institutions may or may not have voting authority for these shares.

The banks may have voting authority to vote on all, some, or no issues. This voting authority may be such that the bank may vote on minor issues but must consult the beneficial owners on major issues such as a merger.

As we have noted, the shares are held in a brokerage firm's name, the broker may or may not have the authority to vote the shares. Stock exchange rules and SEC regulations determine whether the broker may do so. If the broker is not a trustee, the broker must contact the shareholder for voting instructions. Normally, if the broker does not hear from the stockholder at least 15 days before the meeting, he or she may vote the shares (assuming the broker has attempted to contact the shareholder at least 25 days before the meeting). In a contest for control, or when there is a rival insurgent group with counterproposals or candidates, however, the broker may not vote even if he or she has not received instructions from the beneficial owner. A beneficial owner is a broad definition of the legal owners of a security. The beneficial owner has the ultimate power to dispose of the holding. This is generally the party listed on the stock transfer sheets as the owner on the record date.

To expedite the process, the brokerage firm will tabulate the votes from its various proxies and submit its own summary master proxies reflecting the combined votes of its various clients.

Step 3. The Voting Process. Upon receiving the proxies, stockholders may then forward their votes to the designated collector, such as a brokerage firm. The votes are sent to the proxy clerks at the brokerage firms to tabulate them.

The brokerage firm or bank usually keeps a running total of the votes as they are received and submits the vote results shortly before the corporation meeting. When the votes are submitted to the issuing corporation, tabulators appointed by the company count them. Voting inspectors are often used to oversee the tabulation process and help ensure its accuracy. The process takes place in an area that is sometimes referred to as the "snake pit." In a proxy fight, both the issuing corporation and the dissident group frequently have their own proxy solicitors present throughout the voting tabulation process to help ensure that their client's interests are dealt with fairly. Proxy solicitors are alert to any questionable proxies, which they then will challenge.

A proxy might be challenged if the same shares are voted more than once or if it was not signed by the party with voting authority. In cases in which more than one vote has been submitted, the vote with the latest date is usually selected. Major discrepancies in the voting process are usually followed by legal actions in which the losing party sues to invalidate the election.

Voting Analysis[36]

The votes of stockholders are grouped into the following categories:

- *Shares controlled by insurgents and shareholder groups unfriendly to management.* This is the core of the insurgents' support. The greater the number

---

36. This section is adapted from a presentation by Morris J. Kramer, "Corporate Control Techniques: Insurgent Considerations." In James W. Robinson, ed., *Shareholders Meetings and Shareholder Control in Today's Securities Market* (New York: Practicing Law Institute, 1985).

of shares that this group commands, the more likely it is that the proxy fight will be successful.

- *Shares controlled by directors, officers, and employee stock ownership plans (ESOPs).* This category tends to represent the core of management's support. Directors and officers will surely vote with management. Shares held in ESOPs also tend to vote with management because workers may be concerned that a change in control may mean layoffs. In the 1990 proxy battle between Harold Simmons of NL Industries and the Lockheed Corporation, Simmons attributed his defeat in part to the 18.91% of the outstanding shares of Lockheed that were held in the firm's ESOP, which was formed in 1989.[37]

CASE STUDY

HAROLD SIMMONS VERSUS LOCKHEED

An example of one of the proxy contests that took place following the end of the fourth merger wave was the battle between investor Harold Simmons and the Lockheed Corporation. Simmons attempted to take control of Lockheed through the proxy process. Through his company NL Industries, Simmons launched a proxy battle for control of Lockheed Corporation. Using Houston-based NL industries, which owned 19% of Lockheed, he nominated its own slate of directors and submitted a proposal to shareholders to eliminate some antitakeover defenses such as Lockheed's poison pill. This poison pill becomes effective when a shareholder acquires more than 20%.[a] In this instance, however, Simmons failed to convince enough institutional owners of the firm's stock that they should vote for his directors and proposal. As a conciliatory gesture to the insurgents on shareholder rights issues, however, management agreed to take steps to have Lockheed elect to be exempt from the antitakeover provisions of the Delaware antitakeover law. In addition, management, in response to pressure from institutional investors, agreed to allow confidential shareholder voting.[b]

[a]Randall Smith and David Hilder, "Raiders Shorn of Junk Gird for Proxy Fights," *Wall Street Journal,* March 7, 1990, p. C1.
[b]Wartzman and Blumenthal, "Lockheed Wins Proxy Battle with Simmons," *Wall Street Journal,* April 11, 1990, p. A3.

- *Shares controlled by institutions.* As noted previously, large institutions control equity markets; they are by far the largest category of stockholders. Institutions have historically tended to be passive shareholders and have usually voted with management. This situation is starting to change as institutions are becoming more outspoken and are putting more pressure on management to maximize the value of their shareholdings. If the institutions can be convinced that a change in control may greatly increase value, they may vote in favor of the insurgent's position.
- *Shares controlled by brokerage firms.* Certain stock exchange rules, such as those instituted by the New York Stock Exchange and the American Stock Exchange, do not allow brokerage firms to vote the shares held in their name on behalf of

---

37. Rick Wartzman and Karen Blumenthal, "Lockheed Wins Proxy Battle with Simmons," *Wall Street Journal,* April 11, 1990, p. A3.

clients without contacting them to receive voting instructions from the owners of the shares. Voting instructions tend to be required for issues such as mergers or antitakeover amendments. Large amounts of shares tend to be held in street names. Brokerage firms, however, are generally not active voters in proxy fights. The reason for this may be traced to the problems of securing voting instructions, coupled with the fact that one of the brokerage firm's goals is to maximize its commissions and the value of its portfolios. Voting in proxy fights may not pay a return in the foreseeable future. The corporation sends voting materials to the brokerage firms, which in turn are supposed to forward these materials to the "beneficial owners" of the shares. As of 1986, the issuing corporation has been able to send the materials directly to the beneficial owners by asking the brokerage firm for the names and addresses of the owners. These names and addresses are supplied unless the shareholders have asked that they not be given out.

- *Shares controlled by individuals.* Given the larger equity base of many public corporations, this group of stockholders may not constitute a large percentage of the votes. In some cases, however, they may be important. Individual stockholders tend to vote with management. In some instances, major individual shareholders may be the focal point of the tender offer. For example, Kamal Adham, a major stockholder in Financial General Bankshares, Inc., solicited shareholder support for a proxy fight in favor of the approval of an acquisition of Financial General by a company owned by Adham and others.[38] Adham lost the proxy fight, but a plan for the serious consideration of a merger was later adopted.

Costs of a Proxy Fight

A proxy fight may be a less expensive alternative to a tender offer. Tender offers are costly because they offer to buy up to 100% of the outstanding stock at a premium that may be as high as 50%. In a tender offer, the bidder usually has certain stockholdings that may be sold off in the event the tender offer is unsuccessful. The bidder may take a loss unless there is an available buyer, such as a rival bidder or the target corporation. The stock sales, however, may be a way for the bidder to recapture some of the costs of the tender offer. Although a proxy fight does not involve the large capital outlays that tender offers require, it is not without significant costs. The losers in a proxy fight do not have a way to recapture their losses. If the proxy fight is unsuccessful, the costs of the proxy battle are usually not recoverable. In a minority of circumstances, however, the insurgents may recover their costs from the corporation.

The major cost categories of a proxy fight are:

- *Professional fees.* A team of professionals is necessary to carry out a successful proxy fight. This team usually includes proxy solicitors, investment banks, and attorneys. The larger the company and the more contentious the issues, the more professionals involved and the greater the fees.

---

38. "NLT Holders Reject by 5–3 Margin a Plan to Create Group to Study Acquisition Bids," *Wall Street Journal,* May 13, 1982, p. 6.

- *Printing, mailing costs, and "communications costs."* The proxy materials must be printed and distributed to stockholders. A staff may be assembled by the proxy solicitation firm to contact stockholders directly by telephone. This may be supplemented through full-page advertisements in the *Wall Street Journal,* such as the advertisement placed by Lockheed's CEO citing the board of directors' opposition to Harold Simmons's proxy fight (Exhibit 6.10). Brokerage firms must be compensated for the costs of forwarding the proxy materials to stockholders. In major proxy battles companies retain proxy solicitors, such as Georgeson/Shareholders, to assist them with the process.
- *Litigation costs.* Proxy fights, like tender offers, tend to be actively litigated. Both parties incur significant legal fees. For example, the insurgent group may have to sue for access to the stockholder list. The corporation pays management's legal fees, whereas the insurgent group must pay its own legal expenses. Management also has the advantage in this area.
- *Other expenses.* Various other expenses, such as tabulation fees, are associated with the voting process. The tabulation may be done by the issuing company, the company's transfer agent, or a firm that specializes in tabulation work for corporate elections.

Shareholder Wealth Effects of Proxy Contests

Early Research

Dodd and Warner conducted a study of 96 proxy contests for seats on the boards of directors of companies on the New York Stock Exchange and the American Stock Exchange.[39] Their research revealed a number of interesting findings on the impact of proxy contests on the value of stockholders' investments in these firms. They showed that a positive stock price effect is associated with proxy contests. In a 40-day period before and including the announcement of the proxy contest, a positive, abnormal stock price performance of 0.105 was registered. Based on these results, Dodd and Warner concluded that proxy contests result in an increase in value inasmuch as they help facilitate the transfer of resources to more valuable uses.

The positive wealth effects of the Dodd and Warner study were confirmed in later research by DeAngelo and DeAngelo.[40] In a study of 60 proxy contests for board seats, they found an average abnormal shareholder wealth increase equal to 4.85% in a two-day window around the announcement of the dissident activity, whereas an 18.76% increase was associated with a 40-day window, which is the same time period as that of the Dodd and Warner study. DeAngelo and DeAngelo traced the source of the shareholder gains to cases in which the dissident activity led to the sale or liquidation of the company.

---

39. Peter Dodd and Jerrold Warner, "On Corporate Government: A Study of Proxy Contests," *Journal of Financial Economics,* 11(1–4), April 1983, 401–438.
40. Hamj DeAngelo and Linda DeAngelo, "The Role of Proxy Contests in the Governance of Publicly Held Companies," *Journal of Financial Economics,* June 1989, 29–60.

Lockheed Shareholders:

IMPORTANT INFORMATION ABOUT YOUR INVESTMENT
(Part One)

Harold Simmons is a Texas investor who to our knowledge has no experience in the management of an aerospace company. NL Industries, Inc., a company he controls, has launched a proxy fight to replace your Board of Directors with its nominees, including Mr. Simmons. NL Industries is seeking to take control of your company without making an offer to acquire it or announcing any specific plans. Your Board of Directors opposes the election of Harold Simmons and his slate to Lockheed's Board because we believe it would be contrary to the interests of Lockheed shareholders.

Your Board of Directors is committed to taking any and all steps necessary to protect and enhance the value of all shareholders' investment in Lockheed.

We will be communicating with you shortly with additional information about Mr. Simmons and his associates as well as about your company's plans and progress, and we will be providing you with a revised BLUE Proxy Card. We urge you not to sign any proxy card you may receive from Mr. Simmons and his associates. Please sign, date, and return your new BLUE Proxy Card when you receive it!

We think it important, however, for you to be immediately aware of a few facts about Mr. Simmons and his associates:

- Many of those NL Industries has named to its slate have been promised $20,000 each if they are not elected and they are, we believe, personal friends or business associates of Mr. Simmons. None of these nominees has any direct personal investment in Lockheed.

- According to his 13D filings with the Securities and Exchange Commission, Mr. Simmons, who was found by a court to have violated his fiduciary duties under Federal Retirement Law (ERISA) and has been enjoined from further violations until 1992, is currently under investigation by the Securities and Exchange Commission regarding trading in the securities of Lockheed and another company.

- NL Industries has indicated that it intends to propose a shareholder resolution recommending that the Board terminate the company's Shareholder Rights Plan. According to Simmons' public filings, NL's indicated interest in making this proposal is so that it can continue buying Lockheed stock in excess of 20%. The Rights Plan, while restricting certain changes in control without Board approval, is designed in part to protect against the acquisition of control in the marketplace by any shareholder without paying a full and fair price for that right. We oppose NL's proposal because we believe that control of the company rests with ALL the shareholders and that you should reap an economic benefit from any transfer of control through stock acquisitions by anyone. Accordingly, your Board of Directors strongly recommends that you vote AGAINST any proposal NL Industries may make to recommend termination of the Rights Plan.

You, our shareholders, are the owners of Lockheed. We are keenly aware of our fiduciary obligations to you.

1989 was a transition year for Lockheed and your Board of Directors and management are moving aggressively to maximize shareholder value. We will continue to keep you informed of significant developments concerning your investment in Lockheed.

On behalf of your Board of Directors,

Daniel M. Tellep

Daniel M. Tellep
*Chairman of the Board
and Chief Executive Officer*

IMPORTANT

If your shares are held in "Street-Name," only your broker or banker can vote your shares and only upon receipt of your specific instructions. Please contact the person responsible for your account and instruct that individual to vote the new **BLUE Proxy Card** on your behalf in accordance with your Board's recommendations.

If you have any questions or need further assistance, please call our proxy solicitor, *GEORGESON & COMPANY INC.*, at 1-800-223-2064.

EXHIBIT 6.10   *WALL STREET JOURNAL* ANNOUNCEMENT BY LOCKHEED CORPORATION TO ITS SHAREHOLDERS
Source: Reprinted by permission of the Lockheed Corporation.

DeAngelo and DeAngelo attempted to trace the source of the shareholder gains by monitoring the firm for three years after the proxy fights. Fewer than 20% of the companies remained independent and under the same management three years later. At many of the companies, the CEO or president had resigned. In addition, at 15 of the 60 firms they studied, the companies were either sold or liquidated. They actually concluded that many of the gains from proxy fights were related to merger and acquisition activity. The proxy contests may have caused some of these firms to eventually sell the company, which in turn caused shareholders to realize a takeover premium. This is discussed further later in this chapter.

Later Research

A study by Borstadt and Swirlein analyzed 142 companies that traded on the New York and American Stock Exchanges over the period from 1962 to 1986.[41] They learned that dissidents were successful 42% of the time. They determined that shareholders realized just over an 11% rate of return during the contest period. These positive shareholder wealth effects are consistent with the bulk of research in this area, although one study, by Ikenberry and Lakonishok, found negative effects.[42]

More recent research further confirmed the positive shareholder wealth effect of prior studies. In a large study of 270 proxy contests that occurred between 1979 and 1994, Mulherin and Poulsen found that proxy contests help create shareholder value.[43] They traced most of the gains to the acquisition of the firms that occurred around the contest period. Gains were even found, however, when the company was not acquired if that firm experienced management turnover. They found that the new management tended to engage in restructuring, which also created shareholder value. Either way, the proxy contest helped remove poorly performing managers, thus raising shareholder value.

Value of Shareholders' Votes

The value of shareholders' votes was also examined in the Dodd and Warner study. They attempted to test the hypothesis originally proposed by Manne, which stated that a positive stock price effect in proxy fights is associated with the increased value of the votes held by shareholders.[44] This value is perceived by participants in the contest who lobby for the support of shareholders. If their efforts are responsible for some of the increased value of shares, the value should decline after the record date. Shares purchased after the record date may be voted only under restricted and limited circumstances. For the 42 contests in

41. Lisa Borstadt and T. J. Swirlein, "The Efficient Monitoring of Proxy Contests: An Empirical Analysis of Post-Contest Control Changes and Firm Performance," *Journal of Financial Management,* 21, Autumn 1992, 22–34.

42. David Ikenberry and Josef Lakonishok, "Corporate Governance Through the Proxy Contest: Evidence and Implications," *Journal of Business,* 66, July 1993, 405–433.

43. J. Harold Mulherin and Annette B. Poulsen, "Proxy Contests and Corporate Change: Implications for Shareholder Wealth," *Journal of Financial Economics,* 47, 1998, 279–313.

44. Henry Manne, "The Higher Criticism of the Corporation," *Columbia Law Review,* 62, 1962, 399–432.

which they had the specific record date, Dodd and Warner found negative results, which seems to support the Manne vote-value hypothesis.

Nature of the Dissidents and Dissident Campaigns

Research shows that the dissidents are often former managers of the target or those who have prior experience in the target's line of business. The Dodd and Warner study found that only a minority of the proxy contests involved a battle between an outside entity and the target corporation. Almost half of the contests were waged between former insiders who left the company following a policy dispute or other disagreement. DeAngelo and DeAngelo found that in almost 50% of the contests in their sample, the dissident leader had prior experience in the target's line of business. In almost one-third of the cases, the dissident leader was at one time employed by the target company.

Long-Term Effects of Proxy Contests

The DeAngelo and DeAngelo study found that dissidents prevailed in one-third of the contest in their sample, whereas another one-third of the companies had changes in top management within three years of the contest, with most of these changes occurring in the first year. In addition, they found that only 20% of the sample firms remained independent publicly held companies run by the same management team that was in place before the proxy fight. In fact, one-quarter of the companies were either sold or liquidated shortly after the contest.

One of the conclusions of the DeAngelo and DeAngelo study is that once a proxy contest starts, it is more than likely that the company will not remain the same but will undergo some significant changes. It is common that proxy contests result in changes in the managerial structure of the company.

What Determines the Choice of a Tender Offer versus a Proxy Fight?

A study by Sridharan and Reinganum attempted to determine why in some cases a tender offer occurs and in other cases a proxy fight results.[45] They analyzed a sample of 79 tender offers and 38 proxy contests. They found that proxy contests tend to occur more frequently in cases in which the company's performance has been poor as measured by its stock market performance and return on assets. Proxy fights, however, tended to be associated with managerial inefficiency. The capital structure also seemed to be a causal factor as less highly leveraged companies more often were tender offer targets. They theorized that with more equity in the capital structure, there are more shares that may be acquired. In general they found that proxy fight targets are less profitable than targets of tender offers. The poor performance of companies that are the target of proxy fights gives the insurgents a more compelling argument for changing management and enacting other changes.

---

45. Una Sridharan and M. R. Reinganum, "Determinants of the Choice of Hostile Takeover Mechanism: An Empirical Analysis of Takeovers and Proxy Contests," *Financial Management,* 24, Spring 1995, 57–67.

The poor performance of proxy fight targets was also confirmed by Ikenberry and Lakonishok, who found in a sample of 97 election contests "negative abnormal returns and deteriorating operating performance prior to the announcement of the proxy contest."[46]

Combination of a Proxy Fight and a Tender Offer

A proxy fight is sometimes used in conjunction with an offer to buy the target. One classic example occurred on May 1, 1986, when Asher Edelman made an offer to buy Fruehauf. Edelman had bought 5% of Fruehauf and wanted to acquire the entire corporation. He proposed the acquisition to the Fruehauf board of directors, which rejected the offer. Edelman responded by increasing his shareholdings to 9.5% and the bid price to $42 per share.[47] At the annual meeting, Edelman also engaged in a proxy fight. He proposed his own slate of directors, who would, of course, be in favor of approving the bid. Edelman lost the proxy fight but followed with a formal tender offer at $44 per share.

A proxy fight may be an effective ancillary tool when coupled with a tender offer. The hostile bidder may use the proxy fight to effect the approval of a shareholder proposal that would dismantle the target's antitakeover defenses. For example, a bidder could use a proxy fight to have the target dismantle its poison pill or other antitakeover defenses. This would then be followed by a more effective tender offer. Another option available to the bidder and/or insurgent is to have the target agree to elect not to be bound by the prevailing state antitakeover laws.

CASE STUDY

IBM VERSUS LOTUS

The IBM successful tender offer for Lotus Development Corporation is an example of the type of tender offers that took place in the fifth merger wave. They were hostile offers that were financed primarily by equity rather than cash offers that used debt financing, such as those that were more common in the fourth merger wave. On June 6, 1995, the traditionally conservative IBM launched a $3.3 billion, $60-per-share cash tender offer. The aggressive offer of IBM resulted in a quick win, unlike some of the drawn-out takeover battles of the fourth merger wave. The speed of the successful bid was particularly important to this deal because much of Lotus's assets were its skilled personnel along with valued software rather than physical assets. A rancorous contest could mean the loss of key employees. Concern about defections of programmers and other human assets was one of the reasons no more software acquisitions occurred in the 1980s.

After months of discussions with Lotus failed to bear fruit, IBM moved with speed and skill, using acumen derived from the lessons of the 1980s along with new tricks developed in the early 1990s. IBM considered a friendly deal and was going to start with a bear hug, but rejected this plan out of concern that Lotus's chairman, James Manzi, would seek a white knight. Consequently, IBM went with a rich $60-per-share offer, which was a 100% premium above the preannouncement price of $30 per share. This bid was attractive in light of Lotus's slow growth (see Exhibit A). IBM's concern

---

46. Ikenberry and Lakonishok, "Corporate Governance Through the Proxy Contest: Evidence and Implications," p. 405.

47. John Bussey, "Edelman Plans $44-a-Share Bid for Fruehauf," *Wall Street Journal*, June 12, 1986, p. 12.

about personnel defections prompted the company to start with a high preemptive bid rather than risk other bidders coming on the scene. The high bid also made serious resistance by management more difficult to justify. The all-cash offer avoided the delays that assembling the financing may cause.

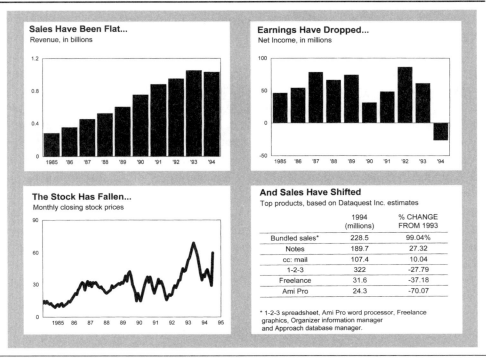

EXHIBIT A   A LOOK AT LOTUS'S DEVELOPMENT

Being concerned about the loss of key personnel but constrained by legal restrictions that limit the bidder's ability to contact target employees, IBM applied some new techniques specific to this industry. IBM placed information about the bid, including a copy of the letter that IBM chairman, Louis Gerstner, sent to Manzi, on the Internet. IBM also had other former members of Lotus's management contact current Lotus managers to "take their temperature."

With the increase in takeovers that occurred in the fifth merger wave, the importance of proxy fights declined somewhat compared with the increased use of tender offers. They still maintain their traditional role as a tool that may be used under certain circumstances to achieve specific goals.

IBM's legal team prepared a lawsuit designed to get Lotus to rescind its poison pill defense. It also took advantage of a clause in Lotus's bylaws that allowed an appeal directly to shareholders if other means were not successful. The public relations campaign and legal maneuvering were all secondary to the high all-cash offer, which they increased to $64 per share before Lotus accepted the $3.53 billion bid, which was at that time the largest computer software deal in history. The deal also was a step in the transformation and adaptation of IBM to changes in the marketplace. With this acquisition IBM acquired valuable software products that it lacked (see Exhibit B). In 2005, IBM took another major step in its transformation when it sold its PC business, having been the founder of the personal computer, to Lenovo.

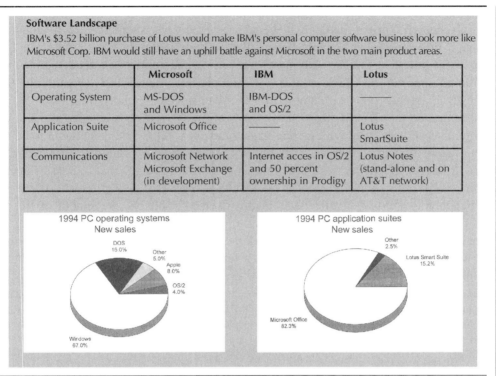

Software Landscape

IBM's $3.52 billion purchase of Lotus would make IBM's personal computer software business look more like Microsoft Corp. IBM would still have an uphill battle against Microsoft in the two main product areas.

	Microsoft	IBM	Lotus
Operating System	MS-DOS and Windows	IBM-DOS and OS/2	———
Application Suite	Microsoft Office	———	Lotus SmartSuite
Communications	Microsoft Network Microsoft Exchange (in development)	Internet acces in OS/2 and 50 percent ownership in Prodigy	Lotus Notes (stand-alone and on AT&T network)

1994 PC operating systems New sales

DOS 16.0%
Other 5.0%
Apple 8.0%
OS/2 4.0%
Windows 67.0%

1994 PC application suites New sales

Other 2.5%
Lotus Smart Suite 15.2%
Microsoft Office 82.3%

EXHIBIT B IBM AND LOTUS'S INDUSTRY POSITION
Source: International Data Corp.

SUMMARY

This chapter discusses the main alternatives available to a hostile bidder: a bear hug, a tender offer, and a proxy fight. A bear hug is an offer made directly to the directors of the target corporation. A bear hug puts pressure of the directors because it carries with it the implication that if the offer is not favorably received, a tender offer will follow. There are several variations of a tender offer, such as the all-cash tender offer and the two-tiered tender offer. The effectiveness of tender offers has varied over time as firms developed better defenses and the availability of financing changed. The regulatory environment has also greatly affected the use of this takeover tool. Laws regulating tender offers not only set forth the rules within which an offer must be structured but also provide strategic opportunities for both the bidder and the target. The use of tender offers grew significantly in both size and number during the 1980s. Large corporations that once considered themselves invulnerable to takeover succumbed to the junk bond–financed tender offers. When the junk bond market declined in the late 1980s, hostile bidders were forced to look elsewhere. Proxy fights, which work through the corporate election proxy, once again became a viable tool. Proxy contests may bring about a change in control or seek more modest goals, such as the enactment of shareholder provisions in the company's corporate charter.

The process of conducting a proxy fight was also described. Bidders have discovered that a successful proxy battle may be a less expensive alternative to a tender offer, although unsuccessful insurgents have little to show at the end of the contest. Bidders have also found that the use of a proxy fight in conjunction with a tender offer presents additional opportunities. Proxy fights, for example, may be used to dismantle the target's defenses, making it more vulnerable to a less-well-financed tender offer.

Research on the shareholder wealth effects of proxy fights has consistently shown that they tend to be associated with increased shareholder wealth. The gains seem to be related to the acquisition of the target company or to management turnover. Even when proxy fights are not directly successful, they may bring about changes that increase shareholder value.

The playing field of hostile deals again reversed itself by the middle of the 1990s, with the tender offer once again becoming a more effective tool for implementing hostile takeovers. With the rebound of the tender offer, now financed more with equity and less with debt, proxy fights again played a less important role. Just as with antitakeover defenses, takeover tactics are continually evolving. Bidders are forced to adapt to the increasingly effective defenses that targets have erected. This process will continue to evolve in the future.

3

GOING PRIVATE TRANSACTIONS AND LEVERAGED BUYOUTS

7

LEVERAGED BUYOUTS

A leveraged buyout (LBO) is a financing technique used by a variety of entities, including the management of a corporation, or outside groups, such as other corporations, partnerships, individuals, or investment groups. Specifically, it is the use of debt to purchase the stock of a corporation, and it frequently involves taking a public company private.

The number of large LBOs increased dramatically in the 1980s, but they first began to occur with some frequency in the 1970s as an outgrowth of the 1960s bull market. Many private corporations took advantage of the high stock prices and chose this time to go public, thereby allowing many entrepreneurs to enjoy windfall gains. Even though some of these firms were not high quality, their stock was quickly absorbed by the growing bull market. When the stock market turned down in the 1970s, the prices of some lower-quality companies fell dramatically. The bulk of this falloff in prices occurred between 1972 and 1974, when the Dow Jones Industrial Average fell from 1036 in 1972 to 578 in 1974. In 1974, the average price-earnings (P/E) ratio was six, which is considered low.

When the opportunity presented itself, managers of some of the companies that went public in the 1960s chose to take their companies private in the 1970s and 1980s. In addition, many conglomerates that had been built up in the 1960s through large-scale acquisitions began to become partially disassembled through selloffs, a process that is called *deconglomeration.* Part of this process took place through the sale of divisions of conglomerates through LBOs. This process was ongoing through the 1980s and is partially responsible for the rising trend in divestitures that occurred during that period.

TERMINOLOGY

There is much overlap in LBOs and going private transactions. A going private deal is where a public company is taken private. Such a transaction is financed with some debt and some equity. When the bulk of the financing comes from debt, this deal can also be referred to as an LBO. When a company sells a business unit, or even the entire company, to a management group, this type of deal is referred to as a management buyout (MBO). Many of these transactions involve a public company divesting a division, and in doing so they sell it to the unit's management as opposed to an outside party. Sometimes they are also referred to as unit management buyouts. When managers rely mainly on borrowed capital to finance the deal, it may also be referred to as a leveraged buyout. Thus we see there is significant overlap in the terms that may be used to describe these transactions.

HISTORICAL TRENDS IN LBOs
Early Origins of LBOs

While the actual term leveraged buyout is a relatively new one, the concept of a debt financed transaction in which a public company goes private is not. One notable example was the LBO of the Ford Motor Company. In 1919, Henry Ford, and his son Edsel, being displeased with having to answer to shareholders who differed with the founder of the auto company on issues such as dividend policy, borrowed what was considered an astronomical sum at that time to take the world's largest automobile company private. The Fords purchased company's shares which they did not own for $106 million of which $75 million was borrowed from a collection of East Coast banks such as Chase Securities of New York, Old Colony Trust, and Bond & Goodwin.[1] The Fords wanted to be free to manufacture and sell their Model Ts at ever-decreasing prices, which would come from reinvesting profits in the company as opposed to distributing them to shareholders. Shareholders such as the Dodge brothers were happy to cash out their positions in the auto giant as they were using their capital to expand their own auto company to compete with Ford, making higher-priced cars. Investors wanted higher profits that could be facilitated by higher prices, but Henry Ford was consumed by making the automobile affordable and attainable for the average American and he needed continually lower prices to bring this about.

It is interesting to note that some of the problems that befell some of the LBOs of the fourth merger wave also affected Ford. When the U.S. economy turned down in the years 1920–21, Ford incurred a cash crunch and many worried it would not be able to service the huge debt load it had taken on in the buyout. Ford responded by a temporary halt in production followed by layoffs and other cost-cutting measures. However, Ford had alternatives at its disposal that most companies do not have. Rather than have to head "hat in hand" to the East Coast bankers whom he despised, Henry Ford exercised rights in his agreements with Ford dealers and shipped them the mounting inventory of cars, even though they did not necessarily need them. This required the dealers to pay for them and the dealers all across the United States headed out for financing, giving the Ford Motor Company the cash infusion it needed. Ironically, Ford got access to the needed cash by its dealers taking out many loans as opposed to Ford seeking distressed financing.

Trends in LBOs: 1980s–2005

The value and number of worldwide LBOs increased dramatically starting in the early 1980s and peaking by the end of the decade (Exhibits 7.1 and 7.2). Prior to then, LBOs were relatively rare. By the mid-1980s, larger companies were starting to become the target of LBOs; the average LBO transaction increased from $39.42 million in 1981 to $137.45 million in 1987. Although LBOs attracted much attention in the 1980s, they were still small in both number and dollar value compared with mergers. For example, in 1987

---

1. Douglas Brinkley, *Wheels for the World* (New York: Penguin, 2003), 241–242.

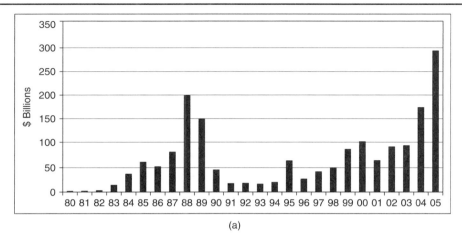

(a)

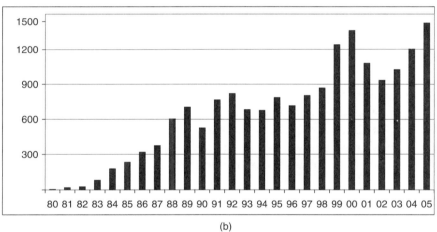

(b)

EXHIBIT 7.1   (a) VALUE OF WORLDWIDE LBOs, 1980–2005; (b) NUMBER OF WORLDWIDE LBOs, 1980–2005
Source: Thomson Financial Securities Data.

there were 3,701 mergers but only 259 LBOs. Leveraged buyouts accounted for only 7% of the total number of transactions. In terms of total value, LBOs accounted for a higher percentage of the total value of transactions. In 1987, LBOs made up 21.3% of the total value of transactions, which shows that the typical LBO tends to have a larger dollar value than the typical merger. Exhibit 7.1 shows that the dollar value of LBOs fell dramatically in 1990 and 1991. This decrease coincided with the decline in the junk bond market that started in late 1988 and the 1990–91 recession that followed a few years later.

The value, and especially the number of worldwide LBOs, increased significantly as we moved through the fifth merger wave. This effect was so pronounced that by 1998, the number of LBOs reached an all-time high. However, in 1999, the number of deals increased approximately 50% over 1998, while in 2000 the number increased again. However, even though the number of deals in 2000 was approximately double the 1980 levels, the total value was only half. This is because the deals of the fifth merger wave are not the mega-LBOs of the fourth wave but smaller and more numerous.

Date Announced	Target Name	Acquiror Name	Rank Value of Deal ($bil.)
10/25/06	RJR Nabisco Inc	Kohlberg Kravis Roberts & Co	25.1
7/24/06	HCA	Investor Group	21.0
11/16/06	Clear Channel	Investor Group	18.7
3/17/06	BAA (Bid No. 1)	Investor Group	17.7
9/16/06	Freescale Semiconductor	Investor Group	17.6
10/2/06	Harrah's Entertainment	Apollo Management Texas Pacific Group	15.1
5/29/06	Kinder Morgan	Investor Group	14.6
6/27/06	Univision Comm.	Investor Group	12.2
3/28/05	SunGuard Data Systems	Investor Group	11.3
1/23/06	Albertson's	Investor Group	11.3

TABLE 7.1 LARGEST WORLDWIDE LBOs

Source: Wall Street Journal, The New York Times, Thomson Financial Securities Data.

By far the largest LBO was the 1988 $24.6 billion RJR Nabisco deal. This food and tobacco company was taken private in a much-acclaimed takeover battle that was won by the buyout firm of Kohlberg Kravis & Roberts (KKR) (Table 7.1). KKR won a bidding war against a rival group that was led by the former chief executive officer (CEO) of the company, Ross Johnson. Johnson was attempting to implement a management buyout but failed when his initial offer put the company in play and he was outbid. Like many other LBOs, however, the deal did not generate gains for the contest winners, and KKR eventually sold off its interest in the company after experiencing disappointing returns.

─── CASE STUDY ───

RJR NABISCO—THE LARGEST LBO OF ALL TIME

The RJR Nabisco leveraged buyout (LBO) is the largest LBO of all time and featured so many colorful characters that it was the subject of a feature film—*Barbarians at the Gate*—which in turn was based on a best-selling book of the same name. The company was a product of a merger between the RJ Reynolds tobacco company and the Nabisco food company.

There were several financial characteristics that made RJR Nabisco an attractive candidate for an LBO. Its cash flows, especially those from its tobacco business, were steady and predictable. The cash flows from both businesses did not vary appreciably with the ups and downs of the business cycles of the economy. In addition, neither business required major capital expenditures, thus allowing room for cash flows to be absorbed with interest obligations. RJR also had another characteristic that made it appealing to LBO dealmakers—it had a low debt level. This meant it had unused debt capacity.

RJR Nabisco had not been performing well prior to the buyout. Its return on assets had been falling while its ability to turn over its inventory had been declining. However, its tobacco and food businesses featured many well-recognized brands. The tobacco business' product line included the

Camel and Winston brands. Its food business featured many products that are household staples and well recognized across the world. The combination of many well-recognized products gave the company a high breakup value that Smith Barney estimated to be in the $85–$92-per-share range compared with the $56 stock price just prior to the initial buyout offer.[a]

The initial offer for the company came from a management group led by CEO Ross Johnson. It was a low-ball $75-per-share offer that the board of directors, which was very close and even beholden to Johnson, was embarrassed by. Johnson faced the conflicts of interest of being a fiduciary for shareholders, charged with the responsibility of maximizing shareholder value, while also being in the position of a bidder trying to acquire the company for the best price possible. The low offer by Ross Johnson, who was backed by Shearson Lehman Hutton and Salomon Brothers, attracted other bidders who quickly saw an undervalued company and responded with their own offers (see Exhibit A).

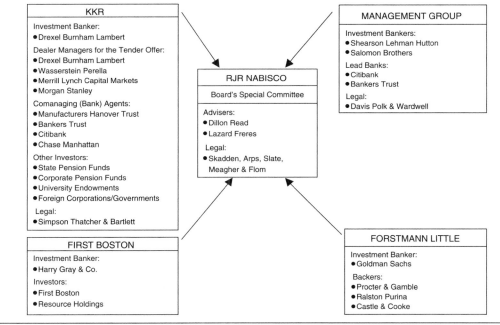

Exhibit A   The Bidding Groups
Source: Allen Michel and Israel Shaked, "RJR Nabisco: A Case Study of a Complex Leveraged Buyout," *Financial Analysts Journal,* September 1991, 23.

After a series of bidding rounds, the board of directors selected Kohlberg Kravis & Roberts's (KKR) offer (see Exhibit B). One unusual aspect of the board's decision-making process is that it took into account a variety of factors beyond just the absolute price. These factors included a promise to keep the company intact and to still have some public share ownership. The Johnson group's offer included plans to sell off assets and use the proceeds to pay down debt. The board also was concerned by the conflicts of interests surrounding the Johnson initial low bid. For KKR they won the bidding contest but the acquisition did not prove to be a financial success. In some ways the case is an example of the winner's curse, as KKR's returns were not impressive.

[a]Allen Michel and Israel Shaked, "RJR Nabisco: A Case Study of a Complex Leveraged Buyout," *Financial Analysts Journal,* September/October 1991, 15–27.

Bidding Date (1988)					
Oct. 19	Nov. 4	Nov. 25	Nov. 29	Dec. 1	Amount/Form of Payment

RJR Management				$112/sh.	$84 Cash $24 Preferred Stock $ 4 Convertible Stock
			$101/sh.		$88 Cash $ 9 Preferred Stock $ 4 Other Security
		$100/sh.			$90 Cash $ 6 Preferred Stock $ 4 New Common Stock
	$92/sh.				$84 Cash $ 8 Debt Securities
	$75/sh.				Bidder did not specify form of payment
KKR Acquisition Group				$109/sh.	$81 Cash $18 Preferred Stock $10 Debentures
		$106/sh.			$80 Cash $18 Preferred Stock $ 8 Convertible Bond
		$94/sh.			$75 Cash $11 Preferred Stock $ 8 Convertible Bond
	$90/sh.				$78 Cash $12 Securities
First Boston		$118/sh.			$110 Notes $ 3 Other Securities $ 5 Warrants

EXHIBIT B THE BIDDING PROCESS

Source: Allen Michel and Israel Shaked, "RJR Nabisco: A Case Study of a Complex Leveraged Buyout," *Financial Analysts Journal,* September 1991, 24.

Globalization of LBOs

Exhibit 7.2 shows the value and number of LBOs in the United States. We see that the number of LBOs in 2005 was higher than its peak in the late 1980s. However, the dollar value of these deals still remains below its peak value in 1988.

Exhibit 7.3 shows that while there were very few LBOs in Europe in the 1980s, the volume of these deals increased dramatically in the late 1990s. In fact, starting in 2001 through 2005, the value of European LBOs exceeded the value of U.S. LBOs. In addition,

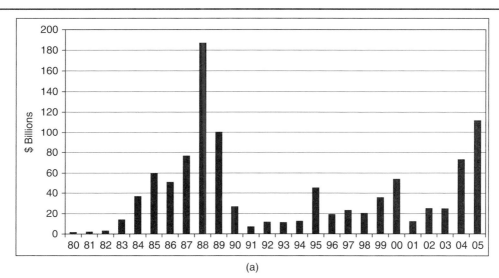

(a)

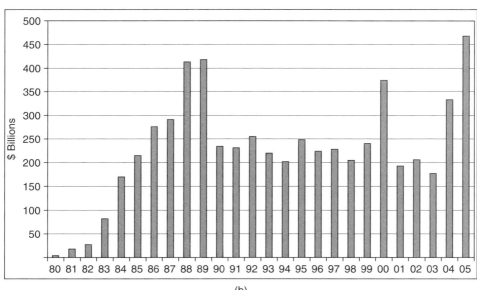

(b)

EXHIBIT 7.2   (a) VALUE OF U.S. LBOs; (b) NUMBER OF U.S. LBOs

Source: Thomson Financial Securities Data.

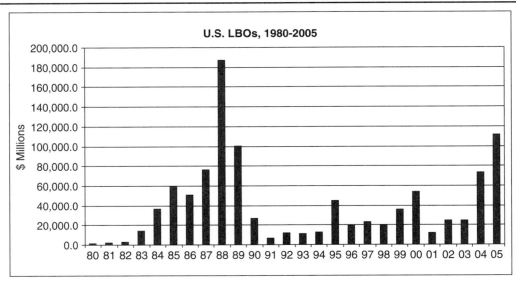

(a)

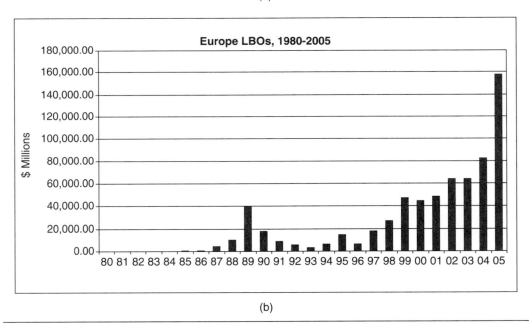

(b)

EXHIBIT 7.3   (a) U.S. LBOs, 1980–2005; (b) EUROPE LBOs, 1980–2005
Source: Thomson Financial Securities Data.

by 2005 the number of LBOs in Europe was roughly double the number that occurred in the United States. In addition, as Exhibit 7.4 shows, the average value of European LBOs was below that of the United States, indicating that more LBOs were completed in Europe but, on average, that were somewhat smaller than the LBOs that took place in the United States.

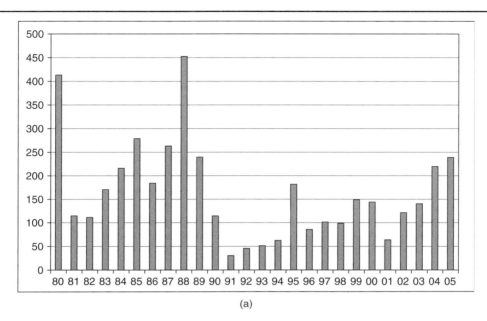

(a)

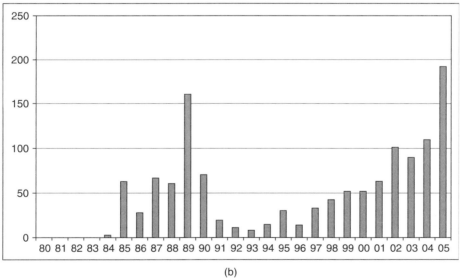

(b)

EXHIBIT 7.4   (a) AVERAGE VALUE OF U.S. LBOs, 1980–2005; (b) AVERAGE VALUE OF EUROPEAN LBOs, 1980–2005

Source: Thomson Financial Securities Data.

While the RJR Nabisco deal remains the largest LBO of all time, we have had a number of mega-LBOs in Europe that are comparable to the largest LBOs that have occurred in the United States. An examination of Exhibit 7.5 shows that most of the largest LBOs in Europe have taken place in 2005, whereas the largest U.S. LBOs are not as concentrated in one time period over recent years.

(a) Ten Largest U.S. LBOs

Date Announced	Target Name	Acquiror Name	Rank Value of Deal ($ Millions)
10/24/88	RJR Nabisco Inc.	Kohlberg Kravis Roberts & Co.	30,598.78
4/11/95	Chrysler Corp.	Tracinda Corp.	21,617.87
3/28/05	SunGard Data Systems Inc.	Investor Group	10,964.92
4/8/85	Unocal Corp.	Investor Group	9,170.90
8/14/89	UAL Corp.	Airline Acquisition Corp.	7,735.00
6/20/05	Cablevision	Investor Group	7,586.62
10/5/89	AMR Corp.	Investor	7,400.00
8/7/89	UAL Corp.	Investor	6,750.00
10/16/85	Beatrice Companies Inc.	BCI Holdings Corp.	6,095.00
3/17/05	Toys "R" Us Inc.	Investor Group	6,005.41

(b) Ten Largest European LBOs

Date Announced	Target Name	Acquiror Name	Rank Value of Deal ($ Millions)
7/11/1989	BAT Industries PLC	Hoylake Investments PLC	20,385.85
11/30/2005	TDC A/S	Nordic Telephone Co ApS	15,648.95
5/26/2005	Wind Telecomunicazioni SpA	Weather Investments Srl	12,799.34
1/16/2006	VNU NV	Investor Group	12,486.37
5/17/2005	Viterra AG	Deutsche Annington Immobilien	7,960.26
3/11/2005	Amadeus Global	Wam Acquisition SA	5,848.89
3/29/2005	ISS A/S	PurusCo AS	5,142.43
7/29/2002	Legrand SA	Investor Group	5,059.72
8/5/2005	ProSiebenSat.1 Media AG	Axel Springer Verlag AG	4,843.93
7/5/2004	GAGFAH-Housing Portfolio	Fortress Deutschland GmbH	4,547.13

EXHIBIT 7.5 TEN LARGEST LBOS: (a) UNITED STATES AND (b) EUROPE

Source: Thomson Financial Securities Data.

CASE STUDY

WIND TELECOMUNICAZIONI $15.6 BILLION BUYOUT: ONE OF EUROPE'S LARGEST LBOs

In May 2005, Weather Investment, an investment firm led by Egyptian businessman Naguib Sawiris, agreed to buy the telecommunications business of the Italian utility Enel SpA. The deal was valued at $15.6 billion, making it one of the largest leveraged buyouts in Europe. The deal was also noteworthy in that it featured another large takeover of a Western business by an emerging markets bidder. That target, Wind Telecommunicazioni, is the second largest fixed telephone company in Italy after Telecom Italia SpA and the third largest Italian mobile company after Telecom SpA and Vodafone Group PLC.[a] The bidding for the Italian telecom company featured various U.S. private equity firms led by the Blackstone Group and Providence Equity Partners. Weather Investments was joined by minority investor Wilber Ross, who is well known for his consolidation acquisitions in the troubled U.S. steel and auto parts industries as well as private equity firm Apax Partners.

In the deal, Weather bought roughly two-thirds of Wind while acquiring an option to buy the remaining shares. The agreement featured some unique reciprocal arrangements, as Enel agreed to use some of the proceeds from the sales of Wind to buy an interest in Weather itself.[b]

The buyout is not one based on eliminating inefficiencies and reducing agency costs. In addition, Wind has stated that it planned on retaining Wind management. Rather, the deal is based on Weather being able to combine this entity with others, which might command a significant percentage of European telecommunications traffic. Whether this will really make a cost-effective investment remains to be seen.

[a]Heather O'Brian, "The $15.1 Billion Deal for Wind Telecomunicazioni Is Europe's Largest Leveraged Buyout Ever, *The Daily Deal,* May 27, 2005.
[a]Ibid.

The LBO business is mainly centered in the United States and Europe. While merger and acquisition (M&A) volume in Asia has increased significantly, LBO volume is comparatively modest (Exhibit 7.6). However, LBO deal volume in Asia has risen markedly from its level in the 1990s. It is reasonable to expect that this trend will continue in the second half of the 2000s.

COSTS OF BEING A PUBLIC COMPANY

Being a public company carries with it certain costs—both monetary and nonmonetary. First, federal securities laws mandate periodic filings with the Securities and Exchange Commission (SEC); for small firms these filings may be a burden both in money and in management time. The magnitude of that burden has increased significantly after the passage of the Sarbanes Oxley Act. One study measured that the cost of being public in 2004 was $14.3 million, which was a 44% increase over the prior year.[2] This may help explain why small- and medium-sized firms may want to go private, but not why large firms go private.

---

2. Thomas E. Hartman, "The Costs of Being Public in the Era of Sarbanes-Oxley," Foley & Lardner LLP Annual Survey, June 16, 2005.

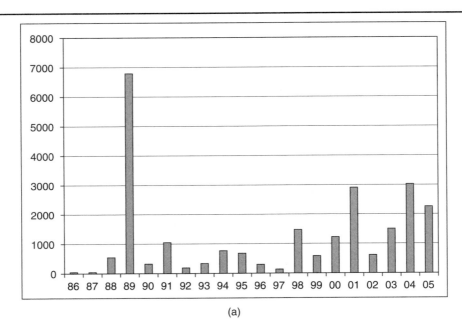

(a)

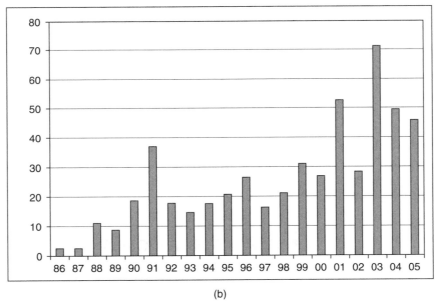

(b)

EXHIBIT 7.6   (a) ASIAN LBO VOLUME; (b) ASIAN NUMBER OF LBOS
Source: Thomson Financial Securities Data.

The costs of maintaining public ownership vary significantly according to the size of the company. Therefore, it is difficult to put forward meaningful averages. These costs include all of the costs associated with doing the necessary filings with the SEC and communicating with shareholders. For smaller companies, the absolute dollar costs are considerably lower than they are for larger companies. However, on a percentage basis, the costs may be more significant for smaller companies than they are for large firms. In addition, public companies have all of the other costs of dealing with shareholders, which some former owners and/or managers who have taken their company public find difficult to accept. These latter costs are more difficult to quantify but they may be even more significant than the direct monetary costs. Owners of public companies want to receive a large payout for part of their shares when they take their company public, but they may find it difficult to accept that the company they have created is only partially owned by them.

MANAGEMENT BUYOUTS

As we have noted, an MBO is a type of LBO that occurs when the management of a company decides it wants to take its publicly held company, or a division of the company, private.[3] We have also noted that many MBOs are deals where a unit of a public company is purchased by managers of that division. Both the dollar volume and number of unit MBOs has risen sharply over the past ten years (see Exhibit 7.7 for value of U.S. MBOs). Some of the same trends that are apparent in the total LBO data are also apparent in the management buyout data. Both the number and dollar value of MBOs fell off sharply after the fourth merger wave ended but recovered as we moved into the fifth wave. However, the dollar value of MBOs never returned to the levels witnessed in the fourth wave while the number of these did come close to the mid-1980 levels by 2003.

These managers in an MBO may invest some of their own capital in the deal, but often other equity capital is provided by investors while the bulk of the funds are borrowed. The purchased entity then becomes a separate company with its own shareholders, board of directors, and management team. While the buying group is insiders in an MBO, and outsiders in an LBO, the process is otherwise not that different. Presumably, however, the buying group in an MBO has better access to information about the company's potential profitability than an outside buying group has. This is one factor that may give an MBO a greater likelihood of success than an LBO. Better information may not be enough. If the parent company is seeking to sell the division because of poor performance, it could be that this poor performance is attributable to management. An MBO leaves the company still in the hands of the same managers, whereas in an LBO the new owners may install their own managers. These new managers may be less tied to prior employees and other assets and may be more willing to implement the changes necessary to turn the company into a profitable entity.

When companies divest divisions, they normally sell them to outside parties. For example, in January 2006, Texas Instruments announced that it was selling its sensors and controls business to the Boston-based private equity firm, Bain Capital, for $3 billion. Only a small percent of the time do they sell them to managers. For example, between 1996 and 2005, only 3.2% percent of all divestitures were unit MBOs. Nonetheless, the numbers are still significant. In 2004, the total dollar value of unit MBOs was $3.5 billion

---

3. Robert L. Kieschnick, "Management Buyouts of Public Corporations: An Analysis of Prior Characteristics," in Yakov Amihud, ed., *Leveraged Management Buyouts* (Homewood, Ill.: Dow Jones Irwin, 1989), pp. 35–38.

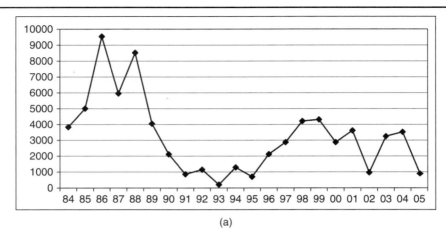

(a)

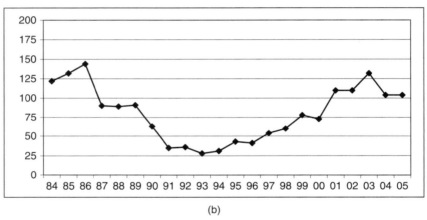

(b)

EXHIBIT 7.7   (a) DOLLAR VALUE OF U.S. UNIT MBOs; (b) NUMBER OF U.S. MBOs
Source: Mergerstat Review 1992, 1998, and 2005.

with the average size of a deal being $33.9 million. By M&A standards, these are comparatively smaller transactions.

CASE STUDY

KINDER MORGAN

In May 2006 the upper management of pipeline company, Kinder Morgan, announced a $13.5 billion buyout. This deal was the largest management buyout in history. Management proposed to contribute just under $3 billion of the total acquisition price. This equity contribution was augmented by a $4.5 billion investment by a group of private equity investors led by Goldman Sachs Capital Partners and the Caryle Group. The buyers planned to assume over $14.5 billion in debt giving the deal an enterprise value of over $22 billion. Kinder Morgan was formed in late 1996 by a collection of assets that were disposed by Enron for approximately $40 million. It is ironic that these assets rose markedly in value while Enron collapsed. The increase in the company's value is principally due to its successful acquisition program the company initiated beginning in 1999.

The diverging fates on Kinder Morgan and Enron was partly attributable to the strategies the two companies pursued. While Enron was a pipeline company, it became a risky energy trading enterprise. Kinder Morgan, on the other hand, stayed in the pipeline business and steadily grew within this industry. With its acquisitions, it became an increasingly larger player in the less risky segment of the industry. Its steady performance also lowered its risk profile, which enabled management to attract private equity investors.

CONFLICTS OF INTEREST IN MANAGEMENT BUYOUTS

A clear conflict of interest may exist in MBOs. Managers are responsible for running the corporation to maximize the value of stockholders' investment and provide them with the highest return possible. These same managers take on a very different role when they are required to present an offer to stockholders to buy the company. We have seen that this was the case when the management of RJR Nabisco presented an offer to stockholders to take Nabisco private in an MBO. This offer was quickly superseded by a competing offer from KKR as well as other responding offers from management.[4] If management truly was attempting to maximize the value of stockholders' investments, why did it choose to advocate an offer that it knew was clearly not in the stockholders' best interests? Many researchers believe that managers cannot serve in this dual, and sometimes conflicting, role as agent for both the buyer and the seller.

One proposed solution to this conflict is neutralized voting, whereby the proponents of a deal do not participate in the approval process. If the proponents are stockholders, their votes would not be not included in the approval process. They may have to partici-pate in the voting process because under some state laws a quorum may not be possible without their participation if they hold a certain number of shares.[5] The appointment of an independent financial advisor to render a fairness opinion is a common second step in this process, which is meant to help reduce the conflicts of interest. Even if these precautionary measures are adopted, certain practical considerations may limit their effec-tiveness. Although those members of the board of directors who may profit from the LBO may not vote for its approval, other members of the board may have a close relationship to them and consider themselves obliged to support the deal. Lawsuits by stockholders suing directors for breach of fiduciary duty have placed limits on this tendency. Fairness opin-ions put forward by investment bankers who have done much business with management or who may have a financial interest in the deal may be of questionable value.

Although these steps are an important attempt to try to reduce some of the conflicts inherent in the MBO process, they do not address the issue of the manager being both the buyer's and the seller's agent. One solution that has been proposed is to have mandated auctions of corporations presented with an MBO.[6]

---

4. See Bryan Burrough and John Helyar, *Barbarians at the Gate: The Fall of RJR Nabisco* (New York: Harper & Row, 1990).
5. Arthur M. Borden, *Going Private* (New York: Law Journal Seminar Press, 1987), pp. 1–6.
6. Louis Lowenstein, *What's Wrong with Wall Street?* (Reading, MA: Addison-Wesley, 1987), p. 184.

According to current case law, directors are not allowed to favor their own bid over another bid once the bidding process has begun. The prohibition on an unfair bidding process was set forth by a number of important court decisions. In *Revlon, Inc. v. MacAndrews & Forbes Holdings, Inc.,* the Delaware Supreme Court ruled that Revlon's directors breached their fiduciary duty in granting a lockup option to white knight Forstmann Little & Co.[7] The court ruled that this constituted an unfair bidding process that favored Forstmann Little & Co. over hostile bidder Pantry Pride.

In *Hanson Trust PLC v. SCM Corporation,* the Second Circuit Court took a similar position on the use of lockup options to favor an LBO by Merrill Lynch instead of a hostile bid by Hanson Trust PLC.[8] Hanson Trust had initially made a tender offer for SCM at $60 per share. In response to Merrill Lynch's LBO offer at $70 per share, Hanson Trust upped its bid to $72. The court ruled that SCM gave preferential treatment to Merrill Lynch by granting lockup options on two SCM divisions to Merrill Lynch.

In *Edelman v. Fruehauf,* the circuit court concluded that the board of directors had decided to make a deal with management and did not properly consider other bids such as the all-cash tender offer by Asher Edelman.[9] The court held that the Fruehauf board of directors did not conduct a fair auction for the company.[10] Although the preceding decisions establish a precedent that an auction for a firm must be conducted fairly, the courts stop short of spelling out the rules for conducting or ending the bidding process. These decisions fall within the purview of the business judgment rule. The law is also unclear regarding when or even if an auction is required. The formation of an independent directors committee may facilitate the auction process.[11] This process is often used when management has proposed a buyout. When faced with a management proposal to take the firm private, the board of directors will usually respond by creating a special committee of independent, nonmanagement directors to ensure that shareholders receive fair, if not maximal, value for their investment. The committee may then decide to have its own valuation formulated, hire independent counsel, and conduct an auction.

Post-Buyout Managerial Ownership

Even when management, as opposed to an outside group, is the buyer of a business unit, other equity is provided by outsiders, so management may not be in control of the postbuyout business. It depends on how much equity capital is needed and how much capital the managers have and are willing to invest in the deal. Using a sample of 76 management buyouts over the period 1980–1986, Kaplan compared the median prebuyout and postbuyout share ownership percentages of the CEOs and all management.[12] He found

7. *Revlon, Inc. v. MacAndrews & Forbes Holdings, Inc.,* 506 A.2d. 173 (Del. Sup. 1986).
8. *Hanson Trust PLC v. SCM Corporation,* 781 F.2d 264 (2d Cir. 1986).
9. *Edelman v. Fruehauf,* 798 F.2d 882, 886–87 (6th Cir. 1986).
10. Lawrence Lederman and Barry A. Bryer, "Representing a Public Company in a Leveraged Transaction," in Yakov Amihud, ed., *Leveraged Management Buyouts* (Homewood, Ill.: Dow Jones Irwin, 1989), pp. 111–174.
11. Joseph Grunfest, "Management Buyouts and Leveraged Buyouts: Are the Critics Right?" in Yakov Amihud, ed., *Leveraged Management Buyouts* (Homewood, Ill.: Dow Jones Irwin, 1989), pp. 241–261.
12. Steven Kaplan, "The Effects of Management Buyouts on Operating Performance and Value,"*Journal of Financial Economics*, 24, 1989, 217–254.

that these percentages rose from 1.4% and 5.9% to 6.4% and 22.6%, respectively. Management ownership more than tripled after the buyout. Theoretically, given their much higher ownership interests, the managers should be better motivated to ensure that the company moves closer to profit-maximizing efficiency levels.

Going Private Premiums and P/Es Offered

Table 7.2 and Exhibit 7.8 compare the median premiums for going private deals and M&As. A couple of trends are immediately apparent. We see that premiums for both going private deals and M&As vary over time. For going private deals, premiums tend to be higher in merger waves than in periods of lower deal volume, whereas M&A premiums have tended to remain stable and have even risen somewhat over time. We also see that the average premium for a going private transaction tends to be lower than

Date	Going Private (%)	M&A (%)
1984	33.7	34.4
1985	25.7	27.7
1986	26.1	29.9
1987	30.9	30.8
1988	26.3	30.9
1989	22.7	29
1990	31.6	32
1991	20	29.4
1992	8.1	34.7
1993	20	33
1994	35	35
1995	19.2	29.2
1996	26.2	27.3
1997	24.5	27.5
1998	20.4	30.1
1999	32.7	34.6
2000	38.7	41.1
2001	52.2	40.5
2002	40	34.4
2003	41.5	31.6
2004	17.2	23.4
2005	22.5	24.1

TABLE 7.2   GOING PRIVATE AND M&A MEDIAN PREMIUMS IN THE UNITED STATES

Source: *Mergerstat Review* 1992, 1998, and 2006.

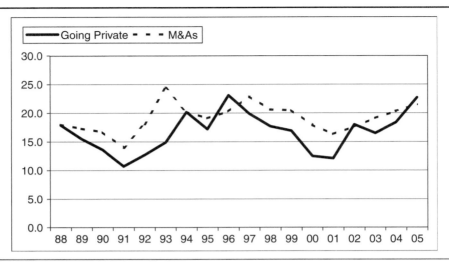

EXHIBIT 7.8   GOING PRIVATE AND M&A P/ES OFFERED IN THE UNITED STATES
Source: Mergerstat Review 1992, 1998, and 2006.

a merger or acquisition. For example, between 1986 and 1989, the average going private premium was 26.5% while the average M&A premium was 30.2%. The average
going private premium fell to 19.9% during the years 1990–1993 while it actually rose
for M&A deals to 32.3%. However, when the fifth merger wave took hold, both going
private and M&A premiums increased with going private premiums rising to 31.1%,
just below M&A premiums, which were 33.2%. In fact, in 2001, going private premiums peaked at 52.2%, which was higher than M&A premiums in that year, which
were 40.5%. Once the fifth wave ended, premiums for both types of deals fell. In
2005, premiums were much lower, 22.5% and 24.1%, respectively, for going private
and M&A deals.

When we compare premiums for these recent years, it is useful to note that studies
focusing on earlier years found higher premiums. For example, DeAngelo, DeAngelo,
and Rice reviewed 72 MBOs during the period 1973–1980 and found average premiums
equal to 56%.

In terms of P/Es offered, the values are similar for both going private transactions and
M&As. Buyers in going private transactions have tended to pay lower premiums than
buyers in M&As (Table 7.2). In addition, Exhibit 7.8 shows that in relation to earnings
per share, the price that is paid in going private deals often is less than in M&As.

Sources of LBO Gains

In Chapter 4 we reviewed some of the various reasons why companies pay premiums and incur some of the expenses of mergers. They pursue these deals for reasons
such as enhancing their growth and realizing synergistic gains, as well as other reasons. Many of these reasons, such as synergies, may not be relevant for LBOs and

MBOs. In MBOs, for example, the company, at least initially, stays independent and does not have the opportunity to combine with another entity and realize synergistic gains. Then what is the source of the gains that allows the acquirer to pay a premium and also incur the financing charges associated with the increased leverage? Research points to several potential sources of these gains, which are discussed in the following sections.

Efficiency Gains

There are several areas in which efficiency gains can manifest themselves in an LBO. The first has to do with agency problems.[13] We discuss agency problems in several places in this text. They arise when the true owners of the company, shareholders, have to elect directors to oversee their interests.[14] These directors select managers who have a fiduciary responsibility to run the company in a manner that will maximize shareholder wealth. However, managers are human and they may pursue their own agenda and seek to further their own gains at shareholder expense. In doing so they may not manage the company in a manner that will maximize profits. Managers may know that if they generate an acceptable return, such as π_{min} in Exhibit 7.9, it would be difficult for shareholders to mount a successful proxy fight and demand their ouster. π_1 could be the average rate of return in the industry. Given that information on potential profitability is asymmetric and management is in a much better position to assess this than shareholders or even the board of directors, managers may know that π_{max} is possible.

This gap between potential profitability, π_{max}, and π_{min}, is depicted in Exhibit 7.9. This is the theoretical gain from eliminating unnecessary costs and selling the output level where marginal revenue equals marginal costs. Managers may be following a different agenda, such as seeking to make the company larger than it optimally should be, so as to maximize their compensation since it is well known that larger companies pay higher compensation to management.[15]

Boards try to install performance-based compensation systems to better align management and shareholder goals.[16] These are far from perfect. In the 1990s, more option- and stock-based incentives were touted as a partial solution to the managerial compensation problem. However, when the various accounting scandals, such as WorldCom, Enron, and Adelphia, arose, critics cited such compensation schemes as one of the main problems. Managers pursued illegal means to try to raise stock prices, which in turn would provide them more stock-based compensation.

Managers who have a good sense of the difference between π_{max} and π_{min} may believe that this difference is sufficiently large to more than offset the costs of doing the deal and

13. Eugene Fama, "Agency Problems and the Theory of the Firm," *Journal of Political Economy,* 7(2), April 1980, 288–307.
14. Michael Jensen and William Meckling, "Theory of the Firm: Managerial Behavior, Agency Costs and Ownership Structure," *Journal of Financial Economics,* 3, October 1976, 305–360.
15. Dennis Mueller, "A Theory of Conglomerate Mergers," *Quarterly Journal of Economics,* 83, 1969, 643–659.
16. Eugene Fama and Michael Jensen, "Separation of Ownership and Control," *Journal of Law and Economics,* 26, 1983, 323–329.

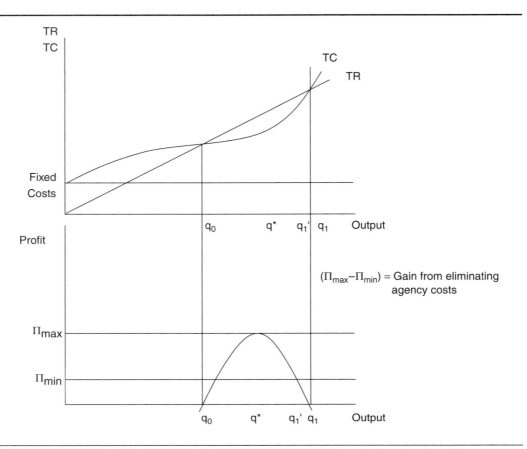

EXHIBIT 7.9   TOTAL COST, TOTAL REVENUES, AND PROFIT FUNCTIONS

paying the service on the debt. This was certainly the case when Ross Johnson pursued his MBO proposal for RJR Nabisco. Unfortunately, his low-ball offer so shocked his very friendly board that they looked to other offers, an auction ensued, and the company ended up being sold to KKR for a much higher price that eliminated many of the gains Johnson foresaw.

There is some evidence that efficiency gains really do occur in buyouts. For example, Harris, Siegel, and Wright examined productivity of 36,000 U.K. manufacturing plants.[17] They compared those that underwent an MBO with those that did not. They found clear increases in efficiency as reflected in output/labor ratios as well as other measures of factor productivity. They also noted that the MBO companies were less efficient than the non-MBO group prior to the buyouts. So these were companies where the potential for gain in the form of increased efficiencies was greater than for those that did not undergo a buyout.

---

17. Richard Harris, Donald Siegel and David Wright, "Assessing the Impact of Management Buyouts on Economic Efficiency: Plant Level Evidence from the United Kingdom," *Rensselaer Working Papers in Economics*, No. 0304, October 2003.

─── Case Study ───

TOYS-R-US GOING PRIVATE

In March 2005, a group led by buyout firm Kohlberg Kravis & Roberts (KKR), Bain Capital, and Vornado Realty Trust agreed to take the number-two U.S. toy retailer private in a $6.6 billion transaction. The buyers offered to pay the Wayne, New Jersey–based retailer $26.75 per share, which was a modest 8% premium above the preannouncement closing price of $24.77.[a] In this deal, the buying group outbid another private equity firm, Cerberus Capital, which had been reported to have also bid for the toy chain. The offer came in response to Toys-R-Us's investment banker, CSFB, sending out materials to 30 potential acquirers.[b]

Toys-R-Us had expanded aggressively over the years into children's products retailing through its Kids-R-Us and Babies-R-Us chains while also expanding internally and moving into online retailing. Unfortunately, the business is highly competitive, which means that its profit margins are not impressive. This is underscored by the fact that one of Toys-R-Us's competitors, KB Toys, Inc., filed for Chapter 11 bankruptcy protection in January 2004. The troubles of this industry were well known to the buying group, as Bain Capital owns KB Toys and KKR had made several retail acquisitions over the years including the Safeway grocery store chain and Fred Meyer, Inc. (which is now owned by Kroger Co.), as well as auto parts retailer Auto Zone.

Toys-R-Us was a very aggressive company that was a pioneer in introducing the superstore concept to an industry that was previously filled with small "mom-and-pop" stores. It is ironic, however, that Wal-Mart, the huge retailer who has caused many smaller retailers to go out of business across the nation, pushed Toys-R-Us to the edge of bankruptcy when it began selling toys at discounted prices below those that previously allowed Toys-R-Us to generate profits.

Toys-R–Us, which had 2004 sales in excess of $11 billion, however, has struggled to be profitable. For example, in the second quarter of 2005 it lost $359 million, which was far greater than the $42 million loss in the second quarter of the prior year. The buyout firm acquired a company that was in an increasingly worsening position. Normally a buyer in a going private deal takes various actions to *improve* profitability so as to justify the financing costs of the deal. Here this group of savvy private equity firms was forced to take dramatic actions to try to breathe life into the troubled retailer.

In the year before the buyout, 2004, the company had implemented a major restructuring program in which it closed 102 of its 146 Kids-R-Us stores. Effectively, it was largely leaving this business. The company's Babies-R-Us chain actually was profitable. This business has a different product mix that includes items such as furniture. The company was able to make money on this business although it had major differences with the toy business. While we have cited many instances of aggressive growth through acquisition strategies, the opposite was the case at Toys-R-Us. The company's rapid internal expansion proved to be too aggressive when large competitors entered its market. However, the 1997 $410 million acquisition of the Baby Superstore allowed the company to move into a new business that remained profitable when its core business's margins fell into the red. The Baby Superstore, found in 1971, went public in 1994 but had trouble one year later and had to restate its results. Toys-R-Us was able to buy the company without paying a significant premium. By 2004, the market valued the company between $1.5 billion and $2.5 billion.[c] When the company started

---

[a]Parija Bhatnager, "Group to Buy Toys 'R' Us for $6.6 B," *CNNMoney.com*, March 17, 2005.
[b]Brenon Daly, "Bain, KKR, Vornado Buy Toys 'R' Us," *The Daily Deal*, March 18, 2005.
[c]Brenon Daly, "Babies May Save Toys 'R' Us," *The Daily Deal*, August 19, 2004.

to pursue radical restructuring in 2004 and 2005, it considered many alternatives including selling off its core business, as a whole or in piecemeal, while just keeping the baby market retailer.

The buyout group continued the company's downsizing program. In January 2005, Toys-R-Us announced that it was closing 87 more stores and eliminating 3,000 jobs.[d] Twelve of the 87 stores were to be converted into Babies-R-Us stores, which held the promise of greater profitability.

[d]"Toys 'R' Us, Inc.: Eighty-Seven Stores in the U.S. Will Be Closed or Converted," *Wall Street Journal*, January 10, 2006.

Tax Benefits

When a company increases its degree of financial leverage, that is, increases the amount of debt relative to equity in its capital structure, it substitutes lower-cost debt capital for equity capital and its weighted average cost of capital usually declines. In general, even on a pretax basis, debt normally has lower costs than equity. That is, normally, equity requires the investors to bear greater risk, and investors require a higher rate of return before they assume this higher risk. In addition, interest payments on debt are tax deductible, thereby lowering the after-tax cost of debt capital.

$$k_d^{at} = (1-t)k_d^{bt} \qquad (7.1)$$

where: k_d^{at} = after-tax cost of debt
t = the company's tax rate
k_d^{bt} = before-tax cost of debt

It is important to remember that when a company undergoes an LBO, the costs of both debt and equity capital generally increase. This is due to the fact that it takes on much more debt, which increases the risk profile of the company. It has more fixed obligations, which increases the probability that it may not be able to service such obligations as they come due. The market responds to this higher risk by requiring a greater risk premium for both debt and equity. Nonetheless, its overall costs of capital, especially after taking into account the tax deductibility of the interest payments, may be lower. This then is a benefit of doing the deal and provides some basis for paying a premium to the equity holders. The question is, how significant are these tax benefits?

The tax benefits from doing deals, and LBOs in particular, have changed over time as a function of new tax laws. Tax benefits put into law in 1981 allowed for aggressive accelerated depreciation. When this is combined with asset step-ups that were also allowed, they provide significant incentives to do leveraged deals. This reason helps explain some of the LBOs that took place in the fourth merger wave. The Tax Reform Act of 1986 eliminated many of these benefits.

A study by Kaplan attempted to quantify the tax benefits that postbuyout firms enjoy.[18] He found that the interest deductions from the debt were almost 30% greater than the premium paid to the selling shareholders. The gains, however, mainly went to selling shareholders and not to the owners of the postbuyout company. "A comparison of the

---

18. Steven Kaplan, "Management Buyouts: Evidence on Taxes As a Source of Value," *Journal of Finance*, 3, July 1989, 611–632.

excess returns earned by pre-buyout and post-buyout investors to several measures of tax benefits is consistent with pre-buyout shareholders receiving most of the potential tax benefits. The returns to post-buyout investors are not related to the tax benefits created by the buyout. This is consistent with a market for corporate control that forces the buyout companies to pay public stockholders tax benefits that are ex-post predictable and obtainable by other bidders."[19]

Kaplan showed that the tax benefits of LBOs are largely predictable and are incorporated in the premium that pre-LBO stockholders receive. This implies that the post-LBO investors need to find other sources of value. Both Kaplan studies imply that any sweeping criticism of LBOs may be unwarranted. That is, the buyout process may create value. Therefore, an evaluation must be made on a case-by-case basis.

Cash Flow versus Asset-based LBOs

As stated previously, LBOs are acquisitions that are financed primarily with debt. They are usually cash transactions in which the cash is borrowed by the acquiring firm. Much of the debt may be secured by the assets of the corporation being taken private. This section provides an overview of the LBO process. The financing of these deals is discussed in greater detail later in this chapter.

The target company's assets are often used to provide collateral for the debt that is going to be incurred to finance the acquisition. Thus, the collateral value of these assets needs to be assessed. This type of lending is often called *asset-based lending.* Firms with assets that have a high collateral value can more easily obtain such loans; thus, LBOs are often easier to conduct in capital-intensive industries—firms that usually have more assets that may be used as collateral than noncapital-intensive firms. It is not surprising, therefore, that Waite and Fridson found that LBO activity during the period they studied was more predominant in manufacturing than in nonmanufacturing industries.[20] Still, LBOs can also be done for firms that do not have an abundance of assets that may be used as collateral. Service industries are one example. They tend not to have as many physical assets with high-asset values that can be used as collateral for loans, but they may still be good LBO candidates if their cash flows are high enough. The high cash flows, as opposed to physical assets, provide the protection for lenders. If the borrower defaults, however, the lenders may not have as many physical assets that can be sold in liquidation. Debt capital providers hope that the cash flows will be so reliable that they will never be facing a liquidation situation. They also are aware that even physical assets can be adversely affected by downturns of a company if they are industry- or even economy-wide downturns.

Cash-flow or unsecured LBOs, as they are sometimes called, tend to have a more long-term focus, with a maturity of 10 to 15 years. In contrast, secured or asset-based LBOs might have a financing maturity of only up to five years. Cash-flow LBOs allow firms that are not in capital-intensive industries to be LBO candidates. This is most important in the

---

19. Steven Kaplan, "Management Buyouts," University of Chicago Working Paper No. 245, p. 44.
20. S. Waite and M. Fridson, "The Credit Quality of Leveraged Buyouts," in *High Performance* (New York: Morgan Stanley, January 1989).

U.S. economy because the United States has become a more service-oriented economy. Many service industries, such as advertising, lack significant physical assets relative to their total revenue but have large cash flows.

Since cash-flow LBOs are generally considered riskier for lenders, they expect to receive a higher return for assuming the additional risk. This higher return may come from a higher interest rate as well as an *equity kicker*. This equity interest often comes in the form of warrants or direct shares in the target. The percentage of ownership may be as little as 10% or as high as 80% of the companies' shares. The percentage is higher when the lender perceives greater risk.

The fact that the loan is not collateralized does not mean that the lenders are not protected by the firm's assets. Unsecured lenders are entitled to receive the proceeds of the sale of the secured assets after full payment has been made to the secured lenders.

Investment Banks and LBOs

As the LBO business has rebounded, investment banks have increasing looked to LBOs to be an important part of the firm's profitability. Investment banks now have separate units dedicated to LBO financing. According to Thompson Financial, as of 2005, the leading investment bank in the LBO business is Citigroup, Inc., followed by Goldman Sachs Group, Inc., Credit Suisse First Boston, J. P. Morgan Chase, USB AG, and Lehman Brothers Holdings, Inc.[21] Investment banks work with private equity firms to help them arrange capital to complete the deal while also enabling them to later cash out their investments so as to return capital to their investors. They may also make money-related financing of the deal such as underwriting high-yield bonds.

Leveraged Recapitalizations as an Alternative to an LBO

In an LBO the shareholders of the company sell their equity ownership to buyers who borrow the bulk of the capital to finance the deal. When the entire equity is sold the prior owners no longer have an equity interest in the company. For closely held businesses this is a way for the sellers to cash out on their investment and exit the business. Sometimes, however, the buyers are unable to raise the full amount. This can be due to a variety of factors including weak market conditions or concerns about the ability of the acquired company to predictably service the required debt. This was the case in 2006, when J. P. Morgan Partners LLC announced that it was buying a significant stake in the Denver-based sandwich chain Quiznos. Over the year prior to this recapitalization several restaurant chains were able to do an IPO or an LBO, and it was anticipated there would be an LBO for Quiznos. In doing a leveraged recapitalization the owners, the Shader family, who valued the chain at $2 billion, would not be able to cash out but would be able to do a partial exit.[22] Media reports asserted that the buyers valued the chain at between $1.3 billion and $1.75 billion.

---

21. Robert Dunn, "Booming LBO Firm Business Is a Boon to Investment Banks," *Wall Street Journal*, August 18, 2004, C4.
22. Lisa Gewirtz, "J. P. Morgan to Buy Quiznos in Recap," *Daily Deal*, March 21, 2006.

FINANCING FOR LEVERAGED BUYOUTS

Two general categories of debt are used in LBOs—secured and unsecured debt—and they are often used together.[23] Secured debt, which is sometimes called *asset-based lending,* may contain two subcategories of debt: senior debt and intermediate-term debt. In some smaller buyouts these two categories are considered one. In larger deals there may be several layers of secured debt, which vary according to the term of the debt and the types of assets used as security. Unsecured debt, which is sometimes known as *subordinated debt* and *junior subordinated debt,* lacks the protection of secured debt, but generally carries a higher return to offset this additional risk.

Secured LBO Financing

Within the category of secured financing, there are two subcategories—senior debt and intermediate-term debt.

Senior Debt

Senior debt consists of loans secured by liens on particular assets of the company. The collateral, which provides the downside risk protection required by lenders, includes physical assets such as land, plant and equipment, accounts receivable, and inventories. The lender projects the level of accounts receivable that the firm would average during the period of the loan. This projection is usually based on the amount of accounts receivable the firm has on its books at the time the loan is closed, as well as the historical level of these assets.

While the percentages vary depending on market conditions, lenders will commonly advance 85% of the value of the accounts receivable and 50% of the value of the target's inventories, excluding the work in progress.[24] Accounts receivable, which are normally collected in short periods such as 30 days, are more valuable than those of longer periods. The lender must make a judgment on the value of the accounts receivable; similar judgments have to be made as to the marketability of inventories. The process of determining the collateral value of the LBO candidate's assets is sometimes called *qualifying* the assets. Assets that do not have collateral value, such as accounts receivable that are unlikely to be collected, are called *unqualified assets.*

Intermediate-Term Debt

Intermediate-term debt is usually subordinate to senior debt. It is often backed up by fixed assets such as land and plant and equipment. The collateral value of these assets is usually based on their liquidation value. Debt backed up by equipment typically has

---

23. For an excellent discussion of the use of secured and unsecured debt in leveraged buyouts, see Stephen C. Diamond, ed., *Leveraged Buyouts* (Homewood, IL: Dow Jones Irwin, 1985), pp. 41–57.
24. Michael R. Dabney, "Asset Based Financing," in Milton Rock, ed., *Mergers and Acquisitions* (New York: McGraw-Hill, 1987), pp. 393–399.

a term of six months to one year.[25] Loans backed up by real estate tend to have a one-
to two-year term. The relationship between the loan amounts and the appraised value
of the assets varies depending on the circumstances of the buyout. Generally, debt can
equal 80% of the appraised value of equipment and 50% of the value of real estate. As
the real estate market rebounded in the 1990s, lenders became willing to advance higher
percentages using real estate as collateral. These percentages will vary depending on the
area of the country and the conditions of the real estate market. The collateral value of
assets, such as equipment and real estate, is based on the auction value of these assets,
not the value they carry on the firm's books. When the auction value is greater than the
book value of the assets, the firm's borrowing capacity is greater than what its balance
sheet would reflect. Lenders look for certain desirable characteristics in borrowers, even
when the borrower has valuable collateral. Some of these factors are discussed in the
following sections.

Desirable Characteristics of Secured Leveraged Buyout Candidates

There are certain characteristics that lenders look for in a prospective LBO candidate.
Some of the more commonly cited features are discussed here.

- *Stable cash flows.* One of the most important characteristics of LBO candidates
  is the existence of regular cash flows as determined by examining the pattern of
  historical cash flows for the company. Statistical measures such as the standard
  deviation may be used to measure this variability. The more erratic the historical
  cash flows, the greater the perceived risk in the deal. Even in cases in which
  the average cash flows exceed the loan payments by a comfortable margin, the
  existence of high variability may worry a lender. Dependable cash flows alone are
  not sufficient to guarantee the success of an LBO.

  The financial difficulties of the Southland Corporation after its $4.9 billion buy-
  out in 1987 is a case in point. The company's main business was the "cash cow"
  7–Eleven convenience chain. Southland's problems emerged when some of the
  7–Eleven cash flows were directed to noncore real estate ventures instead of paying off the buyout debt. This misadventure left the postbuyout Southland on the
  verge of bankruptcy in spite of the firm's sizable cash flows.

  Although historical cash flows are used to project future cash flows, the past
  may be an imperfect guide to the future. Market conditions change and the future
  business environment may be less favorable than what the company's historical
  data reflect. The lender must make a judgment as to whether the past will be
  a reliable indicator of what the future will hold. Lenders and borrowers usually
  construct cash flow projections based on restrictive budgets and new cost structures. Such budget planning takes place for both secured and unsecured LBOs,
  but it is even more critical for cash flow LBOs. These budgets may include lower
  research and development expenditures and labor costs. The target attempts to
  find areas where costs may be cut—at least temporarily. These cost savings may

---

25. Ibid.

be used to meet the loan payments on the LBO debt. The importance of cash flows to LBOs was underscored by a study by Lehn and Poulsen.[26] They showed that buyout premiums were positively related to the firm's free cash flow. That is, the market is willing to pay higher premiums for greater cash flow protection.

- *Stable and experienced management.* Stability is often judged by the length of time management is in place. Lenders feel more secure when management is experienced; that is, if management has been with the firm for a reasonable period of time, it may imply that there is a greater likelihood that management will stay on after the deal is completed. Creditors often judge the ability of management to handle an LBO by the cash flows that were generated by the firms they managed in the past. If their prior management experience was with firms that had significant liquidity problems, lenders will be much more cautious about participating in the buyout.

- *Room for significant cost reductions.* Assuming additional debt to finance an LBO usually imposes additional financial pressures on the target. These pressures may be alleviated somewhat if the target can significantly cut costs in some areas, such as fewer employees, reduced capital expenditures, elimination of redundant facilities, and tighter controls on operating expenses. Lichtenberg and Siegel showed that LBO employee cutbacks were concentrated at the administrative levels of employment, with an average administrative workforce reduction of 16%, while there tended to be minimal cutbacks at the manufacturing level.[27]

- *Equity interest of owners.* The collateral value of assets provides downside risk protection to lenders. The equity investment of the managers or buyers and outside parties also acts as a cushion to protect lenders. The greater the equity cushion, the more likely secured lenders will not have to liquidate the assets. The greater the managers' equity investment, the more likely they will stay with the firm if the going gets tough. Leveraged buyout lenders in the 1990s demanded a much greater equity cushion than they did for the heavy debt deals they financed in the mid-1980s. As conditions improved in the 2000s, however, lending terms became more liberal.

- *Ability to cut costs.* Many LBO candidates are inefficient and need cost restructuring. Leveraged buyout dealmakers work on finding areas where cost can be cut without damaging the business. When these cost cuts are focused on areas of waste or unnecessary expenditures, they may be of great benefit to the LBO candidate. The target may suffer, however, when the cuts are made in areas that will hurt the company in the future. Cuts in research and development, for example, may cause the company to fall behind its competitors and eventually lose market share. Industry factors may determine the extent to which research and product

26. Kenneth Lehn and Annette Poulsen, "Free Cash Flow and Stockholder Gains in Going Private Transactions," *Journal of Finance,* 44, 1989, 771–778.
27. Frank Lichtenberg and Donald Siegel, "The Effects of Takeovers on Employment and Wages of Central Office and Other Personnel," Columbia Graduate School Working Paper #FB-89-05, 1989.

development expenditures may be cut. Reductions are often difficult to implement in rapidly evolving, high-tech industries such as the computer industry. The company may survive the LBO and pay off the debt only to be left behind by its competitors. A good example of a high-tech LBO that should not have been conducted was the 1987 $866 million buyout of defense contractor Tracor, Inc. The company found itself with an unpredictable cash flow after defense industry cutbacks. This, coupled with the capital demands of this high-tech industry, left the firm struggling to meet the LBO debt payments. It eventually had to file Chapter 11 in 1991.

- *Limited debt on the firm's balance sheet.* The lower the amount of debt on the firm's balance sheet relative to the collateral value of the firm's assets, the greater the borrowing capacity of the firm. If the firm's balance sheet is already encumbered by significant financial leverage, it may be more difficult to finance the LBO. The prior debt limits the company's borrowing capacity. Even companies with low pre-LBO debt levels end up exhausting their borrowing capacity after the LBO.

- *Separable, noncore businesses.* If the LBO candidate owns noncore businesses that can be sold off to quickly "pay down" a significant part of the firm's post-LBO debt, the deal may be easier to finance. This may be important for both secured and unsecured LBOs. Problems may occur when debt is incurred based on an unrealistic sales price for noncore divisions. The inability to sell components of the firm on a timely basis, at prices similar to those expected by investment bankers, was one of the main factors that caused the bankruptcy of the Campeau Corporation in 1989. Deals that are dependent on the large-scale selloff of most of the firm's businesses are referred to as *breakup LBOs.*

- *Other factors.* Each LBO candidate has a different product or service and a different history. The existence of unique or intangible factors may provide the impetus for a lender to provide financing when some ambivalence exists. A dynamic, growing, and innovative company may provide lenders with sufficient incentives to overlook some shortcomings. However, these factors, which are sometimes referred to as "the story," only go so far in making up for deficiencies.

Costs of Secured Debt

The costs of senior debt vary depending on market conditions. Senior debt rates are often quoted in relation to other interest rates such as the prime rate. They often range between two and five points above the prime rate for a quality borrower with quality assets. The *prime rate* is the rate that banks charge their best customers. Less creditworthy borrowers have to pay more. Interest rates, in turn, are determined by many economy-wide factors, such as the Federal Reserve's monetary policy or the demand for loanable funds. Therefore, rates on secured LBO financing will be as volatile as other interest rates in the marketplace. However, these rates will also be influenced by the lenders' demand for participation in this type of financing. Inasmuch as this varies, secured LBO rates may fluctuate even more than other rates in the economy.

Sources of Secured Financing

Secured LBO financing is often obtained from the asset-based lending subsidiary of a money center bank. The volume of capital varies depending of the state of the economy and of the LBO business—both of which are interrelated.

Financing Gap

Leveraged buyout lenders are partial to buyouts in which the target company has significant assets that may be used as collateral. However, even then their value may not be sufficient to cover the total purchase cost of the target. In this case, a financing gap exists; that is, the financing needs of the LBO exceed the collateral coverage. At this point the investment bank must seek other sources of financing. These sources may be covered by equity, subordinated debt, or a loan that exceeds the collateral value of the assets.

Equity capital may be raised by offering an ownership interest in the target to outside investors in exchange for financing. *Subordinated debt* is debt that has a secondary claim on the assets used for collateral. As a result of this inferior claim on assets, this debt usually has higher interest costs. Loans beyond the collateral value of the target's assets are often motivated by less tangible forms of security for the lender, such as the existence of dependable cash flows, which make it more likely that the debt payments will be met.

Unsecured LBO Financing

Leveraged buyouts are typically financed by a combination of secured and unsecured debt. The unsecured debt, sometimes referred to as subordinated and junior subordinated debt, is debt that has a secondary claim on the assets of the LBO target—hence the term *subordinated.* The term *mezzanine layer financing* is often applied to this financing because it has both debt and equity characteristics; although it is clearly debt, it is equity-like in that lenders typically receive warrants that may be converted into equity in the target. Warrants are a derivative security offered by the corporation itself. They allow the warrant holder to buy stock in the corporation at a certain price for a defined time period. Unlike call options, which are offered by brokerage firms, when warrants are exercised, the corporation either issues new stock or satisfies the warrant holder's demands by offering treasury stock.

When the warrants are exercised, the share of ownership of the previous equity holders is diluted. This dilution often occurs just at the time the target is becoming profitable. It is then that the warrants become valuable. In an MBO, for example, managers may have held a very high percentage of ownership in the company. If the target becomes profitable in the future, management might have its share of ownership dramatically diluted by exercising the warrants by the junior subordinated lenders. Although such forms of debt may have undesirable characteristics for management, they may be necessary to convince lenders to participate in the LBO without the security of collateral.

It is important to be aware of the role of the warrants in computing the return to the providers of mezzanine layer financing. Their return is more than simply the interest payments they receive. The value of the equity derived from the exercise of the warrants, adjusted for the probability that the firm will be sufficiently profitable to justify exercising of the warrants, needs to be added to the interest payments to compute the return. This analytical process is demonstrated later in this chapter.

In the preceding discussion, mezzanine layer financing was used in conjunction with senior debt to cover the financing gap. However, some LBOs may be financed solely through unsecured financing. This type of LBO lending is not as desirable to some lenders because it lacks the downside risk protection that marketable collateral provides. Most deals include both secured and unsecured lending.

CAPITAL STRUCTURE OF LBOs

After the completion of the deal, the capital structure of a company taken private in an LBO is usually different from its structure before the buyout. The range for the various components of the capital structure for a typical LBO is outlined in Table 7.3. Over time, the percentages accounted for by different financing providers, such as commercial banks, have varied. These banks, for example, began to withdraw from this market after the junk bond market collapsed and the further merger wave ended and the recession of 1990–91 began. They returned to the market in a big way later in the 1990s. The percentages attributed to them are deceptive as banks may sell their participations in these loans to other investors and may not retain the loan in their loan portfolio.

The capital structure does not remain constant after the buyout. The goal of both the company and the lender is to reduce the total debt through debt retirements. After the buyout, the firm is very heavily leveraged. As time passes, the firm's goal should be to retire the debt and return to a more normal capital structure. Companies usually try to retire most of the LBO debt within five to seven years.

The costs of different components of the firm's capital structure vary. Generally, short-term debt costs are lower than long-term debt because of the additional risk imposed by longer-term lending commitments. The longer the term, the greater the opportunity for something to go wrong. Long-term debt is generally less costly than preferred stock,

Securities	Percent of Capitalization (%)	Source
Short-term or intermediate senior debt	5–20	Commercial banks
Long-term senior or subordinate debt	40–80	Life insurance companies, some banks, LBO funds
Preferred stock	10–20	Life insurance companies, venture capital firms, and private equity firms
Common stock	1–20	Life insurance companies, venture capital firms, managers, and private equity firms

TABLE 7.3 LBO CAPITAL STRUCTURE

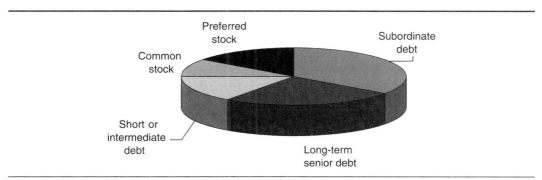

EXHIBIT 7.10   CAPITAL STRUCTURE OF LBOS

which in turn is less expensive to the issuer than common stock. These cost differences are in direct relation to the high degree of risk associated with equity versus debt.

SOURCES OF LBO FINANCING

Exhibit 7.10 shows the participation of the nonbank sources of financing. These sources grew dramatically during the fourth merger wave. They participated in both secured and unsecured financing, and they included different categories of institutional investors, such as life insurance companies and pension funds. Institutional investors actively took part in direct LBO funding or indirectly through an LBO fund. These pools of funds have been developed by private equity firms. The role of private equity funds has become so prominent in M&As and LBOs that a significant portion of Chapter 8 is devoted to these groups of investors.

By investing in LBOs, institutional investors anticipated realizing higher returns than those available from other forms of lending. Also, by pooling the funds, they could achieve broad diversification and the resulting risk reduction. Diversification is designed to limit the exposure to default by any one borrower. Although some institutional investors, such as insurance companies, have tended to be unsecured investors, they often participate in more than one type of LBO financing. This type of financing is sometimes referred to as *vertical strips*. In a vertical strip, investors may participate in several layers of financing within the same deal. For example, they may hold some secured debt and more than one form of unsecured debt as well as some equity.

Types of LBO Risk

LBOs present a variety of risk. The risk of an LBO may be broken down into two main categories: business risk and interest rate risk.

Business risk refers to the risk that the firm going private will not generate sufficient earnings to meet the interest payments and other current obligations of the firm. This risk category takes into account factors such as cyclical downturns in the economy and competitive factors within the industry, such as greater price and nonprice competition. Firms that have very cyclical sales or companies that are in very competitive industries tend not to be good LBO candidates.

Interest rate risk is the risk that interest rates will rise, thus increasing the firm's current obligations. This is important to firms that have more variable rate debt. Interest rate increases could force a firm into bankruptcy even when it experienced greater than anticipated demand and held nonfinancial costs within reasonable bounds. The level of interest rates at the time of the LBO may be a guide to the probability that rates will rise in the future. For example, if interest rates are low at the time of the buyout, interest rate increases may be more likely than if interest rates are at peak levels.

LBOs and the Probability of Bankruptcy

The additional financial leverage and the associated debt service assumed in the financing of leveraged buyouts increase bankruptcy risk. The increase in leverage in LBOs can be significant. Lehn and Poulsen analyzed 284 going private transactions during the period 1980–1987.[28] They showed that the pre-LBO debt-to-equity ratio for a 58-firm subset of their sample was 46%. However, the post-LBO average debt-to-equity ratio rose dramatically to 552%! Companies that are more cyclical and do not have stable and predictable cash flows can be vulnerable to economic downturns after a leveraged buyout.

The fourth merger wave featured many highly leveraged LBO and M&A transactions. When the economy slowed at the end of the 1980s, many of these companies could not service the debt they had assumed in these deals. This gave rise to a number of prominent bankruptcies, some of which are shown in Table 7.4.

Company	Business Description	LBO Year	CH 11 Filing Year
Braniff, Inc.	Airline	1986	1989
Carter Hawley Hale	Department Store	1987	1991
Days Inns	Hotel Chain	1988	1991
Farley, Inc.	Textiles	1988	1991
Federated Stores	Department Store	1988	1990
Greyhound Line	Bus Company	1987	1990
National Gypsum Co.	Building Materials	1986	1990
Resorts Int'l	Casino & Resorts	1989	1990
Revco D.S., Inc.	Drug Store Chain	1986	1988
Southland Corp.	Convenience Stores	1987	1990

TABLE 7.4   SELECTED BANKRUPT LEVERAGED BUYOUTS FROM THE FOURTH MERGER WAVE

Source: The 2002 Bankruptcy Yearbook & Almanac.

28. Kenneth Lehn and Annette Poulson, "Free Cash Flow and Stockholder Gains in Going Private Transactions,"*Journal of Finance*, 44, 1989, 771–788.

RETURNS TO STOCKHOLDERS FROM LBOs

DeAngelo, DeAngelo, and Rice analyzed the gains to both stockholders and management from MBOs of 72 companies that proposed to go private between 1973 and 1980.[29] We have already noted that the premiums paid for their sample was 56%, which was higher than the premium data we have shown for more recent years. They concluded that managers are willing to offer a premium. In the 2000s, however, private equity firms came to dominate the buyout market and they are known to be more careful buyers.

Their research found that an average change in shareholder wealth around the announcement of the deal was 22%. Over a longer time period around the announcement the total shareholder wealth change was approximately 30%. Consistent with the results of the research for M&As generally, the announcement of the bid being withdrawn caused shareholder wealth to decline by 9%.

A study by Travlos and Cornett shows a statistically significant negative correlation between abnormal returns to shareholders and the P/E ratio of the firm relative to the industry.[30] This implies that the lower the P/E ratio, compared with similar firms, the greater probability that the firm is poorly managed. Travlos and Cornett interpret the low P/E ratios as reflecting greater room for improvement through changes such as the reduction of agency costs. Some of these efficiency gains may then be realized by going private. These gains become the source of the buyout premium.

RETURNS TO STOCKHOLDERS FROM DIVISIONAL BUYOUTS

As we have already noted, MBOs area deals where a management group buys a division from the parent company. Many of these transactions have been criticized for not being "arm's-length" deals. Managers of the parent company are often accused of giving preferential treatment to a management bid. The parent company may forsake the auction process and accept management's offer without soliciting other higher offers. One way to see if these transactions are truly in shareholders' interests would be to look at their shareholder wealth effects.

In 1989, Hite and Vetsuypens conducted a study designed to show whether divisional buyouts had adverse effects on the wealth of parent stockholders.[31] Many researchers believe that divisional buyouts may present opportunities for efficiency-related gains as the division becomes removed from the parent company's layers of bureaucracy. This may be a source of value to the managers of the buying group but does not negate the often-cited possibility that a fair price, such as that which might be derived from an auction, was not paid for the division.

29. Harry DeAngelo, Linda DeAngelo, and Eugene Rice, "Going Private: Minority Freezeouts and Stockholder Wealth," *Journal of Law and Economics,* 27(2), October 1984, 367–402. Similar results are found in L. Marais, K. Schipper, and A. Smith, "Wealth Effects of Going Private on Senior Securities," *Journal of Financial Economics,* 23(1), June 1989, 155.

30. Nicholas G. Travlos and M. M. Cornett, "Going Private Buyouts and Determinants of Shareholder Returns," *Journal of Accounting, Auditing and Finance*, no. 8, Winter 1993, 1–25.

31. Galen L. Hite and Michael R. Vetsuypens, "Management Buyouts of Divisions and Stockholder Wealth." *Journal of Finance,* 44(4), September 1989.

Hite and Vetsuypens failed to find any evidence of a reduction in shareholder wealth following divisional buyouts by management. Their results show small, but statistically significant, wealth gains for a two-day period surrounding the buyout announcement. They interpret these results as indicating that division buyouts result in a more efficient allocation of assets. The existence of small wealth gains indicates that shareholders in the parent company shared in some of these gains.

Post-LBO Firm Performance

Several studies have looked at different aspects of postbuyout performance. Long and Ravenscraft surveyed the research literature in this field and have arrived at certain conclusions regarding this research, which we discuss in the following sections.[32]

Overall Operating Performance

Long and Ravenscraft found evidence of improved operating performance, as reflected by cash flow as percent of sales, in companies that underwent LBOs in the 1980s.[33] They found that the more pronounced gains occurred with the LBOs in the early part of the decade. In the latter part of the decade, however, cash flow/sales ratios actually deteriorated while LBO premiums increased. This would imply that the supply of good buyout candidates may have been exhausted but dealmakers, in pursuit of fees and potential profits, went ahead with less desirable LBO candidates.

Employment Effects

Long and Ravenscraft point out that research by Kaplan and Muscarella and Vetsuypens found either negative or no employment effects. Another study by Kitching showed neutral employment effects. It seems that buyouts will either be employment neutral or employment reducing. It would also be reasonable to conclude that the greater the debt service pressures, the more likely management of the postbuyout company will be to cut costs, and labor costs are often a key area that is focused on. When this is combined by the trend of the 1990s and 2000s, where corporations continually seek to become more profitable and efficient, buyout should only provide still another reason to seek greater labor efficiencies.

---

32. Long and Ravenscraft compare the major conclusions of the KKR research with the following studies: William F. Long and David J. Ravenscraft, "The Record of LBO Performance," paper presented at the New York University Conference on Corporate Governance, May 17, 1989; Steven Kaplan, "A Summary of Sources of Value in Management Buyouts," paper presented at the New York University Conference on Management Buyouts, May 20, 1988; Ivan Bull, "Management Performance in Leveraged Buyouts," paper presented at the New York University Conference on Management Buyouts, May 20, 1988; Chris J. Muscarella and Michael R. Vetsuypens, "Efficiency and Organizational Structure: A Study of Reverse LBOs," *Journal of Finance*, 45(5), December 1990, 1389–1414; National Science Foundation, "An Assessment of the Impact of Recent Leveraged Buyouts and Other Restructurings on Industrial Research and Development Expenditures," prepared for the House of Representatives Committee on Energy and Commerce, 1989; James Kitching, "Early Returns on LBOs," *Harvard Business Review*, November/December 1989, 74–81. (The Kitching study was not included in the Long and Ravenscraft review.)
33. William F. Long and David Ravenscraft, "The Aftermath of LBOs," unpublished manuscript, University of North Carolina, April 1991.

Research and Development

The impact of LBOs on research and development (R&D) is less clear. A National Science Foundation study found that "R&D declined between 1986 and 1987 by 12.8% for 8 out of the 200 leading U.S. R&D performing companies which had undergone LBO, buybacks, or other restructuring."[34] A total of 176 firms that were not involved in mergers, LBOs, or other restructurings increased R&D by an average of 5.4%. This observation provides some evidence, albeit weak, that LBOs may be associated with lower R&D expenditures. Once again, if the debt service pressures force major cost cutting, there is no reason to assume that R&D will be immune.

Capital Spending

Kaplan's research shows small declines in capital expenditures, whereas Bull found a 24.7% industry-adjusted decline (21.9% unadjusted) between one year before the LBO and two years afterward. One must be careful about drawing conclusions from these results because they refer to different time periods. The longer the time after the buyout, the lower the debt pressures should be as LBO companies usually try to retire some of the total debt outstanding and thus lower debt service pressures. If an LBO requires that capital expenditures or R&D be curtailed, this policy should be abandoned as the interest payment pressures subside. The longer the time period, the lower the expected capital spending effects.

Effect of LBOs on Prices

Evidence of the impact of LBOs on prices is found in research by Chevalier on the supermarket industry, which underwent a series of major control changes that featured several high-profile LBOs, including those of Safeway ($5.3 billion), Kroger ($4.1 billion leveraged recapitalization), Supermarkets General ($1.8 billion), and Stop & Shop ($1.2 billion).

Chevalier found that, as of the date of her study, 19 of the 50 largest supermarket chains underwent an LBO. She found that these leveraged control deals were associated with price increases in their respective markets. Firms that underwent such LBOs were the high-priced firms in their markets. This industry is a low-margin business and generally not a great candidate for an LBO. If a low-margin company takes on more major costs in the form of interest payments, it is not surprising to see it try to raise prices in response to the greater pressure on its margin caused by the increase in its debt level. The problem with this, however, is that the low margins in this industry are mainly attributable to competitor pressures and the company may not have a great ability to raise prices without incurring a loss of market share.

REVERSE LBOs

A reverse LBO occurs when a company goes private in an LBO only to be taken public again at a later date. This may be done if the buyers who take the company private

---

34. Long and Ravenscraft, "The Record of LBO Performance," p. 2.

believe that it is undervalued, perhaps because of poor management. They may buy the firm and institute various changes, such as replacing senior management and other forms of restructuring. If the new management converts the company into a more profitable private enterprise, it may be able to go through the initial public offer process again.

The opportunity to conduct a successful reverse LBO is greater when the going-private transaction takes place when the stock market is down and the public offering occurs in a bull market.[35] This may make the assets of the LBO candidate undervalued in a poor market and possibly overvalued in the bull market. This reasoning, however, implies that the seller is somewhat naive and does not realize the impact of the short-term market fluctuation.

CASE STUDY

MORTON'S RESTAURANT AND RUTH CHRIS REVERSE LBOS

In July 2002, New York–based private equity firm, Castle Harlan, acquired Morton's steakhouse chain, a public company, for $153.7 million. In this takeover Castle Harlan outbid Carl Icahn for the company. Morton's had been the target of takeover bids and the company ultimately put itself up for sale. The company operated a chain of 61 steakhouses across the United States.

During the period when it was taken private the restaurant chain grew and became a more attractive investment for equity markets. When it filed its registration statements for the initial public offering (IPO) in 2006, Castle Harlan had a sense that the markets would receive the stock offer favorably. This was based on the fact that one of its privately held competitors, Ruth Chris Steakhouse, Inc., which had been taken private in 1999 by Madison Dearborn Partners LLC, went public in August 2005. Madison Dearborn acquired a majority stake in Ruth Chris for $190.3 million, of which $47.1 million was equity it invested.[a] Ruth Chris operated 86 steak houses in the United States as well as in international markets such as Mexico, Hong Kong, and Canada.

The IPO provided Madison Dearborn with a return that was five times its equity investment in Ruth Chris.[b] Castle Harlan indicated that it expected to receive $150 million in the equity offering, which still provided it a reasonable rate of return for its three-year investment.

[a]Kelly Holman, "Ruth Chris to Serve Up $235 M IPO," *Daily Deal*, April 27, 2005.
[b]Kelly Holman, "Morton's Aims to Raise $150 M in IPO," *Daily Deal*, December 5, 2005, p. 1.

Reverse LBO Research

Muscarella and Vetsuypens reviewed 72 reverse LBOs that went public since 1983 and had undergone a buyout.[36] Their study presents a favorable picture of the postbuyout performance of these firms. They found that the ownership structure tended to be concentrated, with management retaining a substantial fraction of the equity. Using traditional accounting measures of performance and financial condition, they found improvements in profitability that were the result of cost reductions as opposed to increased revenues. These results were more dramatic for divisional LBOs than for full firm buyouts. Reductions in capital expenditures were one of the more significant sources of efficiency gains but reduction in staffing was not. Even though the firms increased their leverage to finance

---

35. Leslie Wayne, "Reverse LBOs Bring Riches," *New York Times*, April 23, 1987, p. D1.
36. Chris J. Muscarella and Michael R. Vetsuypens, "Efficiency and Organizational Structure: A Study of Reverse LBOs," *Journal of Finance*, 45(5), December 1990, 1389–1414.

the buyout, management took steps to reduce debt after the buyout. These results imply that the postbuyout firms are in better condition than their prebuyout predecessors. It is not surprising, therefore, that shareholders pay more when the firms go public for the second time compared with the price the company sold for in the LBO. One question arises, however: If the management group is essentially the same before and after the buyout, why did management not enact these increased efficiencies as part of the fiduciary responsibilities for shareholders when they were running the prebuyout company? This criticism may be less relevant for divisional buyouts, in which management may be able to take broader actions because they are not part of a larger bureaucratic structure of a parent company. It is also less relevant for many of the private equity conducted buyouts as the new private equity owners seek to make whatever changes are necessary, including managerial changes, to increase the value of their investment and resell the acquisition.

Holthausen and Larker analyzed the postbuyout accounting and stock price performance of 90 companies that engaged in reverse LBOs from 1983 to 1988.[37] They found that these companies outperformed their industries over the four years following the initial public offering. In addition, they noted that reverse LBOs also increased capital expenditures and working capital levels following the offering. They also noted that when the ownership structure became less concentrated in the hand of managers, firm performance declined.

CASE STUDY

REVERSE LBO OF GIBSON GREETING CARDS

One of the classic reverse LBOs was the buyout of Gibson Greeting Cards, the oldest greetings card company in the United States, by the Wesray Corporation. This buyout firm, led by former Treasury Secretary William Simon and his partner, Raymond Chambers, bought Gibson Greeting Cards from RCA in 1982. They paid $58 million in cash and assumed $22.6 million in liabilities. In May 1983, Wesray took Gibson public in a stock offering valued at $330 million.

Ironically, Gibson Greeting Cards had a troubled financial history after its famous reverse LBO in 1983. In 1995, it held a 10% share of the greeting card market after American Greetings and Hallmark. In 1994, it lost $28.6 million on revenues of $548.8 million.[a] It continued to make financial history in the 1990s when it disclosed in 1994 that it lost $23 million on derivative investments (interest rate swaps). This bad news followed the 1992 bankruptcy of its largest customer, Phar-Mor, Inc. Later in 1994, another of Gibson's large customers, F&M Distributors, Inc., also filed for Chapter 11 bankruptcy. Gibson's retail alignment strategy was highly flawed. While its chief rivals, Hallmark and American Greetings, aligned themselves with leading retailers and garnered the most value shelf space, Gibson moved slowly and was left only with the weaker retailers, many of which ended up going bankrupt.

In 2000 Gibson announced that it was selling the company to its rival American Greetings for $163 million. This is ironic as Gibson rejected a 1996 offer from American Greetings that was almost double this value.

[a]Raju Narisetti and Wendy Bounds, "Sale of Gibson Greetings Inc. Is Considered," *Wall Street Journal* (July 7, 1995), p. A4.

---

37. Robert W. Holthausen and David F. Larker, "The Financial Performance of Reverse Leveraged Buyouts," *Journal of Financial Economics*, 42(3), November 1996, 293–332.

LBO Regulation and Disclosure: SEC Rule 13e-3

SEC Rule 13e-3, which attempted to regulate some of the problems of management self-dealing associated with going private, is an amendment to the Securities Exchange Act of 1934. The rule governs repurchases in going private transactions, and it applies to share repurchases that result in fewer than 300 shareholders or when the previously public company would no longer be listed on public stock exchanges or would no longer be quoted in an interdealer quotation system. The rule requires that the firm going private file a Schedule TO. In Chapter 3 we have already discussed the items that are required to be revealed in this filing. With respect to MBOs, however, the filing must contain information about the alternatives to MBOs that were considered as well as the position of the outside directors.

Leveraged Buyouts as White Knights

Managers in target firms have used LBOs as part of an antitakeover strategy, providing stockholders an offer they may accept instead of the hostile bid. This phenomenon became more commonplace in the fourth merger wave and declined with the overall slowdown in LBO activity in the 1990s.

In a study of 11 MBOs between 1980 and 1984, Shleifer and Vishny found that 6 of the 11 buyouts were responses to hostile threats. These threats came in the form of an outright hostile tender offer or the acquisition of shares with the intention to make a bid for control of the firm.[38]

Leveraged Buyouts, the Position of Other Debt Holders, and Wealth Transfers

One area of interest to many critics in recent years has been the potential impact of the assumption of high amounts of LBO debt, and the associated issuance of junk bonds, on the value of the investment of current bondholders. The fact that bondholders are not part of the approval process has attracted much attention. The additional debt increases the fixed payments that the firm has to make after the buyout. In doing so, it increases the likelihood that the firm will be unable to meet these payments and be forced into receivership.

This problem came to the fore in the RJR Nabisco buyout of November 1988. The value of current bonds dropped sharply after the announcement of the LBO. Some bonds fell as much as 15 points, or $150 for each $1,000 face value amount, in the week the buyout was announced. Although the losses incurred by bondholders drew widespread attention in the RJR Nabisco buyout, bondholders have recognized it as a problem for some time. When the R. H. Macy and Company $3.6 billion buyout proposal was announced in 1985, the stock price rose $16 per share, whereas the price of Macy notes fell more than three points.

---

38. Andrei Shleifer and Robert W. Vishny, "Management's Buyouts as a Response to Market Pressure," in Alan Auerbach, ed., *Mergers and Acquisitions* (Chicago: University of Chicago Press, 1988), pp. 87–103.

Investors who are holding bonds in a corporation that is involved in an LBO see the value and rating of their bonds deteriorate rapidly following the LBO announcement. This has alienated bondholders, particularly institutional investors, who are becoming increasingly vocal. " 'High credit bonds are converted into junk bonds overnight,' fumed John J. Creedon, chief executive officer of Metropolitan Life Insurance Company. 'We think management has a duty to all constituents of the company, including bondholders.' "[39] Metropolitan Life saw its $340 million worth of A-rated RJR bonds downgraded to a junk bond rating for a $40 million loss. The impact of takeover and LBO activity on bonds became so pronounced in the 1980s that the rating agencies often lowered the rating of a firm if it became a takeover or LBO candidate. During the fourth merger wave, the probability of a future LBO became an additional factor that rating agencies took into consideration along with traditional business fundamentals and economic factors.

The state of acrimony between bondholders and RJR Nabisco following the announcement of the LBO led Metropolitan Life Insurance Company to sue Nabisco in a New York State court. Metropolitan's suit alleged that a small group of Nabisco's management sought to enrich themselves at the expense of bondholders who had invested capital in Nabisco in good faith. Opponents of the bondholders contended that the bondholders were seeking to control the operations and decisions of the corporation in a manner that should be reserved only for stockholders. They thought that if bondholders wanted such control, they should have taken the risk of buying stock, not the relatively lower risk bonds.

The conflict between bondholders and stockholders is illustrated in Exhibit 7.11. As the takeover battle for RJR Nabisco heated up during October and November 1988, the value of Nabisco stock rose, as is typical during a takeover contest. However, the

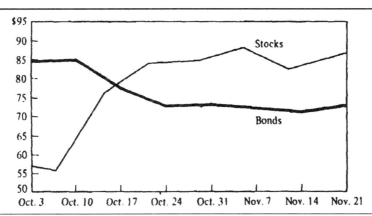

EXHIBIT 7.11   RJR NABISCO BONDS SLIP AS STOCK SOARS: PRICE OF THE 8 3/8 BOND DUE IN 2017 AND THE CLOSING PRICE OF RJR NABISCO STOCK

Source: "Battle Erupts Over Bonds," *New York Times,* November 27, 1988, p. 21. Copyright © 1988 by the New York Times Company. Reprinted by permission.

---

39. "Bondholders Are as Mad as Hell—and No Wonder," *Business Week,* December 5, 1988, p. 28.

value of Nabisco's outstanding bonds declined in response to the market's perception of the added risk and the increased probability of default that the postbuyout Nabisco would have. The fallout was felt throughout the bond market as the value of other bonds declined as a result of the rising concerns that such an event could happen to other bond issuers.

Bondholders contended that buyouts involve a transferal or misappropriation of wealth from bondholders to stockholders; they believe that the board of directors has a fiduciary obligation to bondholders and to stockholders. Others contended that bondholders have to bear "event risk" just like stockholders. They believe that the occurrence of an LBO is another form of event risk that a bondholder must assume when purchasing corporate debt.

On May 31, 1989, a federal judge ruled that an "implied covenant" *did not* exist between the corporation and the RJR Nabisco bondholders, which would prevent the corporation from engaging in actions, such as an LBO, that would dramatically lower the value of the bonds. The court ruled that, to be binding, such agreements had to be in writing.

EMPIRICAL RESEARCH ON WEALTH TRANSFER EFFECTS

There has been much public outcry in the media regarding the losses that bondholders have incurred after going private transactions. Such media coverage implies that there is a general wealth transfer effect from bondholders to equity holders in these transactions. A study by Lehn and Poulsen failed to confirm the existence of such an effect.[40] They found no decrease in value of preferred stock and bonds associated with LBOs. This result, however, was to some extent contradicted by Travlos and Cornett.[41] Although their analysis did reveal a decline in the value of bonds and preferred stock following the announcement of going private proposals, the decline they reported was relatively small.

The limited research in this area fails to provide support for a large wealth transfer effect. The empirical research indicates that if such an effect exists, it is not very significant. The reality of the Nabisco transaction, however, contradicts this conclusion. This seems to imply that these results may not be relevant to very large transactions, such as the Nabisco buyout, in which there is a dramatic change in the bond rating and the financial leverage of the firm. Given the decline in the junk bond market, the supply of such large transactions has been limited. This will reduce the supply of data for additional research on this issue.

---

40. Ken Lehn and Annette Poulsen, "Leveraged Buyouts: Wealth Created or Wealth Distributed," in M. Weidenbaum and K. Chilton, eds., *Public Policy Towards Corporate Takeovers* (New Brunswick, NJ: Transaction Publishers, 1988).

41. Travlos Nicholas and M. M. Cornett, "Going Private Buyouts and Determinants of Shareholder Returns," *Journal of Accounting, Auditing and Finance,* 8(8), Winter 1993.

PROTECTION FOR CREDITORS

After the unfavorable federal court decision in the Metropolitan Life Insurance case, bond purchasers began to demand greater protection against the financial losses resulting from "event risk." In response, they received from bond issuers agreements that would allow them to get back their full principal in the event of a buyout that would lower the value of their debt holdings. The covenants are usually triggered by actions such as the purchase of a block of stock by a hostile bidder or other actions such as a management-led buyout. In return for the added protection, bond buyers pay a somewhat higher interest rate, which is dependent on the issuer's financial condition. The rate may be structured to the magnitude of the rating change.

Much of the protection provided by the covenant agreements is in the form of a poison put allowing the bondholders to sell the bonds back to the issuer at an agreed-upon price. Before the Nabisco case, poison puts were usually confined to privately held company bonds or new issue junk bonds. After the Nabisco bond downgradings, buyers of higher quality public issues demanded some of the same protection once they saw that their bonds could quickly fall into the same categories as the other higher risk issues. Poison puts had also been used as a form of "shark repellent"; that is, companies would issue poison puts as a means of creating a financial obstacle to hostile bidders (see Chapter 5). As we moved into the late 1990s and early 2000s, these protections became less in demand. The fact that the mega-LBO has been around for some time, along with the high volume of LBOs we have seen worldwide, means that these events are already internalized in risk premiums that are built into corporate bonds.

Bankruptcy Proceedings and Pre-LBO Creditors' Interests

If an LBO fails and the company must file for bankruptcy protection, pre-LBO creditors may try to void parts of the deal by seeking to have it treated as a fraudulent conveyance of assets. The pre-LBO creditors may argue that the proceeds of the debt offering were not used for the benefit of the corporation but merely were used to pay a premium to shareholders. Given that such an argument may occur in the future, companies seek to show that, at the time of the LBO, the firm was left with sufficient assets for the protection of creditors and had a reasonable expectation that future cash flows would be sufficient to satisfy both the prior debts and the new debt obligations. The company and lenders may retain a firm to perform a pre-LBO *solvency review* to show that the company was solvent at the time of the deal and had sufficient capital to carry it into the future. This issue is discussed further in Chapter 11.

CASE STUDY

REVCO LBO

On March 11, 1986, Revco received a buyout bid from a management group led by Sidney Dworkin, who was the group's CEO at the time. The bid offered $1.16 billion for the drugstore chain, which at that time was the second largest LBO in this industry. Following the LBO, however, the firm performed below expectations and became one of the first major LBOs to fail. For this reason, along with the fact that this LBO is considered a classic, the Revco going private deal merits further study.

INDUSTRY BACKGROUND

Drugstore sales had been growing rapidly during the ten years before the buyout, increasing at an average annual rate of 11.6% between 1976 and 1986.[a] Sales for the 1987–88 period ran close to the 7.5 to 8.0% range that was projected during the buyout negotiations. In response to growing consumer demand, many drugstore chains opened new outlets. Others expanded by buying other chains. One example was the Rite Aid Corporation's acquisition of the Grey Drug Fair chain, which was owned by the Sherwin-Williams Paint Company.

The pharmaceutical industry instituted many other innovations designed to improve productivity, including the increased use of computers to track and enhance inventory control. However, competitive forces require that the industry be even more efficient. Competition comes from a combination of food and drugstore chains as well as from discount drug chains. Pharmaceuticals is considered one of the two recession-resistant industries in the U.S. economy. (The other is the food industry.) All other factors being constant, a noncyclical firm is a better candidate for an LBO because there is a lower probability that the cash flows will suffer a sudden, unpredictable falloff as a result of a cyclical reduction in demand.

The drugstore industry continued to do well in the two years after the buyout. Sales continued to rise without a significant reduction in profit margins. The increased use of private labels provided firms with higher-margin products that could be sold to consumers at competitive prices. The Revco buyout may have been inspired by the October 1985 LBO of Eckerd Drug Stores, which went private for $1.184 billion. The rise in the number of large LBO offers in the drugstore industry may be attributed to the general well-being of the industry, combined with the decline in interest rates and the cash flow–generating ability of these firms.

REVCO'S POSITION IN THE INDUSTRY

As of August 23, 1986, Revco was the largest drugstore chain in the United States, with 2,049 stores in 30 states. Most of the company's stores were concentrated in Michigan, Ohio, Pennsylvania, North Carolina, South Carolina, Georgia, Virginia, Tennessee, Arizona, and Texas. Although Revco had diversified into other areas, most of its income came from traditional drugstore products. Revco's Odd Lot and Tangible Industries subsidiaries accounted for approximately 5% of its 1986 sales. These subsidiaries are wholesalers of closeout merchandise. Another 5% of its 1986 sales came from generic and private-label drugs and vitamins.

BACKGROUND OF THE REVCO LBO

Revco was formerly Regal D. S., Inc., a Detroit-based drugstore chain. In 1966, the company went public under the name Revco and moved its headquarters to Cleveland, Ohio. It expanded and purchased Carter-Glogau Laboratories, a vitamin manufacturer. Revco also bought the Stanton Corporation, which administered lie detector tests. Revco's CEO, Sidney Dworkin, had been with the firm since 1956, when he joined the company as an accountant. He oversaw Revco's development into one of the largest drugstore chains in the country. By 1983, the company had 1,700 stores in 28 states. Its sales were almost $2 billion, with profits increasing at an impressive 37% per year.

In 1983, vitamins made by Carter-Glogau were blamed for the tragic deaths of 38 infants. As a result, the price of Revco stock fell, and Dworkin feared that the now-undervalued Revco would be

[a]"U.S. Industrial Outlook," U.S. Department of Commerce, Washington, D.C., 1998.

taken over. His defense was to place a large block of stock in what he believed would be friendly hands. In May 1984, Revco bought Odd Lot Trading Company, which had a chain of 70 discount stores, for $113 million in stock. This amounted to 12% of Revco's outstanding shares.

There have been numerous reports of personal conflicts between Dworkin and his new larger stockholders, the previous owners of Odd Lot Trading—Bernard Marden and Isaac Perlmutter.[b] According to these reports, Dworkin favored the close involvement of his two sons in Revco's business operations, a move opposed by Marden and Perlmutter. It is further reported that Marden and Perlmutter threatened to take over Revco. Revco eventually bought back their shares for $98.2 million. The conflict between Dworkin and Marden and Perlmutter, together with the resulting stock buyback, marked the decline of Dworkin's role in Revco. When the board of directors opposed the involvement of Dworkin's sons, he was forced to hire a new president from the outside—William Edwards. The stock buyback put financial pressure on Revco because it was financed by debt. The increased fixed charges associated with the interest payments came at a time when Revco was having trouble keeping the Odd Lot Trading business profitable. By 1985, Revco experienced a loss of $35 million, mainly as a result of a large supply of unsold video cartridges.

Revco's LBO

Dworkin's solution to Revco's financial problems and his declining role in the company was to retain Salomon Brothers and Transcontinental Services Group, which was a European investment group, to arrange an LBO. Dworkin offered the stockholders $36 per share, which was $6 per share higher than the price the stock was trading for four months earlier when the news of the LBO was first announced. However, the LBO offer attracted the interest of the Haft family, who, through their company, the Dart Group, made a higher offer. Dworkin responded by raising his offer to $38.50 per share, or $1.25 billion. The bidding process took seven months to complete before Dworkin's bid was accepted.

The LBO increased Revco's debt four times to $1.3 billion. Revco had planned to pay down the debt by selling off the nondrug businesses. Curiously, Revco also planned to expand at the same time, its goal being to open 100 new stores. This was an unusual move because most LBOs require downsizing and asset sales to pay down the debt. Increasingly concerned about Revco's financial condition, the board of directors favored a new marketing approach, which William Edwards, Revco's president, implemented. This marketing strategy abandoned the everyday low prices that Revco had been known for in favor of weekend specials and promotions. A major thrust of this marketing strategy was to expand Revco's product line to include televisions, furniture, and VCRs. Customers became confused when they saw furniture for sale in stores they had previously known as pharmacies. Revco's profits fell, reflecting the public's negative reaction.

In March 1987, Dworkin was removed as CEO. Edwards made various other attempts to turn the failing company around. For example, he cut prices to clear out inventories, and he rearranged the stores to promote better store traffic. The result was yet more customer confusion, and the company continued to decline. In October 1987, Boake Sells, a former Dayton Hudson president, was appointed CEO and charged with turning Revco around. But this was too little, too late. The 1987 Christmas season was a disaster, with Revco in short supply of many essential and basic products, such as toothpaste, but with stockpiles of televisions and furniture. Cash flow problems became acute as revenues declined while fixed charges remained high.

[b]"Revco: The Anatomy of a Failed Buyout," *Business Week*, October 3, 1998, 58–59.

REVCO'S FINANCIAL CONDITION

Sixteen months after going private through an LBO, Revco became the first of the big LBOs to fail when it missed a $46 million interest payment. In the 1980s, before the LBO, it had shown consistent profitability. Net income remained positive until 1987, when the firm was unable to generate sufficient revenues to meet its higher fixed expenses. To say that sales were not sufficient would be misleading, however. Sales rose in each year before 1987, when they declined to their 1985 levels. However, Revco relied on pre-LBO forecasts, which projected a continually higher sales volume. The 1987 decline in sales should not have forced a firm that was not highly leveraged into bankruptcy, but the pressures of the LBO debt left little room for error. Indeed, the report of the examiner confirmed that the pre-LBO predictions were unrealistically optimistic. This characteristic was symptomatic of other troubled LBOs.

Even before entering the LBO, Revco was not in a very liquid position. One of Revco's problems was its large holdings of nonmarketable inventories. This problem was compounded by the fact that Revco had too high a level of pre-LBO debt. The result was a company that could not meet its overly optimistic sales projections and had to file for bankruptcy.

Revco eventually emerged from Chapter 11 bankruptcy protection in 1992. It wasted no time, however, in getting back into the merger and acquisition business. In April 1994, it purchased the Hook-SupeRx drugstore chain for $600 million, which placed Revco back in the number-three ranking in the drugstore hierarchy behind Walgreen Co. and Rite Aid Corp. In late 1995, however, Rite Aid attempted to purchase Revco for $27.50 per share, or $1.8 billion, to form the largest drugstore chain in the United States with 4,500 outlets. The deal was disallowed in April 1996 by the Federal Trade Commission because of perceived antitrust conflicts.

This opened the door in 1997 for CVS to acquire Revco in a $3.7 billion deal. However, in order to secure antitrust approval, CVS had to agree to sell 114 Revco stores to Eckerd and 6 to Medical Shoppe International. Since the acquisition of Revco, CVS continued to expand through M&As. In a split acquisition in 2004, it bought one half of Eckerd's stores (1,260), along with Eckerd's mail order and pharmacy benefit business, for $2.25 billion. In January 2006, it then bought 700 stores from Albertson's (primarily Osco drug stores). In November 2006, it then made a $21 billion bid for pharmacy benefit manager Caremark. This backward vertical integration strategy raises somewhat similar concerns as the failed forward vertical integration of Merck which had acquired and later divested pharmacy benefit manager Medco.

SUMMARY

An LBO is a financing technique in which the equity of a public corporation is purchased mostly with debt. After the purchase, the public company is taken private. The 1980s witnessed the widespread use of this technique and the participation in the financing of LBOs by many groups of institutional investors. The deals grew larger and larger and were structured by many different layers of secured and unsecured debt as well as by equity. Leveraged buyouts were first known as asset-based lending deals that usually involved firms with significant fixed assets and much unused borrowing capacity. As the major LBO dealmakers heavily promoted the financing technique in the 1980s, cash-flow LBOs of firms that did not have significant assets to be used as collateral but had sizable and steady cash flows became popular. Higher buyout premiums caused more deals to rely on cash-flow coverage rather than on the more traditional asset-based lending.

Stockholders of companies that were taken private reaped large gains, but some of these gains came at the expense of the firms' debtholders, who saw the value of the debt they held decline dramatically. The market value of debt usually fell after the buyout as the debt rating agencies lowered the ratings they gave these securities. Bondholders then sought protection in future debt offerings such as through put options, which allowed the debt to be sold back to the issuer at a specific price after the buyout.

Several of the companies that went private in the 1980s failed by the 1990s. The reasons for their failure were the combined effect of high debt service pressures and the 1990–91 recession and anemic recovery that followed. Large-scale megadeals disappeared from the financial scene, even though LBO investors remained interested in trying to enjoy the high returns that these risky deals may provide. The rising stock market also made going private transactions more expensive.

The LBO business became an international phenomenon during the fifth merger wave. This is particularly the case in Europe, where in 2005 alone we have had many mega-LBOs. Leveraged buyout deal volume is up in the United States but the growth of LBOs in Europe has been very pronounced. In Asia, however, while LBO volume is up, LBOs are still considered mainly a U.S. and European phenomenon.

8

TRENDS IN THE FINANCING OF TAKEOVERS AND GOING PRIVATE TRANSACTIONS INCLUDING HEDGE FUNDS AND PRIVATE EQUITY FUNDS

This chapter features a combination of four loosely related topics. The first concerns how the mix of cash and securities used to finance takeovers has varied over time. An acquiring corporation that is making an offer for another firm has to decide on the mix of cash, debt, and equity that will be used to purchase the target. This is not a unilateral decision, as the total compensation value and mix must be one that the target and its shareholders will accept. While cash and debt seem clearly different, what is designated cash may really be debt where cash was borrowed to finance takeovers. We will see the proportion of cash, debt, and equity used in takeovers has changed over time and there are various factors that determine this mix. In this chapter we will also explore some recent trends that have taken place. For example, we will see how this compensation mix differs internationally.

In addition to the more standard discussion of the mix of various components of compensation used in takeovers, we also will cover some important recent trends related to the financing of M&As. One is the growth of the private equity market. This market has grown internationally and has become a major factor in the M&A business. Private equity firms have often combined together to finance multibillion-dollar takeovers. In the 2000s, these firms have been able to attract large amounts of capital and have very aggressively pursued M&As. Their ability to raise capital has greatly increased in recent years. We will see that, rather than competing with each other, many private equity firms have decided to become partners in deals. This has greatly enhanced the size of transactions they can pursue. In addition, private equity firms have been joined by hedge funds that now compete with private equity firms and other bidders to take over target companies. Hedge funds do outright acquisitions but often they assume large equity stakes and then pressure management to takes steps that will enhance shareholder value.

While the volume of deals rose to unprecedented levels in the fifth merger wave, and still remains high today, bidders finance outright acquisitions and take positions in companies largely without the use of the junk bond market. Junk bond-financed takeovers represent a smaller percent of total takeovers in the 2000s—especially compared with the fourth merger wave. We will explore the reasons for this trend. We will see that one reason is the increased role that leveraged loans have played in takeover financing.

TRENDS IN CASH VERSUS STOCK PERCENTAGE OF TAKEOVER FINANCING

Over the past half century the percent of cash versus stock used to finance takeovers has varied significantly. As Table 8.1 and Exhibit 8.1 show, the cash percentage went from 51% in 1985 to 56% in 1988 but then fell to as low as 22% in 1992. There are several factors that explain this. Companies were performing better in the second half of the 1980s, so cash holdings of companies increased compared to prior years. Some deals listed as cash transactions actually relied on debt financing from sources such as the junk bond market, so that transactions may indicate cash as the form of payment when in fact the bidder is really relying on debt to get the cash to pay the target shareholders. As we will discuss later in this chapter, the role of junk bonds as a financing source changed dramatically as we went through the fifth merger wave.

The percentage of cash used to finance M&As in the United States rose steadily as we moved through the fifth merger wave. However, in contrast with the 1990–91 recession period, when the cash M&A percentage declined significantly as the economy slowed, the cash percentage only declined from 49% in 2000 to 45% in the 2001 recession but then increased to 56% in 2002 and rose to its highest percentage of this two-decade period, 59%, in 2003 and 57% in 2004. The reason for this trend can be seen in Exhibit 8.2, which shows the average cash holdings for S&P 500 companies. Over the past ten years we see that while the growth in these holdings slowed just before and during the 2001 recession, it rose dramatically in the years that followed. The cash M&A payment percentage

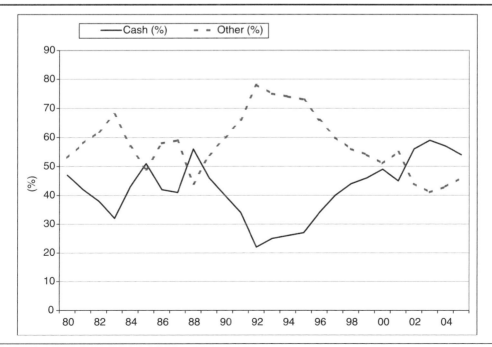

EXHIBIT 8.1 CASH PERCENTAGE OF OFFERS, 1980–2005
Source: Mergerstat Review 2006.

Year	Cash (%)	Stock (%)	Combination (%)	Debt (%)
1980	47	31	21	1
1981	42	34	23	1
1982	38	29	31	2
1983	32	35	33	0
1984	43	26	30	1
1985	51	23	26	0
1986	42	32	26	0
1987	41	34	24	1
1988	56	21	22	1
1989	46	30	23	1
1990	40	31	28	1
1991	34	34	31	1
1992	22	40	37	1
1993	25	40	35	0
1994	26	39	34	1
1995	27	37	36	0
1996	34	37	28	1
1997	40	33	27	0
1998	44	30	26	0
1999	46	30	24	0
2000	49	32	18	1
2001	45	27	27	1
2002	56	22	21	1
2003	59	18	22	1
2004	57	18	24	1
2005	54	19	25	2
Average	42.2	30.1	27.0	0.8
Average 1980–1989	43.8	29.5	25.9	0.8
Average 1990–1999	33.8	35.1	30.6	0.5
Average 2000–2005	53.3	22.7	22.8	1.2

TABLE 8.1 M&A PAYMENT TRENDS: 1980–2004

Sources: Mergerstat Review 1992 and 2006.

responded to this increase by also rising. These factors seem to play a more important explanatory role in determining the tendency to use equity to finance an acquisition.

One recent example of a bid that was partially motivated by large cash holdings was Johnson & Johnson's (J&J) 2005 offer for Guidant. After Boston Scientific kept counterbidding at higher and higher prices, J&J decided the price/value relationship was

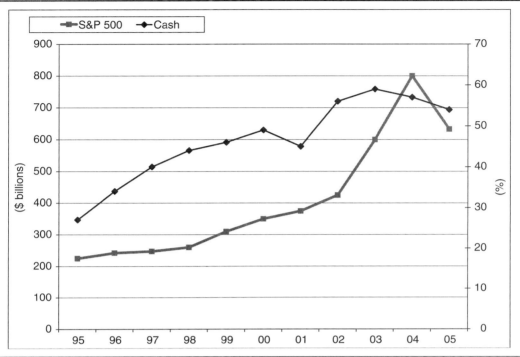

EXHIBIT 8.2 CASH HOLDINGS OF S&P 500 VERSUS CASH PERCENTAGE IN PAYMENT FOR M&AS
Sources: Mergerstat Review 2006 and Standard & Poor's.

no longer beneficial and dropped out of the contest. Over the five year period 2000–2005, J&J's cash holdings had been growing steadily (see Exhibit 8.3). The company faced the decision to either do a major acquisition or return the cash to shareholders either in the form of a dividend or through a share repurchase.[1] J&J shifted its focus from Guidant, and in 2006 acquired Pfizer's consumer products division for $16.6 billion.

On the surface it may seem logical that as the value of the equity of a bidding company rises, the buying power of its stock appreciates. It may be more inclined to use this appreciated "currency" to finance a bid. However, when we consider the fact that the equity of the target also becomes more expensive when the stock market rises, this link becomes questionable. This lack of a relationship becomes clear when we look at Exhibit 8.4, which shows the value of the S&P 500 and the percent of stock used in payment for M&As. As the bull market of the 1990s reached unprecedented heights, the stock M&A percentage actually declined. As we will see later in this chapter, various other factors, beyond just the value of a bidder's stock, play a role in the tendency to do stock-financed deals. The relevant factors include the number of shares owned by management as well as the holdings of institutional investors and other blockholders.

---

1. Some companies with huge cash holdings neither pay dividends nor repurchase their shares. One example is Berkshire Hathaway, which reported $43 billion in cash and cash equivalents in 2005.

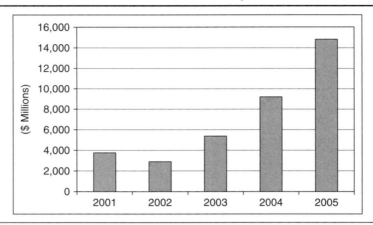

EXHIBIT 8.3   J&J Cash and Cash Equivalents, 2000–2005
Source: J&J Annual Report.

Debt Financing and the Cash Component of Offers

Corporations usually seek to economize on their cash holdings. Cash and other liquid assets pay a comparatively lower return than most long-term assets. Companies, therefore, manage the cash component of their asset structure so as to only maintain cash at levels that will just ensure they will be sufficiently liquid to pay their current obligations as they come due and to have an additional supply of cash and near monies to deal with

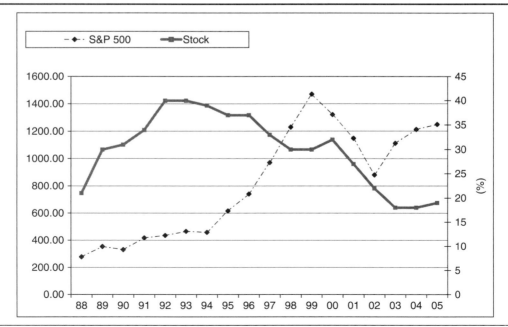

EXHIBIT 8.4   S&P 500 versus Stock Percentage in M&A Payments*
Sources: Mergerstat Review 2006 and Standard & Poor's.

any unforeseen events.[2] As a result, when cash is needed to finance an acquisition, they often resort to debt financing to raise the cash. While stock could be used to generate the cash, debt requires lower flotation costs, thereby giving debt a cost advantage over stock. So we see that cash deals may really mean debt financing.

As seen in Chapter 7, the ability to raise debt financing is influenced by several factors, such as the amount of unencumbered tangible assets as well as the anticipated earnings and cash flows of the bidder. The greater the dollar value of tangible assets and the higher and more stable the projected earnings and cash flows, the greater a company's ability to issue debt and raise cash to finance deals.[3] One aspect that is different about debt capacity evaluation for acquisitions compared with other capital investment decisions is that the assets and cash flows of the target, as well as of the bidder, may enter into the evaluation as the resources that will be available to the combined company if and when the deal is completed.

In some periods companies may have additional cash resources and may choose to accumulate liquid assets if they anticipate a takeover that will require cash. In 2005, for example, the cash holdings of many companies rose to higher than normal levels (see Exhibit 8.2). There are several reasons for the rising cash of U.S. corporations in the mid-2000s. The most basic reason was that the economy continued to improve and corporations began to enjoy higher profits and cash flows. In addition, certain temporary tax law changes allowed U.S. corporations to recapture foreign profits, thereby temporarily raising profits and corporate cash holdings.

International Stock-for-Stock Deals: Currency Issues

When a company in one country seeks to acquire a target in another country, the fact that the shares of the respective firms are denominated in different currencies requires some additional actions on the part of the merging companies. These are usually taken by the bidder issuing depositary receipts in the currency of the target company's country. This was the case in 2000 in the second largest South American deal when Telefonica of Spain acquired two Brazilian telephone companies (Telesp and TSC). The deal, which was a stock-for-stock swap, gave Telefonica a major presence in the Brazilian market. In order to complete the exchange of shares, Telefonica had to issue Brazilian Depository Receipts (BDRs) for the Brazilian target company shareholders, but also American Depositary Receipts (ADRs) for the U.S. investors in both target companies—Telesp and TSC.

SHAREHOLDER WEALTH EFFECTS AND METHODS OF PAYMENT

The choice of compensation paid by the acquirer to target shareholders can itself have important ramifications for the shareholders of both companies. We will see that these effects differ depending on whether we take a short- or long-term perspective.

---

2. See Stephen Ross, Randolph W. Westerfield, and Bradford D. Jordan, *Fundamentals of Corporate Finance* (New York: McGraw Hill, 2003), pp. 673–691.
3. Armen Hovakimian, Tim Opler, and Sheridan Titman, "The Debt-Equity Choice," *Journal of Financial and Quantitative Analysis*, 36, 2001, 1–25.

Target Companies: Short-Term Effects of Method of Payment

Research studies show that the target company valuation effects are greater for cash offers than for stock offers. For example, using a sample of 204 deals, Huang and Walking find that cash offers are associated with substantially higher target returns before and after controlling for the type of acquisition and the amount of resistance.[4] They attribute the higher premiums of cash offers to tax effects. That is, they conclude that the higher premiums are required by shareholders who demand them because they will be forced to incur the costs associated with cash-financed acquisitions. Huang and Walking's finding regarding the higher premiums of cash offers has been confirmed by later research.[5] It is interesting that in a sample of 84 target firms and 123 bidding firms between 1980 and 1988, Sullivan, Johnson, and Hudson found that the higher returns associated with cash offers persisted even after offers were terminated. They interpret this as the market reevaluating firms that are targets of cash offers and placing a higher value on them as a result of the cash offer. When a bidder shows interest in a target, this tends to enhance the market's valuation of that company. It may also attract other bidders to make an offer. This is one of the reasons why bidders request that targets enter into no-shop agreements prior to their making an offer. They know that if they make an offer they may create additional value in the target and they do not want the target to use the value the bidder created against the bidder by inviting other newly interested bidders to compete against the original offeror. New bidders who would be competing against an original cash offer will usually have to also respond with a cash bid as they might be at a competitive disadvantage if they offered securities (depending on the particular issuing company and securities offered).

Acquiring Companies: Short-Term Effects of Method of Payment

As noted previously, acquiring companies tend to show zero or negative returns in response to announcements of takeovers. Chang analyzed the short-term announcement effects on acquiring firms that pursue takeovers of public and privately held companies while also considering how these effects differed for cash versus stock offers.[6]

Using a sample of 281 deals from 1981 to 1992, he found that abnormal returns were approximately zero and not statistically significant for cash takeovers of public companies, whereas returns were a positive and statistically significant 2.64% for stock offers. For private firm takeovers, returns were not statistically significant for cash offers but were a statistically significant −2.46% for stock deals. In conclusion, he found that for cash offers, returns were basically zero and did not vary depending on whether the deal was a public or private acquisition. However, the positive stock price reaction to takeovers of private companies is in sharp contrast to the negative response for public company takeovers. One theory that explains this result is that there may be more monitoring when

---

4. Yen-Sheng Huang and Ralph A. Walking, "Target Abnormal Returns Associated with Acquisition Announcements," *Journal of Financial Economics,* 19, 1987, 329–349.
5. Michael J. Sullivan, Marlin R. H. Johnson, and Carl D. Hudson, "The Role of Medium of Exchange in Merger Offers: Examination of Terminated Merger Proposals," *Financial Management,* 23(3), Autumn 1994, 51–62.
6. Saeyoung Chang, "Takeovers of Privately Held Targets, Methods of Payment, and Bidder Returns," *Journal of Finance,* 53(2), April 1998, 773–784.

stock is given to a few owners of the closely held company. This greater monitoring may reduce adverse agency effects and increase value. When the market perceives this, it reacts with a positive stock price response. As we will see later in this chapter, this conclusion is consistent with other related research on the influence of managerial holdings and those of institutional investors and other blockholders.

Acquiring Companies: Long-Term Effects of Method of Payment

The Chang finding of zero returns for cash offers was contradicted by Loughran and Vijh, who found positive abnormal long-term returns for cash acquisitions but negative abnormal return for stock deals.[7] A major difference between the two studies is that Loughran and Vijh viewed their results from a long-term perspective while Chang focused on short-term announcement effects.

Loughran and Vijh found that over the five-year period following acquisitions, stock deals averaged negative excess returns equal to −25%, whereas for cash tender offers the returns were an average abnormal return of a positive 61.7%! This is a sizable difference. Ghosh's research also provides some support for the long-term effects of the Loughran and Vijh study. He found that performance, as measured by total asset turnover, improved for cash acquisitions but performance measures such as cash flows declined for stock deals.[8] However, when he controlled for the size of the combined companies, which become larger after the deals, the performance difference of stock versus cash deals disappeared. In cash transactions, the firms were larger than those in the stock deal subsample. Ghosh attributes improvements to the larger size of the post-acquisition cash deals compared with stock transactions, which involved relatively smaller combined companies.

Method of Payment and Managerial Ownership

When the shareholdings of a bidder are concentrated so that certain shareholders control a significant percent of the shares and votes of the target, these holdings will be diluted if the bidder issues more shares to finance a bid.[9] Several studies have focused on verifying the extent to which the distribution of holdings is related to the use of stock financing of deals. In a study of 209 M&As in the early 1980s, Amihud, Lev, and Travlos found that the choice of stock versus cash was significantly and negatively related to the size of the shareholdings of managers and directors of the bidder.[10] Their results show that the higher the managerial stock equity ownership the less likely a company will do stock offers. Ghosh and Ruland then extended this work to a sample of 212 M&As over the period 1981 to 1988.[11] They also find that managerial ownership of the bidder was negatively

7. Tim Loughran and Anand M. Vijh, "Do Long Term Shareholders Benefit from Corporate Acquisitions?" *Journal of Finance,* 52(5), December 1997, 1765–1790.
8. Aloke Ghosh, "Does Operating Performance Really Improve Following Corporate Acquisitions?" *Journal of Corporate Finance,* 7, Issue 2, June 2001, 151–178.
9. Rene M. Stulz, "Managerial Control of Voting Rights: Financing Policies and the Market for Corporate Control," *Journal of Financial Economics,* 20, 1988, 25–54.
10. Yakov Amihud, Baruch Lev, and Nicholaos G. Travlos, "Corporate Control and the Choice of Investment Financing: The Case of Corporate Acquisitions," *Journal of Finance,* 45, 1990, 603–616.
11. Aloke Ghosh and William Ruland, "Managerial Ownership, the Method of Payment for Acquisitions and Executive Job Retention," *Journal of Finance,* 53, 1998, 785–798.

related to stock financing of deals. However, the research in this area does not find a linear relationship between stock financing and managerial ownership. Martin, researching a large sample of 846 public but also private acquisitions over the period 1978–1988, also confirmed the inverse relationship between stock financing and managerial ownership over *intermediate* ranges of ownership.[12] He finds that this intermediate ownership range is between 5 and 25%. When acquiring firm management has low or high ownership percentages, managerial ownership is not related to stock financing. For low ownership, managers did not have much control to start off with, so a dilution of the level they had would not change their position significantly. Similarly, when management has a relatively high level of control, they may still be able to command significant control even after their holdings are somewhat diluted through the issuance of stock to effect an acquisition.

The Ghosh and Ruland study also considered the relationship between managerial ownership of the target and the form of payment in deals. They found that stock deals were positively related to the high managerial ownership for the target corporation. They also found that when managerial ownership was high and when the deal was a stock deal, target managers were more likely to stay in the employ of the company after the transaction. We will elaborate on this result a little later in this chapter. As its relates to this discussion, Ghosh and Ruland found that target managerial ownership was the more important factor in determining the form of consideration in bids. Thus it seems that when target management holds a significant percent of the target's stock, they seem to influence the method of payment and demand shares, instead of cash, for their holdings. This implies that they are concerned about influencing control of the combined company, which in turn may better ensure their own employment in the future. When we consider that premiums are often higher in cash deals, target management seems to be considering control along with other factors, such as the tax treatment of the transaction, not just the immediate cash premium they might otherwise receive. Obviously, situations will differ. For some owners of closely held businesses, they may prefer cash as they seek to liquidate their investment and retire. Even in such situations, however, buyers may require that the prior owners stay involved and are only able to gradually cash out their investment.

Method of Payment, Managerial Ownership, and Executive Job Retention

Managers of acquiring companies who value control may want to avoid stock deals because such deals may dilute their control.[13] If this is the case, it may be reasonable to assume that the owners of target companies who value control may prefer stock instead of cash. As noted earlier, Ghosh and Ruland found a "strong positive association between managerial ownership of target firms and the likelihood of acquisitions for stock." They also found that managers in target firms were more likely to retain their positions when they received stock as opposed to cash. When trying to understand this result, keep in mind that hostile deals are more likely to be financed with cash as opposed to stock.

12. Kenneth Martin, "The Method of Payment in Corporate Acquisitions, Investment Opportunities and Managerial Ownership," *Journal of Finance*, 51(4), September 1996, 1227–1246.

13. Yakov Amihud, Baruch Lev, and Nicholas Travlos, "Corporate Control and the Choice of Investment Financing: The Case of Corporate Acquisitions," *Journal of Finance*, 45(2), 603–616.

Cash has a clearly defined value and does not have the potential valuation and liquidity drawbacks that securities offers may have. In general, a sample of cash offers will tend to include more hostile deals than a comparable sample of stock-financed deals. However, hostile bidders will more likely remove target management than friendly bidders. When target management holds a significant number of shares, the bidder has to work to get them to accept the offer. This acceptance will more likely be given when the offer comes with features that meet these shareholders' wants. For target management this may mean staying in the employ of the company after the takeover. When they receive stock in the combined company for their shares, target managers are in a better position to help elect a board that would want to retain their services.

Information Asymmetry, Payment Choice, and Announcement Bidder Performance

Corporate finance has put forward various hypotheses regarding the instances in which management will more likely use stock financing. The theory is that stock financing will more likely be used, as opposed to other financing alternatives such as borrowing, when the stock is overvalued.[14] Because management and directors have better information about the company's future profits and returns opportunities, they are in a better position to evaluate the market's attempt to value the company's expected profits and returns. When they find the market's assessment overoptimistic, they may be more inclined to issue what they consider to be overvalued shares. As applied to acquisitions, the theory assumes that the market is aware of the significance of management's announcement to use stock to finance a deal. Taking this as a negative signal that management believes the stock to be overvalued, the stock price of the bidder should weaken when the deal and its financing choice is announced. This theoretical conclusion is supported by Amihud, Lev, and Travlos, who found that the cases where there were negative bidder returns occurred when managerial ownership is low. The negative market response did not occur when managerial ownership was high. They assume that the market is concluding that when managerial ownership is high, the deal is at least not value reducing. When management has low ownership, the manager's interests may not be well aligned with shareholders and agency conflicts may increase. When companies with low managerial ownership issue stock to finance a deal, the market has less assurance that the deal will be in shareholders' interests and not one that will further management's own agenda.

Institutional Ownership, Blockholders, and Stock Financing

Managerial ownership is not the only factor affecting the use of stock in financing deals. Martin found that institutional holdings were also inversely related to the use of stock to finance deals. He found that companies that have more of their stock held by institutions tend to not use stock as much to finance their acquisitions. These institutions seem to act as a monitor on the willingness of management to liberally use stock to buy targets.

---

14. S. Myers and N. S. Majluf, "Corporate Financing and Investment Decisions When Firms Have Information That Investors Do Not Have," *Journal of Financial Economics*, 13, 1984, 187–221.

Institutions, either directly or indirectly, seem to convey to management they do not want the company to issue more shares, thereby diluting their holdings, in order to acquire other companies. The empirical findings of Martin confirm what has been contended by those such as Jensen, who has opined that higher institutional ownership and blockholdings give these investors an incentive to engage in more close monitoring of management and corporate performance, which, given the incentives and rewards, would not be worthwhile for shareholders with relatively smaller holdings.[15]

PRIVATE EQUITY MARKET

The private equity market is a collection of funds that have raised capital by soliciting investments from various large investors where the funds will be invested in equity positions in companies. When these investments acquire 100% of the outstanding equity of a public company, we have a going private transaction. When the equity is acquired through the use of some of the investment capital of the private equity fund but mainly borrowed funds, we tend to call such a deal a leveraged buyout (LBO). The fact that such deals are very common investments for private equity funds has led some to call these funds LBO funds. However, these firms can certainly use more equity and less debt. The value of using more debt, however, is that the added leverage can amplify positive returns from the deal.

Private equity funds may make other investments such as providing venture capital to nascent businesses. Funds established for this purpose are sometimes called venture capital funds. These investments might exclusively use the fund's capital and not necessarily use borrowed funds. Having such an equity investment, however, may enable the target company itself to have improved access to debt markets after it secured the equity investment from the private equity fund. The fund might take a minority or a majority position in the company. Usually venture capital investments contain incentives, such as stock options, that enable the investor who assumes the risk to enjoy greater profits if the business turns out to be successful.

Private equity funds seek out investments that are undervalued. These could be whole companies that are not trading at values commensurate to what the fund managers think would be possible. They could also be divisions of companies that want to sell the units due to a change in strategy or a need for cash. This was the case in 2002, when the international liquor conglomerate, Diageo, the marketer of brands such as Smirnoff vodka, Guinness beer, and Cuervo tequila, finally came to the realization that there probably was not a lot of synergy between the liquor brands, such as the ones just mentioned and others such as Baileys Irish Cream, and the burgers and fries that are sold at its Burger King division. The Texas Pacific Group and Goldman Sachs Group purchased Burger King from Diageo in 2002 for $1.5 billion.

---

15. Michael C. Jensen, "Corporate Control and the Politics of Finance," *Journal of Applied Corporate Finance*, 4, 1991, 13–33.

Seller versus Private Equity Fund Valuations and Negotiations

In order for private equity firms to generate an acceptable return for their investors, they need to be able to purchase target companies at prices that allow them to achieve a particular hurdle rate. When private equity firms believe that a target has been poorly managed, there may be a greater gap between the value that the private equity firm believes it can readily achieve through the installation of a new management team and the enactment of certain necessary changes in company operations, and the current value of the target based on its unadjusted future cash flows. This gap may provide the basis for some flexibility in negotiations and allow for an agreed-on price. However, when the target has been reasonably well managed and both are aware of the risk-adjusted present value of the company's cash flows, there is less room to provide the seller with the full value of the company while allowing private equity buyers an opportunity to generate a good return on their investment. An example of this occurred in 2006, when the Salt Lake City–based Huntsman Corp., a $13 billion industrial company, broke off negotiations with private equity firm Apollo Management LP. Huntsman, which lost money in 2005, could not come to terms with Apollo at a price that the private equity firm believed made sense. The same result occurred in late 2005, when the grocery store chain Albertson's could not initially agree on terms with a group of private equity buyers. This led the bidders to back away from Albertsons, and later that year a deal was struck with an investment group to sell the company for a revised price of $10.97 billion. Sellers who are seeking to offer their companies to private equity firms have to be willing to accept a price that will allow these firms some room to generate a return with another sale of the business in a few years. While they are certainly not immune from making valuation mistakes, private equity buyers tend to be careful not to overpay as their gains mainly come from the difference between their purchase price and an eventual resale price plus any monies extracted from the company prior to that resale.

Example of a Partial Equity Investment by Private Equity Firm

In January 2006, private equity firm Newbridge Capital Ltd., which is a unit of Texas Pacific Group, purchased $800 million of the equity in the Taiwan-based Taishin Financial Holding Co. Taishin, which is listed on the Taiwan exchange, is that nation's largest credit card issuer. In June 2005, Taishin had acquired a 22% stake in Chang Hwa Commercial Bank. This was one of a series of acquisitions that had been taking place in the Taiwan banking sector, which has been consolidating. Newbridge hopes to capitalize on that consolidation of that sector. In doing so they are leveraging their experience in the Korean banking sector. In the late 1990s, the Korean banking system suffered a series of crises and underwent a restructuring. In 1999, Newbridge had bought the Korean First Bank and later sold its stake in that bank for three times its investment when the bank was sold in 2005 to Standard Chartered PLC for $3.3 billion.[16]

---

16. Laura Santini and Kate Linebaugh, "Newbridge to Pay $800 Million for Taishin Stake," *Wall Street Journal*, January 28–29, 2006, B3.

Example of a Total Acquisition by a Private Equity Firm

As noted, private equity funds seek to find undervalued assets, improve them, and sell them for a higher price. Wilbur Ross, through his private equity firm, Wilbur Ross & Co. LLC, has made this practice a highly skilled art. In the early 2000s, he focused on the troubled steel industry and bought the once-giant LTV Corp. (see case study in Chapter 3 on the conglomerate LTV) and then bought Acme Steel Co., Bethlehem Steel Corp. (another former steel giant), and Weirton Steel Corp. He combined these companies into one steel firm, called International Steel Group (ISG), based in Richfield, Ohio. He then sold the entity to a company that became Mittal Steel. Mittal itself was formed through the acquisition of LNM Holdings by its Netherlands-based sister company, Ispat International NV, for $13.3 billion. This entity then acquired ISG for $4.5 billion, thereby creating the world's largest steel company. Ross's firm has invested $343 million and was reported to have achieved a sevenfold return for his investors.[17]

M&A Opportunities after Private Equity Cash Out

As noted, private equity firms seek to find undervalued opportunities, take corrective actions to improve the market value of the enterprise, and then sell the company. Often the sale is done through an initial public offering (IPO). One might think that after the sale the target is appropriately valued and no further near-term acquisition opportunities exist for the sold company. While normally that is the case, there are numerous examples of companies that are acquired relatively soon after a private equity–inspired IPO. As an example, in August 2005, PanAmSat Holding Corp. announced that it was being sold to Intelsat Ltd. less than six months after KKR and Carlyle took the company public. Similarly, in 2006, the Earle M. Jorgensen Company agreed to merge with Reliance Steel and Aluminum Co. less than a year after Kelso & Co had taken it public in an IPO. The reason why these deals could make sense is that while the IPO may have offered the company at a value that reflected the risk-adjusted present value of its expected cash flows, this value would not include the synergistic benefits that an acquirer might see in the company. These quick-turnaround M&As are certainly not the norm but they are also not uncommon.

Some have been critical of certain private equity buyers which do no more than merely "flip" companies. Such "flippers" try to buy at an attractive price, engage in some cosmetic changes to buttress the financial results and then sell at a higher price without adding any meaningful value to the company. Shareholders in companies that are targets of such offers sometimes have encouraged their boards to reject them based on the belief that their own management can take the same actions as these private equity buyers likely would. This, however, raises the obvious questions as to why management didn't take such value-enhancing actions prior to the arrival of a private equity buyer.

---

17. Renee Cordes and David Carey, "International Steel Group Goes for $4.5 Billion in Cash and Stock to LNM Group," *The Daily Deal,* October 26, 2004.

Firm	Net Revenue ($ Millions)	Market Share (%)
Kohlberg Kravis & Roberts	456	4.9
Blackstone Group	439	4.7
Carlyle Group	368	4.0
Apollo Management	240	2.6
J. P. Morgan Partners	233	2.5
Goldman Sachs Capital Partners	230	2.5
Apax Partners	215	2.3
Morgan Stanley Capital Partners	179	1.9
Warburg Pincus	178	1.9
Bain Capital	176	1.9

TABLE 8.2 LEADING PRIVATE EQUITY FIRMS

Source: Dealogic Revenue Analysis.

Leading Private Equity Firms

A private equity firm may raise capital to build several different funds. Based on an investors' participation in the fund, they will receive a proportion of the return that the fund enjoyed less the management fees for running the fund. Table 8.2 lists some of the leading private equity funds and their net revenues and share of the market.

Private Equity Fund Partnerships and "Club Deals"

Private equity funds may acquire stock in a target company individually or they may combine with other private equity firms to acquire a target. These types of deals are sometimes referred to as club deals. The combinations enable then to spread out the risk. This may be necessary as many funds require that no more than a certain percent, such as 10%, of a fund's assets may be invested in any particular investment. For 100% acquisition, a $10 billion fund, a large private equity firm by any standards, would then be limited to acquisitions no larger than $1 billion if they chose not to utilize debt to complete the transactions. For this reason they may choose to join forces with other private equity firms when they are attempting to complete a large acquisition. This occurred in March 2005, when Silver Lake Partners completed the second largest LBO up to that time when it combined with six other private equity firms to acquire Sunguard Data Systems for $10.8 billion. The other private equity firms who participated in the takeover were the Blackstone Group, Kohlberg Kravis & Roberts, Texas Pacific Group, Goldman Sachs Partners, and Providence Equity Partners.

Private equity firms have become so involved in takeovers that they find themselves forming competing groups or partnerships and bidding against each other for takeover targets. This was the case in 2005, when Kohlberg Kravis & Roberts (KKR) joined forces with Silverlake Partners to acquire Agilent Technologies, Inc.'s semiconductor products business for $2.6 billion in August 2005. This company was spun off by Hewlett-Packard in 1999 as part of a focusing strategy. Agilent itself was pursuing a focusing strategy in

2005 when it decided to try to sell its chip unit and lighting business. The company's CEO, William Sullivan, stated that Agilent, being a diversified company, was "trading at a 25% to 35% discount to" its peers.[18] He believed that giving the company increased focus through selloffs such as this would lower the discount that the market was applying to his company. KKR and Silverlake won the contest in which they were bidding against two other buyout groups: one that featured Bain Capital and Warburg Pincus and another that had Texas Pacific Group, CVC Partners, and Francisco Partners as participants.

When we consider the borrowing power of a private equity fund, or group of funds, the buying capability of these funds has become truly impressive. This is due to the fact that the size of the funds has grown significantly during the 2000s. In March 2005, the Carlyle Group formed a $10 billion fund with approximately three quarters earmarked for U.S. investments and approximately a quarter for European deals. If these monies were leveraged and focused on one or a few transactions, the size of the companies that could be purchased would be much greater than the typical target of a private equity takeover. This was followed later in 2005 by Warburg Pincus, which formed an $8 billion fund, and Goldman Sachs, which formed an $8.5 billion fund. With these funds flush with cash, they helped fuel the post–fifth wave takeover business.

Sales to Other Private Equity Buyers

Another change that has taken place in the private equity business is the willingness of private equity firms to buy companies from other private equity firms. In the past, private equity buyers did not think they could achieve good value by buying a company that was bought some years earlier by another private equity buyer. This changed after the fifth merger wave. In the current market some private equity firms may believe they are capable of taking a company of one size to another higher level. They then may sell this company to another buyer who may believe they have the requisite expertise to take this company to another size level. Each private equity buyer may bring specialized expertise to the target company. The company is then "passed on" to a second private equity buyer as it pursues its growth.

Companies that May be Better in the Hands of "Financial Buyers"

Certain types of companies may be better run when they are under the control of financial buyers such as private equity firms. Public companies face pressure from equities' markets to generate steady returns even when the business is naturally volatile. If these pressures cause a company to make management decisions that sacrifice the long term value of the company, it might be better off being a private company under the control of a financial buyer that has an investment focus that is consistent with the nature of the business.

Private Equity Fund Investors

Private equity firms raise their capital from a variety of sources including institutional investors such as pension funds. These investors have looked to private equity firms as

---

18. Pui-Wing Tam, "Agilent Unveils Broad Restructuring," *Wall Street Journal*, August 16, 2005, p. B8.

a way of achieving higher returns on their portfolio of investments. This became more important when interest rates fell and then the stock market also fell as we moved into the 2000s. These institutional investors may place a portion of their capital with various different private equity funds; thus the portion of their capital devoted to the private equity may be diversified across a few funds. In addition, their overall portfolio is diversified with holdings in many other investment categories such as stock, bonds, and money market investments. The private equity component of their overall portfolio may provide higher returns but would have more risk and be less liquid than their debt and money market investments.

Wealthy individuals are also investors in private equity funds. They also invest some of their capital in private equity funds in pursuit of the higher returns they will hopefully pay. As funds have grown dramatically in size, the percent of total private equity capital provided by individuals has become somewhat less important.

CASE STUDY

PRIVATE EQUITY GOES PUBLIC—KKR IPO

The evolution of the private equity market took a new turn in 2006, when the private equity firm, Kohlberg Kravis & Roberts (KKR), announced a planned $5 billion initial public offering. Historically, private equity firms have raised capital through a network of institutional and individual investors. When one of the pioneers of the private equity field announced it was raising capital for its new investment fund through a public solicitation of shareholders, the markets took notice. However, this was not the first such public offering. This distinction goes to the New York–based Ripplewood private equity firm, which in March 2006 listed its holding company, RHJ International, on the Brussels exchange. The KKR offering is on the Euronext exchange in Amsterdam. The reason why these New York private equity firms went to the European markets to do their IPOs, as opposed to the U.S. securities exchanges, is due to the greater disclosure requirements under U.S. laws. Private equity firms have traditionally avoided disclosure so that competitors do not benefit from such information. When investors receive expected returns, disclosure is usually a non-issue. This would not be the case under U.S. laws.

The fact that these funds are public raises interesting issues regarding the way private equity firms conduct business. Securities markets tend to be quite myopic. They often pressure publicly traded companies to be more short-term oriented and generate near-term returns, sometimes at the expense of long-term growth. However, many private equity investments have a longer focus. It remains to be seen how KKR will respond to this new investment group.

Private Equity Returns and Fees

Thompson Venture Economics has reported that the average rate of return on private equity funds has been 12.5% over the period 1995–2004, which, while consistent with the long-term rate of return on stock of small public companies, has been greater than the average rate of return on large capitalization stocks and bonds over this same ten-year time period.[19] Other data sources, such as Cambridge Associates show average annual

---

19. "Laura Santini, "Ontario Teachers Make Grade with Private Equity Plays," *Wall Street Journal*, August 15, 2005, D1.

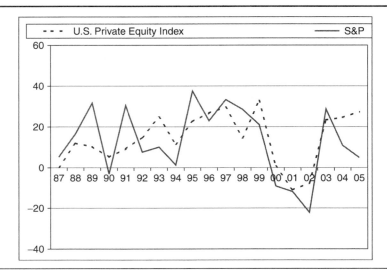

EXHIBIT 8.5   CAMBRIDGE ASSOCIATES PRIVATE EQUITY INDEX VERSUS S&P 500
Source: Cambridge Associates LLC U.S. Private Equity Index and selected benchmark statistics, December 31, 2005.

returns approximately 3% higher. Returns in 2005, however, fell sharply Exhibit 8.5 shows similar rates of return for the past 10 and 20 years, although it also shows that these returns are quite variable. Since these returns were greater than what was available on equity investments in the overall market, managers of private equity firms have charged their investors relatively high fees for the opportunity to invest with the funds. These fees may run from approximately 1 to 2% of total assets to 20% of total profits of the fund or a combination of the two. Venture capital funds may charge a 1.5 to 2.5% fee along with a 20% share of the profits of the fund's investments.[20]

Financial Engineeering and Private Equity Deals in the 2000s

In the 1980s deals that used a relatively small percent of equity and loaded up on relatively less expensive debt were much more common. Often they relied on being able to "bust up" the target and use the proceeds from sales of business units to lessen the leverage. Such deals, sometimes referred to as financial engineering deals, are much less common today. In the 2000s private equity buyers tend to be more knowledgeable about the company and industry and usually have a management team which they believe will enhance the value of the company. It is more unusual to see managers who merely engage in financial manipulations and do not attempt to operationally improve the value of the target.

Dividend Recapitalizations

Private equity firms generate returns from their portfolio companies in more ways than just cashing out the investment when it is sold. In recent years we are seeing private

---

20. Paul Gompers and Joshua Lerner, "An Analysis of Compensation in the Venture Capital Partnership," *Journal of Financial Economics*, 51, 1999, 3–44.

equity firms engaging in "dividend recapitalizations." This is when the private equity firms have companies they have acquired take on more debt, such as through issuing bonds and using the proceeds to pay a dividend to the fund investors. This was the case in September 2004, when KKR had PanAmSat issue $250 million in notes that were used to pay the investors who bought the firm just one month prior for $4.3 billion. In the aforementioned purchase of Burger King by private equity investors, the buyers paid themselves a $400 million special dividend in 2006, which Burger King financed through the assumption of approximately $350 million in debt. In May 2006 Burger King did a $425 million initial public offering which offset the substantial debt the company had taken on to pay the dividend. The combination of the dividend and their share of the private equity proceeds was reported to eventually provide the private equity investors with a 115% return on their three-year-plus investment![21]

Management and Termination Fees

In addition to such dividend recapitalizations, private equity firms sometimes also charge their captive companies management fees in the range of 1 to 2%. These fees are supposed to offset the overhead at the private equity firm but it is also a source of return for these firms. Such firms may also charge the companies fees for having one of their representatives sit on its board. They also may charge a "termination fee" when the company is sold. Not all private equity firms charge such fees and the arrangements vary by firm.

Characteristics of Private Equity Returns

The data shown in Exhibit 8.5 imply that private equity returns do not outperform the market. This was confirmed by Kaplan and Schoar, who examined the LBO fund and venture capital fund returns of private equity firms.[22] They found that gross of fees, both LBO and venture capital fund returns exceeded the S&P 500. However, when fees were also considered, the superior performance of these funds disappeared. One has to remember that low-cost investment vehicles, such as exchange-traded funds as well as regular mutual funds, enable investors to earn the rate of the return of the market at a relatively low cost. Therefore, private equity funds have to do substantially better than the market to justify their comparatively higher fees. There is not much evidence to support these fees.

One characteristic of investment performance that has attracted much attention over the years has been the *persistence* of returns of mutual fund managers. This refers to the likelihood that above-average returns in one period are associated with above-average returns in later periods. Mutual fund managers have not been able to demonstrate much persistence.[23] However, Kaplan and Schoar do find persistence in performance for general managers of one fund and others that they establish.

21. Maxwell Murphy, "Private Investors in Burger King to Get Dividend," *Wall Street Journal*, February 4–5, 2006, B4.
22. Steven N. Kaplan and Antoinette Schoar, "Returns, Persistence and Capital Flows," *Journal of Finance*, 60(4), August 2005, 1791–1823.
23. Mark M. Carhart, Jennifer Carpenter, Andrew Lynch, and Daniel Musto, *Review of Financial Studies*, 15, 2002, 1439–1463.

Kaplan and Schoar also examined capital flows into private equity funds. As expected, fund flows are positively related to fund performance—both on the fund and industry level. However, they found that higher industry performance seems to enable more funds to be formed but many of the funds do not perform as well in the future. That is, better industry performance seems to allow less skilled managers to form new funds that do not exhibit the same performance as those that enabled the industry to grow and allowed them to attract capital. Many of these newly formed funds then go out of existence.

HEDGE FUNDS

Hedge funds were developed as an alternative to open end investment funds or mutual funds. Managers of hedge funds do not make public solicitations to investors in general and as such do not face the public reporting requirements that their mutual fund counterparts do. Since hedge funds do not face as great reporting requirements, investors have more limited access to return data. When returns are high, investors may not care as much about reporting, but when returns fall below expectations investors often want a more complete explanation for the disappointing results. Nonetheless, while industry statistics are somewhat murky, the successful growth of hedge funds is without debate. This industry has been reported to be as large as $1 trillion with as many as 8,000 hedge fund managers active in the United States. Moreover, hedge funds may account for as much as half of all the trading on the New York Stock Exchange.[24] Table 8.3 lists the top ten hedge funds reported by Hedge Fund Research, Inc.

Hedge funds have traditionally employed a variety of aggressive investment strategies. These include short selling, swaps, arbitrage, and employing leverage to increase return potential. Like private equity funds, hedge funds raise capital from institutional investors

Firm	Assets ($ Millions)
Orbis Global Equity	6,345
Highbridge Capital	5,700
Bridgewater Pure Alpha I	5,308
Fairfield Sentry	5,180
Orbis Optimal (U.S.)	4,017
Winton Diversified Futures	4,010
Cerberus International	4,000
Shepherd Investments International A	3,937
King Street Capital	3,609
Ashmore Emerging Markets Liquid Inv.	3,350

TABLE 8.3   TOP TEN HEDGE FUNDS

Source: "Largest hedge funds," *Pensions & Investments*, 33, Issue 26 (December 26, 2005), p. 40.

---

24. Sara Hansard, "Standardized Hedge Fund Reporting Urged," *New York Times*, November 14, 2005, p. 30.

and wealthy individuals. Smaller investors are kept out by the large initial investment requirements combined with the fact that only a limited number of investors are invited to participate. During the early 1990s, hedge funds used to be able to be more selective of the investors they accepted for their funds. The management of some funds had the attitude that they would consider who they wanted to allow to invest in their funds and those investors should be happy with the returns they enjoyed and accept whatever meager disclosure they were given, and that if they did not like it they could be replaced by a long line of investors wanting to take their place. This began to change due to a couple of factors. One was the catastrophic failure of Long Term Capital Management, a firm made popular by the claims that it managed money using the expertise of Nobel prize–winning economists Merton Miller and Myron Scholes.[25] Their expertise did not prevent the fund, which was founded in 1994, from collapsing following the 1998 Russian bond default. The collapse of the fund, which lost $2 billion in one month (20% of its capital), almost brought down many major financial institutions that had lent substantial amounts of money to the fund. The disaster was solved through the intervention of Federal Reserve chairman Alan Greenspan.

Following the failure of Long Term Capital Management, investors began to look more closely at their hedge fund investments. At the same time, however, the growth and proliferation of hedge funds in the 1990s and 2000s continued relatively unabated (see Exhibit 8.6).

Hedge Funds and M&As

As hedge funds began to feel the pressures from competitors to generate high returns they started to look to takeovers—previously the exclusive fund territory of private equity funds. Investors took notice when Edward Lampert, through his hedge fund ESL Investments, did a blockbuster takeover of Kmart in January 2000. Lampert took over Kmart as it was emerging from Chapter 11 bankruptcy protection. In 2004, he then pursued an $11.5 billion merger between Kmart and Sears to form a retail giant that could compete on a more even basis with market leader Wal-Mart. Private equity managers have challenged this entry by asserting that the private equity business is about not just acquiring securities but also overseeing the management of the companies in which the fund takes a position. Hedge funds have been more used to acquiring and trading securities but have generally not been as involved in overseeing the actions of the managers of the companies they acquire positions in. This is one of the main differences between the two types of funds.

Hedge Funds as Sources of M&A Debt Financing

Hedge funds have pursued many different investments areas as they seek to find attractive returns for the capital they have been able to easily raise in recent years. One area they have focused on has been the debt of distressed companies. However, in recent years they have become involved in debt financing of M&As. Commercial banks often originate

25. Roger Lowenstein, *When Genius Failed: The Rise and Fall of Long Term Capital Management* (New York: Random House, 2000).

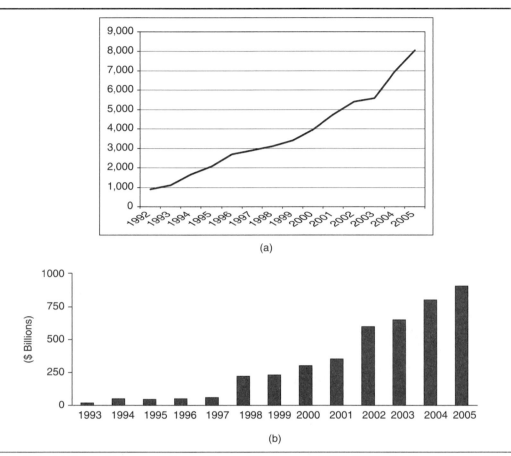

Exhibit 8.6   (a) Total Number of Hedge Funds Worldwide: 1992–2005; (b) Hedge Fund Assets
Worldwide

Source: (a) *Wall Street Journal* and Hennessee Group; (b) *Wall Street Journal.*

M&A debt financing that they syndicate to hedge funds that assume what usually is
second lien debt. The addition of this source of debt financing from hedge funds has
greatly augmented the total capital that is available for M&A financing. This has helped
fuel the resurgence of M&A deals in the mid-2000s.

Hedge Fund Activism and Corporate Governance

Hedge funds have become more activist in recent years in pursuit of greater returns for
the equity investments that they have acquired in public companies. Some hedge fund
managers have become impatient with weak returns that companies may generate and
push for changes, including managerial changes. One of the more notable of these activist
managers is Carl Icahn, who was known in the fourth merger wave as a corporate raider.
He has often been critical of the upper management of major corporations and has been
impatient when companies fail to generate good returns for shareholders.

CASE STUDY

CARL ICAHN—ACTIVIST HEDGE FUND MANAGER

Carl Ichan had been a fixture in the M&A business for the past quarter of a century. He was known to some in the fourth merger wave as a greenmailer, although he would probably consider himself (with good justification) as a shrewd investor who found undervalued companies and took advantage of them. In the 2000s, he acquired a stock position in Time Warner. This company is the product of the merger between AOL and Time Warner—a deal that was the largest merger flop of all time. He used his hedge fund's large stock position to pressure the company to take more aggressive steps to improve shareholder value. He was highly critical of Time Warner's inability to aggressively compete with companies such as Google, Yahoo, and eBay. He claimed that management was more interested in spending many millions on building a corporate fortress at Columbus Circle in Manhattan while floundering in the marketplace. He demanded that the company consider restructuring, including asset sales to become more focused and efficient. In addition, he called for an infusion of better management to "right the ship." It is interesting to note that with all of the clout he commanded in the marketplace, even Icahn had to accept a limited victory given the huge size of Time Warner. The company agreed to some of his initiatives, including a larger stock buyback, but fell short of a major overhaul. However, as we have seen in Chapter 6, when companies are able to initially fend off insurgents in proxy fights, they often pursue some of the very same strategic initiatives that the insurgents recommended after the contest is over, even when they opposed them during the contest.

Hedge Fund Regulation

As we have noted, hedge funds are not closely regulated. They do not have to adhere to the same reporting requirements as investment vehicles such as mutual funds, which make public solicitations and include many investors with much investigation into the level of sophistication of the investor. In order to not have to comply with the reporting requirements set forth in the Investment Company Act of 1940, funds must not have more than 100 investors and have minimum investment thresholds of $250,000 to $1,000,000.

When a new private equity or hedge fund is formed, no performance statistics are available for the fund, which has not even started operation yet. Organizers of these funds like to be able to present what is called "related performance" information. This is usually some historical performance statistics for the performance of the fund managers and funds organized by the same company. However, these are performance statistics covering not only a different time period but also a different fund. This is why the National Association of Securities Dealers (NASD) does not allow its member brokers to distribute related performance materials.[26] This does not prevent the fund managers, who are usually not brokers, from distributing such materials. In doing so they rely on the "user's exemption" from Rule 3a4-1 of the Securities Exchange Act of 1934.[27] However, the Securities and Exchange Commission (SEC) requires that the funds include only qualified purchasers who are individuals with $5 million under investment or an institution with $25 million under management. It is common that private equity funds include only

---

26. Rule 2210 of the NASD's Rules of Conduct.
27. www.whitecase.com/publications.

such qualified investors, but as the number of hedge funds has grown over the past five years, hedge funds have had to reach out to a larger population of investors. They have had to also include "accredited investors," which have minimum net worth of only $1 million and annual income not lower than $200,000. After February 1, 2006, newer rules for hedge funds went into effect that elevate the investor requirements for hedge funds to $1.5 million in net worth while also raising the amount of money under management to $750,000.[28] The SEC adopted a rule that required hedge funds to periodically open their books to regulators, but this rule was struck down in June 2005 by the U. S. Court of Appeals.

There have been calls for increased governmental regulation as a result of some major scandals in the hedge fund industry. One involved the failed Bayou Fund, which reported false returns statistics and deceived investors into thinking the fund was performing acceptably when it was generating large negative returns. Government regulators have long held the position that larger, more sophisticated investors do not need the same regulatory help that smaller investors do as larger investors are in a better position to take care of themselves. However, as noted earlier, in the 2000s, as hedge funds lowered their minimum investments from $1,000,000 or more to $250,000, and some even lower, the field began to feature more entrants and with that came some unscrupulous marketers. Medium-sized investors began to seek some of the same higher returns that have been reported by hedge fund proponents. Unfortunately, investors have little assurance that returns cited by some funds are accurate. For now the regulation in this area of investment is limited and investors need to be on guard.

COMPARISON OF PRIVATE EQUITY FUNDS AND HEDGE FUNDS

The differences between private equity funds and hedge funds used to be clearer but those differences have started to decline as hedge funds began to engage in M&A-related investments that were more the bailiwick of private equity funds. Hedge funds have tended to invest in more short-term and liquid investments than private equity funds. Private equity funds would make a large equity investment in certain companies and hold them for a period of time and then hope to sell the investment at a significant rate of return. Hedge funds vary in the types of investments they make and securities they purchase. They may purchase securities with a short-term investment horizon and often look to sell their investments at the most opportune time even if this means a short holding period.

Hedge fund investors may be able to cash out their investments after a certain initial "lockup" period. Hedge funds that have more liquid assets will normally be able to accommodate such redemption requests. Funds that seek to invest in less liquid investments may require a longer lockup period. Private equity funds, however, make longer term, less liquid investments and are usually not in a position to accede to such requests. As a result, private equity investors must be willing to accept a long-term investment strategy. Their returns will be provided when the private equity fund cashes out its investments, such as when a company it has purchased is sold. However, we have already

---

28. Ibid.

noted some exceptions to this, such as when a private equity firm engages in dividend recapitalizations.

Hedge funds traditionally have not been that active in the operations of the companies they invest in. However, private equity funds normally make large investments in particular companies and play an active role in selecting management and overseeing their performance. Critics of the new-found competition with hedge funds, such as Henry Kravis of KKR contend that hedge funds, such as the group that challenged him in the auction for the energy group of Texas Genco, do not have the skill-set to effectively oversee a major equity investment in a company.[29] However, if M&A investments prove to be a source of high returns for hedge funds, one would expect hedge fund managers to try to adjust their strategies to be consistent with those that will generate the highest returns.

Hedge Fund Fees

Another difference between hedge funds and private equity funds is that while they both may charge similar rates as fees, private equity funds may register gains when an asset is sold based on the difference between the purchase price and the eventual price realized when the equity position is sold. Hedge funds, however, charge fees based on a hypothetical asset price, so when such prices increase they receive a fee, but when they decline they do not give investors a refund.

Funds of Hedge Funds

In both the mutual fund and hedge fund industries we have funds that make investments in several other funds. As such, they are *funds of funds*. For example, Table 8.4 shows that the largest of these funds of funds is UBS Global Asset Management A&O. Given that the hedge fund industry is somewhat fragmented, there is speculation that the industry will be consolidated just like many fragmented industries were consolidated in the fifth merger wave. We are already seeing some funds of funds seeking to acquire other funds or other funds of funds. Being larger would enable these funds of funds to include larger hedge funds as opposed to being a collection of mainly smaller funds. This may prove to be an active area in the remaining half of the 2000s.

HEDGE FUND AND PRIVATE EQUITY FUND CONVERGENCE

While there have been major differences between private equity funds and hedge funds in the past, in recent years these differences have become less apparent. This is mainly due to the fact that many hedge funds are engaging in some of the same equity investments that private equity firms have traditionally focused on. With the proliferation of hedge funds, increased competition has caused diminished investment opportunities. For example, arbitrage opportunities have declined as more hedge funds seek to take advantage of fewer

---

29. Nicholas Ferguson, "No Passing Fad: No Big Deal: Hedge Fund Interest in Private Equity Is Here to Stay," *Financial Times*, October 18, 2004, p. 6.

Fund-of-Hedge-Funds	AUM ($ dollars)	Parent Company
UBS Global Asset Management	26.6	UBS
GAM Multi-Manager	23.3	UBS
Union Bancaire Privee	20.8	UBP
Permal Group	20.4	Legg Mason
HSBC Republic	19.9	HSBC
AMF	18.2	Man Group PLC
Lyxor Asset Management	16.2	Société Générale
Ivy Asset Management	15.3	BNY
Quellos Capital Management	14.9	
Grosvenor Capital Management	14.7	VAM

TABLE 8.4 TOP TEN FUNDS OF HEDGE FUNDS (RANKING AS OF JUNE 2005)

Sources: Hedge Fund Intelligence Ltd., Freeman and Company LLC and *The Deal*, February 6–12, 2006.

pricing differences. This has caused hedge funds to look elsewhere—into the investment arena of private equity funds. In doing so they have begun to make some similar equity investments and thus have become more like private equity funds.

In moving into the private equity fund arena, hedge funds have to approach their business differently. Hedge funds, like mutual funds, seek to report net asset value. However, it is sometimes difficult to put forward accurate monthly values of the equity investments that private equity funds invest in. These values may only be known for certain when the equity is sold. Up to that point their values may be roughly approximated. This is very different from a hedge fund, which purchases securities for which there is an active market and which sells its investments more quickly thereby recording sale values more quickly.

As they have moved into the private equity business, hedge funds have begun to hire managers with private equity experience. Funds such as Cerberus Capital Management and Highfields Capital Management have hired such managers and have made adjustments in their agreements with investors to effectively compete in the private equity business.[30]

Hedge Fund Returns

Depending on the data source that you use, hedge fund returns exceed those of the market. For example, using data from Hennessee, over the period 1987 to 2004, the average annual hedge fund return was 14.04% while the market, as measured by the S&P 500, generated a 12% return and the NASDAQ showed a 10.7% return (see Exhibit 8.7). The Hennessee data also showed the standard deviation of hedge fund returns was lower than that of either of these market measures (9.67 compared to 17.5 and 32.2, respectively). However, we have to consider several factors when evaluating these data.

---

30. Andrew Ross Sorkin, "Why The Buyout Kings Are Running Scared," *New York Times*, August 7, 2005, p. 3.

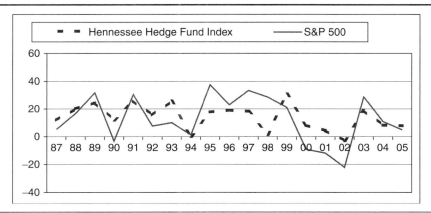

EXHIBIT 8.7 HEDGE FUND RETURNS VERSUS S&P 500
Source: Hennessee Group LLC.

First, hedge fund data are self-reported and companies such as Hennessee are not in a good position, even when they do the best they can to scrupulously investigate and verify the reported rates. Funds that do poorly not report data and might not be included in the hedge fund data set, thus giving the hedge fund data set an upward bias. In addition, we would have to expect higher performance due to the relatively high fees hedge fund managers charge for their management services. Therefore, even if the rate of return were higher, fees such as 1 to 2% plus 20% of profits would also have to be deducted. When this is done, it does not seem that hedge funds have really outperformed the market on a net-of-fees basis.

JUNK BONDS FINANCING OF TAKEOVERS

Junk bonds, also called high-yield bonds, are debt securities that have ratings below investment grade. For rating agencies such as Standard & Poor's, this is a rating of BB or worse. The junk bond market is another financing source that can be used to finance takeovers—especially leveraged takeovers. It played a very important role in the fourth merger wave, but its importance has diminished as we have moved into and out of the fifth merger wave. However, as a result of the development of this market in the 1980s, it remains a very important source of capital for many corporations, although it has reduced importance for takeovers.

History of the Junk Bond Market

Contrary to what some believe, junk bonds are not a recent innovation. They went by the term *low-grade bonds* for decades. In the 1930s and 1940s, they were called "Fallen Angels." In the 1960s, some of the lower-grade debt that was issued to help finance conglomerate acquisitions was referred to as "Chinese Paper." Financier Meshulam Riklis, chief executive officer (CEO) of Rapid American Corporation, states that the term *junk bonds* first originated in a conversation he had with Michael Milken, the former head of Drexel Burnham Lambert's junk bond operation. Riklis claims that when Milken surveyed some of the bonds that Riklis had issued, he exclaimed, "Rik, these are junk!"[31] In the 1920s and 1930s, approximately 17% of all new corporate bond offerings were low-grade/high-yield bonds. A broader range of firms used these securities to finance their growth. The ranks of the high-yield bonds swelled during the 1930s as the Great Depression took its toll on many of America's companies. In 1928, 13% of all outstanding corporate bonds were low-grade bonds; in 1940, this percentage had risen to 42%.[32] Many of the bonds had entered the low-grade class through downgradings from rating agencies. (The rating process is discussed later in this chapter.) As the economy fell deeper and deeper into the depression and firms suffered the impact of declining demand for their goods and services, their ability to service the payments on their outstanding bonds was called into question. This led to a downgrading of the debt. As the overall level of economic demand fell, the revenues of some firms declined so much that they could no longer service the interest and principal payments on the outstanding bonds. As a result, the default rate on these bonds rose to 10%. Investors became disappointed by the rising default rate in a category of securities that they believed was generally low risk. These investors were previously attracted to the bond market by investment characteristics such as dependability of income coupled with low risk of default. As the risk of default rose, low-grade bonds became unpopular.

By the 1940s, the low-grade bond market started to decline as old issues were retired or the issuing corporations entered into some form of bankruptcy. The declining popularity of the low-grade bond market made new issues difficult to market. Between 1944 and 1965, high-yield bonds accounted for only 6.5% of total corporate bond issues. This percentage declined even further as the 1970s began; by the beginning of the decade only 4% of all corporate bonds were low-grade bonds. The low-grade/high-yield bond market's declining popularity preempted access to one form of debt financing to certain groups of borrowers. Many corporations that would have preferred to issue long-term bonds were now forced to borrow from banks in the form of term loans that were generally of shorter maturity than 20- and 30-year corporate bonds. Those that could not borrow from a bank on acceptable terms were forced to forsake expansion or to issue more equity, which had the adverse effect of diluting the shares of ownership for outstanding equity holders. In addition, the rate of return on equity is generally higher than debt. Therefore, equity is a more costly source of capital.

The high-yield/low-grade market began to change in the late 1970s. Lehman Brothers, an investment bank that was itself acquired in the 1980s by Shearson, underwrote a series of new issues of high-yield corporate debt. These bonds were offered by Ling-Temco-Vought (LTV) ($75 million), Zapata Corporation ($75 million), Fuqua Industries ($60 million), and Pan American World Airways ($53 million).[33] This was followed by the entrance of a relatively smaller investment bank, Drexel Burnham Lambert, which started to underwrite issues of low-grade/high-yield debt on a larger scale. The first such

31. Connie Bruck, *The Predators' Ball* (New York: Simon & Schuster, 1988), p. 39.
32. Kevin J. Perry, "The Growing Role of Junk Bonds," *Journal of Applied Corporate Finance,* 1(1), Spring 1988, 37–45.
33. Ibid., p. 44.

issue that Drexel underwrote was a $30 million issue of bonds on Texas International, Inc. in April 1977.[34]

Drexel Burnham Lambert's role in the development was the key to the growth of the low-grade/high-yield bond market. It served as a market maker for junk bonds, as they had begun to be called, which was crucial to the dramatic growth of the market. By 1982, junk bond issuance had grown to $2 billion per year. Just three years later, in 1985, this total had risen to $14.1 billion and then jumped to $31.9 billion in the following year. This was the highest level the market reached in the fourth merger wave. It maintained similar levels until it collapsed in the second half of 1989. After falling to $1.4 billion in 1990, the market rebounded in 1992 and rose to new heights in the first half of the 1990s. Although the market thrived in the 1990s, it took a different form from being a major source of merger and LBO financing source that accounted for its growth in the fourth merger wave.

Why the Junk Bond Market Grew

The junk bond market experienced dramatic and rapid growth in the 1980s, although in the 1990s this growth would seem modest (see Exhibit 8.8). The growth that occurred in the fourth wave was very different from that which occurred later in the 1990s. The fourth wave growth occurred for several reasons. Some of these factors are:

- *Privately placed bonds.* Prior to the late 1970s, high-yield bonds were privately placed with institutional investors. These bonds tended to have unique indenture contracts with varying restrictive covenants that varied based on what different buyers negotiated. This lack of standardized contracts made them difficult to market.

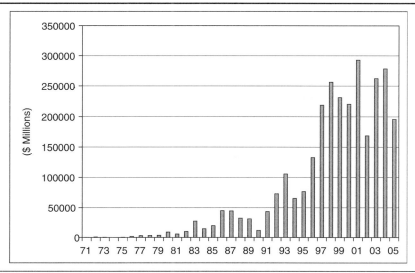

EXHIBIT 8.8   GROWTH OF THE JUNK BOND MARKET, 1980–2005
Source: Thompson Financial Securities Data.

---

34. Harlan D. Platt, *The First Junk Bond* (Armonk, NY: M. E. Sharpe, 1994), p. xiii.

Even more fundamentally, they were not registered with the SEC and could not be publicly traded. This made them somewhat illiquid. Later investment bankers such as Drexel Burnham Lambert would recognize this as an opportunity.

- *Development of market makers.* A major factor leading to the growth of this market was the existence of an active market maker—an entity who serves as an agent of liquidity in facilitating sales between buyers and sellers. Drexel Burnham Lambert became a very active market maker in the junk bond market. Drexel's growth in the 1980s was attributable largely to its involvement in the junk bond market. Therefore, the firm went to great lengths to ensure the growth and vitality of the market.

- *Changing risk perceptions.* Another factor has been the changing risk perceptions of investors toward junk bonds. Investors began to believe that the risks associated with junk bond investments were less than what they once believed. The altered risk perceptions came as a result of active promotion of this financing vehicle by interested parties such as Drexel Burnham Lambert and through academic research. Certain research studies examined the riskiness of junk bonds and reported that the risk of default was far less than was popularly believed. Some of these findings would later be challenged by other studies.

- *Deregulation.* A more relaxed regulatory climate enabled the junk bond market to attract investment capital from traditionally conservative institutional investors such as pension funds and thrift institutions. The 1974 Employee Retirement Income Security Act, and its subsequent interpretations, allowed managers to invest in a broader range of assets, including more risky securities, as long as the portfolio was sufficiently diversified. The Garn–St. Germain Act of 1982 allowed thrift institutions to invest in business loans and corporate bonds. While most thrifts did not invest in corporate bonds, some amassed large portfolios of these securities.

- *Merger demand.* Yet another factor was the expansion of the field of M&As. As the targets of M&As as well as LBOs became increasingly larger, the demand for capital to fund these purchases grew. Investors increasingly relied on the junk bond market to provide a large part of this funding.

Historical Role of Drexel Burnham Lambert

Drexel Burnham Lambert was one of the first investment banks to underwrite new-issue junk bonds and was unique in its efforts to promote the junk bond market as an attractive investment alternative. These efforts were spearheaded by the former manager of Drexel's Beverly Hills office, Michael Milken. Drexel's unique role as a market maker became most apparent in 1986, when bondholders accused Morgan Stanley of failing to make a market for the junk bonds of People Express, which it had previously underwritten. When the price of the bonds fell significantly, Morgan Stanley was reported to have done little to support them.

Morgan Stanley's reported passive stance contrasts strongly with Drexel's aggressive market making in the 1980s. As a result of its involvement in the junk bond market, Drexel progressed from a second-tier investment banking firm to a major first-tier firm. The firm's dominance in the junk bond field during the 1980s made Drexel second only to Salomon Brothers as an underwriting firm.

Drexel made a market for the junk bonds it had underwritten by cultivating a number of buyers who could be depended on to purchase a new offering of junk bonds. The network of buyers for new issues often consisted of previous issuers whose junk bonds were underwritten by Drexel Burnham Lambert. Drexel and Michael Milken used this network to guarantee a demand for new issues of junk bonds. This guarantee often came in the form of a *commitment letter* indicating that the buyer would buy a specific amount of a given issue of junk bonds when they were issued. The commitment fees that the investor might receive were usually less than 1% (i.e., three-quarters of 1%) of the total capital committed. In riskier deals, however, it ranged as high as 2%.

Drexel commanded a dominant 57% of the total market share of new public issues of junk bonds in 1983 and 40 to 50% from 1984 through the beginning of 1987, when its market share began to steadily decline. This was mainly the result of the energetic efforts of other large investment banks, especially Goldman Sachs, Merrill Lynch, First Boston, and Morgan Stanley, to capture part of the lucrative junk bond market. They increased their junk bond resources by expanding their trading, research, and sales staffs. The investment apparently paid off; by the late 1980s each of these banks had captured a significant part of the new public issue junk bond market. Drexel's dominant role in the junk bond market appeared to loosen in 1989 after Milken's indictment. Some firms, hesitant to do business with Drexel, turned to other underwriters. Drexel's end came ingloriously with its Chapter 11 filing in February 1990.

Investment Bankers and Highly Confident Letters

As the size and complexity of the financing packages associated with the deals of the fourth merger wave increased, the need to demonstrate an ability to raise the requisite capital became more important, particularly for bidders who were significantly smaller than their targets. This process was facilitated by the use of a *Highly Confident Letter,* in which the bidder's investment bank states that, based on market conditions and its analysis of the deal, it is highly confident that it can raise the necessary capital to complete the deal. This letter is often attached to tender offer filing documents.

The genesis of the Highly Confident Letter can be traced to Carl Icahn's $4.5 billion bid for Phillips Petroleum in 1985. Icahn's investment banker, Drexel Burnham Lambert, issued a Highly Confident Letter in which it stated, "We are highly confident we can arrange the financing."[35] The letter gave Icahn instant credibility and was a major contributing factor in his success in selling the shares he had acquired back to Phillips without testing the strength of Drexel's letter. Thereafter the Highly Confident Letter became an important part of the takeover business.

Icahn later used the Highly Confident Letter as an essential part of his "takeover tool kit." Armed with the letter and the resulting increased credibility produced by this investment banker's ability to marshal the vast financial resources of the then-strong junk bond market, Icahn had to be taken more seriously. Targets responded to threats from hostile bidders armed with their letters with offers of greenmail.

---

35. Moira Johnson, *Takeover* (New York: Penguin, 1987), p. 147.

Investment Banks and Liquidity of Junk Bond Investments

As noted previously, investment banks, led by the trailblazing role of Drexel Burnham Lambert in the 1980s, served as a market maker for junk bonds. In doing so, they became buyers when holders wanted to sell and sellers when investors wanted to buy. This gave the market liquidity it otherwise would not have had. The enhanced liquidity lowered the risk of these investments and made them more marketable. Another way in which investment banks enhanced the liquidity of these investments was to work with troubled issuers when they appeared to be in danger of defaulting. At one time, Drexel prided itself that issues underwritten by Drexel did not default. Drexel would go to great lengths to ensure that these troubled issuers would not be technically declared in default. Sometimes the default might be prevented by the issuance of a new offering that would be exchanged for the troubled outstanding issue. In cases of more serious liquidity problems, very different types of bonds might be offered in exchange for the bonds that investors were holding. Such bonds might not pay cash interest payments for a period of time while the issuer takes steps to improve its financial condition. One version of such securities is *PIK*, or *payment-in-kind* securities. These bonds do not make cash payments for an initial period, which might range from three to ten years. These bonds came under sharp criticism as the junk bond market began to falter in the late 1980s and investors were being presented with the alternative of exchanging their interest-paying bonds that were about to default for other bonds that would not pay cash interest payments for an extended period of time. Given the poor prospects that security holders with an inferior position in the bankruptcy liquidation hierarchy have, many bondholders reluctantly accepted the exchanges.

Junk Bond Refinancing and Bridge Loans

When companies do a cash acquisition they need the up-front capital to pay the target company shareholders for their shares. They may plan on using high-yield bonds to finance the deal but the seller might not want to exchange its share for the high-yield bonds the buyer would issue. What the buyer then does is to enlist the services of its investment banker, who raises the short-term financing the buyer needs. This financing usually comes in the form of a bridge loan, which can in turn come from various sources. Such was the case when a buyout group led by KKR used a $1.9 billion bridge loan to buy out the Toys-R-Us shareholders. Following completion of the deal, $400 million in high-yield bonds were issued to help pay off the bridge loan. A $1.5 billion loan backed by $1.8 billion in real estate assets was also used to refinance the bridge loan.[36] One trend is that the amount of bridge loans that can be permanently refinanced by high-yield bonds is lower in the 2000s and during the fifth wave than it was at the peak of the fourth merger wave, when buyers would seek to refinance a very substantial part of the bridge loan using junk bonds. The market now wants more security, which is why the bulk of the bridge loan in the Toys-R-Us buyout was secured by real estate assets.

Bridge loans are even more necessary in European buyouts than they are in the United States. European buyers will more likely require up-front cash, whereas in the United

---

36. Vipal Monga, "Turkey Done, Toys Debuts, *The Daily Deal*, November 14, 2005.

States deals can be agreed upon but remain contingent on the necessary financing being secured. This can leave U.S. deals more susceptible to collapse in a market turndown. This happened in 2005, when lenders backed out of underwriting a high-yield bond offering for the $1.8 billion buyout of school materials maker School Specialty, Inc. by private equity firm Bain Capital and Thomas H. Lee Partners LP.[37] Lenders sometimes include a *spread to worst* clause in financing deals if the differential between high-yield bond rates and Treasury Notes goes beyond a given range—say 450 basis points.

Collapse of the Junk Bond Market in the Late 1980s

In spite of its rapid growth in the mid-1980s, the junk bond market collapsed at the end of that decade. Certain major events rocked the junk bond market in the 1980s. They include the bankruptcy of the LTV Corporation and Integrated Resources, and the legal problems of Michael Milken and his investment bank, Drexel Burnham Lambert. These events are discussed in the following sections.

LTV Bankruptcy

The resiliency of the junk bond market was called into question in 1986, when the LTV Corporation defaulted on the high-yield bonds it had issued. The LTV bankruptcy was the largest corporate bankruptcy at that time and represented 56% of the total debt defaulting in 1986.[38] Ma, Rao, and Peterson showed that this event caused a temporary six-month revision in the market's probabilities for default, as reflected by the risk-premium yields on junk bonds. This effect proved transitory, and the market more than fully rebounded afterward. The Ma study indicates that the junk bond market was at that time quite resilient and more than capable of withstanding the shock of a major default.

Financing Failures of 1989

In addition to the bankruptcy of LTV, the junk market was jolted by other critical events. While the LTV bankruptcy was not related to M&As, the failures of other junk bond issuers were directly related to overpriced and overleveraged deals. Large offerings by issuers, such as Campeau Corporation, swelled the market with increased supply. In the first half of 1989, $20 billion worth of junk bonds were offered compared with $9.2 billion for the same period in 1988. Issuers had to offer higher and higher rates to attract investors to buy the risky securities. Campeau Corporation's offering of junk bonds in 1988, led by the investment bank First Boston Corporation, was poorly received even though it provided 16% coupon payments on 12-year bonds and 17.75% coupons on 16-year bonds. In October 1988, First Boston had to withdraw a $1.15 billion junk bond offering as investor demand for the debt-laden concern's securities failed to materialize. The investment bank responded with a $750 million offering that provided higher yields. However, demand was very weak. For example, junk bonds issued by Resorts

37. Bains Out, *The Daily Deal*, October 10, 2005.
38. Christopher K. Ma, Ramesh P. Rao, and Richard L. Peterson, "The Resiliency of the High-Yield Bond Market," *Journal of Finance,* 44(4), September 1989, 1085–1097.

International, Tracor, and Interco declined significantly during this year. The lack of a strong, reliable secondary market made it even more difficult to offer new high-yield bonds. This downturn was a contributing factor in the unraveling of the financing for the buyout of United Airlines in October 1989. Even when reputable issuers, such as Ohio Mattress—maker of Sealy, Stearns, and Foster mattresses—offered 15% interest rates for a proposed $475 million issue in 1989, the market refused to respond. This event become known as the "burning mattress."

Default of Integrated Resources

Integrated Resources, a company built on junk bonds and the most prominent buyer of junk bonds among insurance companies, defaulted in June 1989 and filed for bankruptcy in early 1990. This sent shock waves through the ranks of institutional investors who had helped fuel the growth of the junk bond market.

Bankruptcy of Drexel Burnham Lambert

In its heyday in 1986, Drexel reported pretax annual profits of $1 billion. Only two years later, in late 1988, it pleaded guilty to criminal charges and paid more than $40 million in fines. In 1989, Drexel showed a loss of $40 million.

The immediate cause of Drexel's Chapter 11 bankruptcy filing was a liquidity crisis resulting from the firm's inability to pay short-term loans and commercial paper financing that came due. Securities firms generally rely on short-term capital to finance their securities holdings. Drexel had been the issuer of more than $700 million in commercial paper.[39] When the commercial paper market contracted in 1989, Drexel was forced to pay off more than $575 million, which could not be refinanced through the issues of new commercial paper. Closing the commercial paper market effectively wiped out Drexel's liquidity. With the prior collapse of the junk bond market, Drexel could not seek long-term financing as a substitute. The firm had no recourse but to file for Chapter 11 protection.

Banking Regulation

The savings and loan difficulties of this period led to a regulatory backlash against those institutions that invested heavily in junk bonds. Many of these institutions did so to avoid the disintermediation that came from having to compete for deposits that were leaving savings and loans (S&Ls) in favor of other higher yielding investments. In order to be able to pay higher rates to depositors, S&Ls often invested in high-yield bonds. When the Financial Institutions Reform, Recovery, and Enforcement Act was passed in 1989, banks were forced to mark their junk bond holdings to market values. Many were forced to sell off their junk bond investments into a market in which demand was weak and supply was increasing. This further weakened the junk bond market.

---

39. Affidavit filed by Frederick H. Joseph in Drexel Bankruptcy Filing, printed by the *New York Times,* February 15, 1990, p. D5.

Fate of the Big Junk Bond Issuers

As of the end of the 1990s, we have the opportunity to consider the fate of the major junk bond issuers of the fourth merger wave. According to a study conducted by KDP Investment Advisors, of the 25 largest issuers of junk bond debt between the years 1985 and 1989 and who each had issued a minimum of $1 million in junk bond debt, almost half had defaulted. Sixteen of these 25 companies were acquired. Clearly many of them took on too much debt to withstand the economic downturn that followed at the end of the decade.

Decline in the Use of Junk Bonds as a Source of M&A Financing

The growth of the junk bond market has added a highly combustible fuel to the fires of the fourth merger wave. As described previously, one of the first hostile takeover attempts financed by junk bonds was the attempted bid for Gulf Oil Co. by the celebrated raider T. Boone Pickens. Pickens was president of a relatively small company, Mesa Petroleum. A small oil company by Seven Sisters standards, Mesa was not a serious threat. When Pickens arranged a $2 billion commitment from Drexel Burnham Lambert, as set forth in a Highly Confident Letter, the smaller oil company gained instant credibility. The monies were ultimately to be raised by an offering of junk bonds. The access to such large amounts of financing instantly made Mesa a credible threat. Gulf took the offer seriously and finally agreed to be bought out by a white knight—Chevron. This $13.3 billion deal was the largest U.S. merger at that time and it enabled Chevron/Gulf to become the largest U.S. refiner. In 2001, Chevron would merge with Texaco forming one of the largest oil companies in the world.

Junk bond financing was particularly important for bidders that lacked the internal capital and access to traditional financing sources such as bank loans. The use of junk bond financing to finance acquisitions grew dramatically in 1988, and dramatically collapsed in the years that followed (see Exhibit 8.9). Although the junk bond market recovered in the 1990s, the use of junk bonds to finance larger megadeals did not.

Role of Junk Bond Research in the Growth of the Market in the Fourth Wave

Various studies on junk bonds have been performed that seem to indicate that these securities are not as risky as some investors perceive and may provide returns in excess

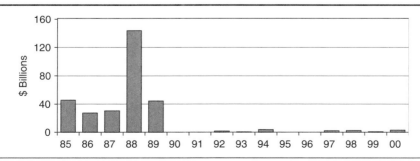

EXHIBIT 8.9   JUNK BONDS USED FOR MERGER AND ACQUISITION FINANCING: 1985–2000
Source: Thomson Financial Securities Data.

of the risk they have. One such study was done by W. Braddock Hickman's National Bureau of Economic Research, which was published in 1958.[40] One of Hickman's main conclusions was that noninvestment-grade bonds showed higher returns than investment-grade bonds, even after taking into account default losses. The time period of his study was from 1900 to 1943. These results were challenged by Fraine, who pointed out that factors such as interest rate fluctuations may have biased Hickman's results.[41] Although Hickman's pro–junk bond results have been widely cited by the securities industry, the contradictory findings of Fraine failed to receive similar attention. Indeed, Michael Milken used Hickman's findings to market high-yield bonds to conservative institutional investors.

The existence of the Hickman research notwithstanding, high-yield bonds remained a difficult sale until the late 1970s. Institutional investors were reluctant to add to their portfolio securities that they considered unduly risky. This attitude started to change with the publication of another major research study that seemed to lend support to the Hickman findings. A study by Altman and Namacher seemed to provide evidence that the default rates of low-rated firms were much lower than was believed.[42] The Altman and Namacher study showed that the average default rate for junk bonds was 2.1%, which was not significantly higher than the default rate on investment-grade securities, which was almost 0%. The Altman and Namacher study revealed that as the time of default approaches, the rating declines. They observed that 13 of 130 (10%) were rated as investment-grade one year before default, whereas only 4 out of 130 (3%) received such a rating six months before default.[43] This implies that the bond rating can be used as a reliable indicator of the likelihood of default.

The Altman and Namacher study had been one of the dominant pieces of research on the default risk of junk bonds. Their results and those of other studies imply that the marketplace is inefficient and pays a return in excess of the risk on these securities.[44] However, the results are affected by the fact that Altman's default measure, the dollar value of bonds in default divided by the total dollar value of high-yield bonds in the market, was very much affected by the rapid growth of this market in the mid-1980s, which to some extent masked the default rate. Bonds that may be risky may not manifest this risk until they have "aged" for a period of time. The Altman and Namacher study did not follow the bonds over their life to see how their risk profile changed as the bonds aged.

A study by Asquith, Mullins, and Wolff (hereafter referred to as Asquith) (Table 8.5)[45] considered the aging effect of junk bonds. He and his co-researchers followed the junk

---

40. W. B. Hickman, *Corporate Bond Quality and Investor Experience* (Princeton, NJ: Princeton University Press), p. 195.

41. Harold G. Fraine and Robert H. Mills, "The Effects of Defaults and Credit Deterioration on Yields of Corporate Bonds," *Journal of Finance,* September 1961, 423–434.

42. Edward I. Altman and Scott A. Namacher, *The Default Rate Experience on High Yield Corporate Debt* (New York: Morgan Stanley & Co., 1985).

43. Ibid.

44. Mark I. Weinstein, "A Curmudgeon View of Junk Bonds," *Journal of Portfolio Management,* Spring 1987, 76–80.

45. Paul Asquith, David Mullins, and Eric Wolff, "Original Issue High Yield Bonds: Aging Analysis of Defaults, Exchanges and Calls," *Journal of Finance,* 44(4), September 1989, 923–952. Also in Patrick A. Gaughan, ed., *Readings in Mergers and Acquisitions* (Cambridge: Basil Blackwell, 1994), pp. 114–144; *Financial Analysts Journal,* September/October 1995, 49–56.

Issue Year	Number Issued	Amount Issued ($ Millions)	Average Issue Amount ($ Millions)	N%	Average Coupon	N%	Average YTM	N%
1977	26	908	34.08	26	10.466	26	10.714	17
1978	51	1,442	28.28	51	11.416	51	11.631	34
1979	41	1,263	30.81	41	12.284	41	12.633	32
1980	37	1,223	33.05	37	13.596	36	14.709	28
1981	24	1,240	51.67	24	14.793	21	17.395	18
1982	41	2,490	60.73	41	13.772	40	16.832	29
1983	74	6,003	81.12	74	12.049	72	13.928	35
1984	104	11,552	113.26	102	14.349	74	15.577	61
1985	145	14,463	99.75	145	13.773	127	14.290	110
1986	200	30,949	154.75	200	12.471	188	12.636	73

TABLE 8.5   FREQUENCY AND MAGNITUDE OF JUNK BOND EXCHANGES

High-yield bonds rated below investment grade at issue date by Moody's and Standard & Poor's. Par value is the customary method used to state the size of the high-yield market.

bonds that were issued in 1977 and 1978 until 1986. In doing so, they offset the impact of the rapidly growing junk bond market that affected the Altman and Namacher results. Their study also commented on the role that exchanges played in understating the true junk bond default rate. When junk bond issuers were in danger of defaulting, investment banks such as Drexel Burnham Lambert sometimes would offer bondholders an exchange of new bonds that might not pay interest right away but that might offer higher interest in the future. Other exchanges involved non-dividend-paying (at least not paying dividends at that time) stock. Bondholders often reluctantly accepted such exchanges as the alternative, default, was less attractive.

The Asquith study also considered the adverse impact that the call-in of bonds had. Many firms that issued junk bonds with relatively higher interest rates took advantage of the decline in interest rates after they were issued. Many junk bonds have call protection for a limited period of time; during that period the bonds may not be called in. At the end of that period the bonds may be called in, as a result of which the bondholders may be deprived of a rate of return superior to other rates available in the market. Asquith and his co-workers reported that 23 to 43% of the bonds issued from 1977 to 1982 were called by November 1, 1988. These calls were a result of the decline in interest rates that started in 1982.

The Asquith study defined defaults to be either a declaration of default by the bond trustee, a bankruptcy filing by the issuer, or the assignment of a D rating by Standard & Poor's. If the bonds were exchanged for other securities that eventually defaulted, this was also considered a default of the original issue. This study showed that, as expected, default rates were higher for "older" issues. For example, bonds issued in 1977 had a cumulative default rate of 33.92%, whereas bonds issued in 1978 had a cumulative default rate equal to 34.26% (Table 8.7).

Issue Year	Number of Issues Exchanged	Amount of Issues Exchanged ($ Millions)	% of Total Issues Exchanged		% of Total Issues Exchanged with No Subsequent Default	
			Number	Amount	Number	Amount
1977	6	281	23.08	30.95	11.54	15.75
1978	10	290	19.61	20.11	7.84	9.02
1979	4	56	9.76	4.43	2.44	1.11
1980	7	212	18.92	17.33	8.11	6.13
1981	6	365	25.00	29.44	20.83	24.19
1982	4	180	9.76	7.23	4.88	0.80
1983	8	820	10.81	13.66	5.41	7.58
1984	7	555	6.86	4.80	6.86	4.80
1985	7	470	4.83	3.25	4.83	3.25
1986	3	480	1.50	1.55	1.00	3.48
Total	62	3,709	8.37	5.19	5.13	3.48

TABLE 8.6   JUNK BOND DEFAULTS

Sources: Paul Asquith, David Mullins and Eric Wolff, "Original Issue High Yield Bonds: Aging Analysis of Defaults, Exchanges and Calls," *Journal of Finance* 44, no. 4 (September 1989), pp. 923–952.

Junk Bond Defaults and Aging

The Asquith study also measured the relationship between defaults and aging. As noted, it showed that default rates were low in the early years after the issuance of a junk bond. They found, for example, that for seven of the ten issue years covered by their study, there were no defaults in the first year. Seven years after issue, however, defaults rose to between 17% and 26%. By years 11 and 12, the default rates increased to greater than one-third for the two relevant issue years, 1977 and 1978 Altman, however, disputes the relationship between aging and defaults and fails to find a discernible pattern that would support this relationship.[46]

Issue Year	Total Issued		Total Defaulted		Cumulative % of Total Default	
	Number	Amount ($ Millions)	Number	Amount ($ Millions)	Number	Amount ($ Millions)
1977	26	908	6	308	23.08	33.92
1978	51	1,442	17	494	33.33	34.26
1979	41	1,263	12	312	29.27	24.70

TABLE 8.7   CUMULATIVE JUNK BOND DEFAULT RATE IN ASQUITH STUDY

---

46. Edward Altman, "Setting the Record Straight on Junk Bonds: A Review of the Research on Default Rates and Returns," *Journal of Applied Corporate Finance*, 3(21), Summer 1990, 82–95. Also in Patrick A. Gaughan, ed., *Readings in Mergers and Acquisitions* (Cambridge: Basil Blackwell, 1994), pp. 185–200.

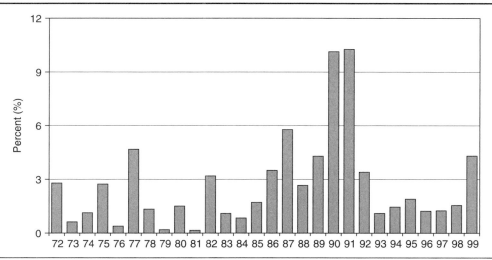

EXHIBIT 8.10   HIGH-YIELD BOND DEFAULT RATES, 1972–1999.
Sources: (1) E. Altman and V. Kishore, "Defaults and Returns on High Yield Bonds: Analysis through 1997," Working Paper Series, Salomon Center for the Study of Financial Institutions, New York University; (2) E. Altman, N. Hukkawala, and V. Kishore, "Defaults and Returns on High Yield Bonds: Lessons from 1999 and Outlook for 2000–2002," *Business Economics,* April 2000.

The Asquith study raises serious questions regarding the riskiness of junk bonds. It contradicts the Altman and Namacher findings, which downplay the riskiness of junk bonds. However, later research by Altman supports the aging factor. For example, Altman and Kishore show that low-rated bonds are less likely to default in the first year of their life but that this probability rises significantly by the third year (see Exhibit 8.10).[47]

Other Junk Bond Research

Wigmore exposed further problems in the junk bond market of the 1980s that went beyond those identified by Asquith.[48] Although the Asquith study pointed out the risk effects of junk bond aging, calls, and exchanges, it did not consider changes in the quality of bonds that were being issued as the junk bond market grew. Asquith focused on bonds that were originally issued in 1977 and 1978. Nonetheless, the consideration of these factors resulted in a high default rate of 34%. Many junk bond critics maintain that as the number of deals financed by junk bonds grew, the quality of junk bonds being issued deteriorated. This criticism was supported by Wigmore.

Wigmore examined a database of 694 publicly underwritten junk bonds issued between 1980 and 1988 (excluding financial institution issues). He measured the quality of the issues by considering ratios such as interest coverage, debt/net tangible assets, and cash flow as a percentage of debt. He found that earnings before interest and taxes (EBIT)

47. Edward Altman and Vellore Kishore, "Report on Defaults and Returns on High Yield Bonds: Analysis through 1997," December 1997. Working Paper, New York University Salomon Center.
48. Barrie Wigmore, "The Decline in Credit Quality of Junk Bond Issues: 1980–1988," in Patrick A. Gaughan, ed., *Readings in Mergers and Acquisitions* (Cambridge: Basil Blackwell, 1994), pp. 171–184.

coverage of interest charges fell from 1.99 in 1980 to 0.71 in 1988. Debt as a percentage of net tangible assets presented a similar picture of deterioration. This ratio rose from 60% in 1980 to 202% in 1988. Cash flow as a percentage of debt fell from 17% in 1980 to 3% in 1988. Wigmore's financial ratios show that the quality of junk bonds issued during the 1980s deteriorated steadily. It is not surprising, therefore, that the junk bond market fell as we approached the late 1980s. The decline of the junk bond market (which is discussed later in this chapter) would be expected as the market rationally responded to a steadily lower quality of issues being offered.

Junk Bond Recovery Rates

It is important to remember that default does not mean a total loss of the investment. Defaulting issuers may renegotiate their obligations, allowing security holders to receive a new payment stream in lieu of the payment they originally agreed to when they bought the bonds.

Researchers define recovery as the price of the bond relative to its issue value either at the time of default or at the end of the reorganization period. Altman and Namacher found an average recovery rate of $41.70 per $100 face value on 700 defaulting bonds from 1978 to 1995.[49] Altman and Kishore, in measuring the recovery rate on 696 defaulted bonds from 1971 to 1995, showed that this recovery rate varied by seniority with senior secured debt averaging 58% of face value, whereas less senior securities averaged lower values.[50] The lowest seniority category they considered, junior subordinated debt, averaged 31% of face value. They also showed significant variation across industry categories. The highest recovery occurred in the public utility sector (70%), whereas other sectors were considerably below that rate. For example, savings institutions showed an average recovery rate of only $9.25.

Conclusion of the Junk Bond Default Research

Even though the Altman research was the target of repeated criticism and opposing studies conducted by well-regarded researchers, the methodology and general conclusions have held up well. Altman openly concedes that in periods when there is a large issuance of junk bonds, the aging effect will tend to suppress the default rate. During the late 1980s and early 1990s, the junk bond market suffered at the same time the criticizing studies were being released. Some people worried that the declining economy and collapsing market marked just the beginning of a trend toward rising default rates. As Exhibit 8.6 shows, however, the resiliency of the junk bond market manifested itself in the years 1992 and thereafter. From 1993 through 1997, the average junk bond default rate equaled 1.39%. The conclusion is that junk bond default rates clearly may be adversely affected by poor economic conditions and declines in this market, but over longer periods the default rates are generally low.

---

49. Edward Altman and Scott Namacher, *Investing in Junk Bonds* (New York: John Wiley & Sons, 1987).
50. Edward Altman and Vellore M. Kishore, "Almost Everything You Wanted to Know about Recoveries on Defaulted Bonds," *Financial Analysts Journal,* November/December 1996, 57–64.

Changing Role of Junk Bond Financing in Takeovers and Corporate Finance

The collapse of the junk bond market in the late 1980s contributed to the end of the fourth merger wave. There were other major factors, such as the slowdown of the economy along with the overall decline of the stock market. Many of the companies that utilized high-yield bonds to finance highly leveraged takeovers ended up defaulting in the 1990s. When the economy began to recover in the early 1990s and companies began to again consider the benefits of rapid growth that M&As provide, many vowed they would never overleverage themselves. Companies insisted that deals have a sound financial structure with more equity and less reliance on debt. Therefore, when the fifth merger wave ensued, high-yield bonds played a much less significant role.

It is also difficult to truly see the ultimate role of junk bonds in M&As as they are used in the refinancing of deals. For example, as we have already noted, a buyer may use a bridge loan to come up with the immediate financing for a deal, while later refinancing the deal in a number of ways including issuing new junk bonds. This was the case in 2005, when a buyout group led by KKR was reported to issue $400 million in high-yield bonds to refinance a bridge loan that it used to take Toys-R-Us private in a $6.6 billion deal.[51] The buying group had taken out a $1.9 billion deal to raise some of the initial capital to complete the transaction. The $400 million in junk bonds is not part of the initial purchase package but is really part of the long-term financing of the deal.

The high-yield bond market grew both in the United States and abroad. New-issue high-yield bonds have become a permanent part of the world of corporate finance, but comparatively less important to M&As than was the case in the 1980s. We still see takeovers that utilize high-yield bond financing but to a much less important degree. However, due to the development of this market, many more corporations can gain access to the comparatively larger financing available from the bond market. This access to greater capital has led to the growth of many medium-sized companies. While M&A played a major role in the development of this market, it has grown on its own without such a heavy reliance on demand from M&As. Its growth has, to a certain extent, been a positive byproduct of the fourth merger wave and that period's use of this source of financing to fuel deals—especially hostile deals.

Leveraged Loan Market as an Alternative to Junk Bond Deal Financing

One of the reasons why the original issue junk bond market grew was that there was a demand for an alternative to bank loans. It is ironic, therefore, that in the 2000s leveraged loans have often replaced junk bond financing as the preferred debt financing source used to complete deals. Exhibit 8.11 shows the decline in high-yield bond issuance over the period 2000–2005 both in the United States and globally. This declining trend is opposite the upward trend in global and U.S. leveraged loans over the same time period. Loans were an important source of financing in the fifth merger wave but declined dramatically when that merger period ended. Since then, though, they have rebounded.

---

51. Vipal Monga, "Turkey Done, Toys Debuts," *The Daily Deal*, November 14, 2005.

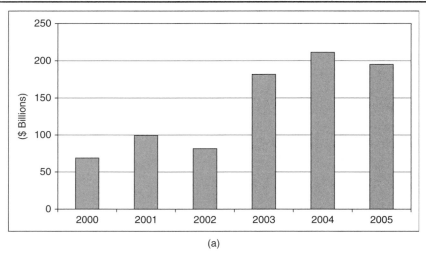

(a)

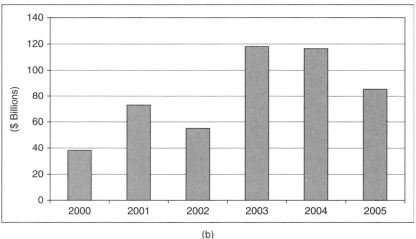

(b)

EXHIBIT 8.11   HIGH-YIELD OFFERINGS: (a) GLOBAL; (b) UNITED STATES.
Sources: The Deal, May 1–7, 2006, p. 32, and Dealogic.

One major difference between the leveraged loan market that now exists compared with the past is that there are now more sources of lending such as hedge funds. These funds provide financing for loans such as second lien debt. This debt is senior debt that has a secondary claim on assets after debt that is held by banks.

Commercial banks may assume loans with the knowledge that they can syndicate the debt to hedge funds. These loans may have a higher claim on the assets of the ultimate borrower and thus offer a lower rate relative to junk bonds, which is attractive to borrowers. Because this market has grown significantly in the mid-2000s, there is an abundant supply of capital that commercial banks know they can tap into to offload the risks of these loans. The availability of this capital makes the loans relatively liquid, which encourages banks to lend. In turn this has caused this supply of debt financing to grow—and often surpass junk bonds as the preferred debt financing source.

Impact of Leveraged Loans on Junk Bond Indenture Contracts

Leveraged loans have moved into competition against junk bonds. In an effort to make junk bonds more competitive, financing providers have tried to adapt the indenture contracts of junk bonds to make them more appealing to bond buyers. Junk bonds may have call options that allow the issuer to call in the bonds when they want to retire the debt or to refinance at more attractive rates. For bonds that have less than 10 years' life to maturity, the call features tend to be approximately halfway through the life of the bond. In response to the competitive pressure from the leveraged loan market, new junk bonds have been offering call provisions as early as one year in the life of the bond.

The indenture covenants of junk bonds may also contain other restrictions that leveraged loans may not have or that may be less restrictive in loans. Junk bond covenants may stipulate certain debt–cash flow levels, whereas leveraged loans may not have such covenants or they may allow for greater ratios of debt to cash flow.

Impact of Sarbanes-Oxley on the Competitiveness of Junk Bond Financing

Junk bonds are publicly issued securities. This means that issuers are then bound by the provisions of the Sarbanes-Oxley Act (this act is discussed in Chapter 12). This adds a layer of reporting and accounting requirements that are not normally present with leveraged loans. Therefore, this law has given leveraged loans another advantage over junk bonds.

Default, Recovery, and Loss Rates: Leveraged Loans versus Junk Bonds

Both junk bonds and leveraged loans have comparable default rates. However, as shown in Table 8.8, the recovery rate is much greater for leveraged loans. As expected, the loss rate for leveraged loans is then much lower. This lower risk profile makes it easier for borrowers to raise debt capital through leveraged loans. It also enables them to get lower rates than what they would with junk bonds.

Expansion of Banks Originating Leveraged Loans

Commercial banks have discovered that by syndicating leveraged loans to buyers of debt, such as hedge funds, they can quickly take the debt off their balance sheet while

| | Three-Year Cumulative Rates | | | | | |
| | Bonds | | | Loans | | |
	Default Rate	Recovery Rate	Loss Rate	Default Rate	Recovery Rate	Loss Rate
Baa	1.6%	37.4	1.0%	1.6%	49.7	0.8%
Ba	5.3%	15.4	4.5%	10.0%	69.6	3.1%
B	21.1%	23.3	16.2%	24.3%	70.3	7.2%
Caa-C	51.7%	22.3	40.1%	59.3%	66.0	20.2%

TABLE 8.8 DEFAULT, RECOVERY, AND LOSS RATES BONDS AND LOANS

Source: "Credit Loss Rates on Similarly Rated Loans and Bonds," Kenneth Emery, Moody's Investor Service Available online: http://www.lsta.org/assets/files/Research_Data.

originating the loans and generating good income from this service. In the early 2000s, in the United States only a few large commercial banks accounted for the bulk of the leveraged loan business. These included banks such as Bank of America and Wells Fargo. However, the rest of the banking industry has responded to the profits with measured risk that are available in this business. This came at a time when hedge funds were eager to participate in this lending. As a result, the number of large commercial bank lenders in this area of finance has significantly increased.

Dealmakers in the mid-2000s noticed that they could not always count on a positive reception from the high-yield bond market, whereas the response was often more favorable in the leveraged loan market. In addition, in the mid-2000s, the junk bond market might ask rates in the 12 to 14% range while the leveraged loan market might quote a rate that is in the range of 200–300 basis points above LIBOR.

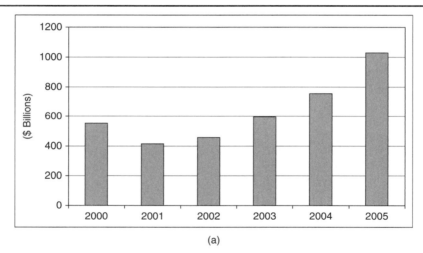

(a)

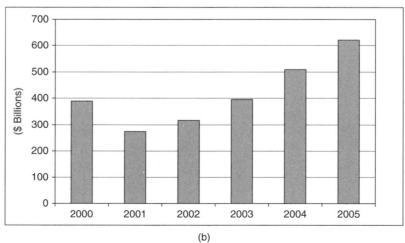

(b)

EXHIBIT 8.12   LEVERAGED LOAN AND BOND ISSUANCE: (a) GLOBAL; (b) UNITED STATES.
Source: The Deal, May 1–7, 2006, p. 32, and Dealogic.

In 1999, regulations that previously limited the ability of banks to underwrite securities were relaxed. This allowed commercial banks to enter underwriting markets such as the junk bond business. Once given the opportunity to enter this arena, commercial banks moved in aggressively and grabbed market share. As of 2005, the leader in this business was the securities units of Bank of America with approximately 12% of the total market.[52] They were followed by J. P. Morgan Chase and Citigroup, Inc. These banks are also leaders in the leveraged loan market; these are loans made to noninvestment-grade borrowers. These loans play an important role in the LBO business as borrowers may look to both sources of debt to complete leveraged takeovers.

STAPLED FINANCING

Another more recent trend in the M&A market is the use by buyers of stapled financing. When a buyer is considering a purchase of a target, one element of uncertainty is the financing that will be needed to complete the deal. Such uncertainty could cause a buyer to pass on a given transaction. In order to maximize the chances of a favorable bid, the investment banks of some targets sometimes offer prearranged financing with specific agreed-on terms. One example was the 2005 auction of Texas Instruments, which was managed by Morgan Stanley. Because it was very familiar with the value of Texas Instruments, Morgan Stanley knew what debt that entity would be able to handle.

Stapled financing became popular during and right after the 2001 recession that followed the downturn in securities markets. The economic contraction made access to capital markets more problematic and helped cool off deal volume. Investment banks, seeking to made deals easier for sellers and buyers, began to prearrange the financing that would be necessary to purchase the target. This became an additional service that they offered that enhanced the total fees they realized from deals. While stapled financing was an innovation brought about to deal with weakness in capital markets, it has grown significantly as the markets improved in the 2000s.

Morgan Stanley claims that it is the first investment bank to provide such a complete package. One of the first deals in which Morgan Stanley used these financing packages involved the auction of Dresser Industries, which was a unit of Halliburton Co. Dresser makes engineering equipment used in the petroleum industry. Morgan Stanley got together with CSFB and was able to arrange the sale of the unit to two private equity buyers, First Reserve Corp. and Odyssey Investment Partners LLC for $1.3 billion.[53] Of this total, $820 million came from a loan package that the two investment banks arranged in advance.

Stapled financing can help facilitate an auction, which tends to result in greater sale prices. By making the financing easier, a potentially greater number of buyers may pursue a given deal. For this reason it may be advantageous for sellers to utilize the services of investment bankers and advisors that also have a strong financing capability.

---

52. Tom Sullivan, "Big Commercial Banks Are Junk Bond Giants: Units of Bank of America, J. P. Morgan Rise to the Top of the Underwriting Ranks," *Wall Street Journal*, July 14, 2005, C4.
53. Vyvyan Tenorio, "A Permanent Staple? Stapled Financing," *The Deal*, May 1–7, 2006, p. 36.

The terms of the stapled financing package may not always be the best for the buyer. The investment banks offering the stapled financing are making the deal easier to finance and seek a fee for this service. However, shrewd buyers, such as private equity firms, who normally have good access to other financing providers, can "shop the loan" to other banks so that they assure themselves they are getting the best terms.

As with other areas of M&A, stapled financing is not without its potential conflicts. Seeking the returns from financing, investment banks may have an incentive to push deals through that may not be in the seller's interests. Sellers need to be aware of their own value so that they do the deal that is in the best interests of their shareholders. Admittedly, they utilize the services of an investment advisor to help them with this process. However, when that advisor is also the stapled financing provider, the seller has to be mindful of the advisor's other interests.

SECURITIZATION AND M&A FINANCING

Securitization has long been used by corporations and financial institutions to enhance the financing needs of companies. For example, a corporation may sell its accounts receivable as well as other receivables to a financial institution that pools these receivables and then issues securities with claims against the contents of the pool. The corporation is then able to quickly liquidate an otherwise less liquid asset.

Private equity firms have developed operating company securitizations as an important financing source for deals. They take specific assets and income streams associated with those assets and direct the income to a financial vehicle that they create. This vehicle then issues securities, asset-backed securities (ABSs), collateralized by this anticipated income. The securitization could be for a collection of assets of a firm or it could be for a whole company (called whole company securitization). The securitization can be used for M&A financing as well as for recapitalization. This recapitalization can be used by a company as an alternative to a sale of the business. It can also be used by a buyer after the acquisition has been completed. This allows the buyer to cash out part or conceivably even all of its investment after the buyout.

The securitization vehicles are typically structured so that the vehicle is separate from the parent company. This lowers the risk of the securities that are issued as they could theoretically be valuable and of high quality even when the issuer is in default. The structure of the deal must be such that the issuer cannot tap into the revenue stream from the dedicated assets as it desires.

Securitizations for deals are easier to do when there is a defined income stream that is readily separable from the overall business of the company. Fashion companies that earn licensing income are an example. Aircraft financing companies that earn lease income are another. Companies that are otherwise risky, and that would have difficulty raising deal financing, can sometimes raise the necessary funds by pursuing securitization financing. This allows the company to isolate a reliable revenue stream and dedicate it to the securitization financing vehicle. In doing so the other risky elements of the business are separated from the revenue stream. When they are added together within the company the combination may be risky and thus raise the rates that the company would have to pay. Separated out, however, they may allow the issuer to raise capital at attractive rates such as AA ratings. This may be much higher than what the overall company would be able to do on its own. In order to do this, though, the company must not have prior loan agreements that prohibit such a separation.

When a buyer can acquire a target at more attractive financing rates, the seller may be able to gain from this in the form of a higher acquisition price. This will more likely be the case when the seller works with an advisor that is familiar with the financing opportunities available in the marketplace. It may be facilitated when there is more than one buyer that has access to such securitized financing.

There is a tremendous amount of innovation and creativity in finance. The high earnings of the field has attracted many bright and creative minds that otherwise might have pursued fields such as mathematics or the sciences. They are continually seeking new ways to generate high returns. In the M&A field, they have even begun to securitize future earnings. For example, lumber companies have securitized the future revenues from timber that will not be cut until sometime in the future.[54] Pharmaceutical companies have been able to do the same for drugs that have yet to find their way through the long R&D and FDA approval process.

Origins of ABSs for M&As

While this financing vehicle has become quite popular in the mid-2000s, it can trace its origins back to the end of the fourth merger wave. In 1989, Michael Milken and Drexel Burnham Lambert assisted a buyout fund, Reliance Capital, which had taken the company private in 1984 and then later public in 1988.[55] In 1989, Drexel helped Days Inn raise $167 million in investment-grade debt by using the franchise fees that Days Inn derived from agreements with its different franchisees. These franchise revenues were directed to a special-purpose entity that issued the securities. This early use of these securitizations did not turn out well as the franchise revenues were not clearly separated from the operating company, which later fell into bankruptcy. However, by the 2000s, other users pursued securitization, such as Triac did with the Arby's food chain. The securities offering was backed by the royalties of the thousands of restaurants that used the Arby's name.

SUMMARY

The mix of cash and securities used to pay for takeover targets has varied over time. The variation in this mix is caused by several factors, but prime among them are the cash holdings of acquirers. When companies have greater available cash, such as when the economy is doing well, they are more inclined to offer cash, which in turn is more appealing to target shareholders. In fact, research studies have shown that acquisition premiums are greater in cash offers.

---

54. Lisa Gerwirtz, "Six Pack Abs," *The Deal*, May 1–7, 2006, p. 48.
55. Times change, but many of the players in the business stay the same. In Chapter 10 we have a case study of a restructuring of Cendant. The CEO of Cendant is Henry Silverman. At the time of this deal Silverman was one of the dealmakers for Reliance. He later went on to be one of the founders of the private equity firm Blackstone Group LP.

Shareholder wealth effects vary depending on the type of consideration used as payment in deals. Research has shown that these effects varied depending on whether a short- or long-term perspective is adopted. These effects also were different depending on the percent of total shares outstanding held by management. One of the reasons for this is information asymmetry. Management has better information about the long-term prospects of the bidder than the market. This affects management decision to offer stock or cash in deals. Another factor affecting this decision is the percent of shares held by institutional investors and large blockholders, whose holdings might be diluted by a stock offering.

Private equity firms are very active in the takeover business. This is not a new phenomenon; it has been going on for many years. However, over the past 15 years their role has become even more pronounced than it was in the fourth merger wave. Such firms are acquiring divisions of parent companies as well as whole firms. They raise capital from institutional and private investors to form funds that they use to acquire equity positions in targets. They seek out undervalued businesses and seek to transform them into more valued assets that can be sold at an attractive multiple of their original investment.

A more recent phenomenon is the pronounced role of hedge funds, which are now more active in takeovers. Hedge funds raise pools of capital that they invest in a variety of ways depending on the strategy the funds espouse. However, in the past 10 to 15 years, some hedge funds have expanded their focus and have moved into the takeover arenas and compete with private equity funds. However, there are significant differences between the two types of investment funds. Private equity funds are normally long-term investors, whereas, in the past, hedge funds have sought quick turnaround from their investments.

While many private equity and hedge funds have made aggressive claims about the returns they provide their investors, research statistics fail to support the claims of many of these funds. Indeed, when fees and costs are deducted from the returns, the returns of many such finds are comparable and not greater than that of the market.

Junk bonds were an important source of financing for takeovers in the fourth merger wave, but their importance has declined over time. The junk bond market grew dramatically during the fourth merger wave and fell precipitously by the end of the 1980s. Its growth enabled the fourth wave to be fundamentally different from any of the previous merger periods. Using the junk bond market, relatively smaller firms were able to make hostile bids for far larger companies. Investors came to regard the junk bond debt used to finance these takeovers as a means to enjoy high returns while they diversified their junk bond holdings to try to lower their risk. The high returns provided by these securities made them popular among a variety of investors, including large institutions such as pension funds, insurance companies, and S&Ls.

The market's view of junk bonds turned downward toward the end of the 1980s. Research studies conducted at the end of that decade contradicted the view of earlier studies, which implied that junk bonds were a relatively safe investment vehicle that provided relatively high yields. These later studies showed that high-yield bonds had high default risk and were of questionable quality. The junk bond market was also rocked by several large defaults and the eventual collapse of its leading market maker, Drexel Burnham Lambert. The absence of Drexel's aggressive market making reduced the liquidity of these securities. In addition, regulatory changes forced some institutions to decrease or eliminate their holdings of high-yield bonds. The big buyouts of the 1980s left a large supply of junk bonds in a market that showed falling demand.

The fall of the junk bond market slowed the pace of mergers and LBOs. The deals that occurred in 1990 relied much more on equity and less on debt. The M&A business was increasingly conducted by well-financed bidders and less by junk bond raiders.

One important byproduct of the use of junk bonds to finance many of the mergers of the fourth merger wave was the introduction of original issue junk bonds to the everyday world of corporate finance. Investors grew accustomed to the high returns these securities offered and quickly learned how to lower their default risk through proper diversification. As a result, less creditworthy corporations now have access to a component of the capital markets that did not exist before. The junk bond market of the fifth merger wave remains vibrant and an important part of the world of corporate finance. It is still relevant to the field of M&As but much less important than it was in the 1980s.

Other financing innovations have taken the place of some of the M&A financing that previously went to the junk bond market. One of these is leveraged loans. These are loans that are usually originated by commercial banks that then syndicate them to buyers such as hedge funds. Hedge funds have looked to these debt investments as they seek more opportunities for the large amount of capital that they as a group have been able to raise. Leveraged loans often are able receive lower interest rates than junk bonds, which have other disadvantages such as Sarbanes-Oxley and restrictive covenants limitations.

Another relatively recent financing innovation in the M&A business has been the use of asset-backed securitizations. Here the revenues from specific assets are directed at a financial vehicle that in turn issues securities that also pay rates that are attractive to the issuer.

9

EMPLOYEE STOCK OWNERSHIP PLANS

A large component of the dramatic growth of employee stock ownership plans (ESOPs) that occurred in the United States in the 1980s is attributable to their role in mergers, acquisitions, and leveraged buyouts (LBOs). Employee stock ownership plans are involved in mergers and LBOs in two main ways: as a financing vehicle for the acquisition of companies (called EBOs), including through LBOs, and as an antitakeover defense. Bidders and employees discovered that they could make a bid for a firm through an ESOP and realize significant tax benefits that would help lower the cost of the buyout. For their part, targets learned that ESOPs could provide them with some assistance with their antitakeover efforts.

Employee stock ownership plans are allowable under the Employee Retirement Income Security Act of 1974 (ERISA), a law that governs the administration and structure of corporate pension plans. The ERISA specified how corporations could utilize ESOPs to provide employee benefits. An ESOP provides a vehicle whereby the employer corporation may make tax deductible contributions of cash or stock into a trust. These trust assets are then allocated in some predetermined manner to the employee participants in the trust. The corporation's contributions to the ESOP are tax deductible. Moreover, the employees are not taxed on the contributions they are entitled to receive until they withdraw them from the ESOP. The contributions are made in direct proportion to each plan participant's compensation. The proportion is based on the ratio of the employee's compensation divided by total compensation. Thus, all employees are paid the same percentage but different absolute amounts.

Participants in an ESOP are required to invest in the employer's stock. They may buy stock in subsidiaries of the employer's corporation if the employer corporation owns more than 50% of the subsidiary's stock. Unlike pension plans, ESOPs do not try to lower the risk level of their assets by diversifying. Although pension plans seek to invest in a variety of assets to lower risk, ESOPs are designed to hold only cash, cash equivalents, or the stock of the employer corporation. The risks of having a very large percent of one's retirement wealth invested in one's employer's assets were underscored by the fallout from the Enron debacle.

HISTORICAL GROWTH OF ESOPs

Employee stock ownership plans were very popular in the United States during the 1920s, when the stock market was rising and Americans widely owned stock. The stock market crash of 1929 and the economic downturn that followed caused the stockholdings of employees to decline dramatically. After the decline in the value of the firm's stock, employees were less willing to take shares in the company as compensation, given the added risk that this form of compensation brought.

In 1974 tax laws were enacted that allowed a qualified retirement plan to borrow for the purpose of purchasing stock. This set the stage for the eventual development of the leveraged ESOPs (LESOPs) that would become more common years later. Nonetheless, ESOP activity was not very significant until the 1980s, when the tax benefits and other advantages of ESOPs began to be explored.

The popularity of ESOPs was also particularly high in the 1980s, especially toward the end of the decade. This increased interest in ESOPs was partly due to improved tax incentives that were enacted in the Tax Reform Act of 1984 and the use of ESOPs as an antitakeover defense. These plans became more relevant in antitakeover strategy after the passage of the Delaware antitakeover statute, which, as discussed in Chapter 3, imposed a three-year delay in actions such as asset sales after takeovers unless the bidder acquired 85% of the target shares. The use of ESOPs as an antitakeover defense, particularly as it relates to the Delaware antitakeover statute, is discussed further later in this chapter.

Exhibit 9.1 shows the growth in the number of ESOP plans from 1974 to 2005. It shows that the number of ESOPs rose exponentially during the 1980s and peaked in 2000 and remained relatively high since then. However, the use of ESOPs as a financing vehicle for LBOs has varied. Table 9.1 lists some of the largest ESOPs.

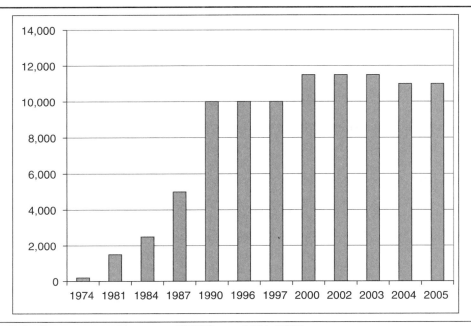

EXHIBIT 9.1 GROWTH IN THE NUMBER OF ESOP PLANS, 1974–2005
Source: ESOP Association.

Company	Location	Number of Participants
Procter and Gamble Co.	Cincinnati, OH	40,000
Lifetouch, Inc	Eden Prairie, MN	26,000
Anheuser-Busch Companies	St. Louis, MO	17,200
Amsted Industries	Chicago, IL	12,500
Parsons Corporation	Pasadena, CA	12,000
Brookshire Brothers	Lufkin, TX	9,000
Ferrell Companies	Liberty, MO	7,400
W.L. Gore Associates	Newark, DE	7,000

TABLE 9.1   REPRESENTATIVE LARGE CORPORATE ESOPs

Note: Based on ESOP Association membership information.
Source: ESOP Association.

TYPES OF PLANS

The two main types of pension plans are defined benefit plans and defined contribution plans.

Defined Benefit Plans

In a defined benefit plan, an employer agrees to pay employees specific benefits upon retirement. These benefits may be defined in terms of a dollar amount per month or a percentage of the previous year's salary, or several years' salary, according to a preset formula. Government workers often have such plans. As employees have begun to live longer while competition forces companies to control costs, many corporations have moved away from defined benefit plans and have switched to defined contribution plans. In 2005 and 2006 defined benefit plans began to draw much public attention as several large corporations froze or ended their costly defined benefit plans.

Defined Contribution Plans

Employers commit to making a substantial and recurring contribution rather than a specific benefit in a defined contribution plan. The employees' benefits depend on the investment performance of the benefit fund. These funds may be managed by a union that oversees the investment of the funds. Defined contribution plans can be riskier for employees, since their benefits will depend on the investment performance of the fund, which is not guaranteed by the employer. Defined contribution plans include Money Purchased Pension Plans, Profit Sharing Plans, 401(k) Plans, and ESOPs. Employee stock ownership plans are a type of defined contribution plan in which the employer contributions are used to invest primarily in employer securities.

CHARACTERISTICS OF ESOPs

In 1986, the General Accounting Office (GAO) conducted a survey of firms that had ESOPs in place. It found that 91% of the respondents indicated that the primary reason for starting an ESOP was to provide benefits to employees; 74% cited tax incentives; and 70% mentioned improved productivity.[1]

Using data derived from the GAO as well as from other sources, however, Corey Rosen found that half the plans were used to buy the company. In approximately one-third of ESOPs, employees owned a majority of the company, and in almost another one-third they owned less than 25% of the firm.[2] Menke & Associates report that approximately 80% of ESOPs own a minority position. Of the 1,500 plans they have installed, the average ESOP ownership was just under 40%. In sum, ESOPs generally own a minority position in the company.

Average Contribution

Employers with ESOPs contribute approximately 8 to 10% of their payroll to the ESOP each year. This is less than the maximum contribution allowable as a tax deduction under the law.[3] For some ESOP firms, such as Menke & Associates, the contributions into ESOPs they form are higher. They report that their average contribution equals 16% of participants' pay, which is significantly higher than the 4 to 5% range for non-ESOP defined contribution plans.

LEVERAGED VERSUS UNLEVERAGED ESOPs

Employee stock ownership plans can be divided into two groups: leveraged and unleveraged. Leveraged ESOPs are those that borrow, whereas unleveraged ESOPs do not borrow. Leveraged ESOPs are of more interest as a vehicle for LBOs.

The size of the contribution that the corporation may make to the ESOP depends on whether it is an LESOP. For ESOPs established after 2001, the contribution limitation for LESOPs is up to 25% of payroll. Unleveraged ESOPs established before this year are limited to a 15% contribution. With LESOPs, the corporation's ESOP borrows to buy the company's stock. The company then makes contributions to the ESOP that are used to pay the principal and interest on the loan. This loan is then amortized and as it is repaid shares are released to employee accounts.

CORPORATE FINANCE USES OF ESOPs

The world of corporate finance has developed several innovative uses for ESOPs. Some of these uses are discussed in the following sections.[4]

Buyouts

Employee stock ownership plans have been widely used as a vehicle to purchase companies. This technique has been used for both private and public firms. Bruner reports that

1. U.S. General Accounting Office, *Employee Stock Ownership Plans: Benefits and Costs of ESOP Tax Incentives for Broadening Stock Ownership* (Washington, D.C.: 1987).
2. Corey Rosen, "The Record of Employee Ownership," *Financial Management,* 19(1), Spring 1990, 39–47.
3. Ibid.
4. The organization of this section partially follows a format presented by Robert F. Bruner, in "Leveraged ESOPs and Corporate Restructuring," *Journal of Applied Corporate Finance,* 1(1), Spring 1988, 54–66.

59% of LESOPs have been used to buy out owners of private companies. Using a LESOP to do a leveraged buyout may place less cash flow pressures on the company compared to a non-ESOP LBO as the company may be able to reduce cash flows by replacing some cash employee compensation payments with stock contributions to the ESOP. There also may be more tax deductions than what would be allowable under a regular LBO. This is due to the fact that both the principal and interest payments are tax deductible. In addition, a LESOP will allow broader employee participation than a management buyout.

Divestitures

Employee stock ownership plans have also been widely used as divestiture and sell-off vehicles. Bruner reports that 37% of the LESOPs have been used as divestiture vehicles. For example, the Hospitals Corporation of America sold off 104 of its 180 hospitals to a new corporation, HealthTrust, which was owned by its employees through an LESOP.[5] As noted earlier, when an LESOP is used to try to finance the acquisition of the divested entity it allows for greater employee participation that what would occur with a management buyout (MBO).

The process of acquiring a divested entity using an ESOP is similar to other ESOP acquisitions. A new company is created, NewCorp, which establishes an ESOP. This ESOP then borrows the funds to purchase NewCorp's shares. These funds are then used to acquire the division whose assets then become part of NewCorp. NewCorp then makes contributions to the ESOP to service the principal and interest payments of the acquisition debt. As with other types of ESOP transactions, both principal and interest payments are tax deductible. When the total amount needed to acquire the divested entity is greater than what is borrowed, then the difference is made up using equity.

Rescue of Failing Companies

The employees of a failing company may use an ESOP as an alternative to bankruptcy. Several examples of this have occurred in the troubled steel industry. The employees of McLouth Steel, for example, exchanged wage concessions for stock in the company in an effort to avoid a second bankruptcy in 1988. However, the company still remained an ill business in a troubled industry and an ESOP could not change these basic facts. Its plants still were outdated and the post-ESOP McLouth did not increase capital expenditures to modernize its facilities. The company went bankrupt in 1995.

Weirton Steel's 1983 rescue is a more favorable example of the ability of an ESOP to rescue a business on the brink of bankruptcy. For a five-year period after the formation of the ESOP the company flourished. The ESOP helped marry management and nonmanagement employees to work together for the betterment of the company. Even in the case of Weirton, however, an ESOP cannot change fundamental problems of an industry. U.S. steel companies have long had difficulty competing with Japanese and other efficient steel producers. Weirton was acquired by Wilber Ross, who combined it with other troubled U.S. steel companies to form ISG. ISG bought most of Weirton's steel operations for

---

5. Ibid.

$253 million in cash while assuming its liabilities and entering into a new agreement with employees. ISG was then sold to Mittal to help form the largest steel company in the world. This company grew even more in 2006 when Mittal merged with Arcelor after a protracted takeover battle.

Raising Capital

An ESOP may also be used to raise new capital for the corporation. The use of an ESOP as an alternative to a public offering of stock is discussed later in this chapter. Bruner reports that 11% of ESOPs have been used for this purpose.

VOTING OF ESOP SHARES

Voting the ESOP shares may be an important issue when the ESOP is used as a tool in mergers and leveraged acquisitions. As noted in Chapter 5, a target corporation may try to use the ESOP as a white squire by placing stock in the plan. It then hopes that the ESOP shares will vote with management on major decisions such as approving mergers and other major transactions. Use of ESOPs as an antitakeover defense is discussed in greater detail later in this chapter. We will see that the voting rights of the shares is an important determinant of the use of the ESOP as an antitakeover defense.

Shares owned by an ESOP are in an Employee Stock Ownership Trust (ESOT) and are not controlled directly by employees compared with shares they might purchase from a broker. The company stock owned by the ESOT is controlled by the board of directors who appoint the ESOP trustees. Thus, the voting power is really with the board of directors, not with the employees. In private companies ESOP shareholders generally have even less voting power. Whether the ESOP employee participants in private corporations retain the right to vote their shares depends on the prevailing state laws, which vary from state to state. Some states provide for limited voting rights, which do not allow full voting privileges for the individual employee shareholders. Employees in private company ESOPs usually do not have the right to vote on major issues, such as elections of the board of directors, unless the owners of the company set up the plan that way.

Approval for the Establishment of an ESOP

Shareholder approval may not always be necessary to establish an ESOP. Companies traded on the New York Stock Exchange, however, are required to receive stockholder approval when an ESOP that will acquire more than 18.5% of the firm's stock is established.

CASH FLOW IMPLICATIONS

As noted previously, cash flows are critically important to the success of an LBO. Employee stock ownership plan contributions positively affect the cash flow of all corporations whether they are involved in an LBO or not.

Let us assume that a corporation makes a $1,000 stock contribution to an ESOP. Because the contribution is in the form of stock, there is no cash outlay. Tax laws allow the corporation a $1,000 tax deduction, which improves the firm's cash flow by the amount of the tax savings. We should not conclude, however, that these cash flow benefits are costless. The benefits may be partially or completely offset by a dilution in the equity holdings of the non-ESOP stockholders. This may be reflected in lower earnings per share.

VALUATION OF STOCK CONTRIBUTED INTO AN ESOP

The cash flow of the corporation may be significantly improved by the tax benefits of the ESOP contribution. In deciding the size of the stock contribution, the company must first determine its value. For public corporations this is clear because there is a readily available market value to use. The problem is less clear for private corporations. It becomes necessary to rely on the various techniques of securities valuation for privately held companies. These methods are discussed in Chapter 14. The services of a business appraiser or an expert in business valuations may be used to determine the securities value. A valuation is particularly important in an LESOP to determine that accurate consideration was paid for the ESOP shares.[6] Stock held in an ESOP must be appraised annually by an independent outside appraiser.

ELIGIBILITY OF ESOPs

The ESOP must fulfill certain requirements to qualify for tax deductibility benefits. It must include all employees 21 years old and over with one year of service during which they have worked 1,000 hours.[7] One exception to this requirement is seasonal industries. The plan should include at least 80% of the eligible employees.

PUT OPTIONS OF ESOPs

Employees may receive a put option to sell their stock back to the employer corporation within 60 days of receiving it. If they do not choose to exercise this option in 60 days, they may receive another 60-day option the following year. Put options may even have a life of up to five years.

The put option is particularly important for departing employees. When employees exercise this option, they almost always ask to be paid in cash as opposed to stock. In S Corporation ESOPs, departing employees may receive only cash and may not receive stock. If a private company with an ESOP decides to go public in the future, the put option may be terminated. This is the case when the ESOP shares are included in the registration statement for going public. The reason for terminating the put option is that it is not necessary given that there is a public market for departing employees to liquidate their holdings.

---

6. Robert Macris, "Leveraged Buyouts: Federal Income Tax Considerations," in Amihud Yikov, ed., *Leveraged Management Buyouts: Causes and Consequences* (Homewood, IL: Dow Jones Irwin, 1989).
7. Robert A. Frisch, *ESOP: The Ultimate Instrument of Succession Panning, 2nd ed.* (Hoboken: NJ: John Wiley & Sons, 2001), p. 55.

DIVIDENDS PAID

Dividends paid by the employer corporation on the ESOP shares are charged against retained earnings. These dividend payments are a tax-deductible expense if they are paid in the following manner:

- Dividends are paid directly to ESOP participants.
- Dividends are paid directly to the ESOP, which distributes them to the ESOP participants within 90 days of the close of the plan year.
- Dividends of the ESOP are used to make payments on an ESOP loan.[8]
- Dividends paid by S Corporation ESOPs are not tax deductible.

ESOPs VERSUS A PUBLIC OFFERING OF STOCK

Let us compare the relative benefit of an ESOP to a public offering of stock. Consider the example of a public offering of stock of $10 million that brings in $10 million, less investment banking fees, legal charges, and other costs associated with the issuance and sale of equity.[9] These costs are often referred to as *floatation costs*. Employee compensation and benefits generally are not affected by such a transaction.

A sale of stock to an ESOP may bring in $10 million without the normal floatation costs of a public offering. However, employee compensation and benefits usually decline because the contributed stock takes the place of some of the compensation and benefits. For example, pension plan contributions could be eliminated. The firm receives a tax deduction on the ESOP contribution, although the pension plan contributions and wages that were paid before the ESOP was established were already tax deductible. If the ESOP incurs interest costs for borrowing the capital needed to purchase the stock, the tax deduction should more than offset the interest payments.

The substitution of an ESOP for parts of the employee benefits package that was in effect before the ESOP was established may present an employee relations problem for the firm. If the pension plan is eliminated, employees may not be eligible to receive the same defined benefits at the time of retirement. With the ESOP, their postretirement income will be a function of the company's financial performance. Employees may not prefer this increase in the uncertainty of their retirement compensation. The employer may have to convince the employees that the company will make substantial contributions to the ESOP. The size of the proposed contributions, plus a favorable track record of financial performance, may persuade employees that they will be better off with the ESOP. Employees may also be favorably impressed by the fact that when stock paid to an ESOP is substituted for wage income, employees enjoy the benefits of a tax shield.

Some privately held companies are reluctant to repurchase the ESOP shares from employee shareholders. Although they have a legal obligation to do so, they may lead

---

8. Myron Scholes and Mark Wolfson, "Employee Stock Ownership Plans and Corporate Restructuring: Myths and Realities," *Financial Management,* 19(1), Spring 1990, 12–28.
9. A $10 million public offering is a relatively small amount and would have, on a percentage basis, relatively high flotation costs compared to larger offerings.

employees to understand that such sales are considered a sign of corporate disloyalty and may reflect badly on the employee who is seeking advancement within the company. This practice reduces the liquidity of part of this employee's compensation. The employee will then have to weigh the increased compensation against this reduced liquidity. In addition to eliminating pension obligations, corporations such as Ralston Purina and Boise Cascade have substituted ESOPs for postretirement health care plans. The corporation will then make contributions of stock into an ESOP. The ESOP in turn will fund the provision of health care benefits to employees. Given the rising cost of health care and the resulting uncertainty vis-à-vis the corporation's future cost structure, firms are eager to find ways to avoid these potential liabilities. Employee stock ownership plans offer them one alternative.

Although this section compares ESOPs with initial public offerings (IPOs), it is important to bear in mind that most ESOPs are private stock transactions in which the owner is seeking personal liquidity and is not intent on accessing capital markets. Many of these companies are not of a sufficiently high profile to be able to go public. The owner uses the ESOP alternative to liquidate part of his holdings in the business while also providing ownership to employees. However, privately held companies that are on the IPO track sometimes use an LESOP as a way to liquidate part of their interest in the business, such as a one-third holding, and then go public at a later date. When the company goes public, some of the proceeds of the public offering may be used to pay off the debt incurred by the LESOP.

CASE STUDY

ESOPs—NO GUARANTEE AGAINST EMPLOYEE UNREST

Part of the theoretical benefits that one tends to assume when contemplating an ESOP is that there will be great increases in worker productivity and a blissful relationship between management and employees. The idea is that after they become "owners," workers will behave differently. The struggles of United Airlines after its employees became partial owners in the company in the 1994 buyout belie this type of thinking.

In 1994, the pilots' and machinists' unions agreed to wage cuts and work rule changes in exchange for a \$4.9 billion loan that was used to buy 55% of the company.[a] These shares would then be distributed to the employees over a seven-year period while the union also received 3 of the 12 seats on the board of directors. Not all unions participated in the buyout. The flight attendants' union, which represented 18,000 employees, the largest employee group, did not think the benefits of ownership were worth the cost.

In 2000, the pilots' union, which owned the largest single percentage of shares in the airline, engaged in a work slowdown that resulted in the cancellation of many flights. Later that year the machinists' union, also major shareholders, followed a similar course of action. Clearly, employee ownership of shares never changed employer–employee relations. Part of the problem was that with the large number of employees, the wages and benefits that workers received far offset the benefits they might have enjoyed from increases in the value of their shares brought about by sacrificing the normal bargaining tools to extract higher wages and benefits from the company. Workers at this highly unionized company could not accept management's plans to have them accept lower

[a]Lawrence Zuckerman, "Divided, an Airline Stumbles," *New York Times,* March 24, 2001, p. C1.

wage growth in exchange for possible increases in the value of equity being held in their retirement accounts. They decided that higher present wages were a greater benefit than potential equity gains they might realize upon retirement.

One of the lessons of this ESOP is that for companies with a large number of employees, especially those with unionized workforces, employee stock ownership may not automatically lead to greater productivity. These gains may be easier to achieve in smaller companies with fewer workers.

While the ESOP buyout of United Airlines did not limit labor troubles, it also did not provide great benefits for employees. United succumbed to the pervasive problems of the airline industry in 2002 and filed for Chapter 11 bankruptcy protection. As is common in many Chapter 11 reorganizations, shareholders, and in this case employee/shareholders, lost the value of their investment in the company. This is ironic as for a while the stock of the company had done well and the employee/shareholders initially benefited following the buyout.

EMPLOYEE RISK AND ESOPs

By accepting part of their compensation in the form of stock in the employer corporation, workers take on an increased risk. They are, in effect, "putting more of their eggs in one basket." If the company fails, employees will lose not only their regular source of income but also perhaps the value of their pension. This occurred in January 1990, when the South Bend Lathe Company was forced to file for bankruptcy under Chapter 7 of the bankruptcy law. Chapter 7 is the part of the law that regulates firms in liquidation. South Bend Lathe, a manufacturing firm established in 1906, was purchased in 1976 by its employees, who owned 100% of the stock. The creditors, who initiated the bankruptcy filing, sought to seize 100% of the firm's stock, which was used as collateral for a loan to one creditor.[10]

Corporations may offset some of this risk by contributing convertible preferred shares instead of shares of common stock. The law requires that the shares be convertible to common stock to be eligible for the plan. Preferred shares have a higher priority than common stock in bankruptcy. If the value of the firm's stock increases, the employees will be able to participate in this growth by converting to shares of common stock. The risk reduction benefits of using preferred stock instead of common stock are limited, given that both preferred stockholders and common stockholders tend to suffer significant losses in bankruptcy proceedings, although preferred stockholders do a little better than common stockholders.

The law does allow employee/shareholders to diversify some of their holdings as they become older. They may diversify from 25 to 100% as they advance in age between the years 55 and 65.[11]

It is important to bear in mind that many successful proponents of ESOPs disagree with this assessment of the risks of ESOPs. For example, Robert Massengill of Menke & Associates indicates that in most of the ESOPs their firm forms, employees do not use any of their own money and do not have their compensation reduced in exchange for the ESOP benefit. When this is combined with the fact that most ESOPs have higher

---

10. Paul Dodson, "Creditors Seek Bankruptcy for S. B. Lathe," *Indiana Tribune*, January 18, 1990, p. 19.
11. Robert A. Frisch, *ESOP: The Ultimate Instrument of Corporate Finance* (Los Angeles: Margate Associates, 1990), pp. 34–35.

contribution rates than other defined contribution plans, employees are ahead of where they would be without the ESOP and have not incurred more risk.

SECURITIES LAWS AND ESOPs

Under federal securities laws, the sale of stock to an ESOP is not considered an issuance of securities to the public. When this stock is issued, it generally comes with a letter stating that it is not subject to a sale to a third party. State corporation laws differ in their treatment of ESOPs. For example, New York laws do not require the registration of the donated securities.

TAX BENEFITS OF LESOPs

One of the more valuable characteristics of LESOPs is their unique tax benefits. These benefits are described in the following sections.

Deductibility of Interest and Principal Payments

If a corporation borrows directly from a bank, only the interest payments are tax deductible. However, if the LESOP borrows from a bank or other lender such as an insurance company, both the interest and the principal payments are tax deductible. This significantly lowers the costs of debt capital.

Other Tax Benefits of ESOPs

Some additional tax benefits of ESOPs are discussed in the following sections.

Employee/Shareholder Benefits

Like other types of pension plans, employee participants in an ESOP are not taxed on the benefits they receive until they actually receive distributions from the ESOP. In a merger or an acquisition, if the target is not a public company, the target shareholders who tender their shares to an acquiring firm's LESOP may elect to defer the gain from the sale of the stock. Target shareholders are eligible for this deferment if certain conditions are met, such as the ESOP holding at least 30% of the value of the outstanding shares after the sale.[12]

Employer Corporation Benefits: Dividend Deduction

In addition to the benefits discussed, an additional tax benefit of ESOPs is that dividends paid to the ESOP generally are tax deductible. This helps avoid the double taxation of corporate income and gives this component of equity some of the same tax benefits that are enjoyed by debt financing. It is even possible to pay no dividends on non-ESOP shares while paying dividends on ESOP stock. This may be done by creating a separate class of stock just for the ESOP that will receive these dividends.

---

12. Coopers & Lybrand, *Business Acquisitions and Leveraged Buyouts* (New York: Coopers & Lybrand, 1989), pp. 181–240.

Ability to Use Loss Carryforwards

The changes in the tax law that took place in 1986 limited the ability of corporations to carry forward losses after control changes. However, this limitation does not apply if an ESOP purchases at least 50% of the equity in the target.

BALANCE SHEET EFFECTS OF ESOPs

The debt that an LESOP incurs must be recorded on the firm's balance sheet. This corresponding reduction in shareholder equity must also be reflected on the firm's financial statements.[13] The shares issued to the ESOP must be counted as outstanding shares for the purpose of computing earnings per share. In doing so, the post-ESOP earnings per share measure captures the equity dilution effects.

DRAWBACKS OF LESOPs

There are certain drawbacks that offset the advantages that have been previously cited. These benefits are discussed in the following sections.

Equity Dilution Effects

The ability of ESOPs to borrow while providing the borrower with attractive tax advantages that lower the ultimate borrowing costs is a clear advantage. However, to compare the after-tax effects of borrowing directly from a bank with those of borrowing through an ESOP would be misleading. When a firm borrows through an ESOP, the employer firm is issuing equity while it is borrowing. From the original stockholders' viewpoint, the result is a dilution of equity. These new equity holders, the firm's employees, will share in any gains that the new debt capital can generate. They will still be expecting to receive returns on their stock even after the loan has been repaid. Therefore, a true analysis of the costs of borrowing through an ESOP is accurate only if the equity dilution effects are considered. This is more difficult to do because the equity dilution costs depend on the firm's future performance, which may be difficult to predict. The true equity dilution effects are based on the productivity of the new "capital," which derives from the ESOP's cost-savings effects.

To reverse the equity dilution effects, the firm must repurchase the newly issued shares at a later date. When it does so, the discounted value of this expenditure may be used to derive a measure of the true costs of borrowing. The ESOP may be structured so that there are smaller equity dilution effects. If the ESOP purchases currently outstanding shares instead of issuing new shares, equity is not diluted.[14]

Distributional Effects of ESOPs

Depending on the price the ESOP pays for the firm's shares, there may be distributional effects associated with the formation of the ESOP. If employees receive shares in the

---

13. Ibid.
14. Joseph Blasi, *Employee Ownership* (Cambridge, MA: Ballinger Publishing, 1988), p. 70.

company at a below-market price, a redistribution of wealth may occur. Employees gain wealth at the expense of nonemployee shareholders. If employees make other sacrifices, such as lower wages or benefits, which offset the gain on the below-market price shares, there may not be any distributional effects.

In a survey of 192 publicly held firms with ESOPs, Chaplinsky and Niehaus found that 48.2% of the firms reported an increase in employee compensation as a result of the ESOP and that 39.3% did not change their compensation. Only 6% reported a decline in employee compensation when the ESOP was adopted.[15]

Because almost half the cases in the Chaplinsky and Niehaus sample reported increases in employee compensation, there may be a redistribution of wealth from nonemployee shareholders to employees. It would be shortsighted, however, to conclude that the total net effect is that nonemployee shareholders lose. Some of the higher employees' compensation may be necessary to offset the increased risk of their total compensation package. In addition, productivity gains may be associated with the fact that employees are now owners of shares in the company.

Loss of Control

Another disadvantage of ESOPs, which is related to the equity dilution effects, is the loss of control by the non-ESOP stockholders. After shares have been issued to the ESOP, the non-ESOP stockholders experience reduced ownership and control of the corporation.

It is more difficult for management to expand its control when an ESOP owns much of the firm's stock. The Tax Reform Act of 1986 contained antidiscrimination provisions requiring that an ESOP's benefits may not be controlled by a small group of managers. This law requires that the percentage of employees who are not highly compensated must comprise at least 70% of the shareholdings controlled by highly compensated employees. Highly compensated employees are defined as those who earn more than $75,000 or those who earn more than $50,000 and who are in the top 20% employee compensation bracket for that company.

Although there may be some loss of control by management, it is important to bear in mind that the shares are held by an ESOP whose trustees hold the voting rights. As noted previously, these trustees are appointed by the board of directors, so the board usually still controls the voting rights. When this is the case, the loss of control may not be very significant.

ESOPs AND CORPORATE PERFORMANCE

Some proponents of ESOPs contend that ESOPs are beneficial for corporations because they help finance capital expenditures and facilitate improvements in labor productivity. Employee stock ownership plans may also enhance worker productivity if the workers view their ownership position as a reason to take a greater interest in their performance. With sufficient financial incentives, workers may be less resistant to productivity-enhancing changes such as mechanization or more efficient work procedures.

---

15. Susan Chaplinsky and Greg Niehaus, "The Role of ESOPs in Takeover Contests," *Journal of Finance*, 49(4), September 1994, 1451–1470.

In a report to the chairman of the U.S. Senate Finance Committee, the GAO found little evidence of such benefits.[16] The study failed to find a perceptible difference in profitability between firms that had ESOPs and those that did not. Apparently, in the first year after adopting an ESOP, firms experienced a temporary increase in profitability; there were no noticeable long-term increases in profitability. The GAO study also compared labor productivity, as measured by the ratio of real value added to real compensation of ESOP firms, with non-ESOP firms. An examination of the productivity trend for ESOP firms appears to show an increase after the adoption of the ESOP. A statistical analysis of this relationship fails to reveal a significant relationship, however.

The GAO findings were contradicted by more recent research. Park and Song examined the long-term performance of firms with ESOPs and found that there was a significant improvement in performance after the adoption of an ESOP.[17] Their analysis of a sample of 232 firms from 1979 to 1989 showed higher market-book ratios and returns on assets. For example, the market-book ratio increased 10.3% in the year the plan was adopted, whereas it increased 24.8% three years after adoption. It is interesting that Park and Song found that the performance improvements were limited to those firms that had large outside blockholders. This is consistent with the thesis that ESOPs have antitakeover attributes that may serve to entrench managers. These researchers theorize that outside blockholders keep management honest, offsetting the management entrenchment effects of ESOPs while allowing the firm to realize the performance-enhancing benefits of the greater employee incentives available with ESOPs.

Blair, Kruse, and Blasi compared the performance of a control group of companies with those that had ESOPs.[18] While their sample was not large, they did find a significant increase in the financial performance, as reflected by stock returns of companies that had ESOPs versus comparable firms that did not. The ESOP group also appeared to be less risky as measured by lower betas. Given their relatively small sample size, one has to be cautious in interpreting the significance of these results but they do provide some support for the assertion that employee ownership may improve financial performance.

Employee Stock Ownership and Corporate Stability

Blair, Kruse, and Blasi studied 27 publicly traded firms that had at least 20% of their stock held by employees in 1983 and compared their performance from that year through 1997 with a control group of 45 firms of similar size and industry classification.[19] They found that the companies with significant employee ownership had more stable management, and were less likely to be acquired, taken private, or fall into bankruptcy. They also failed to find any adverse effects on productivity or firm performance.

---

16. U.S. General Accounting Office, "Employment Stock Ownership Effects: Little Evidence of Effects on Corporate Performance," Report to the Committee on Finance, U.S. Senate, October 1987.
17. Sangsoo Park and Moon H. Song, "Employee Stock Ownership Plans, Firm Performance, and Monitoring by Outside Blockholders," *Financial Management,* 24(4), Winter 1995, 52–65.
18. Margaret M. Blair, Douglas L. Kruse, and Joseph R. Blasi, "Employee Ownership: An Unstable Form or a Stabilizing Force," in Margaret M. Blair and Thomas A. Kochan, eds., *The New Relationship: Human Capital in the American Corporation* (Washington, D.C.: Brookings Institution, 2000).
19. Margaret Blair, Douglas Kruse, and Joseph Blasi, 2000, *op cit.*

Fiduciary Responsibilities and ESOPs

A fiduciary of an ESOP is an individual or other entity that exercises discretionary authority in managing and overseeing the plan. The investment in the employer stock must be "prudent." This is particularly relevant to LBO transactions. The Department of Labor may scrutinize a transaction if a company terminates a pension plan to finance a buyout in which employees receive shares in a now highly leveraged company. It is acceptable that parties other than the employee, such as the employer corporation, receive benefits from formation of the ESOP. If, however, employee welfare is reduced by the transaction in an indisputable manner, the Labor Department may disallow the ESOP.

CASE STUDY

DAN RIVER, INC.—CASE OF A FAILED ESOP[a]

Dan River, Inc., a textile manufacturer in Danville, Virginia, went private in 1983 to prevent being taken over by corporate raider Carl Icahn. As part of the going private transaction, workers agreed to give up their pensions in return for an ESOP. The ESOP gave workers 70% of the stock in the company. The company adopted the ESOP in part to achieve the tax advantages associated with this type of benefit package while avoiding being taken over.

Media reports soon documented workers' disenchantment with their failure to achieve greater voice in the company's affairs even though they were majority owners of the firm. The company did not perform well after the buyout. Table A shows the losses the company had in the three years after the buyout.

Year	Losses
1984	$8.4 million
1985	$32.9 million
1986	$8.1 million

TABLE A   A Dan River Losses

Gains in worker productivity are often cited as one of the potential benefits of ESOPs. Dan River's workers, however, reportedly did not experience any increase in their involvement in determining the company's direction. The public stock offering, for example, did not require the employees' approval even though it would affect their ownership shares. The Dan River case illustrates that employee ownership is not necessarily synonymous with increases in employee morale.

[a]This account is partially based on Dean Foust, "How Dan River Misses the Boat," *Business Week,* October 26, 1987, pp. 34–35.

ESOPs AS AN ANTITAKEOVER DEFENSE

Much of the rising popularity of ESOPs is related to the use of this compensation vehicle as an antitakeover defense rather than because of its tax advantages. Although the antitakeover implications of ESOPs have been discussed in Chapter 5, in the interest of completeness they are reviewed and expanded on here.

A large percentage of U.S. corporations are incorporated in Delaware, where an anti-takeover law became effective December 27, 1987 (see Chapter 3). As noted previously, this law provided that if a bidder purchases more than 15% of a firm's stock, the bidder may not complete the takeover for three years unless:

- The bidder purchases as much as 85% of the target's shares.
- Two-thirds of the shareholders approve the acquisition (excluding the bidder's shares).
- The board of directors and the shareholders decide to exempt themselves from the provisions of the law.

A Delaware corporation can establish an ESOP that may act as its own white squire. The combined holdings of stock in the ESOP plus other "loyal" blocks of stock may prevent a bidder from ever reaching the 85% level necessary to complete the takeover. This defense was used most effectively in the Polaroid–Shamrock Holdings takeover battle in 1988.

In January 1989, the Polaroid court ruling imposed certain qualifications that restrict the indiscriminate use of ESOPs in takeover contests. The court ruled that the ESOP must be planned before the takeover contest. Employee stock ownership plans that are quickly constructed in the midst of a takeover battle, such as in the AT&T–NCR takeover, may be blocked.

Effectiveness of ESOPs as an Antitakeover Defense

Chaplinsky and Niehaus analyzed takeover incidence for targets with and without ESOPs.[20] After controlling for the effects of other relevant factors, such as state takeover laws and other antitakeover defenses, they found that ESOPs significantly reduce the probability of a takeover. Their results show that the defensive attributes of ESOPs compare favorably even with poison pills. However, while poison pills continue to be the most important antitakeover defense in the 2000s, most target companies do not focus much on ESOPs as a source of antitakeover benefits.

Park and Song noticed that the frequency of adoption of antitakeover defenses dropped dramatically after ESOPs were created or expanded.[21] They found that some ESOPs were used as substitutes for other antitakeover defenses such as poison pills.

ESOPs AND SHAREHOLDER WEALTH

Theoretically, ESOPs may have an impact on shareholder wealth in two opposing ways. On the one hand, ESOPs may provide tax benefits to corporations, which can lower their tax liabilities. If tax liabilities are lowered, after-tax profitability is greater and larger

---

20. Susan Chaplinsky and Greg Niehaus, "The Role of ESOPs in Takeover Contests," *Journal of Finance,* 49(4), September 1994, 1451–1470.
21. Sangsoo Park and Moon H. Song, "Employee Stock Ownership Plans, Firm Performance, and Monitoring by Outside Blockholders," *Financial Management,* 24(4), Winter 1995, 52–65.

distributions can be made to shareholders. On the other hand, if the ESOP is used as an antitakeover defense, the probability that shareholders might receive a takeover premium may be reduced because the firm's stock price could decline.

In a study of 165 announcements of the formation of an ESOP, Chang found that 65% of the firms showed positive abnormal returns for a two-day period around the announcement. The average abnormal two-day return was 3.66%.[22] Chang then analyzed the different motives for adopting an ESOP, such as financing an LBO or adopting an antitakeover defense. The impact on shareholder wealth for each of these separate subsamples of ESOP adoptions was considered. For firms that adopted an ESOP to facilitate the financing of an LBO, the average abnormal two-day return was 11.45%. Firms that adopted an ESOP to achieve wage concessions from employees, and thereby improve cash flow, showed an abnormal two-day return of 4.19%. When an ESOP was adopted as an antitakeover defense, a 22.34% average abnormal return was shown.

Chang's results suggest that ESOPs may increase shareholder wealth except when they are used as an antitakeover defense. These results were supported in later research. Dhillon and Ramirez reported that before the Polaroid court ruling, which found that the antitakeover use of ESOPs were legal, ESOPs were associated with positive shareholder wealth effects.[23] After the Polaroid ruling, however, a negative market response was found. The negative effect of the antitakeover defense on shareholder wealth might not be apparent if a longer time period than the two-day window around the announcement were used. If the ESOP results in a better negotiating position for a target, which in turn results in a higher takeover premium, this might not be apparent in the short two-day window. Therefore, although ESOPs that are used as an antitakeover defense may reduce shareholder wealth, further analysis is necessary to prove it.

Not all research studies found statistically significant shareholder wealth effects. Chaplinsky and Niehaus failed to detect a statistically significant stock price reaction to the announcement of the formation of an ESOP.[24] However, they interpret this result, along with their other finding in this study (that ESOPs were an effective defense), as testimony to the beneficial effects of ESOPs because the institution of a potent defense reduces the probability that shareholders will receive a takeover premium. They surmise that this must be offset by higher premiums received by shareholders of companies that have ESOPs and are eventually taken over.

ESOPs AND LBOs

One of the more dynamic ways in which LBOs may be structured involves the innovative use of ESOPs.[25] Louis Kelso of Kelso and Company pioneered the use of this technique to

22. Saeyoung Chang, "Employee Stock Ownership Plans and Shareholder Wealth: An Empirical Investigation," *Financial Management,* 19(1), Spring 1990, 48–58.
23. Upinder S. Dhillon and Gabriel G. Ramirez, "Employee Stock Ownership and Corporate Control: An Empirical Study," *Journal of Banking and Finance,* 18, 1994, 9–26.
24. Susan Chaplinsky and Greg Niehaus, "The Role of ESOPs in Takeover Contests," *Journal of Finance,* 49(4), September 1994, 1451–1470.
25. Robert A. Frisch, *The Magic of ESOPs and LBOs* (New York: Farnsworth Publishing, 1985), p. 12. This book provides a comprehensive treatment of the use of ESOPs to finance LBOs.

purchase firms. (Kelso was also active in convincing legislators, such as Senator Russell Long, former chairman of the Senate Finance Committee, to support provisions of ERISA that would enhance the powers of ESOPs.) Using an ESOP as a corporate finance tool, Kelso helped the employees of a small newspaper chain in Palo Alto, California, Peninsula Newspapers, to buy this business from the retiring owner of the chain.[26] The plan enabled them to buy the company while enjoying significant tax benefits that lowered the cost of the purchase.

In helping to finance an LBO, the ESOP, or more appropriately the LESOP, arranges to borrow funds that will be used to finance the LBO. This may be done through a bank or a group of lenders. The larger the amount of funds required, the more likely the capital will come from a group of lenders. The LESOP borrows a certain amount of money from a bank (or group of lenders). The collateral for this loan will be the stock in the borrowing corporation. The loan may also be guaranteed by the parent corporation in the case of an LBO of a division of a company. The employer corporation makes tax-deductible contributions to the LESOP for the payment of the loan and principal.

Leveraged ESOP-LBO Process

All LBOs are somewhat different but tend to share many common characteristics. For the purposes of exposition, consider the case of a selloff of a division in which the management of the parent company seeks to buy the division through an LBO. The steps by which this transaction could take place, using a LESOP, are:

Step 1. A new company is formed, which will be the division in an independent form.

Step 2. The management of the division, which will constitute the new owners of that part of the parent company, may make an equity investment in the division. Up to this point, the division may be a corporate shell without assets.

Step 3. An ESOP for the new company is established. The ESOP negotiates with a bank or other lenders for a loan.

Step 4. Then the ESOP uses its loan proceeds to purchase newly issued stock of the new company.

Step 5. The new company agrees to make tax-deductible contributions to the ESOP for the repayment of the ESOP's debt. This loan can be guaranteed by the original corporation, if that becomes a condition of the lenders. When the risk level of the new company is perceived to be high, a guarantee is often required.

The deal may also be structured so that the LESOP uses the loan proceeds to purchase stock in the new corporation rather than to purchase assets. Under this scenario, the new corporation uses the proceeds of the sale to buy the assets of the parent corporation.

Employee stock ownership plans may be used to lower the cost of the LBO by taking advantage of the tax deductions allowable under the law. In this way, they are an innovative means of completing an LBO. In a LESOP, the securities that are purchased are placed in a *suspense account*. Shares that are in the suspense account are referred to as

---

26. Joseph S. Schuchert, "The Art of the ESOP Leveraged Buyout," in Stephen C. Diamond, ed., *Leveraged Buyouts* (Homewood, IL: Dow Jones Irwin, 1985), p. 94.

unallocated shares. These securities are allocated to the participants in the ESOP as the loan is repaid. The allocation is based on the compensation relevant to each participating employee

---

CASE STUDY

POLAROID—AN ESOP AS AN ANTITAKEOVER DEFENSE

Polaroid made the first use of an ESOP as an antitakeover defense in response to an unsolicited $40-per-share bid from Shamrock Holdings on July 20, 1988. The ESOP did not provide additional compensation to Polaroid employees. The ESOP was funded through a 5% pay cut and a reduction in certain other employee benefits. The ESOP was structured so that all employees would participate.

> The ESOP borrowed a total of $285 million and received a total of $15 million in cash from Polaroid to purchase 9.7166 million new shares at $30.875 .... The share price to the ESOP was determined more by legal reference than from financial analysis. Legal precedent suggested three possible pricing rules: (i) closing price on the date of the plan approval by the board (July 12); (ii) average between the high and low price on July 12; and (iii) the average share price over a longer time period. Polaroid adopted the lowest price consistent with these rules, rule (ii).[a]

The sale of shares to the ESOP was followed by a share repurchase program that was implemented through a self-tender. A total of 24.5 million shares were repurchased at an average price of $45.918 per share, which resulted in a decline in the number of Polaroid shares outstanding and left the ESOP holding approximately 20% of the firm's stock.[b]

Shamrock Holdings attempted to dismantle the ESOP defense through legal action in the Delaware courts. They took the position that the ESOP was discriminatory in that it was established to prevent Shamrock from purchasing Polaroid. As noted previously, however, the court found that Polaroid's board of directors had considered establishing an ESOP as early as 1985. The court failed to agree with Shamrock's position that the ESOP shares not be considered in computing total shares according to Delaware's antitakeover law. The court thought that because the Polaroid ESOP plan allowed the employees holding shares through the ESOP to vote those shares in the tender offer, these shares should be considered with the other outstanding shares in computing the 85%. Judge Berger stated that the ESOP was "fundamentally fair" and did not advance management's interest over those of the employees.[c] This made it almost impossible for Shamrock to acquire the 85% of total shares necessary to complete the takeover under this law.

Many corporations realized that the cost of establishing a defensive ESOP might be far less than the 14% shareholding that Polaroid used for its ESOP. Many firms already have shares in various pension, savings, and employee benefit plans. These shares may be used as part, if not all, of the necessary 15% to achieve protection under the Delaware law. Chevron, for example, only had to place 5% of its shares in an ESOP because it already had 11% of its stock in company employee benefit plans. Some firms already have 15% of their shares in employee benefit plans, which means that an ESOP may be established without the usual dilution of equity. The firm may be required to alter the voting rights of the shares already in employee benefit plans to allow for the shares to have voting rights if they do not already possess these rights.

[a]Robert F. Bruner and E. Richard Brownlee II, "Leveraged ESOPs, Wealth Transfers and 'Shareholder Neutrality': The Case of Polaroid," *Financial Management,* 19(1), Spring 1990, 63.
[b]Ibid., p. 64.
[c]Keith Hammonds, John Hoerr, and Zachary Schiller, "A New Way to Keep Raiders at Bay," *Business Week,* January 23, 1989, p. 39.

Shamrock Holdings was forced to drop its bid and entered into a ten-year standstill agreement with Polaroid. Shamrock in turn was compensated by Polaroid for some of the expenses it incurred through the bidding process. Polaroid also paid Shamrock Holdings for advertising time on some of the radio stations owned by Shamrock as part of the reimbursement agreement.

Employees played a pivotal role in keeping the company independent. In the years that followed, employees were required to contribute 8% of their pay, whether they wanted to or not, into the company's ESOP. In the years that followed the buyout, the shares of the company rose and fell. As the company's fortunes suffered so did the employee/shareholders' investment. The company fell into bankruptcy, which wiped out the values that had accrued over many years.

Like the United Airlines employee/shareholders, workers assume significant risks when they devote so much of their retirement wealth to the stock of their employer, which also is the provider of their income. The company was sold for $255 million in a bankruptcy restructuring to the venture capital arm of Bank One Corp.

ESOPs versus Management Buyouts

A study by Chaplinsky, Niehaus, and Van de Gucht compared employee buyouts with MBOs.[27] One of their major findings was that employees played a key role in the financing of the acquisition. In addition, they found a number of interesting pre-buyout and post-buyout differences between the two groups:

- Pre-buyout:
  - EBO companies have lower ratio of asset/employees.
  - The stock price performance of EBO was worse than MBOs.
  - EBO companies were more likely to come under takeover pressures.
  - EBO companies were more likely to have overfunded pension plans.
- Post-buyout:
  - EBO companies were more highly leveraged than MBOs (mainly through using bank debt).
  - Reductions in cash compensation occurred in only 2.6% of the MBO cases but existed in 56% of the EBOs.

SUMMARY

Employee stock ownership plans were originally developed to provide benefits to employees. Finance practitioners have discovered, however, that they may also be a highly innovative corporate finance tool. When used as borrowing vehicles by corporations, ESOPs may provide the company with significant cash flow and tax benefits. These cash flow benefits may be enhanced when the company combines the tax benefits with a reduction in outstanding contributions to other benefits programs. Buyers of corporations have realized that this financing tool may give bidders cost advantages in raising the debt capital necessary to finance leveraged acquisitions. Employee stock ownership

---

27. Susan Chaplinsky, Greg Niehaus, and Linda Van de Gucht, "Employee Buyouts: Causes, Structure, and Consequences," *Journal of Financial Economics,* 48(3), June 1998, 283–332.

plans, therefore, may be used by hostile bidders as well as by employee groups interested in acquiring their company.

Although ESOPs may be of great financing benefit to buyers of companies, they also have been instrumental in creating a potent antitakeover defense for corporations. The value of this defense has been underscored by the fact that it has successfully withstood legal challenges. In the Polaroid–Shamrock Holdings decision, the court concluded that, subject to certain qualifications such as the ESOP being planned before the takeover contest, ESOPs are valid when used as a takeover defense.

In addition to providing benefits to buyers of companies and defending corporations in hostile contests, ESOPs also seem to generate positive shareholder wealth effects. Research studies support this conclusion, even though they also find that ESOPs are an effective antitakeover deterrent. This implies that there must be significant benefits that more than offset the lower probability of a takeover when this defense is instituted.

4

CORPORATE RESTRUCTURING

10

CORPORATE RESTRUCTURING

Although the field of mergers and acquisitions (M&As) tends to focus on corporate expansion, companies often have to contract and downsize their operations. This need may arise because a division of the company is performing poorly or simply because it no longer fits into the firm's plans. Restructuring may also be necessary to undo a previous merger or acquisition that was unsuccessful. While we see that many selloffs are motivated by financial pressures brought on by a combination of high leverage and weak economic demand, we also see that the volume of selloffs increases when overall deal volume increases. As such, selloff deal volume tends to follow the ups and down of the economy just like M&A follows the overall pattern of economic fluctuations. This is the case not only in the United States but also in Asia and Europe.

In this chapter, the different types of corporate contraction are considered, and a decision-making methodology for reaching the divestiture decision is developed. The methods used to value acquisition targets are also used by companies to determine whether a particular component of the firm is worth retaining. Both the divesting and the acquiring firms commonly go through a similar type of analysis as they view the transaction from opposite sides. Even though the methods are similar, the two parties may come up with different values because they use different assumptions or have different needs.

This chapter considers the shareholder wealth effects of several forms of corporate restructuring. Corporate contraction may have positive stock price effects when the divested component fails to yield a value to the corporation that is commensurate with its market value. In such instances the corporation may be able to enhance the value of shareholder investments by pursuing a policy of corporate restructuring.

Corporate restructuring can take several different forms: divestitures, equity carve-outs, spinoffs, splitoffs, and splitups. A *divestiture* is a sale of a portion of the firm to an outside party. The selling firm is usually paid in cash, marketable securities, or a combination of the two. An *equity carve-out* is a variation of a divestiture that involves the sale of an equity interest in a subsidiary to outsiders. The sale may not necessarily leave the parent company in control of the subsidiary. The new equity gives the investors shares of ownership in the portion of the selling company that is being divested. In an equity carve-out, a new legal entity is created with a stockholder base that may be different from that of the parent selling company. The divested company has a different management team and is run as a separate firm.

A new legal entity is also created in a standard *spinoff*. Once again, new shares are issued, but here they are distributed to stockholders on a pro rata basis. As a result of the proportional distribution of shares, the stockholder base in the new company is the same as that of the old company. Although the stockholders are initially the same, the spun-off firm has its own management and is run as a separate company. Another difference between a spinoff and a divestiture is that a divestiture involves an infusion of funds into the parent corporation, whereas a spinoff normally does not provide the parent with a cash infusion. In an *exchange offer* new shares in a subsidiary are issued and shareholders in the parent company are given the option to either hold on to their shares or exchange these shares for an equity interest in the new publicly held subsidiary. This type of transaction is somewhat similar to a spinoff in that new shares are issued that represent an equity interest in a subsidiary that is separated from the parent. It is different from a spinoff, however, in that in order the get the newly issued shares, parent company shareholders have to part with their shares.

In a *splitup*, the entire firm is broken up into a series of spinoffs. The end result of this process is that the parent company no longer exists, leaving only the newly formed companies. The stockholders in the companies may be different because stockholders exchange their shares in the parent company for shares in one or more of the units that are spun off.

Sometimes companies do a combination of more than one of these methods of separation. For example, in February 1999, General Motors (GM) did an equity carve-out of just over 17% of its auto products subsidiary, Delphi Automotive Systems. Three months later the remainder of the company was spun off with GM shareholders receiving 0.7 shares of Delphi for each share of GM that they owned. With these transactions GM believed it was exiting the auto parts business. However, the labor agreements GM had with the United Auto Workers left GM with some responsibility for the burdensome wage and benefit payments to Delphi workers. This was problematic when Delphi was forced to file for bankruptcy in 2005.

CASE STUDY

RJR NABISCO RESTRUCTURING

RJR Nabisco announced in 1999 that it was engaging in a dramatic restructuring that would involve divestitures and spinoffs. The parent company, RJR Nabisco Holdings Corp., decided to sell R. J. Reynolds International to Japan Tobacco for almost $8 billion. The tobacco business, long known for impressive cash flows, was already run as separate domestic and international entities. R. J. Reynolds Tobacco, the domestic unit, was then spun off. Part of the reason for the deal was the problems that the domestic tobacco unit had as it faced an ongoing onslaught of litigation in the United States. In addition, the unit was losing market share to a stronger rival—Philip Morris. The U.S. tobacco market is a declining market, and R. J. Reynolds was losing market share in a market that was itself shrinking. In addition, although the tobacco business generates steady cash flow, the litigation liabilities loomed heavy over the company. The international tobacco unit showed more promise, but this promise would have been difficult to realize with the international business tied to the U.S. unit. As part of the restructuring plan, 80% of the food business, Nabisco Holdings Corp., would be owned by Nabisco Group Holdings. The food business was improving, and the company was hoping that the increased focus brought about by the restructuring would enable the company to capitalize on the momentum it was establishing in improving the food business.

Following the restructuring, the stock price of the independent R. J. Reynolds tobacco unit faltered, only to rebound in 2000. The declines in market share began to stabilize at the 24% level, but then deteriorated again due to aggressive discounters, especially those that were not affected by the Master Settlement Agreements, which imposes huge cash flow penalties on the four major U.S. cigarette manufacturers as a result of their legal settlement with the states.

In 2004, R. J. Reynolds, the number-two U.S. cigarette manufacturer, merged with Brown and Williamson, the number-three-ranked company in the industry. The combined company is now called Reynolds American. The fact that this merger was unopposed by the Federal Trade Commission (FTC) underscores the weakness of these two firms. The merger of these two companies, both of which have similar problems in the form of a high volume of litigation and erosion of market share from aggressive discounters, allowed R. J. Reynolds to expand its position in the tobacco business while the sale of its food business to Kraft allowed it to be more focused while allowing Kraft to become even more of a major presence in the international food business.

DIVESTITURES

Most selloffs are simple divestitures. Companies pursue other forms of selloffs, such as a spinoff or an equity carve-out, to achieve other objectives in addition to getting rid of a particular division. These objectives may be to make the transaction tax free, which may call for a spinoff.

The most common form of divestiture involves the sale of a division of the parent company to another firm. The process is a form of contraction for the selling company but a means of expansion for the purchasing corporation. The number of divestitures that took place between 1985 and 2005 is listed in Table 10.1.

Historical Trends

In the late 1960s, during the third merger wave, the number of divestitures and selloffs was relatively small as a percentage of the total number of transactions. Companies were engaging in major expansions at this time, widely using the acquisition of other firms to increase the acquiring company's stock price. This expansion came to an abrupt end following changes in the tax laws and other regulatory measures, along with the stock market decline. Companies then began to reconsider some of the acquisitions that had proved to be poor combinations—a need intensified by the 1974–75 recession. Under the pressure of falling economic demand, companies were forced to sell off divisions to raise funds and improve cash flow. International competition also pressured some of the 1960s conglomerates to become more efficient by selling off prior acquisitions that were not competitive in a world market.

This reversal of the acquisition trend was visible as early as 1971, when divestitures jumped to 42% of total transactions. The trend peaked in 1975, a period of economic recession, when the number of divestitures constituted 54% of all transactions. They remained between 35% and 40% throughout the 1980s. In the fifth merger wave, however, the number of divestitures rose again as downsizing and refocusing became prominent business strategies. When overall deal volume weakened at the end of that wave, divestiture volume also slowed only to rebound again in the 2000s, when M&A activity resumed.

Year	United States			Europe			Asia		
	Value ($ Millions)	Number of Deals	Average	Value ($ Millions)	Number of Deals	Average	Value ($ Millions)	Number of Deals	Average
1985	67,038.4	1,090	61.50	3,305.2	111	29.78	368.0	19	19.37
1986	96,509.6	1,525	63.28	13,748.2	212	64.85	1,013.4	39	25.98
1987	101,319.0	1,310	77.34	18,456.4	430	42.92	6,529.5	80	81.62
1988	144,023.4	1,832	78.62	37,380.1	891	41.95	12,806.3	150	85.38
1989	137,079.0	2,629	52.14	62,792.1	1,173	53.53	14,500.3	165	87.88
1990	93,458.3	2,732	34.21	87,358.7	1,879	46.49	21,359.2	311	68.68
1991	69,233.2	2,654	26.09	73,678.3	3,954	18.63	13,095.3	495	26.46
1992	85,382.8	2,459	34.72	68,653.7	4,106	16.72	12,938.5	372	34.78
1993	95,256.9	2,712	35.12	71,511.2	3,655	19.57	18,981.2	686	27.67
1994	153,446.2	2,957	51.89	64,272.9	3,273	19.64	17,524.2	671	26.12
1995	255,228.9	3,367	75.80	96,925.0	3,862	25.10	36,376.8	893	40.74
1996	196,416.4	3,572	54.99	116,528.5	3,537	32.95	34,512.2	951	36.29
1997	345,006.5	3,592	96.05	175,213.3	3,500	50.06	52,579.5	1,009	52.11
1998	286,066.8	3,668	77.99	215,332.2	3,456	62.31	46,489.2	1,500	30.99
1999	386,415.1	3,274	118.03	322,269.3	4,580	70.36	64,388.8	1,439	44.75
2000	356,651.4	3,075	115.98	378,504.0	5,244	72.18	94,475.9	1,626	58.10
2001	362,471.6	2,793	129.78	216,528.0	4,403	49.18	75,642.4	1,641	46.10
2002	176,126.8	2,745	64.16	221,374.7	3,397	65.17	62,884.4	1,918	32.79
2003	245,166.4	3,096	79.19	208,078.7	3,947	52.72	59,482.7	2,387	24.92
2004	257,710.7	2,893	89.08	274,965.8	3,553	77.39	66,465.1	2,828	23.50
2005	345,634.7	3,041	113.66	369,815.7	3,797	97.40	71,968.0	2,648	27.18

TABLE 10.1 DIVESTITURES IN UNITED STATES, EUROPE, AND ASIA, 1985–2005
Source: Thomson Financial Securities Data.

Many divestitures are the result of selloffs of previous acquisitions. The relationship between acquisitions and subsequent divestitures is shown in Exhibit 10.1. The belief that many divestitures are the undoing of previous acquisitions is seen in the leading trend in the acquisitions curve relative to the divestiture curve. The intense period of merger activity of the late 1960s is reflected in a pronounced peak at this time, followed by a peak in the divestiture curve in the early 1970s. The stock market performance seemed to play a determining role in the volume of divestitures. Linn and Rozeff used regression analysis to show that in years when the stock market fell, such as 1966, 1969, and 1973–74, the rate of divestiture fell below what one would have predicted given the previous merger rates. When the market performed well, periods that usually correspond to when the economy was doing well, the number of divestitures increased.[1] This research

---

1. Scott C. Linn and Michael S. Rozeff, "The Corporate Selloff," *Midland Corporate Finance Journal,* 2(2), Summer 1984, 24.

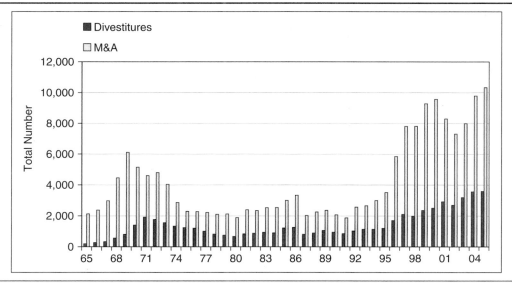

EXHIBIT 10.1 U.S. MERGERS and ACQUISITIONS VERSUS DIVESTITURES, 1965–2005
Source: Mergerstat Review, 1994–1998, 2006.

is also consistent with the rising stock market and increased number of divestitures of the 1990s. Exhibit 10.1 shows that when M&A activity slowed in the late 1980s, the pace of spinoffs and divestitures increased. However, as the fifth merger wave accelerated in the 1990s, the number of selloffs continued to increase, although as a percent of total transactions they declined.

Many critics of corporate acquisitions use the record of the divestitures following poor acquisitions as evidence of ill-conceived expansion planning. These criticisms, which we hear often today, have been voiced for many years. For example, using a sample of 33 companies during the period 1950–1986, Porter shows that these firms divested 53% of the acquisitions that brought the acquiring companies into new industries.[2] Based on this evidence, he concludes that the corporate acquisition record is "dismal." These results were somewhat supported by Ravenscraft and Scherer, who found that 33% of acquisitions made during the 1960s and 1970s were later divested.[3] The track record of many more recent acquisitions also leaves something to be desired.[4]

Global Divestiture Trends

There is a strong similarity among the variations in the volume of divestitures in the United States, Europe, and Asia. However, the value of total divestitures in Europe and

---

2. Michael Porter, "From Competitive Advantage to Corporate Strategy," *Harvard Business Review,* May/June 1987, 43–59.
3. David Ravenscraft and Frederic Scherer, *Mergers, Selloffs and Economic Efficiency* (Washington, D.C.: Brookings Institution, 1987).
4. See Patrick A. Gaughan, *Mergers: What Can Go Wrong and How to Prevent It* (Hoboken, NJ: John Wiley & Sons, 2005).

Asia rose more sharply in the second half of the fifth merger wave than they did in the United States. All three series declined when the economy turned down in 2000–2001; however, they began to increase again in 2003—especially in Europe. (See Exhibits 10.2(a) and (b).) As of the end of 2005, the total value of divestitures in Europe is somewhat greater than in the United States, while deal total and average deal value in Asia is much lower.

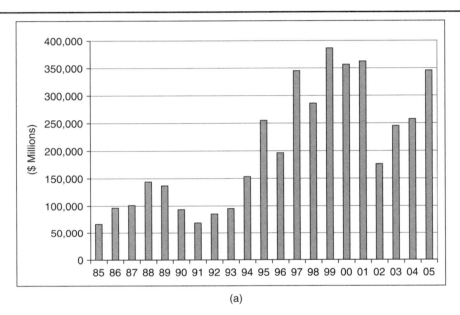

(a)

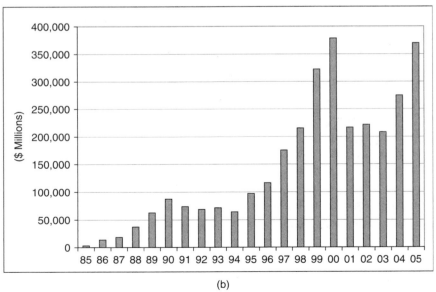

(b)

Exhibit 10.2   (a) U.S. Divestitures, 1985–2005; (b) European Divestitures 1985–2005; (c) Asian Divestitures 1985–2005

Source: Thomson Financial Securities Data.

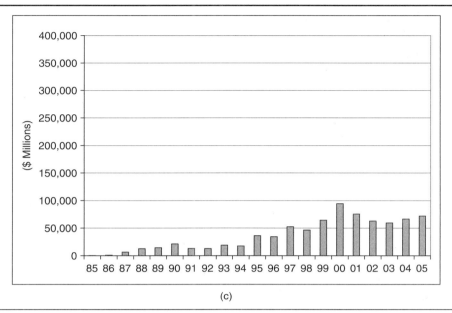

(c)

Exhibit 10.2 *(continued)*

Divestiture Likelihood and Prior Acquisitions

Kaplan and Weisbach analyzed 271 large acquisitions completed between 1971 and 1982.[5] A total of 43.9%, or 119, of these acquisitions were divested by 1982 (Table 10.2). The divested entities were held for an average of seven years. Kaplan and Weisbach investigated the pattern of the divestitures in search for a common motive for some of the selloffs. They found that diversifying acquisitions are four times more likely to be divested than nondiversifying acquisitions. This result supports other evidence, discussed in Chapter 4, that questioned the benefits of acquisition programs. The motives for divestitures, which are discussed in subsequent sections, are summarized in Table 10.3.

Involuntary versus Voluntary Divestitures

A divestiture may be either voluntary or involuntary. An involuntary divestiture may occur when a company receives an unfavorable review by the Justice Department or the Federal Trade Commission (FTC), requiring the company to divest itself of a particular division. For example, in June 1987, in a 4-to-1 vote, the Interstate Commerce Commission (ICC) ruled that the merger of the Santa Fe and Southern Pacific railway systems might reduce competition. Santa Fe had merged with Southern Pacific in 1983 in one of the biggest mergers in railway history. The combined railway was operated together while awaiting an antitrust analysis and ruling from the ICC, which had antitrust jurisdiction for this type of merger. After the ruling, the ICC required Santa Fe–Southern Pacific to submit a

---

5. Steven N. Kaplan and Michael N. Weisbach, "The Success of Acquisitions: Evidence from Divestitures," *Journal of Finance*, 47(1), March 1992, 107–138.

Year	Number of Acquisitions	Median Target Value as Percentage of Acquirer Value	Number Divested	Percentage Divested	Median Years Held
1971	8	36.0	5	62.5	15.6
1972	4	28.9	1	25.0	15.6
1973	9	22.3	7	77.8	11.6
1974	7	19.6	2	28.6	7.7
1975	7	34.1	4	57.1	11.5
1976	16	19.8	8	50.0	8.3
1977	30	26.1	12	40.0	8.8
1978	39	28.0	16	41.0	7.6
1979	45	28.1	23	51.1	6.5
1980	30	25.7	12	40.0	6.3
1981	34	28.4	17	50.0	6.5
1982	42	24.6	12	28.6	4.5
Total	272	25.6	11.9	43.9	7.0

TABLE 10.2   ACQUISITIONS AND DIVESTITURES

Source: Steven N. Kaplan and Michael N. Weisbach. "The Success of Acquisitions: Evidence from Divestitures," *Journal of Finance,* 47(1), March 1992.

divestiture plan within 90 days. The adverse ruling had a depressing effect on Santa Fe's stock price and made the firm a target of a bid by the Henley Group.

Reasons for Voluntary Divestitures

Poor Fit of Division

Voluntary divestitures are more common than involuntary divestitures and are motivated by a variety of reasons. For example, the parent company may want to move out of a

Reason	Number of Divestitures
Change of focus or corporate strategy	43
Unit unprofitable or mistake	22
Sale to finance acquisition or leveraged restructuring	29
Antitrust	2
Need cash	3
To defend against takeover	1
Good Price	3
Divestitures with reasons	103

TABLE 10.3   REASONS FOR DIVERSTITURES

Source: Steven N. Kaplan and Michael N. Weisbach. "The Success of Acquisitions: Evidence from Divestitures," *Journal of Finance,* 47(1), March 1992.

particular line of business that it feels no longer fits into its plans or in which it is unable to operate profitably. This does not mean that another firm, with greater expertise in this line of business, could not profitably manage the division's assets. Sometimes these sales come as a result of the prior acquisition of a company that had divisions that did not fit as well with the acquirer as other divisions that were bought. Divestitures then become part of an efficient market process that reallocates assets to those who will allow them to reach their greatest gain.

CASE STUDY

REFOCUSING THROUGH SALES OF COMPONENTS OF PRIOR ACQUISITIONS—CASE OF TAITTINGER

When a company acquires a diversified target it is often the case that it had some business units that are more appealing than others. This was the case in 2005, when Starwood Capital Group, a real estate company, acquired Taittinger for $3.45 billion. Taittinger is the sixth largest champagne company in that industry. Starwood is known for its diverse hotel properties in an industry that it knows well. However, Taittinger, through its Concorde Group, owned approximately 70 upscale hotels in Europe, such as the Hotel de Crillon in Paris and Hotel Lutetia, as well as the second largest budget hotel chain on the continent—the Evergure Group. These assets were the main appeal of Taittinger to Starwood. In addition to champagne and hotels, Taittinger also owned the famous Baccarat crystal brand. Like a number of other diversified European companies, such as LVMH, the combinations within the corporate entity are only loosely related. This makes them more easily separable.

The Greenwich-based Starwood is run by Barry S. Sternlicht, a shrewd real estate investor/hotel operator. He founded Starwood in 1995 and in a few years he acquired the Westin hotel chain along with ITT (what was left of that conglomerate), which owned the Sheraton and St. Regis chains. He acquired Taittinger knowing that he would be acquiring real estate assets that he felt were quite valuable. He also knew that while he did not want his company in the champagne or crystal business, the brands he was acquiring would command a good value in the market as they were among the leaders in their respective fields. Taittinger, the third oldest champagne house, was founded in 1734 and since 1931 has been controlled by the Taittinger family. This is another example of large European corporations controlled by family interests.

Reverse Synergy

One motive that is often ascribed to M&As is synergy. As described in Chapter 4, synergy refers to the additional gains that may be derived when two forms combine. When synergy exists, the combined entity is worth more than the sum of the parts valued separately. In other words, $2 + 2 = 5$. *Reverse synergy* means that the parts are worth more separately than they are within the parent company's corporate structure. In other words, $4 - 1 = 5$. In such cases, an outside bidder might be able to pay more for a division than what the division is worth to the parent company. For instance, a large parent company is not able to operate a division profitably, whereas a smaller firm, or even the division by itself, might operate more efficiently and therefore earn a higher rate of return.

Reverse synergy occurred in the late 1980s when the Allegis Corporation was forced to sell off its previously acquired companies, Hertz Rent A Car and the Weston and Hilton International hotel chains. Allegis had paid a high price for these acquisitions based on the belief that the synergistic benefits of combining the travel industry companies with United Airlines, its main asset, would more than justify the high prices. When the synergistic benefits failed to materialize, the stock price fell, setting the stage for a hostile bid from the New York investment firm Coniston Partners. Coniston made a bid based on its analysis that the separate parts of Allegis were worth more than the combined entity.

Poor Performance

Companies may want to divest divisions simply because they are not sufficiently profitable. The division could fail to pay a rate of return that exceeds the parent company's *hurdle rate*—the minimum return threshold that a company will use to evaluate projects or the performance of parts of the overall company. A typical hurdle rate could be the firm's cost of capital.

A division could decline for many reasons. The industry as a whole might be in a state of decline. For example, high labor costs, caused by a unionized labor force, may make the division uncompetitive in the world market. This occurred when Swift and Company decided that it would have to sell its fresh meats division in the 1980s. Beset with a high-cost, unionized labor force, this division could not compete with its nonunionized competitors, and Swift and Company decided to sell it off. In the 1990s, GM and Ford tried to do the same with their auto parts business when they spun off Delphi and Visteon. However, these troubled businesses remained tied to the parents through the United Auto Workers labor agreements. GM and Ford remained responsible for the workers at the auto parts companies, and when the businesses encountered financial problems in 2005 the automakers had to bear responsibility.

Management may be reluctant to sell a poorly performing division because they may have to admit that they did a poor job of managing it or, in the case of a prior acquisition, that the purchase was a mistake. They may then hold on to the division for a longer time than would be dictated by its performance.[6]

CASE STUDY

ALTRIA'S SALE OF MILLER BREWING

Altria is the former Philip Morris. For many years the company operated in three main areas: tobacco, food, and beer (they had a small presence in the finance business). Philip Morris is the leading cigarette company in the world and had a U.S. market share in the 50% range. Its brand Marlboro is one of the leading brand names in the world. Philip Morris's tobacco business is divided into two parts: Philip Morris USA and Philip Morris International. The U.S. business is distinctly different from its international business. First, the U.S. business has been the target of over a thousand lawsuits. Second, U.S. tobacco consumption, on a unit basis, has declined at approximately a 2% annual rate for many years. However, the international tobacco business has been quite robust.

While Miller was the second largest U.S. brewer, it lagged behind the Budweiser and Busch brands of market leader Anheuser Busch. The beer business in the United States is highly competitive and

---

6. Arnoud W. A. Boot, "Why Hang on to Losers? Divestitures and Takeovers," *Journal of Finance*, 47(4), September 1992, 1401–1423.

requires major marketing expenditures to build and expand a brand. Despite their best efforts, Miller failed to make the desired contribution to company profits to warrant Altria staying in this business. In July 2002, the company decided to sell Miller to South African Brewers (SAB) in a deal that valued the company at $5.5 billion. SAB assumed $2 billion of Miller's debt while issuing shares to Philip Morris, which would own a little over a third of the combined SAB/Miller.

SAB was at the time of the Miller acquisition the fourth largest brewer in the world. The deal vaulted SAB into the number-two position in the international beer market. We have seen in Chapter 4 that that the number-one and -two position often confers advantages that smaller rivals have difficulty matching. In addition, SAB, which also marketed Pilsner Urquell, now had a major brand in the U.S. market. SAB also planned to use its international clout to help advance the Miller brand in and outside of the United States. This deal was part of SAB's growth through acquisition strategy in which the company expanded into a variety of markets in Eastern Europe and Asia. It also acquired a major international brand in the Italian Pironi Group. However, in terms of international brands, SAB still lacks anything that can rival Heineken and Interbrew's Becks and Stella Artois. Yet, in a relatively short time period, M&As have allowed SAB to be one of the world's largest brewers.

Capital Market Factors

A divestiture may also take place because the postdivestiture firm, as well as the divested division, has greater access to capital markets. The combined corporate structure may be more difficult for investors to categorize. Certain providers of capital might be looking to invest in steel companies but not in pharmaceutical firms. Other investors might seek to invest capital in pharmaceutical companies but may think that the steel industry is too cyclical and has low growth potential. These two groups of investors might not want to invest in a combined steel and pharmaceutical company, but each group might separately invest in a standalone steel or pharmaceutical firm. Divestitures might provide greater access to capital markets for the two firms as separate companies than as a combined corporation.

Similarly, divestitures may create companies in which investors would like to invest but that do not exist in the marketplace. Such companies are sometimes referred to as *pure plays*. Many analysts argue that the market is incomplete and that there is a demand for certain types of firms that is not matched by a supply of securities in the market. The sale of those parts of the parent company that become pure plays helps complete the market.

The separation of divisions facilitates clearer identification and market segmentation for the investment community. For corporate divisions that need capital to grow, the ability to attract new investment funds may be enhanced if the company is an independent entity. Here investors contemplating putting funds into a company can more easily project the future returns when the business is a defined and separate unit as opposed to being housed with a corporate shell that has very different growth prospects. This was particularly the case with GM and its financing unit GMAC. When GM's position in the marketplace worsened in 2005 and 2006, the rating agencies dropped GM's debt rating to junk status. The auto financing business is based on being able to acquire funds at low rates in markets such as the money market through the issuance of commercial paper, and lend monies to car buyers at rates that will be attractive enough to stimulate sales. When GM's ratings fell, this raised GMAC's costs of capital as the two companies were linked. In April 2006, GM agreed to sell 51% of GMAC to Cerberus Capital Management LP for an estimated $14 billion, with $7 billion being paid at the time of closing. The deal required GM to hold on to approximately $20 billion in auto leases. Being partially separated from the auto business also allows GMAC to more aggressively pursue non-auto business. Being too closely tied to the troubled auto business placed GMAC at a competitive disadvantage in capital markets relative to other financing companies that were not burdened with GM's problems.

CASE STUDY

WESTERN UNION 2006 SPINOFF BY FIRST DATA CORP.

In 2006, First Data Corp decided to spin off its Western Union unit rather than keep it housed with the overall First Data corporate umbrella. First Data, which itself was spun off off by American Express in 1992, is a credit card processor. These are companies that process and keep track of credit card charges and provide other related services such as sending out credit cards to consumers. Over the 2004–2005 time period, First Data's core business has suffered significantly as rivals, such as Total Services Systems, aggressively attacked its market share. While its overall financial performance was weak, one bright spot it had was its money transfer business—Western Union. While the credit card processor business was deteriorating, Western Union's business was booming.

It is ironic that Western Union is such a high-growth business as it was founded in 1851. It began as a communications company and built the first trans-Atlantic telegraph. While so many of the companies founded at that time have long gone by the wayside, Western Union continues to *adapt* to a changing marketplace and is thriving. It is now the largest money transfer company in the world with annual revenues of $4 billion. The company does 275 million transactions per year using 271,000 agencies throughout Asia, Europe, Latin America, and the United States.[a] It has been able to fuel its growth throughout a broad international expansion strategy. However, much of the great progress Western Union was making was difficult to see when housed within a mundane credit card processing business. The logical conclusion was to release Western Union in a tax free spinoff to First Data Corp. shareholders and let them realize the benefits of Western Union's anticipated continued success.

[a]Eric Dash, "Western Union, Growing Faster Than Its Parent, Is to Be Spun Off," *New York Times*, January 27, 2006, C3.

Cash Flow Factors

A selloff produces the immediate benefits of an infusion of cash from the sale. The selling firm is selling a long-term asset, which generated a certain cash flow per period, in exchange for a larger payment in the short run. Companies that are under financial duress are often forced to sell off valuable assets to enhance cash flows. Beset with the threat of bankruptcy in the early 1980s, Chrysler Corporation was forced to sell off its prized tank division in an effort to stave off bankruptcy. International Harvester (now known as Navistar) sold its profitable Solar Turbines International Division to Caterpillar Tractor Company, Inc. to realize the immediate proceeds of $505 million. These funds were used to cut Harvester's short-term debt in half.

Cash flow factors also motivated the aforementioned sales of Hertz by Ford in 2005 (see Ford Motor Company Sells Off Hertz case study) as well as the sale by GM of 51% of GMAC in 2006. These divisions were profitable and commanded good prices in the marketplace while bringing much needed cash that these two auto companies used to offset sizable operating losses.

CASE STUDY

FORD MOTOR COMPANY SELLS OFF HERTZ

In the 2000s, both Ford and General Motors (GM) steadily lost market shares to foreign competitors, such as Toyota and Honda. These competitors were not hamstrung by the burdensome labor agreements that Ford and GM were forced to deal with. This allowed Toyota and Honda to establish manufacturing plants in the United States and pay laborers a fraction of the costs that Ford and GM were forced to pay. In addition, both companies face huge "legacy" costs of future pension and health care costs for retired employees. When sales of previously hot vehicles, such as SUVs, turned down as consumer tastes changed, both companies began to incur large losses.

In prior years both Ford and GM had vertically integrated. They built up large suppliers that they eventually spun off as Visteon and Delphi. The union liabilities, however, forced Ford to take back Visteon while GM still maintained responsibilities for Delphi labor costs. As its position began to worsen, Ford was forced to sell off its forward vertical integration unit—Hertz. Hertz is a market leader in the U.S. car rental market. Even though Hertz is the market leader, Ford's sales to Hertz did not generate high profits from these sales, as car rental companies typically buy using large volume discounts that provide low profits for auto manufacturers. The benefit of the high volume purchases, however, while not very profitable, allowed auto manufacturers to maintain market share and keep their plants operating at a high capacity. This was necessary as Ford and GM were forced to make payments to union workers even when they did not need all their capacity. The union compensation commitments to employees became mainly fixed costs for Ford and GM, while these same costs were more variable for foreign auto companies such as Toyota and Honda.

In 2005, Ford decided to sell off Hertz to a consortium of private equity firms including Clayton Dublier & Rice, Carlyle Group, and Merrill Lynch Global Private Equity. The sale of Hertz, which was reported to have an enterprise value of $15 billion, brought a cash infusion into Ford. The benefits of this additional cash provided Ford some respite from financial pressures while it worked on a major restructuring to restore the company to profitability.

Abandoning the Core Business

The sale of a company's core business is a less common reason for a selloff. An example of the sale of a core business was the 1987 sale by Greyhound of its bus business. The sale of a core business is often motivated by management's desire to leave an area that it believes has matured and presents few growth opportunities. The firm usually has already diversified into other more profitable areas, and the sale of the core business may help finance the expansion of these more productive activities. Another example of this was Boise Cascade's decision to sell off its paper manufacturing production business and become an office products retailer through its prior acquisition—OfficeMax. OfficeMax was acquired by Boise Cascade in 2003 for $1.15 billion as part of a vertical integration strategy as Boise Cascade made paper products that are ultimately sold through retailers such as OfficeMax. However, over time the paper production business became less attractive while the retail distribution business gained in appeal.

DIVESTITURE AND SPINOFF PROCESS

Each divestiture is unique and takes place in a different sequence of events. A generalized process is briefly described here.

Step 1. *Divestiture or Spinoff Decision.* The management of the parent company must decide whether a divestiture is the appropriate course of action. This decision can be made only after a thorough financial analysis of the various alternatives has been completed. The method of conducting the financial analysis for a divestiture or spinoff is discussed later in this chapter.

Step 2. *Formulation of a Restructuring Plan.* A restructuring or reorganization plan must be formulated, and an agreement between the parent and the subsidiary may be negotiated. This plan is necessary in the case of a spinoff that will feature a continuing relationship between the parent and the subsidiary. The plan should cover such details as the disposition of the subsidiary's assets and liabilities. In cases in which the subsidiary is to keep certain of its assets while others are to be transferred back to the parent company, the plan may provide a detailed breakdown of the asset disposition. Other issues, such as the retention of employees and the funding of their pension and, possibly, health care liabilities may need to be addressed.

Step 3. *Approval of the Plan by Shareholders.* The extent to which approval of the plan is necessary depends on the significance of the transaction and the relevant state laws. In cases such as a spinoff of a major division of the parent company, stockholder approval may be required. If so, the plan is submitted to the stockholders at a stockholders' meeting, which may be the normally scheduled shareholders' meeting or a special meeting called to consider only this issue. A proxy statement requesting approval of the spinoff is also sent to stockholders. The materials submitted to stockholders may address other issues related to the meeting, such as the amendment of the articles of incorporation.

Step 4. *Registration of Shares.* If the transaction requires the issuance of share, then this stock must be registered with the Securities and Exchange Commission (SEC). As part of the normal registration process, a prospectus, which is part of the registration statement, must be produced. The prospectus must be distributed to all shareholders who receive stock in the spun-off entity.

Step 5. *Completion of the Deal.* After these preliminary steps have been taken, the deal may be consummated. Consideration is exchanged, and the division is separated from the parent company according to a prearranged timetable.

Financial Evaluation of Divestitures

Valuation methods are discussed in Chapter 14. Such methods generally apply to selloffs. The financial evaluation of a subsidiary by a parent company that is contemplating divestiture should proceed in a logical fashion. The following steps form a basis for a general process of evaluation.

Step 1. *Estimation of After-Tax Cash Flows.* The parent company needs to estimate the after-tax cash flows of the division. This analysis should consider the interrelationship between the subsidiary's and the parent company's respective capabilities to generate cash flow. If, for example, the subsidiary's operations are closely related to the parent company's activities, the parent company's cash flows may be positively or negatively affected after the divestiture. Thus, this needs to be factored into the analysis at the beginning of the evaluation process.

Step 2. *Determination of the Division's Relevant Risk-Adjusted Discount Rate.* The present value of the division's after-tax cash flows needs to be calculated. To do so, a division-specific discount rate must be derived, taking into account the risk charac- teristics of the division on a standalone basis. The cost of capital of other firms that are in the same business and approximately the same size may be a good proxy for this discount rate.

Step 3. *Present Value Calculation.* Using the discount rate derived in step 2, we can calculate the present value of each projected after-tax cash flow. The sum of these terms will represent the present value of the income-generating capability of the division by itself.

Step 4. *Deduction of the Market Value of the Division's Liabilities.* Step 3 of this process did not take into account the division's liabilities. The market value of these liabil- ities needs to be deducted from the present value of the after-tax cash flows. The market value is used because the market has in effect already computed the present value calculation in its determination of the current value of these obligations. This results in a net of liability value of the division, which is the value of the division as part of the parent company, assuming it maintains ownership of the division.

$$\text{NOLV} = \sum_{i=1}^{n} \frac{ATCF_i}{(1+k)^i} - \text{MVL}$$

where:

NOLV = the net of liabilities value of the present value of the after-tax cash flows

$ATCF_i$ = the after-tax cash flows

k = the division-specific discount rate

MVL = the market value of the liabilities

The preceding simplified model is presented using a discounted cash flow (DCF) analysis. In Chapter 14 we also discuss other valuation methods such as using comparable multiples. However, for simplicity's sake we also discuss DCF here.

Step 5. *Deduction of the Divestiture Proceeds.* The proceeds that the parent can derive from a sale of the division (DP) are then compared with the value developed in step 4. If the divestiture proceeds, net of selling costs, are higher than the value of keeping the division, the unit should be sold.

DP > NOLV: Sell division.

DP = NOLV: Other factors will control decision.

DP < NOLV: Keep division(unless other factors suggest a sale).

Spinoffs

Spinoffs are one of the more popular forms of corporate downsizing.

Trends in Spinoffs

Spinoffs grew in popularity during the fifth merger wave. This growth was partly fueled by investors' pressure to release internal values that are unrealized in the company's stock price. In the United States, a record level of spinoffs occurred in 1999, while the value of total spinoffs peaked in Europe in 2000 (see Table 10.4). Spinoff volume in Asia peaked in 2001, although the total and average dollar value was well below that in the United States and Europe. While the value of total spinoffs declined in the United States dramatically over the period 1999–2002, the total rose steadily in the years that followed. However, as of the end of 2005 they were still a fraction of their peak 1999 value (see Exhibit 10.3(a)). However, in Europe, the value of total spinoffs declined steadily over the period 2003–2005 while they rose significantly in Asia in 2005 (see Exhibits 10.3(b) and 10.3(c)).

The classic example of a large-scale spinoff is the 1995 ITT $12.4 billion spinoff of the international conglomerate's assets into three separate entities. This spinoff was the

	United States			Europe			Asia		
Year	value ($ Millions)	Number of Deals	Average	value ($ Millions)	Number of Deals	Average	value ($ Millions)	Number of Deals	Average
1985	1,861.0	27	68.93	—	—	—	—	—	—
1986	5,308.5	39	136.12	—	—	—	256.4	3	85.47
1987	4,516.1	31	145.68	.0	2	0.00	.0	5	0.00
1988	10,645.5	50	212.91	.0	7	0.00	.0	1	0.00
1989	10,881.0	46	236.54	3,905.8	9	433.98	119.9	4	29.98
1990	5,742.9	58	99.02	6,227.3	12	518.94	303.6	1	303.60
1991	4,759.9	25	190.40	1,230.8	14	87.91	818.2	5	163.64
1992	17,697.6	55	321.77	7,024.0	10	702.40	34.2	4	8.55
1993	16,584.0	52	318.92	1,726.1	10	172.61	30.3	8	3.79
1994	27,763.8	43	645.67	7.6	6	1.27	.0	4	0.00
1995	104,292.6	71	1468.91	5,676.7	11	516.06	.0	6	0.00
1996	20,816.8	85	244.90	20,460.2	25	818.41	3,175.6	12	264.63
1997	96,805.8	81	1195.13	18,524.5	19	974.97	120.6	7	17.23
1998	53,080.3	75	707.74	23,261.3	38	612.14	394.5	4	98.63
1999	150,232.0	72	2086.56	28,271.3	36	785.31	2,173.2	6	362.20
2000	122,718.2	92	1333.89	51,104.0	59	866.17	4,121.6	21	196.27
2001	40,429.0	40	1010.73	15,840.8	34	465.91	15,568.3	38	409.69
2002	4,835.7	50	96.71	5,852.9	8	731.61	4,118.6	52	79.20
2003	23,894.0	53	450.83	23,003.1	32	718.85	187.4	43	4.36
2004	30,152.5	46	655.49	13,601.4	41	331.74	731.9	32	22.87
2005	46,581.9	60	776.37	5,795.8	43	134.79	3,741.2	29	129.01

TABLE 10.4 SPINOFFS IN UNITED STATES, EUROPE, AND ASIA, 1985–2005

Source: Thomson Financial Securities Data.

culmination of decades of acquisitions that the conglomerate had engaged in, followed by years in which the company's stock price failed to reach the levels that its management hoped to realize.

The ITT spinoff is discussed in detail later in this chapter, in Case Study: ITT— Dissolution of the Quintessential Conglomerate. In recent years we have seen a significant number of prominent breakups, such as the Tyco, Cendant, and Dun & Bradstreet deals.

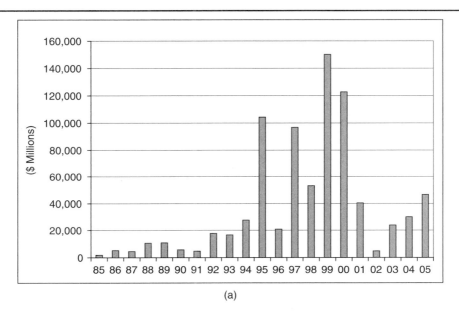

(a)

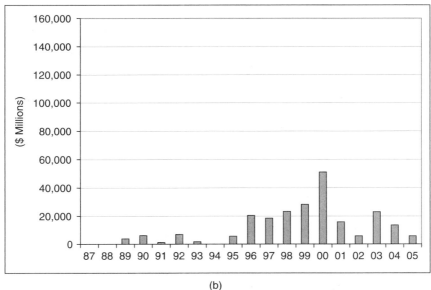

(b)

EXHIBIT 10.3 (a) U.S. SPINOFFS 1985–2005; (b) EUROPEAN SPINOFFS 1985–2005; (c) ASIAN SPINOFFS 1985–2005

Source: Thomson Financial Securities Data.

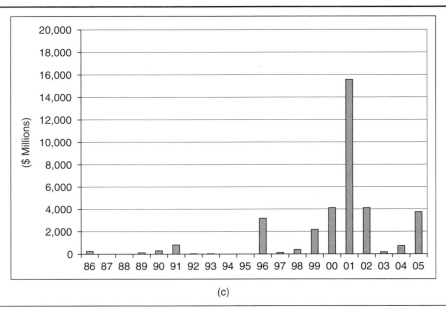

(c)

Exhibit 10.3   *(continued)*

CASE STUDY

EUROPEAN SPINOFFS AND DIVESTITURES OF THE FIFTH WAVE AND BEYOND

European markets underwent major changes in the fifth merger wave. Cross-border deals became more common and regulatory barriers declined. Corporate governance and the obligations on the part of corporations to maximize shareholder value began to take hold of the corporate consciousness. In response, many large European corporations began to look to spinoffs and divestitures as a way to maximize shareholder value. No longer were large European corporations content to hold together a diversified collection of companies that may provide some countercyclical benefits in recessions but that generally resulted in weaker shareholder values. Increased corporate focus, rather than diversification, began to become more important. Toward that end, DaimlerChrysler spun off a 10% interest it had in a telephone network, while Bayer sold off its Agfa unit for almost $4 billion. Other large German conglomerates, such as Veba, listed its Stinnes division as a separate entity on the Frankfurt Exchange. Siemens spun off its Infineon unit for over $5 billion. These corporate restructurings represent a dramatic departure from the traditional European mindset, which was to hold together diversified corporate structures even if it meant an opportunity cost for shareholders. In the 1990s, European corporations began to more carefully consider shareholders' interests while they rethought their traditional management philosophy.

Involuntary Spinoffs

When faced with an adverse regulatory ruling, a firm may decide that a spinoff is the only viable way to comply. The classic example of such an involuntary spinoff was the mammoth spinoff of AT&T's operating companies in 1984. As a result of an antitrust suit originally filed in 1974 by the Justice Department, the government and AT&T reached an agreement providing for the breakup of the large telecommunications company. The agreement, which became effective January 1, 1984, provided for the reorganization of the 22 operating companies within AT&T into 7 regional holding companies. These holding companies would be responsible for local telecommunications service, and the new AT&T would maintain responsibility for long-distance communications.

The spinoff of the 22 operating companies would still allow AT&T shareholders to have the same number of shares in the post-spinoff company. These shares represented ownership rights in a much smaller telecommunications company. For every ten shares that each shareholder had in the original AT&T, shareholders received one share in each of the seven regional holding companies. Those shareholders who had fewer than ten shares received a cash value for their shares rather than shares in the regional holding companies.[7] They would still be shareholders in the post-spinoff AT&T. The spinoff created a major administrative problem. Thousands of workers were hired to process the stock transfers and to handle record keeping. A special administrative center was established in Jacksonville, Florida, to coordinate the paperwork and share distribution.[8]

The 1984 AT&T spinoff is an extreme form of an involuntary spinoff, given the sheer size of the transaction. The spinoff resulted in a dramatic change in the nature of the telecommunications industry in the United States. Most spinoffs, however, are not of this magnitude and are not a response to a regulatory mandate. AT&T made history again in 1995, when it engaged in a three-way splitoff that separated the company into three separate firms. AT&T is a company that had a very troubled M&A history. Its M&A problems culminated in failed acquisitions of cable companies, TCI and Media One, which led to still another breakup of the company. Clearly, AT&T was a "leader" in M&A blunders. The troubles of AT&T are briefly discussed in a case study later in this chapter.

Defensive Spinoffs

Chapter 5 discussed the use of corporate restructuring to defend against hostile takeovers. Companies may choose to spin off divisions to make them less attractive to the bidder. For example, in January 1987, Diamond Shamrock's board of directors approved a restructuring plan that provided for spinning off two core businesses and forming a new entity, called Diamond Shamrock R&M, and distributing R&M stock to its shareholders.[9]

Defensive spinoffs, or other types of selloffs, constitute a drastic takeover defense. They may be challenged in the courts by the bidder and possibly by shareholders. If they are determined to limit the auction process and reduce shareholder value, they may be voided. The wealth effects of these defensive selloffs are discussed later in this chapter.

Tax Consequences of Spinoffs

One of the advantages a spinoff has over other types of selloffs is that the transaction may be structured so that it is tax free. For example, the shares in the regional Bells that

---

7. *AT&T Shareholders Newsletter* (Fourth Quarter, 1982).
8. Ronald J. Kudla and Thomas H. McInish, *Corporate Spin-Offs: Strategy for the 1980s* (Westport, CT: Quorum, 1984), p. 8.
9. James L. Bicksler and Andrew H. Chen, "The Economics of Corporate Restructuring: An Overview," in *The Battle for Corporate Control* (Homewood, IL: Business One Irwin, 1991), pp. 386–387.

stockholders received did not result in additional tax liabilities for those shareholders. The Internal Revenue Service treated the distribution of shares in the AT&T spinoff as neither a gain nor a loss. Voluntary spinoffs are also often treated as nontaxable transactions. If the spinoff occurs for valid business reasons, rather than for the purpose of tax avoidance, Section 355 of the Tax Code allows for the transaction to be nontaxable. Among the Tax Code's requirements for a tax-free spinoff are:

- Both the parent company and the spun-off entity must be in business for at least five years before the restructuring.
- The subsidiary must be at least 80% owned by the parent company.

When the General Utilities Doctrine was in effect, companies could sell off assets without incurring capital gains taxes. With its repeal in the mid-1980s, spinoffs became more popular because they were an alternative that provided a tax-free way to shed assets.

Treatment of Warrants and Convertible Securities

When the parent company has issued warrants or convertible securities, such as convertible debentures, the conversion ratio may have to be adjusted when shares are issued in a spinoff. The spinoff may cause the common stock in the parent company to be less valuable. If the deal is so structured that current common stockholders gain through the distribution of proceeds in the form of a special dividend, warrant holders and convertible security holders may not participate in this gain. After the distribution, the stock price of the parent company may fall, making the expected conversion more difficult because it will be less likely that the price will rise enough to enable the securities to be converted. If this is the case, the conversion prices may need to be adjusted as part of the terms of the deal.

Seller Financing Assistance

Sometimes a seller wants to rid itself of an unattractive division, so it will make an appealing offer to a buyer just more easily to part ways with the unit. This was the case in 2002, when Diegao agreed to guarantee loans that the private equity buyers Bain Capital, Texas Pacific Group, and Goldman Sachs Partners incurred to finance the purchase of its Burger King unit. At the time of the sale the fast-food business was undergoing fierce competition and the buyers were worried that these competitive pressures might adversely affect Burger King's margins and its ability to service acquisition debt. In addition, the ultimate price of $1.5 billion was about three quarters of a billion lower than the price the parties appeared to agree on when they first began negotiations. Following the acquisition, the buyers were able to quickly extract monies from Burger King and then shortly thereafter went public in a reverse LBO. This is an example of the shrewd deals that private equity buyers often conduct.

Allocation of Debt Obligations and Bond Liabilities

When a company decides to do a spinoff, such as when Tyco decided to break itself up into four separate components in 2005, a decision has to be made as to which of the spun-off businesses will assume specific liabilities. Sometimes the answer is obvious. Perhaps the debts were part of a specific business that was acquired. If so, it may be logical that the business maintain these obligations after the spinoff. For Tyco this was not that easy as it had much corporate debt for which there was no specific business unit to which it could be easily attributed. When this is the case, then a decision has to be made as to what a fair allocation would be.

Employee Stock Option Plans

For employees holding shares under an employee stock option plan (ESOP), the number of shares obtainable by option holders may also need to be adjusted after a spinoff. The adjustment is designed to leave the market value of shares that could be obtained after the spinoff at the same level. This is usually done by increasing the number of shares that may be obtained with a given option. Those option-holding employees in the parent company who become employees in the spun-off entity have their stock options changed to become options in the new company. Here again, the goal is to maintain the market value of the shares that may be obtained through conversion of the employee stock options.

CASE STUDY

TELMEX SPINOFF OF CELLULAR AND INTERNATIONAL BUSINESS

In February 2001, Telefonos de Mexico (TelMex), the largest telephone company in Mexico, announced that it was spinning off its cellular and international businesses to its shareholders. The businesses are housed within a new entity called America Movil. Its shares then began trading in Mexico City and Madrid, while its American Depositary Receipts began trading on the New York Stock Exchange and on NASDAQ. The new company immediately became the largest mobile phone provider in Latin America with 12 million subscribers, although 9 million of them are located in Mexico. TelMex shareholders received one share of America Movil for each share of TelMex that they owned. The spinoff was in response to Mexican and international regulatory pressures from the United States, which complained to the World Trade Organization that TelMex unfairly dominated the Mexican telecommunications market. The new company, though, retains strong links to its former parent. Carlos Slim Helu is chairman and controlling shareholder of each entity.

America Movil expanded its area of operations following its separation from TelMex. It expanded throughout South America through a series of acquisitions. In the summer of 2005, it acquired wireless companies in Peru (TIM Peru S.A.C.), Paraguay (Hutchison Telecommunications Paraguay S.A.), and Chile (Smartcom S.A.). The company expanded its grip on the South and Central American markets and was not hampered by the fact that it was no longer a part of its former telecom parent, which held a dominant grip on the Central American telecommunications market.

WEALTH EFFECTS OF SELLOFFS

A major motivating factor for divestitures and spinoffs is the belief that reverse synergy may exist. Divestitures, spinoffs, and equity carve-outs are basically a "downsizing" of the parent firm. Therefore, the smaller firm must be economically more viable by itself than as a part of its parent company. Several research studies have analyzed the impact of spinoffs by examining the effect on the stock prices of both the parent company and the spun-off entity. This effect is then compared with a market index to determine whether the stocks experience extranormal performance that cannot be explained by market movements alone. Spinoffs are a unique opportunity to analyze the effects of the separation because a market exists for both the stock of the parent company and the spun-off entity.

The research in the field of selloffs, whether they are spinoffs or other forms of asset sales such as equity carve-outs, presents a picture of clear benefits for shareholders. This is the case in early studies such as Oppenheimer (1981), Kudla and McInish (1983), and Miles and Rosenfeld (1984), or later studies such as Schipper and Smith (1986), Cusatis, Miles, and Wooldridge (1993), or J. P. Morgan (1995, 1997, 2002). Research from the 1970s through the early 1990s presents a clear pattern of positive shareholder wealth effects from corporate selloffs. This leads to strong conclusions that are not just dependent on trends that prevailed in any one time period (such as in one decade). However, in recent years there is some evidence that the market is not responding as positively to large-scale breakup announcements as it once did. This is also supported by the J. P. Morgan studies that show that the benefits they found in later years were lower than those from their earlier studies.

Early Research

Oppenheimer (1981)

In 1981, Oppenheimer and Company conducted a study of 19 major spinoffs in the 1970s.[10] It was reported that the combined value of the parent company and the spun-off entity was greater than the market value of the parent company before the spinoff in the majority of the cases considered. Of the 19 spun-off companies, 14 companies outperformed the Standard & Poor's 400 Index for 6 months after the spinoff. In addition, a portfolio of these spun-off firms yielded a 440% return during the 1970s. This exceeds a 364% return generated by small company stocks during that decade.[11]

Kudla and McInish (1983)

Kudla and McInish, in a study of six major spinoffs in the 1970s, used residuals as the measure of market-adjusted returns.[12] Their results showed a positive market reaction to the spinoffs. It is interesting that Kudla and McInish showed that the pronounced positive reaction occurred between 15 and 40 weeks before the spinoff. This indicates that the market correctly anticipated the spinoffs long before the actual event. Because the performance of a division may be actively debated in the media or the market well in advance of a decision to sever the division from the parent company, it is not surprising that the market would anticipate the parent company's reaction.

Miles and Rosenfeld (1983)

Miles and Rosenfeld conducted a study of 59 spinoffs between 1963 and 1980, focusing on the impact of the spinoff on the difference between predicted and actual returns.[13]

---

10. "The Sum of the Parts" (New York: Oppenheimer and Co., January 14, 1981).
11. *Stocks, Bills, Bonds and Inflation: 2005* (Chicago: Ibbotson Associates).
12. Ronald Kudla and Thomas McInish, "Valuation Consequences of Corporate Spin-Offs," *Review of Economics and Business Research,* March 1983, 71–77.
13. James Miles and James Rosenfeld, "An Empirical Analysis of the Effects of Spin-Off Announcements on Shareholder Wealth," *Journal of Finance,* 38(5), December 1983, 1597–1606.

Using this method, they filtered out the influence of the market. As did Kudla and McInish, Miles and Rosenfeld found that the effect of the spinoff was positive and internalized in the stock price before the actual spinoff date.

The Miles and Rosenfeld study also revealed that the positive stock price reaction was accompanied by a negative price reaction by the parent company's bonds. In effect, it seems that the wealth-increasing effects for stockholders come at the expense of the bondholders. Some analysts have interpreted this to be the result of the fact that the cash flow from the spun-off entity may no longer be relied on to meet the debt service payments. Another explanation is that, all other factors being constant, larger firms tend to receive higher bond ratings.

Price Effects of Voluntary Selloffs: Summary of Later Research

The Kudla and McInish and Miles and Rosenfeld studies of the early 1980s demonstrate the positive stock price reaction to corporate selloffs. This reaction is supported in later studies. These research findings have been summarized using an expanded version of a table originally compiled by Linn and Rozeff but with the addition of other more recent studies (Table 10.5). The table shows an increase in stockholder wealth resulting from corporate selloffs, with the positive impact on equity values ranging from 0.17 to 2.33%. The equity market clearly concludes that the voluntary selling of a division is a positive development that will result in an increase in the value of the firm's stock.

Shareholder Wealth Effects of Spinoffs: Parent and Subsidiary Effects Evidence

Cusatis, Miles, and Woolridge examined the common stock returns of both spinoffs and their former parent companies. Unlike some prior research studies, which mainly examined the shareholder returns leading up to and including the announcement of the spinoff, the study by Cusatis and co-researchers tracked the companies after the spinoff

Study	Days	Average Abnormal Returns (%)	Period Sampled	Sample Size
Alexander, Benson, and Kampmeyer (1984)	−1 through 0	0.17	1964–73	53
Hite and Owens (1984)	−1 through 0	1.50	1963–79	56
Hite, Owens, and Rogers (1987)	−50 through −5	0.69	1963–81	55
Jain (1985)	−5 through −1	0.70	1976–78	1,107
Klein (1983)	−2 through 0	1.12	1970–79	202
Linn and Rozeff (1984)	−1 through 0	1.45	1977–82	77
Loh, Bezjak, and Toms (1995)	−1 through 0	1.50	1982–87	59
Rosenfeld (1984)	−1 through 0	2.33	1963–81	62

TABLE 10.5 AVERAGE STOCK PRICE EFFECTS OF VOLUNTARY SELLOFFS

to determine what the more long-term wealth effects were. These researchers examined 815 distributions of stock in spun-off firms from 1965 to 1988.

The Cusatis, Miles, and Woolridge research presents a very favorable picture of the postevent performance of spinoffs. Both spinoffs and their parent companies showed positive abnormal returns over a period that ranged between 6 months before and 36 months after the stock distribution date.[14] Another interesting finding of Cusatis and colleagues was that both the spinoff and the parent company *were more active in takeovers* than the control group of comparable firms. This takeover activity may help explain some of the positive shareholder wealth effects. When the firms that were involved in takeovers were removed from the sample, the returns were still positive but not statistically different from zero. This suggests that spinoffs and their parent company are more likely to be involved in takeovers, and when they are, they enable their shareholders to realize takeover premiums.

CASE STUDY

AT&T BREAKUP—ONE OF THE MORE FAMOUS SPINOFFS

AT&T has undergone several restructurings in its history. Before AT&T broke up in 1984, it dominated the local and long distance telecommunications business in the United States. With an eye on more exciting industries, such as the computer business, AT&T parted ways with its "boring" local operating companies. These businesses were spun-off into seven regional operating companies: Ameritech, Bell Atlantic, BellSouth, Nynex, Pacific Telesis, Southwest Bell, and U.S. West. Several of these "Baby Bells" later merged, such as Nynex and Bell Atlantic, which combined to form Verizon, which would eventually became one of the largest telecommunications companies in the United States. AT&T shareholders received one share in each of these regional companies for every ten shares they held in AT&T. They also still owned ten shares in the new AT&T, which would prove to be a company that would engage in some of the more notable merger failures in merger history. Indeed, the surviving AT&T would eventually be acquired by one of its progeny—Southwest Bell.

The AT&T that emerged from the spinoff had the unenviable track record of conducting some of the worst mergers in history. AT&T proved to be a company that had difficulty learning from its mistakes and would proceed to initiate ever larger merger blunders. The spinoff of the operating companies allowed AT&T to enter the computer industry as an antimonopoly consent decree had prohibited it from using revenues from its telecommunications businesses to finance competitive ventures into other industries. When AT&T was unsuccessful with its computer business, it acquired NCR in a hostile acquisition and greatly overpaid after it encountered resistance from the target. Cultural rifts created further problems and AT&T eventually broke itself up into three parts.

Recovering from its wounds received in the fourth merger wave, a new management team decided to outdo their predecessors in the merger flop business. AT&T's management envied the growth and profitability of its progeny such as Verizon. It wished to be able to offer local phone services. Unfortunately, while it was once in this business, it had given it all away in the fourth merger wave so as to be able to enter the computer business, in which it failed. The fifth-wave version of AT&T wanted to gain access to local phone markets and believed that two cable targets, Media

---

14. Patrick J. Cusatis, James A. Miles, and J. Randall Woolridge, "Restructuring through Spinoffs—the Stock Market Evidence," *Journal of Financial Economics*, 33(3), June 1993, 293–311.

One and TCI, would enable it to accomplish this. It also wanted to be a one-stop shop, offering long distance, mobile, local telecommunications plus cable for its customers. Readers know to be wary when management is offering customers a one-stop shop. AT&T announced that it was paying approximately $100 billion for its two cable acquisitions. After it bought the companies (rushing the sellers through without doing its own proper due diligence), it discovered that the acquired local cable lines could not support telecommunications services without a major capital infusion. Once again, AT&T blundered in the M&A area—with each one being larger than the last one. Not long after the deals, AT&T announced it was breaking itself up—again. It is ironic that after this latest M&A debacle and breakup, AT&T was acquired in November 2005 by one of the companies it had previously spunoff, SBC. SBC then assumed the AT&T name.

J. P. Morgan's Spinoffs Studies

J. P. Morgan has conducted a series of studies on spinoffs. They have found that the market rewards companies for doing spinoffs. This is shown in Exhibit 10.4, which shows that the stock price of parent companies rises and increases sharply when companies announce that they are spinning off a division. Exhibit 10.5 shows that these effects have been greater in recent years (1998–2001) than in earlier years (1985–1997). Exhibit 10.6 shows that the larger the spinoff is, the greater this effect is. The J. P. Morgan study also shows that the gains are not restricted only to parent companies (see Exhibit 10.6). Exhibit 10.7 shows that the spinoff subsidiaries enjoy impressive gains over the 18-month study period following the spinoffs. The smaller the spun-off entity, the greater these gains were. Exhibit 10.8 shows that these effects have been greater in 1998–2001 than 1985–1997.

Rationale for a Positive Stock Price Reaction to Selloffs

When a firm decides to sell off a poorly performing division, this asset goes to another owner, who presumably will value it more highly because he or she can utilize this asset more advantageously than the seller. The seller receives cash (or sometimes other

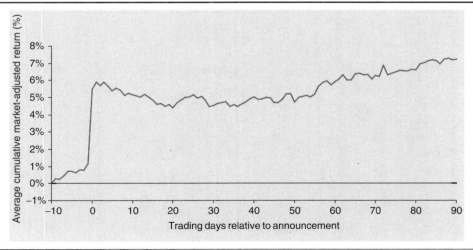

Exhibit 10.4   Parent Company Stock Price Effects of Spinoffs (123 Companies)
Source: J. P. Morgan Spinoffs Study, February 2002.

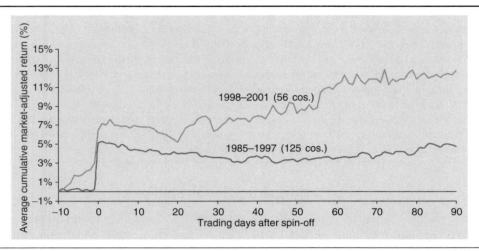

EXHIBIT 10.5 SPINOFF ANNOUNCEMENT EFFECT ON PARENT COMPANY: 1985–1997 versus 1998–2001
Source: J. P. Morgan Spinoffs Study, February 2002.

compensation) in place of the asset. When the market responds positively to this asset reallocation, it is expressing a belief that the firm will use this cash more efficiently than it was utilizing the asset that was sold. Moreover, the asset that was sold may have attracted a premium above market value, which should also cause the market to respond positively.

The selling firm has a few options at its disposal when it is contemplating the disposition of the newly acquired cash. The firm may pay the cash to stockholders in the form of a dividend, or it may repurchase its own shares at a premium. Either option is a way for the selling corporation to give its stockholders an immediate payout. If the seller retains the cash, it will be used for internal investment to expand in one of its current areas of activity or for an acquisition. The choice of another acquisition may give stockholders

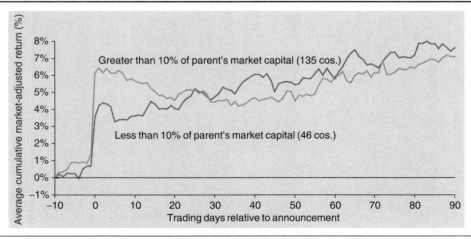

EXHIBIT 10.6 PARENT COMPANY STOCK PRICE EFFECTS OF SPINOFFS, BY SIZE OF TRANSACTION
Source: J. P. Morgan Spinoffs Study, February 2002.

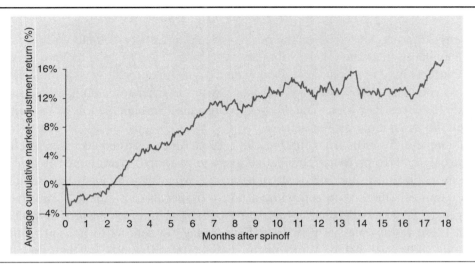

EXHIBIT 10.7 SPUN-OFF SUBSIDIARY STOCK PRICE EFFECT (SPINOFF SUBSIDIARY SHARE PERFORMANCE: FIRST 18 Months; SAMPLE: 190 COMPANIES)

Source: J. P. Morgan Spinoffs Study, February 2002.

cause for concern. The fact that acquisitions may have a dampening effect on stock prices has been documented in some financial research. (See Chapter 4.)

Another argument in favor of the value-increasing effects of selloffs is that the market might find it difficult to evaluate highly diversified companies. The validity of this argument is a matter of considerable debate because it implies that the market is somewhat inefficient. If the market is inefficient in evaluating these types of firms, the sale of one or more divisions might facilitate categorization of the parent company. The greater ease of categorization and evaluation would encourage investors who are looking to invest in certain types of companies.

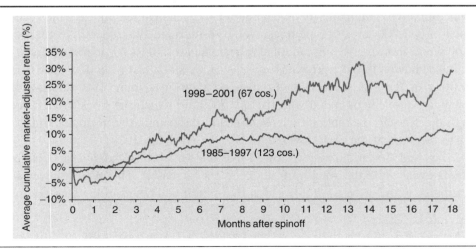

EXHIBIT 10.8 SPINOFF SUBSIDIARY SHARE PERFORMANCE: 1985–1997 VERSUS 1998–2001

Source: J. P. Morgan Spinoffs Study, February 2002.

Wealth Effects of Voluntary Defensive Selloffs

We discussed in previous sections the positive wealth effects of voluntary selloffs. There is some evidence that when these voluntary selloffs are used as an antitakeover defense, positive effects may not exist. Loh, Bezjak, and Toms found positive shareholder wealth effects to voluntary selloffs that are consistent with the other research that has been discussed.[15] However, they found that this positive response was not present when companies used selloffs as an antitakeover defense.

In a sample of 59 firms from 1980 to 1987, 13 of which featured takeover speculation, Loh, Bezjak, and Toms found cumulative average abnormal return equal to 1.5% over a one-day period up to the selloff date. However, when they divided their sample into two subsamples—those with and without takeover speculation—the 13 firms that were the targets of takeover speculation failed to show any significant changes in shareholder wealth. These results suggest that when firms engage in selloffs to prevent themselves from being taken over, the market treats the transactions differently and does not consider it a positive change.

Wealth Effects of Involuntary Selloffs

Most research studies on the effects of selloffs on stockholder wealth conclude that selloffs increase the wealth of parent company stockholders and that the market is somewhat efficient in anticipating the event. Therefore, the stock price reaction occurs in advance of the actual selloff date. The wealth-increasing effects of a selloff of an unwanted or poorly performing subsidiary should be different from those of a parent company being forced to divest itself of a profitable division. This was the case when Santa Fe–Southern Pacific received its unfavorable ruling requiring it to divest itself of the Southern Pacific Railway. As noted previously, the stock price declined and Santa Fe became a takeover target.

In 1981, Kudla and McInish conducted a case study of the effects of the required spinoff of the Louisiana-Pacific Corporation by Georgia-Pacific, the parent company.[16] The spinoff was required by the Federal Trade Commission (FTC), which concluded that the acquisition of 16 companies in the southern part of the United States, which accounted for a total of 673,000 acres of pine trees, would result in an anticompetitive concentration in the plywood industry. Using cumulative residuals to adjust for market effects, Kudla and McInish showed that the price of Georgia-Pacific stock had been declining before the formal filing of the FTC complaint. Louisiana-Pacific was spun off in 1972. However, this downward movement ended with the spinoff, after which the stock price rebounded. Although the stock price rebound was significant, the cumulative residuals did not fully recover to the start of the 1971 level, even as late as March 1974.

The Miles and Rosenfeld study showed that the wealth of bondholders declined after the spinoff even while the wealth of stockholders increased. This was believed to have been attributed to the lower cash flows after the spinoff and the resulting increase in risk to

15. Charmen Loh, Jennifer Russell Bezjak, and Harrison Toms, "Voluntary Corporate Divestitures as Antitakeover Mechanisms," *The Financial Review,* 30(1), February 1995, 41–60.
16. Ronald Kudla and Thomas McInish, "The Microeconomic Consequences of an Involuntary Corporate Spin-Off," *Sloan Management Review,* 22(4), 1981, 41–46.

bondholders. Kudla and McInish attempted to measure the risk effects of the involuntary Louisiana-Pacific spinoff by examining the betas of Georgia-Pacific before and after the spinoff. The betas would then reflect any change in the systematic or undiversifiable risk associated with Georgia-Pacific stock. Kudla and McInish found a large, statistically significant increase in the betas of Georgia-Pacific after the spinoff. They attributed this increase to the market's perception that Georgia-Pacific incurred a decrease in monopoly power after the spinoff and that this caused the firm to be riskier.

The finance research community seems to have reached a consensus that a divestiture that is forced by government mandate, as opposed to a voluntary selloff, will have an adverse effect on the divesting firm's stock price. Ellert's review of 205 defendants in antitrust merger lawsuits showed a 21.86% decline in the value of the equity of these firms during the month the complaint was filed.[17] The issue that the Kudla and McInish study addresses is the timing of that impact and the reversal of the declining trend.

If the antitrust enforcement is effective in reducing the selling firm's monopoly power, this should be reflected in an *increase* in the value of the equity of that firm's competitors. Unfortunately, the antitrust authorities can find little support for their actions in the stock prices of the competitors of divesting firms.[18] The value of the equity of competitors of divesting firms failed to show a significant positive response to mandated selloffs.

Wealth Effects of Selloffs on Buyers

The preceding discussion focused on the wealth effects to stockholders and bondholders of the selling companies. Jain also analyzed the shareholder wealth effects for the buying company.[19] In his large sample event study, which included 304 buyers and 1,062 sellers (not all the buyers were known), he found that buyers earn a statistically significant positive excess return of 0.34%.

Jain's results show that selloffs are good news for both sellers and buyers, although sellers gain more than buyers. It is also interesting that the sales did not seem to take place in an active auction process. In most instances, Jain failed to find more than one bidder coming forward to try to buy the sold-off entity. This raises the question of what the shareholder wealth effects would be if the units were sold in a more auction-like environment.

CASE STUDY

CENDANT—SPLITUP OF A CONGLOMERATE

In October 2005, the board of directors announced that it had approved a proposal to split up Cendant, an $18 billion conglomerate that had been built through a series of acquisitions over many

---

17. James C. Ellert, "Mergers, Antitrust Law Enforcement and the Behavior of Stock Prices," *Journal of Finance*, 31 (1976), pp. 715–732.

18. Robert Stillman, "Examining Antitrust Policy Towards Horizontal Mergers," *Journal of Financial Economics*, 11, 1983, 225–240; and Bjorn E. Eckbo, "Horizontal Mergers, Collusion and Stockholder Wealth," *Journal of Financial Economics*, 11, 1983, 241–274.

19. Prem C. Jain, "Sell-Off Announcements and Shareholder Wealth," *Journal of Finance*, 40(1), March 1985, 209–224.

years. The Cendant of 2005 included real estate companies, Century 21 and Coldwell Banker; car rental businesses Avis, the second largest car rental company in the United States, as well as Budget; hotel chains Days Inn, Ramada, and Super 8; and hotel chains and travel companies Orbitz, Cheaptickets.com, and Galileo International (an international network of travel agents). The company merged with CUC International in 1997, and that deal was a disaster due to the bogus financials of CUC. CUC proved to be one of the bigger financial frauds in history. While the stock price took a difficult short-term hit due to this problem, it recovered due to the fact that the upper management of Cendant, including its CEO Henry Silverman, were not involved in this fraud and were working hard to correct the problem. However, over the years 2003–2005, while the market steadily grew, Cendant stock was weak and even declined (see Exhibit A). Management finally came to the resolution that the market did not understand or like the confusing combination of companies housed within the Cendant corporate structure.

In 2004, Cendant recognized that its conglomerate structure was a problem. It tried to take some steps to correct it while not really admitting that the whole overall structure was problematic. Toward that end, the company parted ways with its mortgage business, PHH Corp.; the Jackson Hewitt Tax Services business; and Wright Express, which is a fleet management company. PHH Corp. was spun off while Cendant did an equity carve-out of its Jackson Hewitt unit. Jackson Hewitt is an example of a business, tax preparation, which is pretty far removed from the other, travel-related businesses housed within Cendant. Its combination with Cendant's other businesses made little sense. The market liked these deals as the stock performance of the carved-out businesses had exceeded that of Cendant.

Before approving the splitup, Cendant's board considered other options such as leveraged recapitalization and more sales of other business units.[a] However, the board finally decided that halfway measures would not fix the problem and that the market wanted more focused businesses, not the

[a]Ryan Chittum, "Cendant to Split into Four Firms," *Wall Street Journal*, October 24, 2005, A3.

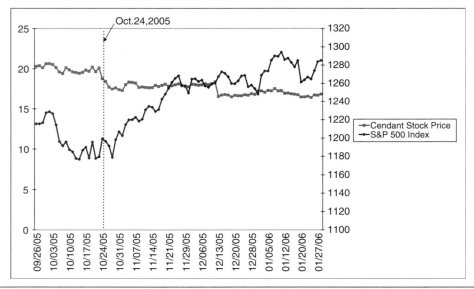

EXHIBIT A CENDANT STOCK PRICE VERSUS S&P 500 INDEX
Source: Yahoo! Finance.

combination that CEO Silverman had put together. The combination may have worked well for Silverman and his personal goals, but not for investors.

THE FOUR NEW BUSINESSES FORMED FROM THE SPLITUP ARE:

1. Travel
2. Car rental
3. Hospitality/hotels
4. Real estate

When we look at the preceding combinations, one can see that the first three have a common travel connection, so one could theorize that there might be synergistic benefits. However, all one has to do is to look back at other attempts to combine such travel businesses, such as what United Airlines tried to do, to discover that extracting synergies from such combinations would be hard. However, one lesson we are always aware of in M&As is that managers and investors have short memories and tend to repeatedly make the same mistakes as were made in the past.

Corporate Focus and Spinoffs

A study of 85 spinoffs between 1975 and 1991 by Daley, Mehrotra, and Sivakumar examined the relationship between spinoffs and corporate focus by comparing the performance of spinoff firms when the parent company and the spun-off entity were in two different Standard Industrial Classification (SIC) codes (cross-industry spinoffs) relative to instances in which both were in the same SIC code (own industry spinoffs).[20] They found improvements in various measures of performance, such as the return on assets, for cross-industry spinoffs but not for own industry deals. They conclude that cross-industry spinoffs create value only when they result in an increase in corporate focus. They attribute the performance improvements to companies removing unrelated businesses and allowing managers to concentrate their efforts on the core business and removing the distraction of noncore entities.

--- CASE STUDY ---

LARGE CORPORATE BREAKUPS OF THE 2000s

In recent years a number of large diversified firms announced plans to break up the company into several separate parts. One was Cendant (see Case Study: Cendant—Splitup of a Conglomerate). Others included Dun & Bradstreet, Sara Lee, Tyco, and Viacom. Sara Lee was not a total corporate breakup but was a large sale of assets that were initially valued at approximately $8.2 billion. The announced asset sale covered just under one-half of Sara Lee's revenues. In the move Sara Lee, whose name we associate with cakes, planned to sell off its coffee, clothing, meat, and direct selling businesses while concentrating on food, drinks, and household products. This was a major move for Sara Lee as Hanes, with its line of T-shirts and underwear, was the company's largest brand. This sale came four years after the company sold off the luxury maker Coach it acquired in 1985. The apparel business also includes Champion and Wonderbra. While the sales announced in early

---

20. Lane Daley, Vikas Mehrotra, and Ranjini Sivakumar, "Corporate Focus and Value Creation: Evidence from Spinoffs," *Journal of Financial Economics*, 45(2), August 1997, 257–281.

2005 improved Sara Lee's focus, the stock trended downward in the year that followed, while the market improved (see Exhibit A).

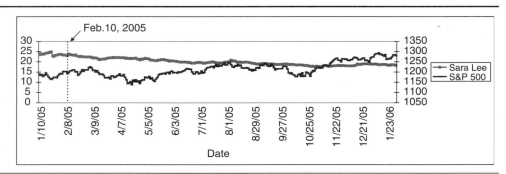

EXHIBIT A   SARA LEE STOCK PRICE COMPARED TO THE MARKET JANUARY 2005–FEBRUARY 2006
Source: Yahoo! Finance.

The picture is somewhat comparable for other large-scale recent breakup announcements. In March 2005, Viacom announced that it was dividing the company into two parts, essentially reversing its acquisition of CBS in September 1999. This announcement came right after the diversified media company announced an $18 billion write-down related to its outdoor advertising business. At that time Viacom's stock was trading in the mid-40s, but by the end of 2005 it was in the low 30s. However, the breakup announcement only gave the company's stock a brief boost and it continued to sag for the remainder of 2005. The company continued to try to find answers to its weak stock price. In February 2006, it announced that the new Viacom would be authorized to conduct a $3 billion stock buyback, which investors preferred to another acquisition, which had been its past strategy. (See Exhibit B.) Unable to admit their error, though, Viacom management continued to defend the acquisition of CBS.

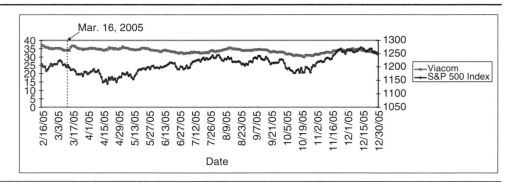

EXHIBIT B   VIACOM STOCK PRICE VERSUS S&P 500 INDEX
Source: Yahoo! Finance.

The stock price performance of Tyco and Dun & Bradstreet also presents a similar picture of negative stock price performance after the breakup announcements. On January 13, 2006, Tyco announced that it was splitting itself up into three parts, thereby parting ways with its electronics ($12 billion in sales) and health care ($12 billion in sales) units. Similarly, in January 1996, Dun &

Bradstreet announced that it would divide itself into three parts that include Cognizant, which does technology research; a media and marketing information entity that includes Neilson Media, A.C. Neilson, and IMS Int'l; and the new Dun & Bradstreet, which provides financial data while also operating Moody's. Just 14 months after this breakup, Cognizant announced that it would break itself up by separating the IMS and Neilson businesses. (See Exhibits C and D.)

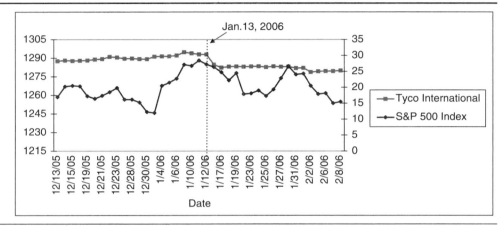

EXHIBIT C   TYCO INTERNATIONAL STOCK PRICE VERSUS S&P 500 INDEX
Source: Yahoo! Finance.

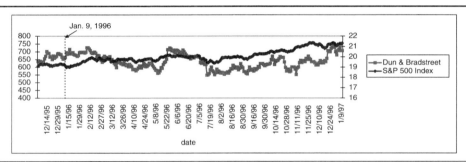

EXHIBIT D   DUN & BRADSTREET STOCK PRICE VERSUS S&P 500 INDEX
Source: Yahoo! Finance.

What does the negative stock price performance of these breakup announcements say? Is it an indictment of breakups? This is not a reasonable conclusion. The breakups were announced in response to weak stock price performances of these inefficient corporate structures. The market did not like the companies before the announcements and continues to have reservations about them afterward. Some of them, such as Viacom, were led by empire-building CEOs, such as Sumner Redstone, who assembled a diverse media conglomerate, based on acquisitions such as Paramount Pictures and CBS, that the market failed to endorse. Even after the breakup, the company remains under the leadership of managers who helped build an empire the market did not like. In the case of Tyco, the breakup of part of the empire the now-imprisoned Dennis Kozlowski built fails to impress the market. These breakups are only partial steps to fixing the deeper problems of these companies. These companies attempted to grow through a strategy based on failed mergers. They need widespread management and strategy changes, not just a quick-fix breakup.

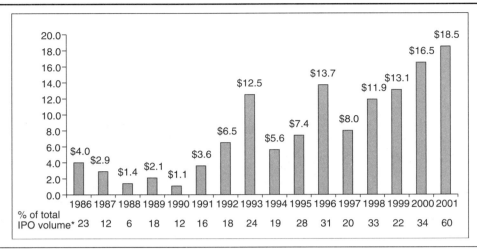

EXHIBIT 10.9   CARVE-OUT VOLUME, 1986–2001

Source: J. P. Morgan Carve-out Study.
*U.S. Carve-outs (principal/amount)/U.S. IPO volume

EQUITY CARVE-OUTS

Equity carve-outs became a popular financing technique in the late 1980s, even though the market for public offerings was poor. Companies such as Enron Corporation, W. R. Grace, Hanson Trust, and Macmillan decided that equity carve-outs provided significant financial advantages over other forms of restructuring. Between 1987 and 1989, the ten largest equity carve-outs totaled $13.92 billion, even though the initial public offering (IPO) market was depressed.[21]

When the fourth merger wave came to an end, equity carve-out volume declined but then rose sharply starting in 1991. The volume of these deals remained relatively high throughout the fifth merger wave (see Exhibit 10.9).

When a parent company conducts an equity carve-out it may sell a 100% interest in the subsidiary, or it may choose to remain in the subsidiary's line of business by selling only a partial interest and keeping the remaining percentage of ownership. This was the case, for example, when the Neoax Corporation chose to sell a 53% ownership in a trucking business that it had acquired in March 1988 in a highly leveraged transaction.[22] Neoax sold this ownership interest in the trucking company, which it had renamed Landstar, for $94 million. The transaction enabled Neoax to maintain a reduced total debt load while providing the firm with the option to regain control of the trucking company in the future. Neoax also received a value for the division that was consistent with its internal valuation analysis, which showed that the entire division was worth $200 million. Efforts to sell the division outright failed to attract offers near this value.

Many firms look to equity carve-outs as a means of reducing their exposure to a riskier line of business. For example, American Express bought the brokerage firm Shearson in

---

21. Susan Jarzombek, "A Way to Put a Spotlight on Unseen Value," *Corporate Finance,* December 1989, 62–64.
22. Ibid.

1981. It later acquired the investment bank Lehman Brothers to form Shearson Lehman. This is a riskier line of business than American Express's traditional credit card operations. American Express later decided that, although it liked the synergy that came with being a diversified financial services company, it wanted to reduce its exposure to the risks of the securities business. In 1987, Amexco, its holding company, sold off a 39% interest in Shearson Lehman. This proved to be fortuitous because the sale preceded the stock market crash, an event that securities firms still had not recovered from by the end of the 1980s. The company would later completely undo these acquisitions. American Express would further streamline its business in 2005, when it spun off its personal finance unit, which became Ameriprise Financial, Inc. This is yet another example of a related business that appeared to have valuable synergies but that in reality did not.

Equity Carve-out Transactions Data: J. P. Morgan Study

In 1998, J. P. Morgan conducted a study of equity carve-out transactions in 1998.[23] They found the market to be quite robust, with equity carve-outs constituting 23% of the total IPO market or a total of $9 billion in 1997. Consistent with the research in this field, they also found a positive stock price reaction for parent companies. This effect was greater for larger carve-outs relative to smaller transactions. One interesting finding of this study was that carve-outs tended not to remain public very long after the transaction. Only approximately 37% remained in their original form three years after the carve-out. Approximately 15% were required by the parent company, whereas 11% were sold to a third party.

Characteristics of Equity Carve-out Firms and the Disposition of Carve-out Proceeds

Allen and McConnell conducted a study of the financial characteristics of firms that undertook equity carve-outs. They analyzed 188 carve-outs between 1978 and 1993.[24] They found that carve-out subsidiaries tended to have poorer operating performance and higher leverage than their industry counterparts. As Table 10.6 shows, pre-carve-out firms

Performance Measure	Pre-Carve-Out Firms	Industry Peers
EBDIT/Interest	2.29	5.42
Long-term debt/Total assets	0.260	0.220
Total debt/Total assets	0.331	0.285
EBDIT/Sales	0.070	0.103

TABLE 10.6   COMPARISON OF PRE-CARVE-OUT FIRMS WITH INDUSTRY PEERS

Source: Jeffrey Allen and John J. McConnell, "Equity Carve Outs and Managerial Discretion," Journal of Finance 53(1), (February 1998) pp. 163–186.

---

23. *J. P. Morgan Equity Carve Out Study,* July 17, 1998.
24. Jeffrey Allen and John J. McConnell, "Equity Carve Outs and Managerial Discretion," *Journal of Finance,* 53(1), February 1998, 163–186.

have lower interest coverage and higher ratios of long-term debt and total debt to total assets. They also had lower ratios of EBDIT (earnings before depreciation, interest, and taxes) to sales and total assets. Allen and McConnell also traced the use of the carve-out proceeds. They found that when the funds were used to pay down debt, the company showed an average excess return of +6.63%, whereas when the funds were retained for investment purposes, the company experienced a −0.01% return.

Equity Carve-outs versus Public Offerings

An equity carve-out, as opposed to a spinoff, brings in new capital to the parent company. Because the acquisition of capital is obviously a motivating factor for this type of selloff, we must investigate why the equity carve-out option may be chosen over a public offering of stock. Katherine Schipper and Abbie Smith conducted a study of equity carve-outs that examined the share price reactions to 76 carve-out announcements. They compared these reactions with previous studies documenting the stock price reactions to public equity offerings.[25] Previous studies have shown that the announcement of seasoned equity offerings results in an abnormal stock return of between 22% and 23% in the periods around the equity offering.[26] In contrast to other equity financing arrangements, Schipper and Smith found that equity carve-outs increase shareholder wealth. Schipper and Smith found that the shareholders of the parent firms experienced average gains of 1.8%. They compared this positive stock price effect with a 23% shareholder loss for a subset of parent firms that engaged in public offerings of common stock or debt.

Schipper and Smith propose that the positive stock price reactions are due to a combination of effects, including better and more defined information available about both the parent and the subsidiary. This is clear to those who have attempted to evaluate the subsidiaries of a publicly held company. The annual reports and other publicly available documents may be very brief and yield little of the data necessary to value the components of a company. When the subsidiary becomes a standalone public company, it publishes more detailed information about its operations because its activities are its only line of business, as opposed to merely being a part of a larger parent company.

Schipper and Smith also point out other possible factors responsible for the positive stock price reaction to equity carve-outs, such as the restructuring and asset management that tend to be associated with equity carve-outs. In addition, divisions may be consolidated into a more efficient form, and managers may work with new compensation incentives. The combination of these and other changes may make the subsidiary a more viable entity as a separate public company. The market's perception of this value may be a source of a premium for the selling company. The parent company, no longer encumbered by a subsidiary that it could not manage as well as another owner might, becomes more valuable when it converts this asset into cash, which it can, it is hoped, invest in more productive areas.

---

25. Katherine Schipper and Abbie Smith, "A Comparison of Equity Carve-Outs and Seasonized Equity Offerings," *Journal of Financial Economics,* 15, January/February 1986, 153–186.
26. For a review of some of this literature and additional research showing that the effects of stock offerings are more negative for industrial firms than for public utilities, see Ronald W. Masulis and Ashok N. Korwar, "Seasonized Equity Offerings," *Journal of Financial Economics,* 15(11), January/February 1986, 91–118.

Equity Carve-outs versus Spinoffs

There are a number of important differences between spinoffs and equity carve-outs. A carve-out results in a new set of shareholders, whereas the same shareholders hold stock in the spun-off entity as in the parent company. There are positive cash flow effects in carve-outs, but spinoffs do not result in initial changes in parent company cash flows. Carve-outs are more expensive to implement and are subject to greater securities law disclosure requirements.

In a study of 91 master limited partnerships (MLPs) that were created between 1981 and 1989, Michaely and Shaw found that for their sample riskier and more highly leveraged firms chose to go the spinoff route rather than to opt for a carve-out.[27] They show in their study that bigger, less leveraged, and more profitable firms chose the carve-out option. They conclude that the equity carve-out versus spinoff decision is determined by access to capital markets. Those companies that have better access, that is, more desirable firms in better financial condition, will choose to market themselves to public markets and enjoy the positive cash flow effects of an equity carve-out. Less desirable firms will be forced to choose the spinoff route. It should be noted that although it may seem that the Michaely and Shaw results contradict those of Allen and McConnell reported earlier, this is not the case. The Allen and McConnell results show a comparison of carve-out firms with industry peers, whereas the Michaely and Shaw study compares firms that did carve-outs with those that did spinoffs.

This study clearly does not explain all spinoff versus equity carve-out decisions. It does not address, for example, the large spinoffs of 1995, such as the ITT and AT&T deals. However, the Michaely and Shaw research results provide much useful insight into other types of transactions.

VOLUNTARY LIQUIDATIONS, OR BUSTUPS

Voluntary liquidations, or bustups, are the most extreme form of corporate restructuring. Corporate liquidations are more often associated with bankruptcy. A company may be liquidated in bankruptcy when all parties concerned recognize that the continuation of the firm in a reorganized form will not enhance its value. The outlook, however, is not as negative for voluntary liquidations. In a voluntary liquidation, the general criterion applied is as follows: If the market value of the firm's assets significantly exceeds the value of the firm's equity, a liquidation may need to be seriously considered. This is not to imply that liquidation should be an alternative in instances of a temporary downturn of the firm's stock. The liquidation option becomes viable only when the firm's stock has been depressed for an extended time. The liquidation option becomes even more likely when the stock prices of other firms in the same industry are not also depressed. In addition, low price-earnings (P/E) ratios may sometimes point to a need to consider the liquidation option. Managers are often reluctant to consider such a drastic step, which would result in their loss of position. They may prefer to sell the entire firm to a single acquirer

27. Roni Michaely and Wayne H. Shaw, "The Choice of Going Public: Spinoffs vs. Carve Outs," *Financial Management,* 24(3), Autumn 1995, 5–21.

rather than pursue liquidation. Stockholders sometimes try to force management's hand by threatening a proxy battle to decide the issue.

Voluntary liquidations may be contrasted with divestitures. A divestiture is generally a single transaction in which a certain part of the firm is sold, whereas a voluntary liquidation is a series of transactions in which all the firm's assets are sold in separate parcels. Tax motives may make a liquidation more attractive than a divestiture. Divestitures may be subject to capital gains taxes, whereas voluntary liquidations may often be structured to receive more preferential tax treatment.

Shareholder Wealth Effects of Voluntary Bustups

Skantz and Marchesini's study of liquidation announcements made by 37 firms from 1970 to 1982 showed an average excess return of 21.4% during the month of the announcement.[28] Hite, Owers, and Rogers found similar positive shareholder wealth effects during the month of the announcement of voluntary liquidations made by the 49 firms in their sample, which covered the years 1966 to 1975.[29] They showed a positive abnormal return in the announcement month equal to 13.62%. Almost half the firms in their sample had been the object of a bid for control within two years of the announcement of the liquidation plan. These bids included a wide range of actions, including leveraged buyouts (LBOs), tender offers, and proxy contests. Moreover, more than 80% of the firms in their sample showed positive abnormal returns. This suggests that the stock market agreed that continued operation of the firm under its prior operating policy will reduce shareholder wealth.

The positive stock market reaction was affirmed by two other studies. Kim and Schatzberg found a 14% positive return for 73 liquidating firms during a 3-day period associated with the liquidation announcement.[30] They revealed that a 3% return was added when shareholders confirmed the transaction. Kim and Schatzberg failed to detect any significant wealth effect, either positive or negative, for the shareholders of the acquiring firms. In a study of 61 publicly traded firms that completed voluntary liquidations between 1970 and 1991, Erwin and McConnell found that voluntary liquidations were associated with an even higher average excess stock return of 20%.[31] They also confirmed the intuitive expectation that firms that decide to voluntarily liquidate face limited growth prospects. The liquidation decision is the rational one because it releases financial resources to be applied to higher yielding alternatives. As suggested previously, these research studies imply that the stock market often agrees that the continued operation of the firm under its prior operating policy will reduce shareholder wealth. This is not surprising because most firms that are considering liquidation are suffering serious problems.

28. Terrence Skantz and Roberto Marchesini, "The Effect of Voluntary Corporate Liquidation on Shareholder Wealth," *Journal of Financial Research,* 10, Spring 1987, 65–75.
29. Gailen Hite, James Owers, and Ronald Rogers, "The Market for Interfirm Asset Sales: Partial Selloffs and Total Liquidations," *Journal of Financial Economics,* 18, June 1987, 229–252.
30. E. Han Kim and John Schatzberg, "Voluntary Corporate Liquidations," *Journal of Financial Economics,* 19(2), December 1987, 311–328.
31. Gayle R. Erwin and John J. McConnell, "To Live or Die? An Empirical Analysis of Piecemeal Voluntary Liquidations," *Journal of Corporate Finance,* 3(4), December 1997, 325–354.

Liquidation then releases the firm's assets to other companies that might be able to realize a higher return on them.

TRACKING STOCKS

In the 1990s, companies began to issue tracking stocks as an alternative to selloffs. A tracking or targeted stock is an equity issue that represents an interest in the earnings of a division of a company. It also is sometimes called *letter stock* or *alphabet stock.* Sometimes when a company acquires other firms but the market prices of the combined entity sell at a discount, the company may try to boost the stock by allowing one or more divisions to trade separately as tracking stocks. AT&T did this with its AT&T Wireless segment.

Tracking stocks were first created in 1984, when General Motors (GM) acquired Electronic Data Systems (EDS). Ross Perot, the colorful CEO of EDS, was concerned that employees, who owned significant shareholdings in the company, would be less motivated if they received shares in slow-growth GM in exchange for their fast-growing shares in EDS. As a solution, they issued Class E shares, which tracked the performance of the EDS division of GM. General Motors also used this mechanism in 1985 when it issued Class H shares, which followed the performance of its Hughes Aircraft division.

Tracking stocks have also been used as a defense measure when a company is confronted with a large and somewhat hostile shareholder. This was the case in 1991, when Carl Ichan, a holder of 13% of USX, demanded that the company spin off the steel division of the company, which owned U.S. Steel and Marathon Oil. As an alternative and less drastic step, the company issued a tracking stock for its steel and oil divisions.

One of the major differences between tracking stocks and selloffs is that a separate legal entity is created in a selloff. With a tracking stock, the shareholder has a legal interest in the earnings of a division, but that division remains part of the overall company. Holders of targeted stock usually still retain their voting rights in the overall company. In some instances, however, such as in the USX case, these voting rights may be adjusted based on the market valuation of the targeted shares.

Tracking stocks do not represent an ownership interest in the assets of the entity being tracked. This may make one wonder why the company does not simply do a spinoff that would give holders shares that have such an interest. However, it may be the case that the transaction would not qualify for tax-free treatment and this would eliminate one of the advantages of a spinoff.

As with announcements of selloffs, the market tends to react positively to announcements of tracking stocks. D'Souza and Jacob found a statistically significant 3.61% stock price reaction within a three-day window of an announcement of proposed tracking stock issues.[32] D'Souza and Jacob tried to determine whether the creation of tracking stocks achieves some of the same benefits that a company would receive if it were a totally independent entity. They examined the correlation between the returns of the tracking stock and the overall firm, as well as the correlation between the returns of the tracking

---

32. Julia D'Souza and John Jacob, "Why Firms Issue Targeted Stock," *Journal of Financial Economics,* 56(3), June 2000, 459–483.

stock and similar firms in the tracking stock's industry. They found a greater correlation between parent firms and tracking stock returns than the returns between the tracking stocks and their industry counterparts. That is, they found that the "firm effect" was greater than the "industry effect." They postulate that the firm effect exists because of all the shared resources and liabilities that exist between the division and the parent company. Clearly, a tracking stock is an intermediate step between being totally independent and staying within the parent company.

MASTER LIMITED PARTNERSHIPS AND SELLOFFS

Master limited partnerships (MLPs) are limited partnerships in which the shares are publicly traded. A limited partnership consists of a general partner and one or more limited partners. The general partner runs the business and bears unlimited liability. This is one of the major disadvantages of this form of business organization compared with a corporation. In a corporation, the owners—the stockholders—are insulated from the company's liabilities. The limited partners in the MLP, however, do not incur the liability exposure of the general partner.

The key advantage of the MLP is its elimination of the corporate layer of taxation. Stockholders in a corporation are taxed twice on their investments: first at the corporate level and then, as distributions in the form of dividends, at the individual level. Master limited partnerships are not taxed as a separate business entity, and the returns to the business flow through to the owners just as they do in other partnerships. This advantage was strengthened by the 1986 Tax Reform Act, which lowered the highest personal income tax bracket to 28% (which is less than the top corporate rate of 34%). This advantage was reduced when the tax law was changed in later years to raise the rate charged in the upper tax bracket.

Corporations have used MLPs to redistribute assets so that their returns are not subject to double taxation. In a *roll-out* MLP, corporations may transfer assets or divisions in separate MLPs. Stockholders in the corporation are then given units of ownership in the MLP while maintaining their shares in the corporation. The income distributed by the MLP is not subject to double taxation.

MLPs may be involved in either spinoffs or equity carve-outs. In a spinoff, assets are directly transferred from the parent company to the MLP. Parent company shareholders receive MLP units on a pro rata basis. In an equity carve-out, the MLP raises cash through a public offering. This cash is then used to purchase assets of the division of the parent company that is being sold off.

MLPs have been popular in the petroleum industry. Oil companies have distributed oil and gas assets into MLPs, allowing the returns to flow through directly to stockholders without double taxation. Initially, start-up businesses may also be structured as MLPs. The MLP may be run by a general partner who receives an income from managing the business. The general partner may or may not own a unit in the MLP. Capital is raised through an initial sale of MLP units to investors.

MLPs are generally held by individuals as opposed to corporations, which are predominantly owned by institutional investors. This trend may be explained by observing several differences between corporations and MLPs. Limited partners in MLPs do not have control, which is an attribute that institutions are starting to value more. Moreover, corporate shareholders are normally taxed on their MLP income as opposed to the exclusion they would qualify for if they were receiving dividends from another corporation. In addition, even institutions that are normally tax exempt may have their MLP income taxed. For these reasons, MLPs are not very attractive to institutions.

CASE STUDY

ITT—DISSOLUTION OF THE QUINTESSENTIAL CONGLOMERATE

On June 13, 1995, the ITT Corporation announced that it would split the giant conglomerate that was constructed during the third merger wave through the acquisition of many dissimilar businesses throughout the world. The transaction was one of the largest of its kind in history. It involved the creation of three separate public companies, each with its own board of directors and each listed on the New York Stock Exchange. Holders of ITT stock received one share of stock in each of the new companies.

The breakup of ITT, once known as the International Telephone and Telegraph company, was an endorsement of the belief that the sum of the parts of the company, as standalone entities, was worth more than the value of them combined under the ITT umbrella. It was difficult to find many commonalities or synergies in ITT's diverse business interests; that is, it is a stretch to say that casinos and hockey teams have much in common with casualty insurance or the hotel business.

One of the clear benefits of splitting the company up was better access to capital.

"We just think that having these three companies acting and operating and being evaluated in their own business environment will provide investors, analysts and those who deploy debt a simpler, more clear way to evaluate us," said the chairman, president and chief executive of ITT, Rand V. Araskog . . . .[a]

The $25 billion conglomerate that was built by Harold Geneen was split into three companies: an insurance company, ITT Hartford; an industrial products firm, ITT Industries; and a casino, hotel, and sports company, ITT Corporation. During the 1960s and 1970s, ITT had acquired more than 250 companies, including Avis Rent A Car, Continental Baking Company, Canteen, Rayonier, Sheraton Hotels, Hartford Insurance Company, and others.[b] ITT sold what was originally its core business in 1986. At that time, it sold its telecommunications operations to Alcatel Alsthom (CGE France).

The three new companies each included divisions that shared common elements for which there might be some synergies. For example, many of the managerial skills and administrative systems necessary to run a hotel are somewhat similar to those of casinos. Within the new ITT Corporation, Sheraton and Ciga hotels were combined. Also included in this company were the Madison Square Garden (MSG) sports arena, along with two of the major users of the arena, the New York Knickerbockers and the New York Rangers. In addition, the company had a partnership arrangement with Cablevision System Corporation—the New York cable television company that offers the MSG cable programming that televises the games of these teams. In 1997, ITT sold Madison Square Garden and its interests in the sports teams to Cablevision.

[a]Stephanie Storm, "ITT the Quintessential Conglomerate, Plans to Split Up," *New York Times,* June 14, 1995, D1.
[b]ITT Company Press Release, June 13, 1995.

The breakup of ITT was typical of the transactions that took place in the mid-1990s, when the pressure to increase efficiency rather than pursue convoluted acquisitions strategies was the way of the day. Whereas the third and fourth merger waves featured many questionable acquisitions, the early to mid-1990s featured more strategic acquisitions, which were closer to two merging companies' core businesses, in addition to the unraveling of many of the poorly conceived deals of earlier periods.

SUMMARY

Corporate restructuring is often warranted when the current structure of the corporation is not yielding values that are consistent with market or management's expectations. It may occur when a given part of a company no longer fits into management's plans. Other restructuring may be necessary when a prior acquisition has not performed up to management's expectations. The decision to sell may be difficult because it requires management to admit that the firm made a mistake when it acquired the asset that is being sold. Once the decision to sell has been made, management must decide how the sale will be implemented.

Managers may consider several of the different options discussed in this chapter, such as a straightforward sale, or divestiture, or the sale of an equity interest in a subsidiary to outsiders, which is an equity carve-out. In both cases, a separate legal entity is created and the divested entity is run by a new management team as a standalone company. An alternative that also results in the creation of a separate legal entity is a spinoff. In a spinoff, shares are issued on a pro rata basis and distributed to the parent company's shareholders, also on a pro rata basis. When the transaction is structured so that shares in the original company are exchanged for shares in the parent firm, the deal is called a splitoff. A splitup occurs when the entire firm is broken up and shareholders exchange their shares in the parent company according to a predetermined formula.

Empirical research has found that a significant number of selloffs are associated with positive shareholder wealth effects for parent company shareholders. This implies that the market agrees that the sale of part of the company will yield a higher return than the continued operation of the division under current operating policies. The market is indicating that the proceeds of the sale of the firm may be used more advantageously than the division that is being sold. The market also has responded with a positive stock price response for shareholders in the divested or spun-off entities. Research results also show positive stock price effects for announcements of voluntary liquidations.

The positive market response to restructuring paints this form of corporate change in a favorable light. Other forms of corporate downsizing, such as large-scale employee layoffs, also are quite common in the 1990s. Although this type of restructuring has been criticized because it is often associated with employee duress, it is partially responsible for the improvement in U.S. productivity in the 1990s. The declining unemployment rate in the economy at a time when the corporate downsizing was ongoing confirms the fact that the firm-specific unemployment associated with downsizing does not result in net unemployment.

11

RESTRUCTURING IN BANKRUPTCY

As noted, merger and acquisition (M&A) volume tends to move with the ups and downs of the economy. This was the case, for example, with both the fourth and fifth merger waves. As with the three prior merger waves, both the fourth and fifth waves ended with downturns in the economy and market. Such economic downturns tend to be associated with lower economic demand, which puts pressure on weaker companies. This pressure may be felt more by those companies that increased their financial leverage due to acquisitions. Thus there is a linkage between certain types of M&As and bankruptcy. However, we discuss bankruptcy for more reasons than just its linkage with M&A volume. This is because bankruptcy is much more than a transaction a company engages in when it is going out of business.

Bankruptcy can be a creative corporate finance tool. Reorganization through the bankruptcy process can in certain instances provide unique benefits that are unattainable through other means. This chapter explores the different forms of bankruptcy in the United States and discusses the circumstances in which a company would use either of the two broad forms of corporate bankruptcy that are available: Chapter 7 and Chapter 11. Chapter 7, liquidation, is appropriate for more severely distressed companies. Chapter 11, reorganization, however, is the more flexible corporate finance tool that allows companies to continue to operate while it explores other forms of restructuring. In addition, Chapter 11 allows the management of bankrupt companies to stay in control while the company pursues reorganization.

TYPES OF BUSINESS FAILURE

Clearly, bankruptcy is a drastic step that is only pursued when other more favorable options are unavailable. A bankruptcy filing is an admission that a company has in some way failed to achieve certain goals. The term *business failure* is somewhat ambiguous and has different meanings, depending on the context and the users. There are two main forms of business failure: economic failure and financial failure. Each has a very different meaning.

Economic Failure

Of the two broad types of business failure, economic failure is the more ambiguous. For example, economic failure could mean that the firm is generating losses; that is, revenues are less than costs. However, depending on the users and the context, economic failure could also mean that the rate of return on investment is less than the cost of capital. It could also mean that the actual returns earned by a firm are less than those that were forecast. These uses of the term are very different and cover situations in which a company could be unprofitable as well as cases in which the company is profitable but not as profitable as was expected.

Financial Failure

Financial failure is less ambiguous than economic failure. Financial failure means that a company cannot meet its current obligations as they come due. The company does not have sufficient liquidity to satisfy its current liabilities. This may occur even when the company has a positive net worth, with the value of its assets exceeding its liabilities.

Costs of Financial Distress

Andrade and Kaplan conducted a study of 31 distressed highly leveraged transactions (HLTs) consisting of management buyouts (MBOs) and leveraged recapitalizations.[1] They focused on firms that were financially but not economically distressed. They traced the causes of the distress to a pre- versus post-HLT leverage, as measured by the median ratio of book value of debt to total capital, 0.21 versus 0.91, and median ratios of earnings before interest, tax, depreciation, and amortization (EBITDA) interest coverage of 7.95 versus 1.16. Their analysis points to the higher leverage as the cause of the financial distress. They then compared the value of the company over a period two months before the HLT until the resolution of the distress. The resolution was defined as the date they either exited Chapter 11, were sold, issued new equity, or were liquidated. They conclude that the changes brought about by the HLTs and the subsequent distress result in an *increase* in value. It is important to note that their conclusions are relevant only to financial distress, not to economic distress.

CAUSES OF BUSINESS FAILURE

Dun & Bradstreet conducted a study of the causes of business failure. They found that the three most common factors, in order of frequency, were economic factors, such as weakness in the industry; financial factors, such as insufficient capitalization; and weaknesses in managerial experience, such as insufficient managerial knowledge (Table 11.1). The last factor highlights the role of management skills in preventing bankruptcy and is one reason workout specialists focus so strongly on managerial skills when they are working on a company turnaround.

Dun & Bradstreet also analyzed the average ages of the businesses that failed (Table 11.2). They found only 10.7% of the failures were in business for one year or less. Just under one-third of the companies were in business for three years or less, whereas 44.3% existed for up to five years.

---

1. Gregor Andrade and Steven N. Kaplan, "How Costly Is Financial (Not Economic) Distress? Evidence from Highly Leveraged Transactions that Became Distressed," *Journal of Finance,* 53(5), October 1998, 1443–1493.

Underlying Causes	Percentage (%)[*]
Economic factors (e.g., industry weakness, insufficient profits)	41.0
Financial factors (e.g., heavy operating expenses, insufficient capital)	32.5
Experience factors (e.g., lack of business knowledge, lack of line experience, lack of managerial experience)	20.6
Neglect (e.g., poor work habits, business conflicts)	2.5
Fraud	1.2
Disaster	1.1
Strategy factors (e.g., receivable difficulties, overexpansion)	1.1
	100.0

TABLE 11.1 CAUSES OF BUSINESS FAILURE

[*] Results are based on primary reason for failure.

Causes of Financial Distress Following Leveraged Recapitalizations

Financial distress and bankruptcy have been linked to many of the highly leveraged deals that took place in the 1980s. As discussed in Chapter 7, leveraged buyouts (LBOs) became popular during this period, along with the use of leveraged recapitalization as an anti-takeover defense. Denis and Denis conducted a study of 29 leveraged recapitalizations that took place between 1984 and 1988.[2] They define leveraged recapitalizations as transactions that use proceeds from new debt obligations to make a payout to shareholders. Their results show that 31% of the firms that completed leveraged recapitalizations encountered financial distress. Contrary to what had been hypothesized by other researchers,

Number of Years in Business	Percentage (%)
One year or less	10.7
Two years	10.1
Three years	8.7
Total three years or less	29.5
Four years	7.8
Five years	7.0
Total five years or less	44.3
Total six to ten years	23.9
Total over ten years	31.8
	100.0

TABLE 11.2 FAILURE BY AGE OF BUSINESS

Source: Dun & Bradstreet Corporation, *Business Failure Record,* 1997.

---

2. David J. Denis and Diane K. Denis, "Causes of Financial Distress Following Leveraged Recapitalizations," *Journal of Financial Economics,* 37, 1995, 129–157.

such as Kaplan and Stein, who had asserted that failures of leveraged transactions were due to overpricing and poor financial structure, Denis and Denis conclude that although these factors are important, the 1990–91 recession and the regulatory factors were the reason some leveraged recapitalizations failed and others did not.[3] They did find that distressed firms had similar but somewhat higher debt levels and lower interest coverage. However, distressed firms required more postdeal cash than nondistressed firms. For example, the cash needs of distressed firms required them to sell an average of 6.3% of their assets, whereas nondistressed firms would have had to sell only 3.6% of their assets. Distressed firms also had to achieve greater postdeal performance improvements. For example, in order to meet the postdeal debt service, distressed firms would have had to have a median increase in operating income of 41.8% compared with 18.9% for nondistressed firms.

Given the reliance on postdeal asset sales, regulatory changes and the recession of 1990–91 played a key role in the failure of the leveraged recapitalizations. These regulatory factors are related to the collapse of the junk bond market. Following the difficulties of this market, certain financial institutions were forced to sell off their junk bond holdings, which hurt the ability of potential junk bond issuers to sell new bonds. This in turn limited the resources available to buyers of assets of companies that engaged in leveraged recapitalizations.

The limited resources lower the values that leveraged recap firms could realize from asset sales (Table 11.3). Many of these firms overestimated the prices they would receive for assets, such as divisions. This error was partially related to not being able to anticipate the dramatic changes that occurred in the junk bond market. The difficulties of the market for assets were compounded by the recession of 1990–91, which made performance improvement more difficult to achieve.

When an economy turns down, debt pressures become more pronounced as cash flows may weaken. In addition, downturns are a poor environment in which to conduct asset sales to pay down debt. The fact that companies got burned after taking on significant M&A-related debt in the fourth wave caused many of them to eschew high leverage in their deal making in the fifth wave. Nonetheless, the initial caution of dealmakers proved to be short lived, as we have seen that fifth-wave M&A blunders far eclipsed those of the 1980s.

BANKRUPTCY TRENDS

Total bankruptcies rose significantly toward the end of the 1980s in direct relation to the performance of the overall economy (Exhibit 11.1). As the economic growth slowed toward the end of the 1980s, bankruptcies, both personal and business, increased. Business bankruptcies increased steadily during this period, hit a 1980s' peak in 1986, declined through 1989, and then rose again as the economy slowed.

---

3. Steven Kaplan and Jeremy Stein, "The Evolution of Buyout Pricing and the Financial Structure of the 1980s," *Quarterly Journal of Economics,* May 1993, 313–357.

Firm Name	Total Asset Sale Shortfall* ($ Millions)	Additional Cash Required in Year of Distress ($ Millions)
Carter Hawley Hale	$612.6	$38.6
Goodyear	489.1	139.5
Harcourt Brace Jovanovich	924.9	243.6
Holiday	35.2	−33.7
Interco	288.5	223.1
Quantum Chemical	140.7	164.4
Standard Brands Paint	0.0	164.4
Swank	0.0	8.3
USG	24.5	351.0
Median	140.7	139.5

TABLE 11.3   A COMPARISON OF THE TOTAL CASH SHORTFALL FROM ASSET SALES AND THE ADDITIONAL CASH REQUIRED TO AVOID DEFAULT IN THE YEAR OF THE FIRST INDICATION OF FINANCIAL DISTRESS FOR THE NINE DISTRESSED FIRMS

The total asset sale shortfall is the sum of the shortfall from completed asset sales and the shortfall from sales not completed. We measure both shortfalls as the difference between the price received for the asset (zero in the case of an asset sale that was not completed) and the expected price as stated in press reports. When this quantity is unavailable, we measure the shortfall as the abnormal return over the three days centered on the announcement of the sale multiplied by the market value of the firm's equity. The additional cash required in the first year of distress is the difference between the firm's interest and principal obligations and its net cash flow (operating income less capital expenditures) for that year.

*Carter Hawley Hale's total shortfall includes $650 million from asset sales not completed. Similarly, Goodyear's total includes $750 million, and Harcourt Brace Jovanovich's includes $33.9 million from sales not completed.

Source: David J. Denis and Diane K. Denis, "Causes of Financial Distress Following Leveraged Recapitalizations," *Journal of Financial Economics* 37, 1995, 129–157.

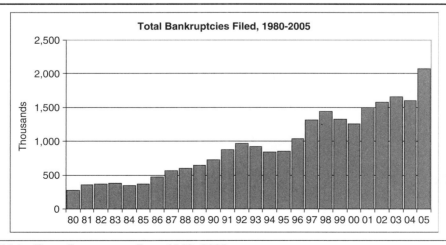

EXHIBIT 11.1   TOTAL BANKRUPTCIES FILED, 1980–2005

Source: BankruptcyData.com, New Generation Research, Administrative Office of the U.S. Courts.

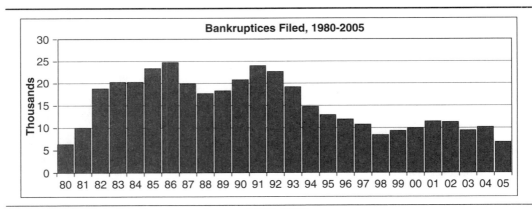

EXHIBIT 11.2 CHAPTER 11 BANKRUPTCY FILLINGS, 1980–2005
Sources: BankruptcyData.com, New Generation Research, and Administrative Office of the U.S. Courts.

The rise in bankruptcies at the end of the fourth merger wave is partially related to the increased use of debt in deals such as LBOs. The increased use of junk bonds to finance takeovers and buyouts put cash flow pressures on companies that they had difficulty meeting when economic demand slowed as we entered the 1990–91 recession and had an initially weak recovery thereafter. However, as the economic expansion picked up steam, filings declined but began to rise in 1999 even as the economy continued another year of expansion. This growth in Chapter 11 filings continued through 2002 and then began to decline as the U.S. economy entered another economic expansion (see Exhibits 11.2 and 11.3). This intuitive procyclical trend in these filings is confirmed by other research.[4]

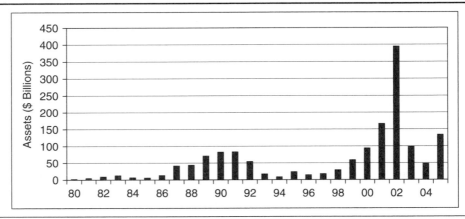

EXHIBIT 11.3 ASSETS OF PUBLIC COMPANIES FILING FOR BANKRUPTCY, 1980–2004
Source: The 2004 Bankruptcy Yearbook & Almanac.

4. Lance Bachmier, Patrick Gaughan and Norman Swanson, "The Volume of Federal Litigation and the Macroeconomy," *International Review of Law & Economics*, 24(2), June 2004, 191–208.

─── CASE STUDY ───

JAPAN'S ECONOMIC TROUBLES AND RISING NUMBER OF BANKRUPTCIES

The Japanese economy struggled mightily during the 1990s while so much of the developed world enjoyed a prolonged economic expansion. Economic growth in Japan declined rapidly when many other countries, such as the United States, went into recession in the period 1990–91. Japan's economy began to recover toward the middle of the 1990s, only to fall into a recession from which it took a number of years to escape (see Exhibits A and B). Unemployment had traditionally been low in Japan but grew dramatically during this period. The Japanese stock market collapsed, falling nearly 75% from its late 1980s high (see Exhibit C). The efforts of the Bank of Japan to try to use expansionary monetary policy only served to be a good case study of why monetary easing is a weak countercyclical tool.

In the years 1950–1970, the Japanese economy grew at a stellar rate; bankruptcy was not much of an issue. However, as the export-oriented Japanese economy began to suffer from aggressive competitors such as South Korea, Taiwan, and China as well as many other nations, Japan's grip on its export markets began to weaken. The Japanese corporate and banking world was in need of a major restructuring, but Japan was slow to respond. This sluggish response help leave Japan mired

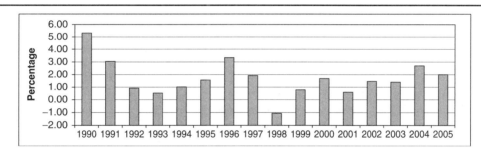

EXHIBIT A   JAPANESE ANNUAL GDP GROWTH, 1990–2005
Source: World Economic Outlook, September 2005.

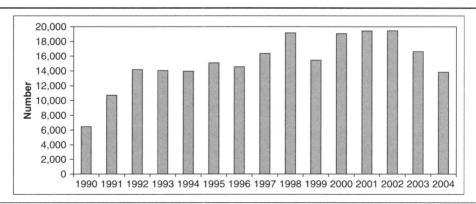

EXHIBIT B   NUMBER OF JAPANESE BANKRUPTCIES, 1990–2004
Source: Japan Statistical Yearbook, www.stat.go.jp/english.

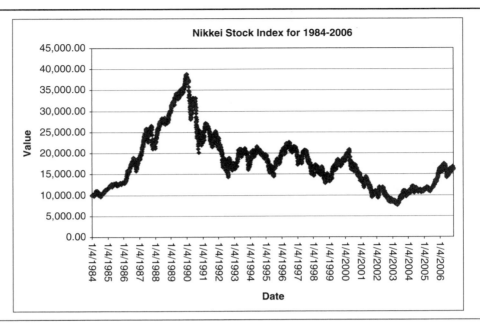

EXHIBIT C NIKKEI STOCK INDEX, 1984–2006

in an economic malaise. Bankruptcy, long avoided due to the special stigma it carried in Japan, became a reality for many Japanese businesses.

The opportunity to file for bankruptcy had been available in Japan for many years. In fact, there are many similarities in Japanese bankruptcy laws due to the fact that the United States had "exported" many of its laws to Japan as part of post–World War II restructuring. Under Japan's civil reorganization laws, companies that file for reorganization continue with current management in place while a court-appointed receiver negotiates with creditors. The court then can appoint a company to acquire the bankrupt business if that is determined to be the best course of action.

Bankruptcies in Japan hit record numbers in the early 2000s as many Japanese companies could not continue to use stop-gap measures to stay alive. For example, in October 2000, the Kyoei Life Insurance Company filed for bankruptcy protection from creditors. At that time it was Japan's largest bankruptcy since World War II. Ironically, the second largest bankruptcy was that of the Chiyoda Mutual Life Insurance Company, one of several Japanese insurance companies that had defaulted before Kyoei. Management of Kyoei claimed that the defaults of other insurers made it increasingly difficult for them to do business because it eroded the confidence of the public. Part of the problem for the industry was that they had issued policies at a time when interest rates were higher. When interest rates fell years later, insurance companies found it difficult to earn the returns that would be needed to meet the policy obligations. The continued weak economy and falling stock and bond markets battered the industry. At the time of this writing, Kyoei had been reported to be in negotiations with the Prudential Insurance Company of America.

Large-scale bankruptcies in Japan spread far outside of the insurance industry. In 2001, Mycal, the country's fourth largest supermarket chain, filed for bankruptcy. In 2002, the largest Japanese bankruptcy was STT Kaihatsu, a golf course company, which proved to be even larger than that of construction company Sato Kogyo. The number of listed companies that failed swelled in 2003. As the real estate bubble exploded in Japan, it took with it many real estate and construction companies, including the Daiwa Construction Company.

Company	($ Billions)	Date Filed
Worldcom, Inc.	103,914,000,000	07/21/02
Enron Corp.	63,392,000,000	12/02/01
Conseco, Inc.	61,392,000,000	12/18/02
Texaco	35,892,000,000	04/12/87
Financial Corp. of America	33,864,000,000	09/09/88
Refco Inc.	33,333,172,000	10/17/05
Global Crossing, Ltd.	30,185,000,000	01/28/02
Pacific Gas and Electric Co.	29,770,000,000	04/06/01
Calpine Corporation	27,216,088,000	12/20/05
UAL Corp.	25,197,000,000	02/09/02
Delta Air Lines, Inc.	21,801,000,000	09/14/05
Adelphia Communications	21,499,000,000	06/25/02
M Corporation	20,228,000,000	03/31/89
Mirant Corporation	19,415,000,000	07/14/03
Delphi Corporation	16,593,000,000	10/08/05

TABLE 11.4 LARGEST U.S. PUBLIC BANKRUPTCIES

Source: BankruptcyData.com, A Division of New Generation Research, Inc.

Fraud-Related Bankruptcies

Table 11.1 shows the causes of bankruptcy based on research by Dun & Bradstreet prior to the huge bankruptcies that occurred at the end of the fifth merger wave. This research shows that only 1.2% of the time fraud is the cause of bankruptcy. This changed in a big way in the 2000s. The two largest U.S. bankruptcies are WorldCom and Enron. Both corporate giants were brought down by management fraud. The list of the largest bankruptcies also includes a number of other fraud-related collapses, including Adelphia and Refco (see Table 11.4). These bankruptcies have led to changes in laws such as the Sarbanes-Oxley Act. While Enron's bankruptcy is not related to M&A, WorldCom's failed merger strategy and the company's inability to achieve organic growth was closely related to its ultimate demise.

Fraud-related bankruptcies were not a U.S.-exclusive phenomenon. In December 2003, the Italian food group, Parmalat Finanziaria SpA, announced that it would file for bankruptcy protection. This bankruptcy shocked the European corporate world when it was revealed that a fraud of this magnitude could take place in a company that was an international household name.

--- CASE STUDY ---

PARMALAT FOOD GIANT FILES BANKRUPTCY

The 2003 bankruptcy filing of Parmalat Finanziaria SpA came after it was revealed that company accounts in the Cayman Islands that were supposed to contain billions of euros were virtually empty but merely based on false documentation. Like some of the major fraud-related bankruptcies that have occurred in the United States, this one came with stories of false accounting, stock market manipulation, and criminal indictments. Once an investigation began it was revealed that Parmalat had double billed many of its distributors and had falsely gained credit from a number of different Italian banks. The Italian dairy had contended it had bank accounts in the Cayman Islands worth just under $5 billion. Research revealed that these accounts did not exist and were based on falsified documents.

It is interesting to note that in the past Italian bankruptcies would take years and mainly be focused on the eventual liquidation of the enterprise. However new bankruptcy laws that are similar to the U.S. Chapter 11 rules have been adopted in Italy. As a result of this a reorganized Parmalat was able to emerge from the reorganization process in about two years. It was not the same company that filed for protection and did not include all the brands for which it was known. The reorganized company had to sell assets to eliminate debt burdens and generate cash flows. However, it did emerge and was re-listed on the Milan exchange.

Comment on Largest Bankruptcies Data

Table 11.4 lists the largest bankruptcies by asset size without an adjustment for inflation. If such an adjustment were made, and all asset values were presented in same year terms, the list would be somewhat similar, but some famous earlier bankruptcies would appear on it. For example, the bankruptcy filing by Penn Central in 1970 listed assets at that time of $6.85 billion. However, this value would equal approximately $40 billion in 2007 dollars.

U.S. BANKRUPTCY LAWS

The Bankruptcy Act of 1978 (the Bankruptcy Code) is the main bankruptcy law of the United States. It organized bankruptcy laws under eight odd-numbered chapters (Table 11.5).

Changes in the U.S. Bankruptcy Laws

The Bankruptcy Act of 1978 has been enhanced by later bankruptcy laws. In 1984, the Bankruptcy Amendments and Federal Judgeship Act established the jurisdiction of the

Chapter	Subject
1	General provisions and definitions
3	Case administration
5	Creditors, debtors, and estates
7	Liquidation
9	Bankruptcies of municipalities
11	Reorganization
13	Bankruptcies of individuals
15	U.S. trustees system

TABLE 11.5 ORGANIZATION OF U.S. BANKRUPTCY LAW

bankruptcy court as a unit of the district courts. This law was in response to a Supreme Court ruling that challenged the jurisdiction of bankruptcy courts. The 1984 law also made it more difficult to immediately void labor contracts in bankruptcy. This was in response to a Supreme Court ruling in the Wilson Foods case, in which the court decided that companies could abrogate existing labor contracts as soon as they filed for bankruptcy. The revised law, which was passed partly because of labor union pressure, requires that a company try to work out a labor agreement before going to the bankruptcy courts. If the sincerity of the efforts of the parties is an issue, a bankruptcy will decide whether each party acted in good faith and under compliance with the law.

The Bankruptcy Reform Act of 1994 enhanced the powers of the bankruptcy courts. The Act gave these courts the right to issue orders that they deem necessary or appropriate to carry out the provisions of the Bankruptcy Code. In October 2005, the Bankruptcy Abuse Prevention and Consumer Protection Act was focused mainly on personal bankruptcy and causes such as credit card abuse. However, the law did contain some changes affecting Chapter 11 filings. We will discuss the rules that relate the length of what is known as the exclusivity period later in this chapter. Other changes related to corporate bankruptcy involved limits on retention bonuses paid to management. Managers receiving such bonuses must prove they have a bona fide job offer at or near the retention bonus. Such a bonus cannot be greater than ten times the average incentives paid to retain nonmanagers.

Another change brought about by the 2005 law is the requirement that the debtor in position has seven months after the filing to accept or reject leases. This is an important requirement for retailers. It forces them to make a long term commitment even though the full reorganization plan may not be finalized and approved. Still another change brought about by the new law is the requirement that the debtor in position pay in full for all goods it received 20 days prior to bankruptcy. This eliminates some of the benefits of doing a Chapter 11 filing.

REORGANIZATION VERSUS LIQUIDATION

The purpose of the reorganization section of the Bankruptcy Code is to allow a *reorganization plan* to be developed that will allow the company to continue to operate. This plan will contain the changes in the company that its designers believe are necessary to convert it to a profitable entity. If a plan to allow the profitable operation of the business cannot be formulated, the company may have to be liquidated, with its assets sold and the proceeds used to satisfy the company's liabilities.

CASE STUDY

WILBER ROSS: FINDING VALUE IN TROUBLED BUSINESSES

Certain investors excel at finding valuable opportunities in troubled businesses. Wilber Ross, a former restructuring advisor at Rothschild, is a leader in the turnaround field. He quickly earned a reputation as a sought-after leader in turnarounds. He formed his own Manhattan-based private equity firm, W. L. Ross & Co., which makes equity investments in firms in dire need of restructuring.

The steel industry in the United States had been troubled since the 1980s, when some of its larger companies proved to be unable to compete internationally due to their burdensome labor cost structure combined with inefficient plants, which caused them to lose market share to rivals from countries such as Japan and South Korea. Ross recognized an opportunity when he entered the steel industry in 2002 by buying a Cleveland steel mill for $325 million. He continued to buy steel companies and combined them into an entity called International Steel Group (ISG). He then took this company public and sold to it Lakshmi Mittal of Mittal Steel ten months later at an attractive 42% premium.[a] With the addition of ISG, Mittal became the largest steel company in the world. Ross's business acumen is underscored by a comparison of the $2.165 billion he paid for the five steel companies that made up ISG, LTV Corp., Bethlehem Steel, Acme Metals, Weirton Steel, and Georgetown Steel, and the $5.1 billion that Mittal paid for them.[b]

Ross also successfully acquired troubled textile businesses. He skillfully acquired Burlington's debt at deeply discounted prices after the textile maker filed for bankruptcy. In 2001, he ended up acquiring the company in bankruptcy for $614 million.

Following up on his success in the steel and textile industries, Ross then set his sights on the troubled auto suppliers industry. This sector has a lot in common with steel and textiles. Each has a high-cost labor force that has difficulty competing in an increasingly international market that has many lower cost competitors. In 2005, Ross formed the International Auto Components Group (IAC), which set about acquiring various different international auto suppliers such as the European operations of Collins and Aikman Corp. If his auto supplier investments turn out like his other large-scale investments in troubled sectors, he will combine several weak businesses into one more efficient company that will be sold at an attractive price.

[a]Heather Timmons, "Mergers Show Steel Industry is Still Worthy of Big Deals," *New York Times*, October 26, 2004, p. 1.
[b]Ibid.

REORGANIZATION PROCESS

Although the Chapter 11 process varies somewhat depending on the particular circumstances of the bankruptcy, most Chapter 11 bankruptcies have certain important common characteristics. These are highlighted next.

Bankruptcy Petition and the Filing

The reorganization process starts with the filing of a bankruptcy *petition for relief* with the bankruptcy court. In the petition, the debtor lists its creditors and security holders. Standard financial statements, including an income statement and balance sheet, are also included. The court then sets a date when the creditors may file their *proofs of claim*. The company then attempts to put together a reorganization plan while it continues its operations. Contrary to what a layperson might think, there is no financial test that is performed by the court at this time to determine whether the debtor is truly financially insolvent.

The petition is usually filed in the federal district in which the debtor has its home office. After the petition is filed, a case number is assigned, a court file is opened, and a bankruptcy judge is assigned to the case.

Filing Location

The most common locations where bankruptcy cases are filed are Delaware and the Southern District of New York. Unlike the decision of where to incorporate, corporations are supposed to file in a district either where they have their headquarters or where they have a substantial percent of their operations. Even though bankruptcy laws are federal laws as opposed to state laws, companies can choose to file their cases in specific local venues within the federal court system. There is some evidence that companies that have reorganized in Delaware have a tendency to refile Chapter 11 in Delaware later on.[5] Others have concluded that there is insufficient evidence that such a displayed preference for Delaware results in any losses for debtors.[6]

Debtor in Possession

After the bankruptcy filing, the bankrupt company is referred to as the *debtor in possession*. This is a new legal entity; however, for all practical purposes, it usually is the same company with the same management and the same employees. From the creditors' point of view, this is one of the problems of the bankruptcy process; that is, the same management that led the company into its financial troubles usually is still running the business while a reorganization plan is being developed.

If the creditors strongly oppose the management of the debtor staying in control of the business, they may petition the court and ask that a trustee and examiner be appointed. For example, if concerns exist about fraudulent actions or incompetence of the debtor's directors or management, the court may agree. A trustee is charged with overseeing the operations of the company while it is in bankruptcy. An examiner may be appointed to investigate specific issues. If the court denies a request for a trustee, an examiner is usually appointed.

Automatic Stay

When the petition is accepted by the court, an automatic stay is granted. This is one of the main benefits the debtor receives in the Chapter 11 process. During the automatic stay, a halt is placed on any prepetition legal proceedings as well as on the enforcement of any prefiling judgment. Creditors are unable to pursue a lien on the debtor's assets or to collect money from the debtor. Parties seeking relief from the stay may petition the court and request a hearing. If the creditors can convince the court that the assets that are being used as collateral for obligations due them are not necessary for the continued operation of the company, or the debtor has no equity interest in the assets, they may be able to get relief from the stay.

Time Line in the Reorganization Process

Table 11.6 shows some of the key events and dates in the Chapter 11 process. Within ten days of filing the Chapter 11 bankruptcy petition, the debtor is required to file a schedule

5. Theodore Eisenberg and Lynn M. Pucki, "Shopping for Judges: An Empirical Analysis of Venue Choice in Large Chapter 11 Reorganizations," *Cornell Law Review,* 1999.
6. David A. Skeel, "What's So Bad About Delaware?" *Vanderbilt Law Review,* 54, March 2001, 309–329.

1. Filing of the Chapter 11 petition
2. Filing a schedule of assets and liabilities
3. Bar date
4. Filing a reorganization plan and disclosure statement
5. Hearing on the disclosure statement
6. Voting on the plan
7. Plan confirmation hearing
8. Effective date of plan/distribution of new claims under the plan

TABLE 11.6 TIME LINE OF KEY EVENTS AND DATES IN A CHAPTER 11 REORGANIZATION

of assets and liabilities with the court. This schedule must include the name and address of each creditor. The next important date is the *bar date,* which is the date when those creditors who have disputed or contingent claims must file a *proof of claim.* A proof of claim is a written statement that sets forth what is owed by the debtor to the particular creditor. Failure to file by the bar date results in forfeiture of the claim. It is automatically assumed, however, that other claimholders have filed a proof of claim. Following the bar date, the next important dates are those associated with the filing and approval of the reorganization plan.

Duration of the Chapter 11 Process

According to New Generation Research, Inc., over the period 1982–2004 the average duration of a Chapter 11 filing was 16.4 months. In more recent years, however, this time period has been getting somewhat shorter. For example, over the period 1996–2000 the average duration was 14 months.

Use of Secured Creditors' Collateral

The Chapter 11 process allows for the use of the secured creditors' collateral by the debtor in possession. Creditors are barred from seizing assets while the stay is in effect. This does not mean that the debtor has free use of the property. The debtor must make some accommodation to the creditors, such as periodic payments (i.e., monthly), for continued use of the assets.

Duties of the Debtor in Possession

After the filing of the petition, the court establishes certain schedules that feature various reporting requirements. For example, the debtor has to file monthly financial statements 15 days after the end of each calendar month. In addition to the court rules as set forth in the federal law, each federal district may have additional reporting requirements. For example, the southern district of New York has local rules that relate to further reporting requirements and the opening of bank accounts.

Creditors' Committees

A creditors' meeting is usually held within 20 to 40 days of the bankruptcy filing. The meeting is called by the U.S. Trustee and is usually held at his or her office. The debtor and its principal officers must be present at this meeting. All creditors may attend this meeting and may ask the debtor specific questions that are of concern to them.

In larger lawsuits, a creditors' committee is formed. This committee is usually composed of the largest creditors, assuming they are interested in being represented. Along with the U.S. Trustee, the creditors' committee monitors the actions of the debtor, ensuring that it does not do anything that would adversely affect the creditors' interests. The creditors' committee may retain counsel, accountants, and other financial experts to represent the creditors' interests during the reorganization process. The fees of professionals are borne by the debtor.

The bigger the bankruptcy, the more likely it is that there may be more committees, such as an equity holders' committee, or different types of creditors' committees, such as a bondholders' committee, representing the various forms of debt that might exist. One example of a megabankruptcy that had several committees was the bankruptcy of the Campeau Corporation, which featured the bankruptcy of Campeau's two major subunits, Federated Department Stores, Inc. and Allied Stores Corp. In this proceeding, there were several committees, including a bondholders' committee and two trade creditors' committees. The court attempted to appoint a cross-section of similarly situated creditors on each committee. In smaller bankruptcies, creditors may have little interest in the committees. In the Campeau bankruptcy, the office of U.S. Trustee Conrad J. Morgenstern was flooded with bondholders who were interested in serving on the committee.

Debtor's Actions and Its Supervision

The debtor may continue to operate the business during the reorganization process. The law requires that the debtor obtain the approval of the bankruptcy court before its takes any extraordinary action that is not part of the normal business operations, such as selling assets or property.

Technically, the supervision of the debtor is the responsibility of the judge and the creditors. They may acquire resources, such as legal and accounting or other financial expert assistance, to help them. Practically, neither the judge nor the creditors usually have the resources or time to closely supervise the debtor. Even if the debtor does something that the creditors do not approve of, the debtor may be able to convince the judge that some actions are necessary for the survival of the company; that is, if the court does not allow the debtor to take these actions, the company may go under. Thus, the judge is put in the difficult position of making this decision with limited information. If the judge rules against the debtor and is wrong, he risks the company's going out of business and all the duress and employee suffering this might cause. For this reason, the debtor is usually granted significant leeway and will be opposed only when its proposed actions are clearly objectionable.

Exclusivity Period

After the filing of the bankruptcy petition and the granting of the automatic stay, only the debtor has the right to file a reorganization plan. This period, which is initially 120 days, is known as the *exclusivity period.* It is rare, however, particularly in larger bankruptcies, to have the plan submitted during that time frame. It is common for the debtor to ask for one or more extensions. Extensions are only granted for cause, but they are not difficult to obtain. However, the Bankruptcy Abuse Prevention and Consumer Protection Act of 2005 placed an absolute limit of 18 months on the exclusivity period.

Obtaining Postpetition Credit

One of the problems a near-bankrupt company has is difficulty obtaining credit. If trade creditors are concerned that a company may become bankrupt, they may cut off all additional credit. For companies that are dependent on such credit to survive, this may mean that a bankruptcy filing is accelerated.

To assist bankrupt companies in acquiring essential credit, the code has given postpetition creditors an elevated priority in the bankruptcy process. That is, postpetition claims have an elevated priority over prepetition claims. It is ironic that creditors may be unwilling to extend credit unless the debtor files for bankruptcy so that the creditor can obtain the elevated priority.

Reorganization Plan

The reorganization plan, which is part of a larger document called the *disclosure statement,* looks like a prospectus. For larger bankruptcies, it is a long document that contains the plans for the turnaround of the company. The plan is submitted to all the creditors and equity holders' committees. The plan is approved when each class of creditor and equity holder approves it. Approval is granted if one-half in number and two-thirds in dollar amount of a given class approve the plan. Once the plan is approved, the dissenters are bound by the details of the plan.

A confirmation hearing follows the attainment of the approval of the plan. The hearing is not intended to be a pro forma proceeding, even if the vote is unanimous. The presiding judge must make a determination that the plan meets the standards set forth by the Bankruptcy Code. After the plan is confirmed, the debtor is discharged of all prepetition claims and other claims up to the date of the confirmation hearing. This does not mean that the reorganized company is a debt-free entity. It simply means that it has new obligations that are different from the prior obligations. Ideally, the postconfirmation capital structure is one that will allow the company to remain sufficiently liquid to meet its new obligations and generate a profit.

Cramdown

The plan may be made binding on all classes of security holders, even if they all do not approve it. This is known as a *cramdown.* The judge may conduct a cramdown if at least one class of creditors approves the plan and the "crammed down" class is not being treated unfairly. In this context, "unfairly" means that no class with inferior claims in the bankruptcy hierarchy is receiving compensation without the higher-up class being paid 100% of its claims. This order of claims is known as the *absolute priority rule,* which states that claims must be settled in full before any junior claims can receive any compensation.

The concept of a cramdown comes from the concern by lawmakers that a small group of creditors could block the approval of a plan to the detriment of the majority of the creditors.[7] By giving the court the ability to cram down a plan, the law reduces the potential for a holdout problem.

Fairness and Feasibility of the Plan

The reorganization plan must be both fair and feasible. Fairness refers to the satisfaction of claims in order of priority, as discussed in the previous section. Feasibility refers to the probability that the postconfirmation company has a reasonable chance of survival. The plan must provide for certain essential features, such as adequate working capital and a reasonable capital structure that does not contain too much debt. Projected revenues must be sufficient to adequately cover the fixed charges associated with the postconfirmation liabilities and other operating expenses.

Partial Satisfaction of Prepetition Claims

The plan will provide a new capital structure that, it is hoped, will be one that the company can adequately service. This will typically feature payment of less than the full amount that was due the claimholders. For example, the Penn Central Railroad, in a bankruptcy process that lasted eight years, produced a confirmed plan that gave holders of secured bonds 10% of their claims in cash. The cash was generated by the sale of assets. The remaining 90% was satisfied by 30% each in new mortgage bonds, preferred stock, and common stock. This provided Penn Central with a lower amount of financial leverage because the secured bond debt was 10% discharged by the cash payment, and 60% was converted to preferred and common equity.

BENEFITS OF THE CHAPTER 11 PROCESS FOR THE DEBTOR

The U.S. Bankruptcy Code provides great benefits to debtors, some of which are listed in Table 11.7. The debtor is left in charge of the business and allowed to operate relatively free of close control. Some people are critical of what they perceive as a process that overly favors the debtor at the expense of the creditors' interests.[8] The law, however, seeks to rehabilitate the debtor so that it may become a viable business and a productive member of the business community.

COMPANY SIZE AND CHAPTER 11 BENEFITS

The fact that debtors enjoy unique benefits while operating under the protection of the bankruptcy process is clear. Smaller companies, however, may not enjoy the same benefits

---

7. Rosemary E. Williams and Daniel P. Jakala, *Bankruptcy Practice Handbook* (Deerfield, IL: Callaghan & Company, 1990), p. 11:54.
8. Lawrence H. Kallen, *Corporate Welfare: The Mega-Bankruptcies of the 80s and 90s* (New York: Lyle Stuart, 1991).

- The ability to restrain creditors from seizing the debtor's property or canceling beneficial contracts and to stay judicial actions against the debtor
- The ability to continue to operate the business effectively without interference from creditors
- The ability to borrow money by granting liens on debtor's assets equal to or superior to the liens of the existing creditors
- The ability to avoid certain transfers that occurred before the filing of the bankruptcy petition
- The cessation of interest accrual on debts that were unsecured as of the filing date
- The ability to propose and negotiate a single plan with all of the debtor's creditors
- The power to bind dissenting creditors to a reorganization plan that meets the Bankruptcy Code standard
- The receipt of a discharge by the bankruptcy court of all prepetition claims treated under the reorganization plan

TABLE 11.7   BENEFITS OF CHAPTER 11 FOR DEBTORS

Source: William A. Slaughter and Linda G. Worton, "Workout or Bankruptcy?" in Dominic DiNapoli, Sanford C. Sigoloff, and Robert F. Cushman, eds., *Workouts and Turnarounds* (Homewood, IL: Business One Irwin, 1991), pp. 72–96.

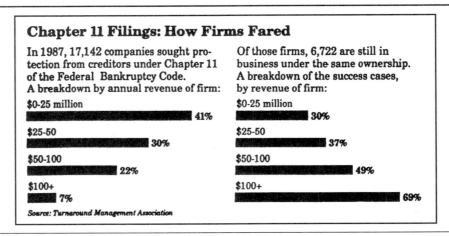

EXHIBIT 11.4   HOW CHAPTER 11 FIRMS FARED BY COMPANY SIZE

that the process bestows on larger counterparts. A study by Turnaround Management Associates showed that the probability of surviving the Chapter 11 process is directly related to the size of the company.[9] Exhibit 11.4 shows that 69% of the larger companies, those with revenues in excess of $100 million, survived the process and were viable afterward, whereas only 30% of the smaller firms, those with revenues under $25 million, were able to do so.

The reason for the size differential in survival rates is that larger companies are in a better position to handle the additional unique demands placed on a Chapter 11 debtor. For example, the bankruptcy process is very demanding on management time. Before the bankruptcy, management presumably was devoting all its time to managing the business, and the business still was not successful. Now management has to devote its time to

---

9.   *Wall Street Journal,* July 14, 1988, p. 29.

managing the business and dealing with the time demands that the bankruptcy litigation imposes. This task may be more difficult for smaller companies, where management is not as deep as in larger firms.

Although the additional expenses of the bankruptcy process may be relatively small compared with a larger company's revenue base, such expenses may be an additional burden that a smaller business cannot handle. For example, Lawrence A. Weiss reports that direct costs average 3.1% of the book value of the debt, plus the market value of the equity.[10] Professional fees may be very high—particularly in larger bankruptcies. For example, in the Johns Manville bankruptcy, professional fees were almost $200 million.[11] For a small firm with a thin capitalization, percentages may be much higher than the average reported by Weiss. For these reasons, Chapter 11 may be an excellent choice for some large companies but may not be a good idea for smaller businesses.

Projections Done in Chapter 11

Before emerging from Chapter 11, a company is required to put forward certain financial and operational projections as part of its reorganization plan. These projections include balance sheets, income statements, and cash flow statements. Michel, Shaked, and McHugh followed 35 Chapter 11 companies from 1989 to 1995.[12] They found that these projections were frequently overstated—sometimes significantly so. For example, they found that actual sales generally lagged projected sales in the first year after emerging from Chapter 11. In some cases the overstatement was as much as 20%.

Postbankruptcy Capital Structure and Success

The capital structure of the postbankruptcy company needs to be one that the company can survive with. It must not have burdensome debt service pressures that will prevent it from being viable in the long run. However, with the long decline of the stock market after the fifth-wave bubble burst, many creditors have become reluctant to accept the comparatively more risky equity and have demanded the security of debt. Unfortunately, the bankrupt company may have found themselves in Chapter 11 simply because they could not handle the degree of leverage they had. For example, American Banknote Corp. had $210.8 million in liabilities prior to filing Chapter 11 and $157.1 million after it came out of reorganization.[13] It is not a surprise that they had to file for Chapter 11 a second time. Another example is Thermadyne Holdings, which has had to file Chapter 11 twice and still has a significant amount of debt. For a company to succeed, it needs a bearable amount of debt and sometimes this may mean a dramatic decline from its prebankruptcy level.

---

10. Lawrence A. Weiss, "Bankruptcy Resolution: Direct Costs and Violation of Priority of Claims," *Journal of Financial Economics,* 27(2), October 1990, 285–314.
11. William Slaughter and Linda Worton, "Workout or Bankruptcy?" in Dominic DiNapoli, Sanford C. Sigoloff, and Robert F. Cushman, eds., *Workouts and Turnarounds* (Homewood, IL: Business One Irwin, 1991), p. 87.
12. Allen Michel, Isreal Shaked, and Christopher McHugh, "After Bankruptcy: Can Ugly Ducklings Turn into Swans?" *Financial Analysts Journal,* 54(3), May/June 1998, 31–40.
13. Ben Fieldler, "Built to Fail," *The Deal,* July 10, 2005, 31–33.

CASE STUDY

REORGANIZATIONS OF GERMANY'S IHR PLATZ

Outside the United States, the debtor in possession is much more limited in its ability to gain protection from creditors while it reorganizes its business. In many countries bankruptcy simply means the liquidation of the business. This may be a societal loss as such companies could possibly be viable if allowed to restructure. Creditors also may gain from a higher payout that they might realize from a reorganized company compared with a liquidated one. Countries are now starting to ease their bankruptcy laws to allow for a more U.S.-style reorganization. For example, Germany changed its bankruptcy law in 1999 to allow bankrupt companies to work out agreements with creditors while management stayed in control of the business as opposed to turning over control to a court-appointed administrator. It takes some time for companies and the business sector to adjust to new laws and consider bankrupt companies potentially viable. However, there are signs that this adjustment process is starting to take place. For example, in 2005, Goldman Sachs's London-based restructuring unit bought up €120 million in bank debt of the insolvent German drug store chain, Ihr Platz. They then reached an agreement with creditors pursuant to the 1999 law, which had been largely unused by German investors. Goldman's experienced restructuring specialists were able to close stores that were no longer viable while it worked out agreements with creditors. In 2006, Goldman pursued a similar strategy with German model train maker Marklin Holding GmbH when it purchased €57 million of its debt.

PREPACKAGED BANKRUPTCY

A new type of bankruptcy emerged in the late 1980s. By 1993, it accounted for one-fifth of all distressed restructurings. During the 1990s, prepackaged bankruptcies accounted for 9.2% of all bankruptcies, while in 2000 they equaled 6.8% of all bankruptcies in that year.

An example of leading prepackaged bankruptcies is shown in Table 11.8. In a prepackaged bankruptcy, the firm negotiates the reorganization plan with its creditors before an actual Chapter 11 filing. Ideally, the debtor would like to have solicited and received an understanding with the creditors that the plan would be approved after the filing. In a prepackaged bankruptcy, the parties try to have the terms of the reorganization plan approved in advance. This is different from the typical Chapter 11 reorganization process, which may feature a time-consuming and expensive plan development and approval process in which the terms and conditions of the plan are agreed to only after a painstaking negotiation process.

The first major prepackaged bankruptcy was the Crystal Oil Company, an oil and natural gas exploration company located in Louisiana.[14] The total time between the bankruptcy filing in 1986 and the company's emergence was only three months. During this time the company negotiated a new capital structure in which it reduced its total indebtedness from $277 million to $129 million.[15] As is typical of such debt restructurings, the creditors received other securities, such as equity and convertible debt and warrants, in exchange for the reduction in the original debt.

---

14. John J. McConnell, "The Economics of Prepackaged Bankruptcy," *Journal of Applied Corporate Finance*, 4(2), September 1991, 93–97.
15. Ibid.

Company	Chapter 11 Date	Confirmation Date
Audio Visual Services	12/17/2001	2/27/2002
Chiquita Brands, International	11/28/2001	3/11/2002
Anacomp, Inc.	10/19/2001	12/12/2001
Regal Cinemas, Inc.	10/11/2001	12/12/2001
Covad Communications	8/15/2001	12/14/2001
Drug Emporium, Inc.	3/26/2001	8/30/2001
Finova Group, Inc.	3/7/2001	8/10/2001
Imperial Sugar Company	1/16/2001	8/7/2001
Decora Industries, Inc.	12/5/2000	
United Artists Theater	9/5/2000	1/22/2001

TABLE 11.8   PREPACKAGED BANKRUPTCY FILINGS: 1995–2001

Source: BankruptcyData.com, A Division of New Generation Research, Inc.

Benefits of Prepackaged Bankruptcy

The completion of the bankruptcy process is usually dramatically shorter in a prepackaged bankruptcy than in the typical Chapter 11 process. Both time and financial resources are saved. This is of great benefit to the distressed debtor, who would prefer to conserve financial resources and spend as little time as possible in the suspended Chapter 11 state.[16] In addition, a prepackaged bankruptcy reduces the holdout problem associated with voluntary nonbankruptcy agreements. In such agreements, the debtor often needs to receive the approval of all the creditors. This is difficult when there are many creditors, particularly many small creditors. One of the ways a voluntary agreement is accomplished is to pay all the small creditors 100% of what they are owed and pay the main creditors, who hold the bulk of the debt, an agreed-upon lower amount.

It was noted previously that approval of a Chapter 11 reorganization plan requires creditors' approval equal to one-half in number and two-thirds in dollar amount. With the imminent threat of a Chapter 11 filing, creditors know that after the filing is made, these voting percentages, as opposed to unanimity, will apply. Therefore, if the threat of a Chapter 11 filing is real, the postbankruptcy voting threshold will become the operative one during the prepackaged negotiation process.

Prevoted versus Postvoted Prepacks

The voting approval for the prepackaged bankruptcy may take place before or after the plan is filed. In a "prevoted prepack" the results of the voting process are filed with the bankruptcy petition and reorganization plan. In a "postvoted prepack" the voting process is overseen by the bankruptcy court after the Chapter 11 filing. In a study of 49

---

16. Critics of the Chapter 11 debtor benefits would disagree. They would contend that some Chapter 11 companies prefer the benefits that protection of the Bankruptcy Code gives them and try to exploit these advantages over their creditors for as long as possible. Therefore, they are not in a hurry to leave the Chapter 11 protection.

prepackaged bankruptcies, Tashjian, Lease, and McConnell found that prevoted prepacks spend less time in bankruptcy court but devote more time to prefiling negotiations.[17] Prevoted prepacks also had lower direct costs as a fraction of assets and had higher recovery rates for nonequity obligations.

Tax Advantages of Prepackaged Bankruptcy

A prepackaged bankruptcy may also provide tax benefits because net operating losses are treated differently in a workout than in a bankruptcy. For example, if a company enters into a voluntary negotiated agreement with debtholders whereby debtholders exchange their debt for equity and the original equity holders now own less than 50% of the company, the company may lose its right to claim net operating losses in its tax filings. The forfeiture of these tax-loss carryforwards may have adverse future cash flow consequences. In bankruptcy, however, if the court rules that the firm was insolvent, as defined by a negative net asset value, the right to claim loss carryforwards may be preserved. Betker estimates that the present value of future taxes saved by restructuring through a prepackaged bankruptcy, as opposed to a workout, is equal to 3% of total assets.[18]

If a debtor company reaches a voluntary agreement whereby creditors agree to cancel a certain percentage of the debt—say, one-third—this amount is treated as income for tax purposes, thus creating a tax liability. A similar debt restructuring in bankruptcy, however, does not create such a tax liability.[19]

CASE STUDY

ONEIDA PREPACKAGED BANKRUPTCY

In 2006, Oneida Ltd., a 124-year-old maker of silverware, ceramic plates, and crystal, did a Chapter 11 filing that included a prepackaged reorganization plan. The company was hurt by changes in the marketplace including a move away from silverware on airlines as well as overall sluggishness in department stores, which is an important distribution channel for the company. The decline in silverware usage on the airlines was tied to the 9/11 attacks in the United States. In response to its financial difficulties, Oneida laid off employees but it still could not service its debt.

Oneida worked to secure commitments for a new financing structure prior to filing for Chapter 11. As part of this process, Oneida received a $40 million debtor-in-possession commitment from J. P. Morgan Chase.[a] J. P. Morgan had refinanced Oneida's debt in 2004, which resulted in the company having two main debt tranches. In this refinancing J. P. Morgan ended up owning 62% of the company in exchange for retiring $30 million of its debt. This debt reduction, however, was not enough to allow the company to stave off bankruptcy. The 2006 prepack provided that holders of the company's

[a]Ben Fidler, "As Promised, Oneida Forks Over Prepack," *The Daily Deal*, March 21, 2006, 5.

---

17. Elizabeth Tashjian, Ronald Lease, and John J. McConnell, "Prepacks: An Empirical Analysis of Prepackaged Bankruptcies," *Journal of Financial Economics*, 40(10), January 1996, 135–162.

18. Brian Betker, "An Empirical Examination of Prepackaged Bankruptcy," *Financial Management*, 24(1), Spring 1995.

19. McConnell, "The Economics of Prepackaged Bankruptcy," pp. 93–97.

tranche B debt would receive new equity in exchange for this debt. The company's tranche A debt was refinanced with an $80 million revolver loan and a $90 million six-year term loan from the Credit Suisse Group.[b]

The Oneida prepack is a useful case study for several reasons, one of which is that it highlights the fact that not all prepacks flow through reorganization quickly and smoothly. Oneida did not have any unsecured debt, thus there was no need for an unsecured creditors committee, making approval seem easier than a typical reorganization. In addition, J. P. Morgan, a holder for both prepetition and postpetition debt, was also the majority shareholder. However, minority shareholders differed with creditors and Morgan regarding the enterprise value, which they placed at approximately $300 million, which was greater than the value of the debt claims, which were $253 million.[c] Minority shareholders then demanded that they be represented by an equity holders' committee that could pursue a distribution of this excess enterprise value. Creditors, on the other hand, estimated an enterprise value of approximately $190 million, which was well below the value of the debt claims.

If the prepack is successful in the long run, it would allow a company with a colorful past to stay alive. Oneida Ltd. was derived from the controversial Oneida Community founded in 1848 by John Humphrey Noyes, who promoted a theology of "perfectionism."[d] This included commune-style living where personal property and monogamous marriage was abolished. In order to support itself the commune started different businesses, and Oneida, Ltd. is an outgrowth of that process.

[b]David Elman, "Oneida to File Chapter 11," *The Daily Deal*, March 14, 2006.
[c]Ben Fidler, "Oneida Case Stalls Over Conflict, Valuation Issues," *The Daily Deal*, April 7, 2006, 1.
[d]William Kates, "From Utopia to Despair, Oneida Ltd. Struggles to Survive," *Associated Press State and Local Wire*, May 15, 2004.

WORKOUTS

A *workout* refers to a negotiated agreement between the debtors and their creditors outside the bankruptcy process. The debtor may try to extend the payment terms, which is called *extension,* or convince creditors to agree to accept a lesser amount than they are owed, which is called *composition.* A workout differs from a prepackaged bankruptcy in that in a workout the debtor either has already violated the terms of the debt agreements or is about to. In a workout, the debtor tries to convince creditors that they would be financially better off with the new terms of a workout agreement than with the terms of a formal bankruptcy.

Benefits of Workouts

The main benefits of workouts are cost savings and flexibility.[20] Workout agreements generally cost less to both the debtor and the creditors in terms of the resources the participants need to devote to the agreement process. In addition, participants in a workout are not burdened by the rules and regulations of Chapter 11 of the Bankruptcy Code. They are free to create their own rules as long as the parties agree to them. They also avoid the public scrutiny, such as from opening accounting records to the public, that would occur in a bankruptcy filing. Workouts may also help the debtor avoid any business

---

20. Slaughter and Worton, "Workout or Bankruptcy?" pp. 72–96.

disruption and loss of employees and overall morale that might occur in a bankruptcy. With these benefits come certain risks. The key risk is the holdout problem discussed previously. If this problem cannot be circumvented, a bankruptcy filing may be the only viable alternative.

Recognizing Better Workout Candidates

Depending on the particular financial circumstances of the company and the personal makeup of the parties involved, a negotiated private settlement outside the bankruptcy process may or may not be possible. Gilson, John, and Lang analyzed 169 debt restructurings from 1978 to 1987 and found that 52.7% of them ended up in bankruptcy.[21] They found that two-day average stock returns around the restructuring announcement equaled 21.6% for successful firms, whereas they were 26.3% for those firms that were not successful in reaching a nonbankruptcy restructuring agreement. This suggests that the market is capable of determining in advance which firms will be able to reach such an agreement.

Evidence on Role of Transactions Costs in Voluntary Restructuring versus Chapter 11 Decision

Gilson analyzed 108 publicly traded companies between 1980 and 1989 that either restructured their debt out of court (57 companies) or reorganized under Chapter 11 (51 companies).[22] He found that the firms that attempt voluntary restructuring outside Chapter 11 were less able to reduce their leverage compared with Chapter 11 firms. He traced the problem to higher transactions costs of voluntary restructuring. Examples of these costs include the credit holdout problem, which makes it difficult to get all creditors to participate in the agreement. This problem is greater for holders of smaller claims, who have an incentive to hold up transactions until they receive preferential treatment. Although a small number of such creditors may not be as much of a problem, the situation becomes very difficult if there are numerous creditors with similar motivations. Other difficulties of voluntary restructuring include the fact that creditors may be less willing to exchange their debt for equity when managers of the company have a significant informational advantage over them. This disadvantage renders creditors less able to assess the value of the equity they would receive in exchange for their debt claims. One additional factor is that institutional holders of debt may simply prefer debt to equity and may not want to voluntarily become an equity holder. These issues become moot when the process moves into Chapter 11 and the position of the debtor improves.

---

21. Stuart C. Gilson, Kose John, and Larry H. P. Lang, "Troubled Debt Restructurings: An Empirical Study of Private Reorganization of Firms in Default," *Journal of Financial Economics,* 27(2), October 1990, 315–354.
22. Stuart Gilson, "Transactions Costs and Capital Structure Choice: Evidence from Financially Distressed Firms," *Journal of Finance,* 52(1), March 1997, 161–196.

─── CASE STUDY ───

SUNBEAM—BANKRUPTCY FOLLOWING A FAILED ACQUISITION PROGRAM

Companies that pursue acquisitions that fail, especially those that incur significant debt to finance the deals, run the risk of going bankrupt. This is one of the extreme penalties that the market imposes for a poor acquisition strategy. Such a fate befell Sunbeam Corp. when it had to file for Chapter 11 bankruptcy protection in the Southern District of New York in February 2001. The company, which marketed Sunbeam appliances, First Alert smoke alarms, and Coleman camping gear, showed negative net worth on its bankruptcy petition though listing assets of $2.96 billion and liabilities of $3.2 billion. The company could not handle the burden of $2.5 billion in debt that it had accumulated, partially from unsuccessful acquisitions.

One of the main sources of financial pressure was a $1.7 billion bank loan that the company had entered into in 1998 to finance three acquisitions. In these deals Sunbeam acquired the Coleman Company, maker of sleeping bags and other camping equipment; Signature Brands, owner of the Mr. Coffee brand; and the First Alert company. The disparate nature of these acquisitions should have presented red flags to investors. The loan was provided by Morgan Stanley Dean Witter, First Union Corp., and the Bank of America; it was then discovered that Sunbeam, led by turnaround artist Albert Dunlop, known as "Chainsaw Al," fresh from his turnaround of the Scott Paper Company, inflated sales by overselling retailers goods they did not want so as to increase short-term revenues.

Sunbeam emerged from Chapter 11 in 2002 as a closely held business under the name American Household, Inc. The company's reorganization plan provided for its debt to be converted into equity. American Household was itself acquired in 2005 by the Rye, New York–based Jarden Corporation for $745.6 million in cash plus the assumption of $100 million in debt.[a]

[a]Terry Brennan, "Sunbeam Files for Chapter 11," *The Daily Deal,* February 7, 2001, p. 2.

Acquisitions Following Bankruptcy

Bidders sometimes can find attractive acquisition opportunities in companies that are in Chapter 11. A reorganization plan can involve finding an acquirer who would take over the bankrupt company. One example is Strouds, Inc., a company that had filed its Chapter 11 bankruptcy petition in September 2000, which announced in March 2001 that the company would be sold to an entity called Strouds Acquisitions Corp., which was controlled by an Orange County investment firm, Cruttenden Partners, and senior management of Strouds. Strouds, a marketer of bed, bath, and other textile products, had suffered in its competition with companies such as Bed Bath & Beyond, Inc. and Linens 'n Things, Inc. Strouds, which was traded on NASDAQ, had 70 stores at the time of its filing and was down to 50 stores as of the date of the acquisition announcement. In this case, buyers of the company considered the $39.5 million acquisition price a good investment. Another example occurred in February 2001, when AMR Corp., the parent of American Airlines, bid $500 million plus assumption of liabilities for the assets of Trans World Airlines (TWA), which was in bankruptcy. TWA's principal asset was its St. Louis hub, which is centrally located in the middle of the United States.

CASE STUDY

LAMPERT ACQUIRES BANKRUPT KMART AND THEN ACQUIRES SEARS

The acquisition of Kmart by Eddie Lampert and his hedge fund, ESL Investments, is a classic example of how acquisition opportunities can arise in the bankruptcy process. Kmart was the third largest retailer in the United States after Wal-Mart and Target. It had over 1,500 stores and 16 distribution centers. Lampert was able to acquire the large but troubled retailer for less than $1 billion. Lampert used the bankruptcy process to become the largest shareholder in the company. He did this by purchasing the company's busted bonds and bank debt and then using the leverage of this position as a creditor to become a controlling equity-holder in the company. As Kmart's troubles became widely discussed in the media, Lampert was able to purchase this debt at attractive prices. The company emerged from bankruptcy in May 2003 with Lampert in charge.

Kmart traces its roots back to the S. S. Kresge variety store chain that was founded in 1899. The first Kmart store was opened in 1962 as a unit of Kresge. At the end of the 1970s, Kmart dwarfed Wal-Mart. However, since then Wal-Mart used aggressive pricing and wise inventory management to steadily attack Kmart's market shares all across the United States. The battle culminated with Kmart's strategic blunder of getting into a price war with Wal-Mart using what Kmart called a ''Blue Light Always'' promotion. Wal-Mart is a very lean retailer and enjoyed significant cost advantages over Kmart. This was a battle that Kmart, with its cost structure, could not win. In January 2002, Kmart had no choice but to file for Chapter 11.

Lampert was able to transform Kmart's troubles into an advantage for him. Prior to Kmart, Lampert had become an approximately 27% shareholder in AutoZone. He used this position to pressure management into making changes that would enhance the value of his and other shareholders' investment. He leveraged his large stock holdings in the company to get a seat on the board and replace the CEO with one more to his own liking (a former Goldman Sachs executive—a firm at which Lampert once worked).

Eddie Lampert showed the influence that a dominant creditor can have on the effectiveness and speed of the reorganization process. When he saw the resources of the company were being drained by inefficient activities, such as paying bankruptcy professionals (reported to be between $10 million and $12 million per month) who may not have an interest in seeing the payment stream end soon, he stepped in and confronted management. Lampert forced the company to exit Chapter 11—a state in which it was becoming too comfortable. He was not as interested in management's reorganization plan as he had his own strategy for the company's future. Once again, we see the role that large blockholders can play in pushing companies in the right direction.

The acquisition of such a large company by a hedge fund is a sign of the changes that are taking place in the M&A business. Hedge fund managers are not just short-term investors looking for a quick return on their purchases. They now have become activist managers and have moved into the arena that was formerly the exclusive bailiwick of private equity firms.

In 2004, Lampert showed that he stands out from other activist hedge fund managers by orchestrating the merger of Kmart with retail giant Sears. The $11.5 billion merger with Sears reflected the waning fortunes of this storied retailer, which was founded in 1893 by Richard Sears (see Case Study: Sears—A Failed Diversification Strategy, Chapter 4). At the time of the deal, Home Depot had risen to become the second-largest retailer behind Wal-Mart (Exhibit A). Both Kmart and Sears experienced declining revenues and profitability while losing market shares to competitors such as Wal-Mart (Exhibits B and C). Kmart was not able to control its problems and fell into bankruptcy. Sears, while certainly not bankrupt, had seen its affinity for malls lead to a steady decline in sales as

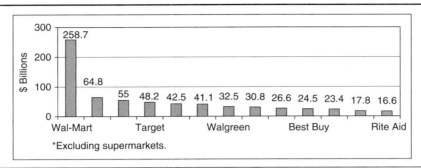

EXHIBIT A U.S. RETAILERS RANKED BY SALES, 2003*

Source: New York Times, November 20, 2004, p. C12.

*Excluding supermarkets.

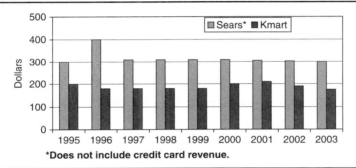

EXHIBIT B ANNUAL SALES PER SQUARE FOOT: SEARS VERSUS KMART

Source: New York Times, November 18, 2004.

*Does not include credit card revenue.

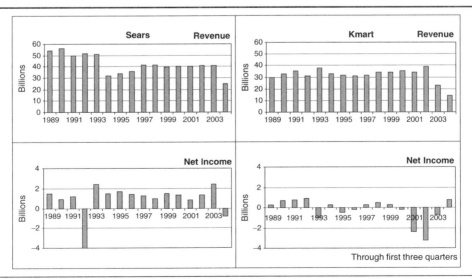

EXHIBIT C SEARS-KMART COMPARATIVE PERFORMANCE PRIOR TO MERGER

Source: New York Times, November 18, 2004.

U.S. consumers increasingly made purchases outside of these suburban malls. Lampert had amassed a significant stock position in Sears and used this holding as leverage to merge the two companies in the hopes of creating one sound business. This is no easy process, as the retail industry is highly competitive and features many notable corporate names that have fallen by the wayside. At least with Lampert overseeing the business, management is not going to get away with "business as usual," as that is what has led to some of these companies' troubles.

CORPORATE CONTROL AND DEFAULT

When a firm defaults, it typically loses control, which is passed to its creditors. Creditors may then acquire seats on the defaulting firm's board of directors and may even require that there be a change in management. Creditors may also receive an ownership position in the debtor in exchange for other consideration, such as a reduction in the amount owed. Gilson analyzed a sample of 111 publicly held companies that experienced significant financial distress between 1979 and 1985.[23] Of this sample, 61 filed for Chapter 11 and 50 restructured their debt privately. He found that banks received an average of 36% of the distressed firm's stock. Gilson found that only 46% and 43% of the predistress directors and chief executive officers (CEOs), respectively, remained in place two years later, when they had either emerged from bankruptcy or reached a negotiated restructuring agreement. It is interesting that directors who resign from distressed boards serve less often than other directors on other boards. As might be expected, very few of the distressed firms were involved in acquisition-related activity during this period.

Leveraged Buyouts and Bankruptcy Proceedings

If a company that has undergone an LBO files for Chapter 11 protection, pre-LBO creditors may try to argue that the transaction was improper and that their potential losses were a result of a deal that allowed shareholders to gain a premium while leaving the firm with insufficient capital to meet its normal postdeal obligations. Creditors may seek to recapture the distribution that the company made to shareholders, alleging that it violated state corporation laws. Under Delaware law, for example, companies are prohibited from repurchasing their shares if their capital is, or will be, impaired as a result of the transaction.[24] In addition to remedies under state law, the creditors may also try to argue that the transaction was a fraudulent transfer of assets and in violation of the U.S. Bankruptcy Code. The company may argue that the business was solvent after the deal and at that time had a reasonable expectation of sufficient future cash flows. As support for its position, it may produce a *solvency opinion* from a firm that analyzed the company's financial condition at the time of the deal and attested to its solvency as well as to the sufficiency of its cash flows.

23. Stuart C. Gilson, "Bankruptcy, Boards, Banks, and Blockholders: Evidence on Changes in Corporate Ownership and Control When Firms Default," *Journal of Financial Economics,* 27(2), October 1990, 355–388.
24. Edward Shea, *The McGraw-Hill Guide to Acquiring and Divesting Businesses* (New York: McGraw-Hill, 1999), p. 430.

Litigation Liabilities and Chapter 11

The litigation explosion in the United States has left many companies facing hundreds and even thousands of lawsuits. Examples include the asbestos and tobacco lawsuits. Unable to meet the financial pressures caused by these lawsuits, companies such as the chemical and building products maker, W. R. Grace, went to bankruptcy court to enable them to keep operating. Grace faced mounting asbestos-related liabilities and looked to Chapter 11 as a way to maintain its viability. Table 11.9 lists some companies that recently have sought bankruptcy protection due to asbestos-related litigation liabilities.

LIQUIDATION

Liquidation is a distressed firm's most drastic alternative, and it is usually pursued only when voluntary agreement and reorganization cannot be successfully implemented. In a liquidation, the company's assets are sold and the proceeds are used to satisfy claims. The sales are made pursuant to the regulations that are set forth under Chapter 7 of the Bankruptcy Code. The priority of satisfaction of claims is as follows:

- Secured creditors (If the amount owed exceeds the proceeds from the sale of the asset, the remainder becomes an unsecured claim.)
- Bankruptcy administrative costs
- Postpetition bankruptcy expenses
- Wages of workers owed for three months before the filing (limit $2,000 per employee)
- Employee benefit plan contributions owed for six months before the filing (limit $2,000 per employee)
- Unsecured customer deposits (limit $900)
- Federal, state, and local taxes
- Unfunded pension liabilities (Limit is 30% book value of preferred and common equity; any remainder becomes an unsecured claim.)
- Unsecured claims
- Preferred stockholders (up to the par value of their stock)
- Common stockholders

INVESTING IN THE SECURITIES OF DISTRESSED COMPANIES

Investing in the securities of distressed companies may offer great profit potential, but only if the buyer is willing to assume significant risks. Distressed securities are defined as the bonds or stocks of companies that have defaulted on their debt obligations or have filed for Chapter 11. The market for these securities grew significantly in the late 1980s through the 1990s. In the early 1970s, it was uncommon to find quotes for the securities of bankrupt firms.[25] This changed in the 1980s, when such quotes were common. Investment

---

25. Dale Morse and Wayne Shaw, "Investing in Bankrupt Companies," *Journal of Finance*, 43(5), December 1988, 1193–1206.

Year	Company	Year	Company
1976	North American Asbestos Corporation	2000	Stone and Webster
1982	UNR Industries		Pittsburgh Corning
	Johns-Manville		Owens Corning Fiberglass
	Amatex Corporation		E.J. Bartells
1983	Waterman Steamship Corp.		Burns & Roe Enterprises
	H & A Construction		Babcock & Wilcox
1984	Wallace & Gale		Armstrong World Industries
1985	Forty-Eight Insulations	2001	W.R. Grace
1986	United States Lines		Washington Group International
	Standard Insulations Inc.		U.S. Mineral
	Prudential Lines		U.S. Gypsum
	Pacor		Swan Transportation
1987	Todd Shipyards		Skinner Engine Company
	Nicolet		G-I Holdings
	Gatke Corp.		Federal Mogul
1988	Chemetron		Eastco Industrial Safety Corporation
	Brunswick Fabrications		Bethlehem Steel
	Asbestec	2002	Western MacArthur
1989	Raytech Corporation		Shook & Fletcher
	Lone Star Steel		Porter Hayden
	Hillsborough Holdings		Plibrico
	Delaware Insulations		North American Refractories (NARCO/RHI)
1990	Celotex		Kaiser Aluminum and Chemical
	National Gypsum		JT Thorpe
1991	Eagle Picher Industries		Harbison Walker
	H.K. Porter Co.		ARTRA (Synkoloid)
1992	Cassiar Mines		A.P. Green
	Kentile Floors		AC&S
1993	American Shipbuilding		A-Best
	Keene Corporation	2003	CE Thurston
1995	Lykes Brothers Steamship		Combustion Engineering
1996	Rock Wool Manufacturing		Congoleum
1998	Atlas Corporation		Kellogg Brown & Root/DII
	Fuller-Austin Insulation		Muralo
	M.H. Detrick	2004	Flintkote
1999	Harnischfeger Industries		Pfizer/Quigley
	Rutland Fire & Clay		Utex Industries

TABLE 11.9   CHAPTER 11 FILING BY COMPANIES WITH ASBESTOS-RELATED LITIGATION LIABILITIES

Source: www.asbestos solution.org

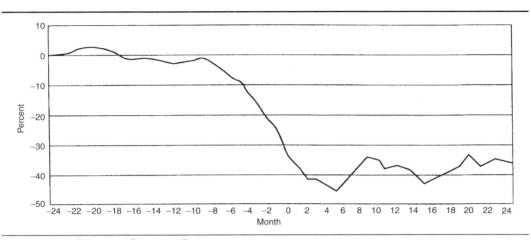

EXHIBIT 11.5 DISTRESSED SECURITIES RETURNS
Source: G. Hradsky and R. Long, "High Yield Default Losses and the Return Performance of Bankrupt Debt," *Financial Analysts Journal,* July/August 1989, 46.

firms dedicated to the distressed securities field began to actively manage distressed securities portfolios.

Hedge funds have long focused on the distressed securities market for undervalued opportunities. We have already seen how Eddie Lampert has used this market as a way of conducting a major acquisition at an attractive price. The business is fraught with risks as securities holders could easily see their investment collapse if the debtor's business deteriorates and is liquidated. Holders of distressed securities try to use the bankruptcy process to convert their discounted bonds and other debt into more valuable investments. They often are able to garner a significant equity stake in a reorganized company that hopefully will have a capital structure that it can live with.

Returns on Distressed Debt Securities

Returns on distressed debt securities have a unique profile. Hradsky and Long found that returns start to become negative approximately 18 months before default as the market internalizes information on the weak condition of the issuer.[26] These returns start to turn sharply negative five months before default and bottom out at approximately −40% around five months after default (Exhibit 11.5). If investors were to buy after default, returns would equal 7.5% over the two-year postdefault period.

Altman created an index of defaulted debt securities covering the period January 1987 through July 1990.[27] As expected, he found highly variable returns, which were as high as 37.9% in 1987 and 26.5% in 1988 but as low as 223.0% in 1989. He

---

26. G. Hradsky and R. Long, "High Yield Default Losses and the Return Performance of Bankrupt Debt," *Financial Analysts Journal,* July/August 1989, 46.
27. Edward I. Altman, "Investing in Distressed Securities," in Dominic DiNapoli, Sanford C. Sigoloff, and Robert F. Cushman, eds., *Workouts and Turnarounds* (Homewood, IL: Business Irwin One, 1991), pp. 663–685.

Monthly Returns Observations, 1987–90				
	Defaulted Debt	**S&P 500 Equity**	**Value Line Equity**	**Merrill Lynch High-Yield**
Defaulted Debt	1.00	0.50	0.59	0.56
S&P 500 Equity	0.50	1.00	0.87	0.56
Value Line Equity	0.59	0.87	1.00	0.69
Merrill Lynch High-Yield	0.56	0.56	0.69	1.00

TABLE 11.10   CORRELATION MATRIX BETWEEN DEFAULTED DEBT SECURITY RETURNS AND VARIOUS EQUITY AND HIGH-YIELD BOND RETURNS

Source: Edward I. Altman, "Investing in Distressed Securities," in Dominic DiNapoli, Sanford C. Sigoloff, and Robert Cushman, eds., *Workouts and Turnarounds* (Homewood, IL: Business One Irwin, 1991), pp. 663–685.

found an average annual rate of return over this period of 10%. This exceeded the high-yield index return for the same period, which was equal to 6.7%. One must be careful drawing long-term conclusions from this short analysis period. However, there is some evidence to support the high-return but high-risk attributes of distressed debt securities.

Altman also analyzed the correlation of the returns on debt securities with those on other major categories of investments. Portfolio theory shows that if there is a low correlation between returns on distressed securities and other potential investment portfolio components, these securities may provide diversification benefits.[28] He found a lower-than-expected correlation, 0.56, between the returns on distressed debt securities and high-yield bonds (Table 11.10). This suggests that managers of high-yield portfolios might want to consider adding distressed debt securities to this nondefaulted high-yield portfolio to increase their overall returns while obtaining some diversification benefits.

Control Opportunities Using Distressed Debt Securities

One of the typical changes that a reorganized company undergoes in the Chapter 11 process is to have its capital structure altered, with some debt being replaced by equity and some, possibly all, prepetition equity disappearing. Debtholders may become equity holders. Buyers of distressed debt securities may actually be seeking to obtain an equity stake in the distressed company when they purchase the debt securities. This has helped fuel the market for *claims trading.* Investors in Chapter 11 companies may buy the claims themselves or purchase components of the bankrupt company as the firm seeks to finance its turnaround or *fund its reorganization plan.*

---

28. For a good discussion of portfolio theory, see Sid Mittra and Chris Gassen, *Investment Analysis and Portfolio Management* (New York: Harcourt Brace Jovanovich, 1981).

The more aggressive of these opportunistic investors are sometimes referred to as *bankruptcy sharks* or *vultures*. They purchase the debt of bankrupt companies with a goal of taking control of the company. The strategy may yield high returns to those who are able to aggressively participate in the reorganization negotiation process to acquire the desired control. Although the securities may be purchased relatively inexpensively, the outcome of the negotiation process, which may be quite lengthy, is very uncertain. For this reason, this type of takeover strategy is particularly risky.

CASE STUDY

CAMPEAU BANKRUPTCY

In January 1988, Campeau Corporation launched a takeover of Federated Stores. The company had a market value of $4.25 billion, with $2.93 billion being equity and $1.33 billion being debt. The purchase price was double the market value of the company ($8.17 billion). The deal was a highly leveraged transaction, with 97% of the total value financed by debt.

In the beginning of 1990, after two years of troubled operations in which the company failed to refinance its takeover debt and bridge loans through the issuance of junk bonds, Campeau filed for Chapter 11 reorganization. Campeau's management of Federated Stores was poor. Under Campeau's reign the company suffered through a difficult Christmas season in 1990, which was also affected by the overall downturn in the economy as the country moved into a recession. In the period between the acquisition and the bankruptcy filing, EBITDA declined. The board of directors took away all operating responsibility from Robert Campeau. The company had excess inventories and had to lower prices in an effort to sell off these inventories while paying down the debt.

During bankruptcy, a management team composed of new CEO Allen Questrom, President James Zimmerman, and CFO Ronald Tysoe increased operating efficiency and raised capital through asset sales while managing to keep most of the management team of this large department store chain mainly intact. They sold off or closed unprofitable stores, streamlined operations, and remodeled stores that needed improvement. Kaplan concludes that the Chapter 11 process worked remarkably well.[a] The process was not costly in terms of a deterioration of value. He compared the value of the postbankrupt company with the preacquisition value. He measured the postbankruptcy value of Federated, net of bankruptcy costs and inclusive of interim cash flows earned during bankruptcy. As Table A shows, the value of the company increased with the acquisition from a preacquisition market value of $4.25 billion to the $8.17 billion value Campeau paid. Using the preceding definition of value, Kaplan computed a $7.81 billion value before an adjustment for market fluctuations. After taking into account market fluctuations, he arrived at a substantially higher value ($11.31 billion).

Kaplan's analysis shows that a leveraged acquisition may increase value even if the company proves not to have sufficient cash flows to service its debt. Campeau's inability to service its debt led to its Chapter 11 filing. However, the Chapter 11 process did not result in a deterioration in value of the bankrupt company. Kaplan does not imply that this is the rule. Rather, he uses the Campeau Chapter 11 reorganization to illustrate that if the process is handled correctly, Chapter 11 does not necessarily result in a loss of company value.

[a]Steven N. Kaplan, "Campeau's Acquisition of Federated Stores," *Journal of Financial Economics,* 35(1), February 1994, 123–136.

Market-adjusted and nominal values[a] of Federated Department Stores (A) post-Campeau, post-Chapter 11, (B) pre-Campeau, and (C) purchase price paid by Campeau Corporation. Post-Campeau, post—Chapter 11 value of Federated equals the sum of asset sales, interim cash flows, and the value of remaining Federated assets. All sales are in billions of dollars.

	Market-Adjusted December 1987	Market-Adjusted February 1992	Nominal
(A) Post-Campeau, post—Chapter 11 Federated market value			
Asset sales[b]	3.77	7.31	4.04
Interim cash flows	0.79	1.52	1.29
Less direct costs of bankruptcy[c]	(0.14)	(0.27)	(0.27)
Value remaining assets	1.41	2.75	2.75
Total	5.85	11.31	7.81
(B) Pre-Campeau Federated market value[d]	4.25	8.25	4.25
(C) Price paid by Campeau for Federated[e]	7.67	14.89	8.17

TABLE A   POST-CAMPEAU FEDERATED VALUE, PRE-CAMPEAU FEDERATED VALUE, AND CAMPEAU PURCHASE PRICE

[a] Market-adjusted values in December 1987 equal the actual values discounted from the month in which they occur to December 31, 1987, by the actual return on the S&P 500. If invested in the S&P 500 on January 1, 1988, the market-adjusted value would equal the actual value in the month the cash flow occurs. The market-adjusted values in February 1992 equal the actual values adjusted from the month in which they occur to February 1992, by the actual return on the S&P 500 over that period.

[b] Asset sales are the value of the divisions sold by Federated from May 1988 to February 1989. These values are detailed in Kaplan (1989).

[c] Interim cash flow equals EBITDA, less capital expenditures, less the increase in net working capital, plus the proceeds from asset sales, less taxes paid.

[d] Pre-Campeau Federated market value on December 31, 1987, equals the sum of the market value of Federated debt.

[e] Purchase price paid by Campeau is the sum of the market value paid for all equity and the fees paid in May 1988 and the book value of Federated debt outstanding on January 30, 1988.

Role of Vulture Investors and the Market for Control of Distressed Firms

Hotchkiss and Mooradian analyzed the role of vulture investors in the governance of 288 firms that defaulted on their debt between 1980 and 1993.[29] Contrary to the reputation that such investors have, Hotchkiss and Mooradian's research found that they had a positive effect on the postdebt operating performance. They found that postrestructuring operating performance was improved relative to the predefault level when the vulture investor becomes CEO or in some way gains control of the company. They attribute this improved performance to enhanced managerial discipline. It is interesting that they also found that a greater percentage of vulture firms were reorganized under Chapter 11 (70.3% for vulture

29. Edith S. Hotchkiss and Robert M. Mooradian, "Vulture Investors and the Market for Control of Distressed Firms," *Journal of Financial Economics*, 43, 1997, 401–432.

firms versus 39% for nonvulture firms), indicating that these investors seek the benefits of the Chapter 11 process more than management.

CASE STUDY

BANKRUPTCY RUSSIAN STYLE—A HOSTILE TAKEOVER TOOL (A UNIQUE SET OF RULES)

In what has been termed legal extortion in the media, politically connected creditors have used the bankruptcy laws to bring about hostile takeovers of relatively healthy companies.[a] Russia enacted a new bankruptcy law in 1998, and it allows a company with as little as $5,000 in debts to be taken over if it is behind in its payments by three months. For Russia, such a position is not unusual because many companies, and the government itself, are regularly behind in payments. Under the bankruptcy laws of most developed countries, companies that are viable can be reorganized, whereas those for which there is no hope are liquidated. In Russia, viable companies are taken over by unscrupulous bidders, who are sometimes competitors.

Under its 1992 bankruptcy law, passed after the collapse of the former Soviet Union, the advantages for debtors were so great that they used the law to avoid paying bills that they could afford to pay. The 1998 version of the law sought to redress this drawback of the 1992 law, but it went too far. The threshold for debt that could trigger a takeover of control of the company was set too low. Takeover artists then used this threshold to buy up the debts of target companies and use them to take control. Hostile bidders used political relationships to help enforce these provisions of the law. As a result, bankruptcies in Russia have soared, creating still another problem for the nascent democracy that is struggling with its belated attempts at capitalism.

[a]Sabrina Tavernise, "Using Bankruptcy as a Takeover Tool," *New York Times,* October 7, 2000, p. C1.

SUMMARY

The world of bankruptcy changed dramatically in the 1980s as companies began to discover the creative corporate finance uses of Chapter 11 of the Bankruptcy Code. Chapter 11 reorganization became a method of corporate restructuring that under certain circumstances can bestow significant benefits to the distressed company. By formulating a reorganization plan, the company may restructure its liabilities and engage in other forms of restructuring, such as selling off assets to fund the plan. The Chapter 11 company obtains an automatic stay after entering Chapter 11, and creditors are held at bay by the court while the debtor and possibly the creditors structure a reorganization plan.

The reorganization plan must be approved by creditors before being approved by the court. Initially, only the debtor may propose a reorganization plan. This time period is called the exclusivity period. At the end of this period, which is initially 120 days but is often extended by the court, the creditors may propose an alternative plan if they oppose aspects of the debtor's plan. The plan must be fair and feasible as determined by the court. If all classes of creditors fail to approve the plan, it may be crammed down on the dissenting class, as long as there is one class that approves it.

Prepackaged bankruptcies became popular in the late 1980s. In a prepackaged bankruptcy, approval of a plan is obtained before entering bankruptcy. The bankruptcy process is significantly shorter in a prepackaged bankruptcy. Therefore, there is less disruption to the debtor's business, and both debtors and creditors may gain from this form of reorganization. There may also be tax advantages that this alternative may pose that are not available in a workout. A workout is a voluntary agreement that does not involve a bankruptcy filing.

Trading in the securities of bankrupt companies, both bonds and equity, may be a high-risk way to implement a takeover. The purchasers of the securities may participate in the bankruptcy process in an effort to win control of the postbankrupt company. Although this method may enable a company to be taken over relatively inexpensively, it is highly unpredictable and fraught with risk for these investors.

12

CORPORATE GOVERNANCE

There has been much discussion of corporate governance in the media over the past decade. Much of this attention has been brought on by accounting scandals such as those that occurred at Enron, Adelphia, and WorldCom. This has led to changes in laws and accounting rules in an effort to achieve more accurate reporting of financial data to markets. However, there has been much less focus on changes in governance related to mergers and acquisitions (M&As). Given the problematic track record of many M&As, there is still a long way to go with this aspect of corporate governance reforms.

In this chapter we discuss how corporations are governed. As part of that process we will examine the role of the board of directors and how they oversee management. We will see how boards are put together and how directors are selected. We will try to identify the characteristics of good boards versus bad boards. We will see that one important factor in differentiating good from bad boards is the extent to which the board is composed of outsiders as opposed to insiders. Abundant research has shown that the makeup of the board, and the director selection process, plays an important role in increasing shareholder value. Such research shows that boards work best when they include more independent directors who are not beholden to the chief executive officer (CEO). By being independent, they are freer to hold management accountable for their decisions and the impact those decisions have on shareholder wealth. Independence may enable them to make objective decisions that are in the interest of shareholders, to whom they have a fiduciary responsibility.

FAILED CORPORATE GOVERNANCE: ACCOUNTING SCANDALS

Failed corporate governance has clearly played a significant role in many of the accounting scandals that have captured the headlines in recent years. In light of the disastrous results, it is easy to conclude that management failed to look after shareholders' interests, while the board failed to make sure that the company was run in a manner that would do so. One of the more extreme cases was the Enron debacle. This company had grown dramatically during the 1990s to be one of the largest companies in the United States. Unfortunately, the favorable financial picture that Enron presented to the market was fueled by fictitious earnings that were partially generated through the use of "special purpose entities" (SPEs) (partnerships formed by the company) to create a false image of a profitable company with much less debt than it actually had.[1] When we consider that each Enron director was paid an average of $380,619 in cash and stock, the seventh highest director compensation of all U.S. companies at that time, one has to wonder why there was not better director oversight.[2]

What is even more troubling is that the Enron scandal was not an isolated event. The cable company Adelphia also reported false results to the markets. As a result, upper management, including John J. Rigas and his son Timothy, were convicted of conspiracy and fraud. Among the acts they were found to engage in was the creation of imaginary customers, whereby the market would be led to believe that the company was larger and growing more rapidly that what was really the case. This is an important valuation issue, as one of the measures used to place a value on a cable company is its number of customers.[3] Still another prominent example of accounting manipulations was the one involving Sunbeam that was led by Al "Chainsaw" Dunlap. He was accused of inflating sales by shipping appliances to customers who would accept the deliveries in warehouses supplied by Sunbeam, even if these deliveries were never actually cash sales.

One accounting scandal that is closely tied to a failed M&A strategy involved World-Com and its convicted CEO, Bernie Ebbers. WorldCom grew dramatically through the fourth and fifth merger waves to become one of the leading telecom companies in the world. This M&A-fueled growth was not sustainable, and Ebbers resorted to other means to create profits that the company did not actually earn. WorldCom was the largest bankruptcy in history. This corporate collapse and others such as Enron gave rise to various regulatory changes, as well as a new focus on corporate governance. Unfortunately, the discussion of corporate governance has focused more on the accounting frauds, and less emphasis has been placed on the need to more closely monitor the M&As that companies may engage in. However, this is an important governance function and an increased focus on this area is needed. In this chapter we will discuss how companies are governed and how that governance process can be improved to result in better M&A strategy. While much of the discussions about WorldCom have focused on the falsified accounting data, insufficient attention has been paid to the shoddy way the company's directors rubber-stamped proposed acquisitions and allowed the process of serial acquisitions to continue long after its benefits had dissipated. The company pursed serial acquisitions to create the false impression of growth when it was actually becoming less profitable. Its CEO, Ebbers, was best at doing deals and terrible at managing a company—especially a large multibillion dollar enterprise. The board should have been aware of this and insisted on Ebbers's turning over the day-to-day management of the firm to someone who would be better able to run such a large company. The directors would eventually personally pay for their negligent efforts when they became the target of civil lawsuits from shareholders.

1. Bethany McLean and Peter Elkind, *The Smartest Guys in the Room: The Amazing Rise and Scandalous Fall of Enron* (New York: Portfolio/Penguin, 2003).
2. Ivan Brick, Oded Palmon, and John K. Wald, "CEO Compensation, Director's Compensation, and Firm Performance: Evidence of Cronyism" unpublished paper, available at SSRN: http://ssrn.com/abstract=303574 or DOI: 10.2139/ssrn.303574.
3. Barry Meier, "2 Guilty in Fraud at Cable Giant," *New York Times*, July 9, 2004, p. 1.

SARBANES-OXLEY ACT

The aforementioned accounting scandals in the United States gave rise to legislation designed to facilitate more accurate financial reporting. This came through the Sarbanes-Oxley Act (SOA, also referred to as SOX), which was enacted in July 2002. The law changed the way companies reported their financial statements and the way they had their financials audited for public release. One of the improvements the law put in place was to reduce opportunities for conflicts of interest. Auditors were limited in their ability to profit from other work, such as consulting, for the company they are auditing. This sought to remove incentives to provide more favorable financial data for the company that might reward them with additional, non-auditing work. Auditors now have to be more independent—a theme that pervades much of the corporate governance reform discussions.

SOA also focused on the role of investment bankers and their relationship with broker-age firms. As part of the rapid changes that have taken place in the financial services and banking industry, financial institutions have become more diversified and it is not unusual to see investment banking and brokerage operations housed within the same "financial supermarket." Merrill Lynch and Citicorp are examples of such diversified institutions. The law focused on conflicts of interest by investment bankers, who may use their position to try to influence research reports that may be issued by a securities operation. It was recognized that there was a potential for conflict through any close association between the marketing investment banking services and the supposedly objective research reports that a securities firm might issue. This has always been a source of conflict for companies that seek to objectively advise clients on the investment benefits of a security while also hoping they would purchase that security from them so that they could derive a commission on the sale. This law did not do away with this potential conflict, but it did put more pressure on companies that might be inclined to deceive investors.

Another major change brought on by SOA is that the CEO and chief financial officer (CFO) have to personally certify the financial statements being released to the market and verify that they are not aware of any material misstatements contained in them. The law requires that the CEO and CFO will forfeit bonuses and compensation if the statements have to be subsequently restated due to material inaccuracies contained in them. The statements themselves also have to provide clearer disclosures, especially with respect to off–balance sheet items that would affect how an investor would interpret the data contained in them. This was designed to prevent Enron-like deceptions through the release of financial statements that were not sufficiently complete.

Section 404 of SOA requires that corporations perform audits of internal controls so as to prevent disasters such as Enron. When the law was first adopted this section received very little attention. However, as companies now have to comply with it, this section has proven to be the most objectionable to corporate America. The audits have to be done pursuant to Auditing Standard Number 2 of the Public Company Accounting Oversight Board (PCAOB). As part of the process companies have to report if they have detected any material weakness in relevant controls and how they are going to address their flaws. In an effort to avoid being found noncompliant, companies may report possible weaknesses even when they do not believe they are a problem. Then when the weaknesses get reported to securities markets, stock prices may decline. This had led some companies to contend that this part of the law has led to much waste with little gain. It is too early to say whether this will be the long-term conclusion of companies. However, it is clear that SOA has added to the costs of being a public company. These costs, many of which are fixed or semi-fixed, are disproportionately borne by smaller public companies. This finding has been supported by a study conducted by the General Accounting Office.

Corporations contended that the problem was not so much the wording of Section 404 but its implementation. Smaller public companies have felt the burden of this section more than larger firms. The adverse effects of public US companies can be seen in a loss of IPO/listing business by NASDAQ and the New York Stock Exchange to the London and Hong Kong Exchanges. US regulators have been somewhat sympathetic and have issued new guidance.

While there has been much media focus in the past few years on corporate governance reform in the United States, other nations have been making important changes in their governance and reporting processes. For example, the Japanese accounting firm, ChuoAoyama PriceWaterhouseCoopers was suspended by Japan's Financial Regulator, the Financial Services Agency. The Agency took this action as a result of false financial reports that were issued by some of that firm's public clients. Japan, an economy in the process of implementing major changes, also changed its corporate law to include some features similar to those that are contained in SOA. For example, the law requires that companies institute internal controls that will help ensure that financial data that are reported are accurate. In addition, The Tokyo Exchange has also been actively de-listing companies that do not provide accurate disclosure to financial markets.

OTHER REGULATORY CHANGES

In addition to those changes brought on by formal laws, the accounting industry responded with its own changes in professional standards. As part of this process the PCAOB was created. This entity is a nonprofit corporation that oversees the auditing of public companies. Each firm doing audits needs to register with PCAOB. This entity also oversees the auditing committee at public companies and requires there be some demonstration of expertise on each public company's auditing committee.

The accounting profession has also devoted new attention to correct inaccurate disclosures. This attention has been focused all the way down to the education and training of accountants, as the profession has learned to place greater focus on more rigorous auditing standards. The various legal and professional changes, however, are not really directed at the governance problems that relate to M&As. These problems are much more difficult to regulate. They are not as obvious as finding false numbers in financial statements. They involve preventing deals that are not in shareholders' interests. Part of this process is making sure that a company pursues its best long-term strategy to maximize shareholder returns. This is not a process that easily lends itself to "regulation." The solution to better M&A governance lies in putting in place better, more vigilant and knowledgeable directors who take their duties seriously and who are willing to closely monitor management to make sure that companies work to advance shareholders' interests.

CORPORATE GOVERNANCE

Corporations are one of three general forms of business organizations: sole proprietorships, partnerships, and corporations. Corporations trace their roots back many centuries as a business form that was designed to encourage the investment of capital into potentially risky ventures such as oceangoing trade that were subject to major risks (e.g., bad weather or theft from those such as pirates). Some of the earliest corporate charters were the Moscovy Company in 1555, the Spanish Company in 1577, and the Dutch East India Company in 1601.[4]

Corporations provide an incentive for shareholders to invest by limiting their exposure to their investment in the entity. Normally the personal assets are shielded from exposure to litigation. This is different from sole proprietorships and partnerships, where the owners' personal assets are at risk. However, in recent years alternatives to simple partnerships have been formed that limit the exposure and liability of partners. As Exhibit 12.1 shows, the most common form of business is corporations and this percentage accounts for the vast majority of the dollar value of businesses.

While limited liability is a benefit, shareholders in corporations face the problem that they have to select others to represent their interests. This is usually done by an election of a board of directors by shareholders. These directors in turn select managers who run the company on a day-to-day basis (see Exhibit 12.2).

Corporate Democracy

Corporate democracy is different from the democratic process that one learns about in political science. Elections for directors are rarely contested. With rare exceptions, shareholders, while the true owners of the company, have only two choices when they receive their ballots for election of directors: vote to approve the slate or throw away their ballots and withhold their vote. Occasionally the withholding of votes has been used to voice displeasure with the board and management. This was the case when a large percentage of Disney's shareholders withheld their support of Michael Eisner, CEO of Disney. This led to the eventual departure of the highly paid Eisner.

In recent years there has been discussion about changing the director voting system from one of plurality to majority voting. In certain embarrassing cases shareholders have been so upset with management and the board that a majority withheld their votes, allowing the slate of directors proposed by the company to "win" without having the support of a majority of the board. This has given rise to many shareholder proposals that would require that directors receive a majority of the votes in order to hold office.

Withholding votes is one option but shareholders who are determined to change the board may pursue a proxy contest. As discussed in Chapter 6, trying to contest an election is expensive and is often unsuccessful for the insurgent. Ballots that are sent out by corporations generally do not feature an alternative slate of candidates. Insurgents who seek to have shareholders vote for their directors have to send out their own ballots and

---

4. Jack Beatty, "Of Huge and Greatness," in Jack Beatty ed., *Colossus* (New York: Broadway Books, 2001), p. 6.

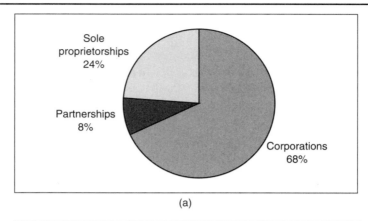

(a)

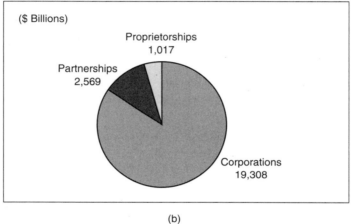

(b)

Exhibit 12.1   (a) Employee Enterprise Establishments; (b) Business Receipts (2001)

Source: (a) "Special Tabulations of 2000 Country Business Patterns," U.S. Census; (b) "Statistical Abstract of the United States: 2001, Business Enterprise," p. 483.

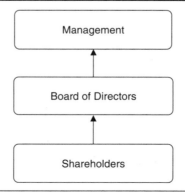

Exhibit 12.2   Flowchart: Management, Directors, and Shareholders

absorb the substantial cost of conducting a campaign to convince shareholders that their views and candidates will better advance shareholders' interests. As a partial solution, William Donaldson, former chairman of the Securities and Exchange Commission (SEC), suggested that institutional investors be able to propose a so-called short slate of directors who could achieve a minority of board seats. This proposal, however, was strongly opposed by corporate America.

Agency Costs

In smaller companies, shareholders may also choose the managers of the company. In this case, there is less of a concern that the managers will take actions that are not in the best interests of shareholders. In large companies, however, shareholders hold a relatively small percent of the total shares outstanding. When shareholders own a portfolio of assets, with their equity positions in any given company constituting a relatively small percent of their total assets, they do not have a big incentive to oversee the operations of the company. In addition, even if they wanted to, as the shareholders' percent of total shares outstanding declines, shareholders have less ability to influence the operations of the company—even if they wanted to devote time to doing so. For this reason, shareholders must trust that managers will really run the business in a manner that maximizes shareholder wealth. One of the concerns that shareholders have is that managers will pursue their own personal goals and will not run the company in a manner that will maximize shareholder wealth. If managers do pursue policies that shareholders oppose, their relatively small share holdings often do not allow them to take actions to effectively oppose management. Shareholders have to put their trust in the board of directors and hope that they will look after their collective interests when they monitor management. This is the essence of the board's fiduciary duties. When directors are insufficiently diligent and do not require managers to act in shareholders' interests, they violate their fiduciary duties.

The topic of agency costs was popular in the 1970s and 1980s. Yet it is ironic that it remains in the forefront as we go through the 2000s. This seems to be a function of human nature and the inability of some to put their ethical obligations ahead of their own personal ambitions. The position of a director is not a full-time position and directors pursue other work including possibly serving on other boards. One survey of directors reported that on average there were 5.6 board meetings per year and that they devoted an average of 19 hours per month on board issues.[5] The challenge of board members is to make sure that the time they allocate to monitoring managers is sufficient to allow them to ensure that management runs the company in a way that maximizes shareholder wealth.

Since directors are not generally monitoring the company on a daily basis, they use periodic updates from management and monitor their performance as reflected in various financial statements such as quarterly reports. Even with such reporting, there is opportunity for the managers, the agents of the shareholders, to pursue their own self-interest at the expense of shareholders. When this occurs, the owners of the company are said

---

5. "What Do Directors Think" Study: 2003, *Corporate Board Member,* July 2003.

to incur agency costs. Shareholders will never be able to eliminate agency costs and it will always exist to some level. The goal is to limit it to some minimal or acceptable level. One of the solutions that has been used to try to control agency costs is to create incentives for managers to act in the interests of shareholders. This is sometimes done by giving management shares or stock options that would enable them to profit when shareholder values increase, thereby aligning the interests of both managers and shareholders.[6] According to a 2006 annual survey of CEO compensation done by Mercer Consulting, 192 of the CEOs cashed in options in 2005 that had a median value of $3,493,400.[7] Occasionally, the value of the grants rises to much greater heights. In 2005, the CEO of Capital One cashed in options equal to $249.27 million.[8] Another of the more extreme cases of profiting from exercising options was Disney's Michael Eisner, who in 1997 exercised over $500 million in options in Disney.

For a while option grants were touted as the solution to the agency costs problem. However, with the various highly publicized accounting scandals of the late 1990s and 2000s, many have questioned the large offerings of stock options. Option grants are given by the board with the details of the grant being handled by the board's compensation committee. At some companies there have been questions about the timing of the option grants, which sometimes come too close to upward movements in the stock price to be coincidental. In addition, some companies have given option grant recipients the right to select the date when options are granted. Normally options do not vest for a period of time, such as a year or more, and have an exercise price of the closing stock price on the day the grant is given. Therefore, the date that the options are officially granted can make a big difference in their value. This whole issue has come under increased scrutiny in recent years.

As a result of concerns about the appropriateness of some option grants to managers, this method of reducing agency costs has become somewhat less popular. To some extent, this solution became more of a problem than the problem it was designed to solve.

CEO Compensation and Agency Costs

The recent accounting scandals have attracted even more attention to what was already a major source of concern—the high compensation of the CEOs of U.S. companies. Many questioned whether these CEOs really were generating value for shareholders consistent with the high compensation they withdrew from these firms. The compensation of U.S. CEOs seems particularly high when compared with their counterparts in Europe and Asia. The difference in these compensation levels can be readily seen in data compiled by Towers Perrin that shows that the average CEO compensation at 365 of the largest publicly trading corporations was $13.1 million in 2000. In this particular study of very large U.S. corporations, CEO compensation was 531 times the average employee's compensation, and in the country with the second highest multiple, Brazil, it was 57 times.

6. Michael Jensen and W.H. Meckling, "The Theory of the Firm: Managerial Behavior, Agency Costs and Ownership Structure," *Journal of Financial Economics,* 3, 1976, 305–360.
7. Joann Lublin, "Adding it All Up," *Wall Street Journal,* April 10, 2006, R1.
8. Ibid.

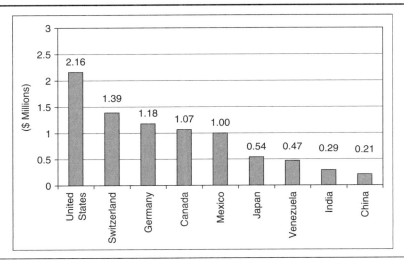

EXHIBIT 12.3 INTERNATIONAL COMPARATIVE CEO COMPENSATION
Source: Lauren Etter, "Are CEOs Worth Their Weight in Gold?", *Wall Street Journal,* January 21–22, 2006.

Compared to developed economies such as the United Kingdom it was 25 times greater, while in Germany it was 11 times, and in Japan the multiple was 10.[9] However, other more recent surveys by Towers Perrin portray a smaller but still very significant gap. When considering large companies in general, but not necessarily the very largest, Towers Perrin found that the average U.S. CEO received $2.2 million, whereas their British counterparts earned half that much.[10] Part of the reason for this is that corporate reforms were adopted in Britain that required that shareholders vote annually on executive compensation. When we consider that institutional investors wield significant power at some British corporations, it is not hard to understand why executive compensation seems under better control in that nation.

The cross-country CEO compensation level differences have been demonstrated in other research. For example, surveys have documented the magnitude of the differences between CEO compensation in the United States compared with the rest of the developed world. Canyon and Murphy found that CEOs in 500 of the largest corporations in the United Kingdom earned in the aggregate £330 million and £74 million from exercising options, whereas the top 500 CEOs in the United States earned £3.2 billion and £2 billion from exercising options.[11] Still other surveys, using different data, show somewhat less dramatic differences in CEO compensation levels, but the fact that CEO compensation in the United States is far above that of other major countries remains (Exhibit 12.3).[12]

---

9. Business Week Online, "Spreading the Yankee Way of Pay," April 18, 2001.
10. Joanna L. Ossinger, "Poorer Relations: When it Comes to CEO Pay, Why Are the British So Different?", *Wall Street Journal*, April 10, 2006, R6.
11. Martin J. Canyon and Kevin Murphy, "The Prince and the Pauper? CEO Pay in the United States and the United Kingdom," *The Economic Journal,* 110, November 2000, F640–F671.
12. Laura Etter, "Are CEOs Worth Their Weight in Gold?", *Wall Street Journal,* January 21, 2006, A7.

The differences between the compensation levels of U.S. CEOs and their counterparts in other parts of the world cannot be explained by cost-of-living factors. The fact that the U.S. economy is the richest in the world still does not explain these large compensation differences, as the gap in the CEO compensation is far in excess of the relative differences in the size of the economies. Moreover, although a larger economy may have more large corporations than a smaller economy, other reasons must be found for the fact that at comparably sized companies across different countries, the U.S. CEO earns a far greater compensation. Given that CEOs have become accustomed to earning the highest compensation in the world by international standards, shareholders in these companies have a right to expect superior performance in exchange. Indeed, if it could be shown that U.S. CEOs generated increased shareholder value commensurate with their higher compensation level, shareholders would not have cause to complain. It is only when the value of their investment does not benefit from the high pay that they give their CEOs that shareholders have reason to be upset.

If U.S. shareholders often do not receive sufficient benefits from the higher compensation they pay their CEOs, then this raises questions regarding how effective the corporate governance process is in controlling the financial benefits that CEOs seem to be extracting from the company without a comparable gain for shareholders. A study by Core, Holthausen, and Larker provides some insight into the relationship between CEO compensation and the makeup of boards.[13] They examined 205 large corporations over a three-year period in 14 different industries. They related the different levels of CEO compensation to different characteristics of boards.

Implicit in their analysis, Core, Holthausen, and Larker assumed that larger boards were less effective and more susceptible to CEO influence.[14] This conclusion is intuitive, as at a larger board each director constitutes a smaller percent of the total board and commands a smaller percent of the total votes needed to approve board decisions. Additionally, Core, Holthausen, and Larker also looked at the percent of outside directors on boards as well as the number of "gray" directors. These were directors who receive other compensation or benefits beyond the director payment that directors receive for serving on the board. In addition, the study's authors also assumed that if the director was appointed to the board after the CEO was in place, then the CEO played a role in that decision. Their analysis also highlighted interlocked directors, as those directors may be weaker from a corporate governance perspective (interlocked boards will be discussed in greater detail later in this chapter). They also assigned a negative value to CEOs being older (over 70) and being on too many other boards.[15]

Core, Holthausen, and Larker are consistent with human nature. Their research showed an inverse relationship between CEO compensation and the percentage of outside directors on the board. They also found that CEO compensation was positively related to board size as well as to the number of members of the board who were appointed by the CEO.

---

13. John E. Core, Robert W. Holtausen, and David Larker, *Journal of Financial Economics*, 51, 1999, 371–406.
14. David Yermack, "Higher Market Valuation of Companies with a Small Board of Directors," *Journal of Financial Economics*, 40, 1996, 185–211.
15. A. Shivdasani, "Board Composition, Ownership Structure and Hostile Takeovers, *Journal of Accounting and Economics*, 16, 1993, 167–198.

CEO compensation was also greater for the directors who were gray, over age 69, or who served on three or more boards. There was also an inverse relationship between CEO compensation and the size of the share holdings of the CEO. In addition, they also found that CEO compensation was lower when there were external blockholders who owned 5% or more of the outstanding shares. These external blockholders had sufficient power to try to keep the CEO's pursuit of higher personal compensation in check. The lower the size of the holdings of the largest shareholders, the less likely they will have the power, or the incentive, to hold the CEO in check. Earlier in this book we have seen the important role large blockholders can play in preventing value-reducing deals.

Managerial Compensation, Mergers, and Takeovers

Managers often personally gain from M&As. That is, many CEOs and other senior management have employment agreements that provide them with large payouts upon changes of control. Sometimes such agreements are called golden parachutes. An example of such payouts is the change of control provisions in Caesar's Entertainment's CEO, Wallace R. Barr's employment agreement, which has been reported to provide total compensation of almost $20 million in accelerated options and stock awards.[16] In early July 2004, Harrah's announced that it would acquire Caesar's for $5.2 billion. Usually shareholders do not have a lot to say against such large payouts. In theory, target shareholders may stand to gain from the premiums offered by a bidder. However, target management may stand to lose their positions and their compensation if there is a change in control and the bidder replaces them. Employment agreements that provide financial benefits for managers who pursue changes in control that may result in the termination of their positions may help shareholders receive a wealth increasing control premium. However, it may not always work in the way outlined in the theory. Sometimes managers may promote deals that will create a situation where they receive the payout even if the deals are not the best move for shareholders at the time. This seemed to be the position of the California Public Employees Retirement System (CALPERS) when it voted against the 2004 merger of two health care companies—Amthem, Inc. and WellPoint Health Networks. Total executive compensation from the change of control provisions equaled approximately $200 million. Leonard Schaeffer, WellPoint's CEO, alone was to receive $47 million in various severance agreements. The deal was eventually completed in November 2004 at a $20.88 billion value.

The issue is important due to the pivotal role that a target CEO may play in negotiating his or her own postmerger position and compensation. While it probably shouldn't be part of the premerger negotiating process, it is well known that it is. As an example, it has been reported that the breakdown of the merger negotiations in the fourth merger wave between American Home Products (now called Wyeth) and Monsanto was the result of neither CEO being willing to relinquish control of the merged company to the other.[17] These issues should be secondary to the impact the deal would have on shareholder

---

16. Gretchen Morgenson, "No Wonder CEOs Love Those Mergers," *New York Times,* July 18, 2004, Sec. 3, p. 1.
17. Thomas M. Burton and Elyse Tanouye, *Wall Street Journal,* October 13, 1998, p. B1.

wealth. CEOs should consider the impact on shareholders well before the impact on their own careers. Placing their careers and positions ahead of shareholders' interests is a violation of their fiduciary obligations to shareholders. However, to deny that this occurs in practice is to be naïve. This is one of many areas that need to be addressed in corporate governance reform as it relates to M&As. Hartzell, Ofek, and Yermack analyzed 311 primarily friendly transactions over the period 1995–1997.[18] They found that target CEOs enjoyed mean wealth increases between $8 million and $11 million. The bulk of these financial gains came from increases in stock and options as well as from golden parachute payments. Some CEOs even receive last-minute increases in their golden parachute agreements—presumably in exchange for promoting the deal. They also found that about one-half of the CEOs became officers in the buying entity although their departure rates over the three years following the merger were very high. Even for these exits, however, the former target CEO received enhanced compensation.

The Hartzell, Ofek, and Yermack study cannot be used, however, to definitely determine if the bountiful compensation enjoyed by target CEOs comes at the expense of target shareholders. In order to come up with a reliable measure of the target shareholder wealth effects, they would need to also be able to consider a sample of both completed and rejected deals, so that we would be able to include the effects of the premiums that target shareholders receive as well as to try to measure the "lost premiums" from those deals that did not go through because target CEOs could not come up with a sufficiently rich compensation package for them to accept the proposal.

One of the potential limiting factors that hinders unscrupulous managers from expanding their own compensation beyond what would be prudent is the threat of takeovers. Managers who extract excessive benefits from their own companies or who pursue a strategy that enriches themselves, as opposed to shareholders, may create an opportunity for an outside bidder to acquire the company in a hostile takeover and correct this inefficiency. Agrawal and Knoeber examined a sample of 450 corporations and looked at the compensation of their CEOs.[19] They divided their sample into two subgroups, where the CEO either was or was not protected by an employment agreement or golden parachute that would provide him or her with protection from removal by a hostile bidder. The bidder could remove the CEO following an acquisition, but the CEO's short-term compensation might not be affected that much. Their results showed what they referred to as a *competition effect*. This occurs when managers receive lower compensation when there is a greater threat of takeover. They also found what they termed a *risk effect*—that managers tend to demand more compensation when they are employed by companies that are more likely to be takeover targets.

18. Jay Hartzell, Eli Ofek, and David Yermack, "What's In It for Me? CEOs Whose Firms Are Acquired," NYU Working Paper, August 2002.
19. Anup Agrawal and Charles R. Knowber, "Managerial Compensation and the Threat of Takeover," *Journal of Financial Economics*, 47, 1998, 219–239.

Clearly takeovers are an event that managers are mindful of and that may keep them honest.

CASE STUDY

HEWLETT-PACKARD–COMPAQ MERGER—SHAREHOLDERS LOSE, CEOs GAIN

In February 2005, the board of Hewlett-Packard (HP) announced that it had terminated the employment of its colorful CEO, Carly Fiorina. Fiorina, formerly of AT&T and Lucent, had orchestrated the $25 billion stock-financed merger between Compaq and HP in September 2001. This merger was strongly opposed by leading shareholders such as Walter Hewlett, son of the company's founder. Fiorina barely won shareholder approval of the deal. When we look back on the merger, we see that the concerns of the market and opposing shareholders were well founded. The gains that she projected when the operations of the rival computer makers were combined never materialized. While revenues at HP rose steadily over her tenure, profitability had been weak. Fiorina caused the company to move even more deeply into the PC business, which it had not been able to manage profitably, unlike its rival Dell.

She was not content to focus on HP's more successful business segments such as printers. Instead she expanded into areas where it would command a larger market share—but not make a meaningful contribution to shareholder value. In merging with Compaq, it was adding a company that also had similar troubles. Compaq itself was the product of a prior merger between Compaq and Digital Equipment. However, the PC business is very unusual in that it exists in a *deflationary* market with industry competitors having to often reduce prices of their products while their costs are often rising. This is a very difficult environment in which to be successful. It is noteworthy that the founder of the PC, IBM, sold its PC business in 2005 to Chinese computer manufacturer Lenovo.

The acquisitive Fiorina was replaced by Mark Hurd, who immediately changed the focus at HP from doing megadeals to being a lower-costs company and emphasizing the company's strength in areas such as printers. It is too early to tell how successful this very reasonable strategy is, but early results show promise. Hurd separated the printer and PC businesses and focused on dealing with the PC unit's problems. He has cut costs and managed to purchase components, such as chips, cheaper by playing chipmakers, AMD and Intel, against each other. He has also developed better relationships with retailers, while Dell has started to suffer from its lack of a retail distribution system.

It is ironic that while shareholders have suffered under Fiorina's reign, she profited handsomely from her five-year stint at the company. At the time of her dismissal, it was estimated that she would enjoy a severance package in excess of $20 million. In addition, Michael Capellas, the former CEO of Compaq, who served as president of the postmerger HP, received in excess of $15 million when he left, even though he was only with the combined entity for a relatively short period. The merger was the most significant action that Fiorina orchestrated at HP and it was a clear failure. When CEOs receive great rewards for eroding shareholder value, there are few incentives for them to pursue different strategies. One solution would be to tie CEO compensation to the achievement of specific targets. If a CEO very aggressively pushes a major merger in which the success is predicated on the achievement of certain measurable performance targets, then let the board only agree if the CEO's compensation and bonuses are also tied to the achievement of those targets. This should be particularly true for deals that face strong opposition as this one did. If the CEO does not agree to performance-based compensation tied to such major corporate gambles, then maybe the likelihood of these goals being achieved is questionable.

Compensation Characteristics of Boards That Are More Likely to Keep Agency Costs in Check

We can use the findings of the Core, Holthausen, and Larker study to highlight some of the characteristics of boards that will be in a better position to keep agency costs in control. These characteristics are:

- Fewer or no gray directors
- Fewer inside board members
- Fewer interlocked directorships
- Board members who were selected with minimal CEO influence
- Board members who serve on fewer boards
- Boards that are not too large

These desirable board characteristics are supported by other research beyond the Core, Holthausen, and Larker study. In the following section we will focus on two board characteristics and other research that sheds light on their impact on shareholder wealth.

Management Perks, Agency Costs, and Firm Value

Management perks have clear direct costs that are measurable, but there is some evidence that indicates that such expenses may have costs well beyond these direct costs. A study by Yermack looked at certain high-profile perks such as use of corporate aircraft and showed that companies that disclosed such managerial perks tended to underperform annual market benchmarks by 4%. His study analyzed 237 large corporations over the years 1993–2002. The magnitude of the aggregate dollar underperformance was significantly greater than the actual monetary costs of the specific perks. One explanation is that the market takes the revelation of the perks as an indication of corporate waste and management that may not be running the company in a manner that will maximize shareholder value. Clearly, for large corporations, corporate aircraft may be more efficient than scheduled airlines. It is unlikely that investors disagree. However, they are concerned not with necessary corporate transportations but with signs that might be indicative of symptomatic waste and a lack of concern about management's fiduciary obligations. This was alleged to be the case at the Arkansas-based Acxiom Corp., which became the target of a 2006 proxy battle led by its largest shareholder, ValueAct Capital. ValueAct alleged that Acxiom's CEO spent millions of the company's money to sponsor NASCAR cars and trucks.[20] He then had the company lease a Falcon jet that he repeatedly used to fly back and forth to NASCAR events. When these uses of company resources became intolerable, ValueAct believed it had no choice but to start a proxy battle.

CASE STUDY

RJR NABISCO AND THE PERKS OF ITS DIRECTORS

While management is known to enjoy perks, directors have long also enjoyed such benefits. When directors are beholden to the individuals they have to manage, it is more difficult for them to be

---

20. Gretchen Morgenson, "Gentlemen, Start Your Proxy Fight," *New York Times*, May 14, 2006, 3.1.

objective. The case of RJR Nabisco of the 1980s is an example of extreme perks that made it difficult for the company's board to oversee its extravagant managers. Ross Johnson became CEO of Nabisco in 1984. Nabisco would merge with Reynolds tobacco in 1985. Clearly the tobacco business and food products have little in common other than they are both consumer products that are eventually sold through some of the same retail outlets. Johnson became CEO of the combined entity a year after the merger. The perks of his board have been detailed in Burrough and Helyar's *Barbarians at the Gate: The Fall of RJR Nabisco.*[a] In their book they describe how one board member, Bob Schaeberle, enjoyed "a six year $100,000 a year contract for ill defined duties." Another director, Juanita Kerps, was a professor at Duke and had enjoyed various benefits from being on the Reynolds board. The benefits were not limited to her but also extended to her university—Duke. When Johnson took the reigns of the combined company, Burrough and Helyar point out how he continued to bestow perks on the professor. They noted how she was given $2 million to endow two chairs at the university. How this helped sell cigarettes or food products remains a mystery.

RJR Nabisco had a fleet of corporate aircraft that had been referred to as the *RJR Air Force.* Burrough and Helyar describe how when Johnson took the reigns of the combined company he changed the policies for usage of corporate aircraft and allowed board members to use the planes for personal needs. Being the busy CEO he took it upon himself to personally arrange free transportation for his directors. "I sometimes feel like the director of transportation," he once sighed, after arranging another director's flight. "But I know if I am there for them they will be there for me." It is not surprising that when he, as CEO of the company and a fiduciary for shareholders, decided to make an offer to take the company private, he proceeded with a low-ball offer that even shocked his own loyal directors.

[a]Bryan Burrough and John Helyar, *Barbarians at the Gate: The Fall of RJR Nabisco* (New York: Collins Business, 1990 and 2003).

Interlocking Boards

In an interlocked board, directors sit on each other's boards. In one variant of this, the CEO of one company may sit on the board of another firm that has its CEO sitting on his or her board. One can only imagine that this cozy situation will not result in closer CEO oversight. Once again, this is what one would expect based on human nature. This expectation is supported by research findings such as those of Hallock, who analyzed a dataset of 9,804 director seats covering 7,519 individuals and 700 large U.S. companies.[21] He found that 20% of the companies in his sample were interlocked. He defined interlocked to be where any current or retired employee of one company sat on another company's board where the same situation was the case for the other company. He found that approximately 8% of CEOs are reciprocally interlocked with another CEO.

In addition to quantifying the frequency of interlocked boards, Hallock's study also provided other interesting results. He noted that in his sample, interlocked companies tended to be larger than noninterlocked firms. In addition, CEOs of interlocked companies tend to earn significantly higher compensation. This implies that CEOs stand to gain when their boards are interlocked. In his study he controlled for firm characteristics, such as firm size, and found that pay gap could not account for all of the difference. Research seems

---

21. Kevin Hallock, "Reciprocally Interlocked Boards of Directors and Executive Compensation," *Journal of Financial and Quantitative Analysis,* 32(3), September 1997, 331–344.

to show that interlocking boards are not desirable. If we assume that there is a sufficiently abundant supply of potential directors, we wonder why they exist 20% of the time.

Independence of Directors

Boards have two groups of directors: inside and outside board members. Inside board members are also management employees of the company. These board members may include the CEO as well as certain other senior members of management whose input may be useful in board deliberations. While it is often the case that the CEO is also the chairperson of the board, we are starting to see more examples of the two positions being separated. One 2005 survey of S&P 500 companies by Russell Reynolds Associates showed that this is the case 29% of the time compared with 21% five years earlier.[22]

A 2003 survey conducted by *Corporate Board Member* found that the average number of inside directors is 2.7 while the average number of outside directors is 7.2, giving an average size of a board of 10 directors.[23] This same survey found that 70% of the time the CEO does not sit on the board, which is consistent with the recent Russell Reynolds results. Certain rules require a certain percentage of outside directors be on a company's board. For example, the New York Stock Exchange (NYSE) requires that a majority of directors be independent for companies listed on this exchange.

Research findings provide convincing support for the belief that the more outside directors are on the board, the more likely the board will make decisions that are in shareholders' interests. This body of research also indicates that shareholders will realize greater gains if their companies are taken over when their boards contain more outside directors.[24] Another study by Rosenstein and Wyatt noted that stock prices of companies tend to increase when an outside director is added to a board.[25] The market has indicated a clear preference for outside control of the board and it usually is concerned when boards fall under the control of management.

It is reasonable to conclude that boards in which insiders have limited influence will be able to make tough decisions involving managers and their performance. Such boards are more likely to be able to make a change in upper management when current managers fail to generate the performance that shareholders may be expecting. This was readily apparent in the removal of Robert Stempel from the CEO position at General Motors (GM) in 1992. In this managerial change, John Smale led the board of GM. Smale held great stature in the corporate world from his years of being CEO of Procter & Gamble. When he asserted that GM would benefit from a change at the helm, his recommendation was taken very seriously. This theme was also apparent in other prominent CEO overthrows. For example, Robert Morrow, CEO of Amoco, led the ouster of Paul Lego of Westinghouse. The same was the case when James Burke, former CEO of Johnson & Johnson, led the overthrow of IBM CEO John Akers. Each of these situations has some important common

22. Claudia Duetsch, "Fewer Chiefs Also Serving as Chairman," *New York Times*, March 17, 2006, C13.
23. "What Directors Think Research Study," *Corporate Board Member*, July 2003.
24. J. Cooter, A. Shivdasni, and A. Zenner, "Do Independent Directors Enhance Target Shareholder Wealth During Tender Offers?", *Journal of Financial Economics*, 43, 1997, 195–218.
25. S. Rosenstein and J. Wyatt, "Outside Directors, Boards Independence and Shareholder Wealth," *Journal of Financial Economics*, 26, 1990, 175–192.

characteristics. In each case the situation called for a change at the wheel. In all of these removals of high-profile CEOs, the company was lagging behind where it should have been and the position of CEO was a prominent one that was very much in the public eye. In these situations the markets had been critical of the company's performance, and thus indirectly, if not directly, of the performance of the CEO. The market and the media put pressure on the board to take decisive action and make changes at the helm. In each instance the board members, and chairman in particular, were prominent corporate figures.

When decisive action is needed and where the performance of management needs to be critically reviewed, outside boards will be in a better position to implement such an objective review. However, we have to understand that there are good reasons why boards have certain managers on them. These management board members can provide useful insight of the performance of the company that other, outside directors may lack. However, we would not want a board composed solely of such directors. Indeed, much can be said for a mixed board composed not just of insider and outside directors but of outside directors of diverse backgrounds who can bring a wide range of expertise and experience to the management monitoring process. Outside, and especially some prominent outside directors, can play a key role when action such as removal of an incumbent CEO is needed.

A study by Weisbach showed that boards with a greater percent of outside directors were more likely to discipline their CEO for performing poorly than those where insiders played a more prominent role.[26] Inside-dominated boards may simply be too close to the CEO and may be reluctant to make decisions that may have adverse effects on their co-managers. Outside board member directors are often less close to the CEO and can react more objectively. However, exceptions to this are interlocking directorships that may have outsiders with reciprocal relationships on each other's boards. These interlocking board members should not be considered in the same light as other outside directors.

CASE STUDY

COCA-COLA'S PROPOSED ACQUISITION OF QUAKER OATS*

While it seems that many boards simply rubber-stamp M&As proposed by their CEOs, some boards have the foresight and the courage to stand up to the CEO and question proposed deals. This was the case when a $15.75 billion offer for Quaker Oats was proposed to Coca-Cola Company's board of directors in November 2001. Quaker Oats had a certain appeal to Coca-Cola because it included its popular Gatorade line, which might fit in well with Coke's other soft drink products. Gatorade commands more than 80% of the sports drink market, whereas Coke's own Powerade brand accounted for just over 10% of that market. The whole sports drink business had grown significantly, and Powerade had a distant second position to the leader Gatorade, and Coke was having great difficulty gaining ground on the leader. Acquiring Gatorade through an acquisition of Quaker Oats could have been a quick solution to this problem. However, the acquisition also

*Source: Patrick A. Gaughan, *Mergers: What Can Go Wrong and How to Prevent It* (Hoboken, NJ: John Wiley & Sons, 2005), pp. 237–239.

---

26. Michael Weisbach, "Outside Directors and CEO Turnover," *Journal of Financial Economics*, 37, 1988, 159–188.

presented another problem because Coke most likely would have been forced by antitrust regulators to divest Powerade in order to have the deal approved.

Coke was not the first bidder for Quaker Oats. On November 1, 2000, Pepsi made an initial offer for Quaker following negotiations between Robert Enrico, Pepsi's CEO, and Robert Morrison, Quaker's CEO. However, after Quaker could not get Pepsi to agree on improved terms, including a stock collar provision, negotiations between Pepsi and Quaker broke down. Quaker was then in play, and other potential bidders, such as Coke and French food giant Group Danone, expressed interest in the U.S. food company. Both companies made competing bids, which featured improved terms over Pepsi's bid, yet Pepsi held fast and declined to exceed its prior offer. Coke's CEO assured Quaker Oats that he had been keeping his board apprised of the bid's progress and had asked and received agreement from Quaker to exclusively negotiate with just Coke. Coke's CEO, Douglas Daft, however, did not count on the negative response of the market to the deal (see Exhibit A).[a] The board, however, was mindful of the market, and after a long meeting on November 21, 2000, they forced Daft to go back to Quaker Oats and inform them that Coke was pulling out of the negotiations. The market loved this, and the stock price immediately rose. Pepsi eventually acquired Quaker Oats in August 2001 for $13 billion.

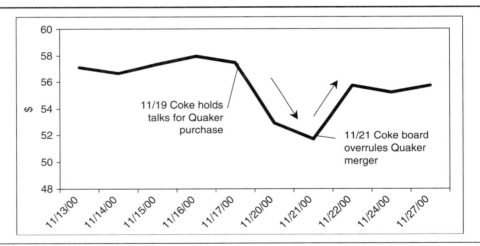

EXHIBIT A   COKE'S STOCK PRICE RESPONSE TO QUAKER OATS BID

Source: finance.yahoo.com.

There were some clear problems with the deal that Coke's board obviously paid attention to. As already noted, the market did not like the proposed acquisition, and it voiced its displeasure by dropping its valuation of Coke's stock. In the years before the Coke bid, the company had experienced problems with other failed acquisitions, and the spotlight was on its merger strategy. Right at the start, management faced an uphill battle. Another problem with the deal was that the acquisition would require Coke to be able to effectively manage the components of Quaker Oats' business that was outside of Coke's soft and sports drink business lines. These were Quaker's food brands, which included Captain Crunch cereals, Rice-A-Roni, and Aunt Jemima pancakes, as well as other snack products such as rice cakes and granola bars. Some of Quaker's brands were impressive, but they were a little far afield from Coke's core business. Another problem with the

[a]Pepsi's Bid for Quaker Oats (B), Harvard Business School, 9-801-459, August 5, 2002.

deal was its defensive nature. Coke's bid was in response to Pepsi's original offer. Such defensive responses are not the best motive for a merger or acquisition.

One of the reasons why the Coke board stood up to this proposal lies in the nature of its board and their relationship with the CEO. Coke had a CEO, Robert Goizueta, who was highly acclaimed. Unfortunately, after many successful years at the helm of the soft drink giant, Goizueta passed away in October 1997 at a relatively young age. He was succeeded by Douglas Investor, who resigned at the end of 1999 and was replaced by Douglas Daft, who was well thought of but could not draw on the track record of success that Goizueta enjoyed. Perhaps if Goizueta had brought this deal to the board, they might have considered it more seriously. Nonetheless, there is little reason to believe that they would have ultimately approved it no matter who brought the deal because they considered it generally flawed.

Coke's board featured some leading business figures, including the renowned Warren Buffett, who is considered by many to be one of the market's shrewdest investors, as well as a new CEO who was looking to make a make for himself. This board, however, would have none of it. In 2006, Buffett announced he would step down from Coke's board. This is a void that will be hard to fill.

The board of directors is one of the last lines of defense against poorly conceived merger strategies. In order for it to work with maximum effectiveness, the board needs to be knowledgeable and strong willed. However, it is not enough that a board be composed of individuals who are strong willed and capable of standing up to the management leaders of the company. Knowledge of the industry and the company's operations are also essential to being an effective director. Management, who runs the company on a day-to-day basis, should have a distinct advantage over board members who are engaged full-time in other activities, such as running their own companies, and have not invested nearly as much time as management in studying the company. However, there is a certain minimum level of knowledge that the board must have in order for it to function properly. When considering the commitment of billions of dollars in merger costs, the board needs to get whatever resources it needs to be able to effectively evaluate management's proposals. If this means retaining outside consultants to study the proposal in depth, then this should be done. This is sometimes difficult to do because the proposals may be time sensitive and require a quick response. Nonetheless, the board must apply all of the necessary resources to reach an enlightened and impartial decision. The bigger the deal, the more work and research the board needs to do. However, in the case of Coke's offer for Quaker Oats, the board's studied response was clear and strong. In properly exercising their fiduciary responsibilities, they saved shareholders from a possibly costly acquisition.

New Bright Line Standards for Directors

Both the SEC and the NYSE have enacted what are called "bright line" standards for defining director independence. They were conceptualized in the wake of Enron, and it took some time before they eventually came to affect public companies. The new rules require that a majority of directors and board members sitting on key board committees must be independent. They have certain specific tests that when applied bar certain people from being considered independent. For example, directors who have received more than $100,000 from a company over the prior three years may not be considered independent (the SEC limit is $60,000). The NYSE has gone beyond such tests and focuses on more broadly defined "material" relationships that may be more subtle than what can be defined under direct compensation. However, even if a relationship is determined by the company to be immaterial it needs to still provide shareholders with an explanation of why it believes it is immaterial so that shareholders can make their own judgment about the relationship.

Compensation, Board Size, and Corporate Governance

The size of a board plays an important role in how effectively it may oversee management. Boards that are relatively large tend to be better at corporate governance. Kini, Krackaw, and Mian found that board size tended to shrink after tender offers for firms that were not performing well.[27] This implies that disciplinary takeovers, or at least the threat of such takeovers, tends to reduce the size of boards to that which the market believes may be more effective. When companies receive such hostile bids, they may be good buys for the bidder, which sees the company as relatively cheap when its market value is compared with the bidder's perception of its intrinsic value. The company may respond by taking various actions that will make it become less vulnerable to a takeover. The Kini, Krackaw, and Mian study implies that among these actions may be reductions in the board size.

Yermack attempted to determine if there was a relationship between the market valuation of companies and board size. He analyzed a sample of 452 large U.S. corporations over the period 1984–1991. The average board size for his sample was 12 directors.[28] Yermack found that there was an inverse relationship between market value, as measured by Tobin's q, and the size of the board of directors (Exhibit 12.4). Smaller boards were associated with higher market values and larger boards tended to be associated with lower valuations. The higher valuations often come from relatively smaller boards that have fewer than ten members. He also looked at other performance measures such as operating efficiency and profitability measures and found that they were also inversely associated with board size. He also found that smaller boards were more likely to replace a CEO following a period of poor performance. In addition, Yermack also found some evidence that CEO compensation was more closely linked to performance, especially poor performance, when boards are smaller. Based on these results, boards need to be kept to a certain size beyond which the efficiency and ability to carry out their corporate governance functions seems to deteriorate. CEOs may personally benefit in the form of higher compensation when boards are larger but shareholders may suffer.

Do companies adopt antitakeover defenses to avoid the disciplinary pressure of the takeover market? Are certain types of boards more likely to adopt such defenses?

A study by Brickley, Terry and Coles found that board compensation affected the likelihood that a company would adopt a poison pill defense.[29] The Brickley, et al. study analyzed the role that the composition of the board might play in any negative reaction the market might have to the adoption of poison pills by 247 companies over the period 1984–1986. This was a period where prior research had shown that the negative market

---

27. Omesh Kini, William Krackaw, and Shehzad Mian, "Corporate Takeovers, Firm Performance and Board Composition," *Journal of Corporate Finance,* 1, 1995, 383–412.

28. David Yermack, "Higher Market Valuation of Companies with a Small Board of Directors," *Journal of Financial Economics,* 40, 1996, 185–211.

29. James A. Brickley, Jeffrey L. Terry, and Rory L. Coles, "Outside Directors and the Adoption of Poison Pills," *Journal of Financial Economics,* 35, 1994, 371–390.

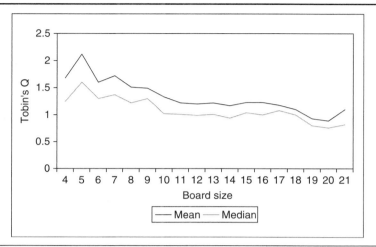

EXHIBIT 12.4 BOARD SIZE AND TOBIN'S Q: SAMPLE MEANS AND MEDIANS

Source: D. Yermack, "Higher Market Valuation of Companies with a Small Board of Directors," *Journal of Financial Economics,* 40, 1996, 185–211.

Sample means and medians of Tobin's Q for different sizes of boards of directors. The sample consists of 3,438 annual observations for 452 firms between 1984 and 1991. Companies are included in the sample if they are reanked by Forbes magazine as one of the 500 largest U.S. public corporations at least four times during the eight-year sample period. Utility and financial companies are excluded. Data for board size is gathered from proxy statements filed by companies near the start of each fiscal year. Tobin's Q is estimated at the end of each fiscal year as Market value of assets/Replacement cost of assets. The estimation of Q follows the qPW specification of Perfect and Wiles (1994), which is described more fully in the text.

reaction to poison pills was the greatest. They found a statistically significant positive relation between the stock market's reaction to the adoption of poison pills and the percent of the board accounted for by outside directors. The market's reaction was positive when the board was dominated by outsiders and negative when it was dominated by insider board members. This implies that the market tended to believe that when an outside-dominated board adopted a strong antitakeover defense like a poison pill, they did so to advance shareholder wealth. However, when an insider-dominated board took the same action, the market seemed to believe that they were doing this to entrench managers and insulate them from the disciplinary forces of the takeover market. The market was also saying that it believes that outside directors represent shareholders interests better than insider directors.

CASE STUDY

HOLLINGER INTERNATIONAL*

The 2004 probe of Hollinger International into what it referred to as a "corporate kleptocracy" was released at the end of the summer 2004. The report issued by a special committee of the Hollinger board of directors found that the company's CEO, Conrad Black, and ex-president, David Radler,

*Source: Patrick A. Gaughan, *Mergers: What Can Go Wrong and How to Prevent It* (Hoboken, NJ: John Wiley & Sons, 2005), pp. 225–227.

"siphoned off more than $400 million through aggressive looting of the publishing company."[a] Hollinger International is a publishing company that publishes various newspapers including the *Chicago Sun Times* and the *Jerusalem Post*. Black controlled Hollinger through a holding company he owned, Ravelston, which owned 78% of the stock of a Canadian company, Hollinger, Inc., which in turn owned 68% of the voting shares in Hollinger International. Through his control of a 68% interest in Hollinger International, Black was able to effectively influence the board of directors.

One astounding finding of the report was that the total cash taken equaled "95.2% of Hollinger's entire adjusted net income during the period 1997–2003!"[b] The probe of the activities of Hollinger's CEO and ex-president was headed by former SEC chairman Richard Breeden and was filed with the federal courts and the SEC. Black and Radler engaged in lavish spending that included $24,950 for "summer drinks," $3,530 for silverware for their corporate jet, which they put to regular personal use, thousands of dollars for handbags, tickets for the theater and opera, as well as very generous donations made by the company to charities and establishments favored by Black and his wife, columnist Barbara Black. The couple threw lavish dinner parties for friends including Henry Kissinger, who was, coincidentally, on the board of directors. Birthday parties for Mrs. Black were thrown at the company's expense. One such party for 80 guests cost the company $42,870. Other examples of looting of the company were a ten-day vacation to Bora Bora at a cost of $250,000 and refurbishing work on Black's Rolls-Royce, which cost $90,000.[c] Black and Radler took compensation from the company in several ways, including $218 million in management fees that they derived over the period 1997–2003. Management fees were paid to Ravelston while Hollinger International also paid "noncompete" fees to other entities controlled by Ravelston. In addition, Hollinger sold newspaper businesses to entities controlled by Lord Black and his associates for below market values. These included the sale of the *Monmouth Times*, in Monmouth Lakes, California, which went for "$1 when there was a competing bid of $1.25 million."[d]

The report called the board and the audit committee's monitoring of payments such as these management fees "inept." The board of directors included some very prominent names in international diplomacy. Among its members were former secretary of state, Henry Kissinger, as well as former assistant secretary of defense in the Reagan administration, Richard Perle, and James Thompson, former governor of Illinois who headed the company's audit committee. While such political figures may be world renowned, it is not clear what special expertise they brought to the board of directors of a publishing company. Clearly, if one wanted to talk foreign affairs at a board meeting, this was probably a board that could have an enlightening discussion on such topics. If it was corporate oversight you were looking for, the track record of these directors was dismal at best. The report of the special committee particularly singled out Perle for "repeatedly breaching his fiduciary duties as a member of the executive committee of the board, by authorizing unfair related party transactions that enabled Black and Radler to evade disclosure to the audit committee. The report calls on Perle to return $3 million in compensation he received from the company."[e]

Hollinger's use of former political figures as directors of corporations is not unusual. However, it is not clear why specialized expertise they bring to overseeing corporations. Many have worked in the public sector, isolated from the pressures of running an organization to turn a profits, much if not all of their careers. Often their leading expertise is to market themselves to the public to gain votes.

[a]Mark Heinzl and Christopher J. Chipello, "Report Slams Hollinger's Black for Corporate Kleptocracy," *Wall Street Journal*, September 1, 2004, p. 1.
[b]Ibid.
[c]Geraldine Fabricant, "Hollinger Files Stinging Report on Ex-Officials," *New York Times*, September 1, 2004, p. 1.
[d]Ibid.
[e]Op. cit., Heinzl and Chipello, p. A4.

Hollinger's board also included friends and family members. For example, Lord Black's wife, Barbara Amiel Black, was on the board along with family friend Marie-Josee Kravis, the wife of financier Henry Kravis of Kohlberg, Kravis & Roberts. Clearly, Black pushed the appointment of directors to an extreme. This became possible because Black controlled the votes required to place individuals on the board. The hand-picked board appeared to have been kept in the dark, as Black could keep them, but they did not go to any great lengths to remove themselves from any clouds that he surrounded them with. They were being taken care of very well by Black and Hollinger and did not seem to want to rock the boat. The following passage from the *Wall Street Journal* that describes one Hollinger board meeting is instructive of the atmosphere in Holllinger's board room:

> Gathered around a mahogany table in a boardroom high above Manhattan's Park Avenue, eight directors of the newspaper publisher, owner of the Chicago Sun Times and the Jerusalem Post, dined on grilled tuna and chicken served on royal blue Bernardaud china, according to two attendees. Marie-Josee Kravis, wife of financier Henry Kravis, chatted about world affairs with Lord Black and A. Alfred Taubman, then chairman of Sotheby's. Turning to business, the board rapidly approved a series of transactions, according to the minutes and a report later commissioned by Hollinger. The board awarded a private company, controlled by Lord Black, $38 million in "management fees" as part of a move by Lord Black's team to essentially outsource the company's management to itself. It agreed to sell two profitable community newspapers to another private company controlled by Lord Black and Hollinger executives for $1 apiece. The board also gave Lord Black and his colleagues a cut of profits from a Hollinger Internet unit. Finally, the directors gave themselves a raise. The meeting lasted about an hour and a half, according to minutes and two directors who were present."[f]

One lesson we can learn from the Hollinger scandal is that a board should not be too close to the CEO, and definitely should not be picked by the CEO. The board needs to be somewhat at arm's length from those whom they will be monitoring. If they are indebted to the CEO, then how objective will they be in pursuing the interests of shareholders?

[f]Frank, Robert, and Elena Cherney, "Lord Black Board: A-List Cast Played Acquiescent Role," *Wall Street Journal*, September 27, 2004, p. 1.

CEO Compensation and Power

Common sense tells us that if CEOs have greater power, many will use it to increase their own compensation. Research seems to support this assumption. One study by Cyert, Kang, and Kumar considered a sample of 1,648 small and large companies. The average CEO in their study was 55 years of age, and had served in that position for an average of eight years.[30] They also found that in 70% of the cases the CEO was also the board chairman. In addition they noted that equity ownership of the largest shareholder and the board was negatively correlated with CEO compensation. This is consistent with the findings of the Core, Holthausen, and Larker study, wherein they noted that CEO compensation was lower when there were large equity blockholders. Interestingly, Cyert et al found that equity ownership of the members of the board was more important than board size in keeping CEO compensation under control than the size of the board or the percent of outside directors. When board members have their own capital at risk, they seem to do a better job of monitoring the CEO and reviewing how much of the potential profits of the business the CEO extracts in the form of compensation. Once again, these findings are quite intuitive.

---

30. Richard M. Cyert, Sok-Hyon Kang, and Pravenn Kumar, "Corporate Governance, Takeovers and Top-Management Compensation: Theory and Evidence," *Management Science*, 48(4), April 2002, 453–469.

There is another force that can help keep CEOs in check and that is the takeover market. Bertrand and Mullainathan found that when a company is allowed to install antitakeover defenses that insulate the company from takeovers, CEO compensation tends to be higher.[31] Therefore, there are both internal and external forces that monitor the CEO and ensure that he or she runs the company in a manner consistent with shareholders' goals. The process is far from perfect, but research seems to imply that it often works in a somewhat satisfactory manner, although it can benefit from improvement.

Disciplinary Takeovers, Company Performance, CEOs, and Boards

The board of directors, as fiduciaries of shareholders, monitor the performance of the company and management, including the CEO. This is the internal process we have referred to earlier. When this process fails to yield acceptable results, external forces may come into play. This is often done through disciplinary takeovers of poorly performing companies. Kini, Krackaw, and Mian analyzed a sample of 244 tender offers and looked at the effects that these hostile bids had on CEO and director turnover.[32] They found an inverse relationship between posttakeover CEO turnover and pretakeover performance. Companies that yielded poor performance prior to the takeover were more likely to have their CEO replaced. However, this finding was not in certain types of cases. It was the case when the companies had insider-dominated boards but not the case when the boards were dominated by outside directors. This finding seems to imply that when the board was composed mainly of outsiders, the problem was not the CEO; otherwise the outsiders on the board would have already changed the CEO.

The Kini, Kracaw, and Mian study also found that board composition tended to be changed following disciplinary takeovers. Boards that were previously dominated by insiders were changed and the number of insiders reduced. This implies that the bidders identified the composition of the board, and the large number of insiders, as a potential source of problems the company may have had. In making these changes, the takeover market altered board composition. However, this is an expensive way of making such changes.

There is some evidence that the effect of disciplinary takeovers is greatest in more active takeover markets. Mikkelson and Partch found a greater rate of CEO, president, and board chair turnover for companies that were performing poorly in an active takeover market relative to a less active takeover market.[33] Specifically, they found that 33% of the companies in the "poor performer" sample experienced complete turnover of the CEO, president, and board chair during the 1984–1986 time period, which were years within the fourth merger wave. This was almost double the 17% rate they found for comparable performing companies during the less active 1989–1993 time period. Takeovers can serve an important role in eliminating poor managers. It is important to note that this can take

---

31. M. Bertrand and S. Mullainathan, "Is There Discretion in Wage Setting? A Test Using Takeover Legislation," *Rand Journal of Economics,* 30, 1999, 535–554.
32. Omesh Kini, William Kracaw, and Shehzad Mian, "Corporate Takeovers, Firm Performance and Board Composition," *Journal of Corporate Finance,* 1, 1995, 383–412.
33. Wayne H. Mikkelson and M. Megan Partch, "The Decline of Takeovers and Disciplinary Managerial Turnover," *Journal of Financial Economics,* 44, 1997, 205–228.

place even if the company is not taken over. Directors are aware of the intensity of the takeover market and some will act before the company actually receives an unwanted bid. However, this study implies that they may monitor and change the CEO more aggressively in an active takeover market. This has been confirmed by other research that shows that management turnover is greater when companies are actually taken over.[34] The threat of a takeover alone can bring about turnover of top management.[35] This implies that active takeover markets can be good for corporate governance. Conversely, it also implies that a sluggish takeover market may not be best for shareholders interested in improving corporate governance.

Merger Strategy and Corporate Governance

Having discussed corporate governance in this chapter, we will focus on the relationship between corporate governance and merger strategy. We will try to determine whether better corporate governance means that companies will carry out more or fewer deals. How does the quality of corporate governance affect the types of deals that are done and the shareholders' returns that these transactions generate? These are the issues that we will focus on for the rest of this chapter.

Do Boards Reward CEOs for Initiating Acquisitions and Mergers?

It is well known that many deals do not fare well; one wonders why boards are so willing to approve M&A proposals. Ironically, there is even evidence that boards actually encourage CEOs to pursue such deals. A study was conducted by Grinstein and Hribar of 327 large M&As that occurred during the fifth merger wave period, 1993–1999.[36] They examined proxy statements that broke down CEO compensation into individual components with an eye toward identifying which companies attributed part of the CEO's compensation to his or her ability to complete M&As. They found that in 39% of cases they considered the compensation committee cited completion of a deal as the reason they provided certain compensation. In other instances companies awarded bonuses following deals even though they did not specify that the bonuses were for deals. This implies that the real percentage of boards that gave bonuses for mergers was even higher than the 39% that overtly cited this as a reason.

Consistent with much other research in M&A, Grinstein and Hribar noted that bidder announcement period returns were negative for the companies included in their sample. However, they found that the negative reaction was greatest in cases when the CEOs have the greatest corporate power as reflected by the CEO also being head of the board of directors. The market often seems to not only dislike acquisitions but it really dislikes deals done by CEOs whose power is less constrained by the board of directors. The market seems to prefer more power limitations on the CEO and will penalize companies

34. K. J. Martin and J. J. McConnell, "Corporate Performance, Corporate Takeovers and Management Turnover," *Journal of Finance*, 46, 1991, 671–687.

35. D. J. Denis and D. K. Denis, "Ownership Structure and Top Management Turnover, *Journal of Financial Economics*, 45, 1997, 193–222.

36. Yaniv Grinstein and Paul Hribar, "CEO Compensation and Incentives: Evidence from M&A Bonuses," *Journal of Financial Economics*, 2003, 535–554.

less for doing acquisitions when they know that there is a group of directors who are potentially capable of preventing CEOs from doing deals that might not be in the best interest of the company. Whether the board actually does this is another issue.

Grinstein and Hribar not only found that the market reacted more negatively to deals done by CEOs with more power, but they also noted that managers of companies who had more power got higher bonuses and tended to do bigger deals. Their power was less checked and they seemed to personally gain from this situation—at the expense of shareholders.

CASE STUDY

SOVEREIGN BANK'S M&A GROWTH STRATEGY AND SHAREHOLDERS' INTERESTS

Over the period 1995–2005, Pennsylvania-based Sovereign bank grew exponentially through 27 different M&As. The company grew from a bank with approximately 1,500 employees and 120 offices, to a financial institution with just under 10,000 employees and over 730 offices. However, CEO Jay Sidhu's growth-through-M&As strategy was not well received by certain large, money manager shareholders, who preferred that bank focus more on increasing shareholder returns as opposed to increased size. This caused the bank's largest shareholder, San Diego–based money manager Relational Investors, LLP, to launch a proxy fight in October 2005 to gain seats on the bank's board from which it could take a more active role in framing the company's strategy. The conflict between large institutional investors and the bank's CEO came to a head when Sidhu announced that Sovereign would acquire Independence Bank for $3.6 billion but would finance the deal by selling 19.8% of its stock to Spain's largest bank, the 148-year-old Banco Santander Central Hispano, SA, for $2.4 billion. Santander has been active in M&As, having completed what was at that time the largest cross-border acquisition in European history—the $15.4 billion acquisition of the United Kingdom's Abbey National Bank. One of the side effects of this deal that irked dissident shareholders was the dilution of their equity and voting power. Institutional investors such as Relational petitioned the NYSE to require that the deal be brought to shareholders for their voting approval. The stock exchange, however, declined to require this. The market, however, voiced its displeasure with a decline in Sovereign's market capitalization.

In March 2006, Relational Investors and Sovereign reached an agreement in which Relational would get to place a representative on Sovereign's board and Sovereign would add another outside director. Relational, in turn, dropped its lawsuit. Later in 2006, Sidhu resigned. The conflict between Relational and Sovereign is a good example of the important counterbalancing role large blockholders, as well as hedge funds, can play in monitoring management.

CEO Compensation and Diversification Strategies

In Chapter 4 we saw that diversification strategies generally cause the shareholders of companies pursuing such strategies to lose value. There are some examples of diversified companies who generated significant gains for shareholders such as GE. In addition, we have also discussed in Chapter 4 the fact that not all diversifications are the same, with related diversifications yielding better performance than unrelated diversifying deals. In spite of the dubious track record of diversifications, it is surprising to see that companies pay their CEOs a diversification premium—meaning that research has shown the CEOs of diversified companies earn on average 13% more than CEOs of companies that operate in only one line of business. There is some evidence that eventually diversification strategies lead to lower CEO compensation, but the process of correcting the CEO compensation level seems to be slow.[37] Boards seem to be slow to stop diversification deals recommended by CEOs and penalize them after the fact in the form of lower compensation.

Agency Costs and Diversification Strategies

Agency costs may help explain the tendency of some CEOs and their companies to engage in diversifying M&As. Management may be pursuing a merger strategy that generates gains for themselves even though such a strategy may not be the one that is in the best interest of shareholders. That is, the agents of the owners, the managers, derive private benefits that are greater than their own private costs from doing these deals. Diversifying deals may provide managers greater prestige and what economists call "psychic income." They may also generate other direct monetary gains such as higher compensation that is paid to management of larger companies. Denis, Denis, and Sarin analyzed a sample of 933 firms starting in 1984.[38] They examined the degree of ownership held by managers and related this to the tendency of managers with different percents of equity ownership to engage in diversifying deals, which research has shown often tend to reduce shareholder value. They found that diversification, moving the company into other business segments, was more likely to reduce shareholder values when CEO ownership was lower (e.g., less than 5% of the outstanding shares). Such deals, however, had a mild positive effect when the CEO's ownership shares were greater than 5%. Similar effects were found when they looked at the combined share percentages owned by overall management. They also found that there was a strong relation between decreases in diversification and external control threats. Almost one in five of the decreases in diversification, such as selling off diversified divisions, were preceded by a takeover bid. In other words, decreases in diversification were associated with market pressure. This implies that often management may not be willing to sell off prior acquisitions that reduced shareholder value until they were faced with an outside bidder that may be taking advantage of reduced stock values relative to the underlying value of the divisions if they were sold separately on the market. If the diversification strategy reduced value, it made the company vulnerable to a takeover and when the takeover threats materialized, management financially responded by refocusing.

The agency costs hypothesis can partially explain the tendency of some companies to engage in diversifying deals. This hypothesis is also consistent with the reaction of management to outside threats. However, we do not have to just rely on outside market forces to limit these costs. Boards are in a good position to prevent deals that will reduce shareholder value. Directors need to be aware of the track record of certain types of deals and make sure that management and the CEO do not get to complete them. They also need to be aware of the company's own track record of deals. Some companies, such as AT&T and Daimler, had a very poor M&A track record. Boards of such companies need to be especially wary.

---

37. Nancy L. Rose and Andrea Shepard, "Firm Diversification and CEO Compensation: Managerial Ability or Executive Entrenchment," *Rand Journal of Economics,* 28(3), Autumn 1997, 489–514.

38. David J. Denis, Diane K. Denis, and Atulya Sarin, "Agency Problems, Equity Ownership and Corporate Diversification," *Journal of Finance*, 52(1), March 1997, 135–160.

Interests of Directors and M&As

Directors are fiduciaries for shareholders and as such they have the responsibility to oversee the management and direction of the company so that the goals of shareholder wealth maximization are pursued. However, it would be naïve for us to ignore the fact that directors are human and also consider what is in their own interests. How are directors affected by takeovers? Directors of target companies are usually not retained after the takeover by a company. The bidding company already has a board of directors and there is usually no place or need for the target's directors. Therefore, the target directors know that the takeover will normally bring an end to their directorships. This may or may not be an important issue to them—depending on their own personal circumstances.

The personal adverse financial impact to a target director as a result of approving a merger or hostile takeover has been documented in a study by Harford, who considered 1,091 directors of Fortune 1000 companies over the period 1988–1991.[39] As expected, he remarked that directors of target companies were rarely retained after the merger or acquisition. However, what was especially interesting was the fact that such directors were less likely to get another director's post in the future. This is the case for both inside and outside directors. Harford also found that directors of poorly performing companies whose companies were, nonetheless, able to be acquired do not seem to suffer a reduced frequency of future directorships. Conversely, directors of poorly performing companies that mounted antitakeover defenses that successfully prevented takeovers were less likely to be directors of companies in the future. These findings are remarkable as they imply that the market for directors seems to be pretty efficient in weeding out those directors who may place their own interests ahead of those of shareholders.

Managerial Compensation and Firm Size

It has long been postulated by economists that managers run companies in a manner that is more consistent with revenue maximization than profit maximization.[40] This is based on the purported relationship between managerial compensation and firm size. The optimal firm size may be less than that which would maximize revenues. The reason why researchers theorize that management would want to have a larger than optimal company is the positive relationship between firm size and managerial compensation. Senior management of larger companies tend to earn more than their smaller corporate counterparts.[41] Lambert, Larker, and Weigelt have showed that this positive association exists for most major levels of management such as:

- Corporate CEO: the manager with the greatest authority in the company
- Group CEO: a manager who has authority for various different subgroups within the overall corporation
- Subgroup CEO: senior manager of one of the individual subgroups

---

39. Jarrad Harford, "Takeover Bids and Target Director Incentives: The Impact of a Bid on Director's Wealth and Board Seats," *Journal of Financial Economics,* 69, 2003, 51–83.
40. William Baumol, *Business Behavior: Value and Growth* (New York: McMillan, 1959), p. 46.
41. S. Finkelstein and D. Hambrick, ""Chief Executive Compensation: A Study of the Intersection of Markets and Political Processes," *Strategic Management Journal,* 10, 1989, 121–134.

- Divisional CEO: senior manager of a division or corporate unit
- Plant manager: senior manager of a cost center[42]

The Lambert, Larker, and Weigelt results for these broad categories of management may help explain why there may not be as much managerial resistance to the recommendations of very senior management who advocate transactions that result in greater corporate size but not necessarily greater profitability. Their findings are not unique to this field of research. In general, research in this area tends to show that there is a good relationship between company size and executive compensation but a poor one between compensation and corporate performance.[43]

Corporate Control Decisions and Their Shareholder Wealth Effects

Does the nature of management's compensation agreements affect the likelihood that managers will pursue M&As? If this is the case, then does the market react differently when these deals are pursued by managers who receive a significant percent of their compensation from equity-based components? Dutta, Dutta, and Raman analyzed a sample of 1,719 acquisitions made by U.S. companies over the period 1993–1998.[44] This was a time period where there were large increases in stock option–based compensation for senior executives. Therefore, it is an excellent time period to test market reactions as a function of the extent to which the managers pursing the deals will gain in a similar manner to shareholders. If the deals are value-reducing to shareholders, then managers would stand to personally lose from such deals. They found that companies with managers having high equity-based compensation tended to receive positive stock market responses to the announcement of their acquisitions while those with lower equity-based manager compensation tended to receive negative reactions. The market seemed to assume that given the financial impact that these deals would have on the equity holdings of managers, they would not pursue them if they were not wealth enhancing for shareholders.

Dutta, Dutta, and Raman also looked at the size of the takeover premium paid by acquiring firms. When managers had their own wealth at risk, due to the impact that a premium may have on their equity-based compensation, were the premiums they offered different? Interestingly, they found that companies with higher equity-based compensation tended to pay lower premiums. Once again, when managers are playing with their own money, to some extent, they are more frugal with exchanging premiums whereas when they are playing with "house money"—shareholder wealth—they will tend to be more generous and more liberally give away corporate wealth when they do not personally lose from such largesse. Dutta, Dutta, and Raman also found that high equity-based compensation managers tended to acquire targets with higher growth opportunities than their lower equity-based counterparts did. That is, they tended to acquire companies with

42. Richard A. Lambert, David F. Larker, and Keith Weigelt, "How Sensitive Is Executive Compensation to Organizational Size?", *Strategic Management Journal*, 12(5), July 1991, 395–402.
43. H. L. Tosi and L. R. Gomez-Mejia, "The Decoupling of CEO Pay and Performance: An Agency Theory Perspective," *Administrative Science Quarterly*, 34, 1989, 169–189.
44. Sanip Dutta, Mai Iskandar-Dutta, and Kartik Raman, "Executive Compensation and Corporate Acquisition Decisions," *Journal of Finance*, 56(6), December 2001, 2299–2336.

a greater likelihood of generating equity-based gains for both themselves and shareholders. Moreover, they found that lower equity-based compensation managers/companies significantly underperformed their higher equity-based counterparts.

The Dutta, Dutta, and Raman study implies that if management's interests are aligned with shareholders', they tend to do better deals and pay less. It also seems to be reasonable to assume that such managers may try harder to pursue value-reducing deals. The market is aware of this and reacts more positively when such managers announce deals but penalize acquiring shareholders when they, and their board of directors, allow managers to push deals when they do not have their own compensation at risk.

Does Better Corporate Governance Increase Firm Value?

We have already answered the above question in a piecemeal fashion by looking at specific governance issues, such as director independence, and noted that research finds a clear linkage between better governance and firm value. Many of these studies use short-term-oriented event studies to ascertain the effects of specific governance elements. We have already discussed how such studies can be quite telling when it comes to determining long-term effects. However, a study by Gomers, Ishii, and Metrick used a governance index (G) to test the shareholder wealth effects of a collection of governance factors.[45] They created their index using 24 corporate governance measures for 1,500 large companies over the 1990s. The data were culled from the Investor Responsibility Research Center's database of corporate charter provisions. Among these are antigreenmail and classified board provision, poison pills, golden parachutes, and many others. They found that corporate governance was closely related to value of firms as measured by Tobin's Q. The way they constructed their index, lower G values were indicative of better governance. Not only did lower G values result in higher Qs, but the relationship got significantly stronger as the researchers traced their sample over the 1990s. They found that at the beginning of the decade, a one-point increase in G was associated with a 2.2 percentage decrease in Q values. By the end of the 1990s, a one-point increase in G was associated with an 11.4% decrease in Q values. This implies that not only is corporate governance inextricably linked to firm values, the relationship has become stronger over time.

Executive Compensation and Postacquisition Performance

Is the compensation of senior management affected by the success or failure of acquisition programs? For companies that pursue large-volume acquisition programs, with M&As being an integral part of their growth strategy, linking managerial compensation to the success of those deals makes good sense. Schmidt and Fowler analyzed a sample of 127 companies, of which 41 were bidders that used tender offers to make acquisitions, 51 were nontender offer acquirers, and 35 were control firms.[46] Consistent with research

45. Paul Gomers, Joy Ishii, and Andrew Metrick, "Corporate Governance and Equity Prices," *Quarterly Journal of Economics*, February 2003, 107–155.
46. Dennis R. Schmidt and Karen L. Fowler, "Post-Acquisitions Financial Performance and Executive Compensation," *Strategic Management Journal*, 11(7), November/December 1990, 559–569.

previously discussed, bidder companies, those that would more likely be involved in initiating hostile takeovers, showed a significant decrease in postacquisition shareholder returns. This was not the case for acquirers who did not use tender offers, as well as for the control group. Also interesting from a corporate governance perspective was that both bidders and acquirers showed higher managerial compensation than the control group. Takeovers pay "dividends" for management in the form of higher compensation even though they may generate losses for shareholders of those companies that use tender offers and hostile takeovers to pursue the acquisition strategy. Takeovers may enhance the personal wealth of managers but they may not be in the interests of shareholders. It is for this reason that boards have to be extra diligent when overseeing managers who may be acquisition-minded. There is greater risk of shareholder losses and managers, in effect, gaining at shareholder expense. For this reason, the board needs to make extra sure the deals will truly maximize shareholder wealth and not just provide financial and psychic income for managers.

Mergers of Equals and Corporate Governance

In mergers of equals, two companies combine in a friendly deal that is the product of extensive negotiations between the management teams of both companies and especially between the CEOs of both firms. Research shows that bidders (normally the larger of the two companies) do better in mergers of equals while targets do worse when compared with more traditional M&As. This was the case in a study by Wulf, who showed that bidder shareholders enjoyed more of the gains in these types of takeovers.[47] She pointed to the negotiation process between the management and directors of the respective companies as being an important factor that explains why mergers-of-equals deals have different relative financial effects for target and bidder shareholders.[48] Wulf found that the abnormal returns that target shareholders received were lower when target directors received equal or even greater control of the combined entity! This result raises corporate governance concerns. Are target directors, fiduciaries for target shareholders, trading off returns for their shareholders just so they can gain positions in and control of the combined entity? We have to also acknowledge that such positions come with compensation that is important to these directors. If it were not important they would be serving for free, and that is not consistent with the way the corporate world is overseen.

Another very interesting finding of the Wulf study, and one that has important ramifications for corporate governance, is that shared corporate governance was more common for larger and more poorly performing target companies and ones that were in industries that were undergoing restructuring. CEOs of target companies that may not have been doing well or that are in industries that are consolidating may pursue mergers of equals so as to prevent a bid that might not provide them with any continued control. They may see a friendly merger-of-equals deal as their best option even though it may be self-serving and not in the best interests of shareholders.

---

47. Julie Wulf, "Do CEOs in Mergers Trade Power for Premiums? Evidence from Mergers of Equals," University of Pennsylvania Working Paper, June 2001.
48. Ibid.

─── CASE STUDY ───

WORLDCOM—GOOD MERGER PLAN GONE OUT OF CONTROL*

WorldCom is an excellent example of a good M&A idea that was pushed too far and ended up killing the company that was built through such mergers. Mergers enabled the company to grow to a size where it could compete effectively with the largest telecommunications companies in the U.S. market. At one time WorldCom was one of the better M&A success stories. However, this great story of corporate growth all came to a crashing end.

WORLDCOM'S M&A HISTORY

WorldCom traces it roots to a small telecommunications reseller called LDDS. The telecom resale business grew in the wake of the breakup of AT&T, which allowed other companies to come in and compete with the venerable telecom giant. At that time, AT&T offered price breaks for bulk buying of minutes on the AT&T long-distance network. Companies, including many small firms, would commit to buying bulk minutes from AT&T and then passing along some of the discount that they would receive to customers they would solicit. These customers would be able to receive lower rates than they might get on their own. As a result, a whole industry of resellers grew. However, such companies were limited in the profit opportunities they would enjoy as they would have to incur switching and access costs at both the origination and end of a call. The reseller industry eventually grew into subgroups, switchless and switch resellers, as some of the resellers purchased their own switches so that they could avoid some of the costs they would incur going to and from the long-distance network. The industry grew through M&As and one of the companies that used this method to grow was a Mississippi-based reseller—LDDS Communications. The head of that company was Bernie Ebbers, who was far from being a major figure in the dealmaking business.

The idea for what would become WorldCom can be traced back to 1983, when Ebbers and a few friends met at a diner in Hattiesburg, Mississippi, to discuss the concept of forming a long-distance company now that the breakup of AT&T was moving toward a reality. Ebbers was initially an investor in the business, but he took the reigns when the company began to perform poorly. Within six months he took this losing operation and moved it to profitability. In doing so he showed that he had the management skills to run a small business efficiently. Years later he would demonstrate that these same management skills could not be translated to a multibillion-dollar telecommunications business. Ebbers would show that he could very effectively build a large company through M&As. However, when it came to running such an enterprise profitably, he failed.

The business went on to grow and in 1989 it went public through an acquisition with the already public Advantage Companies. As a result of this deal, LDDS now had operations in 11 different states—mainly in the South and Midwest of the United States. The next major step in LDDS's history was a 1993 three-way deal in which LDDS would merge with Metromedia Communications and Resurgens Communications Group. Each of these companies was a full-service long-distance firm. Ebbers had established momentum in his growth-through-M&As strategy and he would not be slowed. LDDS was still a comparatively small company compared with giants such as AT&T and MCI. However, there was no denying the company's meteoric growth path. Ebbers continued on this path when on the last day of 1994 he completed the acquisition of IDB Communications Corp, and on January 5, 1995, the acquisition of the WilTel Network Services took place. The IDB deal moved LDDS more clearly into the international telecommunications market as that company had more than 200 operating agreements in foreign countries. WilTel operated a national digital

*Source: Patrick A. Gaughan, *Mergers: What Can Go Wrong and How to Prevent It* (Hoboken, NJ: John Wiley & Sons, 2005), pp. 237–239.

fiber-optic network and was one of only four companies in the United States to do so. Using this network, LDDS would be able to transfer some of its traffic and save outside network costs. With these deals LDDS then changed its name to WorldCom, as it considered itself a major U.S. telecommunications company but also a presence in the world telecom market. M&A had now helped the company continue with its exponential growth, as shown in Exhibits A through C.

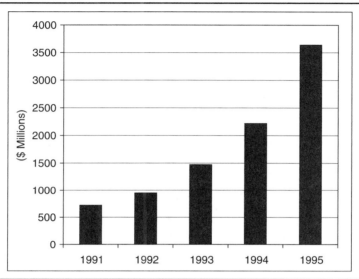

Exhibit A   Worldcom Revenues: 1991–1995
Source: WorldCom Annual Report.

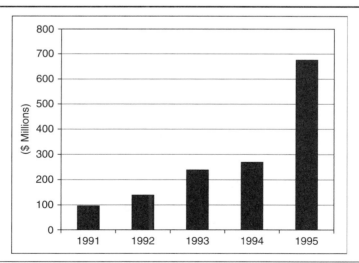

Exhibit B   Worldcom Operating Income
Source: WorldCom Annual Report.

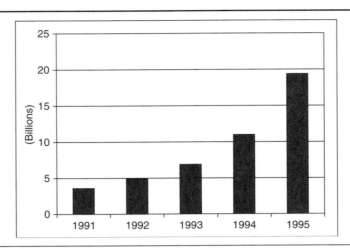

EXHIBIT C WORLDCOM MINUTES BILLED
Source: WorldCom Annual Report.

In December 1996, WorldCom completed its first megamerger when it merged with MFS Communications in a deal that was valued at approximately $14 billion. This deal brought several valuable capabilities to WorldCom. For one, MFS had various local networks throughout the United States as well as in Europe. For another, the deal brought with it UUNet, which was a major Internet service provider, thus expanding the package of services that WorldCom could offer customers. However, Ebbers was not content to sit on his laurels. He was determined to make WorldCom an industry leader. He continued in 1997 to seek out other merger partners to help him fulfill this dream.

At the beginning of 1998, WorldCom completed three more deals. They were the mergers with BrooksFiber, a company in the local exchange business, Compuserve, and ANS Communications, Inc. Compuserve was acquired from H&R Block. This sale by H&R Block was the undoing of a failed prior deal as H&R did not derive significant benefits from its ownership of Compuserve. However, in the fall of 1998, WorldCom announced a deal that would vault the company to a leadership position in the world telecommunications business. In September 1998, WorldCom merged with MCI in a transaction valued at $40 billion. By 1999, the company would have revenues of over $37 billion—with the growth coming from M&As as opposed to organic processes. As rapidly as the company was growing in the early 1990s, the end of the decade made that progress seem modest (see Exhibit D). However, while the revenue growth over the period 1995–1998 was impressive, profits were not, although they appeared to move in the right direction in 1999.

The MCI deal put WorldCom on a new level. However, Ebbers was not satisfied to stay put. His expertise was doing deals and he sought out even more deals. He reached an agreement to acquire Sprint in a $155 billion stock transaction. However, right away antitrust concerns began to materialize. The market was skeptical that the Justice Department would approve the acquisition and this skepticism proved warranted as in July 2000 the Justice Department stopped the deal. By this time, however, the stock had already begun the slide from which it would never recover until the company had to file for bankruptcy. Amazingly, Ebbers kept right on doing deals. In July 2001, WorldCom announced that it was acquiring Intermedia Communications.

While Ebbers seemed to keep trying to grow the company through deals virtually right up to the end of his tenure with the company, an irreversible slide had now begun. The Securities and Exchange Commission (SEC), fresh from dealing with major accounting frauds such as Enron and Adelphia,

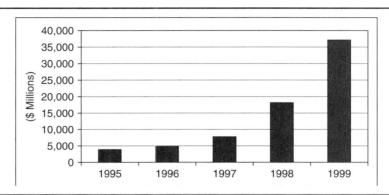

EXHIBIT D   WORLDCOM REVENUES: 1995–1999
Source: WorldCom Annual Report 2000.

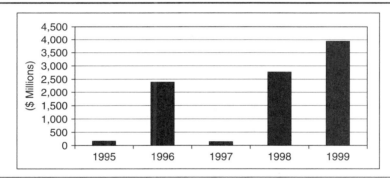

EXHIBIT E   WORLDCOM NET INCOME: 1995–1999

now began an investigation into WorldCom's accounting practices. It questioned the company's revenue recognition and other accounting practices. It appeared that many of the revenues and profits that the company was booking were fictitious. Ebbers was forced to resign from the company on April 30, 2002. The demise of WorldCom resulted in the largest corporate bankruptcy in history. From this bankruptcy a new company, now called only MCI, would emerge.

WHAT WENT WRONG WITH WORLDCOM'S STRATEGY?

This is a very broad question. However, we can provide a short answer and say the company and its CEO followed an excellent growth-through-mergers strategy. Probably all the way through the MCI deal, the strategy was working, although even then some questions began to arise. Ebbers was great at doing deals and building up his company to be a leading player in the world telecommunications business. The telecommunications industry has natural economies of scale that can be exploited through growth. His performance at achieving growth through mergers has to rank up there with leaders in U.S. business history. So where did it all go wrong? It went wrong in several ways. The obvious one was the accounting manipulations and other alleged improprieties. However, from a strategy perspective, the problem was that Ebbers and the company could not turn off the M&A acquisition binge. This really was what Ebbers was good at. However, he also proved that he was

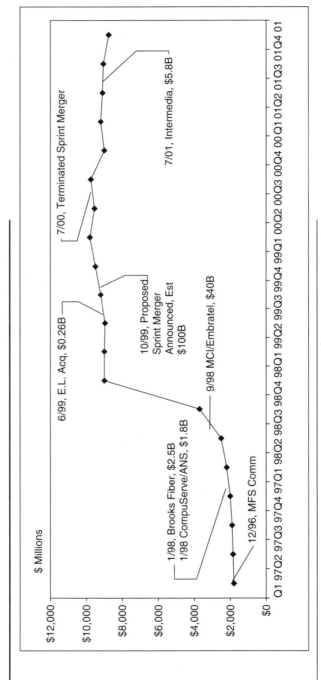

$ Millions

$12,000
$10,000
$8,000
$6,000
$4,000
$2,000
$0

Q1 97Q2 97Q3 97Q4 97Q1 98Q2 98Q3 98Q4 98Q1 99Q2 99Q3 99Q4 99Q1 00Q2 00Q3 00Q4 00 Q1 01Q2 01Q3 01Q4 01

6/99, E.L. Acq, $0.26B

7/00, Terminated Sprint Merger

7/01, Intermedia, $5.8B

10/99, Proposed Sprint Merger Announced, Est $100B

9/98 MCI/Embratel, $40B

1/98, Brooks Fiber, $2.5B
1/98 CompuServe/ANS, $1.8B

12/96, MFS Comm

Exhibit F Worldcom quarterly revenue growth and key acquisitions

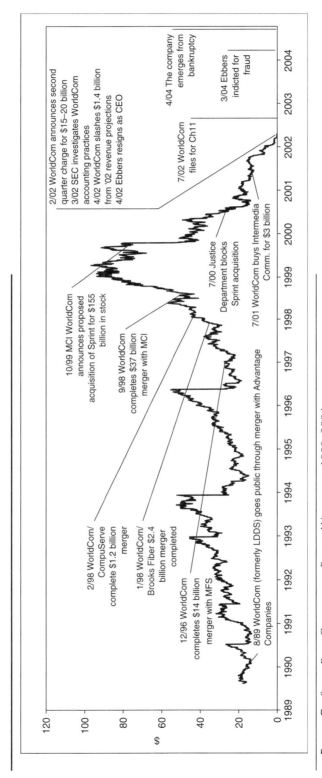

EXHIBIT G STOCK PRICE GROWTH AND FALL AT WORLDCOM: 1989–2004
Source: Center for Research in Security Prices.

not good at managing a large company on a day-to-day basis. Reports of him micromanaging minutiae at company headquarters are quite amusing as the following passage relates:

> It was billed as strategy meeting not to miss. WorldCom, Inc. senior executives from around the globe gathered two months ago at the telecom giant's headquarters in Clinton, Miss. They had to come to hear CEO Bernard J. Ebbers reveal his grand vision for rescuing a company mired in debt, sluggish growth, and rising controversy about its accounting practices. What executives heard instead was their boss thundering about the theft of coffee in the company's break room.

> How did Ebbers know? Because he had matched brewing filters with bags, and at the end of the month, filters outnumbered bags. Henceforth Ebbers commanded, his executives would follow a checklist of priorities now referred to as Bernie's seven points of light. They would count coffee bags, make sure no lights were left on at the end of the day, and save cooling costs in the summer by turning the thermostat up four degrees, say three former and current executives. Bernie is running a $40 billion company as if it were still his own mom and pop business, says one WorldCom exec who attended the meeting. He doesn't know how to grow the company, just save pennies.[a]

Other reports state that Ebbers installed video cameras outside company facilities to record the length of employee smoking breaks. Still other reports talk about his approving expenditures above $5,000 and of personally reviewing all press releases the company would issue. Running a large company was not what Ebbers was good at. The skills that one needs to run a small company, or to do creative and aggressive deals, are not the same skills that one needs to manage a multibillion-dollar company. Indeed, with the exception of his grand-scale dealmaking, Ebbers gave all the signs of being a small-company CEO. Managing a business as though it was a small, closely held enterprise also contributed to his own personal woes. Prior to his resignation from the company, Ebbers borrowed $366 million from the company to bail him out when personal loans he had taken had come due and he would have had to sell some of his WorldCom shares at a time when the price was not favorable. It is not usual for CEOs of closely held companies to cause the company to function for their own personal benefit. However, when a company is mainly owned by public shareholders, it has to be run for their benefit and it is no longer the founding shareholder/CEO's personal fiefdom.

Ebbers and his management also did a poor job of managing the capital structure of the telecom giant. The company had assumed significant amounts of debt that had by 2002 risen to $30 billion. In that year interest payments were $172 million but were scheduled to rise dramatically to $1.7 billion in 2003 and $2.6 billion in 2004.[b] In addition, investment bankers were reporting that the company had negative cash flow in 2001. This was not a time to have a major increase in debt service pressures when the company's market shares and cash flows were under pressure. The company had over a billion in cash on hand and had a line of credit with banks of up to $8 billion. However, credit lines regularly come up for renewal and a bank will reexamine a company's liquidity position at such times. WorldCom was heading for a liquidity crisis and dealmaker Ebbers had no answer. The wrong man was at the wheel and he kept the company on course for disaster.

When it is clear that the company has gotten all it is going to get out of a growth-through-M&A strategy, and the company is at an efficient size, then the dealmaking process needs to be, at least temporarily, turned off. At that point organic growth needs to be the focus, not more deals. The board let shareholders down by not stopping Ebbers and putting in place someone else to run the business. Ebbers was allowed the run the company right into bankruptcy. The outcome is a sad one as the growth Ebbers achieved was so impressive, but many will now know him

[a]Charles Haddad and Steve Rosenbush, "Woe Is WorldCom," *Business Week,* May 6, 2002, 86.
[b]Haddad and Rosenbush op cit.

only for allegations of improprieties and the bankruptcy of the company. Who knows what would have happened had the board been vigilant and asked him to step aside before they got close to bankruptcy? Would a good manager have been able to maintain and grow the business Ebbers built?

One factor that helped allow Berbie Ebbers to stand unopposed was the fact that there was no major blockholder who would stand up and insist that the board of directors better represent shareholders' interests. These failures can be contrasted with a notable corporate governance success from many years gone by. The case is GM, which was run by a CEO who shared many of the same positive and negative traits of Bernie Ebbers. GM was built by the great dealmaker, Willie Durant. His great skill, like Ebbers's, was doing deals and combining companies. Also like Ebbers, he was not good at managing and could not create a management structure at GM that would maintain profitability in the face of frantic dealmaking. Unlike Ebbers, Durant knew he had some shortcomings in managing and he convinced the great Walter Chrysler to postpone his plans to start his own company and to run GM instead. However, Chrysler could not endure Durant's disruptive and chaotic dealmaking and left to form his own very successful auto company.

Fortunately for GM, it had an outspoken large shareholder, Pierre DuPont, who insisted on making sure that the company would be profitable—not just ever larger. DuPont became convinced that Durant had outlived his usefulness and that his constant dealmaking had to stop. He had a showdown with Durant in 1916. By then GM was the second largest auto company in the United States but was a troubled concern, DuPont insisted that Durant resign. DuPont replaced him with the great manager, Albert Sloan (after whom the Sloan school at MIT is named). Ironically, Durant built one of the largest companies in the world but died a poor man.

Lessons of the WorldCom Strategy

- *Dealmaking CEOs need to be controlled by the board.* There will come at time that dealmaking may need to be paused and possibly stopped. Acquisitive CEOs need to be held in check. They also need to demonstrate that they can run a company and do something other than acquisitions.
- *Dealmaking and managing are two different skills.* Some managers are capable of doing both. Some are better at one than the other. Boards need to put in place the right people with the right skills. Having a dealmaker in place greatly increases the likelihood that deals will be made. If that is not what is needed, then get someone else in the leadership position.

SUMMARY

The corporate governance process has received great attention in recent years. Much of this attention has centered on financial fraud and manipulations of data contained in statements disseminated to the public. Various reforms, such as those that have been required pursuant to SOA, have been implemented to address these governance problems. However, insufficient attention has been paid to limitations in the corporate governance process as they relate to M&As. The track record of many M&As has been poor and many of these can be related to breakdowns in the oversight process. This is an additional area where corporate governance reforms could be helpful.

Boards of directors are the main force that needs to monitor management and the CEO and ensure that the company is run in a manner that maximizes shareholder wealth. When the board is more independent and less close to the CEO, corporate governance seems to work best. But when the board is closely aligned with the CEO, the monitoring process does not work as well. There is abundant evidence that shows that when CEOs are unchecked, some will tend to pursue their own goals. Sometimes these goals will be increased compensation and perks. Other times they will be manifested in the building of a larger corporate empire that may be motivated by CEO hubris and not shareholder interests. Independent boards, and ones that are not interlocked, work best in holding such CEOs in check.

Research studies have analyzed the role of boards and CEOs in better performing M&As and better oversight in general. From this research we are able to conclude that "busy" directors who sit on many boards are not in shareholders' interests. Neither are the "gray" directors, who benefit from the association with the corporation in ways other than the direct fees they are paid to serve on the board. In addition, interlocked boards, where directors have reciprocal relationships with each other's boards, are also not in shareholders' interests. Boards in which directors are motivated, diligent, and independent tend to do the oversight job the best.

13

JOINT VENTURES AND STRATEGIC ALLIANCES

As we have seen, a merger with, or an acquisition of, another company can be a costly endeavor but may provide great gains for the companies pursing the deal. It may also be the case, however, that many of the gains that the participants hoped to achieve could be realized without having to do a merger or an acquisition. It may be possible that these gains can be achieved with a joint venture or a strategic alliance. In this chapter we will explore these two options as alternatives to mergers and acquisitions (M&As). We will consider their respective benefits and costs and then compare these to M&As. We will see that in certain instances, companies are better off with an alliance or joint venture but in other cases such deals will not achieve a company's goals and it will have to focus on M&As.

As with our discussions of M&As, we will review the shareholder wealth effects of both joint ventures and strategic alliances. We will see that the studies of the market's initial reaction, like those of M&As, can provide great insight to whether a deal will ultimately be beneficial.

CONTRACTUAL AGREEMENTS

Even before discussing joint ventures and strategic alliances, we should first consider a simpler alternative to an alliance or joint venture—a contractual agreement between the parties. If the goals of the relationship are specific and can be readily set forth in an enforceable contract between the parties, then this may be the least costly and most efficient solution. As an example, consider a company that is concerned about sources of supply and is contemplating an acquisition of a supplier to lower the risk of availability of inputs for its production process. It is possible that these risk-lowering benefits could be achieved by a long-term contractual agreement between the company and a supplier. The company may not need to create a strategic alliance or a joint venture to get a supplier to commit to providing specific products and services. However, when the products in question are not readily available and require a specific development commitment on the part of the supplier, a contract may or may not suffice. If the process is even more complicated and involves the parties exchanging valuable and proprietary information as well as a buyer providing funding for the supplier to engage in a long-term and uncertain development process, such as what often occurs between biotechnology and pharmaceutical firms, then a contract may not be enough and either a strategic alliance or a joint venture may be needed, if not an outright merger or acquisition. We would expect to have a contractual agreement with a strategic alliance or joint venture, but most contracts between businesses are not strategic alliances or joint ventures. Thus strategic alliances and joint ventures involve agreements that go beyond the usual contractual relationships with businesses. They are more complicated and require more detailed roles and commitments between the parties.

COMPARING STRATEGIC ALLIANCES AND JOINT VENTURES WITH MERGERS AND ACQUISITIONS

Strategic alliances feature less involvement between the alliance partners than joint ventures, which in turn are also a lesser commitment than a merger or acquisition. In terms of investment of capital, control, and the cost of reversal, Exhibit 13.1 shows that strategic alliance is the lowest on this scale, followed by joint venture and then M&A.

JOINT VENTURES

In a joint venture, two or more companies combine certain assets and work toward jointly achieving a business objective. Usually the time period of this combination is defined and limited in duration. This is another difference between joint ventures and M&As because the latter involves an indefinite period unless it is a specialized deal where a company is acquired with the planned goal of selling it within a limited time period. There are many recent examples of private equity firms buying public companies, taking them private with the goal of improving the business, and then putting them up for sale at a higher price than they paid. However, in this chapter we consider very different types of transactions.

The companies involved in a joint venture maintain their own separate business operations and continue to exist apart as they did before the joint venture. This venture is then formally created as a business entity such as a separate corporation or partnership. A formal agreement among the venture participants sets forth the extent to which they each will exercise control over the venture's activities and will participate in the entity's profits or losses. Presumably this will be a road map that each can follow to assess the venture's progress toward achieving its goals.

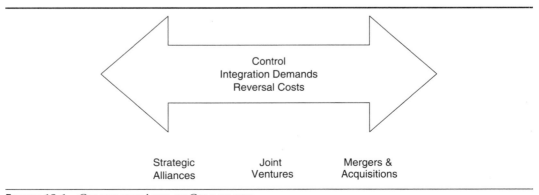

EXHIBIT 13.1 COMPARATIVE LEVEL OF COMMITMENT

Joint ventures can be used for a wide variety of business purposes. Perhaps two companies have specialized resources that when combined can be used to create or market a specific product. For example, one could be a traditional pharmaceutical manufacturer while the other might be a biotechnology firm. The pharmaceutical company may want to utilize the research and development (R&D) resources of the biotech business to develop a particular drug for the treatment of some ailment. If this is the goal, buying the biotech business, which may be involved in many other areas in which the drug manufacturers are not interested, may be an expensive way of gaining the research capability it needs to develop the drug. The drug manufacturers may have in place a widespread marketing network that would be able to rapidly capture market share when the product is eventually developed. In this case, both parties bring resources to the table and, for this one particular venture, each can gain from the other's resources. The solution may be a joint venture in which the two businesses come together for this one activity and may not necessarily do anything else together in the future. Of course, if this venture worked out well, they might pursue other joint efforts.

Joint ventures may be a way for two potential merger partners to assess how well they work together. Cultural differences between two companies may become apparent when they are involved in a joint venture or strategic alliance. If these differences are problematic, the business dealing usually can be curtailed at comparatively lower costs in a joint venture or strategic alliance compared with a merger or acquisition that may erode shareholder value.

Motives for Joint Ventures

If we consider that a merger or acquisition is a combining of the resources of two different companies, then a joint venture is a different process that, to some extent, may achieve the same goals. The motives for joint ventures are varied, but the following list provides a few examples that often occur:

- *Enhance research and development capabilities.* A company, such as a pharmaceutical company, may enter into a joint venture with another business that has some specific capability that it needs to further its R&D process. On the other hand, the R&D capability may be so important that a company may want to "luck it up" and do an outright acquisition. This was the case in 2006 when Merck purchased the biotech Sirna Therapeutics for $1.1 billion. The deal gave Merck access to Sirna's promising RNAi gene technology.
- *Gain access to key supplies.* Two or more companies may form a joint venture so they can have a better source of supplies for their production process. Such supplies could range from joint exploration for oil by petroleum companies to joint training programs for workers.
- *Enhance distribution systems.* Two companies may enter into a joint venture agreement that will enable one or both of them to have an enhanced distribution network for their products. One company could be a manufacturer of a product but lacks a distribution system including an established sales force that the other possesses.

- *Gain access to foreign market.* International joint ventures may enable companies that operate in different countries to work together to achieve gains in one or more countries. Such international joint ventures are common in the automobile industry. An example occurred in November 2006 when Renault announced it entered into a joint venture with the conglomerate, Mahindra and Mahindra. The two agreed to work together to build an automobile plant to makes cars for the rapidly growing Indian auto market. Renault is an "old hand" at joint ventures having done others with companies such as Japanese automaker Nissan Motors.

CASE STUDY

FEDEX AND TDW—JOINT VENTURE AS A PRECURSOR TO AN ACQUISITION

A joint venture can allow a company to "sample" a takeover target and learn about its strengths and weaknesses. Entering into a joint venture with another firm allows each company to see how the two work together. It also allows the one that would be the acquirer to get a sense of just how real the synergies are. This is much easier and less costly to do in a joint venture than it is in an acquisition. An example of this occurred when Federal Express decided in 2006 to buy out the 50% stake of its venture partner Tianjin Datain W. Group Co. Ltd. (TDW). The two companies formed an international express delivery venture in 1999. Federal Express bought TDW's stake in the venture as well as TDW's domestic delivery business in China. The experience working with TDW had been favorable and Federal Express wanted to move strongly into the Chinese delivery market that its rivals, UPS and Deutsche Post AG's DHL unit, were actively pursuing. The Chinese market is one of the most rapidly growing in the world, and trade is a key component of this growth. Trade in turn intensively utilizes delivery services.

Each of FedEx's two rivals had formed partnerships with Chinese shipping companies. UPS had established a partnership with Yangtze River Express Airline Co. Ltd. and DHL had established a partnership with China National Trade Transportation Corp. (Sinotrans). FedEx first entered the Chinese market in 1984. The acquisition of TDW gave FedEx 6,000 employees in China—almost all of whom are Chinese. FedEx hopes to use this entity as a base for rapid expansion into this market.[a]

[a]*Daily Deal,* January 24, 2006, p. 1.

Regulation and Joint Ventures

Simply because two companies form a joint venture instead of doing a formal merger or acquisition does not exempt them from some of the same regulatory scrutiny they might face if they merged or one was acquired by the other. This is definitely the case for antitrust laws. The anticompetitive provisions of the Sherman Act and the Clayton Act can be also applied to joint ventures, where the effect of the venture on the market is to reduce competition. The cases of the Justice Department or the Federal Trade Commission challenging joint ventures are less common than their challenges of M&As. However, in theory the same laws look at the business combination and its impact on the degree of competition in the market. Keep in mind that when a company enters into a joint venture or a strategic alliance, it cannot be doing so to circumvent antitrust laws, and those laws still apply. Another point to also remember is that if the antitrust authorities found a venture to be anticompetitive, it usually can be terminated at a lower cost than a merger or acquisition of a business that has been fully integrated into the parent company.

Shareholder Wealth Effects of Joint Ventures

In Chapter 3, as well as elsewhere, shareholder wealth effects of corporation combinations were examined. It was found that the market responses to acquisition announcements are often not positive, and target shareholders often do not do well. When target shareholders receive their premium, assuming it is not in stock and they do not hold those shares for an extended period, they have measurable gains. In light of these M&A shareholder wealth effects, the logical question that arises is "How do shareholders do in joint ventures?"

McConnell and Nantell did a study of 136 joint ventures involving 210 U.S. companies over the period 1972–1979.[1] The joint ventures were in a variety of industries, with the most common being real estate development (18/136%) and television and motion pictures (14/136%). The study was an announcement period, short-term-oriented study that compares with many of the event studies that have been conducted for M&A announcements. It is important to bear in mind, however, that when we say short-term-oriented, the market is adjusting to the announcement in the short term, such as during an event window of three days before and after a joint venture announcement, but this adjustment reflects the market's anticipation of the long-term effects of the benefits and costs of the venture. The reaction occurs in a short time period, but it is attempting to reflect or forecast long-term effects. This is different from a long-term study, which looks at the financial impact of an event after the fact, when we have had the benefit of the passage of a number of years.

The McConnell and Nantell study showed that shareholders in companies entering into joint ventures enjoyed announcement period returns of 0.73%. They found similar results when some of the industries such as real estate were removed from the sample. They also found that the gains were fairly evenly distributed across venture participants. When the authors tried to convert that seemingly small percentage return to a dollar amount, they found it corresponded to an average value of $4.8 million.

The McConnell and Nantell study supports the idea that, when considering the shareholder wealth effects, joint ventures are a viable alternative to a merger or an acquisition. Whether they may accomplish what a company wants to achieve with an M&A is going to be determined on a case-by-case basis. However, while it also varies depending on the circumstances, one cannot argue that joint ventures lack some of the aggregate positive shareholder wealth effects that M&As provide. One thing that a joint venture will not provide, and for acquirers this is a good thing, is a large buyout premium for target shareholders. Without that premium, the opportunities for management to make bad decisions by overpaying may be more limited. They may still be able to negotiate poor terms for their own companies, but the opportunities for large financial losses *may* be more limited.

---

1.   John J. McConnell and Timothy J. Nantell, "Corporate Combinations and Common Stock Returns: The Case of Joint Ventures," *Journal of Finance*, 40(2), June 1985, 519–536.

The McConnell and Nantell findings of positive shareholder wealth effects for joint ventures were supported by the research of Woolridge and Snow, who analyzed a sample of 767 announcements of strategic investment decisions involving 248 companies operating in 102 industries.[2] These strategic investment decisions included joint ventures as well as R&D projects and major capital investments. Their methodology featured an examination of the stock market reaction to the announcement of these decisions. In general they found positive stock market responses to these various announcements. When the sample was divided into subsamples for the different types of announcements, they were able to determine that the shareholder wealth effects were positive for joint venture announcements. These results are consistent with the McConnell and Nantell findings.

Shareholder Wealth Effects by Type of Venture

While the McConnell and Nantell study looked at the shareholder wealth effects by type of industry, it did not differentiate these effects by type of venture. Johnson and Houston analyzed a sample of 191 joint ventures over the period 1991–1995.[3] They divided their sample into vertical joint ventures (55%) and horizontal joint ventures (45%). They defined *vertical joint ventures* as transactions between buyers and suppliers. *Horizontal joint ventures* are transactions between companies that are in the same general line of business and that may use the products from the venture to sell to their own customers or to create an output that can be sold to the same group. The results showed average positive gains from joint ventures equal to 1.67%. For horizontal joint ventures, it appears that the gains are shared by the venture participants. The average returns for vertical joint ventures were somewhat higher—2.67%. However, what is particularly interesting when they looked at the vertical sample was that the gains did not accrue to both parties. Suppliers gained an average of 5%, with 70% of the returns being positive, while buyers received an average return of only 0.32%, which was not statistically significant and of which only 53% of the returns were even positive. For vertical joint ventures, the biggest winners were suppliers, who were able to capture the bulk of the gains, while the market did not see major benefits for buyers.

Johnson and Houston recognized that when two companies entered into a joint venture, especially a vertical venture that showed the greater gains, the venture participants could have entered into a contract as opposed to a joint venture. Why did they choose the venture alternative? Johnson and Houston analyzed a sample of announcements of contracts and also found positive shareholder wealth effects with such announcements. However, they found that companies enter into joint ventures, as opposed to contracts, when transaction costs are high. They describe some of these transaction costs as "hold-up hazards." This could occur, for example, if a supplier had to make buyer-specific investments, such as investments in certain machinery and capital goods needed to produce the buyer-specific

2. J. Randall Woolridge and Charles C. Snow, "Stock Market Reaction to Strategic Investment Decisions," *Strategic Management Journal,* 11(5), September 1990, 353–363.

3. Shane Johnson and Mark Houston, "A Reexamination of the Motives and Gains in Joint Ventures," *Journal of Financial and Quantitative Analysis,* 35(1), March 2000, 67–85.

products. Although a contract may provide some temporary protection to the supplier over the contract period, once this period is over, the supplier may be vulnerable unless this capital equipment could be redeployed to another buyer. For these types of transactions, Johnson and Houston saw benefits for joint ventures that mere contracts could not provide.

Restructuring and Joint Ventures

Sometimes a company may be able to pursue restructuring or a selloff through the use of a joint venture. Consider a company that wants to divest itself of a division but is having difficulty finding a suitable buyer for 100% of the company that would provide a sufficient value to make the company sell off the division. One alternative would be to sell off part of the company and in effect run the division as a jointly owned entity. If the goal of the company doing the partial sale is really to be able to do a 100% sale, it may negotiate terms with the partial buyer, whereby that buyer would be able to purchase the remaining shares in the division at some point in the future based on the occurrence of certain events. Such events might be the division achieving certain performance goals. If this occurs, the seller would, in stages, have found its buyer. That buyer is able to utilize the capabilities of the business unit without, at least initially, having to do a 100% acquisition. If it buys control of the target, it may be able to enter into whatever agreement it needs while saving on the costs of a 100% acquisition. If it finds that the relationship is rewarding, it may then want to be a 100% shareholder and not have to share in the ownership of the company. The seller may also be able to add terms to the original agreement that state that if certain targets are met, the buyer is bound to complete the purchase and buy the remaining shares as of some date.

Potential Problems with Joint Ventures

Many potential problems can arise with joint ventures. They are certainly not a cure for all of the ills of M&As. This is obvious from the fact that we continue to do so many M&As, and if joint ventures were the solution, we would see more of them instead of M&As. The potential problems with joint ventures are as varied as the types of ventures. They may fail because the venture partners do not work well together. There may be disagreements between the participants, which may get in the way of accomplishing the venture's goals. The venture may require participants to share intellectual property or other proprietary knowledge, and they may be reluctant to do so or one venture partner may be using such information in a way that was not intended by the other venture participant. The participants may not see themselves as fully committed as they might if the activities of the venture were part of the overall business. This lack of full commitment may prevent the venture from achieving its goals. Other problems may be that the venture simply does not accomplish what it set out to accomplish. We will see that many of these same problems can occur with strategic alliances as well.

Strategic Alliances

Strategic alliances are less formal associations between companies compared with joint ventures. In a joint venture, a separate entity is often created, whereas in a strategic alliance the agreement and the relationship are less formal. Such alliances are common in various different industries, including the pharmaceutical, airline, and computer industries. Airlines that serve different geographic markets often form alliances or airline partner agreements. Under such agreements, they remain separate airlines but share routes. This enables them to be able to keep a customer who wants to fly beyond the range of a given airline's routes. Each airline alliance partner can market the entire route, and the same flights may be marketed under different flight numbers for each partner. With such alliances, the various partners may be able to provide customers with a global network. In addition, as various companies in an industry form such alliances, this puts pressures on competitors to follow suit so they are not at a disadvantage because of a smaller network.

Enhancing R&D is a major reason why companies form strategic alliances. Robinson reports a National Science Foundation study that indicated that one company in ten that was involved in R&D financed such work outside of the company.[4] Robinson and Stuart also report a survey from the Pharmaceutical Research and Manufacturers of America, which suggested that approximately "25% of the $26 billion in U.S.-based, industrially financed, pharmaceutical R&D that occurred in 2000 took place in over 700 collaborative agreements with outside organizations."[5] An example of such an agreement is the alliance between Novartis, a Swiss-based pharmaceutical company, and Vertex, a biotechnology research company, whereby Novartis made various payments, including an initial payment of $600 million and additional payments of $200,000 staggered over six years, in exchange for the rights to market various pharmaceutical products. With such agreements, pharmaceutical companies can gain access to technology provided by biotech firms that may not be available to the drug companies. As technological change accelerates in the pharmaceutical industry, the methods of developing drugs also change. In recent years, the way in which pharmaceutical companies create new drugs has changed, and many of these companies have lacked some of the capabilities and expertise to conduct more modern research. Drug manufacturers need access to research capabilities that biotech companies have and that they may not be able to develop quickly in the time frame they need to stay competitive with other drug companies, which may have such capabilities in-house or through other alliances with biotech companies.

GOVERNANCE OF STRATEGIC ALLIANCES

When a company acquires another company, the governance process is hierarchical in the sense that the acquirer pays for and receives the right to control the target. It governs the target—hopefully in a manner that facilities growth of the wealth of the acquirer's shareholders. The governance of strategic alliances is bilateral and is determined by the agreement the alliance partners enters into as well as by factors such as the nonlegal commitment of the alliance partners to make the alliance succeed. In entering into such

---

4. David Robinson, "Strategic Alliances and the Boundaries of the Firm," Working Paper, Columbia University, Graduate School of Business, November 2001.
5. David Robinson and Toby Stuart, "Financial Contracting in Biotech Strategic Alliances," Working Paper, Columbia University, Graduate School of Business, February 2002.

an agreement, the alliance participants seek to lower some of the various costs that might exist if they had a looser arrangement. This does not mean that they will not have opportunities for strategic behavior. Depending on the type of alliance entered into, a significant degree of trust may be needed between the partners. If the success of the alliance requires that they share confidential information, then the parties must be confident that this valuable intellectual property will not be used inappropriately. If this proves to be a concern, it may inhibit the success of the alliance because the parties may be reluctant to share what needs to be shared in order to have complete success.

There has been much discussion in the economic and financial literature on the assignment of control rights in joint ventures.[6] This assignment is important in alliances involving the development of new technologies. Aghion and Triole point out that two factors should govern the allocation of control rights, and we add a third.

1. The degree to which there may be an underinvestment of either party that could have an adverse effect on the success of the alliance
2. The relative bargaining parties of the two partners
   We can add another factor as follows:
3. The extent to which one party may engage in opportunistic behavior, which can have an adverse effect on the outcomes

Lerner and Merges describe a case study involving pharmaceutical company Eli Lilly and the Repligen Corporation, a biotechnology company. They worked together on a project involving monoclonal antibody treatments of inflammation:

> In the negotiations there were three areas where control rights were in dispute. The first was the management of clinical trials: which drugs would be pursued and when. A second was the control over the marketing strategy, an area in which Lilly had extensive experience and Repligen only a slight acquaintance. Finally, both parties wished to undertake the process development and ultimate manufacturing of the drug. Repligen, in fact, had recently acquired a cell culture facility and the key personnel that went with it.
> The final agreement appeared to assign control rights to the parties with the greatest discretion to behave opportunistically. Repligen was allowed a great deal of flexibility in developing the lead product candidate (where it had the greatest experience), but tangential product development activities would only be supported when precise milestones were reached. Lilly was assigned control over all aspects of marketing; while Repligen was assigned all manufacturing control rights, unless it encountered severe difficulties with regulators.[7]

Lerner and Merges did an empirical study of 200 contracts/alliances between biotechnology companies and sponsoring firms. They found results that were consistent with the previous case study they described in their paper. They found that, in general, control rights were assigned to the smaller alliance partner as an increasing function of their financial health. It seems that in the drug development industry, it may be optimal for control rights to be assigned to the smaller company, but the limiting factor may be its own financial condition. Smaller companies that are in better financial condition are in

6. Phillipe Aghion and Jean Triole, "On the Management of Innovation," Quarterly Journal of Economics, 109, 1994, 1185–1207.
7. Josh Lerner and Robert P. Merges, "The Control of Strategic Alliances: An Empirical Analysis of Biotechnology Collaborations," NBER Working Paper No. 6014, April 1997.

a stronger bargaining position and also are less risky alliance partners. Larger pharmaceutical companies may be less able to force their terms on a financially sound smaller biotech company. They also may have more confidence in a financially sound but smaller biotech company and may worry less about its being able to do what it agreed to do.

Shareholder Wealth Effects of Strategic Alliances

Just as we have with joint ventures, we will look at the shareholder wealth effects of strategic alliances. Chan, Kensinger, Keown, and Martin looked at the shareholder wealth effects of 345 strategic alliances over the period 1983–1992.[8] Almost one-half of their sample involved alliances for marketing and distribution purposes. For the overall group, they found positive abnormal returns equal to 0.64%. This is somewhat comparable to what was seen with the research of McConnell and Nantell for joint ventures. The Chan, Kensinger, Keown, and Martin study also found no evidence of significant transfers of wealth between alliance partners. This implies that there was no evidence that one partner was gaining at the expense of another. This result supports strategic alliances as an alternative to M&As—*in the limited circumstances where it is appropriate.*

Shareholder Wealth Effects by Type of Alliance

Chan, Kensinger, Keown, and Martin looked at how the shareholder wealth effects varied by type of alliance. They separated their sample into horizontal and nonhorizontal alliances. They defined horizontal alliances as those involving partners with the same three-digit SIC code. They found that horizontal alliances that involved the transfer of technology provided the highest cumulative abnormal return—3.54%. This may help explain why strategic alliances occur so often between technologically oriented companies. Nonhorizontal alliances that were done to enter a new market provided a positive but lower return—1.45%. Other nonhorizontal alliances failed to show significant returns. Another study conducted by Das, Sen, and Sengupta also looked at the types of alliances that might be successful, as reflected by their initial announcement shareholder wealth effects.[9] They were able to show how the announcement effects varied by type of alliance as well as by firm profitability and relative size of the alliance participants. They discovered that technological alliances were associated with greater announcement returns than marketing alliances. These are two of the more common types of alliances. In his research of 4,192 alliances, Hagedoorn has previously shown that, as expected, technological alliances were more common in high-growth sectors, whereas marketing alliances were more common in mature industries.[10] Das, Sen, and Sengupta also showed that the abnormal returns were negatively correlated with both the size of the alliance partners and their profitability. We see that the market is concluding that larger and more profitable

8. Su Han Chan, John W. Kensinger, Arthur Keown, and John D. Martin, "Do Strategic Alliances Create Value?" *Journal of Financial Economics,* 46(2), November 1997, 199–221.
9. Somnath Das, Pradyot K. Sen, and Sanjit Sengupta, "Impact of Strategic Alliances on Firm Valuation," *Academy of Management Journal,* 41(1), February 1988, 27–41.
10. J. Hagedoorn, "Understanding the Rationale of Strategic Technology Partnering: Interorganizational Modes of Cooperation and Sectoral Differences," *Strategic Management Journal,* 14, 1993, 371–385.

partners will capture fewer of the gains from the alliance. Stated alternatively, the market sees greater benefits for smaller and less profitable businesses to partner with larger and more profitable companies. The smaller and less profitable companies seem to have more to gain from strategic alliances. This does not imply that the partnerships are not also good for larger companies. Given that they are bigger and their profits are greater, it would be reasonable to expect that when such companies partner with smaller firms, they have less to gain because the impact of that alliance will have a smaller impact on the overall business of the larger company. That larger company may enter into several such alliances, and the aggregate effect of all of these alliances may make the difference less.

CASE STUDY

WYETH AND PROGENICS COLLABORATE ON DRUG DEVELOPMENT

In December 2005, Wyeth Corp (formerly American Home Products) and Progenics announced that the two companies would collaborate on the development of a drug that would deal with the opioid-induced side effects of certain pain medications. Wyeth is a Madison, New Jersey—based pharmaceutical company that, like all other major drug companies, is seeking to expand its product line. Progenics Pharmaceuticals, Inc. is a Tarrytown, New York–based biopharmaceutical company. It is well known that many opioid products that are used to treat pain, such as after major surgery, may have adverse gastrointestinal side effects. The two companies see this as a sizable market.

Progenics developed a product called methylnaltrexone (MNTX), which, with further refinement, could fill the void in this market. As part of their agreement, Wyeth agreed to provide Progenics with an up-front payment of $60 million and as much as $356.5 million based on Progenics achieving certain milestones in the development process. Wyeth also agreed to pay Progenics royalties on sales while also being responsible for further development costs. Progenics has initially developed the subcutaneous and oral versions of the product that were in Phase 3 and Phase 2 trials as of the date of the agreement. In order to have both the Federal Drug Administration–approved injectable and oral versions of the product, Progenics relies on the greater financial resources of the much larger Wyeth. In addition, Wyeth will bring its considerable marketing resources to bear to ensure that, when available, the product will fully exploit the potential market.

What Determines the Success of Strategic Alliances?

What factors determine whether a strategic alliance is going to be a success? Which types of alliances are more likely to be successful and which will be more difficult to pull off? A study that focused on this issue was conducted by Kale, Dyer, and Singh.[11] They analyzed a sample of 78 companies that reported on 1,572 alliances that had been established for at least two years. As of the study date, approximately 12% of the alliances were already terminated. The researchers surveyed managers within the firm, who responded to questions designed to elicit responses on the degree of success of the alliances. They found that firms that had more experience with alliances were more likely to be successful in future alliances. This means that there is a learning curve, and companies do better at alliances the more they do them. This result is intuitive. They also found that companies

---

11. Prashant Kale, Jeffrey H. Dyer, and Harbir Singh, "Alliance Capability, Stock Market Response and Long-Term Alliance Success: The Role of the Alliance Function," *Strategic Management Journal*, 23, 2002, 747–767.

that had a dedicated alliance function, such as a department and department head dedicated to overseeing alliances that the company entered into, were more likely to be successful with their alliances. An example would be companies that have a Vice President or Director of Strategic Alliances position. They found that Hewlett-Packard and Eli Lilly, for example, had such positions. It would also be reasonable to assume that if a given company established such a position, it would be more likely to engage in alliances than companies that did not have one. The reported success rate of companies with a dedicated alliance function was 68%, compared with a 50% rate for those without these positions. Interestingly, the market reacted more positively for alliance announcements for those companies that had such dedicated alliance functions (1.35% compared to 0.18%). The other interesting product of this research is that it shows a consistency between the initial market response and long-term results—in this case as applied to alliances. This is one of many pieces of evidence that allows us to take the results of studies of the short-term announcement effects for various events, such as mergers, acquisitions, joint ventures, and alliances, seriously because they seem to correlate well with long-term research results.

SUMMARY

Joint ventures and strategic alliances can be a less drastic and less expensive alternative to a merger or acquisition. Sometimes a prospective acquirer may really want to control only certain aspects of a potential target's business. If it can get the other company to form a joint venture with it or if it can get that firm to enter into a strategic alliance, then it may be able to achieve all it wants without the costs of a merger or acquisition. Usually such arrangements can be discontinued with less effort and costs than reversing a merger or acquisition. However, joint ventures are more formal arrangements than strategic alliances and may feature a greater level of commitment.

When we review the research literature on joint ventures and strategic alliances, we see that the announcements of such ventures and alliances tend to be associated with positive shareholder wealth effects for the participants. Vertical joint ventures showed higher gains than horizontal ventures. Research has also showed that for horizontal joint ventures, shareholder gains are shared by the venture participants. However, for vertical deals, this was not the case. In vertical joint ventures, the bulk of the gains went to suppliers, while buyers did not realize many of these gains.

Strategic alliances also show their own positive shareholder wealth effects, so they also are a favorable alternative. Certain companies seem to do better with strategic alliances than others. Companies that have had significant experience with such alliances seem to do better with them than those that have not. Similarly, companies that have a dedicated alliance position or department do better than those that do not have such a position.

Before approving a merger or acquisition, management and the board of directors needs to make sure that either of these two less drastic alternatives would not accomplish the same goals at a lesser cost. When this is the case, the deal planning needs to be redirected toward one of these possibilities.

14

VALUATION

The importance of a systematic valuation process became more apparent for corporate America during the fourth merger wave, when many companies found themselves the targets of friendly or unfriendly offers. Even companies that had not been targets had to determine their proper value in the event that such a bid might materialize. To exercise due diligence, the board of directors must fully and properly evaluate an offer and compare this price with its own internal valuation of the firm. The need to perform this evaluation as diligently as possible was emphasized in the 1980 bid for the Trans Union Corporation by Jay Pritzker and the Marmon Corporation.

In September 1980, Jerome Van Gorkom, chairman and chief executive officer of Trans Union, suggested to Jay Pritzker that Pritzker make a $55 a share merger bid for Trans Union, which would be merged with the Marmon Group, a company controlled by Pritzker. Van Gorkom called a board of directors meeting on September 20, 1980, on a one-day notice. Most of the directors had not been advised of the purpose of the meeting. The meeting featured a 20-minute presentation on the Pritzker bid and the terms of the offer. The offer allowed Trans Union to accept competing bids for 90 days. Some directors thought that the $55 offer would be considered only the beginning of the range of the value of the company. After a two-hour discussion, the directors agreed to the terms of the offer and a merger agreement was executed.

The Trans Union directors were sued by the stockholders, who considered the offer inadequate. A Delaware court found that the decision to sell the company for $55 was not an informed business judgment:

> The directors (1) did not adequately inform themselves as to Van Gorkom's role in forcing the "sale" of the Company and in the per share purchase price; (2) were uninformed as to the intrinsic value of the Company; and (3) given these circumstances, at a minimum, were grossly negligent in approving the "sale" of the Company upon two hours consideration, without prior notice, and without the exigency of a crisis or emergency.

The court was also impressed with other deficiencies in the board of directors' decision-making process. Among them was the fact that the board did not even have a copy of the merger agreement to review at a meeting convened for the explicit purpose of deciding on the merger. The board members therefore did not read the amendments to the agreement, and they did not request an outside valuation study of the merger offer.[1] Based on these facts, the case seems to be one of clear negligence on the part of the directors. However, there is evidence that the directors had conducted an analysis of the value of the firm before the meeting in which they approved the offer. In fact, the directors had been monitoring the firm's financial condition for several years before the Pritzker bid. Their defense also included the following factors:

> The directors' key defense was the "substantial" premium in Pritzker's $55 offer over Trans Union's market price of $38 per share. The merger price offered to the shareholders represented a premium of 62 percent over the average of the high and low prices at which Trans Union had traded in 1980, a premium of 48 percent over the last closing price, and a premium of 39 percent over the highest price at which the stock had traded at any time during the prior six years. They offered several other defenses as well. First, the market test period provided opportunity for other offers. Second, the board's collective experience was adequate to determine the reasonableness of the Pritzker offer. Third, their attorney, Brennan, advised them that they might be sued if they rejected the Pritzker proposal. Lastly, there was the stockholders' overwhelming vote approving the merger[2]

The directors' defense clearly had some merit, as reflected in the opinions of the two dissenting justices, who saw adequate evidence that the directors had studied the value of Trans Union for an extended period of time before the directors' meeting and were in a position to determine whether the offer was inadequate.

The board of directors also considered the comments of Donald Romans, Trans Union's chief financial officer, who had stated that the $55 offer was at the beginning of the range within which an adequate value of Trans Union lay. Romans's analysis was prepared to determine whether Trans Union could service the necessary debt to fund the leveraged buyout (LBO) he was contemplating. The court had not, however, considered his analysis sufficient to approve a merger because it was not a valuation study. This ruling is significant because it affirms the need for a formal valuation analysis in all mergers, acquisitions, and LBOs. Ultimately, then, the *Smith v. Van Gorkom* decision is important because it set forth, under the business judgment rule, the responsibilities of directors of public companies to have a thorough and complete valuation analysis conducted by an objective party, such as an investment bank or valuation firm. Following *Smith v. Van Gorkom,* even the more financially adept directors seek to get themselves off the hook by having an outside valuation firm or investment bank issue a "fairness opinion" expressing their belief that the offer is adequate. What is also significant about the *Smith v. Van Gorkom* decision was that the court was more impressed with the decision-making process that the directors engaged in than with the ultimate decision that they made. When compared with the usual standards to which merger offers are held, such as the size of the merger premium relative to recent or industry averages or what the offer price was relative to historical stock prices, the offer

1. Stanley Foster Read and Alexandra Reed Lajoux, *The Art of M&A: A Merger Acquisition Buyout Guide*, 2nd ed. (New York: John Wiley & Sons, 1995), pp. 662–663.
2. Arthur Fleisher, Geoffrey C. Hazard Jr., and Miriam Z. Klipper, Board Games (Boston: Little, Brown, 1988), pp. 31–32.

seemed to be a good one for shareholders. The soundness of the decision was not enough for the court, however, when it was the result of a process that the court found to be deficient.

Following *Smith v. Van Gorkom* the demand for fairness opinions rose significantly. While such opinions may help get directors off the hook they raise their own concerns. It is common that firms such as investment banks will issue fairness opinions involving transactions from which they stand to profit. This raises concerns of conflicts of interest. This is another area that M&A governance reform needs to address. In addition, fairness opinions really do not state that the price is the best value for the company. Rather they merely state that the price is "fair."

VALUATION METHODS: SCIENCE OR ART?

The methods and data considered in the valuation of businesses vary widely. In some respects, business valuation is as much an art as it is a science. It is exact and scientific in that there are standard methods and hard data to consider in the formulation of valuation. However, several different methods may be employed in a given evaluation. The methods may provide different business values and thus give the impression that the general methodology lacks systematic rigor.

The naive reader may infer that the valuation of businesses may be an overly subjective process. A closer examination of the methodology, however, reveals that objective valuations can be achieved. The variability of values is natural, given that we are considering the market for a business in which different participants may place varied values on the same business or collection of assets because the anticipated uses of these businesses or assets may be different in different hands.

In this chapter we will discuss the main methods of business valuation. We will consider the methods that are used to value both public and private companies. Many of the techniques used to value both types of companies are similar. For example, the selection of the discount rate and comparable multiples are clearly relevant to valuing both public and private companies. But some techniques, such as the marketability discount, may be more relevant to the valuation of closely held businesses.

MANAGING VALUE AS AN ANTITAKEOVER DEFENSE

The intensified takeover pressures that managers experienced in the fourth merger wave gave them a great incentive to increase the value of their firms so as to reduce their vulnerability to a takeover. Firms with a falling stock price but marketable assets are vulnerable to a takeover. Those with high liquid assets are even more vulnerable. Managers have found that adopting a management strategy that will boost the stock price makes the firm a more expensive target. With an increased stock price, raiders have trouble convincing stockholders that management is doing a bad job and that there are more value-enhancing ways to run the company.

An increase in stock price reduces the effectiveness of several takeover tactics. It makes a tender offer more difficult by raising the cost of control, and it decreases the effectiveness of a proxy fight because it is harder to garner the requisite number of votes from other shareholders when management has increased the value of their investment. Some supporters of takeovers maintain that the pressures placed on management have benefited shareholders by forcing management to take actions that maximize the value of their investment. The stock price has become a report card of management performance. Managers now have to regularly monitor the market's valuation of their actions. This marks a significant change in the way corporations were run in earlier years, when managers kept the stock price in mind but did not make it a factor in most of their major decisions. For this reason, among others, valuation has been placed in the forefront of corporation management.

BENCHMARKS OF VALUE

The analysis presented in this chapter provides several different methods of valuing a company. Their accuracy can be tested through a basic sensibility check, which can be performed by comparing the resulting values with certain benchmarks that indicate the *floor value* of the company. The floor value is the normal minimum value that the company should command in the marketplace. Some of these benchmarks are described in the following sections.

Book Value

Book value is the per-share dollar value that would be received if the assets were liquidated for the values at which the assets are kept on the books, minus the monies that must be paid to liquidate the liabilities and preferred stock. Book value is sometimes also called shareholders' equity, net worth, or net asset value. Book value tends not to be an accurate measure of a company's value. It merely reflects the values at which the assets are held on the books. If these historical balance sheet values are not consistent with the true value of the company's assets, book value will not be as relevant to the company's valuation.

One use of book value is to provide a floor value, with the true value of the company being some amount higher. The evaluator's role is to determine how much higher the true value of the company is. In some cases, however, the company may be worth less than the book value. Although this is not common, a company may have many uncertain liabilities, such as pending litigation, which may make its value less than the book value. Book value may also contain intangibles, such as goodwill, so it may also be useful to look at tangible book value, which excludes such components.

Sales prices of companies can be expressed as multiples of book values. These multiples tend to vary by industry. Depending on the current trends in the industry, there is a certain average value that can be used to gauge the current market price of potential targets. If firms in the industry are priced at a certain average value, such as selling at six times the book value, and the firm in question is selling for only two times the book value, this might be an indicator of an undervalued situation. Book value is a preliminary indicator that takeover artists use to find undervalued firms.

Liquidation Value

Liquidation value is another benchmark of the company's floor value. It is a measure of the per-share value that would be derived if the firm's assets were liquidated and all liabilities and preferred stock as well as liquidation costs were paid. Liquidation value may be a more realistic measure than book value. If accurately computed, it may be a more accurate indicator of the true value of the firm's assets in that to some extent it reflects the market value of the assets. However, it may underestimate the true market value because in a liquidation assets may sell at "fire sale" prices. Liquidation value does not directly measure the earning power of the firm's assets. These assets may have different values depending on the user. If the firm is using its assets very efficiently, the company's value may be well in excess of the liquidation value.

Discounted Future Cash Flows or Net Present Value Approach

When the investment that is required to purchase the target firm is deducted from the discounted future cash flows or earnings, this amount becomes the net present value. This concept is similar to net present value calculations used for capital budgeting (equation 14.1). These techniques are covered in most corporate finance textbooks.

The discounted future cash flows approach to valuing a business is based on projecting the magnitude of the future monetary benefits that a business will generate. These annual benefits, which may be defined in terms of earnings or cash flows, are then discounted back to present value to determine the current value of the future benefits. Readers may be familiar with the discounting process from capital budgeting, where net present value (NPV) is used to determine whether a project is financially worth pursuing:

$$NPV = I_0 - \sum_{i=1}^{n} \frac{FB_1}{(1+r)} + \ldots = \frac{FB_n}{(1+r)^n} \tag{14.1}$$

where:

FB_i = future benefit in year i

r = discount rate

I_0 = investment at time 0

When earnings are used instead of cash flows, the particular earnings measure utilized may differ depending on the user, but most earnings-oriented models use some version of adjusted operating income such as earnings before interest, taxes, depreciation, and amortization (EBITDA).

The cash flows or earnings must be adjusted before constructing a projection so that the projected benefits are equal to the value that a buyer would derive. For example, adjustments such as the elimination of excessive officers' compensation must be made to the base that is used for the projection.

One of the key decisions in using the discounted cash flows (DCF) approach is to select the proper discount rate. This rate must be one that reflects the perceived level of risk in the target company. We will discuss the computation of discount rate a little later in this chapter.

When we use DCF to value a business we do the valuation in a two-part process. Part one is to value the cash flows that have been specifically forecasted for a period over which the evaluator feels comfortable about the accuracy of the forecast. Typically this is five years in length. The second part of the process values the remaining cash flows as a perpetuity. The value of these remaining cash flows is sometimes referred to as *continuing value*. The longer the specific forecast period, the smaller the continuing value. The value of the business (BV) is equal to the sum of these amounts (equation 14.2):

$$BV = \text{Value derived from the specific forecast period} + \text{Value of remaining cash flows} \quad (14.2)$$

This value can then be computed as follows:

$$BV = \frac{FCF_1}{(1+r)} + \frac{FCF_2}{(1+r)^2} + \cdots + \frac{FCF_5}{(1+r)^5} + \frac{\frac{FCF_6}{(r-g)}}{(1+r)^5} \quad (14.3)$$

where:

BV = value of the business
FCF_i = free cash flows in the ith period
g = the growth rate in future cash flows after the fifth year

The numerators of all the fractions are free cash flows. Note that after the fifth year the values of all the future cash flows are measured by treating them as a perpetuity that is growing at a certain rate, g. This perpetuity or future stream of cash flows of indefinite length is valued using the process of capitalization. This process is explained subsequently because it is also used as a separate method of valuing businesses. However, the first step is to project free cash flows for the sixth year. This may be done by multiplying the fifth year's cash flows, FCF_5, by $(1 + g)$. The resulting value is then divided by the capitalization rate to obtain the present value of all cash flows from year 6 and thereafter. This is the value as of the beginning of year 6. We then compute the present value of that amount by dividing it by $(1 + r)^5$. This is the present value in year 0 of all future cash flows for year 6 and thereafter. This amount is sometimes referred to as the *residual*. It is then added to the other five present value amounts computed for the first five years to arrive at a value of the business.

Continuing Value

The continuing value (CV) represents the value that the business could be expected to be sold for at the end of the specific forecast period. We have measured this value by treating it as a perpetuity and capitalizing the remaining cash flows, which we assumed were going to grow at a certain growth rate. Another way to arrive at the continuing value would be to apply an *exit multiple*. If we use an exit multiple for the continuing value, we need to make sure it is a multiple that we expect to apply during the exit period. For example, if a higher multiple is relevant as of the date of acquisition due to the company being in an initial high-growth phase of its life cycle, perhaps a lower multiple, consistent with mature firms in that industry, would be more relevant as an exit multiple.

It should be noted that when measuring the continuing value using the perpetuity calculation, the value that results is quite sensitive to the growth rate that is used. Different growth rate assumptions can change the resulting value significantly. As an example let us assume that the FCF at the end of the specific forecast period is $10,000,000 and we are using an 11% discount rate. Applying a 6% growth rate results in:

$$CV_1 = \$10,000,000(1.06)/(0.11 - 0.06) = \$212,000,000 \qquad (14.4)$$

If we used just a 1% lower growth rate, 5%, the resulting value is:

$$CV_2 = \$10,000,000(1.05)/(0.11 - 0.05) = \$175,000,000 \qquad (14.5)$$

The extra 1% in the growth rate from 5% to 6% increased the continuing value by 21% (remember this value still has to be discounted back to year 0 terms). This is why the assumptions about the continuing growth of the company after the end of the specific forecast period are important to the overall value of the company. As we will discuss in the Quaker Oats–Snapple case study that follows, flawed growth rate assumptions can result in disastrous overpayment.

CASE STUDY

QUAKER OATS' ACQUISITION OF SNAPPLE

A classic example of overpaying was the acquisition of Snapple by Quaker Oats. In 1994, Quaker Oats had acquired Snapple for $1.7 billion. Just three years later, in March 1997, Quaker Oats announced that it was selling Snapple for $300 million to Triac Cos. Now *that* is value creation for you! The market reacted positively to this admission of an acquisition mistake when on March 27, 1997, Quaker Oats stock closed at $37.75—up 25 cents.

How did Quaker Oats, a well-known and established company with major consumer brands, make such a huge error? Clearly it overvalued Snapple and thought that its growth, which before the acquisition had been impressive, would continue. Snapple used its prior growth to demand a high premium, as it should have done. Quaker should have more realistically evaluated Snapple's growth prospects and used a more modest growth rate when it valued the company.

At the time that Quaker made its rich offer for Snapple, many analysts questioned it and thought that Quaker was overpaying. The word at the time was that Quaker might be overpaying by about as much as $1 billion. But Quaker was not buying Snapple in a vacuum, and it was already successful in the soft or recreational drinks business with its Gatorade line. Gatorade was and still is a successful beverage and has carved out its own niche in this business that is separate and distinct from giants such as Coke and Pepsi. To a large extent, Snapple had already done the same thing. However, with the familiarity it already had with the beverage business through its experience with Gatorade, Quaker Oats should have known better. It would be one thing for Quaker Oats to have had no experience with this business and make such a mistake. While that would not have made the misvaluation excusable, Quaker's experience in the sector makes the misvaluation even harder to explain.

Quaker Oats is an established company with a 100-year history in business. It has a diverse product line that ranges from pancakes and cereals to juices and sports drinks. Quaker had already done well with its Gatorade acquisition. One author reported, however, that the success of this acquisition for Quaker's CEO, William Smithburg, was based on luck and impulsive decision making rather than shrewd acquisition planning.[a] He was reported to have bought this company based on "his taste buds" rather than a more serious market and valuation analysis. Regardless of his reasoning, however, the Gatorade purchase was a big success. The business cost Quaker $220 million, and it grew it into a $1 billion company. Based on this success, Quaker's board gave Smithburg more free rein for other acquisitions, and it was here that both he and the board made an error.

The Quaker Oats–Snapple debacle was compounded by the manner in which the deal was financed. In order to raise the capital to afford the Snapple acquisition, Quaker sold its "highly successful pet and bean divisions" to "raise $110 million of the $1.8 billion price tag."[b] It sacrificed a profitable, albeit boring, business, to purchase an overpriced and mature business.

Triac was a company with its own acquisition history. It was run by Nelson Peltz and Peter May. Peltz was well known in the world of M&As, having led Triangle Industries, which was involved in some well-known leveraged transactions working with Drexel Burnham Lambert and Michael Milken in the fourth merger wave. Triangle grew from acquiring stakes in several can-making companies, consolidating them, and eventually selling them to a French company for $1.26 billion. More recently Peltz is know for his aggressive proxy fight for a presence on the board of Heinz Corp.

Quaker made more errors than just overpaying. After it bought Snapple, it changed its advertising and marketing campaign. Before its sale, Snapple used an odd set of advertisements that featured a Snapple employee named Wendy Kaufman. When Quaker bought Snapple, it changed this campaign to one that directly positioned Snapple behind Coke and Pepsi. This campaign, however, did little to help Snapple grow enough to justify its rich price.

In 2000, Triac packaged together its beverage operations, which included RC Cola, Mistic, and Snapple, and sold them to Cadbury for $1 billion plus the assumption of $420 million of debt. This was a great deal for Triac when one considers that it invested only $75 million in equity for Snapple and borrowed the rest of the $300 million. The fact that Cadbury paid $1.4 billion for this business in 2000 is ironic in that it passed on the Snapple acquisition a few years earlier because it believed that the business was too troubled to justify a much lower price than what it eventually paid.[c]

Why did Quaker Oats overpay? One factor that is clear is that it believed there was more growth potential in the Snapple business than what was really there. To review the reasonableness of Quaker Oats' assessment of Snapple's growth potential, one can consider the distribution into the market that Snapple already enjoyed in 1997. Snapple had grown impressively before that year. It had a high growth rate to show potential buyers. Buyers, however, needed to assess whether that growth was sustainable. One way to do so would be to determine how many more food outlets Snapple could get into and how much more product it could sell at those that it had managed to get distribution into. Was it already in most of the food stores that it would be able to get into in the U.S. market? Could it really increase sales significantly at the outlets it was already in? If it was at a maturity position, in a noncarbonated beverage market that was growing significantly but where the growth was slowing, then this needed to be incorporated into the valuation model using either a lower growth rate for a DCF model or a lower multiple for a comparable multiples model. That is, if historical growth rates were extrapolated, this would result in an overvaluation. Obviously, Quaker Oats was using inflated growth parameters when it significantly overpaid for Snapple.

[a]P. C. Nutt, *Technology Forecasting and Social Change*, 2004, 239–265.
[b]Ibid., p. 245.
[c]Constance Hays, "Cadbury Schweppes to Buy Snapple Drinks Line," *New York Times*, September 19, 2000, C1.

Adjustments to DCF Enterprise Value

In computing enterprise value using DCF we are implicitly including only those assets that contribute to the generation of free cash flows. If the company owns other assets that have a positive market value but that do not contribute to cash flow generation, then the value of these assets needs to be added to the enterprise value that has been computed using DCF. An example is real estate assets that are not involved in the operations of the business.

Arriving at Equity Value Using Enterprise Value

When we use DCF to arrive at enterprise value we compute the value of the equity by deducting the value of the liabilities from the total enterprise value. However, we may have to make other adjustments to the debt value that is found on the balance sheet. Two areas of sometimes significant liabilities that may not be on the balance sheet are unfunded pension liabilities and contingent liabilities. For companies that have defined benefit pension plans, such as automakers General Motors and Ford, they may have unfunded pension and health liabilities that are not fully recorded on the balance sheet. In addition, the company may have contingent liabilities, such as litigation-related liabilities, that may be difficult to measure. We know, however, that these liabilities can be significant. For example, when ABB acquired Combustion Engineering in 1989 for $1.6 billion in cash plus assumed debt, it did not anticipate the true magnitude of that company's asbestos liabilities.

Defining Free Cash Flows

Free cash flows are those cash flows, as measured by EBITDA, that are available to all capital providers, both equityholders as well as debtholders, after necessary deductions have been made for the capital expenditures (CE) that are needed to maintain the continuity of the cash flow stream in the future. These expenditures are made to replace capital that may have been depleted through the company's operating activities. While the term free cash flows (FCF) has been defined differently by some users, many also deduct any necessary changes in working capital (CWC) as well as cash taxes paid (CTP) (equation 14.6):

$$FCF = EBITDA - CE - CWC - CTP \qquad (14.6)$$

Free cash flow reflects the cash from a business that is available to make payments to shareholders and long term debt holders. Therefore, it reflects the monies that generate value for these investors.

Free Cash Flow Theory of Mergers, Acquisitions, and Leveraged Buyouts

Some researchers believe that a firm's amount of free cash flows may determine whether it is going to engage in takeovers. The theory implies that managers of firms that have unused borrowing capacity and ample free cash flows are more likely to engage in takeovers. Managers use the cash resources to acquire other firms instead of paying the monies to stockholders in the form of higher dividends.

Jensen contends that many of these mergers result in "low benefits or even value destroying mergers. Diversification programs generally fit this category and the theory predicts that they will generate lower total gains."[3] According to Jensen, these mergers are more likely to occur in industries that are in a period of retrenchment but that nonetheless have large cash flows. When the mergers are horizontal, they may create value because the payment of cash to the stockholders of the target firm is a way in which cash is leaving the company. However, in Jensen's view, mergers outside the industry may have low or even negative returns because the managers will be running a company in an industry that may be outside their area of managerial expertise. As an example, Jensen cites tobacco firms, which are experiencing a gradual decline in demand as society becomes more aware of the link between tobacco consumption and disease. The gradual decline in demand notwithstanding, tobacco companies still have large free cash flows to invest. Jensen's theory would then imply that diversifying acquisitions such as Philip Morris's (now called Altria) acquisition of General Foods and R. J. Reynolds's acquisition of Nabisco are more likely to have negative productivity effects. While that may be true in many such instances, in the case of Philip Morris, the company used cash flows from the tobacco business to build a very successful food business that lacked the health concerns and litigation exposure of tobacco.

Industries that have high free cash flows and limited growth opportunities are sometimes considered good LBO candidates. This is supported by a study by Opler and Titman of 180 firms that undertook LBOs between 1980 and 1990.[4] They found that companies that did LBOs had relatively high cash flows and poor investment opportunities (as reflected by low Tobin's Qs). These results are consistent with those reported by Lehn and Poulsen, who investigated the role of free cash flows in going private transactions.[5] They found that going private companies had more free cash flows than a control group.

The presence of high free cash flows makes an LBO possible. It also creates opportunities for many of the leveraged recapitalizations that are being done by private equity firms, which acquire targets, increase leverage, and use the proceeds to quickly withdraw value from the target. Without excess target cash flows this would not be possible.

The free cash flow theory of takeovers assumes that managers have the ability to use free cash flows for their own purposes. The greater the agency costs, the more likely this will occur. With companies with high free cash flows that have managers that are shielded by high monitoring and agency costs, managers may pursue their own corporate agenda as opposed to shareholder wealth maximization.[6] Robert Hanson investigated the free cash flow theory of takeovers and found that high cash flow target firms receive higher than average abnormal returns.[7] His research showed that during the 1970s, cash

3. Arthur Fleisher, Geoffrey C. Hazard Jr., and Miriam Z. Klipper, Board Games (Boston: Little, Brown, 1988), 31–32.
4. Tim Opler and Sheridan Titman, "The Determinants of Leveraged Buyout Activity: Free Cash Flow vs. Financial Distress Costs," *Journal of Finance,* 48(5), December 1993, 1985–2000.
5. Kenneth Lehn and Anne Poulsen, "Free Cash Flow and Shareholder Gains in Going Private Transactions," *Journal of Finance* 44, July 1989, 771–787.
6. Randall Morck, Andrei Shleifer, and Robert W. Vishny, "Do Managerial Objectives Drive Acquisitions?" *Journal of Finance,* 45, March 1990, 31–48.
7. Robert C. Hanson, "Tender Offers and Free Cash Flow," *The Financial Review.* 27(2), May 1992, 185–209.

flow–rich bidding firms pursued low benefit takeovers. However, in the 1980s, high free cash flow firms became targets of tender offers themselves as the market pursued the valuable free cash flows. In the 1990s and 2000s, private equity firms sought out undervalued companies with high cash flows and acquired them often using leverage that could be readily serviced by the cash flows of the target.

Accuracy of Discounted Cash Flows: Evidence from Highly Leveraged Transactions

Kaplan and Ruback conducted a study of 51 highly leveraged transactions (HLTs) between 1983 and 1989, in which they compared the market value of the transactions with the discounted using cash flow forecasts in an effort to ascertain the accuracy of the forecasts relative to the actual purchase price.[8] Of the 51 transactions, 43 were management buyouts and 8 were recapitalizations. They found that the median estimates of the DCF were within 10% of the market values of the transactions. It is interesting that they compared the accuracy of the DCF forecasts with that of other valuation methods, such as comparable multiples from transactions in similar industries. The results showed that the DCF valuation performed at least as well, if not better, than comparable methods. When they added the comparable data to their model, however, the explanatory power of the DCF estimates improved. This suggests that using information from *both* methods would result in better valuations than using just one.

The importance of the Kaplan and Ruback study is that it reinforces the superiority of DCF to other valuation methods while recognizing the value of other methods, such as comparables, in enhancing a valuation. It further affirms the validity of DCF methods as they are currently used in the valuation of public and closely held firms.

Choice of the Discount Rate

The choice of the appropriate discount rate to calculate the present value of the future projected cash flows requires that the riskiness of the target and the volatility of its cash flows be assessed. As is true of other forms of capital investment, an acquisition is a risky endeavor. The target's cash flows are focused on as they are the cash flows that reflect the value of the investment that is about to be made by the acquirer. The discounting process gives us a means of internalizing our judgments about the risk of an acquisition within the discount rate.

If a project were judged to be without risk, the appropriate discount rate would be the rate offered on Treasury bills, which are short-term government securities with a maturity of up to one year. Treasury bonds, the longer-term version of U.S. government securities, may also have zero default risk, but they carry interest rate risk. Interest rate risk is the risk that interest rates may rise above the rate that the investor receives from the Treasury bond. Although the investor is guaranteed the predetermined coupon payments, these coupon payments will not necessarily be invested at the same rate of interest. If

---

8. Steven N. Kaplan and Richard S. Ruback, "The Valuation of Cash Flow Forecasts: An Empirical Analysis," *Journal of Finance*, 50(4), September 1995, 1059–1093.

they are not, the investment's proceeds will not be compounded at the rate of interest offered on the Treasury bond.

The riskier the investment, the higher the discount rate that should be used; the higher the discount rate, the lower the present value of the projected cash flows. However, a firm methodology for matching the risk with the discount rate needs to be established.

Cost of Capital and the Discount Rate

One guide to selecting the proper discount rate is to consider the cost of capital. This measure is useful in capital budgeting because only one firm is involved. The cost of capital for a given company can be generally derived through:

$$CC = \sum_{i=1}^{n} w_i k_i \tag{14.7}$$

where:

CC = the firm's cost of capital

w_i = the weight assigned to the particular k_i. This weight is the percentage of the total capital mix of the firm that this source of capital accounts for.

k_i = the rate for this source of capital

Let us consider a simple example of a firm whose capital structure is composed of 50% debt and 50% equity. The weights for each source are 0.50. If the debt rate is 9% and the rate of return on equity is 15%, the cost of capital can be computed as follows:

$$CC = 0.50(0.09) + 0.50(0.15) + 0.045 + 0.075 = 0.12 \text{ or } 12\% \tag{14.8}$$

The target may have a very different risk profile than the acquirer. This is why the target's cost of capital may be more relevant to the computation of the discount rate than the acquirer's. This is then used as the discount rate for the firm when using DCF. As the analysis is expanded to make the cost of capital reflect the true capital costs of the firm, all the various components of the capital mix must be considered. Therefore, if the firm has preferred stock outstanding as well as different forms of debt, such as secured bonds, unsecured debentures, and bank loans, each needs to be considered separately in the new, expanded version of equation 14.8.

Cost of Debt

The after-tax debt rate reflects the true cost of debt, given the fact that debt is a tax-deductible expense. The after-tax rate of debt can be determined as follows:

$$k^t = k_d(1 - t) \tag{14.9}$$

where:

k^t = the after-tax cost of debt

k_d = the pretax cost of debt

t = the actual corporate tax rate for the firm

One question that often arises is what tax rate should be used to compute the after-tax cost of debt. Some analysts simply use the statutory corporate rate as there may be uncertainty as to what rate a given corporation may actually pay. However, it is important to note that many corporations may pay a different rate. John Graham has provided a methodology for how such rates can be determined.[9]

Cost of Preferred Stock

Because preferred stock dividends are usually fixed, preferred stock shares some of the characteristics of debt securities. Therefore, preferred stock is often considered a fixed-income security. The cost of preferred stock to the issuer can be determined by first focusing on the dividends that have to be paid each period relative to the proceeds derived by the issuer. These proceeds should be net of floatation costs. Let us consider a firm that has issued 8% preferred stock with a par value of $100. Let us further assume that floatation costs are 2.0% of the par value. This suggests a net of proceeds value of $98. The annual dividends are $8, or 8% of the $100 par value. (Dividends are annualized for simplicity.) The cost can be determined as follows:

$$\text{Cost of preferred stock} = D_p/P_n = \$8/\$98 = 8.16\% \qquad (14.10)$$

The consideration of floatation costs should also be applied to all publicly issued securities. For the sake of brevity, we consider only floatation costs for preferred stock.

Cost of Common Stock

Many rules determine the cost to the corporation of the common stock it has issued. One of the simplest methods is to calculate the historical rate of return on equity for the stock over a given time period. A 5- to 10-year historical period is often chosen. The time period selected would have to be placed in perspective by considering the corporation's growth to see whether it represents the company's current and expected condition.

If the company is a start-up company with little available history, proxy firms should be used. Proxy firms are similar to the company being analyzed but they have more historical rate of return data available. The rate of return on equity for proxy firms is used in place of the company being analyzed.

Another method that is sometimes employed is the beta risk measure, which is derived from the capital asset pricing model. This measure allows us to consider the riskiness of the company and to use this risk level to determine the appropriate rate of return on the company's equity. The beta can be derived from the following expression:

$$R_i = R_{RF} + \beta_i(R_M - R_{RF}) \qquad (14.11)$$

where:

R_i = the rate of return on equity for security i

R_{RF} = the risk-free rate. The Treasury bill rate is typically used as the risk-free rate of interest.

β_i = the beta for security i

---

9. John Graham, "Debt and the Marginal Tax Rate," *Journal of Financial Economics*, 41, May 1996, 41–73 and John Graham, "Proxies for the Corporate Marginal Tax Rate," *Journal of Financial Economics*, 42, October 1996, 187–221.

$$R_M = \text{the rate of return for the market}$$
$$(R_M - R_{RF}) = \text{the market risk premium}$$

Beta is derived from a regression analysis in which the variability of the market's return is compared with the variability of the security's return. From this analysis, a beta for the firm is derived, which can be used to weigh the risk premium. This weighed risk premium is then specific to the firm being analyzed. This method of measuring the cost of capital makes good conceptual sense but is not commonly used in daily merger analysis.

The rate of return on equity can also be measured by directly projecting the dividend flow. This calculation is easy in the case of preferred stock because the dividends are generally fixed. The following equation, derived from the Gordon model discussed previously, demonstrates the relationship between the stock price and dividends:

$$P_s = D_i / (k_e - g) \tag{14.12}$$

where:

P_s = the price of the firm's stock
D_i = the dividend paid in period i (i.e., the next quarter)
k_e = the capitalization rate for this stock
g = the growth rate of dividends

We can manipulate the preceding equation to solve for k_e:

$$k_e = D_i / P_0 + g \tag{14.13}$$

Consider the example of a firm whose common stock is currently selling for $40 per share. Annual dividends are $3, and the expected growth in dividends is 7% per year. (For simplicity's sake, dividends are considered annually, even though they may be paid quarterly.) The capitalization rate can be calculated as follows:

$$k_e = \$3(1.07)/\$40 + 0.07 = 15\% \tag{14.14}$$

The capitalization rate can be used as a measure of the firm's cost of equity capital.

A simple guideline in deriving the cost of equity is to consider that the rate of equity is generally 4% to 6% higher than the rate of debt. The rate of debt may be clear if the firm does not have many different types of debt. In this case, the debt rate is given, and 4% to 6% can simply be added to derive the rate for equity.

Another way to look at the appropriate rate on equity is to consider the long term risk premium. This is the difference between the long term average rate on risk-free T-bills and the rate on equities. Historically this has been between 6% and 7%. However, there has been much debate regarding whether the appropriate risk premium should be lower given what some see as one-time factors and institutional changes which would make the difference in return on these securities to be less in the future than it has been in the past.[10]

---

10. Jeremy J. Siegel, "The Shrinking Equity Premium," *Journal of Portfolio Management*," 26 (1), Fall 1999, 10–17 and Eugene Fama and Kenneth French, "The Equity Premium," *Journal of Finance*, 57 (2) April 2002, 637–659, as well as Ravi Jagannathan, Ellen R. McGRattan and Anna Scherbina, "The Declining U.S. Equity Premium," *Federal Reserve Bank of Minneapolis Quarterly Review*, 24 (4), Fall 2000, 3–19.

Acquirer's Hurdle Rate

In discussing the cost of capital we have indicated that we would focus more on the targets costs of capital rather than the acquirers. However, the buyer may also want to do the analysis using its own *hurdle rate*. This is the rate of return that it requires that its investments generate. This in turn may be equal to the acquirer's own cost of capital. One problem that arises in using such a rate is that if the target's cash flows have a higher volatility or risk than the acquirer's, the use of the hurdle rate may not fully capture all of the risk in the acquisition. However, this issue becomes somewhat moot if the two companies operate in the same industry and have a somewhat similar risk profile.

HOW THE MARKET DETERMINES DISCOUNT RATES

As should now be clear, no set discount rate exists; many different interest rates are available to choose from. The overall market for capital consists of many submarkets. The rate within each market is determined by that market's supply and demand for capital. Markets are differentiated on the basis of risk level. For example, the market for debt capital contains many different gradations of debt that vary according to their risk level. The market for secured debt offers a lower rate of return than the market for unsecured debt. Within each of the secured and unsecured categories are other gradations, each of which has its own interest rate. The historical relationship between the broad categories of capital can be seen in Table 14.1.

Discount Rate and Risk

The greater the risk associated with a given earnings stream, the higher the discount rate that will be used. If the projected cash flow or income stream is considered highly likely, a lower discount rate should be used. For high-risk cash flow or income streams, a risk premium is added, which increases the discount rate. The use of a higher discount rate lowers the present value of each annual projected income amount.

	1926–2005 Rate (%)	1981–2005 Rate (%)	1990–2005 Rate (%)
Inflation	3.0	3.4	2.8
Treasury Bills	3.7	5.7	4.1
Long-term Treasury Bonds	5.5	11.1	9.2
Long-term Corporate Bonds	5.9	11.0	8.9
Common Stock of Large Corporations	10.4	12.5	10.5
Common Stock of Small Corporations	12.6	13.9	14.2

TABLE 14.1 RATES OF RETURN AND INFLATION, 1926–2005 AND 1981–2005

Source: Stocks, Bonds, Bills and Inflation 2006 Yearbook.

Cross-Border Acquisitions and Risk

Investing in foreign countries brings with it a new element that varies depending on the market. The acquirer may face the worry that the foreign government may take actions that will limit the ability of the acquirer to access the cash flows that are generated in the foreign market. These actions range from changing tax rates to imposing additional regulations to even nationalization of businesses. When governments are not stable, potential acquirers may not be able to predict what type of government will be in control over the life of the investment. A good recent example is Venezuela, which has had a dramatic change in control with a less pro-business government in office. This government had threatened to take control of the petroleum industry investments that U.S. oil companies had made in that country.

Obviously some countries are more risky than others. This needs to be a factor that is incorporated into the discount rate. Markets that are in a state of transition, such as Russia and China, can be hard to predict. Investments in less stable markets will usually

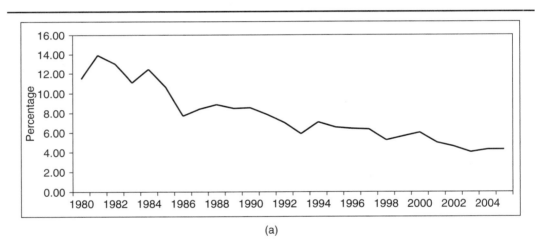

(a)

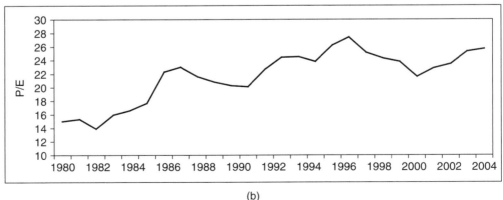

(b)

EXHIBIT 14.1   (a) YIELD ON LONG-TERM TREASURIES; (b) AVERAGE ANNUAL ACQUISITION P/E MULTIPLE

Sources: Economic Report of the President, February 2006, and *Mergerstat Review* 1991 and 2006.

warrant a higher risk premium. Countries can increase the value of their businesses and attract more foreign capital by lowering their risk profile, thereby enabling businesses to better predict the cash flows they may expect to gain access to.

Changing Interest Rates and Acquisition Prices: Evidence from the Fifth Merger Wave

Lower interest rates tend to result in lower discount rates. Short-term fluctuations may not change the discount rate that one would use in a valuation, but changes in long-term rates that persist for an extended period of time should have an influence. Such was the case in the fifth merger wave, where interest rates fell and the average price of acquisitions rose. This is demonstrated in Exhibits 14.1(a) and (b), which show that as the average yield on long-term Treasury bonds declined, the average acquisition prices rose. Long-term Treasuries are used as a base on which a risk premium is applied to arrive at a risk-adjusted discount rate. When interest rates fall for an extended period of time, evaluators lower their discount rates, resulting in higher acquisition values. This is not to imply, however, that interest rates are the only factor determining acquisition prices. They are but one of several important factors that need to be considered.

CASE STUDY

APPLYING THE DISCOUNTED CASH FLOW METHOD OF BUSINESS VALUATION?

This case study applies the discounted cash flow method of business valuation to a company that has $2.5 billion in sales in 2006. Sales are expected to grow at declining rates of growth over the next five years from 10% in 2007 to a maturity growth rate of 6% (g) after the fifth year. For the purposes of this simple example we define free cash flow as the difference between net operating income after tax (NOPAT) and new net capital expenditures:

$$\text{NOPAT} = \text{Earnings Before Interest \& Taxes(EBIT) } (1 - \text{tax rate})$$
$$\text{FCF} = \text{NOPAT} - \text{New net capital expenditures}$$

The discount rate is taken to be the weighted average costs of capital for the company, which this case study assumes is 12% (r). The capitalization rate that is used to compute the terminal value of the company after year 5 is the difference between this rate and the long-term growth rate:

$$\text{WACC} = r = 12\% \text{ and } k = \text{Capitalization rate} = r - g = 12\% - 6\% = 6\%$$

The enterprise value of the company is the present value of its future projected cash flows. This value is computed as the sum of the present value of the individually projected cash flows for the first five years and the capitalized terminal value. This value is computed as follows:

$$\text{Terminal value} = \text{FCF}_6 / (r - g)$$

It is important to remember that this terminal value is itself a year 5 value because it is the value of the company's cash flows that are projected to be received after year 5. Therefore, it must be brought to present value by dividing it by the PVIF applicable to year 5 or $1/(1.12)^5$:

Valuation Equation:

$$\frac{\text{FCF}_1}{(1+k)_1} + \frac{\text{FCF}_2}{(1+k)_2} + \cdots + \frac{\text{FCF}_5}{(1+k)_5} + \frac{\text{FCF}_6/(r-g)}{(1+k)_5}$$

Assumptions: Sales Growth: Growth at 10% per year declining by 5 and 6% thereafter:
Shares outstanding (mil): 40

	Years				
	1	2	3	4	5
Sales growth rate	10.0%	9.5%	9.0%	8.0%	7.0%
After-tax operating margin	6.0%	6.0%	6.0%	6.0%	6.0%
Net op. cap. exp. %/sales	5.0%	5.0%	5.0%	5.0%	5.0%
Weighted Average Cost Capital (WACC)	12.0%				
Long run growth rate	6.0%				
Sales Base Level - 2006:	2,500				

Free Cash Flows (1–5)

Sales (mil $)	2,750.0	3,011.3	3,282.3	3,544.8	3,793.0
NOPAT	165.0	180.7	196.9	212.7	227.6
Net operating capital expenditures	137.5	150.6	164.1	177.2	189.6
Free Cash Flows (FCFs)	27.5	30.1	32.8	35.4	37.9
Present Value of FCFs	24.6	24.0	23.4	22.5	21.5

Terminal Value Calculation		**Total Enterprise Value**	
Free Cash Flow Year 6	40.2	Present Value of FCF's (years 1–5)	116.0
Term. Value of Company in Year 5	670.1	Present Value Company's Terminal Value	380.2
Present Value of Terminal Value	380.2	Total Enterprise Value	496.2
		Deduct market value of debt & preferred	100.0
		Total Value Common Equity	396.2
		Shares Outstanding	40.0
		Price of Share of Stock	**9.9**

Source: Patrick A. Gaughan, Measuring Business Interruption Losses and Other Commercial Damages (Hoboken, NJ: John Wiley & Sons, 2004), pp. 281–282.

Real Options in Valuation

In the past decade the DCF analysis that is used in capital budgeting as well as in business valuation came under attack for its lack of flexibility. Capital investments normally carry with them various options or alternatives that may affect the value of the investment over their life. In the context of capital budgeting these options, which allow for modification of the value of an investment over time, are referred to as *real options*. Many options or alternatives are relevent to most capital investments, but some of the more common are the options to postpone or delay, the options to grow or even to abandon an investment. In the context of M&As, the options could be postponing a proposed acquisition or selling off all a division. Capital projects typically also feature many different growth options that allow a company to take steps and incur costs that may speed up or slow the growth of the cash flows from a proposed deal. In an acquisition context, this could involve a decision to invest capital in an acquired business in the hope that the target's growth can be increased.

Simply creating one projection of future cash flows without considering the many different options that can be pursued over the life of the investment or acquisition presents a limited picture of the wide range of alternatives that can occur or could be pursued. This limitation has long been considered by theoreticians and practitioners in the field of capital budgeting and they have used various tools to try to augment simple net present value computations.

In an effort to arrive at business values that explicitly incorporate the alternatives of various projected cash flows researchers and practitioners applied models that are derived from the Nobel Prize winning option pricing model (OPM) used to value financial options. While the analysis today has reached quite sophisticated levels, the original 1973 Black-Scholes option pricing model (see equations 14.15 through 14.17) can be successfully employed to show the real option approach. The model is still a mainstay in the valuation of options. For a call option:

$$C = SN(d_1) - Ee^{-rt}N(d_2) \tag{14.15}$$

$$d_1 = \frac{\ln(S/X) + rt}{\sigma\sqrt{t}} + \frac{1}{2}\sigma\sqrt{t} \tag{14.16}$$

$$d_2 = d_1 - \sigma\sqrt{t} \tag{14.17}$$

Table 14.2 shows the five parameters that are used in the typical Black-Scholes calculation and their equivalent if this model were applied to business valuation.

To demonstrate the use of this model in an acquisition situation let's assume that Big Pharma Corp. (BPC) contemplates the acquisition of a medium size biotech company (BIOT) that conducts research in an area that is important to BPC. Based on a DCF analysis the value of the BIOT would be $500 million given the projected cash flows and a weighted cost of capital (WACC) of 12%. However, BIOT demands a price of $750 million. BIOT argues that its research into a new drug has a potential DCF value of $1 billion three years form now if an investment of $1.2 billion will be made. The management of the BPC is quite puzzled of why a seemingly negative NPV project in future would give more value to BIOT, and, in fact, is prepared to lower their offer for the biotech company. BIOT responds that the new drug DCF value has a standard deviation of 70% and claims that this gives the required value to his company as long as the 3 year T-note has a yield of 5%. BIOT's CFO explains to BPC that this growth potential is analogous to a call option with a current value of the stock of $1 billion discounted for three periods at 12% (BIOT's WACC) which is approximately $712 million. He proceeds to use the call model (see equations 14.5–14.7) where S is $712 million, the excercise

Call Option Parameter	Symbol	Business Real Option Parameter
Underlying stock price	S	Present Value of Future Cash Flows
Exercise price	E	Investment
Volatility of the stock price	σ	Volatility of the cash flows
Risk-free rate	r	Risk-free rate
Time for option's expiration	t	Time for option's expiration

TABLE 14.2 Black Scholes Call Option versus Business Real Option Parameters

price E is $1.2 billion, the maturity of the option is 3 years, the risk free rate is 5% and the volatility is 70%. Doing the computation with these inputs the CFO obtains a value for the growth potential of BIOT of $253 million. Therefore, he maintains that the asking price of $750 million is more than justified.

Some have criticized the application of models, such as the Black Scholes model, to the problem of valuing a business. They contend that such models are difficult for valuation practitioners to use. The inputs are complex to estimate and business values are not as straight forward candidates for such models as they are for securities. This is generally true. However, critics are missing the point of the exercise. By trying to develop more realistic models that provide greater flexibility, we are seeking to advance the simplistic nature of business valuation methodology so as to arrive at models that will incorporate more factors, such as the natural variability of cash flows, that are not captured by simplistic valuation methods. We are not saying that the basic Black-Scholes model would be a sufficient approach to value businesses. Rather it is merely introduced so that further thought can be given to developing newer and richer valuation methods that go beyond basic DCF valuation.

Comparable Multiples

Comparable multiples are regularly used to value businesses. They are a quick and easy method to come up with a value for a company. Like DCF they can be used to value both public and closely held businesses. There are two basic steps in using comparable multiple analysis: (1) selecting the correct multiple and then (2) applying it to the relevant earnings base. We will see that there are abundant areas for judgment and subjectivity in the selection of these two parameters.

Common multiples that are used are price-earnings multiples, so-called P/E ratios, price-to-book, enterprise value to EBITDA, price to revenues, as well as other combinations. Usually some normalized value of these measures is used, especially when the levels of the values fluctuate greatly. Once the multiple is derived, it is then applied to either the current year or an estimate of the next year's value of the base selected. Perhaps the most commonly cited multiple is the P/E ratio, which is the ratio of a company's stock price (P) divided by its earnings per share (EPS). When we multiply a derived P/E ratio by a target company's EPS, we get an estimated stock price. For example, let us say that we have analyzed 10 comparable companies and have found that the average P/E ratio is 17. We can then multiply this value by the target company's EPS, which we assume in this example is $3: $17 \times \$3 = \$41$. When the multiples are derived from an analysis of historical earnings, they are referred to as *trailing multiples*. When they are based on forecasts of future earnings, they are called *forward multiples*.

Other commonly used multiples are EBITDA multiples—sometimes called cash flow multiples because EBITDA is sometimes used as a proxy for cash flows. We usually obtain EBITDA multiples by dividing enterprise value, including the sum of equity and debt capital, by a given company's EBITDA level. This is done for our group of comparable companies to derive our average value. That value is then applied to the target company's

EBITDA value to obtain its enterprise value. We then back out the debt of the target from this value to get the value of its equity.

Establishing Comparability

When we use comparable multiples, one obvious key issue is comparability. Are the comparable companies from which we derived the multiple truly similar to the target being valued? Are they more valuable or less valuable? If, for example, the company being valued is a troubled concern, then it may not be worth the same multiple of other, more healthy, companies in the same industry. The target's difficulties should be reflected not only in a lower earnings base but also in lower comparable multiples, which might reflect lower earnings growth in the future.

Comparable multiples are forward-looking measures. For example, a buyer may pay seven times EBITDA not for access to the past EBITDA level but for future cash flows. When the market establishes specific acquisition multiples for different companies that have been purchased in the industry, it is making a statement about the ability of those companies to generate future cash flows. When using such multiples comparability is key. It is more than just saying that a company being acquired shares the same Standard Industrial Classification (SIC) or North American Industry Classification System (NAICS) code and is in the same industry. It is a more specific examination of comparability. Finding multiples for companies in the same business as the target is a first step, not the final step, in the comparability process. Having established a range based on prior acquisitions and the multiples that were paid, the evaluator needs then to see how the target compares with those companies from which the average multiple was derived. If the target has many features that would enhance its future earning power, then perhaps a higher multiple should apply. It is likely that the buyer is aware of this and may be asking for such a multiple. If it is not, either the buyer is naïve or this assessment of higher than average future earning power may be misguided.

Dealing with Outliers

Users of industry multiples should know which companies entered into the computation of the average. It is useful to be aware of the degree of dispersion. It may be the case that many of the companies in the industry have multiples very different from the average. If one or two outliers have skewed the average, then we need to consider whether they should be eliminated. If the outliers are very different from the company being evaluated, then there may be a good case for eliminating the outliers from the computation of the average.

CASE STUDY

USE OF COMPARABLE MULTIPLES TO DETERMINE ENTERPRISE VALUE

Enterprise value is a broad measure that reflects the value of the capital, both debt and equity, that has been invested in the company. In this case study, we will measure enterprise value using comparable multiples derived from similar businesses that have been sold before the current valuation. As previously noted, comparable multiples are applied to specific performance measures. Some common performance measurements are as follows:

- EBITDA: earnings before interest, taxes, depreciation, and amortization
- EBIT: earnings before interest and taxes
- Net income: earnings after interest and taxes
- Free cash flow: operational cash flow less capital expenditures

The example depicted in Exhibit A uses an EBITDA performance measurement. This is used as a base in Exhibit A, which shows how an enterprise value/EBITDA multiple may be computed.

Net Income	$2,000,000
Taxes	700,000
Interest	250,000
Depreciation and amortization	150,000
EBITDA	$3,100,000
Equity acquisition price	12,000,000
Interest bearing debt	2,500,000
Total enterprise value	14,500,000
Multiple	4.68

Exhibit A   EBITDA Multiple

Exhibit A illustrates the relationship between total enterprise value ($14,500,000) and EBITDA ($3,100,000). The application of the multiple indicated to the EBITDA performance of a target company to be acquired will result in an estimate of total enterprise value. Equity value can then be determined by deducting interest-bearing debt from total enterprise value.

Exhibit B, however, shows how such a multiple can be derived from other comparable historical transactions.

	Court Company	Rotary Company	Bay Products	Western Manufacturing
Net Income	748,125	304,000	776,000	2,374,000
Taxes	785,625	110,000	400,000	1,411,000
Interest	48,750	45,000	182,000	1,407,000
Depreciation/Amortization	458,125	233,000	392,000	3,498,000
EBITDA	2,040,625	692,000	1,750,000	8,690,000
Equity Acquisition Price	14,052,000	4,600,000	14,600,000	54,300,000
Interest Bearing Debt	498,000	1,863,000	2,616,000	15,954,000
Total Enterprise Value	14,550,000	6,463,000	17,216,000	70,254,000
Multiple	7.13	9.34	9.84	8.08
Average EBITDA Multiple	8.60			
Weighted Average EBITDA Multiple	8.24			

Exhibit B   OCI, Inc., Summary of Acquisitions

An example of the application of comparable multiple valuation can be illustrated in the following case. We are attempting to determine the appropriate value of Wilson Company, which is being acquired by OCI, Inc. OCI has made several acquisitions over the past years (see Exhibit B). Historically, OCI has paid between 7 and 10 times EBITDA, averaging 8.6 times on an unweighted basis or 8.24 times on a weighted basis, depending on the size of the transaction.

We can apply this multiple to the financial results of the Wilson Company, the target acquisition, to determine an approximate value to be assigned to the Wilson acquisition (see Exhibit C). It should be pointed out that the results of Wilson's historical financial performance should be adjusted for nonrecurring or unusual items, which are not anticipated in the future. The valuation results in an enterprise value of $33.2 million and an equity value, after deducting liabilities of approximately $9 million, of $24.2 million.

Net income	$1,539.000
Taxes	928,000
Interest	374,000
Depreciation and amortization	1,194,000
EBITDA	$4,035,000
Average Multiple	8.24
Total enterprise value	33,248,400
Interest bearing debt	8,990,000
Total equity value	$24,258,400

Exhibit C   Valuation of Wilson Company

Using P/E Multiples

P/E multiples are a very often cited measure of value. Like other multiples, such as EBITDA multiples, one needs to be aware of the subtleties. As noted before, we can have trailing or forward multiples. When using multiples to value a business we need to make sure that they are applied to *permanent* income. This is income that excludes nonrecurring, one-time earnings. For example, gain from sales of assets may not be relevant to future performance and should be excluded. As discussed earlier, we also need to differentiate between trailing and forward multiples. In the context of P/E multiples, a *trailing multiple* would be a recent stock price divided by earnings in the last full accounting period, such as the last year. A *forward multiple* would be the current stock price divided by forecasted earnings. Such forecasts may be either projected by the evaluator or derived from a commercial source. Vendors such as Zachs Investment Research market forecasts. However, for companies that have had stable earnings, constructing a forecast by applying the company's own historical earnings growth to the last year's earnings level may provide a usable forecasted value.

Keep in mind that multiples vary by industry. This is intuitive as industries vary in their expected earnings growth. Table 14.3 shows selected P/E acquisition multiples for different industries. We can see that there is a significant degree of cross-industry variation.

Industry	P/E
Agricultural Production	18.2
Comm. & Broadcasting	21.4
Financial Services	28.0
Manufacturing	17.5
Natural Resources	30.3
Other Services	29.5
Real Estate	33.3
Retail	23.4
Transportation	23.6
Utilities	22.6
Wholesale & Distribution	23.6
Average 1995–2005	25.7**

TABLE 14.3   ACQUISITION MULTIPLES: AVERAGE P/E* BY
                 INDUSTRY, 2005

*Excludes P/E multiples less than 0 and greater than 100.
**Weighted Average
Source: Mergerstat Review, 2006.

CASE STUDY

MATTEL'S ACQUISITION OF THE LEARNING COMPANY—OVERPAYING THROUGH FLAWED DUE DILIGENCE AND POOR STRATEGY

The case of Mattel's acquisition of the Learning Company is a classic example of overpaying caused by poor due diligence and a flawed strategy. Mattel is a major player in the toy business and markets leading brand names such as Barbie. The company grew into this leadership position partly through a series of strategic acquisitions. This included acquiring major toy companies such as Tyco Toys and Fisher Price. These horizontal acquisitions of competitors expanded the company's product line while increasing its market share.

In 1997, a new executive took the helm at the toy company—Jill Barad. She quickly gained notoriety and became one of the better-known female executives in the United States. Her fame peaked when she appeared on the cover of *Business Week*. Following taking control of the toy company, she began to pursue her own acquisitions and in 1999 committed the company to buy a very different type of business. Mattel paid $3.5 billion for the Learning Company, which was in the educational software business. The idea behind the strategy was that toys are becoming more computerized and the products that the Learning Company marketed were sold to a similar audience as Mattel's product line sold to. Skeptics were concerned that the similarities between the product lines of the two companies were hard to see. This was confirmed in 2000 when Mattel sold off the Learning Company for virtually nothing. The business had lost money for Mattel and, when overall poor performance forced the company to refocus, the company decided to cut its losses and part ways with the Learning Company.

VALUATION OF THE TARGET'S EQUITY

In conducting a valuation of a public company, the value of the debt is usually a fairly straightforward exercise. The valuation of the target's equity is the more challenging part of the process. For public companies, however, there is a market for the target's stock and the values that a company's stock trades at in this market may be helpful in determining the value that should be paid for a target's equity in an acquisition. However, the bidder would not simply adopt the current price at the time an offer is being made. Several adjustments might have to be made. One would be a time variation adjustment that simply addresses the fact that the current price might not be representative of the long-term historical prices at which the stock traded. It could be that the market is in a temporary downturn. The bidder may want to use the temporarily low price, but it is unlikely that the seller would accept this. The difference between the near-term historical average price and the current price would provide some room for negotiations between the parties. In addition, the price of the stock at a moment in time does not reflect a control premium that normally accompanies acquisition offers.

TAKEOVERS AND CONTROL PREMIUMS

When a company makes a bid for a target's stock, one way to assess the offer is to examine the magnitude of the control premium. There is a major difference between the price of a single share quoted on an organized exchange and the price of a 51% block of stock that will give the buyer effective control of the company. When a buyer buys a controlling interest in a target company, it receives a combined package of two "goods" in one: the investment features normally associated with ownership of a share of stock and the right to control and change the company's direction. Control allows the buyer to use the target's assets in a manner that will maximize the value of the acquirer's stock. This additional control characteristic commands its own price. Therefore, the buyer of a controlling block of stock must pay a control premium.

The comparative value of a controlling interest relative to a minority interest can be seen by examining the data in Table 14.4 and Exhibit 14.2. In each of the years shown (1982–2004), the controlling interest commanded a higher value, although, as with the P/Es offered shown in Table 14.3, there is a good deal of cross-industry variation.

Supply and Demand Factors and Takeover Prices

The basic forces of supply and demand affect the prices at which a company's stock may sell in a takeover contest. The amount of the target's stock is fixed at any moment in time. This assumes that the target is not going to take actions that will increase or decrease its outstanding shares in an effort to thwart an unwelcome bid. When a new bidder buys a large block of stock, the price of the target's stock may go up (Exhibit 14.3). Because the supply of the target's stock outstanding is fixed, at any moment in time the supply curve for those shares is vertical at the quantity denoting that number of shares. D_B represents the market demand for the target's shares before the acquirer's bid. The impact of the additional demand by the acquirer is shown by the shift of the demand curve to the right of D_A.

Industry	Premium
Agricultural Production	19.8
Comm. & Broadcasting	15.5
Financial Services	31.3
Manufacturing	37.9
Natural Resources	78.3
Other Services	32.7
Real Estate	33.1
Retail	27.0
Transportation	28.3
Utilities	32.5
Wholesale & Distribution	48.7
All Industry Average	34.5**

TABLE 14.4   AVERAGE PREMIUM* BY INDUSTRY, 2005

*Excludes negative premiums.
**Weighted average
Source: Mergerstat Review, 2006.

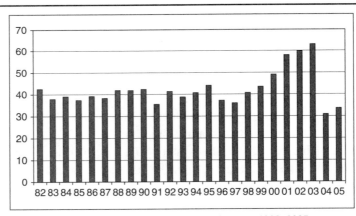

Note: Average percent premium for controlling interest, 1982–2005.

EXHIBIT 14.2   CONTROL PREMIUM: 1982–2006
Source: Mergerstat Review, 1994 and 2006.

The analysis demonstrated in Exhibit 14.3 is not the complete story. In addition to the control feature, which by itself will add value to the target's share price, there may be some offsetting effects. These offsetting effects may come in the form of quantity-purchased discounts that often accompany large block purchases. When institutional investors purchase large blocks of stock, they are often able to negotiate a quantity discount from the seller, which may be another institution such as an insurance company or a pension fund.

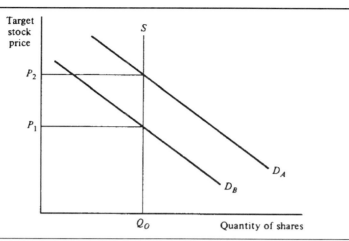

EXHIBIT 14.3 DEMAND PRICE EFFECTS

Holthausen, Leftwich, and Mayers found that for seller-initiated transactions, buyers receive temporary price concessions that are related to the size of the block.[11] For buyer-initiated transactions, the buyer is given a premium that is also a function of the size of the block. For cases in which the acquirer initiates the bid, the Holthausen, Leftwich, and Mayers study supports the demand-driven price adjustment shown in Exhibit 14.3. The offsetting effects discussed previously may come into play in cases in which the target is putting itself up for sale. Even when it does exist, this effect may not be observable because the control premium may more than totally offset it.

The Holthausen study does not focus on large blocks bought for mergers. Its focus is on the block trading that is a normal part of securities markets. It is useful, however, because it indicates how the size of the block itself affects the purchase price.

Finally, in our discussion we said the supply of target shares is fixed. It is true that unless the target issues more shares or purchases some of its own stock, the number of outstanding shares is fixed. However, at any moment in time only a percent of the total shares outstanding are traded, while the remaining amount is being held by investors who have a long-term focus. Major events, such as takeover bids, can attract some of these inactive shares into the market, thus changing the nature of the supply curve.

MARKETABILITY OF THE STOCK

The marketability of common stock varies considerably. The equity of publicly held companies is traded on organized exchanges and on the over-the-counter (OTC) market. Securities that are traded on the New York Stock Exchange (NYSE) are generally considered quite liquid. Stocks that are traded on smaller exchanges, such as the regional exchanges, may not have the same liquidity. The *OTC* is a trading system wherein securities are bought and sold through a network of brokers and dealers who trade through

---

11. Robert W. Holthausen, Richard W. Leftwich, and David Mayers. "The Effect of Larger Block Transactions on Security Prices," *Journal of Financial Economics,* 19, 1987.

the National Association of Security Dealers' Automated Quotations (NASDAQ) computerized network. In the past this market was for smaller companies, but in recent years NASDAQ has grown in importance and features many large companies. However, companies that trade on NASDAQ vary in size and trading volume. The over-the-market securities that are seldom traded are not kept on the NASDAQ computer network. Prices on these securities are available through the *pink sheets,* which appear daily and are made available through the National Quotation Bureau.

The market on which the security is traded is an important consideration in the valuation process. The broader the market and the greater the daily trading volume, the more liquid the security. This means that if you want to sell the stock, you have a better opportunity to sell a larger amount of stock without depressing the price significantly when it is actively traded on an organized exchange. If the stock is a seldom-traded security on the OTC market, however, the price quoted may be less reliable. A seller may not be able to sell a large block of stock for anywhere near the last price quoted on the pink sheets. The exact value of the stock may not be determinable until offers for the block have been made.

The "thinness" of the market is a major determinant of the liquidity of the security. Lack of liquidity is another element of risk that must be factored into the stock price. The liquidity or marketability risk can be factored into the risk premium that is used to value the projected cash flows.

Market thinness can be judged by looking at the number of *float shares* —the number of shares available for trading. Small companies on the OTC market may have only a small percentage of their shares traded, whereas most of the shares may be rarely traded. When the number of float shares is small compared with the total shares outstanding, the valuation provided by the market may not be very useful. Moreover, when the number of float shares is small, any sudden increase in trading volume can greatly affect the stock price. This is another element of risk that needs to be considered.

A related influence on the price a buyer may be willing to pay for an OTC-traded security is the concentration of securities in the hands of certain groups. The companies traded on the OTC market frequently have large blocks of stock concentrated in the hands of a small group of individuals. Some of these companies may be firms that have recently gone public and have large blocks of stock owned by family members. European companies, for example, tend to have a much higher percent of shares held by large blockholders such as founding families. Such a concentration makes the likelihood of a successful takeover by an outside party less probable unless it is a friendly transaction. The greater the concentration of securities in the hands of parties opposed to a takeover, the more problematic and costly a takeover may be.

CASE STUDY

TIME-WARNER-PARAMOUNT—CASH FLOW VERSUS EARNINGS VALUATIONS

In June 1989, Time, Inc. made a bid for Warner Communications, Inc., which was followed by a bid by Paramount Communications, Inc., for Time, Inc. Both combinations—Time-Warner and

Paramount-Time—would result in a highly leveraged company that would generate few earnings. Paramount took on $8 billion in debt to complete a $14 billion acquisition of Warner. This, however, did not make the company valueless in the eyes of its bidders. Paramount offered $12.2 billion, or $200 per share, for Time, Inc. The key to the target's value was the cash flow–generating capacity of the media assets that these communications giants commanded.

"What's significant is that Time, one of America's leading companies, is putting a stamp of approval on cash flow valuations as opposed to earnings valuations," said Bernard Gallagher, vice president and treasurer of the Philadelphia-based Comcast Corporation, the nation's third largest cable company. "Paramount, Time and Warner, all traditional earnings oriented companies, are now saying that earnings aren't nearly as important as combining and building assets that will generate cash in the future."[a]

The cash flow method of analyzing companies gained in popularity in the fourth merger wave. Here companies with reliable cash flows discovered that they could do transactions using a lot of leverage and be able to find capital providers even though they tended to not have as many hard assets as traditional borrowers. Good examples were cable companies such as the then-Denver-based cable giant Tele-Communications, Inc. (TCI). The cash flows from their subscriber base provided these firms with reliable cash flows with which to service debt. Other cable companies learned from TCI, and the industry consolidated as cable companies built national networks.[b] The valuation of TCI and Media One, another cable company, became an important issue some years later when AT&T paid handsomely for these companies based upon a belief that synergies with AT&T's telecom business would enhance the cash flows the combined companies generated. This analysis proved highly flawed.

The presence of high cash flows is not enough to ensure profitability. The $8 billion Time borrowed to finance the merger with Warner left the combined firm, which became the world's largest media company at that time, with $11 billion of debt. As with many of the leveraged transactions of the fourth merger wave, the pressure of interest payments on this debt took its toll on the firm's profitability. Time-Warner posted a $432 million loss for 1989.

It is ironic that Time turned down a substantial offer from Paramount, based on the belief of Time's management that the price of Time-Warner stock would eventually rise to $200 per share. This decision was questioned when in early 1990 Time-Warner's stock was trading as low as $96.125 per share, less than half management's projections.[c] This transaction, however, would prove to be one of many megaentertainment deals that would take place in the 1990s as this industry underwent significant restructuring. Time-Warner, a company that included many valuable assets, would rebound well from the initial falloff following the merger and would go on to grow in the fifth merger wave and become a valuable company for its investors. This value-creation process came to a crashing halt with its disastrous merger with AOL. AOL shareholders ended up owning the majority of the combined AOL-Time-Warner based on a speculative valuation of the company's stock. They gained at the expense of Time-Warner shareholders, who incurred major losses as a result of the poor dealmaking of their company's management.

[a]"Time's Warner Bid Reflects Emphasis on Value of Cash Flow, Not Earnings," *Wall Street Journal,* 27, June 1989, p. A2.
[b]Ibid.
[c]David Hilder, "Time Warner Holders Fret As Stock Sinks," *Wall Street Journal,* February 7, 1990, p. 21.

Data Reliability and Fraudulent Inaccuracies

Perhaps the worst scenario for acquirers is fraudulent misrepresentation of earnings. This was the case when Cendant Corp. reported in 1998 that its earnings were overstated. As discussed in Chapter 10, Cendant is a franchisor of Ramada hotels, Coldwell Banker real estate, and Avis Rent A Car, and a marketer of membership clubs. It was formed with the December 1997 merger of HFS, Inc. and CUC International, Inc. The company was forced to report that CUC International deliberately inflated revenues and decreased expenses. Among the issues raised were the treatment of revenues from offered memberships for which customers may ask for a full refund. In its restated data, the company reported revenues reflecting a high 50% cancellation rate. Various estimates of the inflated profits ranged from $500 to $640 million. The deliberate falsification of financial statements is an acquisition nightmare scenario. Cendant survived this accounting debacle. It was a one-time event that the market understood and thought the company could overcome. The market was less sanguine about the company's diversification strategy, and the company eventually relented and agreed to break itself up into separate component companies.

Role of Arbitragers and Impact on Prices

When a company is rumored to be the object of a takeover, the target's stock becomes concentrated in the hands of risk arbitragers, which are institutions that gamble on the probability that a company will eventually be taken over. When this occurs, the holders of the shares, including the arbitragers, will receive a premium. As arbitragers accumulate stock, upward pressure is put on its price. This effect will tend to offset any large block discounts that institutions may receive. The net effect of the arbitrage buying is to increase the price while also increasing the probability that the company will be taken over. As we have discussed in Chapter 6, the likelihood of a takeover is increased because now more shares will be concentrated in the hands of fewer investors, making large block purchases easier. In addition, given that arbitragers are simply looking to realize a good return on their investment as quickly as possible, they are very willing sellers if the price is right. A committed buyer, therefore, can be aided by risk arbitrage activities.

Valuation Effects of Mergers and Acquisitions

Numerous studies have considered the valuation effects of mergers and acquisitions. Many of these studies were done in the early 1980s. Their results, however, also apply to later time periods. Some more recent research, such as studies that consider the magnitude of returns over longer time periods as well as studies that look at the impact of the medium of exchange on returns, are discussed later in this chapter.[12]

Many of these research studies consider the impact of bids over a relatively short-term window, which may be several months before and after a bid. Proponents of the positive effects of mergers contend that it takes many years for the bidder's acquisition plans to come to fruition. Researchers, however, respond that the market has the long-term experience of many prior acquisitions and that it draws on this information when evaluating bids. In addition, it is difficult to conduct long-term studies that filter out the effects of a specific transaction from many events and other transactions that may

---

12. It is important to note that the fact that research studies may be dated several years earlier does not mean that their findings no longer apply. It is difficult to publish research that uses a similar methodology and reaches the same conclusions as studies published a decade earlier. Generally, only if their findings differ in some significant aspect will journal referees and editors accept a new version of prior research.

occur over a longer time period. Nonetheless there are some that look at various financial measures over an extended time period after deals.

These studies on the valuation effects of M&As have five general conclusions:

1. *Target shareholders earn positive returns from merger agreements.* Several studies have shown that for friendly, negotiated bids, target common stockholders earn statistically significant positive abnormal returns.[13] The source of this return can be traced to the premiums that target shareholders receive.

2. *Target shareholders may earn even higher significant positive returns from tender offers.* Target common shareholders of hostile bids that are tender offers also receive statistically significant positive returns.[14] The hostile bidding process may create a competitive environment, which may increase the acquiring firm's bid and cause target shareholder returns to be even higher than what would have occurred in a friendly transaction.

3. *Target bondholders and preferred stockholders gain from takeovers.* Both target preferred stockholders and preferred bondholders gain from being acquired.[15] Given that bidders tend to be larger than targets, the addition of the bidder and its assets as another source of protection should lower the risk of preferred stocks and bonds, thus making them more valuable. Like the target common stockholder effects, this is an intuitive conclusion.

4. *Acquiring firm shareholders tend to earn zero or negative returns from mergers.* Acquiring firm stockholders tend not to do well when their companies engage in acquisitions. These effects are either statistically insignificant or somewhat negative. Presumably, this reflects the fact that markets are skeptical that the bidder can enjoy synergistic gains that more than offset the fact that it is paying a premium for the target. The fact that the bidder's stock response is small compared with that of the target is due to the fact that bidders tend to be larger than targets.

5. *Acquiring firm shareholders tend to earn little or no returns from tender offers.* Returns to acquiring firm shareholders following hostile bids are not impressive. There is some evidence that there may be a response that ranges from mildly positive to zero.

What Types of Acquiring Firms Tend to Perform the Poorest?

Given that acquiring firms often perform poorly in M&As, the question arises as to what types of firms do the worst and which do better. Rau and Vermaelen analyzed a sample of

---

13. Debra K. Dennis and John J. McConnell, "Corporate Mergers and Security Returns," *Journal of Financial Economics,* 16(2), June 1986, 143–187; Paul Asquith, "Merger Bids, Uncertainty and Stockholder Returns," *Journal of Financial Economics,* 11, April 1983, 51–83; Paul Asquith and E. Han Kim, "The Impact of Merger Bids on Participating Firm's Security Holders," *Journal of Finance,* 37, 1982, 121–139; and Peter Dodd, "Merger Proposals, Management Discretion and Shareholder Wealth," *Journal of Financial Economics,* 8(2), June 1980, 105–138.

14. Michael Bradley, Anand Desai, and E. Han Kim, "The Rationale Behind Interfirm Tender Offers," *Journal of Financial Economics,* 11(1–4), April 1983, 183–206.

15. Debra K. Dennis and John J. McConnell, "Corporate Mergers and Security Returns," *Journal of Financial Economics,* 16(2), June 1986, 143–187.

3,169 mergers and 348 tender offers between 1980 and 1991.[16] They compared glamour firms, companies with low book to market ratios and high past earnings and cash flow growth, with value firms, companies with higher book to market ratios and poorer prior performance. The results of their research showed that glamour firms underperformed value companies. They attribute the relatively poorer performance of glamour firms to factors such as hubris. They also noted that glamour firms tended to more frequently pay with stock. This is understandable because their stock is more highly valued than that of so-called value firms.

Control Premiums and Target Shareholder Returns

Given that the control premium is the source of the positive returns reported for target shareholders, it is useful to consider how these premiums vary under different circumstances. In the next section, we discuss the trends in these premiums over time, how they vary when the stock market varies, and how they may be different for strategic versus nonstrategic deals and for mergers of equals. Next we consider whether the market places a value on control independent of takeovers.

Historical Trends in Merger Premiums

Merger premiums vary over time. When we look back at the two most recent merger waves we see that during the initial and middle part of the waves, merger premiums were actually below average. It is interesting to note that, when we consider the research by Moeller, Schlingemann, and Stulz, which showed that toward the end of the fifth merger wave acquirers incurred huge shareholder losses, the two phenomena can be linked.[17] As we will discuss below, premiums in latter part of both the fourth and fifth merger waves rose (see Exhibit 14.3). While these premiums declined when the fourth wave came to an end and the economy entered a recession, merger premiums rose sharply even after the fifth wave came to an end. In fact, 2002 and 2003 featured premiums of 59.7% and 62.3%, respectively, even though the merger wave was only beginning to rise again after a hiatus after the end of the fifth wave.

Stock Market Activity and Merger Premiums

The normal ups and downs of the stock market cause stock prices to rise and fall more than may be explained by variations in their earnings or dividends.[18] This causes some stock to be overpriced at times and underpriced at other times. Managers know that in a bear market their stock price may be below the long-term value of the firm. Believing

---

16. P. Raghavendra Rau and Theo Vermaelen, "Glamor, Value and the Post-Acquisition Performance of Acquiring Firms," *Journal of Financial Economics*, 49(2), August 1998, 223–253.

17. Sara B. Moeller, Frederick P. Schlingemann, and Rene Stulz, "Wealth Destruction on a Massive Scale: A Study of Acquiring Firm Returns in the Recent Merger Wave," *Journal of Finance*, 60, April 2005, 757–783.

18. Robert Shiller used this relationship to show that security markets are not perpetually efficient, as some researchers would like to believe. More relevant, markets can be efficient, which means they respond quickly to new information, but they may not always be rational and often may be incorrect in how they process this new information. They may overreact and then reverse direction. See Robert Shiller, "Do Stock Prices Move Too Much to Be Explained by Subsequent Changes in Dividends?" *American Economic Review*, 71, 1981, 421–426.

that their stock price is only temporarily undervalued, managers are inclined to resist selling in bear markets unless a higher than average premium is forthcoming. Similarly, in bull markets, such as in the period 1994–1997, bidders are less inclined to pay the same average premium, knowing that the market has overpriced most stock already. During this period the average takeover premiums declined, which is what we would expect (see Table 14.5). However, as the market continued to rise in the latter part of the 1990s, premiums began to rise with it. That is, target stock prices continued to rise sharply, even though the earning power of these same companies would reasonably not rise proportionately. Instead of tempering the premiums offered, as bidders did in 1994–1997, bidders began to offer even higher premiums on top of the overly inflated stock prices! It is not surprising that Moeller, Schlingemann, and Stulz's research shows that during the period 1998–2001, acquiring firm shareholders lost a total of $240 billion!

Determinants of Acquisition Premiums

The magnitude of acquisition premiums is often attributed to a combination of the bidder's estimate of the acquisition gains and the strength of the target's bargaining position. The acquisition gains may come from a variety of sources, including anticipated synergistic benefits derived from combining the bidder and the target, or the target being underpriced or poorly managed. The bidder's bargaining position may also be affected by several factors, including the presence of other bidders and the strength of the target's antitakeover defenses. Varaiya analyzed the role of these various factors in determining acquisition premiums in 77 deals between 1975 and 1980.[19] He found significant support for the role of competitive forces in the auction process and antitakeover measures in determining premiums but mixed results for the role of anticipated benefits.

Premiums from Strategic Mergers

Roach investigated whether the size of the control premium is greater for strategic mergers versus those transactions that lack such a strategic focus.[20] Nonstrategic acquisitions have been criticized as deals that add little value to the acquiring firm. In theory, if strategic deals are more valuable, the seller should be in a better position to demand higher premiums. In a study of 1,446 transactions between 1992 and 1997, Roach failed to find any difference in the control premium for those deals in which the merging companies have the same or different SIC codes. This implies that strategic focus is not a determinant of merger premiums.

Premiums and Mergers of Equals

The findings of the Roach study are consistent with the absence of a significant premium in some of the large telecommunications megamergers that occurred in 1998. The deal between GTE Corp. and Bell Atlantic (later Verizon) is a good example. If the transaction

19. Nikhil P. Varaiya, "Determinants of Premiums in Acquisition Transactions," *Managerial and Decision Economics*, 8, 1987, 175–184.
20. George R. Roach, "Control Premiums and Strategic Mergers," *Business Valuation Review*, June 1998, 42–49.

Year	DJIA	Average Premium
1978	805.00	46.2
1979	838.70	49.9
1980	964.00	49.9
1981	875.00	48.0
1982	1,046.50	47.4
1983	1,258.60	37.7
1984	1,211.60	37.9
1985	1,546.70	37.1
1986	1,896.00	38.2
1987	1,938.80	38.3
1988	2,168.60	41.9
1989	2,753.20	41.0
1990	2,633.70	42.0
1991	3,168.80	35.1
1992	3,301.10	41.0
1993	3,754.10	38.7
1994	3,834.40	41.9
1995	5,117.10	44.7
1996	6,448.30	36.6
1997	7,908.30	35.7
1998	9,181.40	40.7
1999	11,497.10	43.3
2000	10,786.90	49.2
2001	10,021.50	57.2
2002	8,341.63	59.7
2003	10,453.92	62.3
2004	10,783.00	30.7
2005	10,717.50	34.5
Average 1978–2005	—	43.1

TABLE 14.5 PERCENT PREMIUM PAID OVER MARKET PRICE, 1978–2005
Sources: Yahoo Finance, and *Mergerstat Review,* 2006.

is considered an acquisition by Bell Atlantic, GTE shareholders were understandably disappointed when they received only 1.22 shares of Bell Atlantic for each share of their company, as GTE shares closed at $55.13 shortly after the deal was announced, whereas Bell Atlantic shares closed at $44.32. When one considers the fact that GTE had a higher P/E, a faster revenue growth rate, and a share price that was as high as $64, the offer was not impressive from GTE's point of view. GTE management, however, defended the deal as a "merger of equals." This view, however, is consistent with the Delaware court's position that stock-for-stock mergers are not changes in control. Based on this legal view, a control premium may not be in order. One lesson that was learned in the Time-Warner–Viacom–QVC takeover contest was that such deals can quickly turn into acquisitions if a third suitor enters the fray and makes an acquisition bid with an attractive premium.

The debate of whether a control premium is warranted came to a head in the wake of a lawsuit brought by Kirk Kerkorian and his Tracinda Corp., which was a large shareholder in Chrysler Corporation. The 1998 merger between Chrysler and Daimler Benz was termed at the time as a merger of equals.[21] However, particularly as the financial troubles at Chrysler became apparent, Daimler proved to be the dominant party. Chrysler executives were supplanted by Daimler managers, who took control of the former Chrysler operation. Kerkorian sued because he considered the deal was a takeover and as such he and other shareholders were entitled to a takeover premium. The court, however, failed to agree with his position. The court's ruling was not consistent with Daimler's CEO Jurgen Schremp's own comments in the *Financial Times*:

> We had to go a roundabout way but it had to be done for psychological reasons. If I had gone and said that Chrysler would be a division everybody on their side would have said "There is no way we'll do a deal."[22]

Does the Market Value Control Independent of Takeovers?

Having cited the abundant evidence supporting the existence of a control premium in takeovers, we should determine whether control provides a premium in the absence of takeovers. In a study designed to measure the premium paid for control, Lease, McConnell, and Mikkelson sought to determine whether capital markets place a separate value on control.[23]

The Lease study examined the market prices of common stocks of 30 companies with classes of common stock that pay identical dividends but differ significantly in their voting rights. One group had substantially greater voting rights on issues related to the control of the firm, such as the election of directors. The two groups of securities provided the same opportunities for financial gain and differed only in their voting rights and the opportunities to control the company's future. Their results showed that for 26 firms that had no voting preferred stock outstanding, the superior voting common stock traded at a premium relative to the other classes of common stock. The average premium they found was 5.44%. It is important to remember that this is not inconsistent with the premiums cited previously because these other premiums are found in takeovers. This is expected, however, because the companies included in the Lease study were not involved in takeovers.

21. See case study in Patrick A. Gaughan, *Mergers: What Can Go Wrong and How to Prevent It* (Hoboken: John Wiley & Sons, 2005), pp. 306–316.
22. Andrew Ross Sorkin, "A TransAtlantic Merger of Equals? Not Exactly," *New York Times*, April 10, 2006.
23. Ronald C. Lease, John J. McConnell, and Wayne H. Mikkelson, "The Market Value of Control in Publicly Traded Corporations," *Journal of Financial Economics*, 11, April 1983, 439–471.

Four of the 30 firms considered in the study showed that the superior voting rights common stock traded at a discount relative to the other class of common stock. These firms differed from the other 26, however, in that they had a more complex capital structure that featured preferred stock with voting rights. Given the existence of this type of voting preferred stock, these four firms are not as comparable to the other 26 clear-cut cases. Another study that focused on specific industries, such as the banking industry, found control premiums in the range of 50 to 70%.[24]

VALUATION OF STOCK-FOR-STOCK EXCHANGES

In this section we will go through a basic discussion of valuation in stock-for-stock exchanges. Prior to beginning our discussion of valuation we need to address some background issues.

Stock-for-Stock Exchanges and Auctions

Some companies are reluctant to initiate merger discussions for a stock-for-stock swap based on concerns that the combination might be viewed as a sale of one or both of the companies. If this were the case, then other bidders might approach the companies and seek to have an auction. Such was the case in the 1989, when Time, Inc. made an offer for Warner Communications. The announcement of a friendly stock-for-stock swap merger between Time and Warner Communications brought an unwanted bid by Paramount, Inc. Paramount demanded that the companies be put for sale to the highest bidder. Paramount's position was that the announcement of the bid by Time and Warner required an auction. The Delaware court ruling, however, failed to agree. The court's position was that an auction was not required. The Delaware decision has great significance for friendly stock-for-stock mergers. After that decision, management and directors have more leeway in agreeing to such transactions by relying on the business judgment rule. Proponents of such deals may take the position that they have a long-term plan for the corporation that is in the best interests of stockholders, and they may choose not to accept a hostile bid from another firm. This paves the way for more stock-financed friendly mergers and acquisitions.

Tax Incentives for Stock versus Cash Transactions

The tax laws provide that stock-for-stock exchanges may be treated as tax-free reorganizations.[25] This means the stock that target stockholders receive will *not* be taxed until the shares are sold. Target stockholders are thus able to postpone being taxed on the consideration that is received for the shares in the target company until the new shares in the acquirer are sold. One tax disadvantage of a reorganization is that the acquirer may

---

24. Larry G. Meeker and O. Maurice Joy, "Price Premiums for Controlling Shares of Closely Held Bank Stock," *Journal of Business*, 53, 1980, 297–314.

25. Alan J. Auerbach and David Reishus, "The Impact of Taxation on Mergers and Acquisitions," in *Mergers and Acquisitions*, Alan J. Auerbach, ed. (Chicago: National Bureau of Economic Research, 1987), pp. 69–85.

not utilize other tax benefits that would be allowable if the transaction were not a reorganization, such as if it were financed by cash. If the transaction were not a reorganization, other tax advantages, such as the ability to step up the asset base or utilize unused tax credits that the target might possess, would be available. It is also possible to receive debt in exchange for the target's shares. For example, the target stockholders could receive debt as part of an installment sale of the target. In this case, the deferred payments are not taxed until they are actually received.[26] The seller can accumulate interest, tax free, on the unreceived portions of the sale price.

Risk Effects: Stock versus Cash

In cash deals target shareholders immediately realize their gains, whereas acquiring firm shareholders assume the risk that the synergistic gains will offset the premiums paid and other costs of the acquisitions. In a stock deal the shareholders of both companies share the risk that the deal will be successful. In Chapter 8 we have discussed the relative merits and valuation effects of stock-versus-cash deals.

Legal Issues in Stock-Financed Transactions

Buyers seeking to finance an acquisition through the use of securities must be mindful of the registration requirements of the Securities and Exchange Commission (SEC) that are set forth in the Securities Act of 1933. Sellers prefer registered securities that can be readily sold in the market. However, buyers may prefer to offer unregistered securities. One reason buyers may prefer unregistered securities is the cost of the registration process, which is expensive in terms of both professional fees and management time. The registration process may also require the buyer to make public information it may not want to reveal to other parties, such as competitors. In addition, the registration process may impose impediments on the buyer that may inhibit its ability to take certain actions lest they necessitate an amendment in the registration statement filed with the SEC.

It may be possible for the parties to negotiate an agreement that allows the buyer to take advantage of certain exemptions to the registration requirements. The buyer may try to qualify for an exemption on the grounds that the securities being offered to purchase the target company do not constitute a public offering. Although the attainment of this nonpublic offering exemption is often not a certainty, it may have a significant effect on the costs of the total transaction from the buyer's viewpoint, as well as on the value the seller places on the consideration being offered by the buyer.

EXCHANGE RATIO

The exchange ratio is the number of the acquirer's shares that are offered for each share of the target. The number of shares offered depends on the valuation of the target by the

---

26. Alan J. Auerbach and David Reishus, "Taxes and the Merger Decision," in *Knights, Raiders, and Targets*, John C. Coffee Jr., Louis Lowenstein, and Susan Rose Ackerman, eds. (New York: Oxford University Press, 1988), pp. 300–313.

	United Communications	Dynamic Entertainment
Present earnings	$50,000,000	$10,000,000
Shares outstanding	5,000,000	2,000,000
Earnings per share	10	5
Stock price	150	50
P/E ratio	15	10

TABLE 14.6 UNITED COMMUNICATIONS AND DYNAMIC ENTERTAINMENT:
COMPARATIVE FINANCIAL CONDITION

acquirer. For example, in April 2006, Alcatel and Lucent announced a stock-for-stock merger in which each Lucent shareholder would receive 0.1952 of an Alcatel American depository share for each share of Lucent they owned.

To arrive at the exchange ratio both the acquirer and the target conduct a valuation of the target, and from this process the acquirer determines the maximum price it is willing to pay while the target determines the minimum it is willing to accept. Within this range, the actual agreement price will depend on each party's other investment opportunities and relative bargaining abilities. Based on a valuation of the target, the acquirer determines the per-share price it is offering to pay. The exchange ratio is determined by dividing the per-share offer price by the market price of the acquirer's shares. Let us consider the example of United Communications, which has made an offer for Dynamic Entertainment (Table 14.6).

Let us assume that, based on its valuation of Dynamic, United Communications has determined that it is willing to offer $65 per share for Dynamic. This is a 30% premium above the premerger market price of Dynamic. In terms of United's shares, the $65 offer is equivalent to United's $65/$150 share.

$$\text{Exchange ratio} = \text{Offer price/Share price of acquirer} = \$65/\$150 = 0.43 \text{ shares}$$

Based on the preceding data, United Communications can calculate the total number of shares that it will have to offer to complete a bid for 100% of Dynamic Entertainment. Total shares that United Communications will have to issue:

$$= [(\text{Offer price})(\text{Total outstanding shares of target})]/\text{Price of acquirer}$$

$$= [(\$65)(2,000,000)]/\$150 = 866,666.67$$

Earnings per Share of the Surviving Company

Calculating the EPS of the surviving company reveals the impact of the merger on the acquirer's EPS:

$$\text{Combined earnings} = \$50,000,000 + \$10,000,000$$

$$\text{Total shares outstanding} = 5,000,000 + 866,666.67$$

United Communications' Impact on EPS—$65 Offer

Premerger EPS	Postmerger EPS
$10.00	$10.23

United Communications will experience an increase in its EPS if the deal is completed. Let us see the impact on EPS if a higher price is offered for Dynamic Entertainment.

Let us assume that Dynamic Entertainment rejects the first offer of $65 per share. In addition, assume that this rejection is based partly on Dynamic's own internal analysis showing the value of Dynamic to be at least $75. Dynamic also believes that its value to United is well in excess of $75. Based on some hard bargaining, United brings a $90 offer to the table.

To see the impact on the surviving company's EPS, we will have to redo the preceding analysis using this higher offer price:

$$\text{Exchange ratio} = \text{Offer price}/\text{Share price of acquirer}$$

$$= \$90/\$150 = 0.60 \text{ shares}$$

Total shares that United Communications will have to issue:

$$= [(\text{Offer price})(\text{Total outstanding shares of target})]/\text{Price of acquirer}$$

$$= [(\$90)(2,000,000)]/\$150 = 1,200,000$$

United Communications' Impact on EPS—$90 Offer

Premerger EPS	Postmerger EPS
$10.00	$9.68

United Communications' EPS declined following the higher offer of $90. This is an example of dilution in EPS.

Criteria for Dilution in EPS

Dilution in EPS will occur any time the P/E ratio paid for the target exceeds the P/E ratio of the company doing the acquiring. The P/E ratio paid is calculated by dividing the EPS of the target into the per-share offer price. This is as follows:

$$\text{P/E ratio paid} = \$65/\$5 = \$13 < \$15$$

Offer price $65

In the case of the $65 offer, the P/E ratio paid was less than the P/E ratio of the acquirer, and there was no dilution in EPS. Exhibit 14.4 shows the variation in the

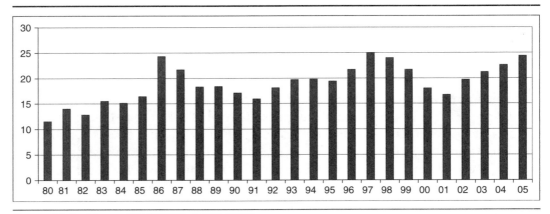

Exhibit 14.4   Median P/E Offered: 1980–2005
Source: Mergerstat Review, 1994, 1998, 2001, 2005, and 2006.

P/E paid for public companies. It shows how these premiums rose in the fourth and fifth merger waves.

$$\text{Offer price } \$90$$

$$\text{P/E ratio paid} = \$90/\$5 = \$18$$

In the case of the \$90 offer, the P/E ratio paid was greater than the P/E ratio of the acquirer, and there was a dilution in EPS.

Highest Offer Price without Dilution in EPS

We can determine the maximum offer price that will not result in a dilution in EPS by solving for P' in the following expression:

$$\text{Maximum nondilution offer price}(P')$$

$$\$15 = P/\$5$$

$$P = \$75$$

Solving for P', we see that the maximum offer price that will not result in a dilution in EPS is \$75. This does not mean that the acquirer will not offer a price in excess of \$75 per share. A firm might be willing to incur an initial dilution in EPS to achieve certain benefits, such as synergies, which will result in an eventual increase in per share earnings. This can be seen in the trend in EPS in Table 14.7.

An examination of Table 14.7 reveals that although United Communications would incur an initial \$0.32 dilution in EPS, United would quickly surpass its premerger EPS level. Let us assume that United had a historical 4% growth in EPS before the merger. In other words, United's rate of growth in EPS was only equal to the rate of inflation. Presumably, United was interested in Dynamic Entertainment in order to achieve a higher rate of growth. Let us also assume that a premerger analysis convinced United that it would be able to achieve a 5% rate of growth after it acquired Dynamic Entertainment.

Years	Without Merger (4% growth) ($)	With Merger (5% growth) ($)
0	10.00	9.68
1	10.40	10.16
2	10.82	10.67
3	11.25	11.21
4	11.70	11.77
5	12.17	12.35
6	12.66	12.97
7	13.16	13.62
8	13.69	14.30

TABLE 14.7   EARNINGS PER SHARE WITH AND WITHOUT MERGER, UNITED COMMUNICATIONS

Based on a 5% rate of growth, it is clear that United Communications would achieve a higher EPS level by the fourth year. A more precise estimate of the breakeven point can be determined as follows:

$$\$10(1.04)^t = \$9.68(1.05)^t \tag{14.18}$$

where t equals the breakeven time period.

Solving for t, we get:

$$\frac{\$10}{\$9.68} = \frac{(1.05)^t}{(1.04)^t}$$

$$0.033 = (1.05/1.04)^t$$

$$\log(1.033) = t\log(1.05/1.04)$$

$$0.01412 = (0.004156)$$

The firm may have a ceiling on the maximum amount of time it may be willing to wait until it breaks even with respect to EPS. If United Communications is willing to wait approximately 3.25 years to break even, it may agree to the merger at the higher price of $90. If United thinks that this is too long to wait, it may agree only at a lower price or it may look for other merger candidates.

Factors That Influence Initial Changes in Earnings per Share

The amount of change in EPS is a function of two main factors:

1. *Differential in P/E ratios.* Rule: The higher the P/E ratio of the acquirer relative to the target, the greater the increase in EPS of the acquirer.
2. *Relative size of the two firms as measured by earnings.* Rule: The larger the earnings of the target relative to the acquirer, the greater the increase in the acquirer's EPS.

The first factor has already been explained, but the role of the relative size of the two firms needs to be explored. For the sake of this discussion, let us assume that earnings are an acceptable measure of value. Because EPS is the ratio of earnings divided by the number of outstanding shares, the greater the addition to the earnings of the surviving firm that is accounted for by the addition of the target's earnings, the greater the EPS of the surviving firm. This is a commonsense proposition.

We can combine the effect of both factors to say that the higher the P/E ratio of the acquirer relative to the target and the greater the earnings of the target relative to the acquirer, the greater the increase in the combined company's EPS. The opposite also follows. The combined effect of the P/E ratio differential and the relative earnings of the two firms can be seen in Exhibit 14.5.

Bootstrapping Earnings per Share

Bootstrapping EPS refers to the corporation's ability to increase its EPS through the purchase of other companies. These earnings were prevalent during the third merger wave of the late 1960s. During this time, the market was not efficient in its valuation of conglomerates. These conglomerates were able to experience an increase in EPS and stock prices simply by acquiring other firms.

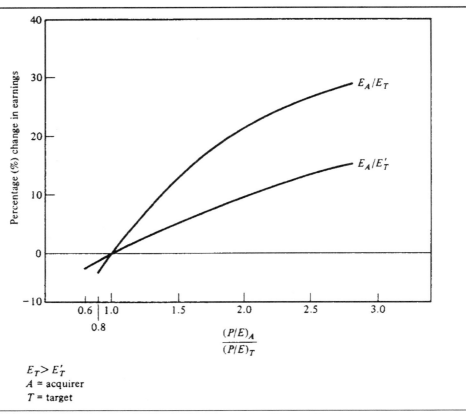

EXHIBIT 14.5 COMBINED EFFECT OF P/E RATIO DIFFERENTIAL AND RELATIVE EARNINGS

Earnings	60,000,000.00
Shares outstanding	5,866,666.67
EPS	10.23
P/E ratio	15.00
Stock price	153.45

TABLE 14.8 UNITED COMMUNICATIONS' POSTMERGER FINANCIAL CONDITION

In the case of United Communications' acquisition of Dynamic Entertainment, United issued 866,666.67 shares of stock based on a $65 offer price. This results in 5,866,667.67 total shares of United Communications outstanding (Table 14.8).

With the offer price of $65 per share, United Communications can offer Dynamic Entertainment a 30% premium above its premerger price of $50 and still experience an increase in EPS. If we assume that the market will apply the same EPS to United before and after the merger, the stock price has to rise. This can be seen from the following expression:

$$P/E = P/EPS \tag{14.19}$$

$$15 = P/\$10.23$$

$$P = \$153.45$$

United Communications' postmerger stock price has risen to $153.45 as a result of boot-strapping EPS. Two conditions are necessary for bootstrapping EPS to occur:

1. *The P/E ratio must not decline following the merger.* This implies that the market must be willing to apply at least the premerger P/E ratio after the merger. If the market decides that the combined firm is not as valuable, per dollar of earnings, there may be a market correction and the P/E ratio may fall. In the third merger wave, the market was slow to reevaluate the growing conglomerates and apply a lower P/E ratio.

2. *The acquirer must have a higher P/E ratio than the target.* If these two condi-tions prevail, companies with higher P/E ratios can acquire companies with lower P/E ratios and experience growth in EPS. This gives the acquiring company an incentive to continue with further acquisitions and have even greater increase in EPS. The process will continue to work as long as the stock market continues to value the acquiring company with the same P/E ratio. This occurred during the late 1960s. The movement came to an end when the market corrected itself as it questioned many of the acquisitions that appeared to lack synergistic benefits.

Postmerger P/E Ratio

If the market is efficient, bootstrapping EPS is not possible. The postmerger P/E ratio will be a weighted average of the premerger P/E ratios. This can be calculated using the following expression:

$$\frac{P}{E_{A+B}} = \frac{(P_A \times S_A) + (P_B \times S_B)}{E_A + E_B} \tag{14.20}$$

where:

$\frac{P}{E_{A+B}}$ = the postmerger P/E ratio

P_A = the premerger stock price of Company A

P_B = the premerger stock price of Company B

S_A = the number of outstanding shares of Company A

S_B = the number of outstanding shares of Company B

E_A = the earnings of Company A

E_B = the earnings of Company B

Using the preceding expression, we can calculate United Communication's postmerger P/E ratio after the stock-for-stock acquisition of Dynamic Entertainment. We will calculate this ratio based on the $65 initial offer that required the issuance of 866,666.67 shares:

$$\frac{P}{E_{U+D}} = \frac{(P_U \times S_U) + (P_D \times S_U)}{E_U + E_D}$$

$$\frac{P}{E_{A+B}} = \frac{(\$150 \times 5,000,000) + (\$50 \times 2,000,000)}{50,000,000 + \$10,000,000} \tag{14.21}$$

$$= \frac{\$750,000,000 - \$100,000,000}{\$60,000,000} = \frac{\$850,000}{\$60,000} = 14.17$$

Without the bootstrapping effect, the P/E ratio of the combined firm falls relative to United Communications' premerger P/E ratio. The resulting P/E ratio is a blended combination of United's P/E ratio (15) and Dynamic's lower P/E ratio (10).

CASE STUDY

AMERISOURCE–BERGEN BRUNSWIG STOCK-FOR-STOCK MERGER

In March 2001, two of the largest U.S. drug distributors announced a merger that would (assuming it is approved) result in a combined capitalization of approximately $5 billion. AmeriSource had $11.6 billion in revenues in 2000, while Bergen Brunswig generated almost $23 billion over the same time. Despite the big difference in size, as measured by revenues, AmeriSource was considered to be the acquirer. In 2000, AmeriSource generated net income of $99 million and Bergen lost $752 million. Bergen Brunswig's financial difficulties can be traced to problems with prior acquisitions.

Under the initially announced terms of the deal, AmeriSource shareholders would own 51% of the shares in the combined company. Each share of Bergen would be valued at 0.37 shares of the combined entity, while each share of common stock of AmeriSource would equal one share in the new firm. Before the deal, Bergen had 136.1 million fully diluted shares outstanding. Using the pre-deal closing stock price of AmeriSource of $44.48 and an exchange ratio of 0.37 shares in the combined company for each share of Bergen, the target is valued as follows:

> Number of Bergen shares × Exchange ratio × Value of AmeriSource shares
> 136.1 million shares × 0.37 × $44.48 = $2.44 billion = Value of Bergen
> Number of AmeriSource shares × Pre − deal value of AmeriSource shares
> 52.4 million shares × $44.48 = $2.33 billion
> Approximate combined equity value = $5 billion
> AmeriSource shareholder's percent : 51%; Bergen shareholder's percent : 49%

FIXED NUMBER OF SHARES VERSUS FIXED VALUE

A buyer in a stock-for-stock transaction can offer either a fixed number of shares in its company or a specific dollar value. When the number of shares is fixed, its value can vary as the stock price of the acquirer varies. The value the seller receives and the buyer provides then varies depending on movements in the bidder's stock price. A buyer, however, can simply offer a fixed value, and the actual number of shares may vary as the stock price of the acquirer varies. The uncertainty caused by a fixed number of shares can be reduced through a *collar agreement.* Such an agreement usually stipulates that if the stock price goes above or below a certain value, there will be an adjustment in the exchange ratio.

The collar agreement may tolerate small movements in the stock price without causing changes in the exchange ratio. A certain threshold is established beyond which the exchange ratio has to be adjusted. The existence of a collar agreement in a merger is usually a point of negotiation. It is more important if the stock of one or both of the participants tends to be volatile. If both firms are in the same industry, market movements in each stock might offset each other. However, many collar agreements allow the bidder to walk away from a deal if its stock price moves higher than range for its stock set forth in the collar. This adds an element of uncertainty that is important for the parties to the transactions but also to risk arbitragers.

INTERNATIONAL TAKEOVERS AND STOCK-FOR-STOCK TRANSACTIONS

One complication that can occur with international takeovers is that target company shareholders may not want to hold shares in the acquiring corporation. This often is the case for U.S. shareholders who receive shares in European corporations. Displaying a preference for U.S. stock, target company shareholders may sell their shares in the acquiring company. When these shares return to the acquiring company's market, they can cause its stock price to decline. Such a decline could effectively increase the costs of the acquisition for the bidder. This phenomenon is sometimes referred to as *domestic market flowback.*

DESIRABLE FINANCIAL CHARACTERISTICS OF TARGETS

Acquirers can use the following characteristics as financial screens:

* *Rapidly growing cash flows and earnings.* A pattern of rising cash flows and earnings is the most desirable characteristic. The future cash flows are the most direct benefit the buyer derives from an acquisition. Therefore, a rising historical trend in these values may be an indicator of higher levels in the future.

- *Low price relative to earnings.* A P/E that is low compared with its level over the past two to three years suggests that the company may be relatively inexpensive. A low P/E ratio is generally considered a desirable characteristic in a target. The lower the P/E ratio, the lower the price that will be paid to acquire the target's earning power. Because of market fluctuations, the P/E ratio of a firm or an industry category may go up and down. In addition, the market fluctuates up and down. A falling stock price that is not caused by a reduction in the potential target's earning power may present a temporary undervaluation and an acquisition opportunity. An acquirer can measure the extent of the undervaluation by comparing the P/E ratio with the previous level over the preceding three years. A low level can mean undervaluation due to changes in investor preferences or it can reflect a change in the firm's ability to generate income in the future. The lowest value in three years is an indicator of one of the two; it is the analyst's job to decide which one it is. (Although the prior discussion is framed in terms of a P/E ratio, it also applies to a pre–cash flow ratio.)
- *Market value less than book value.* Book value is a more reliable measure of value in certain industries. Industries that tend to have more liquid assets also tend to have more useful book values. Finance companies and banks are examples of firms that have a large percentage of liquid assets. Even in industries in which assets may be less liquid, such as in firms that have large real estate holdings, however, book value can be put to use as a floor value. This was the case in Campeau Corporation's acquisition of Federated Stores in 1988. Both firms had large real estate holdings and marketable divisions and store chains. The combined market value of these assets and the estimated market value of the divisions on a per-share basis made Federated a vulnerable target. In retrospect, the estimated value of the divisions proved to be greater than their market value when they were offered for sale.
- *High liquidity.* A target company's own liquidity can be used to help finance its own acquisitions. High liquidity ratios relative to industry averages are a reflection of this condition. The additional liquidity is even more applicable for debt-financed takeovers, where the liquidity of the target may be an important factor in the target's ability to pay for its own financing after the merger.
- *Low leverage.* Low leverage ratios, such as the debt ratio and debt-equity ratio, are desirable because this shows a lower level of risk as well as added debt capacity that can be used to finance the takeover. The more cyclical the industry, the more important it is to keep leverage within a manageable range.

Valuation of Private Businesses

Closely held businesses vary tremendously in size. Many think of closely held businesses as small businesses. This is not true. For example, the largest closely held company in the United States is Koch Industries. In November 2005, Koch acquired the publicly held Georgia Pacific for $13.2 billion. The deal gave the company total annual revenues of $80 billion, which enabled it to overtake Cargill as the largest closely held company in the United States. Large closely held companies are much more common in Europe. One example is Bertelsmann, the giant German media conglomerate controlled by the

Mohn family since the 1800s. It has revenues in excess of $20 billion from a variety of sources including broadcast and TV services, book and magazine publishing, and recorded music. In May 2006, the company contemplated going public but instead decided to buy out the 25% equity stake held by the Belgian investment firm, Groupe Bruxelles Lambert.

The valuation models that we have already discussed can be readily applied to value closely held businesses. However, certain adjustments may have to be made. These adjustments are warranted based on the differences between public and private companies.

A major difference between public and private business valuations centers on the availability and reliability of financial data.[27] Some of these differences are caused by the efforts of firms, particularly private businesses, to minimize taxable income. Another factor is the requirement that public firms disclose certain financial data in a specific manner, whereas private firms do not face such requirements.

Reported Taxable Income

Public and private corporations are subject to different requirements with regard to the declaration of taxable income. Owners of closely held businesses take every opportunity to keep taxable income low and therefore have a lower tax obligation. Although public firms also want to minimize their taxes, privately held businesses have greater means available to do so than their public counterparts. Because of these efforts to minimize taxable income, private companies may issue less reliable financial data than public firms. Therefore, analysts may not be able to rely on the reported income of privately held firms to reflect their true profitability and earning power.

With regard to declaring income, public and private corporations have dramatically different objectives. Public corporations have several outside constraints that provide strong incentives to declare a higher taxable income. One of these constraints is the pressure applied by stockholders, the true "owners" of the corporation, to have a regular flow of dividends. Because dividends are paid out of taxable income, the public corporation's ability to minimize taxable income is limited.

Public Corporations and the Reporting of Income

Like their private counterparts, public corporations want to minimize taxes, but given their dividend obligations toward stockholders, public corporations have fewer opportunities to do so. They do not have as much ability to manipulate their reported income, primarily because of the accounting review requirements that the shareholder reporting process imposes on them.

In preparing financial statements, there are three levels of accounting reports: compilation, review, and audited statements. The compilation is the least rigorous of the three, whereas audited financial statements require an independent analysis of the company's financial records. Public corporations are required to prepare audited financial statements

---

27. This section is drawn from Patrick A. Gaughan and Henry Fuentes, "Taxable Income and Lost Profits Litigation," *Journal of Forensic Economics*, IV(1), Winter 1990, 55–64.

for their annual reports. These audit requirements are enforced by the SEC subject to the requirements of the Securities Exchange Act of 1934. The SEC does not accept a review or a compilation statement for a 10K report. A review is acceptable for a 10Q quarterly report. However, a compilation is not acceptable for use in preparing either of these types of published financial reports. Because the reported income contained in published financial statements is subject to audit, the profit numbers tend to be more reliable than those that appear in the financial statements of private firms, which generally are not audited. The lack of required audit scrutiny is one reason the reported profit levels may lack validity. The lack of an audit requirement allows private firms to manipulate their reported income levels to minimize taxable income. It is in this area that public and private corporations tend to have two very different agendas. Public firms may want to demonstrate higher reported profits to impress stockholders. Stockholders may become more impressed when these reported profits are translated into higher dividend payments or increased stock prices.

Private corporations are subject to neither the government's public disclosure requirements nor the constraints and pressures of public securities markets. Free to utilize every opportunity to show a smaller taxable income, they therefore have a lower tax bill. A private corporation can reduce taxable income in two ways. The first is to have lower reported revenues, and the second is to show higher costs. The first approach is more common for small businesses, particularly cash businesses, which sometimes show a smaller than actual level of reported income. This is occasionally done through deliberately inaccurate record keeping. In addition to being illegal, this practice creates obvious problems for the evaluators.

If there is a reason to believe that a company's revenues have been underreported, an estimate of the actual revenues may be reconstructed. This sometimes occurs in litigation involving minority stockholders who are suing for their share in a business. The actual revenue levels can be reconstructed from activity and volume measures, such as materials and inputs purchased, which can be translated into sales of final outputs.

The most common form of income manipulation for purposes of minimizing taxes is giving higher than normal compensation, benefits, and perquisites to officers. The entrepreneurs of closely held companies may withdraw a disproportionate amount of income from the company relative to total revenues. Furthermore, entrepreneurial owners may list a variety of extraordinary personal benefits on the corporation's books as expenses. Although these expenses may be legitimate tax deductions, they really are another form of compensation to the owner. Any measure of the closely held corporation's profitability that does not take into account these less overt forms of return to the owners will fall short of measuring the business's actual profitability. Evaluators of closely held businesses often have to *recast the income statement* to reflect the true earning power of the business. This may involve adding back, after an adjustment for tax effects, costs that are really a form of compensation for the owners.

Factors to Consider When Valuing Closely Held Businesses

One set of factors that is often cited in valuing private firms is Revenue Ruling 59–60. This ruling sets forth various factors that tax courts consider in a valuation of the stock of closely held businesses for gift and estate purposes. These factors are:

- Nature and history of the business
- Condition of the economy and the industry
- Book value of the company and its financial condition
- Earnings capacity of the company
- Dividend-paying capacity
- Existence of goodwill or other intangibles
- Other sales of stock
- Prices of comparable stock

Evaluators of closely held businesses should be aware of the factors that are set forth in Revenue Ruling 59–60 because these are often-cited standards for the valuation of the stock of closely held companies. The inclusion of certain factors such as both earnings and dividend-paying capacity may be questionable because dividend-paying capacity presumably is a function of earnings capacity. Industry analysis and a macroeconomic and possibly regional economic analysis are important enough to be treated as separate components of the valuation process. Putting a lot of weight on book value, a measure that may not accurately reflect the value of the company, is questionable. Revenue Ruling 59–60 also fails to mention other benchmarks, such as liquidation value, which may be worth considering along with book value. Taking these issues into consideration, this revenue ruling is important to be aware of but should not be the exclusive list of factors that are considered.

Acquisition Multiples

The stock of public companies is marketable, whereas the stock of closely held companies generally lacks a broad market. For this reason acquisition multiples of closely held companies are generally lower than those of public companies. Table 14.9 shows that the median P/E offered for public companies over the period 1995–2005 was 21, whereas the median P/E multiple for closely held companies was only 17.1.

Adjustments to Valuation Methods

We have noted that the same methods used to value public businesses can be applied to the valuation of closely held companies. In some ways it is easier to value a public company because there is a market that regularly values the equity of these companies. However, for private businesses there are various transactions databases that provide data on purchase prices of acquisitions and multiples that the companies sold for. They are organized by industry and size so that evaluators can get a list of comparable transactions and derive average multiples that can be applied to place a value on closely held businesses.

Since there is a much greater abundance of data on public companies than there is on closely held businesses, we may want to use multiples from market trading of public firms to value closely held businesses. That is, we may want to take an average industry P/E ratio and use it to value a closely held company. Before we do so we need to make certain adjustments before this value can be used. Various research studies have attempted to measure the *marketability discount* that should be applied to public stock prices and

Year	Public P/E	Private P/E
1995	19.4	15.5
1996	21.7	17.7
1997	25.0	17.0
1998	24.0	16.0
1999	21.7	18.4
2000	18.0	16.0
2001	16.7	15.3
2002	19.7	16.6
2003	21.2	19.4
2004	22.6	19.0
2005	24.4	16.9
Average 1995–2005	21.3	17.1

TABLE 14.9   MEDIAN P/E* OFFERED: PUBLIC VS. PRIVATE 1995–2005
* Excludes negative P/E multiples and P/E multiples larger than 100.
Source: Mergerstat Review, 2006.

multiples to make them relevant to closely held companies. Many of them analyzed the difference between the prices that restricted (nontradable to the public on the market) shares trade for in private sales and the market prices of those shares. Much of that research was initially done in the 1970s.[28] Later studies compared the prices that shares of closely held companies sold for prior to companies going public with IPO prices after the company went public. Those studies were first done in the 1980s.[29] These various studies put forward a wide range of marketability discounts that supports a discount in the one-third range.

Minority Discounts

A second discount might also be needed, depending on the percentage of ownership the privately held stock position constitutes. This is because control is an additional valuable characteristic that a majority position possesses that is not present in a minority holding. A minority shareholder is often at the mercy of majority shareholders. The holder of a minority position can elect only a minority of the directors, and possibly

---

28. *Institutional Investor Study Report of the Securities and Exchange Commission* (Washington, D.C.: U.S. Government Printing Office), Document No. 93-64, March 10, 1971; Milton Gelman, "An Economist-Financial Analyst's Approach to Valuing Stock of a Closely Held Company," *Journal of Taxation*, June 1972; Robert E. Moroney, "Most Courts Overvalue Closely Held Stocks," *Taxes*, 51(3), March 1973, 144–154; Robert R. Trout, "Estimation of the Discount Associated with the Transfer of Restricted Securities," *Taxes*, 55, June 1977, 381–385; J. Michael Maher, "Discounts for Lack of Marketability for Closely Held Business Interests," *Taxes*, 54(9), September 1976, 562–571.

29. John D. Emory, "The Value of Marketability as Illustrated in Initial Public Offerings of Common Stock," *Business Valuation News*, September 1985, 21–24; and John D. Emory, "The Value of Marketability as Illustrated in Initial Public Offerings of Common Stock," *Business Valuation Review*, December 1986.

none of the directors, depending on whether the corporation is incorporated in a state that allows cumulative voting. Majority shareholders and minority shareholders each possess proportionate rights to dividends distribution, but a majority shareholder possesses the right to control the actions of the corporations in addition to these dividend claims. This is an additional valuable characteristic, and an additional premium must be paid for it.

If the valuation of the closely held company was done using transaction data that featured the acquisition of control of the various companies considered, then these data need to be adjusted to eliminate the added value that entered into these data to eliminate the part of the multiple that accounted for control.[30]

A guide to the appropriate minority discount is the magnitude of the average control premium. Table 14.10 shows that the average control premium between 1980 and 2004 was 42.8%. This premium can be used to compute the appropriate minority discount using the following formula:

$$\text{Minority discount} = 1 - [1/(1 + \text{Average premium})] \qquad (14.22)$$

Using the average control premium of 42.8%, we get an implied minority discount of 30%.

Applying Marketability and Minority Discounts

Let us assume that a value of $50 per share has been computed for a 20% ownership position in a closely held firm. Assuming 33% marketability and minority discounts, the value of this stock position equals:

Unadjusted value	$50/share
Less 33% marketability discount	$33.50
Less 33% minority discount	$22.45

The $22.45-per-share value is the value of a nonmarketable minority position in this closely held business.

Valuation Research on Takeovers of Privately Held Companies

Although there is an abundance of published research on the valuation effects of takeovers of public companies, there is limited research for closely held businesses. This is because data are readily available on public companies but they are much harder to come by for private firms. One study by Chang analyzed the stock price reaction of public bidding firms when they acquire private companies.[31] In a study of 281 merger proposals between 1981 and 1992, which did not include any tender offers, Chang found that bidding firms did not experience any abnormal returns for cash offers but did show positive abnormal returns for stock offers. The positive returns for stock offers contrast with some research on stock acquisitions of public companies that feature negative returns.

30. Shannon P. Pratt, Robert Rielly, and Robert Scheihs, *Valuing a Business* (New York: McGraw Hill, 2000), pp. 353–355.
31. Saeyoung Chang, "Takeovers of Privately Held Targets, Methods of Payment, and Bidder Returns," *Journal of Finance* 53(2), April 1998, 773–784.

Year	Average Control Premium Offer (%)	Implied Minority Discount (%)
1980	49.9	33.3
1981	48.0	32.4
1982	47.4	32.2
1983	37.7	27.4
1984	37.9	27.5
1985	37.1	27.1
1986	38.2	27.6
1987	38.3	27.7
1988	41.9	29.5
1989	41.0	29.1
1990	42.0	29.6
1991	35.1	26.0
1992	41.0	29.1
1993	38.7	27.9
1994	41.9	29.5
1995	44.7	30.9
1996	36.6	26.8
1997	35.7	26.3
1998	40.7	28.9
1999	43.3	30.2
2000	49.1	32.9
2001	58.0	36.7
2002	59.8	37.4
2003	63.0	38.7
2004	30.9	23.6
2005	34.5	25.7
Average	42.8	29.8

TABLE 14.10   AVERAGE CONTROL PREMIUMS AND IMPLIED
                  DISCOUNTS

Source: Mergerstat Review, 2006.

Chang compared the stock offers with private equity placements because the closely held targets typically were owned by a small number of shareholders. These positive returns are consistent with the research on the returns to companies that issue stock in private placements.[32]

---

32. Michael Hertzel and Richard L. Smith, "Market Discounts and Shareholders Gains for Placing Private Equity," *Journal of Finance 48*, June 1993, 459–485.

One possible explanation for the positive stock response for public acquirers is that there may be more monitoring when stock is given to a few owners of the closely held company. This greater monitoring may reduce adverse agency effects and increase value. When the market perceives this, it reacts with a positive stock price response.

SUMMARY

The variety of different financial techniques available to value publicly held companies were explored in this chapter. Primary among these are DCF and comparable multiple valuations. In DCF analysis FCFs are projected for a specific period into the future. After that specific forecast period the remaining cash flows are valued as perpetuity. This value is called the continuing value. Both the continuing value and the specific forecasted value are brought to present value through the application of a risk-adjusted discount rate. The more specific years that are forecasted the lower the continuing value. The values that are arrived at are influenced by the size of the risk premium built into the discount rate. The greater the premium and discount rate the lower the value of the business.

Comparable multiples may be used to value a target by arriving at a comparable ratio and then applying it to the relevant financial measure of the target. For example, an analyst may select certain comparable transactions and then derive a multiple, such as a P/E multiple, which is applied to the earnings of the target. Key to doing this type of valuation is to make sure that the companies that are selected to derive a multiple are truly comparable.

An abundance of research studies have attempted to trace the valuations effects of M & As. These studies show that stockholders of target companies clearly earn statistically significant positive abnormal returns. Shareholders in bidding firms tend not to do as well. Research studies indicate that although they can earn slightly positive returns, they often realize zero or negative returns. Many of these studies are short-term oriented. However, research on the long-term effects of M&As on bidding shareholders, and shareholders who may have received stock in their shares of the target, also paints an unimpressive picture. Given the many benefits that may be derived from well-planned mergers, readers should not conclude that companies should avoid mergers and acquisitions. Rather, these studies should give rise to a need for greater caution and more thorough premerger planning.

Research studies also focused on the medium of payment. The analysis for stock-for-stock offers is different from that for cash offers. The relative value of the stock of both firms needs to be considered in stock-for-stock deals. Factors such as the dilution of EPS must be considered to do a thorough analysis. The agreed-upon relative stock values can then be "locked in" by a collar agreement that would adjust the stock amounts on either side of the deal according to market fluctuations in the stock prices of both firms.

Valuation analysis can be an intricate process that requires a well-rounded knowledge of finance and other related fields. To construct a reliable analysis, much due diligence analysis needs to be done. The lessons of some of the merger failures of the fourth merger wave point to deficiencies in this type of analysis.

APPENDIX

In 2006, VNU, a Dutch media and market research company, received a $9 billion bid from a group of private equity firms including the Blackstone Group and the Carlyle Group. The board of directors endorsed the offer but some shareholders, including Knight Vinke Asset Management, which owns 20% of the company, expressed their opposition believing that a higher price could be received. As part of its efforts to obtain the support of shareholders, VNU provided shareholders with a detailed analysis that presented its reasoning. This included fairness opinions of two valuation firms: Credit Suisse Group and Rothschild & Sons Ltd. Following is an excerpt from Credit Suisse's fairness opinion. It shows how they used discounted cash flow and comparable analysis to arrive at a range of values for VNU.

Discounted Cash Flow Analysis

Using a DCF analysis, Credit Suisse calculated a range of estimated net present values of both the consolidated, unlevered, after-tax free cash flows that VNU could generate over calendar years 2006 through 2010 and the terminal value at 2010. These cash flows were based on internal forecasts of VNU's management (as described more fully in this Offer Memorandum under the heading "Certain Projections"). "Present value" refers to the current value of future cash flows or amounts and is obtained by discounting those future cash flows or amounts by a discount rate that takes into account macroeconomic assumptions, the cost of capital, and other appropriate factors.

"Terminal value" refers to the value of all future cash flows from an asset at a particular point in time in the future. In the first instance, Credit Suisse did not give effect to the value of the estimated cost savings projected by VNU management pursuant to VNU management's proposed "Project Forward" cost savings initiative. Credit Suisse then calculated a range of estimated terminal values for VNU by multiplying VNU's estimated 2010 EBITDA by selected multiples ranging from 10.0× to 11.0×. The estimated after-tax free cash flows and terminal values were then discounted to the present value using discount rates ranging from 8.5% to 9.5%. Thereafter, Credit Suisse calculated a range of per-share values by making certain adjustments, including adjustments to reflect the Company's year-end 2005 net debt, preferred stock, associates/joint ventures, minority interests, and certain other liabilities in order to derive an implied equity value reference range for the company and then dividing those amounts by the number of fully diluted shares of the Company.

Separately, Credit Suisse used a DCF analysis to calculate a range of estimated net present values of management's projected estimated cost savings for calendar years 2006 through 2010 based upon VNU management's proposed "Project Forward" cost savings initiative, including the estimated pre-tax costs projected to achieve such savings (as described more fully in this Offer Memorandum under the heading "Certain Projections"). This analysis was based on discount rates ranging from 8.5% to 12.5% and a terminal value based on cash flows in perpetuity growing at annual rates ranging from 0.0% to

1.0% This analysis indicated at the midpoint of these assumptions an implied per-share value of approximately €2.25.

The implied values per VNU ordinary share including cost savings were calculated by adding the implied per share DCF value of the "Project Forward" cost savings initiative to the implied values per VNU ordinary share calculated as described above. This analysis indicated the following implied per-share equity value reference ranges for VNU:

- Discounted Cash Flow Scenario Implied Per-Share Equity Reference Range for VNU
- Excluding "Project Forward" Estimated Cost Savings €24.75–€28.25
- Including "Project Forward" Estimated Cost Savings €27.00–€30.50

Credit Suisse also performed a sensitivity analysis on the estimated "Project Forward" cost savings in order to assess the potential impact of variations in the amount of cost savings realized by assuming full run-rate cost savings in calendar year 2008 of €125 million, €175 million, and €225 million, assuming the same ramp up in cost savings during calendar years 2006 and 2007 as in the "Project Forward" cost savings initiative as provided by VNU management. This analysis was based on discount rates ranging from 8.5% to 12.5% and a terminal value based on cash flows in perpetuity growing at an annual rate of 0.5%. This analysis indicated an implied per-share value range of approximately €1.75 to €3.75.

Other Factors

Sum-of-the-Parts Breakup Analysis

Credit Suisse's opinion addressed only the fairness from a financial point of view to the holders of the ordinary shares of VNU of the consideration to be received by such holders pursuant to the Offer and did not address the merits of a potential alternative transaction involving a breakup of VNU or other alternative transactions or strategies that may be available to VNU. At the request of the Supervisory Board, in order to assist the Supervisory Board in evaluating the offer, Credit Suisse also considered financial analyses regarding a possible transaction pursuant to which the Company's business information businesses would be sold and each of its Marketing Information and Media Measurement and Information units would be separated into independent public companies. In connection with such analyses, among other things, VNU management advised Credit Suisse, and Credit Suisse assumed without independent verification, that (i) the sale of the Business Information U.S. unit would result in a tax liability of approximately €380 million to €400 million (based on Credit Suisse's estimated valuation analysis described below); (ii) the sale of the Business Information Europe unit for cash would result in approximately €320 million to €370 million of proceeds, without any tax liability incurred; (iii) the separation of the Marketing Information and Media Measurement and Information units would be effected through a tax-free separation; (iv) certain pro forma annualized cost savings (without giving effect to the pre-tax costs to achieve such savings) would be realized at each of the Marketing Information and Media Measurement and Information units in the amount of €15–20 million and €50–60 million, respectively;

(v) approximately €73 million of after-tax costs would be required to achieve such savings; (vi) all corporate overhead would be eliminated, although €15 million in standalone, public company expenses were assumed to be required at the Marketing Information and Media Measurement and Information units; and (vii) there would be transaction expenses and costs associated with the transactions contemplated by this analysis of €150 million. Credit Suisse was informed that a breakup of the Company would also likely result in a significant increase in the effective tax rates for each of the Marketing Information and Media Measurement and Information units, although this impact was not factored into the analysis.

Sale of Business Information U.S. for Cash

Using publicly available information, Credit Suisse also reviewed the transaction multiples of several merger and acquisition transactions, which involved targets that Credit Suisse deemed similar to the Business Information U.S. unit. Credit Suisse noted that the transactions identified below were deemed the most relevant for purposes of its analysis.

Acquiror Targets

> PBI Media Holdings, Inc. (an entity controlled by Primedia Inc.'s business information unit, Wasserstein & Co., LP)
> J. P. Morgan Partners, LLC Hanley Wood LLC
> Apprise Media LLC Canon Communications
> VNU N.V. Miller Freeman USA

Credit Suisse compared transaction values in the selected transactions as multiples of the target companies' expected EBITDA for the year during which each transaction was announced. Transaction multiples for the selected transactions, including the transaction involving VNU, were based on publicly available financial information at the time of the announcement of the relevant transaction and research analysts' estimates for EBITDA. Estimated data for the Business Information U.S. unit were based on internal management forecasts. Credit Suisse then applied a range of multiples derived from the selected transactions to estimate 2006 EBITDA for the Business Information U.S. unit. This analysis indicated an implied range of enterprise values, before giving effect to tax liabilities associated with the sale of the Business Information U.S. unit, of €1,150 million to €1,200 million based on a reference multiple range of $11.5 \times -12.0 \times$ estimated 2006 EBITDA.

Public Market Valuation for Media Measurement and Information

Using publicly available information, Credit Suisse reviewed the enterprise values and calendar year 2006 estimated EBITDA multiples of the following three selected publicly traded companies it deemed similar to the Media Measurement and Information unit: Arbitron, Inc., GfK AG, and Ipsos SA. Credit Suisse compared enterprise values (defined as equity value plus net debt plus minority interest and preferred stock) as multiples of estimated 2006 EBITDA. Multiples were based on closing market prices on March

3, 2006. Estimated data for the selected companies were based on publicly available research analysts' estimates. Estimated data for the Media Measurement and Information unit were based on internal VNU management forecasts, and accounted for pro-forma cost savings. Credit Suisse then applied a range of multiples of estimated 2006 EBITDA for the selected companies described above to estimated 2006 EBITDA of the Media Measurement and Information unit (excluding NetRatings, Inc. estimated 2006 EBITDA of €1 million). This analysis indicated an implied range of enterprise values (excluding NetRatings, Inc.) of approximately €3,605 million to €3,970 million based on a reference multiple range of 12.0×–13.0× estimated pro forma 2006 EBITDA.

Public Market Valuation for Marketing Information

Using publicly available information, Credit Suisse reviewed the enterprise values and calendar year 2006 estimated EBITDA multiples of the following five selected publicly traded companies it deemed similar to Marketing Information: IMS Health Inc., Taylor Nelson Sofres plc, Wolters Kluwer NV, Thomson Corporation, and Reed Elsevier plc. Credit Suisse compared enterprise values (defined as equity value plus net debt plus minority interest and preferred stock) as multiples of estimated 2006 EBITDA. Multiples were based on closing market prices on March 3, 2006. Estimated data for the selected companies were based on publicly available research analysts' estimates. Estimated data for the Marketing Information unit were based on internal VNU management forecasts, and accounted for pro-forma cost savings. Credit Suisse then applied a range of multiples of estimated 2006 for the selected companies described above to estimated 2006 EBITDA of the Marketing Information unit.

This analysis indicated an implied range of enterprise values of €3,150 million to €3,600 million based on a reference multiple range of 9.0×–10.0× estimated pro forma 2006 EBITDA.

Based on its analysis, Credit Suisse calculated an aggregate enterprise value €7,844 million to €8,741 million based on the after-tax cash proceeds from the cash sale of the Business Information U.S. and Europe units and the public market enterprise value of each of the Media Measurement and Information unit and the Marketing Information unit. Thereafter, Credit Suisse calculated a range of per-share values by making certain adjustments to the aggregate enterprise value to account for certain factors, including subtracting (x) net debt, preferred stock and certain other liabilities of €1,302 million (excluding NetRatings, Inc. year-end cash), after-tax cost to achieve savings and transaction costs and expenses associated with the transactions (as described above), and, at the direction of VNU, adding (y) market value of €226 million for VNU's 61% stake in NetRatings, Inc. and (z) book value of €170 million with respect to other minority interests (excluding NetRatings, Inc.) held by VNU and its associates/joint ventures.

The sum-of-the-parts breakup analysis indicated an implied per-share equity value reference range for VNU of €25.90–€29.35.

15

TAX ISSUES

Depending on the method used to finance the transaction, certain mergers, acquisitions, and restructuring may be tax free. Some firms may use their tax benefits as assets in establishing the correct price that they might command in the marketplace. For this reason, tax considerations are important as both the motivation for a transaction and the valuation of a company. Part of the tax benefits from a transaction may derive from tax synergy, whereby one of the firms involved in a merger may not be able to fully utilize its tax shields. When combined with the merger partner, however, the tax shields may offset income. Some of these gains may come from unused net operating losses, which may be used by a more profitable merger partner. Tax reform, however, has limited the ability of firms to sell these net operating losses through mergers.

Other sources of tax benefits in mergers may arise from a market value of depreciable assets, which is greater than the value at which these assets are kept on the target's books. The acquiring firm that is able to step up the basis of these assets in accordance with the purchase price may finally realize tax savings.

This chapter discusses the mechanics of realizing some of the tax benefits through mergers. It also reviews the research studies that attempt to determine the importance of tax effects as a motivating factor for mergers and leveraged buyouts (LBOs) and examines the different accounting treatments that may be applied to a merger or an acquisition. These methods, which are regulated by tax laws, affect the importance of taxes in the overall merger valuation. It will be seen that various reforms in tax laws have diminished the role that taxes play in mergers and acquisitions. However, taxes may still be an important consideration that both the seller and buyer must carefully weigh before completing a transaction.

FINANCIAL ACCOUNTING

Until 2001, there were two alternative accounting treatments for mergers and acquisitions: pooling and the purchase method. The main difference between them is the value that the combined firm's balance sheet places on the assets of the acquired firm, as well as the depreciation allowances and charges against income following the merger. After much debate, however, the accounting profession eliminated pooling. All mergers must now be accounted for under the purchase method. In eliminating pooling, the United States came more into conformance with the accounting standards of most of the industrialized world.

Purchase Method

Under purchase method, the transaction is recorded at its fair market value. Fair market value is defined as the total amount paid for the acquisition, including related costs of the acquisition, such as legal and accounting fees, broker's commission, and the like. If the acquisition is consummated with stock, then the acquisition price is based on the fair market value of the stock.

Assets that are acquired are assigned part of the overall cost of the acquisition based on their fair market value as of the acquisition. Any excess value that cannot be allocated to specific assets is then assigned to *goodwill*.

Goodwill is amortized over a period not exceeding 40 years by a charge against consolidated net earnings. Amortization of goodwill is deductible for tax purposes over a 15-year period if acquired after August 10, 1993. Amortization of goodwill for acquisition prior to August 10, 1993, is not deductible for tax purposes.

Under the purchase method the acquiring company is entitled to income of the acquired company only from the date of purchase. Prior retained earnings of the acquired company are not allowed to be brought forward to the consolidated entity.

Effect of Accounting Treatment on Stock Prices

Although the purchase method does permit the creation of tax-deductible expenses, the choice of method (when there was a choice) did not itself create any value. The accounting treatment does not produce synergistic effects or other benefits that would affect the combined firm's cash flows. Therefore, if the securities markets are efficient with regard to accounting methods, these paper changes should not affect security prices. Hong, Mandelker, and Kaplan found that stock prices were unaffected by the choice of acquisition accounting.[1]

TAXABLE VERSUS TAX-FREE TRANSACTIONS

A merger or an acquisition may be either a taxable transaction or a tax-free transaction. The tax status of a transaction may affect the value of the transaction from the viewpoint of both the buyer and the seller. A tax-free transaction is known as a tax-free reorganization. The term *tax-free* is a misnomer because the tax is not eliminated but will be realized when a later taxable transaction occurs.

Tax-Free Reorganizations

There are several different types of tax-free reorganizations. Each is discussed below.

Type A Reorganization

For a transaction to qualify as a tax-free reorganization, it must be structured in certain ways.[2] One way is a type A reorganization, which is considered a more flexible tax-free

---

1. H. Hong, G. Mandelker, and R. S. Kaplan, "Pooling vs. Purchase: The Effects of Accounting for Mergers on Stock Prices," *Accounting Review*, 53, January 1978, 31–47.
2. For a good description of the tax-free reorganizations, see George Rodoff, "Tax Consequences to Shareholders in an Acquisitive Reorganization," in Steven James Lee and Robert Douglas Coleman, eds., *Handbook of Mergers, Acquisitions and Buyouts* (Englewood Cliffs, NJ: Prentice-Hall, 1981), pp. 359–379.

reorganization technique than some of the others that are discussed in the following sections. In contrast to a type B reorganization, a type A reorganization allows the buyer to use either voting stock or nonvoting stock, common stock or preferred stock, or even other securities. It also permits the buyer to use more cash in the total consideration because the law does not stipulate a maximum amount of cash that may be used. At least 50% of the consideration, however, must be stock in the acquiring corporation. In addition, in a type A reorganization, the acquiring corporation may choose not to purchase all the target's assets. For example, the deal could be structured to allow the target to sell off certain assets separately and exclude them from this transaction.

In cases in which at least 50% of the bidder's stock is used as the consideration, but other considerations are used, such as cash, debt, or nonequity securities, the transaction may be partially taxable. Capital gains taxes must be paid on those shares that were exchanged for nonequity consideration, whereas taxes are deferred for those shares that were exchanged for stock. Rights and warrants that are convertible into the bidding firm's equity securities are generally classified as taxable.[3]

A type A reorganization must fulfill the continuity of interests requirement. That is, the shareholders in the acquired company must receive enough stock in the acquiring firm that they have a continuing financial interest in the buyer.[4]

Type B Reorganization

A type B merger or reorganization requires that the acquiring corporation use mainly its own voting common stock as the consideration for purchase of the target corporation's common stock. Cash must constitute no more than 20% of the total consideration, and at least 80% of the target's stock must be paid for by voting stock in the acquirer. In this type of transaction, the acquiring corporation must buy at least 80% of the stock of the target, although the purchase of 100% is more common. Target company shareholders may not be given the option to opt for cash as opposed to stock, where the effect could be that less than 80% of stock could be used. The presentation of this option, even if at least 80% of stock is actually used, disallows the type B reorganization.

Following the purchase of the target's stock, the target becomes a subsidiary of the acquiring corporation. In both type A and type B reorganizations, the transactions are viewed, from a tax regulatory point of view, as merely a continuation of the original corporate entities in a reorganized form. Therefore, these transactions are not taxed because they are not considered true sales.

It is possible to have a *creeping type B reorganization,* in which the stock is purchased in several transactions over a period of time. To qualify as a type B reorganization, however, the stock purchases must be part of an overall plan to acquire the target company. The plan itself must be implemented over 12 months or less. In a creeping type B reorganization, only stock may be used as consideration. It is acceptable for the acquiring

---

3. Cathy M. Niden, "Acquisition Premia: Further Evidence on the Effects of Payment Method and Acquisition Method," paper presented at the American Economics Association annual meeting, December 1989.
4. Joseph Morris, *Mergers and Acquisitions: Business Strategies for Accountants* (New York: John Wiley & Sons, 1995), pp. 254–255.

company to have bought some stock in the target with cash in the past as long as the purchases were not part of the acquisition plan.

Type C Reorganization

In a type C reorganization, the acquiring corporation must purchase 80% of the fair market value of the target's *assets.* Cash may be used only if at least 80% of the fair market value of the target's assets has been purchased using the voting stock of the acquiring corporation. As a result of the transaction, the target company usually must liquidate.

One advantage of a type C reorganization is that the acquiring company may not need to receive approval of its shareholders in such an asset purchase. Of course, target shareholders must approve this type of control transaction.

Type D Reorganization

There are two kinds of type D reorganizations. One type covers acquisitions, and the other covers restructuring. In an acquisitive type D reorganization, the acquiring company receives 80% of the stock in the target in exchange for voting stock in the acquiring company. Shareholders in the acquiring company become controlling shareholders in the target.

Divisive type D reorganizations cover spinoffs, splitups, and splitoffs. As discussed in Chapter 10, one or more corporations are formed in a spinoff, with the stock in the new companies being distributed to the original company shareholders according to some predetermined formula. In a splitoff, a component of the original company is separated from the parent company, and shareholders in the original company may exchange their shares for shares in the new entity. In a splitup, the original company ceases to exist, and one or more new companies are formed from the original business.

There are some additional requirements that a divisive type D reorganization must fulfill to qualify as tax free. For example, the distribution of shares must not be for the purpose of tax avoidance. Both the parent company and the spun-off entity must be in business for at least five years before the spinoff.

TAX CONSEQUENCES OF A STOCK-FOR-STOCK EXCHANGE

Target stockholders who receive the stock of the acquiring corporation in exchange for their common stock are not immediately taxed on the consideration they receive. Taxes must be paid only if the stock is eventually sold. Given the time value of money, this postponement of tax payments clearly has value. If cash is included in the transaction, this cash may be taxed to the extent that it represents a gain on the sale of stock.

Taxable Purchases of Stock

As noted, consideration other than stock, such as cash or debt securities, may result in a tax liability for the target shareholders. This tax liability applies only to a gain that might be realized from sale of the stock. If the stock is sold at a loss, no tax liability results.

Taxable Purchases of Assets

A tax liability may also result when the acquiring corporation purchases the assets of the target using consideration other than stock in the acquiring corporation. The potential tax liability is measured by comparing the purchase price of the assets with the adjusted basis of these assets.

Taxable versus Partially Taxable Transactions

A transaction may be partially taxable if the consideration is a combination of stock and cash. The stock consideration may not be taxed but the cash is taxed. Therefore, the percentage of the transaction that is taxable depends on the relative percentages of stock and cash.

Tax Loss Carryforwards

A tax loss or tax credit carryover was a more important motive for mergers and acquisitions in prior years, such as the early 1980s, than it is today. In fact, at one time companies advertised the availability of such tax gains to motivate a sale. The Tax Code, however, has been changed to prevent such tax-motivated transactions.

The tax losses of target corporations can be used to offset a limited amount of the acquiring corporation's future income. These tax losses can be used to offset future income for a maximum of 15 years or until the tax loss is exhausted. Before 1981, the maximum period was five years. Only tax losses for the previous three years can be used to offset future income.

Tax loss carryforwards may motivate mergers and acquisitions in two ways. A company that has earned profits may find value in the tax losses of a target corporation that can be used to offset the income it plans to earn. However, the tax losses realized by a company that has lost money can be used in the purchase of a profitable company. Although tax benefits may be an important factor in determining whether a merger will take place, they may not be the sole motivating one. A merger may not be structured solely for tax purposes. The goal of the merger must be to maximize the profitability of the acquiring corporation.

An acquiring corporation may not make unrestricted use of the tax loss carryforwards that it receives through an acquisition. The primary restrictions include the requirement that the acquirer must continue to operate the preacquisition business of the company in a net loss position. The acquirer must also give up any tax savings from a change in the asset basis of the "loss company" that might otherwise have occurred in a taxable acquisition.[5] For an example of tax loss carryforwards, see Table 15.1.

As shown in Table 15.1, the acquiring corporation expects to earn $500 million in each of the next two years. (All dollar amounts shown in the table are in thousands of dollars.) It has acquired a company that has a tax loss of $600 million. The acquirer may use this tax loss to offset all the projected income for the year following the acquisition. In addition, $100 million is still available to offset income earned in the following year. The value of this tax loss is seen by the income after taxes in the first year of $500 million

---

5. Mark J. Warshawsky, "Determinants of Corporate Merger Activity: A Review of the Literature," Staff Study No. 152, Board of Governors of the Federal Reserve System, April 1987, p. 5.

Taxes and Income without the Merger ($ Thousands)		
	Year I	Year II
Taxable income	500,000	500,000
Taxes (40%)	200,000	200,000
Income after taxes	300,000	300,000

Taxes and Income with the Merger ($ Thousands)		
	Year I	Year II
Income before tax loss	500,000	500,000
Tax loss carryforward	500,000	100,000
Taxable income	0	400,000
Taxes (40%)	0	160,000
Income after taxes	500,000	340,000

TABLE 15.1   EXAMPLE OF TAX LOSS CARRYFORWARDS

with the merger, as opposed to $300 million without the merger. In addition, income after taxes is $40 million higher in the second year after the merger. This income must be discounted to reflect the present value of these amounts. They are then used in the valuation process when the purchase price of the target is determined.

An example of the gains that an acquirer may reap from merging with a target that has incurred past operating losses is the 2006 Alcatel SA–Lucent Technologies, Inc. merger. When the telecom bubble burst in 2000, Lucent accumulated many billions of dollars of losses; while the company returned to profitability in 2003, it still did not use up all of its net operating loss tax credits. The size of these credits has been reported to be as high as $3.5 billion.[6] The tax credits can be applied to U.S. profits by the merged company for many years in the future. This means that it will be able to enjoy significant postmerger profits without having to pay U.S. taxes. Alcatel also has net operating loss credits, and the merger with Lucent, a company that derives most of its business in the U.S. market, better enables Alcatel to use its own credits.

Tax Loss Carryforward Research

A number of research studies have sought to estimate the present value of tax loss carryforwards. These tax benefits may be less than their "face value," not only because of the time value of money but also because they might expire without being fully utilized. Estimates of these values have been developed by Auerbach and Poterba and by Altshuler and Auerbach.[7] These research studies indicate that the two offsetting factors of deferral and expiration reduce the tax benefits to half their face value.

6. Jesse Drucker and Sara Silver, "Alcatel Stands to Reap Tax Benefit on Merger," *Wall Street Journal*, April 26, 2006, C3.

7. Alan Auerbach and James Poterba, "Tax Loss Carry Forwards and Corporate Tax Incentives," in Martin Feldstein, ed., *The Effect of Taxation on Capital Accumulation* (Chicago: University of Chicago Press, 1987); Roseanne Altshuler and Alan Auerbach, "The Importance of Tax Law Asymmetries: An Economic Analysis," National

Acquiring Firm's Treatment of Target's Tax Benefits

In tax-free acquisitions, target firms may provide tax benefits through NOL carryforwards and unused investment and foreign tax credits. In taxable acquisitions, the acquiring firm may derive tax benefits in the form of depreciation deductions that are derived from a step-up in the basis of assets. The acquiring firm or target may be affected by the cost of the depreciation recapture tax, which reflects the accumulated depreciation for assets that are sold. The extent of this effect is a function of the negotiations between the acquirer and the target. These effects are summarized in Table 15.2 according to the tax status of the acquisition.

ASSET BASIS STEP-UP

Tax advantages may arise in an acquisition when a target corporation carries assets on its books with a basis for tax purposes that is a fraction of the assets' replacement cost or market value. These assets could be more valuable for tax purposes if they were owned by another corporation, which could increase their tax basis after the acquisition and gain

These are the tax provisions in effect before the Tax Reform Act of 1986. The relevant sections of the Internal Revenue Code are given in parentheses.

Target Firm's Tax Attribute	Tax Status of Acquisition	
	Tax Free	**Taxable**
Tax basis on assets after acquisition	Basis transfers to acquiring firm unchanged [Secs. 358 and 362(b)]	Basis is revalued (stepped-up) at acquiring firm's cost [Sec. 1012]
Depreciation recapture taxes	The excess of cumulative accelerated depreciation over cumulative straight-line depreciation is deferred until a subsequent taxable transaction occurs [Secs. 354 and 361]	The excess of cumulative accelerated depreciation over cumulative straight-line depreciation is subject to tax at ordinary income rates, payable by the target firm [Secs. 1245 and 1250]
Net operating loss carryforward	Carryforward transfers to acquiring firm [Sec. 381]. [Secs. 368(a)(1), 382, and 269]*	Carryforward ceases to exist upon acquisition and is not available to acquiring firm
Unused investment and foreign tax credits	Credit transfer to acquiring firm [Sec. 381], subject to restrictions [Secs. 368(a)(1), 382, and 269]*	Credits cease to exist upon acquisition and are not available to acquiring firm

TABLE 15.2   Acquiring Firm's Treatment of Target Firm's Tax Attributes by Tax Status of Acquisition

*Section 381 does not apply to type B reorganizations, one of the types of tax-free acquisitions.
Source: Carla Hayn, "Tax Attributes as Determinants of Shareholder Gains in Corporate Acquisitions," *Journal of Financial Economics,* 23, 1989.

Bureau of Economic Research Working Paper No. 2279, National Bureau of Economic Research, Cambridge, MA, 1987.

additional depreciation benefits. The tax basis for the acquiring corporation is the cost or purchase price of the assets. The acquiring corporation may use this higher asset basis to shelter income.

The Tax Reform Act of 1986 has also reduced some tax benefits. The selling corporation now incurs a greater tax liability on asset sales, which reduces the seller's incentive to participate in the transaction. Moreover, research seeking to find the existence of *asset basis step-up* as a motivating factor for mergers and acquisitions before the Tax Reform Act of 1986 did not find asset basis step-up to be a significant motivating factor.[8]

CHANGES IN THE TAX LAWS

General Utilities Doctrine

Until its repeal with the Tax Reform Act of 1986, the General Utilities Doctrine allowed preferential treatment for "disincorporating" or liquidating corporations.[9] According to this doctrine, the sale of corporate assets and a liquidating distribution to shareholders were exempt from capital gains taxation. These distributions could occur, for example, following the acquisition of one corporation by another. The acquiring corporation could then sell off the assets of the acquired corporation and distribute the proceeds to shareholders without incurring capital gains tax liability to the corporation. These tax-free liquidating distributions could also occur without an acquisition, such as when a firm chose to sell off certain assets and distribute the proceeds to shareholders.

Assets sales were often structured by establishing separate subsidiary corporations. An acquired corporation could be purchased and its assets distributed into one or more subsidiaries. These subsidiaries would contain the assets that the acquiring corporation was not interested in keeping.[10] The assets that would be retained would be put into the parent corporation or into a separate subsidiary. The stock of the subsidiaries containing the unwanted assets could then be sold without incurring a significant tax liability. With the repeal of the General Utilities Doctrine, the gains or losses from an acquisition must be attributed to the acquiring corporation. The opportunities to avoid such tax liabilities were narrowed with the passage of the Tax Reform Act of 1986. They were further narrowed by the 1987 and 1988 tax acts.

Elimination of the Morris Trust

The Morris Trust is named after a 1966 tax court decision, *Commissioner v. Morris Trust.* This decision established certain variants of spinoffs as tax free. Using a Morris Trust, a company could spin off component businesses that it did not want to keep. In a second set preplanned transaction, the spun off business is merged into an acquirer's business in a

---

8. Alan J. Auerbach and David Reishus, "The Impact of Taxation on Mergers and Acquisitions," in Alan J. Auerbach, ed., *Mergers and Acquisitions* (Chicago: National Bureau of Economic Research, University of Chicago Press, 1988), pp. 69–88.
9. *General Utilities v. Helvering,* 296 U.S. 200 (1935).
10. George B. Pompan, "Federal Income Tax Considerations," in *Mergers and Acquisitions: Back-to-Basics Techniques for the 90s,* 2nd ed. (New York: John Wiley & Sons, 1994), pp. 198–202.

tax-free stock transaction. The final result is that shareholders in the selling company end up with shares in both their own company and the company of the acquirer. Companies have creatively used these vehicles to borrow money through a subsidiary, spin it off, and later sell it while having the buyer agree to pay the loan. The selling parent company keeps the cash from the loan. The tax law was changed in 1997 to eliminate the tax-free status of a preplanned spinoff and subsequent sale, although if the deal is not preplanned it still may be possible to be tax free.

Real Estate Investment Trusts

Real estate investment trusts (REITs) are publicly traded, passive investment vehicles that pay little or no federal taxes. The rebound of the real estate market in the mid-1990s enhanced the popularity of REITs. REITs consist of two entities in one: a management firm that manages real estate assets and an investment vehicle. Although they are supposed to be separate, their shares are paired and trade as one. Real estate investment trusts typically purchase property and rent it to a management firm. The management firm pays out its cash flow from properties to the investment vehicle, where it is treated as tax-free rent. Real estate investment trusts must distribute 95% of their earnings to shareholders, who then pay taxes on these monies at the individual level. Real estate assets such as hotels and shopping malls are often included in such investment vehicles. By combining them under the REIT umbrella, a real estate portfolio acquires tax benefits and liquidity. One of the more famous REITs is Starwood Hotels and Resorts Worldwide, Inc. There has been much debate about reducing the tax benefits of REITs, but such discussions have not resulted in changes in the laws that relate to REITs.

Given that REITs are required to pay out 90% of their earnings, they are not considered good for companies that have good growth prospects. The market's confirmation of this came in April 1998, when Corrections Corporation of America, the nation's largest commercial operator of prisons, announced that it would merge into CCA Prison Realty Trust, which is a REIT that would be the surviving entity. In response to the announcement, the stock prices of both companies fell. Shareholders in Corrections Corporation of America were more interested in growth and believed that being in a REIT would limit growth prospects.

ROLE OF TAXES IN THE MERGER DECISION

Auerbach and Reishus examined a sample of 318 mergers and acquisitions that occurred between 1968 and 1983. Approximately two-thirds of these mergers were in the manufacturing sector, with the average acquiring firm approximately 10 times larger than the acquired company. They found that a significant percentage of the companies in their sample had various constraints on their ability to use their tax benefits. Nonetheless, many of the companies realized tax benefits as a result of merging. The average gain was 10.5% of the acquiring firm's market value.[11]

---

11. Alan J. Auerbach and David Reishus, "Taxes and the Merger Decision," in John C. Coffee Jr., Louis Lowenstein, and Susan Rose Ackerman, eds., *Knights, Raiders and Targets* (New York: Oxford University Press, 1988), pp. 300–313.

Scholes and Wolfson studied the number of mergers and acquisitions for various times, including the periods before 1981, between 1981 and 1986, and after 1986.[12] The 1981 Tax Act provided various tax incentives for mergers and other forms of restructuring. Some of these were eliminated in the tax reforms that were part of the 1986 Tax Act. They attribute part of the intensified level of merger activity to tax motives that were put in place with the 1981 act and eliminated by the 1986 act.

Hayn analyzed 640 successful acquisitions between 1970 and 1985.[13] In her sample she noted that 54% were taxable, 18% were partially taxable, and 28% were tax free. There were 279 tender offers in her sample, and the majority of them (64%) were taxable. Mergers, however, varied in tax status. Of the 361 mergers in her sample, 39% were tax free, whereas 46% were taxable and the remainder were partially taxable.

Hayn researched the role that the tax attributes of transactions played in determining abnormal returns for targets and acquirers. First, she noted that tax-free status is a prerequisite of certain deals. Targets that do not receive such a status may decline to continue with the deal and may look to other bidders who can structure the transaction so that such a status is attained. Specifically she found that "potential tax benefits stemming from net operating loss carryforwards and unused tax credits positively affect announcement period returns of firms involved in tax-free acquisitions, and capital gains and the step-up in the acquired assets basis affects returns of firms involved in taxable acquisitions."[14]

Effects of Increased Leverage

Interest payments on debt are a tax-deductible expense, whereas dividend payments from equity ownership are not. The existence of a tax advantage for debt is an incentive to have greater use of debt, as opposed to equity, as the means of exchange in mergers and acquisitions.

The leverage argument suggests that the acquiring firm has a suboptimal debt-equity ratio and has not sufficiently used debt in its capital mix. The argument goes on to put forward mergers and acquisitions as a means whereby companies can achieve greater utilization of debt. An overly simplistic test of this hypothesis would be to look at the debt-equity ratios before and after various mergers and acquisitions. This test is considered overly simplistic because the acquiring corporation might retain earnings for one or more years before an acquisition in anticipation of the takeover. After the takeover, which might be financed with internal funds and borrowed capital, there would be a sudden increase in the debt-equity ratio. This jump in the debt-equity ratio may be offset by a gradual reduction over the years following the acquisition as the firm moves to a long-term debt-equity ratio that it considers optimal.

The tax deductibility of interest payments is not an incentive to merge; rather, it is an incentive to increase the potential acquiring firm's borrowing and alter its capital structure. This may be done in a much more cost-effective manner by issuing bonds

12. Myron Scholes and Mark A. Wolfson, *Taxes and Business Strategy* (Englewood Cliffs, NJ: Prentice-Hall, 1992).
13. Carla Hayn, "Tax Attributes as Determinants of Shareholder Gains in Corporate Acquisitions," *Journal of Financial Economics* 23, 1989, 121–153.
14. Ibid., p. 148.

or directly borrowing from a lender than through the costly process of engaging in an acquisition.

Auerbach and Reishus found that, contrary to popular belief, firms that merge more frequently do not borrow more than firms that have exhibited less tendency to merge.[15] They also discovered that the long-term debt-equity ratios of firms in their sample increased from 25.4% to only 26.7% after the mergers, which took place at a time when debt-equity ratios were increasing throughout the economy. The Auerbach and Reishus result may be less relevant to many of the private equity deals we are seeing in the 2000s. Many private equity firms are acquiring targets with unused debt capacity and engaging in leveraged recapitalizations. In these deals they acquire a target in a going private transaction, increase its debt, and take some or all of the debt proceeds as a dividend. The acquired corporation then has a more levered capital structure that in turn provides tax benefits to the corporation at the expense of a higher risk profile. A somewhat similar situation is discussed in the following when we describe Kaplan's research on the tax effects of management buyouts.

TAXES AS A SOURCE OF VALUE IN MANAGEMENT BUYOUTS

Taxes have quite a different role in management buyouts (MBOs) than they have in mergers and acquisitions. Kaplan measured the value of tax benefits for 76 MBOs between 1980 and 1986.[16] In this sample of MBOs, the average premium was 42.3% above the market price two months before the initial announcement of the buyout. The median ratio of debt to total capital rose from 18.8% before the buyouts to 87.8% afterward. Kaplan found that the value of increased interest and depreciation deductions ranged between 21.0% and 142.6% of the premium paid to prebuyout shareholders. A regression analysis relating the total tax deductions generated by the buyout to the premium available to prebuyout shareholders suggested that total tax deductions are an important determining variable. The t statistics equal to 5.9 indicated that total tax deductions were a highly significant explanatory variable. Kaplan's regression results were as follows:

$$\text{Buyout premiums} = f(\text{Total tax deductions}) \qquad (15.1)$$

$$\text{MAP} = -0.13 + 0.76 \times \text{Total tax deductions}$$

$$(1.5) \quad (5.9)$$

where:

$\text{MAP} = \text{Market-adjusted premium (t statistics are in parentheses)}$

$R^2 = 0.31$

$N = 75 \text{ (number of observations)}$

---

15. Ibid., p. 80.
16. Steven Kaplan, "Management Buyouts: Evidence on Taxes as Source of Value," *Journal of Finance* 44(3), July 1989, 611–632.

Leveraged Buyouts and Tax Revenues

Critics of LBOs contend that the tax deductibility of the debt used to finance these transactions causes a loss in tax revenues for the U.S. Treasury. These critics assert that, in effect, taxpayers are absorbing some of the financing costs of the LBOs. Jensen, Kaplan, and Stiglin, however, argue that LBOs result in *positive* tax revenues for the U.S. Treasury. They cite factors such as the increased efficiency of post-LBO firms, which increases taxable income; tax payments on capital gains to shareholders; tax payments on the interest income; and capital gains taxes paid on post-LBO asset sales to support their position. Jensen and colleagues attempted to measure these factors for a typical LBO.

For a typical LBO of $500 million, Jensen and associates estimated that incremental tax revenues equal $226.9 million, with incremental tax losses equal to $116.9 million, resulting in a net positive incremental tax revenue equal to $110 million. Scholes and Wolfson criticized some of the assumptions used by Jensen and colleagues.[17] For example, they focused on the assumption that the LBO would cause an increased value of the company and its shares. They contend that it is reasonable that some of these gains would have occurred anyway. They also point out that some of the capital gains preceding the LBO would have resulted in capital gains for shareholders, some of whom would have sold their shares even without the LBO. These criticisms and others they point out would change the conclusions of the Jensen study. Scholes and Wolfson do not go so far as to say that their suggested refinements would have wiped out all the positive net incremental tax revenues noted by Jensen and colleagues. They simply state that the result would be different and probably lower, but that it remains an open and controversial issue.

MISCELLANEOUS TAX ISSUES

Taxes and Golden Parachutes

The Internal Revenue Code imposes a 20% excise tax on excess parachute payments. Deductions for such excess payments are not allowed. The excess amount of such compensation is defined as that amount that is greater than the compensation during a five-year base period. There are some exceptions, such as when it can be established that the payments were reasonable in relation to the specific services that were provided.

Taxes and Termination Fees

Termination fees paid by a winning bidder, such as the $1.8 billion paid by Pfizer to American Home Products (now Wyeth) after Pfizer's successful bid for Warner Lambert in 2000, may be tax deductible. This arises out of a 1994 decision by a federal court in which monies paid to an unsuccessful white knight were found to be deductible if they were a separate transaction, that is, separate from the transaction that was eventually consummated.[18] The transactions are regarded mutually exclusive if only one can be

---

17. Steven Kaplan, "Management Buyouts: Evidence on Taxes as Source of Value," *Journal of Finance* 44(3), July 1989, 611–632.
18. *United States v. Federated Department Stores* 171 Bankr (603 S. D. Ohio 1994).

completed, which is normally the case when a buyer outbids a company that had already entered into a termination fee agreement with a target.[19]

Taxes and Greenmail

As noted in Chapter 5, penalties have been imposed on the receipt of greenmail payments. The Internal Revenue Service imposes a tax equal to 50% of the gain on such payments.

SUMMARY

The various ways in which taxes may play a role in mergers and acquisitions were addressed in this chapter. It was seen that the tax impact of a transaction is a function of the accounting treatment applied to the deal, which in turn is regulated by tax laws. Tax law changes, such as those that occurred in 1986, have reduced the initiative to merge with and acquire companies simply to realize tax gains.

Acquisitions are accounted for in the United States using the purchase method, which is consistent with the way they are accounted for in most nations. Under this method the costs of an acquisition are allocated to specific assets acquired according to their fair market value. Any excess cost that cannot be allocated to specific assets is then treated as goodwill.

Clearly, taxes must be carefully examined in any merger, acquisition, or LBO because they are important in evaluating the target firm and the overall cost of the acquisition. Some potential sellers will not sell unless they receive the desired tax consequence. Recent research has shown that tax benefits from net operating loss carryforwards and unused tax credits positively affect returns of companies involved in tax-free acquisitions. This research has also shown that capital gains and asset basis step-up also affect returns of companies involved in taxable acquisitions.

There is also evidence that taxes play an important role in LBOs. However, readers should be cautious in interpreting these research results. Simply demonstrating that taxes are a determinant of returns does not mean that tax effects are the prime reason for a deal. These studies have shown that taxes are one of several factors that influence returns. It would be reasonable to conclude that taxes normally play a secondary but still important role in determining mergers and acquisitions.

---

19. Robert Willens, "Guidant Eyes Tax Cut for Breakup Fee," *Daily Deal*, March 9, 2006, p. 5.

GLOSSARY

Abnormal return   In event studies, the part of the return that is not predicted by factors such as the market.

Absolute priority rule   The hierarchy whereby claims are satisfied in corporate liquidation.

Acquisition   The purchase of an entire company or a controlling interest in a company.

Agency problem   The conflict of interest that exists between owners of firms (shareholders) and their agents (management).

Alphabet stock   See Tracking stock.

Antigreenmail amendment   A corporate charter amendment that prohibits targeted share purchases at a premium from an outside shareholder without the approval of nonparticipating shareholders.

Antitakeover amendment   A corporate charter amendment that is intended to make takeovers more difficult and/or expensive for an unwanted bidder.

Any-or-all tender offer   A tender offer for an unspecified number of shares in a target company.

Appraisal rights   The rights of shareholders to obtain an independent valuation of their shares to determine the appropriate value. Shareholders may pursue these rights in litigation.

Back-end rights plan   A type of poison pill antitakeover defense whereby shareholders are issued a rights dividend that is exercisable in the event that a hostile bidder purchases a certain number of shares. Upon the occurrence of that event, shareholders may then exchange their rights combined with their shares for a certain amount of cash and/or other securities equal to a value that is set by the target. In doing so, the target's board, in effect, establishes a minimum price for the company's stock.

Bear hug   An offer made directly to the board of directors of a target company. Usually made to increase the pressure on the target with the threat that a tender offer may follow.

Beta   A risk measure derived from the capital asset pricing model. It quantifies the systematic risk of a security.

Bidder   The acquiring firm.

Blended price   The weighted average price that is set in a two-tiered tender offer.

Board out clause   An antitakeover provision that allows the board of directors to decide when a supermajority provision is effective.

Business judgment rule   The legal principle that assumes the board of directors is acting in the best interests of shareholders unless it can be clearly established that it is not. If that is established, the board would be in violation of its fiduciary duty to shareholders.

Bustup fees   The payments that the target gives the bidder if the target decides to cancel the transaction.

Bustup takeover   A takeover in which an acquisition is followed by the sale of certain, or even all, of the assets of the target company. This is sometimes done to pay down the debt used to finance a leveraged acquisition.

Capital asset pricing model   A financial model that computes a security's rate of return as a function of the risk-free rate and a market premium that is weighted by the security's beta.

Capital budgeting   A project analysis in which a project's receipts and outlays are valued over a project's life.

Cash flow LBO   Leveraged buyout in which the debt financing relies more on the expectation of projected cash flows than on the collateral protection of the target's assets.

Casual pass   When a bidder makes an informal overture to the management of the target expressing interest in an acquisition.

Celler-Kefauver Act   A 1950 amendment to the Clayton Act that modified Section 7 of that act to make the acquisition of assets, not just the stock, of a company an antitrust violation when the deal has anti-competitive results. This amendment also made "anticompetitive" vertical and conglomerate mergers an antitrust violation.

Chapter 7   The part of the bankruptcy law that provides for the liquidation of corporations.

Chapter 11   The part of the bankruptcy law that provides for the reorganization of a bankrupt company.

Chinese wall   The imaginary barrier separating the investment banking, arbitrage, and securities trading activities within a financial institution such as an investment bank.

Classified board   Also called a staggered board. An antitakeover measure that separates the firm's board of directors into different classes with different voting rights. The goal is to make acquisition of voting rights more difficult.

Clayton Act   A federal antitrust law passed in 1914. Section 7, which is most relevant to mergers and acquisitions, prohibits the acquisition of stock and assets of a company when the effect is to lessen competition.

Coercive tender offer   A tender offer that exerts pressure on target shareholders to tender early. This pressure may come in the form of preferential compensation for early tendering shareholders. Changes in securities laws have limited the effectiveness of such tender offers.

Coinsurance effect   Where cash flows of two combining companies are not perfectly correlated so that the volatility of the combined firm's cash flows exhibits less variability.

Collar agreement   Agreed-upon adjustments in the number of shares offered in a stock-for-stock exchange to account for fluctuations in stock prices before the completion of the deal.

Concentration ratios   Measures of the percentage of total industry revenues accounted for by a certain number of firms, usually the top four or eight.

Conglomerate   A combination of unrelated firms.

Cramdown   A situation that occurs when a reorganization plan is approved even when some classes of creditors do not approve it. At least one class of creditors needs to approve the plan for there to be a cramdown.

Cumulative abnormal return   The sum of daily abnormal returns over a certain period in an event study.

Cumulative voting rights   When shareholders have the right to pool their votes to concentrate them on the election of one or more directors rather than apply their votes to the election of all directors.

Dead hand provisions   Antitakeover measure that gives the power to redeem a poison pill to the directors who were on the target's board of directors before the takeover attempt.

Debtor in possession   A term used to refer to a bankrupt company in a Chapter 11 proceeding.

Deconglomerization   The process of taking apart a conglomerate through various sell-offs.

Dissident   A shareholder, or group of shareholders, who oppose current management and may try to use the proxy process to gain control of the company or to try to get the company to take certain actions, such as payment of certain dividends. Dissidents often try to have their representatives placed on the board of directors.

Diversification   In mergers and acquisitions, a term that refers to buying companies or assets outside the companies' current lines of business.

Divestiture   The sale of a component of the company, such as a division.

Dual classification   The creation of two classes of common stock, with the goal of concentrating more voting rights in the hands of management.

Economies of scale   The reduction of a company's average costs due to increasing output and spreading out fixed costs over higher output levels.

Economies of scope   The ability of a firm to utilize one set of inputs to provide a broader range of outputs or services.

Employee stock ownership plan (ESOP)   A type of pension plan in which the assets of the plan are the stock of the company.

Equity carve-out The issuance of equity in a division or part of a parent company that then becomes a separate company.

ESOP See Employee stock ownership plan.

Exclusivity period The time period during the initial days after a Chapter 11 filing when only the debtor can put forward a reorganization plan. It is initially 120 days, but the time period is often extended.

Fair price provision An antitakeover charter amendment that requires the payment of a certain minimum price for the shares of the target. It increases the bidder's cost of a takeover and makes coercive actions, such as two-tiered tender offers, less effective.

Fallen angel A bond originally issued with an investment-grade rating that had its rating fall below the investment-grade level, BB or lower, into the junk bond category.

Flip-in poison pill plan Shareholders are issued rights to acquire stock in the target at a significant discount, usually 50%.

Flip-over poison pill plan The most commonly used poison pill antitakeover defense, in which shareholders are issued rights to purchase common stock in a bidding firm's company at a significant discount, usually 50%.

Free cash flow hypothesis Theory put forward by Michael Jensen, which asserts that the assumption of debt used to finance leveraged takeovers will absorb discretionary cash flows and help eliminate the agency problem between management and shareholders. It is assumed that with the higher debt service obligations, management would apply the company's cash flows to activities that are in management's interest and not necessarily in shareholders' interests.

Front end-loaded tender offers A tender offer in which the compensation of a first tier is superior to a later second tier. Such offers are designed to be coercive and cause shareholders to tender early.

General Utilities Doctrine A component of the Tax Code that provided tax benefits for the sale of assets or liquidating distributions. It was repealed by the Tax Reform Act of 1986.

Going private When a public corporation becomes privately held. This is usually done through a leveraged buyout.

Golden parachute Employment contract of upper management that provides a larger payout upon the occurrence of certain control transactions, such as a certain percentage share purchase by an outside entity or when there is a tender offer for a certain percentage of the company's shares.

Greenmail The payment of a premium above current market price for the shares held by a certain shareholder, with the goal of eliminating that shareholder as a threat to the company's independence.

Hart-Scott-Rodino Antitrust Improvements Act of 1976 A law that requires a bidding company to file with the Federal Trade Commission and the Justice Department and receive antitrust approval from one of these entities before completing a takeover.

Herfindahl-Hirschman (HH) Index The sum of the squares of the market shares of companies in a given industry. It is a measure of industry concentration and is more sensitive to the effects of mergers than simple market shares.

Highly Confident Letter A letter issued by an investment bank indicating that it is confident that it can raise the necessary financing for a takeover.

High-yield bond Another name for a junk bond.

Holding company A company that owns the stock of other corporations. A holding company may not engage in actual operations of its own but merely manages various operating units that it owns an interest in.

Horizontal equity A principle of equal treatment for all shareholders such as in tender offers. Front end-loaded tender offers violate this principle.

Horizontal integration A merger of firms selling a similar product or service.

Hubris hypothesis A theory by Richard Roll that asserts that managers in acquiring companies believe that their valuations of targets may be superior to the market. This hubris causes them to overpay and overestimate the gains from acquisitions.

Initial public offering (IPO) The first offering of the common stock to the public by a closely held company.

In play When the market believes that a company may be taken over. At this time, the stock becomes concentrated in the hands of arbitragers and the company becomes vulnerable to a takeover and the target of a bid.

Investment Company Act of 1940 One of several pieces of federal legislation passed after the October 1929 stock market crash and the Great Depression. This law regulated the activities and reporting requirements of investment companies, which are firms whose principal business is the trading and management of securities.

Joint venture When companies jointly pursue a certain business activity.

Junk bond High-yield bonds that receive a rating from Standard & Poor's (or other agency) of BB or below. Such bonds are riskier than investment-grade bonds, which have higher ratings.

LBO See Leveraged buyout.

LBO funds A pool of investment capital that invests in various leveraged buyouts seeking to realize the high returns potentially available in LBOs while lowering risk through diversification.

Letter stock See Tracking stock.

Lerner Index Developed by Abba Lerner, the index measures market power as the difference between price and marginal cost relative to price.

Leveraged buyout (LBO) The purchase of a company that is financed primarily by debt. However, the term is more often applied to debt-financed going-private transactions.

Leveraged ESOP An employee stock ownership plan in which the purchase of shares is financed by debt. The principal and interest payments may be tax deductible.

Liquidation The sale of all of a company's assets whereby the firm ceases to exist.

Lockup option An option to buy certain valuable assets or stock in the target, which it issues to a friendly party. If the option limits the bidding process, it could be legally challenged.

Management buyout (MBO) A going-private transaction in which the management of a company or division of a company takes the company or division private.

Management entrenchment hypothesis Proposes that nonparticipating shareholders experience reduced wealth when management takes actions to deter attempts to take control of the corporation.

Marketability discount A discount applied to the value of some securities, such as securities in closely held companies, based on their comparatively lower liquidity.

Market flowback The depressing stock price effect in the domestic stock market of an acquirer when it purchases a foreign company using its own stock as consideration.

Market model A method that is used in event studies. Regression analysis is used to compute the return that is attributable to market forces. It is used to compute "excess returns" that may be attributable to the occurrence of an event.

Market power Although this term is used differently in different contexts, one definition used in an industrial organization is the ability to set and maintain price above competitive levels.

Master limited partnership (MLP) A limited partnership whose shares are publicly traded. Its key advantage is that it eliminates the layer of corporate taxation because MLPs are taxed like partnerships, not corporations.

Mezzanine layer financing Subordinated debt financing that is often used in leveraged buyouts. It is debt but also has equity-like characteristics in that the debt securities are often accompanied by "equity kickers."

Minority discount A discount applied to the value of equity securities based on a lack of control.

MLP See Master limited partnership.

Monopoly An industry structure that is characterized by one seller.

Morris Trust Using a Morris Trust, a company could spin off component businesses that it did not want to keep while in a second set, preplanned transaction the spun-off business is merged into an acquirer's business in a tax-free stock transaction. The end result is that shareholders in the selling company end up with shares in both their own company and that of the acquirer.

NASDAQ   National Association of Securities Dealers Automated Quotations. It is the trading system for the over-the-counter market.

Net operating loss carryover   Tax benefits that allow companies to use net operating losses in certain years to offset taxable income in other years.

Net present value (NPV)   A capital budgeting technique that combines the present value of cash inflows of a project with the present value of investment outlays.

No-shop provisions   Where a seller agrees not to solicit or enter into sale agreements with any other bidders.

Note purchase rights   Another name for back-end poison pill plans.

Oligopoly   Industry structure characterized by a small number of sellers (i.e., 3–12).

Pac-Man defense   One of the more extreme antitakeover defenses. It refers to a situation in which a target makes a counteroffer for the bidder.

Partial tender offer   A tender offer for less than all of a target's outstanding shares.

Perfect competition   An industry structure characterized by certain conditions, including many buyers and sellers, homogeneous products, perfect information, easy entry and exit, and no barriers to entry. The existence of these conditions implies that each seller is a price taker.

PIK debt securities   Bonds that may pay bondholders compensation in a form other than cash.

Poison pill   A right issued by a corporation as a preventative antitakeover defense. It allows right holders to purchase shares in either their own company or the combined target and bidder companies at a discount, usually 50%. This discount may make the takeover prohibitively expensive.

Poison put   A provision added to bond indenture contracts that allows bondholders to sell or "put" their bonds back to the issuing corporation at a predetermined exercise price. Poison puts became popular in the LBO era of the 1980s, when bond prices plummeted in response to the increased debt loads of post-LBO companies and the subsequent downgrading of the debt.

Preferred stock plans   Early version of poison pills that used preferred stock as opposed to rights.

Prepackaged bankruptcy   In a prepackaged bankruptcy, the debtor negotiates the reorganization plan with its creditors before an actual Chapter 11 filing.

Proxy contest   When a dissident shareholder or group of shareholders try to take control of the board of directors or use the process to enact certain changes in the activities of the company.

Pure plays   Companies that operate within clearly defined market boundaries.

Rabbi trusts   Where monies to fund golden parachutes are sometimes put.

Real estate investment trusts (REITs)   Publicly traded, passive investment vehicles that pay little or no federal taxes.

Recapitalization plan   The alteration of the capital structure of a company that adds debt and may reduce equity. It often is used as an antitakeover device when a target uses it as an alternative offer to a hostile bid. It often involves assuming considerable debt and paying a superdividend to target shareholders.

Restructuring charges   Also referred to as big bath write-offs. In a merger context it refers to a company's taking large write-offs following an acquisition, which lowers current income but may carry the implication that future income may be higher.

Reverse LBO   Companies that go public after having gone private in an LBO.

Reverse synergy $4_-1 = 5$; where, following a sell-off, the remaining parts of a company are more valuable than the original parent business.

Revlon duties   Legal principle that actions, such as antitakeover measures, that promote a value maximizing auction process are allowable whereas those that thwart it are not.

Roll-up acquisitions   An acquisition program that features multiple acquisitions of smaller companies by a larger consolidator.

Schedule 13D   The document that is required by the Williams Act to be filed with the SEC within 10 days of acquiring 5% or more of a public company's outstanding shares. This filing discloses certain information, including the purchaser's identity and intentions, as well as other related information, such as financing sources, in the case of a planned takeover.

Schedule 14D   The document that, pursuant to the Williams Act, must be filed with the SEC by the initiator of a tender offer. This filing discloses information on the identity of the bidder, specifics of the offer, and other relevant information, such as sources of financing and postacquisition plans.

Scorched-earth defense   An antitakeover defense that has such an adverse effect on the target that it renders it undesirable to bidders.

Securities Act of 1933   The first of the federal securities laws of the 1930s. It provided for the registration of publicly traded securities.

Securities Exchange Act of 1934   The federal law that established the Securities and Exchange Commission. It also added further regulations for securities markets. The law has been amended several times since its initial passage. One of the amendments that is relevant to mergers is the Williams Act of 1968.

Sell-off   A general term describing a sale of a part of a company. It also includes other more specific transactions, such as divestitures or spin-offs.

Shareholder interests hypothesis   It implies that stockholder wealth rises when management takes actions to prevent changes in control.

Shark repellent   Another name for an antitakeover defense.

Shelf registration rule   SEC Rule 415 that allows companies to register, in advance, shares they may want to offer in the future.

Sherman Act of 1890   The major piece of federal antitrust legislation. It contains two principal sections Section 1 prohibits all contracts and combinations in restraint of trade; Section 2 prohibits monopolization and attempts at monopolization.

Spin-off   A type of sell-off in which a parent company distributes shares on a pro rata basis to its shareholders. These new shares give shareholders ownership rights in a division or part of the parent company that is sold off.

Split-off   A type of sell-off in which shareholders of a parent company exchange their shares in the parent company for shares in the sold off entity.

Split-up   When the parent company spins off all of its component parts and ceases to exist.

Staggered board   Also called a classified board. This is an antitakeover measure in which the election of directors is split in separate periods so that only a percentage of the total number of directors come up for election in a given year. It is designed to make taking control of the board of directors more difficult.

Stakeholder   Any entity that is affected by the actions of a company, which may include shareholders, management, workers, communities, consumers, and so on.

Standstill agreement   An agreement that a potential hostile bidder enters into with the target corporation whereby the bidder agrees, in exchange for some consideration, not to purchase more than an agreed-upon number of shares.

Strategic alliance   A more flexible alternative to a joint venture whereby certain companies agree to pursue certain common activities and interests.

Stock parking   The attempt to evade the disclosure requirements of securities law by keeping shares in names other than the true owner.

Street sweeps   Open-market purchases of a target's stock that are not tender offers and therefore are not subject to the requirements of the Williams Act.

Supermajority provision   A preventative antitakeover defense that amends the corporate charter to require a higher majority, such as two-thirds or even more, to approve certain transactions such as mergers.

Synergy   2_2_5; a combination of businesses in which the combined entity is more valuable than the sum of the parts.

Targeted share repurchase   Refers to repurchase of stock of a large shareholder, such as a hostile bidder. It usually is done at a premium over market prices. This type of transaction is also referred to as greenmail.

Targeted stock   See Tracking stock.

Tax-free reorganizations   Types of business combinations in which shareholders do not incur tax liabilities. There are four types—A, B, C, and D—which differ in various ways, including the amount of stock and/or cash that is offered.

Tender offer   An offer made directly to shareholders. One of the more common ways hostile takeovers are implemented.

Tracking stock   An issuance of equity that represents an interest in the earnings of a division of a company.

Two-tiered tender offer   Tender offers in which the bidder offers a superior first-tier price for a maximum number of shares while it offers to acquire the remaining shares in the second tier at a lower price.

Unocal standard   The legal principle that reasonable defensive measures that are consistent with the business judgment rule are legally acceptable.

Vertical merger   A merger of companies that operate at different levels or stages of the production process in the same industry. For example, a company with large oil reserves buying a pipeline company for a gasoline retailer is an example of forward integration. A consumer electronics retail chain that buys a brand name manufacturer would be an example of backward integration.

Voting plans   A variation on the poison pill defense theme. They allow preferred stockholders to have supervoting rights if a bidder acquires a certain percentage of the target's stock. They are designed to prevent a bidder from getting voting control of the target.

White knight   A more acceptable buyer that a target of a hostile bid may approach.

White squire   A friendly company or investor that purchases an interest in the target of a hostile bid. The target may do this to make a takeover more difficult.

Williams Act of 1968   An amendment of the Securities and Exchange Act of 1934 that regulates tender offers and other takeover-related actions, such as larger share purchases.

Winner's curse   This is the ironic hypothesis that states that bidders who overestimate the value of a target will most likely win a contest. This is due to the fact that they will be more inclined to overpay and outbid rivals who more accurately value the target.

Workout   A workout refers to a negotiated agreement between the debtors and its creditors outside the bankruptcy process.

INDEX

A

Abnormal returns, 253–256
Accountants, 15, 16, 482
Accounting
  and corporate governance, 482
  goodwill, 589
  manipulation and incentive to
    merge, 44, 45
  scandals, 479, 480, 486
  treatment for M&As, 588, 589
Acquisition premiums. *See* Premiums
Agency costs, 485–489, 492, 505, 506
Alphabet stock, 439
Antitakeover defenses, 58, 171, 233
  active, 197–233
  change in control of board of
    directors, 83
  employee stock ownership plans, 392,
    393, 396, 397
  management entrenchment hypothesis
    versus stockholder interests
    hypothesis, 172, 173
  preventative, 173–196
Antitakeover legislation, 58, 92–98, 116
Antitrust law, 100, 116
  antitrust conflict as takeover
    defense, 226
  Celler-Kefauver Act, 40, 41, 103, 116
  Clayton Act, 36, 37, 40, 41, 97,
    101–103, 116
  enforcement, 32–34, 36, 37, 40–42, 46,
    107–113, 418, 419
  Europe, 114, 115
  Federal Trade Commission Act, 102,
    103
  government opposition to proposed
    acquisition, 105, 106

  Hart-Scott-Rodino Act. *See*
    Hart-Scott-Rodino Antitrust
    Improvements Act
  international mergers, 107
  litigation as antitakeover defense, 227
  premerger review, 104, 105
  Sherman Act, 32, 33, 36, 37, 100–102,
    116
  state laws, 97, 116
  21st Century Acquisition Reform and
    Improvement Act of 2000, 104
Approval procedures for mergers, 21, 22
Arbitrage, 16–18, 57, 180, 239, 261–263,
  560, 575
Articles for merger or consolidation, 21
Asia
  bankruptcies, 449, 450
  divestiture trends, 405–407
  executive compensation,
    486
  and fifth merger wave, 63
  golden shares, 192
  leveraged buyouts, 295, 329
  privatization of state-owned
    enterprises, 65, 66
  spinoffs, 416, 417
  takeover regulation, 88–90
  trends in M&As, 6, 8, 9
Asset acquisition, 23, 592, 594, 595
Asset-backed securities (ABSs), 374, 375,
  377
Asset-based (secured) lending, 307,
  309–315, 328
Asset selloffs, 25, 225–227
Assumption of liabilities, 25, 213,
  216–219, 226, 322, 420, 421, 467
Attorneys, 15, 16, 22, 99,
  247

Auction process, 92, 98, 116, 180, 183,
    207, 211–213, 229, 231, 233, 243,
    245, 247, 299, 300, 304, 317, 373,
    419, 429, 563, 566
Audits, 577, 578
Automobile industry, vertical
    integration, 156, 157

B
Back-end plans, 178
Backward integration, 154
Banking industry, 4, 6, 61, 129–132, 362
Bankruptcy, 443, 477, 478
    acquisition opportunities, 467, 468
    business failure, 443–446
    and corporate control, 470, 471
    distressed securities, investing
        in, 471–477
    ESOP as alternative to, 382, 383
    filing for, 443, 454–456
    fraud related, 451, 452
    fraudulent transfers, 470
    Japan, 449, 450
    laws, 452, 453
    and leveraged buyouts (LBOs), 316,
        325–328, 445, 448, 470
    liquidations (Chapter 7), 437, 443,
        452–454, 471
    and litigation liabilities, 471, 472
    petition, 454
    prepackaged, 462–465, 477
    reorganization (Chapter 11), 443, 444,
        448, 453–467, 470–472, 474–478
    risk of and debt-coinsurance, 133, 134
    and roll-up acquisitions, 153
    sharks (vultures), 475–477
    tax consequences, 464, 478
    trends, 446–452
    workouts, 444, 464–466, 478
Base equity price, 12
Bear hugs, 234, 237–240, 281
Best price rule, 83
Beta, 543
Black-Scholes option pricing model, 549,
    550

Blank check preferred stock, 179, 208,
    233
Board of directors
    and agency costs, 485, 492, 493
    and approval of M&As, 503, 504
    bright line standards, 497,
        498
    compensation issues, 480, 488, 489,
        492, 493, 497, 498, 501
    control of after tender offer, 83
    and corporate performance,
        502, 503, 507
    elections, 263, 264
    independence, 256, 257, 494–498, 508,
        517, 518
    interlocking, 488, 492–495, 518
    merger approval procedures, 21, 22
    and need for formal valuation, 531–533
    perks, 492, 493
    personal interests and M&As, 485, 506
    proxy contests for seats on, 268
    size of, 488, 494, 498, 499, 501
    staggered terms, 185, 186, 233
Board out clauses, 186, 187
Boesky, Ivan, 57, 99, 261
Bondholders, wealth transfer effects,
    322–324
Book value, 534, 535, 576, 579
Bootstrap effect, 46, 572–574
Breakup fees, 211, 212
Bridge loans, 360, 361
Brokerage firm purchase exception, 106
Business combination provision, state
    antitakeover laws, 95, 96, 116
Business failure, 443–446
Business judgment rule, 22, 91, 92, 98,
    194, 223, 224, 233, 531, 532
Bustups, 437, 438
Buyers, 429

C
Capital structure
    changes, 197, 213–225, 233, 458, 459,
        461, 462, 473, 474
    leveraged buyouts (LBOs), 314, 315

Cash flow leveraged buyout. *See* Leveraged buyouts (LBOs)
Cash flows, 536, 539–541, 545, 548–551, 558, 559, 575, 576, 583, 584–587. *See also* Discounted cash flow (DCF)
Cash-out statutes, 95, 116
Cash repurchase tender offers, 25
Cash transactions, 14, 331–335, 566, 567, 583
Casual pass, 237
Celler-Kefauver Act, 40, 41, 103, 116
Central America, 6, 10, 11, 63, 65, 66
Certificate of merger or consolidation, 21
Chewable pills, 180
Chief executive officer compensation. *See* Executive compensation
China, 6, 89, 90
Chinese Paper, 355
Chinese wall, 17
Clayton Act, 36, 37, 40, 41, 97, 101–103, 116
Closed-end investment companies, 25
Closely-held businesses, 25, 550, 576–583
Club deals, 343, 344
Coinsurance, 133, 134, 140, 141
Collective bargaining agreements, 24
Committee on Foreign Investment in the United States (CFIUS), 84
Common stock, cost of, 543, 544
Comparable multiple analysis, 533, 541, 550–553, 583
Concentration ratios, 109
Conflicts of interest, 22, 299–301
Conglomerate mergers, 13, 37, 40, 46, 47
Consolidation, 12, 61–63, 152–154
Consolidators, 62
Consumer surplus, 147, 148
Continuing value (CV), 536, 537, 583
Contracts, 519, 520
Control rights and strategic alliances, 527
Control share provision, state antitakeover laws, 95, 116
Convergence of interests hypothesis, 172

Convertible securities, 45, 46, 106, 208, 420
Corporate charter amendments, 184–192, 233, 266
Corporate governance, 479–518. *See also* Management
  and accounting profession, 479, 481, 482
  and accounting scandals, 479–481, 486
  agency costs, 485–489, 492, 493, 505
  board of directors. *See* Board of directors
  corporate democracy, 483, 485
  disciplinary takeovers, 498, 499, 502, 503
  executive compensation. *See* Executive compensation
  insiders, 494, 495, 499, 502
  and merger strategy, 503–518
  and mergers of equals, 509
  and Sarbanes-Oxley Act. *See* Sarbanes-Oxley Act
Corporate raiders, 57, 67, 68, 237, 239. *See also* Icahn, Carl; Pickens, T. Boone
Corporate restructuring, 225–227, 233, 442
  defined, 18
  divestitures. *See* Divestitures
  equity carve-outs. *See* Equity carve-outs
  exchange offers, 402
  generally, 18, 19
  and joint ventures, 525
  spinoffs. *See* Spinoffs
  splitoffs, 401
  splitups, 401, 402
Cost of capital, 135, 166, 542
Cost of debt, 542, 543
Cost restructuring, 18, 19
Creditors
  and bankruptcy, 454–466, 470, 471, 477, 478
  and leveraged buyouts, 311, 325–328

Creeping acquisitions, 106, 242
Currency valuation, 59, 121, 335

D
De facto mergers, 24
Dead hand provisions, 179
Deadweight loss, 147–149
Deal structures, 24
Debt, assumption of, 217–219, 420, 421
Debt coinsurance, 133, 134
Debt financing, 334, 335
Delaware, 12, 23, 34, 88, 89, 91, 92, 95,
    96, 179–181, 185, 196, 199, 203, 204
Depositories, 247, 267, 268
Deregulation, 6, 56, 59, 61, 129–132,
    151, 358
Disclosures, 20, 21, 51, 70–72, 75–78,
    86, 206, 222, 227, 228, 236, 258,
    259, 322, 481–483, 578
Discount rate, 533, 535, 537, 541, 542,
    545–555, 583, 584–587
Discounted cash flow (DCF), 535, 536,
    538–542, 547–550, 583–587
Discounts, 142, 143, 556, 560, 566,
    579–583
Diseconomies of scale, 127, 128
Dissenting shareholders rights, 23
Distressed securities, 471–477
Distribution channels, 164, 166, 521, 528
Diversification, 40–43, 136–145, 504, 505
Divestitures, 18, 109, 382, 401–415, 438
Dividends
    on ESOP shares, 385
    liquidating, 25
    and poison pills, 178, 179
    preferred stock, 178
    recapitalizations, 346, 347
    and share repurchases, 201
    superdividends, 213, 233
Domestic market flowback, 575
Downsizing, 18, 19, 421, 442. *See also*
    Spinoffs
Drexel Burnham Lambert, 57, 99, 100,
    250, 356–363, 365, 375, 376
Dual capitalization, 189–191, 233

E
Earnings before taxes, interest, taxes,
    depreciation and amortization
    (EBITDA), 444, 535, 539, 550–553,
    584, 586, 587
Earnings per share (EPS), 188, 302, 389,
    550, 568–575, 583
Economies of scale, 36, 62, 126–129,
    134, 135, 152, 165
Economies of scope, 129, 165
EDGAR (Electronic Data Gathering and
    Retrieval), 72
Efficiency gains, 303, 304, 317, 320
Eight Factor Test, 80–82, 240, 241
Emerging markets, 66
Employee stock ownership plans
    (ESOPs), 378, 397, 398
    as antitakeover defense, 392, 393, 396,
        397
    balance sheet effects, 389
    as bankruptcy alternative, 382, 383
    buyouts, 381, 382
    and cash flow, 383, 384
    contributions to, 381
    and corporate performance, 390–392
    divestitures, 382
    dividend payments, 385
    eligibility requirements, 384
    and employee morale, 386, 387,
        390–392
    employee risk, 387, 388
    fiduciary responsibilities, 392
    growth of, 378–380
    leveraged, 379–382, 384, 388–390,
        394–396
    and leveraged buyouts, 378, 381,
        394–396
    and management buyouts, 397
    public stock offering compared, 385,
        386
    put options, 384
    reasons for, 380, 381
    and recapitalization, 214
    securities laws, 388

and share issuance, 220, 221
shareholder approval for, 383
shareholder wealth, effect on, 393, 394
as source of capital, 383
and spinoffs, 421
stock contribution, valuation of, 384
tax benefits, 388, 389
types of, 380
unleveraged, 381
voting rights, 383, 390
and Williams Act requirements, 75
Enterprise value, 12, 539
Equity carve-outs, 18, 19, 401–403, 434–437, 442
Equity financing, 43, 44, 331–335, 339
Equity kicker, 308
Equity restructuring, 189–191
Escape clauses, 79, 186, 187
Europe
bridge loans, 360, 361
divestiture trends, 405–407
executive compensation, 486–488
and fifth merger wave, 63
fraud-related bankruptcies, 451, 452
golden shares, 192
leveraged buyouts, 291–295, 329
merger and acquisition trends, 3–7
privatization of state-owned enterprises, 65, 66
protectionism, 67
spinoffs, 416–418
takeover regulation, 85–88
takeover tactics and shareholder concentration, 205, 206
tender offer regulation, 248
European Union (EU)
merger regulation, 114
takeover regulation, 86, 87
Evergreen agreement, 194
Exchange offer, 402
Exchange ratio, 14, 567–575

Executive compensation, 162, 163, 192–196, 486–491, 493, 498, 501–505, 508, 509

F
Fair price provision, 94, 116, 188, 189, 233, 248, 249
Fairness opinions, 21, 22, 532, 533
Fallen Angels, 355
Family businesses, 39. *See also* Closely-held businesses
Federal Trade Commission Act, 102, 116
Federal Trade Commission (FTC), 102, 103, 106
Fees
hedge funds, 355
investment banks and bankers, 15, 16, 22, 57, 58
private equity firms, 347
termination, 211, 212, 599, 600
topping fees, 211, 212
Fiduciary duties, 91, 159, 194, 199, 211, 220, 232, 233, 236, 299, 300, 303, 321, 324, 392, 480, 485, 486, 490, 492, 502, 506, 509
Financial characteristics of targets, 575, 576
Financial printers as insiders, 99
Financial restructuring, 19
Financial statements, 560, 577, 578
Financial synergy, 124, 125, 133–136
Financing, 14, 375–377
cash versus stock, 331–334
debt financing, 334, 335
equity financing, 43, 44
generally, 14, 330
hedge funds, 348–355
institutional investors, effect of, 339, 340
international deals, 335
junk bonds. *See* Junk bonds
leveraged buyouts, 309–316
payment method, effects of, 335–340
private equity market, 340–348, 352–355

Financing, *(continued)*
   securitization, 374, 375, 377
   seller financing and spinoffs, 420
   shareholder wealth effects, 335–340
   stapled, 373, 374
5% test (merger guidelines), 112
5% threshold (Williams Act), 72, 75, 82,
   116, 187, 236, 245, 258, 259, 267
Flip-in poison pills, 177, 178, 233
Flip-over poison pills, 173–176, 178,
   233
Flipping companies, 342
Form 8K, 70
Form S-1, 70
Form S-4, 70
Forward integration, 154, 155
Forward triangular mergers, 24
Forwarding agent, 247
401(k) plans, 380
Franchises, 375
Fraud
   and bankruptcy, 451, 452, 470
   and misrepresentation of earnings, 559,
   560
Free cash flows, 536, 539–541, 547, 548,
   584
Freezeouts, 23
Front end-loaded tender offers, 248

G
General Utilities Doctrine, 595
Glamour firms, 253, 562
Go-go years, 44
Going private, 17, 18, 225, 226, 285, 295,
   301, 302, 305, 315–317, 320,
   322–326, 329
Golden handcuffs, 195
Golden parachutes, 192–196, 599
Golden shares, 192
Goodwill, 589
Governance. *See* Corporate governance
Greenmail, 57, 191, 197, 198–203, 223,
   233, 239, 259, 600
Growth as motive for M&As, 14,
   117–123, 165

H
Hart-Scott-Rodino Antitrust Improvements
   Act, 83, 103–107, 116, 244
Hedge funds, 180, 198, 202, 345,
   348–355, 370–372, 376, 377
Herfindahl-Hirschman (HH)
   Index, 110–112
High-yield bonds. *See* Junk bonds
Highly Confident Letters, 359
Holding companies, 26–28, 39
Holdouts, 23, 261
Hong Kong, 6
Horizontal integration, 145–154, 165
Horizontal mergers, 13, 30, 36, 41
Hostile takeovers, 19, 46–61, 234,
   236–240. *See also* Tender offers
Hubris hypothesis, 157–162, 166,
   562
Hurdle rate, 410, 545

I
Icahn, Carl, 53, 96, 198, 199, 202,
   237–239, 265, 266, 270, 320, 350,
   351, 359, 392
Income reporting, 577, 578
Initial public offerings (IPOs), 342, 385,
   386, 436
   special purchase acquisition vehicles
   (SPACs), 27, 28
Inside information, 17, 261
Insider trading, regulation of, 98–100
Insiders and corporate governance, 494,
   495, 499, 502
Institutional investors, 14, 18, 75, 167,
   173, 184, 205, 242, 264–266, 315,
   323, 328, 339, 340, 344, 345, 348,
   357, 358, 364, 376, 556
Interest, 316, 541, 547, 597
Internal transfer price, 155
International mergers and acquisitions, 58,
   61, 63–68, 107, 120–123, 335, 546,
   547, 575
International securities laws, 85–90
Investment banks and bankers
   arbitrage departments, 17

Chinese wall, 17
fairness opinions, 22
fees, 15, 16, 22, 57, 58
as insiders, 99
and junk bonds, 360
leveraged buyouts, 299, 308, 312, 313
and merger waves, 39, 43, 57, 58, 62
role of, 15, 16
tender offers, 246
Investment companies, 25
Investment Company Act of 1940, 25,
351
Investment exception to Hart-Scott-Rodino
Act, 106

J
Joint ventures, 519–527, 530
Junior subordinated debt, 309, 313
Junk bonds, 17, 57, 58, 60, 67, 68, 330,
331, 355–361, 363–366, 369–373,
376, 377
collapse of market, 17, 59, 99, 100,
250, 263, 281, 287, 361–369, 377,
446, 448
and leveraged buyouts (LBOs), 287,
314, 322–325
Just say no defense, 230, 231
Justice Department, 107–113

L
LBO. *See* Leveraged buyouts (LBOs)
Leading industry position, 136, 137
Lerner Index, 147
Letter of Transmittal, 82
Letter stock, 439
Leverage ratios, 576
Leveraged buyouts (LBOs), 68, 225, 226,
285, 328, 329
asset-based (secured) lending, 307,
309–315, 328
and bankruptcy, 316, 325–328, 445,
448, 470
capital structure, 314, 315

cash-flow (unsecured LBOs), 307, 308,
310, 313
and costs of being public
company, 295–297
defined, 17
divisional, 317, 318, 320, 321
and ESOPs, 378, 381, 394–396
financing, 309–316
and fourth merger wave, 58, 286, 287,
297, 306, 315, 316, 322, 323
gains, sources of, 302–308
globalization, 291–295
going private. *See* Going private
and investment banks, 299, 308, 312,
313
and junk bonds, 287, 314, 322–325
and LESOPs, 382
management buyout, 285, 297–304,
313, 317, 322
performance, 318–321
and private equity funds, 315, 340
recapitalization compared, 215, 216,
308
regulation and disclosure,
322
reverse, 319–321
risk, 306, 308, 309, 314–316, 324, 325
shareholder returns, 317–319
tax consequences, 306, 307, 599
trends, 286–290
wealth transfer effects,
322–324
as white knights, 322
Leveraged employee stock ownership
plans (LESOPs), 379–382, 384,
388–390, 394–396
Leveraged loans, 369–373, 377
Leveraged recapitalizations, 215, 216, 308
Lipton, Martin, 174, 230
Liquidating dividends, 25
Liquidation, 226, 227, 437, 443, 452–454,
471, 535
Liquidity, 152, 360, 376, 444, 557, 558,
576, 596

Litigation
  as antitakeover defense, 227–229,
    233
  liabilities and bankruptcy, 471, 472
  takeover battles, 197
Lockup transactions, 209–211, 226

M
Management
  and agency costs, 485–489, 492, 505
  compensation, 489, 490, 504,
    506–509
  perks, 486, 492, 493
  proposals, proxy contests, 268
  and tender offers, 245, 246
Management buyouts (MBOs), 17, 58,
    285, 297–304, 313, 317, 322, 382,
    397, 598
Management entrenchment
    hypothesis, 172, 173
Managerialism, 159
Market concentration, 42, 109
Market power, 146, 147, 149–152
Market share, 109
Marketability of stock, 533, 557–559,
    579–581
Master limited partnerships, 440, 441
Material adverse change clause, 20
Megamergers, 30, 54–56, 60, 68
Merger defined, 12
Merger waves
  causes of, 29, 30
  fifth wave, 3, 4, 59–66, 234, 287, 297,
    302, 329, 377, 418, 547
  first wave, 30–36, 67
  fourth wave, 3, 15, 16, 39, 53–59, 67,
    234, 263, 264, 286, 287, 297, 306,
    315, 316, 322, 323, 350, 351,
    363–366, 369, 377, 434, 443, 446,
    448
  international, 63
  and leveraged buyouts, 17, 18
  and merger premiums, 562, 563
  1940's, 39, 40
  1970's, 47–53

second wave, 36–39, 67
  third wave, 17, 40–47, 67
Mergers of equals, 509, 562–565
Mergerstat, 12
Mezzanine layer financing, 313, 314
Milken, Michael, 99, 100, 355, 356, 358,
    359, 375
Minority discount, 580–582
Minority shareholder freezeouts, 23
Money purchase plans, 380
Monopolies, 30, 36, 37, 101, 145–147,
    149–152, 165
Morris Trust, 595, 596
Motives for mergers and acquisitions
  distribution channels, 164,
    166
  diversification, 136–145
  generally, 14
  growth, 117–123, 165
  horizontal integration,
    145–154
  hubris hypothesis, 157–161
  management improvement,
    163, 166
  research and development
    improvement, 164–166
  synergy, 124–136
  tax benefits, 165
  vertical integration, 154–157
Mutual funds, 25, 347, 348, 353

N
NASDAQ, 85, 558
National Association of Securities Dealers
    (NASD), 21, 75, 78, 351, 558
National security, threats to, 84, 85
Negotiations, 19–21, 341
Net acquisition value (NAV), 124
Net present value, 535, 536
New York Stock Exchange (NYSE), 85,
    494, 497, 557
No action letter, 269
No hand provisions, 180
No-shop provisions, 212, 213
Note purchase rights plans, 178

O

Offer to Purchase, 82

Oligopoly, 36, 146, 149

Open-end investment companies, 25

Open market purchases, 241, 242, 258–261

Operating synergy, 124–133

Option exception to Hart-Scott-Rodino Act, 106

Over-the-counter (OTC) market, 557, 558

P

Pac-Man defense, 197, 229, 230, 232, 233

Partial tender offers, 79, 249, 250

Paying agent, 82

Payment, methods of, 335–340. *See also* Financing

Payment-in-kind (PIK) securities, 360

Pension funds, 180, 184. *See also* Institutional investors

Pickens, T. Boone, 53, 91, 207, 223, 224, 229, 239, 363

Poison pills, 88, 173–184, 216, 233, 393

Poison puts, 184, 325

Portfolio management, 137, 138

Preferred stock, 174, 175, 179, 208, 543

Premiums
  acquisition, 132, 133, 563
  cash offers, 375
  control premium, 555–557, 563, 565, 566, 581
  and director independence, 256, 257
  equals, mergers of, 563–565
  going private, 301, 302, 305
  historical trends, 562
  poison pills, effect of, 182, 183
  risk, 544, 545, 547, 558, 583
  and role of arbitragers, 560
  and stock market activity, 562, 563
  strategic mergers, 563
  and synergy, 132, 133

Press releases, 76, 80

Price-earnings ratio (P/E), 43, 44, 46, 64, 285, 301, 302, 317, 550, 553, 554, 564, 569–574, 576, 579, 580, 583

Price elasticity, 112

Price-fixing, 37

Private companies. *See* Closely-held businesses

Private equity firms, 17, 18, 347, 374–376

Private equity funds
  and hedge funds, 352–355
  leveraged buyouts (LBOs), 315, 340

Private equity market, 330, 340–348

Privatization of state-owned enterprises, 65, 66, 68

Producer surplus, 147, 148

Profit sharing plans, 380

Proxy fights, 191, 234, 235, 261, 263–282

Proxy solicitations, 21, 85

Proxy voting, 265–268

Public Utility Holding Company Act (PUHCA), 38, 84

Pure plays, 411

Put options, 184, 384

Pyramid holding companies, 39

R

Rabbi trusts, 194

Real estate investment trusts (REITs), 596

Recapitalization, 197, 215, 216, 233, 308, 311, 346, 347

Regulation M-A, 75

Regulatory framework, 69, 522, 523

Reincorporation, 196, 233

Reorganization in bankruptcy. *See* Bankruptcy

Research and development (R&D), 164–166, 319, 521, 524, 526

Reverse leveraged buyouts (LBOs), 319–321

Reverse mergers, 25, 26

Reverse subsidiary merger, 12

Reverse triangular mergers, 24

Revlon duties, 91, 92, 98, 115, 116, 231

Risk
  arbitrage, 17, 560, 575
  of bankruptcy, 133, 134
  beta measure, 543

Risk (*continued*)
  business risk, 315
  and choice of discount rate, 541
  and discount rate, 541, 542, 545–547
  and ESOPs, 387, 388
  event risk, 324, 325
  interest rate, 316, 541
  international acquisitions, 546, 547
  junk bonds, 363–366
  lack of liquidity, 558
  leveraged buyouts. *See* Leveraged
    buyouts (LBOs)
  premium. *See* Premiums
  stock versus cash transactions, 567
Roll-out, 440
Roll-up acquisitions, 62, 152–154
Russia, tender offer rules, 88

S
Sarbanes-Oxley Act, 295, 371, 377, 451,
    481, 482, 517
Saturday-night special, 51
Scorched earth defense, 218
Securities Act of 1933, 71
Securities and Exchange Commission
    (SEC)
  audit requirements, 577, 578
  bright line standards for directors, 497,
    498
  EDGAR database, 72
  Form 8K, 70
  Form S-1, 70
  Form S-4, 70
  hedge fund regulation, 351, 352
  no action letters, 269
  proxy contests, regulation of, 268, 269
  proxy statements, 69
  and regulation of public utilities, 38
  Rule 14a-6, proxy materials, 85
  Rule 10b-5, insider trading, 98, 99
  Rule 10b-13, purchases outside of
    tender offer, 83
  Rule 14d-6, oversubscribed partial
    tender offer, 79
  Rule 14d-7, withdrawal rights, 79

Rule 14d-9, 223
Rule 14d-10, type of consideration, 83
Rule 13e-1, self-tenders, 223
Rule 13e-3, repurchases in going
    private transactions, 322
Schedule 14A, 21, 85, 268, 269
Schedule 13D, 72, 76
Schedule 14D-9, 77, 78, 223
Schedule 13E-3, 322
Schedule 13G, 75
Schedule TO, 75–77, 116, 241, 242,
    245, 259, 322
stock-financed transactions, registration
    requirements, 567
Securities Exchange Act of 1934, 70, 84,
    116, 223, 268, 269, 351
Securities transactions, 14, 244
Securitization financing, 374, 375, 377
Self-tender offer, 222–224
Selloffs, 18, 403, 421–431, 439, 440, 442,
    525. *See also* Divestitures; Equity
    carve-outs; Spinoffs
Shadow pill, 180
Share repurchases, 201, 221–223. *See
    also* Greenmail
Shareholder activism, 270
Shareholder appraisal rights, 23
Shareholder approval, 21, 22, 25
Shareholder interests hypothesis, 172
Shareholder wealth
  conglomerates, effect of, 142
  and corporate control, 506–509, 517
  diversification, effect of, 42, 43, 141,
    142
  dual capitalizations, effect of, 190, 191
  employee stock ownership plans, effect
    of, 393, 394
  fair price provisions, effect of, 188, 189
  fifth merger wave, effect of, 63–65, 68
  golden parachutes, effect of, 193
  greenmail, effect of, 200, 201
  international mergers, effect of, 122
  joint ventures, effect of, 523–525, 528,
    530

leveraged buyouts, 317, 318, 322–324

litigation, effect of, 228, 229

methods of payment, effect of, 335–340, 376

poison pills, effect of, 180–184

proxy fights, effect of, 275, 277, 283

recapitalization plans, effect of, 217

reincorporation, effect of, 196

selloffs, effect of, 421–429

standstill agreements, effect of, 203, 204

state antitakeover laws, effect of, 97

strategic alliances, effect of, 528–530

supermajority provisions, effect of, 187, 188

tender offers, effect of, 253–258

two-tiered tender offers, effect of, 248, 249

and valuation effects of M&As, 540, 560–562, 567, 583

voluntary liquidations, effect of, 438

white knight bids, effect of, 206, 207

Shark repellents, 173, 325

Shelf registration rule, 219

Shell corporations, 23–26, 258

Sherman Act, 32, 33, 36, 37, 100–102, 116

Short-form mergers, 22, 23

Silver parachutes, 194

Slow hand provisions, 179, 180

Smith v. Van Gorkom, 22, 531–533

South America, 6, 10–11, 63, 65, 66

Special purchase acquisition vehicles (SPACs), 27, 28

Spinoffs, 18, 401–403, 413–421, 424, 425, 431, 437, 442

Splitoffs, 401

Splitups, 401, 402

Standstill agreements, 197, 203–205, 224, 233

Stapled financing, 373, 374

State law

antitakeover legislation, 58, 95, 96, 116

antitrust law, 97, 116

blue sky laws, 244

and ESOPs, 388

mergers and acquisitions, 21

State of incorporation, changing, 196, 233

Statutory mergers defined, 12

Stock exchanges

de-listing target after takeover, 84

NASDAQ, 85, 558

New York Stock Exchange, 85, 482, 494, 497, 557

regulations, 85

Schedule 14D-9, 77, 78

Stock-for-stock exchanges, 335, 565–575, 583, 584, 591–594

Stock held in street names, 267, 268

Stock market crashes, 39

Stockholders' meeting, 266

Strategic alliances, 519–522, 525–530

Strategic mergers, 60, 68, 98

Street sweeps, 258–262

Stub, 213

Subordinated debt, 309, 313, 314

Subsidiary mergers defined, 12

Successor liability, 24

Supermajority provisions, 186–188, 258

Synergy, 14, 117, 124–136, 409, 410, 421

T

Takeovers, 12, 35, 58, 197. *See also* Hostile takeovers

Tax consequences, 588

after-tax debt rate, 542, 543

asset basis step-up, 594, 595

General Utilities Doctrine, 595

golden parachutes, 599

greenmail payments, 202, 600

leveraged buyouts, 306, 307, 599

leveraged employee stock ownership plans, 388, 389

loss carryforward, 592–594

management buyouts, 598

master limited partnerships, 440, 441

and merger decision, 596–598

Morris Trust, 595, 596

prepackaged bankruptcy, 464

Tax consequences, *(continued)*
  real estate investment trusts
      (REITs), 596
  spinoffs, 419, 420
  stock and cash transactions, 592
  stock-for-stock exchange, 591–594
  stock versus cash transactions, 566,
      567, 592
  tax-free exchanges, 165
  tax-free reorganizations, 589–591,
      594
Tax issues
  changes in tax laws, 595,
      596
  income reporting, 577, 578
  tax benefits as motive for M&As, 165,
      166
  valuation of closely-held business, 578,
      579
Tender offers, 69, 79–85, 234, 235,
    240–258, 260, 261, 278, 279, 281.
    See also Williams Act
Termination fees, 211, 212, 599, 600
Three-piece suitor, 250
Time-Warner-Paramount, 98
Tobin's q, 142, 172
Toe-hold share accumulations, 236,
    237
Topping fees, 211, 212
Tracking stocks, 439, 440
Trading patterns, 173
Trends in financing, 330–377
Trends in mergers and acquisitions, 3–11,
    286–290, 403–407, 416–418
Triangular deal structure, 24
Trust funds doctrine, 24
Trusts
  and first merger wave, 33, 34
  Morris Trust, 595, 596
  rabbi trusts, 194
  real estate investment trusts
      (REITs), 596
  utility trusts, 38
Two-tiered tender offers, 248, 249

Types of mergers, 13

U
Unocal standard, 91, 223, 224

V
Valuation
  analysis, 20
  and antitakeover defenses, 533, 534
  and arbitragers, 560
  and Black-Scholes option pricing
      model, 549, 550
  book value, 534
  closely-held businesses, 533, 541, 550,
      576–583
  comparable multiples, 538, 541,
      550–553, 583
  continuing value, 536, 537
  and control premiums. *See* Premiums
  cost of capital, 542
  cost of common stock, 543, 544
  cost of debt, 542, 543
  cost of preferred stock, 543
  data reliability, 559, 560
  discount rate, 545–547
  discounted cash flow method, 535, 536,
      538, 539, 541, 542, 547–550,
      583–585
  effects of M&As, 560, 561
  enterprise value, 539
  exchange ratio, 567–575
  experts, role of, 15, 16
  fraudulent misrepresentation, 559, 560
  free cash flows, 539–541
  glamour firms versus value
      companies, 562
  hurdle rate, 545
  and interest rates, 547
  and liability of board of
      directors, 531–533
  liquidation value, 535
  and marketability of stock, 557–559
  methods, 533
  net present value, 535, 536
  outliers, 551

P/E multiples, 546, 553, 554, 579, 580, 583

and real options, 548–550

Smith v. Van Gorkom, 531–533

stock contributed to ESOP, 384

stock-for-stock exchanges, 565–575

sum-of-the-parts breakup analysis, 585–587

of target's equity, 539, 551, 553, 555

Venture capital, 340

Vertical integration, 37, 154–157, 165, 166

Vertical mergers defined, 13

Voting plans, 178

Voting process, 265–268

Voting rights, ESOP shares, 383, 390

W

Warrants, 106, 308, 313, 314, 420

Welfare loss, 147–149

Wellman v. Dickinson, 80–82, 240, 241

White knights, 197, 205–209, 212, 214, 243, 258, 259, 322

White squires, 197, 208–213, 220, 222

Wholly owned subsidiaries, 26

Williams Act, 46, 69–84, 116, 240, 242–244, 246, 259

Winner's curse hypothesis, 161–163, 166

Withdrawal rights, 79

Workforce restructuring, 18

WorldCom, 479, 480, 510–517